Secondary School Teaching
A Guide to Methods and Resources
Planning for Competence

Richard D. Kellough
Noreen G. Kellough
California State University at Sacramento

Merrill,
an imprint of Prentice Hall

Upper Saddle River, New Jersey   Columbus, Ohio

Library of Congress Cataloging-in-Publication Data

Kellough, Richard D. (Richard Dean)
    Secondary school teaching : a guide to methods and resources :
planning for competence / Richard D. Kellough, Noreen G. Kellough.
      p.   cm.
    Rev. ed. of: A resource guide for secondary school teaching /
Eugene C. Kim, Richard D. Kellough, 6th ed. ©1995.
    Includes bibliographical references and indexes.
    ISBN 0–13–618059–0
    1. High school teaching—United States. 2. Education, Secondary
—United States. 3. Curriculum planning—United States. 4. High
school teachers—Training of—United States. 5. Effective teaching—
United States. I. Kellough, Noreen G. II. Kim, Eugene C.
Resource guide for secondary school teaching. III. Title.
LB1737.U6K47   1999   98-9788
373.1102—dc21   CIP

Editor: Debra A. Stollenwerk
Production Editor: Mary Harlan
Photo Coordinator: Sandy Lenahan
Design Coordinator: Karrie M. Converse
Production Coordination and Text Design: Betsy Keefer
Cover art: © Diana Ong/Superstock
Cover Designer: Russ Maselli
Production Manager: Pamela D. Bennett
Illustrations: Carlisle Communications, Ltd.
Director of Marketing: Kevin Flanagan
Marketing Manager: Suzanne Stanton
Marketing Coordinator: Krista Groshong

This book was set in ITC Garamond by Carlisle Communications, Ltd., and was printed and bound by Courier/Kendallville, Inc.
The cover was printed by Phoenix Color Corp.

©1999 by Prentice-Hall, Inc.
Upper Saddle River, New Jersey 07458

Photo credits: pages 1 and 167, Scott Cunningham/Merrill; page 273, Anthony Magnacca/Merrill; page 415, Anne Vega/Merrill.

Printed in the United States of America

10 9 8 7 6 5 4 3

ISBN: 0-13-618059-0

PRENTICE-HALL INTERNATIONAL (UK) LIMITED, *LONDON*
PRENTICE-HALL OF AUSTRALIA PTY. LIMITED, *SYDNEY*
PRENTICE-HALL CANADA INC., *TORONTO*
PRENTICE-HALL HISPANOAMERICANA, S.A., *MEXICO*
PRENTICE-HALL OF INDIA PRIVATE LIMITED, *NEW DELHI*
PRENTICE-HALL OF JAPAN, INC., *TOKYO*
PEARSON EDUCATION ASIA PTE. LTD., *SINGAPORE*
EDITORA PRENTICE-HALL DO BRASIL, LTDA., *RIO DE JANEIRO*

Preface

The purpose of *Secondary School Teaching: A Guide to Methods and Resources: Planning for Competence* is to provide a practical and concise guide for college and university students who are preparing to become competent secondary school teachers. Others who may find it useful are experienced teachers who want to continue developing their teaching skills and curriculum specialists and school administrators who want a current, practical, and concise text of methods, guidelines, and resources for teaching grades 7 to 12. This book follows and replaces the sixth and final edition of *A Resource Guide for Secondary School Teaching: Planning for Competence.*

OUR BELIEFS: HOW AND WHERE THEY ARE REFLECTED IN THIS BOOK

In preparing this book, we saw our task not as making the teaching job easier for you—effective teaching is never easy—but as improving your teaching effectiveness and providing relevant guidelines and current resources. You may choose from these resources and build upon what works best for you. Nobody can tell you what will work with your students; you will know them best. We do share what we believe to be the best of practice, the most useful of recent research findings, and the richest of experiences. The boldface statements present our beliefs and explain how they are embraced in this resource guide.

The best learning occurs when the learner actively participates in the process, which includes having ownership in both the process and the product of the learning. Consequently, this resource guide is designed to engage you in hands-on and minds-on learning about effective teaching. For example, rather than finding a chapter devoted to an exposition of the important topic of cooperative learning, in each chapter you will become involved in cooperative and collaborative learning. In essence, via the exercises found in every chapter, you will practice cooperative learning, talk about it, practice it some more, and finally, through the process of doing it, learn a great deal about it. This resource guide *involves* you in it.

The best strategies for learning about secondary school teaching are those that model the strategies used in exemplary teaching of adolescents. As you will learn, integrated learning is the cornerstone of effective teaching for the twenty-first century, and that is a premise upon which this resource guide is designed.

To be most effective, any teacher, regardless of grade level and subject, must use an eclectic style in teaching. Rather than focusing your attention on particular models of teaching, we emphasize the importance of an eclectic model—that is, one in which you select and integrate the best from various instructional approaches. For example, sometimes you will want to use a direct, expository approach, perhaps by lecturing; more often you will want to use an indirect, social-interactive, or student-centered approach, perhaps through project-based learning. This resource guide provides guidelines to help you not only decide which approach to use at a particular time but also develop your skill in using specific approaches.

Learning should be active, pleasant, fun, meaningful, and productive. Our desire is to present this book in an enthusiastic, positive, and cognitive-humanistic way, in part by providing rich experiences in social-interactive learning. How this is done is perhaps best exemplified by the active learning exercises found throughout the book. Exercises were developed to ensure that you become an active participant in learning the methods and procedures that are most appropriate in facilitating the learning of active, responsive secondary school students.

Teaching skills can be learned. In medicine, certain knowledge and skills must be learned and developed before the student physician is licensed to practice with patients. In law, certain knowledge and skills must be learned and developed before the law student is licensed to practice in a courtroom. So it is in teacher preparation: knowledge and skills must be learned and developed before the teacher candidate is licensed to practice the art and science of teaching young people. We would never allow just any person to treat our child's illness or to defend us in a legal case; the professional education of teachers is no less important! Receiving a professional education on how to teach young people is absolutely necessary, and certain aspects of that education must precede any interaction with students if teachers are to become truly competent professionals.

ORGANIZATION OF THIS BOOK: AN OVERVIEW

Developmental components are involved in becoming a competent teacher. This book is organized around four developmental components: *why, what, how,* and *how well.* Each of the four parts of this resource guide clearly reflects one of those components. Each part is introduced with objectives and with reflective thoughts relevant to topics addressed in its chapters. The adjacent concept map illustrates how these four developmental elements are divided. Each chapter, in turn, begins with a brief introduction to that chapter followed by its major learning objectives.

Throughout, we provide information useful for the teacher as a decision maker. We also provide numerous exercises for practicing the handling of concepts in ways that facilitate metacognitive thinking. All exercises require the student-user to deal in some descriptive, analytical, or self-reflective manner with text concepts and actual practice. Most of the exercises are adaptable for cooperative or collaborative group processing.

PART I: ORIENTATION TO TEACHING AND LEARNING IN TODAY'S SECONDARY SCHOOLS

The three chapters of Part I reflect the *why* component—the reality and challenge of secondary school teaching today.

Chapter 1 presents an overview of that reality and challenge and provides specific guidelines for meeting the challenge. ***Regardless of their individual differences, all students must have equal opportunity to participate and learn in the classroom.*** Beginning in the first chapter, this belief is reflected throughout this resource guide, sometimes in a very direct fashion and other times indirectly. This attention to details in showing an overall sensitivity to diversity is intended to model not only our belief but also how to be inclusive to people of diverse backgrounds in many ways.

Chapter 2 reflects the expectations, responsibilities, and behaviors that are characteristic of competent and effective secondary school teachers.

Chapter 3, about the classroom learning environment, presents important information and guidelines to effectively plan and implement any instructional plan. You must know your students and have and maintain their attention. Thus, guidelines for accomplishing that are presented in Chapter 3.

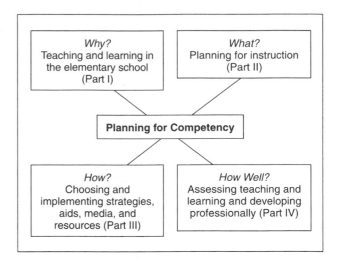

PART II: PLANNING FOR INSTRUCTION

Effective teaching is performance based and criterion referenced. This resource guide is constructed in this manner. Because we believe that teaching, indeed living, must allow for serendipity, encourage the intuitive, and foster the most creative aspects of one's thinking, we cannot always be specific about what students will learn as a result of our instruction, and hence the occasional ambiguity must be expected. The two chapters of Part II reflect the planning, or *what,* component.

Chapter 4, on the rationale for planning and selecting the content of the curriculum, provides information about the national curriculum standards and the state and local documents that guide content selection, the preparation of goals and objectives, and how to use those in planning. It also includes guidelines on using textbooks and dealing with controversial issues.

Chapter 5 presents specific information about integrating subjects of the curriculum and guidelines for preparing units and lessons.

PART III: CHOOSING AND IMPLEMENTING INSTRUCTIONAL STRATEGIES, AIDS, MEDIA, AND RESOURCES

Although it is very difficult to predict what secondary school students of today will need to know to be productive citizens in the middle of the twenty-first century, we believe they will always need to know how to learn, how to read, how to communicate effectively and work together cooperatively, and how to think productively. We believe that young people need skills in how to gain knowledge and how to process information, and they need learning experiences that foster effective communication and productive, cooperative behaviors. We hope all young people feel good about themselves, about others, and about their teachers, schools, and communities. We emphasize the importance of helping students to develop those skills, feelings, and attitudes. Teachers of all grades and subjects share in the responsibility for teaching skills in reading, writing, thinking, working cooperatively, and communicating effectively. This responsibility is reflected throughout this book.

The appropriate teaching methods for reaching these goals incorporate thoughtful planning, acceptance of the uniqueness of each individual, honesty, trust, sharing, risking, collaboration, communication, and cooperation. Furthermore, we believe students best learn these skills and values from teachers who model the same. Our book is faithful to that hope and to that end.

Part III, the *how* component, is presented in five chapters. Throughout the book, but particularly in the chapters of Part III, we emphasize the importance of students' use of visual and technological tools to access information and to make sense of it.

Chapter 6 provides a succinct presentation of important theoretical considerations for the selection of instructional strategies and learning activities. Chapter 7 addresses the strategy of questioning, with an emphasis on the encouragement of questions formulated and investigated by students. Chapter 8 presents guidelines for grouping students, using project-centered teaching, learning from assignments and homework, ensuring classroom equity, and writing across the curriculum. Chapter 9 presents guidelines for using teacher talk, demonstrations, direct teaching of thinking, discovery and inquiry, and educational games. Chapter 10 focuses on the selection and use of media, aids, and resources, tools that are intricately interwoven with teaching and learning.

PART IV: ASSESSMENT AND CONTINUING PROFESSIONAL DEVELOPMENT

In two chapters, Part IV addresses the fourth component of teaching and learning—*how well* the students are learning and how well the teacher is teaching.

Chapter 11 focuses on the assessment of what students know or think they know before, during, and after the instructional experience. It also provides practical guidelines for parent-teacher collaboration and for grading and reporting student achievement.

Chapter 12, the final chapter, focuses on how well the teacher is doing—the assessment of teaching effectiveness. Additionally, it includes guidelines for student teaching, for finding a teaching position, and for continued professional growth. These guidelines, as with this resource guide in general, will be useful as references for years beyond the methods course.

FEATURES OF THE TEXT

To achieve professional competency, you need guided learning, guided practice, productive feedback, encouragement, and positive reinforcement. To provide you with the resources and encouragement to make you an effective and confident teacher, this resource guide is organized with the following features.

- *Advance organizers.* The objectives and reflective thoughts at the beginning of each part and the objectives found at the beginning of each chapter serve as advance organizers; that is, they establish a mind-set.
- *Exercises for active learning.* Found within each chapter, all exercises require you to deal in some descriptive, analytical, or self-reflective manner with text concepts and actual practice. Each is designed to encourage continual assessment of and reflection on your progress in building your competencies and skill development for teaching and involve you in collaborative and cooperative learning. Since some exercises necessitate a school visit, an early review of the exercises will need to be done so you can plan your visits and work schedule. In fact, because certain exercises build upon previous ones or suggest that help be obtained from teachers in the field, it is advised that all exercises be reviewed at the beginning of your course. It is unlikely that all exercises in this book could be (or should be) completed in a one-semester course, so it will have to be decided which exercises will be done.
- *Perforated pages.* Pages of the resource guide are perforated for easy removal of the exercises. Exercises and some forms that are likely to be removed begin on separate pages so that they can be torn out without disturbing text.
- *Performance assessment.* Assessment of your developing competencies is encouraged by four micro peer teaching exercises found in Chapters 7 (Exercise 7.6), 9 (Exercises 9.1 and 9.3), and 12 (Exercise 12.1), plus an initial one suggested in Questions for Class Discussion in Chapter 1.
- *Situational case studies, teaching vignettes, and questions for class discussion.* For extended class discussions, situational case studies are presented in Chapter 3; teaching vignettes are distributed in several locations, such as "Precious Moment in Teaching" (Chapter 5) and "Late Homework Paper and an At-Risk Student" (Chapter 8); and Questions for Class Discussion appear at the end of each chapter.

- *Motivational teaching strategies and ideas*. More than 100 ideas for lessons, interdisciplinary teaching, transcultural studies, and student projects are presented in the final section of Chapter 8.
- *Outstanding practices and exemplary programs*. To let you gain further insight or to visit exemplary programs, schools recognized as having exemplary programs are identified throughout the text.
- *Suggested readings*. At the conclusion of each chapter are additional sources, both current and classic, to deepen and broaden your understanding of particular topics.
- *Appendix*. The appendix displays additional unit and lesson plans for various subjects.
- *Glossary*. The text concludes with a glossary of terms, a name index, and a subject index.
- *Instructor's guide*. The Instructor's Manual addresses each chapter of the resource guide in three ways: a detailed outline of the chapter, chapter notes containing additional information or suggestions about particular content, and examination questions and answers.

ACKNOWLEDGMENTS

We would never have been able to complete this book had it not been for the valued help of many individuals, including former students in our classes and teachers who have shared their experiences with us, administrators and colleagues who have talked and debated with us, and authors and publishers who have graciously granted permission to reprint materials and who are acknowledged in the book. To each we offer our warmest thanks.

Although we take full responsibility for any errors or omissions in this book, we are deeply appreciative to others for their cogent comments and important contributions that led to the development of this book. We thank James Dick, University of Nebraska at Omaha; Cynthia E. Ledbetter, University of Texas at Dallas; Robert L. Mulder, Pacific Lutheran University; and Helen Rallis, University of Minnesota, Duluth.

We express our deepest admiration for and appreciation to the highly competent professionals at Merrill/Prentice Hall with whom we have had a long and rewarding relationship, especially to Jeff Johnston, Vice President and Publisher, for believing in us and supporting us in even the most difficult moments an author can have, and to Senior Editor Debbie Stollenwerk, whose professional knowledge and talent, bright confidence, positive demeanor, and sense of humor helped to make writing this book an enjoyable event for us.

We are indeed indebted and grateful to all the people in our lives, now and in the past, who have interacted with us and reinforced what we have known since the days we began our careers as teachers: teaching is the most rewarding profession of all.

Richard D. Kellough
Noreen G. Kellough

Brief Contents

Contents

PART

I

ORIENTATION TO TEACHING AND LEARNING IN TODAY'S SECONDARY SCHOOLS

Part I assists you with:

- Guidelines for establishing and maintaining a safe and effective classroom learning environment.

- Guidelines for getting the school year off to a good beginning.

- Guidelines for working in a multicultural classroom.

- Your knowledge of legal guidelines for the classroom teacher.

- Your recognition of the value of multicultural education.

- Your understanding of the expectations, responsibilities, competencies, and facilitating behaviors of a secondary school classroom teacher.

- Your understanding of the importance of home, school, and community partnerships.

- Your understanding of the realities of secondary school teaching today.

- Your understanding of instructional practices that are developmentally appropriate for specific groups of learners.

Reflective Thoughts

During one school year, you will make literally thousands of decisions, many of which can and will affect the lives of students for years to come. You may see this as an awesome responsibility, which it is.

A teacher who, for all students, uses only one style of teaching in the same classroom setting day after day is shortchanging students who learn better another way.

Traditional teaching techniques—such as the lecture, which assumes that students are homogeneous in terms of background, knowledge, motivation, learning styles, and facility with the English language—are ineffective in many of today's secondary school classrooms.

Like intelligences, teaching style is neither absolutely inherited nor fixed. Your teaching style will change, develop, and emerge throughout your career.

The bad news is that most of us are not born with innate teaching skills; the good news is that teaching skills can be learned and steadily improved.

As a classroom teacher, you cannot solve all the ailments of society, but you do have an opportunity and the responsibility to make all students feel welcome, respected, and wanted.

A nontraditional school schedule alone—without quality individualized attention to the individual needs of the students—seems to be of no value in addressing the needs of students who are at risk of dropping out of school.

Chapter

1

Teaching and Learning in Today's Secondary Schools

You have probably begun reading this book because you are interested in a career in secondary school teaching. Whether you are in your early twenties and starting your first career or older and beginning a new career, this book is for you—that is, for any person interested in becoming a secondary school classroom teacher.

If you are now in a program of teacher preparation, then perhaps near the completion of the program you will be offered your first teaching contract. If that happens, you will be excited and eager to sign the contract and begin your new career. Yet after the initial excitement, you will have time to reflect. Many questions will then begin to form in your mind. If in a multiple-school district, to which school will I be assigned? Will it be a comprehensive high school, a junior high school, or a middle school? Will it be a traditional school, or will it be a magnet school, that is, a school that specializes in a particular academic area, such as business and technology, the performing arts, science and mathematics, history and international relations, or international studies?[1] Or will it be a fundamental school, that is, a school that specializes in teaching basic skills? Or a charter school, that is, a school that is "an autonomous educational entity operating under a charter, or contract, that has been negotiated between the organizers, who create and operate the school, and a sponsor, who oversees the provisions of the charter"?[2] Or a partnership school, that is, a school that has entered into a partnership agreement with community business and industry to link school studies with the workplace? Or a tech prep high school, that is, one that has a curriculum that is articulated from grades 9 to 12 to the first two years of college, leading to an associate of applied science degree?[3] Or a school designated as a community learning center, so named because of its profound engagement with community life, a focus on lifelong learning, and the personal learning plan that each student works from?[4] Or a full-service school, offering quality education and comprehensive social services all under one roof,[5] and so on?[6]

---

1. See K. Checkley, "Magnet Schools: Designed to Provide Equity and Choice," *Education Update* 39(2):1, 3, 8 (March 1997). At Brien McMahon High School (Norwalk, CT), for example, The Center for Japanese Study Abroad is a magnet program that allows students in a school-within-a-school program to become proficient in the Japanese language through an interdisciplinary Japanese studies curriculum that includes economics, literature, arts, and music and to obtain firsthand knowledge of the Japanese culture through home and school experience in Japan. See W. Jassey, *Center for Japanese Study Abroad* (Bloomington, IN: Fastback 386, Phi Delta Kappa Educational Foundation, 1995).

2. L. A. Mulholland and L. A. Bierlein, *Understanding Charter Schools* (Bloomington, IN: Fastback 383, Phi Delta Kappa Educational Foundation, 1995), p. 7. Since the first in 1991, charter school legislation has been passed in more than half the states. See the several articles about charter schools in the theme issues of *Phi Delta Kappan* 78(1) (September 1996) and *Educational Leadership* 54(2) (October 1996).

3. See J. E. Green and R. A. Weaver, *Tech Prep: A Strategy for School Reform* (Bloomington, IN: Fastback 363, Phi Delta Kappa Educational Foundation, 1994).

4. For information about community learning centers, contact Designs for Learning, 2550 University Avenue West, Suite 347N, St. Paul, MN 55114-1052, phone 612-645-0200.

5. See J. G. Dryfoos, "Full-Service Schools," *Educational Leadership* 53(7):18–23 (April 1996).

6. See the theme issues "The New Alternative Schools," *Educational Leadership* 52(1) (September 1994), and "Self-Renewing Schools," *Educational Leadership* 52(7) (April 1995).

Will it be a school that has its start in the fall, as is traditional, or will it be a year-round school? (From 1985 to 1995, the number of schools that changed to a year-round program increased from 410 in 16 states to more than 2,200 in 37 states.[7]) Which subjects will I be assigned to teach? What specific grade levels will I have? How many different preparations will I have? Will I be a member of a teaching team? Will I have core curriculum teaching responsibilities? What supervision responsibilities might I have? What will the students be like? What will their parents or guardians be like? How will I get along with the rest of the faculty? What textbooks will I use, and when can I expect to see them? Will I be using a media program? How should I prepare? How *can* I prepare when there are so many unanswered questions? What school district policies do I need to learn about now? What support services can I expect? How extensive are the school's rules and regulations? Will my teaching assignment be split between departments? Will the department chairperson like me? Will there be an orientation for new and beginning teachers? How can I prepare for students I know nothing about?

Those questions, and many others, are often the focus of long, concentrated thinking by teachers. To guide you through this initial experience and to help answer some of your questions, this chapter offers a first glimpse into today's world of secondary school teaching by discussing school organization, secondary school students, teachers, administrators, and parents or guardians. The complexity of this active and ever-changing world means that no one could cover everything that needs to be said to every teacher. But, because it is necessary to start somewhere, we begin with an overview. Enjoy your quest in becoming the best teacher you can be.

The material in the three chapters of Part I provides a basis for your planning and selection of learning activities presented in subsequent chapters. Specifically, upon completion of this first chapter, you should be able to

1. Define *secondary school,* and describe similarities and differences between the middle school, junior high school, and high school.
2. Describe the middle school concept and its contributions to secondary education.
3. Describe the purposes and characteristics of the "house" concept.
4. Define the term *school restructuring;* identify the common purpose of current school restructuring and reform efforts; identify the premise upon which various secondary school restructuring approaches are based.

5. Describe today's concept of teaching and learning and how it differs from the concept of the recent past.
6. Describe techniques for working effectively with specific groups of learners.
7. Describe trends, problems, and issues in secondary education today.

Before going further, let us define what is meant by the term *secondary school. A secondary school is any school that houses students in some combination of what traditionally have been known as grades 7 through 12.* However, as you shall learn, some middle schools, which may have students at the eighth-grade level, also house students in grade 6 and even grade 5. So, for this resource guide, our definition of secondary school includes middle schools, junior high schools, and high schools.

Now, let's begin your quest for understanding by considering some significant characteristics of today's secondary schools, beginning with orientation meetings for teachers.

ORIENTATION MEETINGS

As a beginning teacher, you will likely be expected to participate in a series of orientation meetings for new and beginning teachers, meetings designed to help you get off to a good beginning. Some school districts start the academic year with a districtwide orientation, whereas others schedule on-site orientations at each school. Many school districts do both, with perhaps a districtwide morning meeting followed by on-site meetings in the afternoon. Of course, the scheduling and planning of orientation meetings will vary district by district and school by school. The objectives for all orientation meetings, however, should be similar. As a beginning teacher, you will be encouraged to do the following:

1. Become familiar with the district's (or school's) written statement of its beliefs and goals—its statement of mission or philosophy—and what that statement means to the people affiliated with the district or school. For example, for a middle school, the mission statement might be similar to this:

   The mission of Harriet Eddy Middle School is to promote academic excellence and responsible citizenship, provide a transition into the high school experience and create lifelong learners who function successfully in an ever changing world.

   And, for a high school, it may resemble this:

   Davis High School integrates an active and committed community of learners. Through a challenging curriculum with diverse opportunities, students are empow-

7. See C. Ballinger, "Prisoners No More," *Educational Leadership* 53(3):28–31 (November 1995).

ered to: think analytically, communicate effectively, express themselves aesthetically, and appreciate the importance of a healthy life style. As informed and ethical members of the greater community, our graduates are equipped to participate in a complex and dynamic society with creativity, courage, compassion, and resilience.[8]

2. Meet other teachers and establish new collegial friendships and professional relationships.

3. Become familiar with the policies of the school and district. Numerous policies often cover a wide range. There are policies for procedures relating to injuries of students at school; for natural disasters, such as earthquakes and severe storms; for allowing students to take prescribed medications; for finding nonprescribed drugs, other controlled substances, and weapons; for parking on campus; for leaving campus during the school day; for class conduct; for school programs, off-campus field trips, and parties in the classroom; for grading practices; for completing absentee and tardy forms; for sending students to the office; and for chaperoning and sponsoring student activities. And these examples are just the beginning.

4. Become familiar with the myriad forms that teachers must fill out. There are forms for injuries at school, for textbook loans, for key loans, for attendance and tardiness, for student academic grade deficiencies, for sponsoring student activities, for field trips, and for referrals of students for misbehavior, to name just a few.

5. Become familiar with the approved curriculum that defines what teachers are to teach and what students are to learn. This means that you must familiarize yourself with the courses of study, curriculum guides, resource units, teacher's manuals, student textbooks, and supplementary materials—all of which should reflect the school's philosophy and approved curriculum.

6. Become familiar with the school or district plan for monitoring, assessing, and supervising implementation of the curriculum.

7. Study available resource materials and equipment, as well as procedures for reserving and using them on certain dates.

8. Become familiar with the school library/media resource center, its personnel, and its procedures.

9. Meet district and school personnel and become familiar with the many services that support you in the classroom.

10. Become familiar with campus security personnel, resource officers, and other ancillary personnel and their functions and locations.

11. Prepare the classroom for instruction.

As a student in a program for teacher preparation, you may be expected to participate in an orientation meeting at your college or university. The meeting may be held at the beginning of the program or just before the beginning of your field experiences, or possibly at both times. Perhaps this meeting will be a function of one of your college or university courses. You will receive your school assignment, the name of the school and the school district, the school's location, the date when you should report to that assignment, the name of your cooperating teacher(s), the grade level(s), the subject(s), and perhaps the name of your college or university supervisor. You will probably be encouraged to follow many of the 11 items or objectives just listed as well as to meet other teacher candidates.

When you arrive at your assigned school and after introductions have been made, you should begin to become familiar with the school campus and the way that the school is organized. Walk around the campus, perhaps with a copy of the school map, and learn the location of your classroom. Also locate the nearest restrooms for girls, for boys, and for faculty men or women. You may be lent one or several keys—one for the classroom, one for the faculty restroom, and perhaps one for a faculty workroom. Become familiar with such areas as the teacher's workroom, the faculty room, and the faculty lunchroom. (These rooms may or may not be in a single area. A large comprehensive school may have several faculty rooms scattered about the campus.)

Thoroughly investigate this campus environment. Where do students eat lunch? Is there a multipurpose room, a room used for lunch as well as for educational purposes? Where is the nurse's room? Is there a school nurse? When is the nurse available? Where is the nearest first-aid and emergency equipment? How do you notify maintenance personnel quickly and efficiently? Where are the written procedures for fire drills and other emergencies? Where is information about the school's emergency warning system? Is a plan posted in a conspicuous place for all to see? Where are the various administrative offices? Where are the counseling and guidance offices? Is there an office of student activities? Where are the library, media center, resources room, gymnasium, and auditorium? Where are textbooks stored, and how are they checked out and distributed? Where is the attendance office? Are there resource specialists, and if so, what are their functions and where are their offices located?

At an orientation session, you may meet the department or division chairperson or the interdisciplinary

---

8. Source: Student handbooks of Harriet Eddy Middle School (Elk Grove, CA) and Davis High School (Davis, CA).

team leader and members of that team. How can you discover where those persons are to be found at various times during the school day? Where are teaching and laboratory supplies kept, and how do you obtain them? Have you located your faculty mailbox and the place to check in or out when you arrive at school or leave at the end of the day? What procedures do you follow if you are absent because of illness or if you know you are going to be late? Do you have the necessary phone numbers? Not least in importance, if you drive an automobile to school, where do you park? Otherwise, what is the best local transportation available for getting to school each day?

After you become familiar with the campus and obtain answers to some of your more urgent questions, you will want to focus your attention on the various school schedules and particularly your own teaching schedule.

TODAY'S SECONDARY SCHOOLS

The rapid and dramatic changes occurring throughout modern society, as well as what has been learned in recent years about intelligence and learning, are reflected in the equally rapid and dramatic changes occurring in today's secondary schools. The school in which you soon will be teaching may bear little resemblance to the secondary school from which you graduated—in its curriculum, its student body, its methods of instruction, or its physical appearance.

The School Year: Conventional and Year-Round Schedules

School years vary from state to state, from district to district, and from school to school. Most school years begin in late August or early September and continue through late May or mid-June, though some schools operate on a year-round schedule. With year-round operation, a teacher might teach for three-quarters of the year and be off for one-quarter or teach in a 45/15 program, which means nine weeks of school (45 days) "on track" followed by three weeks of school (15 days) "off track" throughout the year. In the 45/15 arrangement, teachers and students are on tracks, referred to as A Track, B Track, and so on, with starting and ending times that vary depending on the track and time of year.

Most schools operate five days a week, though some are open for just four days. Whether school follows a year-round schedule or not, for teachers and students in the United States the school year still approximates 180 days. The school day usually begins at about 8:00 a.m. and lasts until about 3:00 or 4:00

p.m. In crowded schools, beginning and ending times of the school day may be staggered. With a staggered start, some students and teachers start as early as 7:15 a.m. and end at about 2:30 p.m., and others begin at 9:00 a.m. and continue until 4:00 p.m. In many secondary schools, the first and last periods of the day are scheduled with classes that are optional for students; those periods are often called *zero periods*. District and state laws vary, but generally teachers are expected to be in the classroom no less than 15 minutes prior to the start of school and to remain in their classrooms no less than 15 minutes after dismissal of students.

Teaching Teams

Traditionally, secondary school teachers taught their subjects five or six times each day, in their own classrooms, and were fairly isolated from other teachers and school activities—not unlike the parallel play of preschool children, who play side by side but not together. In many schools, that is still the case. Increasingly, however, secondary school teachers are finding themselves members of a collaborative team in which several teachers from different subject areas work together to plan and implement the curriculum for a common group of students. (A distinction must be made between teaching teams and team teaching; **team teaching** refers to two or more teachers simultaneously providing instruction to students in the same classroom. Members of a teaching team may participate in team teaching.)

The teaching team may comprise only a few teachers, for example, teachers who teach English and world history to the same group of eleventh-grade students; they may meet periodically to plan a curriculum and learning activities around a common theme, such as the Elizabethan era. Sometimes teaching teams comprise one teacher each from English/language arts, mathematics, science, and history/social studies. These four subject areas are known as the **core curriculum.** In addition to the core subject teachers, specialty-area teachers may be part of the team, including teachers of physical education, teachers of the visual and performing arts, and even special education teachers and at-risk specialty personnel or school counselors. In addition, some teams may invite a community-resource person to be a member. Because the core and specialty subjects cross different disciplines of study, these teams are commonly called interdisciplinary teaching teams or simply **interdisciplinary teams.**

The School-Within-a-School Concept

An interdisciplinary teaching team and its common group of students can be thought of as a school-within-a-school (also called a village, pod, family, or house), where each team of teachers is assigned each day to the same group of 90 to 150 students for a common block of time. Within this block of time, teachers on the team are responsible for the many professional decisions necessary, such as how school can be made meaningful to students' lives, what specific responsibilities each teacher has each day, what guidance activities need to be implemented, which individual students need special attention, and how students will be grouped for instruction. Members of such a team become "students of their students" and thereby build the curriculum and instruction around their students' interests, perspectives, and perceptions. Because they "turn on" learning, their classrooms become exciting places to be and to learn. (In contrast, "symptoms of turned-off learning include students' seeming inability to grasp concepts, to exert effort, or to display enthusiasm; repeated lateness or absence; boredom; and work that is sloppy or of poor quality.")[9]

The house concept helps students make important and meaningful connections among disciplines. It also provides them with both peer and adult group identification, which provides an important sense of belonging. (In some schools, using an arrangement called **looping** or *banding,* students and teachers of a house remain together as a group for the three or four years a student is at that school.) There are many advantages of being a member of a teaching team in a school-within-a-school environment. The combined thinking of several teachers creates an expanded pool of ideas, enhances individual capacities for handling complex problems, and provides intellectual stimulation and emotional support; the synergism of talents produces an energy that has a positive impact on the instructional program; a beginning teacher who joins a team has the benefit of support from more experienced teammates; when a team member is absent, other members of the team work closely with the substitute, resulting in less loss of instructional time for students; and more and better planning for students occurs as teachers discuss, argue, and reach agreement on behavioral expectations, curriculum emphasis, instructional approaches, and materials.[10]

For an interdisciplinary team to plan most effectively and efficiently, members must meet together frequently. This is best accomplished when they share a **common planning time;** a minimum of four hours a week is recommended. This means that *in addition* to

each member's daily preparation period, members of a team share a common planning time to plan curriculum and to discuss the progress and needs of individual students.

Each teaching team assigns a member to be the lead teacher, or teacher leader. The lead teacher organizes the meetings and facilitates discussions during the common planning time. This teacher also acts as a liaison with the administration to ensure that the team has the necessary resources to put its plans into action. A team's lead teacher (or another member designated by the team) may also serve on the school leadership team, which consists of a group of teachers and administrators, and sometimes students, designated by the principal or elected by the faculty (and student body) to assist in the leadership of the school.

School Schedules

For many secondary school teachers, the school day consists of the traditional six or seven periods, each period lasting 45 to 60 minutes. One of these periods is a preparation period, referred to sometimes as the conference, planning, or free period. This traditional or conventional schedule includes teaching three or four classes before lunch and three or four following lunch.

When a teacher's preparation period falls during either the first or the final period of the day—or just before or after lunch—the teacher is still expected to be present on the campus during that time in order to be available for conferences with students, parents, guardians, counselors, other teachers, or administrators. Most teachers are quite busy during their preparation periods, reading and grading student papers, preparing class materials, meeting in conferences, or preparing teaching tools.

To allow for more instructional flexibility and to accommodate common planning time for teachers, many schools use some form of **block scheduling.** Blocks of time ranging from 70 to 140 or more minutes replace the traditional structure of 45- to 60-minute classes. The sample block schedule in Figure 1.1 shows the assignment of teachers to different classes. Compare that block schedule with a conventional schedule shown in Figure 1.2. The sample student schedule in Figure 1.3 illustrates how a seventh grader in a school that uses block scheduling might be assigned to different classes on different days.[11] Often, no bells ring to

---

9. The phrases *students of their students* and *turn on learning* are from C. A. Grant and C. E. Sleeter, *Turning on Learning* (Upper Saddle River, NJ: Prentice Hall, 1989), p. 2.

10. R. J. McCarthy, *Initiating Restructuring at the School Site* (Bloomington, IN: Fastback 324, Phi Delta Kappa Educational Foundation, 1991), p. 11.

11. For various sample schedules, see R. L. Canady and M. D. Rettig, "The Power of Innovative Scheduling," *Educational Leadership* 53(3):4-10 (November 1995).

Teacher	Advisor-Advisee	Block 1		Block 2		Block 3		Block 4	
		M W F	T Th	M W F	T Th	M W F	T Th	M W F	T Th
A	yes	Sci–6	Sci–6	Plan time	Plan time	Sci–6	Sci–6	Reading–6	Exploratory–6
B	yes	Eng–6	Eng–6	Plan time	Plan time	Eng–6	Eng–6	Reading–6	Exploratory–6
C	yes	SS–6	SS–6	Plan time	Plan time	SS–6	SS–6	Reading–6	Exploratory–6
D	yes	Mth–6	Mth–6	Plan time	Plan time	Mth–6	Mth–6	Reading–6	Exploratory–6
E	yes	Eng–7	Eng–7	Eng–7	Eng–7	Plan time	Plan time	Speech	Exploratory–6
F	yes	Sci–7	Sci–7	Sci–7	Sci–7	Plan time	Plan time	Reading–7	Exploratory–6
G	yes	SS–7	SS–7	SS–7	SS–7	Plan time	Plan time	Reading–7	Exploratory–6
H	yes	Pre Alg–7	Mth–7	Mth–7	Mth–7	Plan time	Plan time	Reading–7	Exploratory–6
I	yes	Plan time	Plan time	SS–8	SS–8	SS–8	SS–8	Reading–7	Exploratory–7
J	yes	Plan time	Plan time	Alg I–8	Pre Alg–7	Pre Alg–8	Mth–8	Mth–8	Pre Alg–8
K	yes	Plan time	Plan time	Sci–8	Sci–8	Sci–8	Sci–8	Intramurals	Sci–8
L	yes	Plan time	Plan time	Eng–8	Eng–8	Eng–8	Speech	Eng–8	Eng–8
M	yes	Computer	Computer	Home Ec–8	Home Ec–8	Plan time	Plan time	Home Ec–8	Exploratory–7
N	yes					Shop–8	Shop–8	Shop–8	Exploratory–7
O	yes							Spanish–8	Exploratory–7
P	yes	Plan time	Plan time	Art–6	Art–6	Art–7	Art–7	Art–8	Exploratory–7
Q	no						Art–8		
R	no	LD	LD	LD	LD	LD	LD	Plan time	Plan time

Figure 1.1
Sample block schedule.

signal movement from one block to the next. Instead, teachers dismiss their classes with verbal instructions to students. When the school building is so designed, or if the blocks are planned appropriately, students move only a short distance between classes, such as just across the hall or next door. Proximity of team members' classrooms can facilitate coordination of instruction, allow more flexibility in scheduling, and promote productive collaboration between colleagues. Classrooms scattered about the school campus, as in traditional school structures, are less likely to facilitate a cohesive learning environment.[12]

Using what is called a *5 × 7 block plan,* the school year at Skyline High School (Longmont, CO) consists of three 12-week trimesters and each school day is divided into five 70-minute class periods.[13]

Some schools (especially in the states of Colorado, Florida, Illinois, Maryland, Minnesota, North Carolina, Pennsylvania, South Carolina, Texas, and Virginia) use a *4 × 4 block plan,* where students take four 90-minute *macroperiods* (or *macroclasses*) each day, each semester, for the four years they attend high school. Taking eight classes a year allows a student in four years to complete 32 credits, rather than the

---

12. J. Valentine et al., *Leadership in Middle Level Education* (Reston, VA: National Association of Secondary School Principals, 1993), p. 53.

13. T. Stumpf, "A Colorado High School's Un-Rocky Road to Trimesters," *Educational Leadership* 53(3):16–19 (November 1995).

Teacher Number	0	1	2	3	4	5	6	7	8	9
1		50 P30 ENG 11Y P	31 P30 ENG 10Y P			32 P30 ENG 10Y P	51 P30 ENG 11Y P	52 P30 ENG 11Y P	1061 P30 TA ENG F	
2			712 29 ROPFDS3HRY	1155 29 ROPFDS2HRY	1200 29 ROPFDS1HRF		586 29 NUTRSCI 1F	585 31 H/INT DES	625 29 TA CAFE F	
			713 29 ROPFDS2HRY	1286 29 ROPFDS2HRY			588 29 NUTRSCI 2F	1156 31 ADVINTDESF		
6		345 P43 SPANISH 2 P	346 P43 SPANISH 2 P		332 43 SPANISH 1 P		347 43 SPANISH 2 P	349 43 SPANISH 2 P	1063 43 TAF/LAN F	
TEACH 2000								447 GYM ADAPT PE Y		
								448 GYM ADAPT PE F		
3						309 80 APE/PSCI P	311 80 ADVANSCI P		1065 80 TA APPSCIF	
4		562 07 KYBD 1A F	563 07 KYBD 1A F	553 19 ACCTG 1 Y		567 07 KYBD 1A F	564 07 KYBD 1A F		1067 07 TA BUS F	
				565 17 KYBD 1A F						
				573 19 RCRDKEEP P						
5		320 P33 SPANISH 1 P	321 P33 SPANISH 1 P	322 P33 SPANISH 1 P		349 P33 SPANISH 3 P	350 P33 SPANISH 3 P	334 P33 SPANISH 1 P	1069 P33 TAF/LAN F	
7		11 14 ENG 9Y P	12 14 ENG 9Y P	13 14 ENG 9Y P		14 14 ENG 9Y P		15 14 ENG 9Y P	1071 14 TA ENG F	
10		202 P39 ALGEBRA1 P	203 P39 ALGEBRA1 P	194 P39 MATH A Y	549 78 DR PROD 1 F		193 P39 MATH A Y		1073 P39 TA MATH F	
					551 78 DR PROD 2 F					
14					131 46 WRLD HIST P		154 47 US HISTY P	155 47 US HISTY P		
					807 46 WRLD HST F					
20			732 P26 SDCSCIE/PY	731 P25 SOC MATH Y	734 P26 SDCSCILIFY			741 P26 SDCSTDSKLF	1075 P26 TA SP ED F	
			733 P26 SDCSCIP/EY	1051 P25 RSP MATH Y	760 P26 SDLLIFSCIY			743 P26 SDCSTDSKLY		
			784 P26 RSPPSCIP/E	1093 P25 SDL MATH Y	783 P26 RSPLIFSCIY			1153 P26 RSPSTDSKLS		
			785 P26 RSPPSCIE/P							
			1036 P26 SDLPSCIE/P							
25		33 P38 ENG 10Y P	67 P38 ENG 11 Y H	1006 P38 ENG 10Y P			69 P38 ENG 11 Y H	1007 P38 ENG 10Y P	1077 P38 TA ENG F	
43		253 P02 PSCIP/EY P		250 P08 PSCIP/EY P	270 28 BIOLOG Y P	271 28 BIOLOG Y P		251 P08 PSCIP/EY P	1079 28 TA SCI F	
		868 P02 PHYSSCIF P		863 P08 EARTHSCF P				864 P08 EARTHSCF P		
46									1299 AT 0 TA CNSLR F	
48		16 15 ENG 9Y P		17 04 ENG 9Y P	18 04 ENG 9Y P		19 04 ENG 9Y P	20 04 ENG 9Y P	1081 04 TA ENG F	
50			735 61 SDC GOV F	737 61 SDCUSHST Y	738 61 SDCWHIST Y			745 61 SDC W GEOG	1083 61 TA SP ED F	
			739 61 SDC CONECON	749 61 SDLUSHST Y	777 61 RSPW HST Y			747 61 SDC W GEOG		
			750 61 SDL GOVT	778 61 RSPUSHST Y				779 61 RSP WGEOGF		
			752 61 SDL ECON							
			775 61 RSPCONECON							
			781 61 RSP GOV F							
60		315 82 FAB W/METL	318 82 AG MECH 3Y	316 82 DESIMPLE P	312 90 ADVANSCI P				621 82 TA APPSCI F	

Figure 1.2
A conventional high school teacher's schedule.

Figure 1.3
Sample seventh-grade student schedule.

WEEK SCHEDULE A

		Mon Wed Fri	Tu Thur
7:45–8:10		Advisory	Advisory
8:10–9:35	1st Block	Social studies	Mathematics
9:35–11:35	2nd Block	English	Science
11:35–1:00	3rd Block	General music (1/2) P.E./Health (1/2)	Art (1st half) P.E./Health (1/2)
1:00–2:25	4th Block	Reading	Exploratory

WEEK SCHEDULE B

		Mon Wed Fri	Tu Thur
7:45–8:10		Advisory	Advisory
8:10–9:35	1st Block	Mathematics	Social studies
9:35–11:35	2nd Block	Science	English
11:35–1:00	3rd Block	Art (1/2) P.E./Health (1/2)	General music (1st half) P.E./Health (1/2)
1:00–2:25	4th Block	Exploratory	Reading

traditional 24 or 28.[14] Using macroperiods lengthens the time each day students are in a course while simultaneously reducing the number of courses taken at one time. The extended period, or macroperiod, allows the teacher to supervise and assist students with assignments and project work as well as with their reading, writing, thinking, and study skills. Macroperiods provide more time for learning activities, such as projects, that might otherwise be difficult or impossible to accomplish in shorter class periods.

Under still another plan, students take just one four-hour class for 30 days, or two two-hour macroclasses for 60 days. At Laguna Creek High School (Elk Grove, CA), for example, a teacher meets only two 140-minute classes each day for six weeks, which at that school is one trimester.

Nonconventional School Scheduling: Advantages and Disadvantages

Consistently reported in the research of schools using block scheduling, where students and teachers work together in longer but fewer classes at a time, are greater satisfaction among teachers and administrators and improvement in both the behavior and the learning of students. Students do more writing, pursue issues in greater depth, enjoy classes more, feel more challenged, and gain deeper understandings. In addition, teachers get to know the students better and are therefore able to respond to a student's needs with greater care.[15]

There are other reported benefits of the block plans over a traditional six- or seven-period daily schedule. (1) In one school year the total hours of instruction are significantly greater. (2) Each teacher teaches fewer courses during a semester and is responsible for fewer students; therefore, student-teacher interaction is more productive and the school climate is positive with fewer discipline problems. (3) Because planning periods are longer, there is more time for teachers to plan and to interact with parents. (4) More students can take advanced placement (AP) classes.

There are also benefits to taxpayers. During one school year teachers teach more courses and potentially more students, thereby decreasing the number of faculty needed. Also, fewer textbooks are needed. For example, instead of all sophomores taking history for an entire year, half of them take it the first semester and half the second, thereby reducing the number of textbooks needed by one-half.[16]

Block scheduling arrangements often produce serendipitous benefits. For example, students may not

---

14. C. M. Edwards, Jr., "The 4 × 4 Plan," and J. O'Neil, "Finding Time to Learn," *Educational Leadership* 53(3):20–22 and 11–15, respectively (November 1995).

15. S. Willis, "Are Longer Classes Better?" *ASCD Update* 35(3):3 (March 1993).

16. See the several articles in the theme issue, "Productive Use of Time and Space," *Educational Leadership* 53(3) (November 1995).

have to carry as many books and may go to their lockers fewer times a day to exchange textbooks and materials between blocks. In many secondary schools, except perhaps in physical education and vocational education, student lockers are not used at all. Because students are not roaming halls for three to five minutes five or six times a day, teachers can more easily supervise unstructured time and thereby have better control over the hidden or unplanned curriculum. (The **hidden curriculum** is the accepted or implied values and attitudes and the unwritten rules of behavior students must learn to participate and to be able to succeed in school.[17]) Also, the reduction of bell ringing from as many as eight times a day to perhaps only two or three times a day or not at all creates less disturbance.

Nontraditional school schedules are not without their problems. The following problems sometimes arise when using block scheduling: (1) content coverage in a course may be less than that in traditional classes, and some teachers and parents have a problem with that; (2) there may be a mismatch between content actually covered and that expected by state-mandated tests and on the dates those tests are given to students; (3) community relations problems may occur if students are out of school and off campus at nontraditional times.

Using a *modified block schedule,* some schools have successfully combined schedules, thus satisfying teachers who prefer block scheduling as well as those who prefer a traditional schedule. A modified block schedule can provide both traditional 40-minute periods that meet daily (sometimes preferred especially by teachers of mathematics and foreign languages) and longer blocks. A modified block schedule centers on seven or eight 40- or 45-minute periods per day but also provides alternate longer blocks. In a modified block schedule all students might start the day with a 30- or 40-minute first period, which serves as a homeroom or advisor/advisee time. From there some students continue the morning by attending traditional-length periods and others move into a morning block class. Throughout the day, teachers and students may pass from block classes to those of traditional length or vice versa. North DeSoto High School (Stonewall, LA), for example, uses a *flexible block schedule.* The daily schedule is a seven-period day with all seven classes meeting on Monday. Periods one through four meet for 75 minutes, and periods five through seven meet for 30 minutes on Mondays. Periods one through four meet for 105 minutes each

on Tuesdays and Thursdays, and periods five through seven meet for 120 minutes each on Wednesdays and Fridays. A special 30-minute period after lunch provides an opportunity for students to attend club meetings or pep rallies, to make up tests, and to receive guidance and counseling or tutorial help.[18]

School Reform and Restructuring

Nontraditional scheduling is part of the effort to restructure schools in order to deliver quality learning to all students. Sometimes it may appear that more energy is devoted to organizational change (*how* the curriculum is delivered) than to school curriculum (*what* is taught). School organization has a direct effect on what students learn; if it didn't, educators wouldn't be spending so much valuable time trying to restructure their schools to effect the most productive delivery of the curriculum—both the planned and the hidden curriculum.

Organizational changes are referred to today as *school restructuring,* a term that has a variety of connotations, including site-based management, collaborative decision making, school choice, personalized learning, integrated curricula, and collegial staffing. School restructuring has been defined as "activities that change fundamental assumptions, practices, and relationships, both within the organization and between the organization and the outside world, in ways leading to improved learning outcomes."[19] No matter how it is defined, educators agree on the following point: the design and functions of schools should reflect the needs of young people who will be in the work force in the twenty-first century, rather than the needs of the nineteenth century. As emphasized by Villars, too many schools are still designed like factories, organized like factories, and run like factories. The purpose of school reform efforts and of school restructuring is to move from that factory model to a more personalized redesign that better reflects the current needs of all students.[20]

From the Industrial Age to the Information Age

Exemplified by efforts mentioned in the preceding discussion, the redesigning of schools into "houses," each with an interdisciplinary team of teachers plus

17. See Chapter 3 of H. Hernández, *Multicultural Education: A Teacher's Guide to Content and Process* (Upper Saddle River, NJ: Prentice Hall, 1989), pp. 45–76, and K. Ryan, "Mining the Values in the Curriculum," *Educational Leadership* 51(3):16–18 (November 1993).

18. Source for North DeSoto High School schedule: Southern Regional Educational Board, *1995 Outstanding Practices* (Atlanta, GA: Southern Regional Educational Board, 1995), p. 22. By permission.

19. D. T. Conley, "Restructuring: In Search of a Definition," *Principal* 72(3):12 (January 1993).

20. J. Villars, *Restructuring Through School Design* (Bloomington, IN: Fastback 322, Phi Delta Kappa Educational Foundation, 1991), pp. 12–13.

School Emphases of the Industrial Age	School Emphases Needed for the Information Age
1. Top-down organizational structure at state, district levels.	1. Decentralization of decision making; participative management; reduction of federal/state regulations; decisions made closest to where action is carried out; clear accountability.
2. Conventional K–12 curriculum (ages 6–18); proliferation of course titles and fragmented curricula; textbook oriented.	2. Earlier, more flexible entry ages (entry on one's birthday at age 4, 5, or 6); age clustering for instruction (4–7, 8–12, 13–15); simplified core curriculum (less is more); integrative/transdisciplinary approaches; continuing education options; global emphasis on world as interdependent community.
3. Fragmented learning time.	3. Flexible scheduling; variable time blocks.
4. Teacher isolation in planning and instruction; limited planning time.	4. Staff organized as teams for planning and instruction; block of time for team/individual planning.
5. Community involvement in school activities.	5. Community/school shared ownership and accountability for carrying out school's purposes.
6. Classroom (cell) model of organization, by age-grade level.	6. House model design, learning task spaces, multiage and multiyear student cohort families; school as experiential place.
7. Tracking and ability grouping.	7. Personalized programming for every student; varied groupings based on task demands and student interests.
8. Minimal teacher expectations and parental aspirations for disadvantaged/at-risk students.	8. High expectations for optimal learning of every student.
9. Promotion based on time spent in school, with little evidence of true accomplishment.	9. Promotion based on performance, using obtainable outcomes with agreed-on standards.
10. Teaching emphasis on low cognitive skills, short-term memory tasks.	10. Teaching emphasis on higher-order reasoning, problem-solving skills.
11. Student as passive consumer of information.	11. Students as active participants in formulating and accomplishing relevant (real-life) objectives.
12. Impersonal student-teacher relationships; emotional flatness of classroom.	12. Teacher as mentor, coach, learning facilitator, providing timely feedback to improve student performance; concern for affective needs of students.
13. Flatness in teachers' salary, few professional growth options.	13. Differential staffing; salary based on roles and responsibilities.
14. Piecemeal tinkering of present structure; focus on maintaining status quo.	14. Systemic approach to organizational change that transforms school.

Figure 1.4
Changes in school emphasis needed for demands of the information age. (*Source:* Adapted from Jerry Villars, *Restructuring Through School Redesign.* [Bloomington, IN: Fastback 322, Phi Delta Kappa Educational Foundation, 1991], pp. 16–18. By permission of the Phi Delta Kappa Educational Foundation.)

additional support personnel, represents a movement that is becoming increasingly common across the country. (Throughout this resource guide we identify schools and their efforts and successes.) This movement is from what has been referred to as a "system of schooling" rooted in the "Industrial Age" toward a design more in touch with the emerging demands of the new millennium, or the "Information Age."[21] The intention of this redesign is that schools will better address the needs and capabilities of each unique student. A number of specific recommended changes, many of which are occurring, are shown in Figure 1.4. As a teacher in the twenty-first century, you will undoubtedly help accomplish many of those changes.

21. Villars, p. 41.

Table 1.1. Summary of Differences Between Junior High and Exemplary Middle Schools

	Junior High School	*Middle School*
Most common grade span	7–8 or 7–9	6–8
Scheduling	Traditional	Flexible, usually block
Subject organization	Departmentalized	Integrated and thematic; interdisciplinary, usually language arts, math, science, and social studies
Guidance/counseling	Separate advising by full-time counselor on individual or "as needed" basis	Adviser-advisee relation between teacher and student within a home base or homeroom
Exploratory curriculum	Electives by individual choice	Common "wheel" of experiences for all students
Teachers	Subject-centered; grades 7–12 certification	Interdisciplinary teams; student-centered; grades K–8 or 6–8 certification
Instruction	Traditional; lecture; skills and repetition	Thematic units; discovery techniques; "learning how to learn" study skills
Athletics	Interscholastic sports emphasizing competition	Intramural programs emphasizing participation

Middle Schools and Junior High Schools

Upon receipt of your teaching certification, you may or may not be certified to teach at the middle school level. In some states a secondary school credential certifies a person to teach a particular subject at any grade level, K through 12. In other states such a credential qualifies a person to teach only grades 7 through 12. In yet other states a middle school teaching credential is received only after successfully completing a teacher preparation program specifically designed to prepare teachers for that level. Although 33 of the 50 states have middle school certification, only about 11 percent of middle school teachers have that certification. Sixty-three percent have secondary credentials, and 26 percent hold elementary credentials. These 1992 data compare with 1981 data that showed that 80 percent of middle-level teachers held secondary credentials, 11 percent held middle-level credentials, and only 9 percent held elementary credentials. The trend toward the holding of elementary credentials by middle-level teachers is probably reflective of the increase in the number of middle schools housing grades 5 and 6.[22]

You should note that there are two sometimes quite different types of schools, both of which are called middle schools. One is the traditional junior high school with perhaps a few minor changes, such as having its name changed to "middle school." The second is the exemplary middle school, which is, as shown in Table 1.1, quite different from the traditional

junior high school. To understand the significance of the middle school, certain background information may prove helpful.

Origin, Evolution, and Contributions of the Middle School

Used historically from about 1880, the term *junior high school* most commonly refers to schools having grades 7 and 8 or grades 7, 8, and 9, in which a program is designed to approximate the type of education commonly found in traditional high schools. Thus, a junior high school might be considered a "not-quite-yet-but-trying-to-be" high school. Students graduating from a junior high school often would then move on to a *senior high school*.

The term *middle school* gained favor as a result of the movement away from the concept of "junior" high school. Brooks and Edwards identify at least three reasons for the reorganization away from the concept of junior high school and the adoption of a middle school education: (1) to provide a program specifically designed for children in this age group, (2) to set up a better transition between the elementary school and the high school, and (3) to move grade 9 to the high school.[23] Although any combination of grades 5 through 9 may be included in a middle school, the most common configuration is grades 6 through 8. Sixth

---

22. Valentine et al., pp. 30–31.

23. K. Brooks and F. Edwards, *The Middle School in Transition: A Research Report on the Status of the Middle School Movement* (Lexington, KY: College of Education, University of Kentucky, 1978).

graders, and even fifth graders, are increasingly becoming a part of middle schools, whereas ninth graders are continuing to be excluded.[24] The trend continues. For example, in California the number of middle schools that include sixth-graders doubled during the decade 1987–1997. Grades 6 to 8 is now the most common grade span inclusion of middle schools in that state.

The term *middle-level education* identifies school organizations based on a philosophy that incorporates curricula and instructional practices specifically designed to meet the needs of children aged 10 to 15. This philosophy is often referred to as the *middle school concept*. The notion that greater and more specific attention should be given to the special needs of young adolescents became known as the *middle school movement*. The middle school movement began to grow in the 1960s, especially with the publication of several books.[25]

Youngsters of middle school age have been given various nomenclatures, including *transescent, preadolescent, preteen, prepubescent, in-betweenager,* and *tweenager.* Eichhorn called this developmental phase *transescence,* defined as follows:

> [Transescence is] the stage of development which begins before the onset of puberty and extends through the early stages of adolescence. Since puberty does not occur for all precisely at the same chronological age in human development, the transescent designation is based on the many physical, social, emotional, and intellectual changes in body chemistry that appear before the time at which the body gains a practical degree of stabilization over these complex pubescent changes.[26]

Although the term used is perhaps inconsequential, some understanding of the various developmental stages associated with this group of youngsters is essential if an educational program and its instruction are to be appropriately tailored to address their needs. That understanding is addressed later in this chapter.

Students at Risk of Not Finishing School

The term *at risk,* is used to identify students who have a high probability of not finishing school. It has been estimated that by the year 2020, the majority of students in the public schools in this country will be at risk.[27] Five categories of factors that cause a child to

be at risk of dropping out of school have been identified: (1) personal pain (exemplified by drugs, physical and psychological abuse, suspension from school), (2) academic failure (exemplified by low grades, academic failure, absences, low self-esteem), (3) family tragedy (exemplified by parent illness or death, health problems), (4) family socioeconomic situation (exemplified by low income, negativism, lack of education), and (5) family instability (exemplified by moving, separation, divorce).[28] Many young people, at any one time, have risk factors from more than one of these categories. A modified school schedule alone, without quality, individualized attention to each student, may be of no value in addressing the needs of students who are at risk of not finishing school.

The restructuring of school schedules, then, represents only one aspect of efforts to help all students achieve. The following other strategies (including attitudes) are important:

1. All teachers and staff should have the perception that all students can learn, although not all students need the same amount of time to learn the same thing.
2. High expectations should be maintained for all students, although not necessarily identical expectations.
3. Individualized attention should be given and scheduling and learning plans created to help students learn in a manner best suited to them. Research clearly points out that achievement increases, students learn more, and students enjoy learning and remember more of what they have learned when individual learning styles and capacities are identified and accommodated. Learning-style traits are known that significantly discriminate between students who are at risk of dropping out of school and students who perform well, discussed in Learning Modalities and Learning Styles in Chapter 2.
4. Parents and guardians should be engaged as partners in their children's education.
5. Extra time and guided attention should be given to basic skills, such as those of thinking, writing, and reading, rather than to rote memory.
6. Specialist teachers and smaller classes should be employed.
7. Peer tutoring and cross-age coaching are useful.
8. Attention to and guidance in the development of coping skills are important.[29]

24. Valentine et al., p. 19.
25. See W. M. Alexander, "The Junior High: A Changing View," in G. Hass and K. Wiles (eds.), *Readings in Curriculum* (Boston: Allyn and Bacon, 1965); D. H. Eichhorn, *The Middle School* (New York: The Center for Applied Research in Education, 1966); and W. M. Alexander, *The Emergent Middle School* (New York: Holt, Rinehart and Winston, 1969).
26. D. H. Eichhorn, *The Middle School* (New York: The Center for Applied Research in Education, 1966), p. 3.
27. R. J. Rossi and S. C. Stringfield, "What We Must Do for Students Placed at Risk," *Phi Delta Kappan* 77(1):73–76 (September 1995).

28. P. L. Tiedt and I. M. Tiedt, *Multicultural Teaching: A Handbook of Activities, Information, and Resources,* 4th ed. (Boston: Allyn and Bacon, 1995), p. 37.
29. See, for example, Tiedt and Tiedt, pp. 37–38; C. Dixon, et al., *Gifted and At Risk* (Bloomington, IN: Fastback 398, Phi Delta Kappa Educational Foundation, 1996), p. 21; and E. S. Foster-Harrison, *Peer Tutoring for K–12 Success* (Bloomington, IN: Fastback 415, Phi Delta Kappa International, 1997).

STUDENTS

The bell rings and the students enter your classroom, a kaleidoscope of personalities, all peerless, each a bundle of eccentricities, different concentrations, different experiences, dispositions, and capacities, differing proficiencies in the use of the English language, different challenges. What a challenge this is—to understand and to teach 30 or so unique individuals, all at once, and to do it for six hours a day, five days a week, 180 days a year! What a challenge it is today to be a secondary school teacher.

The Challenge

Students differ in many ways: physical characteristics, interests, intellectual ability, learning capacities, motor ability, social skills, aptitudes and talents, experience, ideals, attitudes, needs, ambitions, dreams, and hopes. Having long recognized the importance of these individual differences, educators have made many attempts to develop systematic programs of individualized instruction. In the 1920s there were "programmed" workbooks. The 1960s brought a multitude of plans, such as IPI (Individually Prescribed Instruction), IGE (Individually Guided Education), and PLAN (Program for Learning in Accordance with Needs). The 1970s saw the development and growth in popularity of individual learning packages and the Individualized Educational Program (IEP) for students who have disabilities and special needs. Although some of these efforts did not survive the test of time, others met with more success; some have been refined and are still being used. Today, for example, some schools are reporting success in using IEPs for all students.

Furthermore, for a variety of reasons (e.g., learning styles and learning capacities, modality preferences, information-processing habits, motivational factors, and physiological factors), all persons learn in their own ways and at their own rates. Interests, background, innate and acquired abilities, and a myriad of other influences shape how and what a person will learn. From any particular learning experience no two students ever learn exactly the same thing.

There is a rapidly growing knowledge base and interest in the psychological factors of learning and in the possibility of matching students and instructional treatments.[30] A related need is to increase our knowledge about strategies for teaching the number of students from diverse cultural backgrounds and whose primary language may not be English. Consider the following from Banks and Banks:

> Cultural diversity in U.S. schools has deepened considerably during the last two decades. The aging of the mainstream population and the influx of immigrants to the U.S. since the Immigration Reform Act of 1965 have resulted in a rapid rise in the percentage of ethnic, cultural, language, and religious minorities in the nation's schools. One out of three U.S. students will be an ethnic minority by the turn of the century. The civil rights movement of the 1960s and 1970s and the resulting national legislation have increased cultural diversity within the schools and have also made educators more sensitive to the special educational needs of various groups of students, such as females, the disabled, the poor, and students from various language groups.

Today, most teachers have students in their classroom from various ethnic, cultural, religious, language, and social-class groups. They are also likely to have one or more exceptional students in their classes. Such students may be handicapped, gifted, or both. Teachers should be aware of the many needs of students from diverse groups and also sensitive to the special characteristics and needs of female and male students. It is also important for teachers to keep in mind that most students belong to several of these groups . . . (although) for many students one group identification is much more important than all the others.[31]

Multicultural Education

Central to the concept of multicultural education is the recognition and acceptance of students from a great variety of backgrounds. Multicultural education, however, is more than a concept. It is also an educational reform movement and a process with a major goal of changing the structure of educational institutions so that male and female students, exceptional students, and students who are members of diverse racial, ethnic, and cultural groups will have an equal chance to achieve academically in school.[32]

This variety of individual differences among students requires that teachers use teaching strategies and tactics that accommodate those differences. In order to teach students who are different from you, you need skills in (1) establishing a classroom climate in which all students feel welcome, (2) providing a classroom environment in which all students feel that they are welcome and can learn, (3) building upon students' learning styles, capacities, and modalities, (4) using techniques that emphasize cooperative and social-interactive learning and that deemphasize competitive

30. See, for example, R. J. Sternberg, "What Does It Mean to Be Smart?" *Educational Leadership* 54(6):20–24 (March 1997).

31. J. A. Banks and C. A. McGee Banks (eds.), *Multicultural Education: Issues and Perspectives* (Boston: Allyn & Bacon, 1989), p. xi.

32. Banks and Banks, p. 1.

learning, and (5) employing strategies and techniques that have proven successful for students of specific differences. The last skill mentioned is the focus of the next section.

To help you meet the challenge inherent in today's teaching, a wealth of information is available. As a credentialed teacher you are expected to know it all, or at least to know where you can find all necessary information, and to review it when needed. Certain information you have stored in long-term memory will surface and become useful at the most unexpected times. While concerned about all students' safety and physical well-being, you will want to remain sensitive to each student's attitudes, values, social adjustment, emotional well-being, and cognitive development. You must be prepared not only to teach one or more subjects but also to do it effectively with students of different cultural backgrounds, diverse linguistic abilities, and different learning styles, as well as with students who have been identified as having special needs. It is, indeed, a challenge! The statistics given in the paragraphs that follow make even more clear this challenge.

Approximately one-half of the students in the United States will spend some years being raised by a single parent. The traditional two-parent, two-child family now constitutes only about 6 percent of U.S. households. Between one-fourth and one-third of U.S. students go home after school to places devoid of adult supervision. On any given day, it has been estimated that as many as 300,000 children have no place to call home.

In the nation's largest school systems, minority enrollment levels range from 70 to 96 percent. In just a few years, by the year 2010, minority youths in the school-age population throughout the United States will average close to 40 percent. By the year 2050, the nation's population is predicted to increase to 383 million (from today's approximately 252 million). That population boom will be led by Hispanics and Asian Americans, with the nation's white population much less a factor. However, the increase in interracial marriages and interracial babies may challenge current conceptions of multiculturalism and race.[33]

The United States truly is a multilingual, multiethnic, multicultural country. In most states and the District of Columbia, Spanish is now the second most common language, after English. In recent years, the fastest-growing language has been Mon-Khmer, spoken by Cambodians (Figure 1.5).

Of students aged 5 to 7, approximately one of every six speaks a language other than English at home. Many of those students have only limited proficiency in the English language (i.e., conversational speaking ability only). However, limited English proficiency (LEP) is not always their only problem, albeit a huge one, in adjusting to school. For example, immigrant children from Asia, who statistically have tended to excel in school, are increasingly more apt to be from rural and impoverished countries and are therefore, as well as having language adjustments, increasingly likely to have many of the problems associated with poor, disadvantaged youth.[34]

In many large school districts, as many as 100 languages are represented, with as many as 20 or more different primary languages found in some classrooms. But an increasing ethnic, cultural, and linguistic diversity is no longer limited to large metropolitan areas. Increasing diversity is affecting schools across the country, from traditionally homogeneous suburbs to small-town America.

By the time you are reading this book, the number of new immigrants probably has reached 1,000,000 annually, up from the approximately 500,000 annually in 1990 and 972,000 in 1993. The language diversity of students in the school poses special problems for teachers, who use language as a major vehicle for teaching and learning. The overall picture that emerges is a rapidly changing, diverse student population that challenges teaching skills. Teachers who traditionally have used direct instruction (discussed in Chapter 6) as the dominant teaching mode have done so with the assumption that their students were relatively homogeneous in terms of experience, background, knowledge, motivation, and facility with the English language. However, this assumption cannot be made today in classrooms of such cultural, ethnic, and linguistic diversity. *As a teacher for the twenty-first century, you must be knowledgeable of and skilled in using teaching strategies that recognize, celebrate, and build upon that diversity.* In a nutshell, that is the challenge you must meet. The section that follows will help you begin your repertoire of strategies and skill development necessary to meet that challenge.

MEETING THE CHALLENGE: PROVIDING FOR STUDENT DIFFERENCES

From research and practical experience have come a variety of instructional techniques that do make a difference. First consider the following general guide-

---

33. L. Baines, "Future Schlock," *Phi Delta Kappan* 78(7):497 (March 1997).

34. W. Dunn, "Educating Diversity," *American Demographics,* April 1993, p. 40.

Figure 1.5
Most common foreign languages spoken at home in the United States. (*Source:* U.S. Census Bureau survey report number CPH-L-133, "Language Spoken at Home and Ability to Speak English for United States, Regions and States: 1990," Population Division, Statistical Information Office, Census Bureau, Washington, DC.)

Language	Total Speakers Over 5 Years Old in 1990	Percentage Change Since 1980
Spanish	17,339,172	50
French	1,702,176	8
German	1,547,049	−4
Italian	1,308,648	−20
Chinese	1,249,213	98
Tagalog	843,251	87
Polish	723,483	−12
Korean	626,478	127
Vietnamese	507,069	150
Portuguese	429,860	19
Japanese	427,657	25
Greek	388,260	−5
Arabic	355,150	57
Hindi, Urdu, and related	331,484	155
Russian	241,798	39
Yiddish	213,064	−34
Thai	206,266	132
Persian	201,865	85
French Creole	187,658	654
Armenian	149,649	46
Navajo	148,530	21
Hungarian	147,902	−18
Hebrew	144,292	46
Dutch	142,684	−3
Mon-Khmer	127,441	676

lines, most of which are discussed in further detail in later chapters as designated.

Instructional Practice That Provides for Student Differences: General Guidelines

Consider the recommendations that follow and refer to them during the preactive phase of your instruction. (The preactive phase of instruction is discussed at the beginning of Chapter 2.)

- As frequently as is appropriate, plan the learning activities so that they follow a step-by-step sequence from concrete to abstract. (Chapter 6)
- Collaboratively plan with students challenging and engaging classroom learning activities and assignments. (Throughout)
- Concentrate on using student-centered instruction, by using project-centered learning, discovery and inquiry strategies, simulations, and role-play. (Chapters 8 and 9)
- Establish multiple learning centers within the classroom. (Chapter 8)
- Maintain high expectations, although not necessarily identical, for every student; establish high standards

and teach toward them without wavering. (Chapter 3 and throughout)
- Make learning meaningful by integrating learning with life, academic subjects with vocational, helping each student successfully make the transitions from one level of learning to the next, one level of schooling to the next, and from school to life. (Throughout)
- Provide a structured learning environment with regular and understood procedures. (Chapter 3)
- Provide ongoing and frequent monitoring of individual student learning (formative assessment). (Chapters 5, 11, and others)
- Provide learning experiences that are consistent with what is known about various ways of learning and knowing. (Chapters 2, 6, and others)
- Provide variations in meaningful assignments, with optional due dates, that are based on individual student abilities and interests. (Chapter 8)
- Use direct instruction to teach the development of observation, generalization, and other thinking and learning skills. (Chapter 9)
- Use reciprocal peer coaching and cross-age tutoring. (Chapter 8)

- Use small-group and cooperative learning strategies. (Chapter 8)
- Use multilevel instruction. (Chapter 2 and others)
- Use interactive computer programs and multimedia. (Chapter 10)

Appropriate Practice for Specific Learners

Because social awareness is such an important and integral part of a student's experience, many exemplary school programs and much of their practices are geared toward some type of social interaction. Indeed, learning is a social enterprise among learners and their teachers. Although many of today's successful instructional methods rely heavily on social learning activities and interpersonal relationships, each teacher must be aware of and sensitive to individual student differences. For working with specific learners, consider the guidelines that follow and refer to these guidelines during your preactive phase of instruction.

Recognizing and Working with Students with Special Needs

Students with special needs (referred to also as exceptional students) include those with disabling conditions or impairments in any one or more of the following categories: learning, speech or language, mental, emotional, visual, auditory, orthopedic, or other medical needs. To the extent possible, students with special needs must be educated with their peers in the regular classroom. Public Law 94-142, the Education of the Handicapped Act (EHA) of 1975, mandates that all children have the right to a full and free public education, as well as to nondiscriminatory assessment. (Public Law 94-142 was amended in 1986 by P.L. 99-457 and again in 1990 by P.L. 101-476, at which time its name was changed to Individuals with Disabilities Education Act—IDEA.) Emphasizing normalization of the educational environment for students with disabilities, this legislation requires provision of the least restrictive environment (LRE) for these students. An LRE is an environment that is as normal as possible.

Students identified as having special needs may be placed in the regular classroom for the entire school day, called full inclusion (as is the trend[35]). (The term *inclusion* has largely replaced use of an earlier and similar term, *mainstreaming*.) Those students may also be in a regular classroom the greater part of the school day, called partial inclusion, or only for designated periods. Although there is no single, universally accepted definition, it is generally agreed that *inclusion is a commitment to educate each special needs child in the school and, when appropriate, in the class that child would have attended had the child not had a disability*. The underlying assumption "is that inclusion is a way of life, a way of living together, based on a belief that each individual is valued and does belong."[36] As a classroom teacher you will need information and skills specific to teaching learners with special needs who are included in your classes.

Generally speaking, teaching students who have special needs as opposed to other students requires more care, greater skill, more attention to individual needs, and an even greater understanding of the students. The challenges of teaching students with special needs in the regular classroom are great enough that to do it well you need specialized training beyond the general guidelines presented here. At some point in your teacher preparation you should take one or more courses in working with the special needs learner who is included in the regular classroom.

When a student with special needs is placed in your classroom, your task is to deal directly with the differences between this student and other students in your classroom. To do this, you should develop an understanding of the general characteristics of different types of special needs learners, identify the student's unique needs relative to your classroom, and design lessons that teach to different needs at the same time (**multilevel teaching,** or **multitasking,** as discussed in Chapter 2 and elsewhere). Remember that just because a student has been identified as having one or more special needs does not preclude that person from being gifted or talented.

Because of a concern for problems of the special needs child, Congress stipulated in P.L. 94-142 that an Individualized Educational Program (IEP) be devised annually for each special needs child. According to that law, an IEP is developed for each student each year by a team that includes special education teachers, the child's parents or guardians, and the classroom teachers. The IEP contains a statement of the student's present educational levels, the educational goals for the

35. For a review of the history of special education, see R. Schattman and J. Benay, "Inclusive Practices Transform Special Education in the 1990s," *School Administrator* 49(2):8–12 (February 1992). See also Chapter 2 of R. A. Villa and J. S. Thousand (eds.), *Creating an Inclusive School* (Alexandria, VA: Association for Supervision and Curriculum Development, 1995); articles about inclusion in *Phi Delta Kappan* 77(4) (December 1995); about attention deficit disorder in *Phi Delta Kappan* 77(6) (February 1996);

about working with students with disabilities in *Educational Leadership* 53(5) (February 1996); and T. P. Lombardi and B. L. Ludlow, *Trends Shaping the Future of Special Education* (Bloomington, IN: Fastback 409, Phi Delta Kappa Educational Foundation, 1996).
36. T. P. Lombardi, *Responsible Inclusion of Students with Disabilities* (Bloomington, IN: Fastback 373, Phi Delta Kappa Educational Foundation, 1994), p. 7.

year, specifications for the services to be provided and the extent to which the student should be expected to take part in the regular educational program, and the evaluative criteria for the services to be provided. Consultation by special and skilled support personnel is essential in all IEP models. A consultant works directly with teachers or with students and parents. As a classroom teacher, you may play an active role in preparing the specifications for the special needs students assigned to your classroom, as well as assume major responsibility for implementing the program.

Guidelines for Working with Students with Special Needs in the Regular Classroom

Guidelines for working with special needs learners who are wholly or partially included in a regular education classroom follow. Although these guidelines are important for teaching all students, they are especially important for working with special needs students.

Familiarize yourself with exactly what the special needs of each learner are. Privately ask the special needs student whether there is anything he would like for you to know about him and what you specifically can do to facilitate his learning while in your class.

Adapt and modify materials and procedures to the special needs of each student. For example, a student who has extreme difficulty sitting still for more than a few minutes will need planned changes in learning activities. When establishing student seating arrangements in the classroom, give preference to students according to their special needs. Try to incorporate into lessons activities that engage all learning modalities—visual, auditory, tactile, and kinesthetic (discussed in Chapters 2 and 6). Be flexible in your classroom procedures. For example, allow the use of tape recorders for note taking and test taking when students have trouble with the written language.

Break complex learning into simpler components, moving from the most concrete to the abstract rather than the other way around. Check frequently for student understanding of instructions and procedures and for comprehension of content. Use computers and other self-correcting materials for drill and practice and for provision of immediate and private feedback to the student.

Define the learning objectives in behavioral terms (discussed in Chapter 5). This helps to provide high structure and clear expectations.

Develop your withitness (discussed in Chapters 2 and 3). Be aware of everything that is going on in the classroom, at all times, monitoring students for signs of restlessness, frustration, anxiety, and off-task behaviors. Be ready to reassign individual learners to different activities as the situation warrants.

Have students maintain assignments for the week or some other period of time in a folder that is kept in their notebooks. Post assignments in a special place on the bulletin board, and frequently remind students of these and their deadlines.

Maintain consistency in your expectations and in your responses. Special needs learners particularly can become frustrated when they do not understand a teacher's expectations and when they cannot depend on a teacher's reactions.

Plan interesting activities that bridge learning, that is, activities that help the students connect what is being learned with their real world. Learning that connects what is being learned with the real world helps to motivate students and to keep them on task.

Plan questions and questioning sequences and write them into your lesson plans (discussed in Chapter 7). Plan questions that you ask special needs learners so that they are likely to answer them with confidence. Use signals to let students know that you are likely to call on them in class (e.g., prolonged eye contact or mentioning your intention to the student before class begins). After asking a question, give the student adequate time to think and respond. Then, after the student responds, build upon the student's response to indicate that the student's contribution was important.

Provide for and teach toward student success. Offer students activities and experiences that ensure success and mastery at some level. Use of student portfolios (discussed in Chapter 11) can give evidence of progress and help in building student confidence. To help build student self-esteem, make every effort to capitalize on students' strengths and to provide opportunities for success in a supportive classroom environment (see Chapter 3).

Provide guided or coached practice. Provide time in class for students to work on assignments and projects. During this time, you can monitor the work of each student while looking for misconceptions, thus ensuring that students get started on the right track (discussed in Chapter 5).

Provide help in the organization of students' learning. For example, give instruction in the organization of notes and notebooks. Have a three-hole punch available in the classroom so that students can put papers into their notebooks immediately, thus avoiding disorganization and loss of papers. During class presentations use an overhead projector with transparencies; students who need more time can then copy material from the transparencies. Ask students to read their notes aloud to each other in small groups, thereby aiding their recall and understanding and encouraging them to take notes for meaning rather than for rote learning.

Teach students the correct procedures for everything (discussed in Chapter 3).

Encourage and provide for peer support, peer tutoring or coaching, and cross-age teaching (discussed in Chapter 8). Ensure that the special needs learner is included in all class activities to the fullest extent possible.[37]

Recognizing and Working with Students of Diversity and Differences

A teaching credential authorizes you to teach in any public school throughout a state and, in some instances, throughout a region that consists of several states. That means you could find yourself teaching in a school that is ethnically, culturally, linguistically, and socioeconomically diverse. It will be important for you to determine the language and nationality groups represented by the students in your classroom.

A major problem for recent immigrant students, as well as some ethnic groups, is learning a second (or third or fourth) language. Although in many schools it is not uncommon for more than half the students to come from homes where the native language is not English, standard English is a necessity in most communities of this country if a person is to become vocationally successful and enjoy a full life. Learning to communicate reasonably well in English can take an immigrant student at least a year and probably longer; some authorities say it takes three to seven years. By default, then, an increasing number of teachers are teachers of English language learning. Success in teaching students who have limited English proficiency (LEP) requires the use of hands-on learning and cooperative learning (discussed in Chapters 6 and 8).

Numerous programs are specially designed for working with English as a second language (ESL) learners. Most ESL programs use the acronym LEP with 5 number levels:

- LEP 1 is non–English-speaking, although the student may understand single sentences and speak only simple words or phrases in English.
- LEP 2 is used for the student who speaks, reads, and writes English only with considerable help.
- LEP 3 is used for the student who understands spoken English rather well but is considerably below age/grade level in reading and writing skills.
- LEP 4 is for the student who speaks and understands English with acceptable proficiency and whose reading and writing skills are near age/grade level.
- LEP 5, sometimes designated FEP (fluent English proficient), is for the student who is fully fluent in English, although the student's overall academic achievement may still be low because of language or cultural differences.[38]

Some schools use a pullout approach, where the student's school time is divided between special bilingual classes and regular classrooms. In some schools, LEP students are placed in academic classrooms that use a simplified or "sheltered" English approach, sometimes called a bilingual immersion approach or a cognitive academic language learning approach (CALLA).[39] Regardless of the program, specific techniques used in working with ESL students include:

- Allowing more time for learning activities than one normally would.
- Allowing time for translation by a classroom aide or by a classmate and allowing time for discussion to clarify meaning, encouraging the students to transfer into English what they already know in their native language.
- Avoiding jargon or idioms that might be misunderstood.
- Dividing complex or extended language discourse into smaller, more manageable units.
- Giving directions in a variety of ways.
- Giving special attention to key words that convey meaning and writing them on the board.
- Reading written directions aloud and then writing them on the board.
- Speaking clearly and naturally but at a slower than normal pace.
- Using a variety of examples and observable models.
- Using simplified vocabulary but without talking down to students.[40]

Additional Guidelines for Working with Language Minority Students

While they are becoming literate in English-language usage, LEP students can learn the same curriculum in the various disciplines as native English-speaking students.[41] To help you work effectively with LEP students, additional guidelines are presented here. Although these guidelines are important for teaching

---

37. See L. Farlow, "A Quartet of Success Stories: How to Make Inclusion Work," *Educational Leadership* 53(5):51–55 (April 1996), and other articles in the theme issue of "Students with Special Needs."

38. D. R. Walling, *English as a Second Language: 25 Questions and Answers* (Bloomington, IN: Fastback 347, Phi Delta Kappa Educational Foundation, 1993), pp. 12–13. By permission of the Phi Delta Kappa Educational Foundation.

39. See R. Gersten, "The Double Demands of Teaching English Language Learners," *Educational Leadership* 53(5):18–22 (February 1996).

40. Walling, p. 26. Adapted by permission of the Phi Delta Kappa Educational Foundation.

41. C. Minicucci et al., "School Reform and Student Diversity," *Phi Delta Kappan* 77(1):77–80 (September 1995).

all students, they are especially important when working with language minority students.

Present instruction that is concrete and includes the most direct learning experiences possible. Use the most concrete (least abstract) forms of instruction (see Chapter 6).

Build upon (or connect with) what the students already have experienced and know. Building upon what students already know, or think they know, helps them to connect their knowledge and construct their understandings.

Encourage student writing. One way is by using student journals (see Chapter 8). Two kinds of journals are appropriate when working with LEP students: dialogue journals and response journals. In dialogue journals students write anything that is on their minds, usually on the right page. Teachers, parents, and classmates then respond on the left page, thereby "talking with" the journal writers. In response journals students write (record) their responses to what they are reading or studying.[42]

Help students learn the vocabulary. Assist the LEP students in learning two vocabulary sets: the regular English vocabulary needed for learning and the new vocabulary introduced by the subject content. For example, while learning science a student is dealing with both the regular English-language vocabulary and the special vocabulary of science.

Involve parents, guardians, or older siblings. Students whose primary language is not English may have other differences about which you will also need to become knowledgeable. These differences are related to culture, customs, family life, and expectations. To be most successful in working with language minority students, you should learn as much as possible about each student. To this end it can be valuable to solicit the help of the student's parent, guardian, or even an older sibling. Parents (or guardians) of new immigrant children are usually truly concerned about the education of their children and may be very interested in cooperating with you in any way possible. In one study of eight schools recognized for their exemplary practices with language-minority students, the schools were recognized for being "parent friendly," that is, for welcoming parents in a variety of innovative ways.[43]

Learn as much as possible about the student's native language. At the start of a science lesson to middle school students, all of whom were Hispanic, one teacher, for example, told the class they were going to use a model and asked them what the Spanish word for

model was. Then, for the rest of the lesson she used the Spanish word rather than the English word *model*. This example of reciprocal teaching helped establish rapport with the students, demonstrating to the students that she was interested in them and their language.

Plan for and use all learning modalities. In working with language minority students, you need to use multisensory approaches, learning activities that involve students in auditory, visual, tactile, and kinesthetic learning modalities.

Use small-group cooperative learning. Cooperative learning strategies are particularly effective with language minority students because they provide opportunities for students to produce language in a setting that is less threatening than is speaking before the entire class.[44]

Use the benefits afforded by modern technology. For example, computer networking allows the language minority students to write and communicate with peers from around the world as well as to participate in "publishing" their classroom work. (See Chapters 5 and 11.)

Additional Guidelines for Working with Students of Diverse Backgrounds

To be compatible with and be able to teach students who come from backgrounds different from yours, you need to believe that all students *can* learn, regardless of gender, social class, physical characteristics, language, and ethnic or cultural backgrounds. You also need to develop special skills, presented in the following guidelines and discussed in detail in other chapters. To work successfully and most effectively with students of diverse backgrounds, you should:

- Build the learning around students' individual learning styles (Chapter 2).
- Communicate positively with every student and with the student's parents or guardians, learning as much as you can about the student and the student's culture and encouraging family members to participate in the student's learning. Involve parents, guardians, and other members of the community in the educational program so that all have a sense of ownership and responsibility and feel positive about the school program (discussed later in this chapter and in Chapter 11).
- Establish a classroom climate in which each student feels she can learn and wants to learn (Chapter 3).
- Establish and maintain high expectations, although not necessarily the same expectations, for each student. Both you and your students must understand that intelligence is not a fixed entity but a set of characteristics that can be developed through a feeling of "I can" and with proper coaching.

---

42. See K. M. Johns and C. Espinoza, *Mainstreaming Language Minority Children in Reading and Writing* (Bloomington, IN: Fastback 340, Phi Delta Kappa Educational Foundation, 1992).

43. Minicucci et al., p. 78.

44. Minicucci et al., p. 78.

- Involve students in understanding and in making important decisions about their own learning so that they feel ownership (i.e., a sense of empowerment and connectedness) of that learning.
- Personalize learning for each student, much like what is done by using the IEP with special needs learners.
- Provide learning activities adapted to individual students.
- Teach to individuals by using a variety of strategies to achieve an objective or by using several objectives at the same time (multilevel teaching).
- Use techniques that emphasize collaborative and cooperative learning and deemphasize competitive learning.

Recognizing and Working with Students Who Are Gifted

Sometimes neglected in the regular classroom are the students who have special talents. There is no singularly accepted method for identification of these students. For placement in special classes or programs for the gifted and talented, school districts traditionally used standard intelligence quotient (IQ) testing. On the other hand, gifted young people sometimes are unrecognized, and they also are sometimes among the students most at risk of dropping out of school.[45] Studies indicate that between 10 and 20 percent of students who do not complete high school are students who are in the range of being intellectually gifted.[46]

To work most effectively with gifted learners, you must first identify their giftedness. The following types of students and the problems they may have—that is, personal behaviors that may identify them as being gifted but academically disabled, bored, and alienated—may assist you in understanding who is gifted.

- *Antisocial* students, alienated by their differences from peers, may become bored and impatient troublemakers.
- *Creative, high achievers* often feel isolated, weird, and deeply depressed.
- *Divergent thinkers* can develop self-esteem problems when they provide answers that are logical to them but seem unusual to their classmates. They may have only a few peer friends.

- *Perfectionists* may exhibit compulsive behaviors because they feel as though their value comes from their accomplishments. When their accomplishments do not live up to their own expectations or those of their parents or teachers, anxiety and feelings of inadequacy arise. When other students do not live up to the gifted student's high standards, alienation from those students is probable.
- *Sensitive* students who also are gifted may become easily depressed because they are more aware of their surroundings and of their differences.
- *Students with special needs* may be gifted. Attention deficit disorder, dyslexia, hyperactivity, and other learning disorders sometimes mask giftedness.
- *Underachievers* can also be gifted students but fail in their studies because they learn in ways that have never been challenged by classroom teachers. Although often expected to excel in everything they do, most gifted students can be underachievers in some areas. Having high expectations of themselves, underachievers tend to be highly critical of themselves, develop low self-esteem, and can become indifferent and even hostile.[47]

Providing Meaningful Curriculum Options

Students who are gifted in some way need a challenging learning environment.[48] Although grouping and tracking students into classes based on interest and demonstrated ability are still widely practiced, an overwhelming abundance of sources in the literature adamantly opposes the homogeneous grouping of students according to ability, or **curriculum tracking,** as it has long been known.[49] Grouping and tracking do not seem to increase overall achievement of learning, but they do promote inequity.[50] Although most research studies conclude that tracking as has been traditionally practiced should be discontinued because of its discriminatory and damaging effects on students, many schools continue using it. They may do this either directly, by counseling students into classes according to evidence of ability and the degree of academic rigor of the program, or indirectly, by designating certain classes and programs as "college prep" and

45. C. Dixon, L. Mains, and M. J. Reeves, *Gifted and At Risk* (Bloomington, IN: Fastback 398, Phi Delta Kappa Educational Foundation, 1996), p. 7.

46. S. B. Rimm, "Underachievement Syndrome: A National Epidemic," in N. Colangelo and G. A. Davis (eds.), *Handbook of Gifted Education,* 2nd ed. (Needham Heights, MA: Allyn & Bacon, 1997), p. 416.

47. Adapted from Dixon, Mains, and Reeves, pp. 9–12. By permission of the Phi Delta Kappa Educational Foundation.

48. K. B. Rogers and R. D. Kimpston, "Acceleration, What We Do vs. What We Know," *Educational Leadership* 50(2):58–61 (October 1992), p. 58.

49. See Valentine, pp. 56–60.

50. See J. Oakes et al., "Equity Lessons from Detracking Schools," in A. Hargreaves (ed.), *Rethinking Educational Change with Heart and Mind* (Alexandria, VA: ASCD 1997 Yearbook, Association for Supervision and Curriculum Development, 1997), pp. 43–72.

others as "non–college prep" and allowing students some degree of latitude to choose, either partly or wholly, from one or the other.[51]

Because of research about how students learn and about intelligences (as discussed in Chapter 2), the trend today is to assume that each student, to some degree and in some area of learning and doing, has the potential for giftedness and to provide sufficient curriculum options so each student can reach those potentials. Clearly, achievement in school increases and students learn more, enjoy learning, and remember more of what they have learned when individual learning capacities, styles, and modalities are identified and accommodated.[52]

To provide relevant curriculum options, a trend is to eliminate from the curriculum what have traditionally been the lower and general curriculum tracks and instead provide curriculum options that try to ensure success for all students. Most experts agree that secondary schools should be "organized around non-tracked, thematic programs of student design to prepare all students for entry into both higher education and high-skill employment through intellectually rigorous practical education."[53]

While attempting to diminish the discriminatory and damaging effects on students believed to be caused by tracking and homogeneous ability grouping, educators have devised and are refining numerous other seemingly more productive ways of attending to student differences, of providing a more challenging learning environment, and of stimulating the talents and motivation of each student. These methods are shown in Figure 1.6, most of which are discussed throughout this resource guide. Check the Index for topic locations.

Guidelines for Working with Gifted Students

When working in the regular classroom with students who have special intellectual gifts and talents, you should:

- Emphasize skills in critical thinking, problem solving, and inquiry.
- Identify and showcase the students' special gifts or talents.

---

51. For a research-based argument for the elimination of or severe reduction in the use of tracking and ability grouping as traditionally practiced, see A. Gamoran, "Is Ability Grouping Equitable?" *Educational Leadership* 50(2):11–17 (October 1992) and other related articles in that issue. For patterns of grouping students in middle-level schools, see Valentine, 1993, pp. 56–60.

52. Dixon, Mains, and Reeves, p. 21.

53. See, for example, S. Goldberger and R. Kazis, "Revitalizing High Schools," *Phi Delta Kappan* 77(8):550 (April 1996), and A. Penn and D. Williams, *Integrating Academic and Vocational Education: A Model for Secondary Schools* (Alexandria, VA: Association for Supervision and Curriculum Development, 1997).

- Allowing a student to attend a high school class while still in middle school or to attend college classes while still in high school
- Allowing a student to skip a grade, thereby accelerating the time a student passes through the grades
- Community service project learning
- Cooperative learning in the classroom
- Individualized educational plans and instruction
- Integrating new technologies into the curriculum
- Interdisciplinary teaming and thematic instruction
- Nongraded or multiage grouping
- Peer and cross-age teaching
- Preparing students simultaneously for the workplace and postsecondary education
- Problem-centered learning
- Specialized schools and block schedules
- Within-class and across discipline student-centered projects

Figure 1.6
Productive ways of attending to student differences, of providing a more challenging learning environment, and of stimulating the talents and motivation of each student.

- Involve the students in selecting and planning activities, encouraging the development of the students' leadership skills.
- Use curriculum compacting, a process that allows a student who already knows the material to pursue enriched or accelerated study. Plan and provide optional and voluntary enrichment activities. Self-instructional packages, learning centers, special projects, and computer and multimedia activities are excellent tools for provision of enriched learning activities.
- Plan assignments and activities that challenge the students to the fullest of their abilities. This does *not* mean overloading them with homework. Rather, carefully plan so that the students' time spent on assignments and activities is quality time on meaningful learning.
- Provide in-class seminars for students to discuss topics and problems that they are pursuing individually or as members of a learning team.
- Provide independent and dyad learning opportunities. Gifted and talented students often prefer to work alone or with another gifted student.
- Use preassessments (diagnostic evaluation) for reading level and subject content achievement so that you are better able to prescribe objectives and activities for each student.
- Work with individual students in some planning of their own objectives and activities for learning.

Recognizing and Working with Students Who Take More Time But Are Willing to Try

Secondary school students who are slower to learn typically fall into one of two categories: those who try to learn but simply need more time to do it and those who do not try, referred to variously as underachievers, recalcitrant learners, or reluctant learners. The same teaching strategies do not always work well for both categories of students, making life difficult for a teacher of 30 students, half who try and half who don't.[54] It is worse still for a teacher of 30 students of various types—some who try but need time, one or two who are academically talented, a few who are LEP students, and several who not only seem unwilling to try but who are also disruptive in the classroom.

Remember that just because a student is slow to learn doesn't mean that the student is less intelligent; some students just plain take longer, for any number of reasons. The following guidelines may be helpful when working with a slow student who has indicated willingness to try:

- Adjust your instruction to the student's preferred learning style, which may be different from yours.
- Be less concerned with the amount of content coverage than with the student's successful understanding of content that is covered.
- Discover something the student does exceptionally well, or a special interest, and try to build on that.
- Emphasize basic communication skills, such as speaking, listening, reading, and writing, to ensure that the student's skills in these areas are sufficient for learning the intended content.
- Help the student learn content in small sequential steps with frequent comprehension checks.
- If necessary, help the student to improve his or her reading skills, such as pronunciation, word meanings, and comprehension.
- If using a single textbook, be certain that the reading level is adequate for the student; if it is not, use other more appropriate reading materials for that student.
- Maximize the use of in-class, on-task work and cooperative learning, with close monitoring of the student's progress. Avoid relying much on successful completion of traditional out-of-class assignments unless the student gets coached guidance by you before leaving your classroom.

---

54. R. D. Kellough, "The Humanistic Approach: An Experiment in the Teaching of Biology to Slow Learners in High School—An Experiment in Classroom Experimentation," *Science Education* 54(3):253–262 (1970).

- Vary the instructional strategies, using a variety of activities to engage the visual, verbal, tactile, and kinesthetic modalities.
- When appropriate, use frequent positive reinforcement, with the intention of increasing the student's self-esteem.

Recognizing and Working with Recalcitrant Students

For working with recalcitrant learners you can use many of the same guidelines from the preceding list, but you should understand that the reasons for these students' behaviors may be quite different from those for slow learners who are willing to try. Slower-learning students who are willing to try are simply that—slower learning. They may be slow because of their learning style or because of genetic reasons, or a combination of the two. But they can and will learn. Recalcitrant learners, on the other hand, may be generally quick and bright thinkers but reluctant even to try because of a history of failure, a history of boredom with school, a poor self-concept, severe personal problems that distract from school, or any variety and combination of reasons, many of which are psychological in nature.

Whatever the case, you need to know that a student identified as being a slow or recalcitrant learner might, in fact, be quite gifted or talented in some way but because of personal problems may have a history of increasingly poor school attendance, poor attention to schoolwork, and an attitude problem. Consider the following guidelines when working with recalcitrant learners:

- At the beginning, learn as much about each student as you can. Be cautious in how you do it, though, because many of these students will be suspicious of any genuine interest in them shown by you. Be businesslike, trusting, genuinely interested, and patient. A second caution is although you learn as much as possible about each student, what has happened in the past is that—past history. Use it not as ammunition, something to be held against the student, but as insight to help you work more productively with the student.
- Avoid lecturing to these students; it won't work.
- Early in the school term, preferably with the help of adult volunteers (e.g., professional community members as mentors have worked well at helping change the student's attitude from rebellion to one of hope, challenge, and success), work out an Individual Educational Program (IEP) with each student.
- Engage the students in learning by using interactive media, such as via the Internet.

- Engage the students in active learning with real-world problem solving and perhaps community service projects.
- Forget about trying to cover everything about the subject being taught. Concentrate instead on student learning of some things well. A good procedure is to use thematic teaching and divide the theme into short segments. Because school attendance for these students is sometimes sporadic, try to individualize their assignments so that they can pick up where they left off and move through the course in an orderly fashion even when they have been absent excessively. Make sure that each student experiences learning success.
- Help students develop their studying and learning skills, such as concentrating, remembering, and comprehension. Mnemonics, for example, is a device these students respond to positively, and they are often quick to devise their own. (For examples, see section D of Chapter 9.)
- If using a single textbook, be certain that the reading level is appropriate; if it is not, select other more appropriate reading materials for that student.
- Make sure your classroom procedures and rules are understood at the beginning of the school term and be consistent about enforcing them.
- Maximize the use of in-class, on-task work and cooperative learning, with close monitoring of the student's progress. Do not rely on successful completion of traditional out-of-class assignments unless the student gets coached guidance from you before leaving your classroom.
- Use simple language in the classroom. Be less concerned about the words the students use and the way they use them and more concerned about the ideas they are expressing. Let the students use their own idioms without carping on grammar and syntax. Always take care, though, to use proper and professional English yourself.
- When appropriate, use frequent positive reinforcement, with the intention of increasing the student's sense of personal worth. When using praise for reinforcement, however, be sure to praise the deed rather than the student (see discussion of using praise in Chapter 2).

For additional guidelines for working with students who are at risk, see Learning Modalities and Learning Styles in Chapter 2.

Attitude Development

Reminiscent of the 1930s and the late 1960s, there is a resurgence of national interest in the development of students' values, especially those of honesty, kindness, respect, and responsibility. Today this interest is in what is called "character education."[55] Whether defined as ethics, citizenship, moral values, or personal development, character education has long been a part of public education in this country.[56] Stimulated by a perceived need to reduce students' antisocial behaviors and to produce more respectful and responsible citizens, many schools and districts today are developing curricula in character education with the ultimate goal of "developing mature adults capable of responsible citizenship and moral action."[57]

Teachers can teach toward positive character development in two general ways: by providing a conducive classroom atmosphere where students actively and positively share in the decision making and by being models that students can emulate. Acquiring knowledge and developing understanding can enhance the learning of attitudes. Nevertheless, changing an attitude is often a long and tedious process, requiring the commitment of the teacher and the provision of numerous experiences that will guide students to new convictions. Here are some specific techniques:

- Build a sense of community in the classroom, with shared goals, optimism, cooperative efforts, and clearly identified and practiced procedures for reaching those goals. (See Chapter 3.)
- Collaboratively plan with students action- and community-oriented projects that relate to curriculum themes, and solicit parent and community members to assist in projects. (See Chapter 8.)
- Teach students to negotiate; practice and develop skills in conflict resolution.[58]
- Have students research and present their viewpoint by advocating a particular stance on a controversial issue.[59]
- Share and highlight examples of class and individual cooperation in serving the classroom, school, and community.

---

55. See, for example, A. Kohn, "How Not to Teach Values: A Critical Look at Character Education," *Phi Delta Kappan* 78(6):429–439 (February 1997).
56. K. Burrett and T. Rusnak, *Integrated Character Education* (Bloomington, IN: Fastback 351, Phi Delta Kappa Educational Foundation, 1993); T. Lickona, "The Return of Character Education," *Educational Leadership* 51(3):6–11 (November 1993); and E. A. Wynne and K. Ryan, *Reclaiming Our Schools: A Handbook on Teaching Character, Academics, and Discipline* (Upper Saddle River, NJ: Prentice Hall, 1993).
57. Burrett and Rusnak, p. 15.
58. See D. W. Johnson and R. T. Johnson, *Reducing School Violence Through Conflict Resolution* (Alexandria, VA: Association for Supervision and Curriculum Development, 1995).
59. See Chapter 11 of Johnson and Johnson, pp. 104–111.

- Make student service projects visible in the school and community.[60]
- Promote higher-order thinking about value issues through the development of skills in questioning.
- Sensitize students to issues through role play, simulations, and creative drama.

Adolescent Years: The Time of Growing Up

The years of adolescence, ages 10 to 18, are years of rapid change, the time of growing up. Historically, young adolescents between the ages of 10 and 15 have represented a particularly troublesome age for many teachers. This is the age of middle school and junior high school students. Because boys and girls do not change overnight just because they have graduated from middle school to high school, an awareness of the general characteristics of young adolescents provides understanding not only of them but also, by inference, of older adolescents—students of high school age.

Developmental Characteristics of Young Adolescents and Their Implications for Developmentally Appropriate Practice

From many years of experience and research, experts have come to accept certain precepts about young adolescents. These are developmental characteristics of young adolescents regardless of their individual genetic or cultural differences. Subsequently, these characteristics are presented in five developmental categories: intellectual, physical, psychological, social, and moral and ethical.[61] Each category is accompanied by practices that are developmentally appropriate, especially, although not exclusively, for middle-level curriculum and instruction.[62]

It is well known that even older high school students (as well as college students and adults) will revert to young adolescent behaviors, especially when confronted with perplexing and stressful situations. Some researchers refer to this mental phenomenon as *downshifting*.[63]

The following conditions can induce situational downshifting, creating conditions under which the search for meaningful learning and understanding is sabotaged: (1) prespecified "correct" outcomes have been established for the learner; (2) what is learned does not connect well with what students already know or think they know; (3) rewards and/or punishments are externally controlled and relatively immediate; (4) time lines are too restrictive and inflexible; and (5) the work to be done is relatively unfamiliar, with little or no support available for doing it.[64]

Intellectual Development

Young adolescents tend to:

1. Be egocentric; argue to convince others; exhibit independent, critical thought.
2. Be intellectually at risk; that is, they face decisions that have the potential to effect major academic values with lifelong consequences.
3. Be intensely curious.
4. Consider academic goals as a secondary level of priority, whereas personal-social concerns dominate thoughts and activities.
5. Display a wide range of individual intellectual development as their minds experience change from the concrete-manipulatory stage to the capacity for abstract thought. This change makes possible:
   a. Ability to project thought into the future, to expect, and to formulate goals.
   b. Analysis of the power of a political ideology.
   c. Appreciation for the elegance of mathematical logic expressed in symbols.
   d. Consideration of ideas contrary to fact.
   e. Insight into the nuances of poetic metaphor and musical notation.
   f. Insight into the sources of previously unquestioned attitudes, behaviors, and values.
   g. Interpretation of larger concepts and generalizations of traditional wisdom expressed through sayings, axioms, and aphorisms.
   h. Propositional thought.
   i. Reasoning with hypotheses involving two or more variables.
6. Experience the phenomenon of **metacognition**—that is, the ability to think about one's thinking and to know what one knows and does not know.
7. Exhibit strong willingness to learn what they consider to be useful and enjoy using skills to solve real-life problems.
8. Prefer active over passive learning experiences; favor interaction with peers during learning activities.

60. See J. Van Til, "Facing Inequality and the End of Work," *Educational Leadership* 54(6):78–81 (March 1997).
61. These characteristics were adapted from *Caught in the Middle: Educational Reform for Young Adolescents in California Public Schools* (Sacramento, CA: California State Department of Education, 1987), pp. 144–148. See also "Characteristics of Young Adolescents," in *This We Believe: Developmentally Responsive Middle Level Schools* (Columbus, OH: National Middle School Association, 1995), pp. 35–40.
62. The implications are adapted from J. Wiles and J. Bondi, *The Essential Middle School*, 2nd ed. (Upper Saddle River, NJ: Prentice Hall, 1993), pp. 29–34. By permission of Prentice Hall.
63. See J. Abbott, "To Be Intelligent," and C. R. Pool, "Maximizing Learning: A Conversation with Renate Nummela Caine," *Educational Leadership* 54(6):6–10 and 11–15 (respectively) (March 1997).

64. R. Nummela Caine and G. Caine, *Education on the Edge of Possibility* (Alexandria, VA: Association for Supervision and Curriculum Development, 1997), pp. 41–42.

IMPLICATIONS FOR DEVELOPMENTALLY APPROPRIATE PRACTICE. Regarding the intellectual development of young adolescents, developmentally appropriate actions include:

- The use of a wide variety of approaches and materials for instruction.
- Individualized subjects. Skill grouping is flexible. Students are treated at their own intellectual levels, providing immediate rather than remote goals.
- A program of learning that is exciting and meaningful, that encourages physical movement, with small-group discussions, learning centers, and creative dramatics.
- Curricula organized around real-life concepts (e.g., conflict, competition, peer-group influence). Activities in formal and informal situations that are designed to improve reasoning powers. Studies of the community and environment are particularly relevant to this age level.
- Organized discussions of ideas and feelings in peer groups to facilitate self-understanding. Provision of experiences for individuals to express themselves by writing and participating in dramatic productions.
- Opportunities for enjoyable studies in the arts. Encouragement of self-expression in all subjects.

Physical Development
Young adolescents tend to:

1. Be concerned about their physical appearance.
2. Be physically at risk; major causes of death are homicide, suicide, accident, and leukemia.
3. Experience accelerated physical development marked by increases in weight, height, heart size, lung capacity, and muscular strength.
4. Experience biological development five years sooner than adolescents of the nineteenth century; since then, the average age of menarche has dropped from 17 to 12 years of age.
5. Experience bone growth faster than muscle development; uneven muscle/bone development results in lack of coordination and awkwardness; bones may lack protection of covering muscles and supporting tendons.
6. Experience fluctuations in basal metabolism, which at times can cause either extreme restlessness or listlessness.
7. Face responsibility for sexual behavior before full emotional and social maturity has occurred.
8. Have ravenous appetites and peculiar tastes; may overtax digestive system with large quantities of improper foods.
9. Lack physical health; have poor levels of endurance, strength, and flexibility; as a group they are fatter and less healthy than older or younger groups.
10. Mature at varying rates of speed. Girls are often taller than boys for the first two years of early adolescence and are ordinarily more physically developed than boys.
11. Reflect a wide range of individual differences that begin to appear in prepubertal and pubertal stages of development. Boys tend to lag behind girls at this stage, and there are marked individual differences in physical development for both boys and girls. The greatest variation in physiological development and size occurs at about age 13.
12. Show changes in body contour, including temporarily large noses, protruding ears, long arms; have posture problems.

IMPLICATIONS FOR DEVELOPMENTALLY APPROPRIATE PRACTICE. Regarding the physical development of young adolescents, developmentally appropriate actions include:

- A health and science curriculum that emphasizes self-understanding about body changes. Guidance counseling and community resource persons to help students understand what is happening to their bodies.
- Adaptive physical education classes to build physical coordination. Equipment to help students develop their small and large muscles.
- Opportunities for interaction among students of different ages, but with an avoidance of situations in which physical development can be compared (e.g., communal showers).
- Emphasis on intramural programs rather than interscholastic athletics.
- Provision for daily exercise and a place where students can be children by playing and being noisy for short periods.
- Encouragement of activities such as special-interest classes and hands-on activities.
- Allowing students to move around physically in classes rather than to sit for long periods of passive work.
- Snacks to satisfy between-meal hunger as well as nutritional guidance specific to this age group.

Psychological Development
Young adolescents tend to:

1. Be easily offended and are sensitive to criticism of personal shortcomings.
2. Be erratic and inconsistent in their behavior; anxiety and fear are contrasted with periods of bravado; feelings shift between superiority and inferiority.
3. Be moody, restless; often feel self-conscious and alienated; lack self-esteem; are introspective.
4. Be optimistic, hopeful.

5. Be psychologically at risk; at no other point in human development is an individual likely to meet so much diversity in relation to self and others.
6. Be searching for adult identity and acceptance even in the midst of intense peer-group relationships.
7. Be searching to form a conscious sense of individual uniqueness—"Who am I?"
8. Be vulnerable to naive opinions, one-sided arguments.
9. Exaggerate simple occurrences and believe that personal problems, experiences, and feelings are unique to themselves.
10. Have an emerging sense of humor based on increased intellectual ability to see abstract relationships; appreciate the double entendre.
11. Have chemical and hormonal imbalances, which often trigger emotions that are frightening and poorly understood; may regress to more childish behavior patterns at this point.

IMPLICATIONS FOR DEVELOPMENTALLY APPROPRIATE PRACTICE. Regarding the psychological development of young adolescents, developmentally appropriate actions include:

- Encouragement of self-assessment.
- Activities designed to allow students to play out their emotions.
- Helping students to understand their feelings of superiority and inferiority.
- Avoiding the pressuring of students by adults in the school to explain their emotions. Occasional child-like behavior is not ridiculed. Sarcasm by adults is avoided.
- Encouragement of students to assume leadership in group discussions and to experience frequent success and recognition for personal efforts and achievement.
- A general atmosphere of friendliness, relaxation, concern, and group cohesiveness.
- Numerous opportunities to release emotional stress.
- Use of sociodrama to enable students to see themselves as others see them.
- Readings that deal with problems similar to their own to help them see that many of their problems are not unique.

Social Development
Young adolescents tend to:

1. Act out unusual or drastic behavior at times; may be aggressive, daring, boisterous, argumentative.
2. Be confused and frightened by new school settings that are large and impersonal.
3. Be fiercely loyal to peer-group values; sometimes cruel or insensitive to those outside the peer group.

4. Be impacted by the high level of mobility in society; may become anxious and disoriented when peer-group ties are broken because of family relocation.
5. Be rebellious toward parents but still strongly dependent on parental values; want to make their own choices, but the authority of the family is a critical factor in final decisions.
6. Be socially at risk. Adult values are largely shaped conceptually during adolescence; negative interactions with peers, parents, and teachers may compromise ideals and commitments.
7. Challenge authority figures; test limits of acceptable behavior.
8. Experience low-risk trust relationships with adults who show lack of sensitivity to adolescent characteristics and needs.
9. Experience often traumatic conflicts because of conflicting loyalties to peer group and family.
10. Refer to peers as sources for standards and models of behavior. Media heroes and heroines are also singularly important in shaping both behavior and fashion.
11. Sense the negative impact of adolescent behaviors on parents and teachers; realize the thin edge between tolerance and rejection. Feelings of adult rejection can drive the adolescent into the relatively secure social environment of the peer group.
12. Strive to define sex role characteristics; search to set up positive social relationships with members of the same and opposite sex.
13. Want to know and feel that significant adults, including parents and teachers, love and accept them; need frequent affirmation.

IMPLICATIONS FOR DEVELOPMENTALLY APPROPRIATE PRACTICE. Regarding the social development of young adolescents, developmentally appropriate actions include:

- An active student government that allows students to establish their own standards and guidelines for dress and behavior.
- Plans that encourage students to engage in service activities (e.g., peer tutoring and community projects).
- Flexible teaching patterns so students can interact with a variety of adults with whom they identify.
- Large-group activities rather than boy-girl events.

Moral and Ethical Development
Young adolescents tend to:

1. Ask broad, unanswerable questions about the meaning of life; not expect absolute answers but are turned off by trivial adult responses.

2. Be at risk in the development of moral and ethical choices and behaviors; depend on the influences of home and church for moral and ethical development; explore the moral and ethical issues that are met in the curriculum, in the media, and in daily interactions with their families and peer groups.
3. Be idealistic; have a strong sense of fairness in human relationships.
4. Be reflective, introspective, and analytical about their thoughts and feelings.
5. Experience thoughts and feelings of awe and wonder related to their expanding intellectual and emotional awareness.
6. Face hard moral and ethical questions for which they are unprepared to cope.

IMPLICATIONS FOR DEVELOPMENTALLY APPROPRIATE PRACTICE.   Regarding the moral and ethical development of young adolescents, developmentally appropriate actions include:

- Encouraging mature value systems by providing opportunities for students to examine options of behavior and to study consequences of various actions.
- Providing opportunities for students to accept responsibility in setting standards for behavior.
- Helping students to develop values when solving their problems.

When planning curriculum and devising instructional methods, middle school teachers and curriculum developers must take into account these common characteristics and their implications for developmentally appropriate practice. From their studies of schools, researchers conclude that the curricula of exemplary middle schools are designed around the following categories of needs: competence and achievement; self-exploration and definition; social interaction with peers and adults; physical activity; meaningful participation in school and community; routine, limits, and structure; diversity; and opportunities to explore concepts, values, and decision making and generate ideas from concrete experiences.[65]

When you have obtained the understandings and skills necessary to work effectively with young adolescents as well as students with special needs, cultural diversity, limited proficiency in English, and intellectual gifts and talents, you can then effectively teach all students. It is likely that you will have students who fit many of these categories in your first classroom. Techniques for effectively working with groups of students of varying group size and skill levels are presented in Part III.

Now, to reflect on your own school experiences and to interview one or more secondary school students to learn more about their experiences, do Exercises 1.1 and 1.2.

---

65. Robert L. Gilstrap, Cathy Bierman, and Thomas R. McKnight, *Improving Instruction in Middle Schools* (Bloomington, IN: Fastback 331, Phi Delta Kappa Educational Foundation, 1992), p. 17.

EXERCISE 1.1
Reflecting Upon My Own Secondary School Experiences

Instructions: The purpose of this exercise is to share with others in your class your reflections on your own secondary school experiences.

1. What secondary schools did you attend? Where? When? Were they public or private? _____

_____

_____

_____

_____

2. What do you remember most from your secondary school experiences? _____

_____

_____

_____

_____

3. What do you remember most about your teachers? _____

_____

_____

_____

_____

4. What do you remember most about the other students? _____

_____

_____

_____

_____

5. What do you remember most about your overall school life? _____

_____

_____

_____

_____

6. What grade (or class) do you specifically recall with fondness? Why? _____

_____

_____

_____

_____

_____

7. What grade (or class) would you particularly like to forget? Why? _____

_____

_____

_____

_____

_____

8. What do you recall about peer and parental pressures? _____

_____

_____

_____

_____

_____

_____

9. What do you recall about your own feelings during those years? _____

_____

_____

_____

_____

_____

_____

10. Is there any other aspect of your life as a secondary school student you wish to share with others? _____

_____

_____

_____

_____

_____

EXERCISE 1.2
Interviewing a Secondary School Student

Instructions: The purpose of this exercise is to gain insight into a secondary school student's perceptions of his own school experiences. Visit a school and interview one or more students. You may select any type of secondary school, such as a middle school, junior high, or high school. Use the question format that follows. You may want to make duplicates of this form to use with each student interviewed. You will probably find that it is best to interview one student at a time, privately. Share the results of your interviews with others in your class.

1. Name and location of school: _____

   _____

   _____

2. Date of interview: _____

3. How old are you (interviewee)? _____

4. What grade are you in? _____

5. What other schools have you attended? _____

   _____

   _____

   _____

6. With whom do you live (parent or guardian)? How many adults are in your home? _____

   _____

   _____

7. What do you like most about this school? _____

   _____

   _____

   _____

8. Is there anything that you dislike about this school? _____

   _____

   _____

   _____

9. What do you like the most about your teachers this year? _____

   _____

   _____

   _____

   _____

10. Is there anything you dislike about your teachers? _____

_____

_____

_____

11. What do you like about the other students at this school? _____

_____

_____

_____

12. Is there anything you dislike about the other students? _____

_____

_____

_____

13. What has been your favorite class at this school? Why? _____

_____

_____

_____

14. What has been your least favorite class? Why? _____

_____

_____

_____

15. Have you received any guidance or counseling while attending this school? _____

_____

_____

_____

16. What do you hope to do when your schooling is all done? _____

_____

_____

_____

17. Is there anything else you can tell me that will help me understand your experiences and
     feelings about being a student at this school? _____

_____

_____

_____

TEACHERS

Secondary school teachers represent myriad individual personalities—perhaps impossible to capture in generalizations. Let us imagine that a teaching colleague mentions that Pat Washington, in Room 17, is a "fantastic teacher," "one of the best teachers in the district," "super," and "magnificent." What might be some of the characteristics you would expect to see in Pat's teaching behaviors?

We can expect Pat to (1) know the curriculum and how best to teach it, (2) be enthusiastic, motivated, and well organized, (3) show effective interpersonal skills, and (4) be warm, caring, and nurturing toward all students.

Students need teachers who are well organized and who know how to establish and manage an active and supportive learning environment (the topic of Chapter 3), even with its multiple instructional demands. Students respond best to teachers who provide leadership and who enjoy their function as role models, advisers, mentors, and reflective decision makers.

Professional Teachers Assume Responsibility for Instructional Decisions and Their Outcomes

During any school day you will make hundreds of decisions, many of them instantaneously. In addition, you will have already made many decisions to prepare for the teaching day. During one school year a teacher makes literally thousands of decisions, many of which can and will affect the lives of their students for years to come. For you this should seem to be an awesome responsibility, which indeed it is.

Initially, of course, you will make errors in judgment, but you will also learn that secondary school students are fairly resilient, and that experts are available who can guide you to help ensure that the students are not damaged severely by your mistakes. You can learn from your errors. Keep in mind that the sheer number of decisions you make each day will mean that not all of them will be the best ones that could have been made had you had more time and better resources for planning.

Although pedagogy is based on scientific principles, good classroom teaching is as much an art as it is a science. Few rules apply to every teaching situation. In fact, decisions about the selection of content, instructional objectives and materials, teaching strategies, a teacher's response to student misbehavior, and the selection of techniques for assessment of the learning experiences are all the result of subjective judgments. Although many decisions are made at a somewhat unhurried pace when you are planning for your instruction, many others will be made intuitively and immediately. Once the school

day has begun, there is rarely time for making carefully thought-out judgments. At your best, you base your decisions on your teaching style, which, in turn, is based on your knowledge of school policies, pedagogical research, the curriculum, and the unique characteristics of the students in your classroom. You will also base your decisions on instinct, common sense, and reflective judgment. The better your understanding and experience with schools, the content, and the students, and the more time you give for careful reflection, the more likely it will be that your decisions will result in the students' meeting the educational goals. You will reflect upon, conceptualize, and apply understandings from one teaching experience to the next. As your understanding about your classroom experiences accumulates, your

---

- Admonishes behaviors rather than personalities.
- Advocates a school of problem solvers rather than of blamers and faultfinders.
- Ensures a base of community support for the school, its students, its faculty, and its mission.
- Emphasizes the importance of making everyone feel like a winner.
- Encourages people when they have made a mistake to say "I'm sorry," rather than making them feel compelled to cover their mistakes.
- Ensures that school policies are closely and collaboratively defined and clearly communicated.
- Ensures that staff and students receive proper and timely recognition for their achievements.
- Ensures that teachers' administrative chores and classroom interruptions are limited to those that are critical to student learning and effective functioning of the school (see Exercise 1.3).
- Establishes a climate in which teachers and students share the responsibility for determining the appropriate use of time and facilities.
- Follows up promptly on recommendations, concerns, and complaints.
- Fosters professional growth and development for teachers, with opportunities for visitations, demonstrations, conferences, workshops, and projects.
- Has a vision of what a good school is and strives to bring that vision to life—school improvement is the effective principal's constant theme.
- Involves teachers, parents, and students in decision making and goal setting.
- Is an advocate for teachers and students.
- Is positive in her outlook.
- Keeps everyone well informed of events and successes.
- Spends time each day with students.

Figure 1.7
Characteristics of the exemplary school principal.

teaching will become more routinized, predictable, and refined. The topic of reflective decision making, teacher competencies, and teacher facilitating behaviors is presented more fully in Chapter 2; for now let us consider the chief administrator in charge of everything at the school site—the school principal.

THE PRINCIPAL CAN MAKE A DIFFERENCE

One person significantly responsible for the success of any school is its principal. What are the characteristics of an effective school principal? Perhaps foremost is that the principal has a vision of what a good school is and strives to bring that vision to life—school improvement is the effective principal's constant theme. In addition, the school principal establishes a climate in which teachers and students share the responsibility for determining the appropriate use of time and facili-

ties. Other characteristics of an effective secondary school principal are listed in Figure 1.7.

In addition to the school principal, there are vice- or assistant principals, persons with specific responsibilities and oversight functions, such as student activities, school discipline and security, and curriculum and instruction. Sometimes teachers who are department or division chairs, or designated team leaders, may also perform administrative functions. The principal, however, has (or should have) the final responsibility for everything that happens at the school. As a new or visiting member of the faculty, one of your tasks is to become familiar with the administrative organization of your school and district.

Now, using the formats of Exercises 1.3, 1.4, and 1.5, observe a classroom for interruptions, and interview one or more secondary school teachers and a school administrator to learn more of the reality of secondary school teaching today.

EXERCISE 1.3

Observing a Secondary School Classroom for Frequency of External Interruptions

Instructions: It is disconcerting to know how often teachers and students learning in classrooms of some schools are interrupted by announcements from over the intercom, a phone call, or a visitor at the door. After all, no one would even consider interrupting a surgeon during the most climatic moment of an open-heart operation or a defense attorney at the climax of her summation, but it seems far too often that teachers are interrupted just at the moment they have their students in the palm of their hand at a critical point in a lesson. Once student attention and that teachable moment are lost because of an interruption, it is nearly impossible to recapture. School administrators and office personnel must sometimes be reminded that the most important activity in the school is teaching, so the act of teaching must not be frivolously interrupted. In our opinion, except for absolutely critical reasons, teachers should never be interrupted after the first five minutes of a class period and before the last five minutes. That policy should be established and rigidly adhered to. Otherwise, after many years of being a student, students will feel that what is going on in the classroom is the least important activity at the school. No wonder then that it is so difficult for teachers in some schools to gain student attention and respect. That respect must start from the central school office. Because the turn-around and refocus must somehow begin now, we have added this exercise to this resource guide. Arrange to visit a secondary school classroom and observe for classroom interruptions created from outside the classroom.

1. School and class visited: _____

2. Time (start and end of class period): _____

3. Interruptions (Tally for each interruption.)

   Intercom: _____

   Phone: _____

   Visitor at door: _____

   Emergency drill: _____

   Other (specify): _____

4. Total number of interruptions: _____

5. Share and compare your results with those of your classmates. _____

   _____

   _____

   _____

   _____

   _____

   _____

For Your Notes

EXERCISE 1.4
Interviewing a Teacher

Instructions: The purpose of this exercise is to gain insight into the experiences of secondary school teachers. Interview one or more teachers, perhaps one who is relatively new to the classroom and one who has been teaching for ten or more years, or one who is teaching at the junior high or middle school level and another who is teaching at the high school level. Use the following questions. You may duplicate blank copies of this form. Share the results with others in your class.

1. Name and location of school: _____

2. Grade span of school: _____

3. Date of interview: _____

4. Name and grade level (and/or subject of teacher): _____

5. In which area(s) of the school's curriculum do you work? _____

_____

_____

_____

_____

6. Why did you select teaching as a career? _____

_____

_____

_____

_____

_____

_____

7. Why are you teaching at this level? _____

_____

_____

_____

8. What preparation or training did you have? _____

_____

_____

_____

_____

9. What advice about preparation can you offer me? _____

_____

_____

_____

_____

10. What do you like most about teaching? _____

_____

_____

_____

_____

11. What do you like least about teaching? _____

_____

_____

_____

_____

12. What do I most need to know to be an effective classroom teacher? _____

_____

_____

_____

_____

13. What do you consider two of the most important characteristics to be a competent secondary school teacher? _____

_____

_____

_____

_____

14. What other specific advice do you have for those of us entering teaching at this level? _____

_____

_____

_____

_____

EXERCISE 1.5
Interviewing a Principal

Instructions: The purpose of this exercise is to gain information about secondary schools by interviewing a principal (or a vice-principal, if necessary). Use the question format that follows. You may choose any type of secondary school. Appointments should be arranged in advance. Follow-up thank-you letters are recommended. Share the results of your interview with others in your class. (Since school administrators are quite busy, an alternative to the strategy here would be to invite one or more administrators to your class for a discussion.)

1. Name and location of school: _____

2. Grade span of school: _____

3. Date of interview: _____

4. What is your official title? What are your official functions? _____

_____

_____

_____

_____

_____

5. How did you get this job? _____

_____

_____

_____

_____

_____

_____

6. What other administrators are on your staff? _____

_____

_____

_____

_____

_____

7. Which administrators are you responsible to? _____

_____

_____

_____

_____

_____

8. What are your teachers' administrative functions? _____
_____
_____
_____

9. Do you intend to remain at this school for the rest of your career? _____
_____
_____

10. What do you like about your job? _____
_____
_____
_____

11. What do you dislike about your job? _____
_____
_____
_____

12. What is your school's mission? _____
_____
_____
_____

13. What are some of your school's most recent accomplishments that you are most proud of?
_____
_____
_____
_____

14. What are your school's most pressing problems? Is building maintenance one? _____
_____
_____
_____
_____

15. What can you tell me (us) about your school's home-school-community partnership activities?

_____

_____

_____

_____

16. What can you tell me (us) about your school's curriculum? Are the students involved in making decisions about any aspects of the curriculum? _____

_____

_____

_____

_____

17. What are your school's campus security measures? Are they different today than, say, ten years ago? If so, in what respect? _____

_____

_____

_____

_____

18. What influences from society affect your students? _____

_____

_____

_____

_____

19. What do you see in the future of schools such as yours? _____

_____

_____

_____

_____

20. What advice can you give me (us) about my (our) preparation to teach middle school or high school? Is there anything else you would like me (us) to know about schools, teaching, students, or the community relationship with the schools? _____

_____

_____

_____

_____

For Your Notes

HOME, SCHOOL, AND COMMUNITY PARTNERSHIPS

In the final decade of the twentieth century, educators have enhanced the partnerships between the home, school, and community to promote the success of students. Although traditionally many teachers do effectively involve parents and guardians in their children's schoolwork, too many families still have little positive interaction with the schools their children attend. Later, especially in Chapter 11, specific suggestions are offered about ways teachers can communicate and collaborate with parents or guardians. These suggestions include making time for parent conferences; sending positive messages home about a student's learning or behavior; seeing that the student's portfolio is shared with parents or guardians; and communicating with parents about specific ways they can help with their child's learning. Sometimes a teacher might send a weekly assessment checklist home to parents or guardians as a report on the student's work for that week (see Figures 11.10 and 11.13 of Chapter 11). A weekly report communicates to parents improvements the student is making in schoolwork and exactly where more effort may be needed.

Research indicates that parental involvement in a child's education has a positive impact on a child's achievement at school.[66] Title I of the Improving America's Schools Act of 1994 offers guidelines that emphasize both quality and quantity family involvement in the schools. When parents of at-risk students get involved, the child benefits with more consistent attendance at school, more positive attitudes and actions, better grades, and higher test scores. Guidelines from Title I clearly emphasize that parents should be included as partners in the educational program. They also stress that teachers and administrators should inform parents about their child's progress, the school's family involvement policy, any programs in which family members can participate, and the school-parent compact that is required under the Title I guidelines.

Some states, districts, and local schools have adopted formal policies about home and community partnerships. School and administrative efforts to foster parent and community involvement include (1) student-teacher-parent contracts and weekly assignment calendars, (2) home visitor programs, (3) involvement of community leaders in the classroom as mentors, aides, and role models, and (4) workshops for parents. Some schools have homework hot line programs through which students and parents can, by phone or computer modem, obtain help with homework.

When school principals were given a list of 15 community groups or organizations and asked to assess the influence each group had exerted on their school in the past two years, they chose the parent-teacher organization (PTO) or parent-teacher association (PTA) as the most influential.[67] In recognition of the positive effect that parent and family involvement has on student achievement and success, in 1997 the National PTA released *National Standards for Parent/Family Involvement Programs*.[68] If you have not recently attended a school open house and a parent-teacher-student organization meeting, do so now, using Exercises 1.6 and 1.7 while there.

66. R. C. Burns, *Parents and Schools: From Visitors to Partners* (Washington, DC: National Education Association, 1993).

67. Valentine, p. 98.
68. For a copy of the standards, write to the National PTA, 330 N. Wabash Avenue, Suite 210-0, Chicago, IL 60611-3690. Phone 312-0670-6782; fax 312-670-6783.

EXERCISE 1.6

Attending an Open House or a Back-to-School Night

What happens when a school holds an open house (usually in the spring) or a back-to-school night (usually in the fall)? As part of your teacher education program, you may be expected to participate in these activities. This exercise will provide an opportunity to observe the educational and community-related activities planned for such special events.

Instructions: The purpose of this exercise is to visit a school to observe an open house or a back-to-school night. If you want to visit more than one school, you may duplicate this form. Share your observations with others in your class.

1. Name and location of school: _____

_____

2. Grade span of school: _____

3. Date of visit: _____

4. What exhibits did you see? _____

_____

_____

5. What presentations did you hear? By whom? Were they effective? How did the audience

respond? _____

_____

_____

_____

_____

6. What displays of student work did you see? _____

_____

_____

_____

7. Whom did you meet? Principal? Teachers? Parents or guardians? Grandparents? Students?

Clerical staff? _____

_____

_____

8. What questions were asked by parents? Of whom? _____

_____

_____

_____

9. What comments were made? By whom? _____

_____

_____

10. How did parents and teachers respond to one another? _____

_____

_____

11. What evidence was there that teachers and students had worked together to prepare for the event? _____

_____

_____

_____

12. Did the educators show self-confidence, optimism, enthusiasm, and clarity in expressing the school's expectations, and did they describe their programs and goals in a way visitors could understand? _____

_____

_____

_____

13. Would you like to have been a student in this school? Why or why not? _____

_____

_____

_____

14. Would you like to be a teacher in this school? Why or why not? _____

_____

_____

_____

15. Would you be satisfied if your own child were a student in this school? Why or why not?

_____

_____

_____

16. What other observations about this visit would you like to share? _____

_____

_____

_____

_____

EXERCISE 1.7
Attending a Parent-Teacher or Parent-Teacher-Student Organization Meeting

Parents and teachers are usually supportive of one another and are linked together by their common interests in the academic achievement of the children and in the total development—social, physical, psychological, intellectual, moral, and ethical—of each child. To show this mutual support and interest, they often form parent-teacher or parent-teacher-student organizations.

Instructions: The purpose of this exercise is to attend a meeting of a parent-teacher or parent-teacher-student group, recording your observations on the form that follows. Share your findings with others in your class.

1. Name and location of school: _____

   _____

2. Grade span of school: _____

3. Date of visit: _____

4. Type of organization: _____

5. Number of parents in attendance: _____

6. Number of teachers in attendance: _____

7. Number of administrators in attendance: _____

8. The meeting agenda: _____

   _____

   _____

   _____

   _____

   _____

   _____

   _____

9. The group's interests as related to the school: _____

   _____

   _____

   _____

   _____

   _____

   _____

   _____

   _____

10. Educational issues raised: _____

_____

_____

_____

_____

_____

_____

_____

11. General attitudes of members: _____

_____

_____

_____

_____

_____

_____

_____

12. Fundraising projects proposed: _____

_____

_____

_____

_____

_____

_____

_____

13. Other observations: _____

_____

_____

_____

_____

_____

_____

_____

_____

THE EMERGENT OVERALL PICTURE

Certainly, no facet of education receives more attention from the media, causes more concern among parents and teachers, or gets larger headlines than a decline (factual or fanciful) in students' achievement in the public schools.[69] Reports are issued, polls taken, debates organized, and blue-ribbon panels formed. Community members write letters to local editors about it, news editors devote editorial space to it, television anchors comment about it, and documentaries and specials focus on it in full color. We read "Schools Shortchanged," and "Education Fever: Pupils Catching It, Experts Say," and "Students Play Catch-Up on Basic Skills," and so on. What initiated this attention that began nearly a quarter-century ago and continues today? We are not sure, but it has never been matched in its political interest and participation, and it has affected and continues to affect both the public schools and programs in higher education that are directly or indirectly related to teacher preparation and certification.

Never were so many reports about education published in such a short time as there were in 1983 and 1984 (a few of which are listed in the suggested readings at the end of this chapter). More than 120 national studies were published during just those two years, and the interest continues.[70]

Important Actions Resulting from National Reports

In response to the reports, educators and politicians acted. Around the nation, their actions resulted in the following:

- Changes in standards for teacher certification.[71]
- Emphasis on education for cultural diversity and ways of teaching language minority students.
- Emphasis on helping students make effective transitions from one level of schooling to the next and from school to life, with an increased focus on helping students make connections between what is being learned and real life, as well as connections between subjects in the curriculum and between academics and vocations.
- Emphasis on raising test scores, reducing dropout rates, increasing class time, and changing curricula.
- Federally enacted Goals 2000: Educate America Act and the development of national education standards for all major subject areas (see Chapter 5).
- Formation of school-home-community partnerships.
- New "basics" required for a high school diploma.
- School restructuring to provide more meaningful curriculum options.

Key Trends and Practices Today

Key trends and practices today are listed in Figure 1.8.

- Dividing the student body and faculty into smaller groups, that is, the "school-within-a-school" concept, and using nontraditional scheduling and teaching teams.
- Eliminating curriculum tracking and instead providing meaningful curriculum options.
- Facilitating students' social skills as they interact, relate to one another, solve meaningful problems, and develop relationships and peaceful friendships.
- Facilitating the development of students' values as related to their families, the community, and schools.
- Holding high expectations, although not necessarily the same expectations, for all students by establishing goals and assessing results against those goals.

(continued)

Figure 1.8
Key trends and practices in today's secondary schools.

---

69. For an interesting and informative discussion about media coverage of education in the United States, see Chapter 1, "A Question of Confidence," in S. Elam, *How America Views Its Schools* (Bloomington, IN: Phi Delta Kappa Educational Foundation, 1995).
70. G. W. Bracey labels the 1983 publication, *A Nation At Risk,* a "masterpiece of propaganda." See G. W. Bracey, "A Nation of Learners: Nostalgia and Amnesia," *Educational Leadership* 54(5):53–57 (February 1997).
71. Model standards describing what prospective teachers should know and be able to do in order to receive a teaching license were prepared and released in 1992 by the Interstate New Teacher Assessment and Support Consortium (INTASC), a project of the Council of Chief State School Officers (CCSSO), in a document titled *Model Standards for Beginning Teacher Licensing and Development.* Representatives of at least 36 states and professional associations— including the National Education Association (NEA), the American Federation of Teachers (AFT), the American Association of Colleges

for Teacher Education (AACTE), and the National Council for the Accreditation of Teacher Education (NCATE)—compose the group. The standards are performance-based and revolve around a common core of principles of knowledge and skills that cut across disciplines. The INTASC standards were developed to be compatible with the National Board for Professional Teaching Standards (NBPTS). For copies of the INTASC document, contact CCSSO, One Massachusetts Avenue NW, Suite 700, Washington, DC 20001; phone 202-3367-7048. You may want to identify other lists of competencies and to compare the ten common standards of the INTASC document with the 22 competencies that we identify in Chapter 2 of this resource guide and with the 22 "components of professional practice" in C. Danielson, Enhancing Professional Practice: A Framework for Teaching (Alexandria, VA: Association for Supervision and Curriculum Development, 1996). Figure 1.2 (pp. 10–11) of Danielson shows a correlation of the INTASC standards with Danielson's framework of teaching components.

- Integrating the curriculum, especially with the language arts, and introducing reading, thinking, and writing across the curriculum.
- Introducing the Internet and using it in the classroom as a communication tool and learning resource.
- Involving communities in the schools by developing community learning centers and involving parents and guardians in school decision making.
- Involving students in self-assessment.
- Making multicultural education work for all students.
- Providing students with the time and the opportunity to think and be creative, rather than simply memorizing and repeating information.
- Using heterogeneous grouping and cooperative learning, peer coaching, and cross-age tutoring as instructional strategies.
- Using occupations to contextualize learning and instruction to vitalize a school-to-work transition.

Figure 1.8 *(continued)*

Critical Problems and Issues That Plague the Nation's Schools as We Enter a New Millennium

As we close out the 1990s and enter a new millennium, major problems and issues plague our nation's schools, some of which are listed in Figure 1.9. Some of these are discussed in subsequent chapters (see the Index for topic locations). Perhaps you and members of your class can identify other issues and problems faced by our nation's schools.[72]

When compared with traditional instruction, one of the characteristics of exemplary instruction today is the teacher's encouragement of dialogue among students in the classroom, to discuss and to explore their own ideas. As said in the Preface, modeling the very behaviors we expect of teachers and students in the classroom is a constant theme throughout this resource guide. One purpose of Exercise 1.8 is, in a similar fashion, to start that dialogue. Do Exercise 1.8 now.

---

72. A useful resource for understanding current major issues in education is D. R. Walling (ed.), *Hot Buttons: Unraveling 10 Controversial Issues in Education* (Bloomington, IN: Phi Delta Kappa International, 1997).

- Continuing controversy over books and their content.
- Continuing, long-running controversy over values, morality, and sexuality education.
- Controversy created by the concept of teaching less content but teaching it better.
- Controversy over the development of a national curriculum.
- Controversy over the development of national performance-based assessment standards and strategies.
- Continuing controversy over the elimination of traditional ability grouping or tracking.
- Lack of facilities to house the influx of students and the lack of money to repair existing facilities.
- Potential for crime and violence on school campuses.
- Scarcity of minority teachers to serve as role models for minority students.
- School security and the related problem of weapons, crime, violence, and drugs on school campuses and in school neighborhoods.
- Sexual harassment of students, mostly from other students but sometimes from school employees.
- Shortage of qualified teachers.
- Teaching and assessing for higher-order thinking skills.
- The education of teachers to work effectively with students who may be too overwhelmed by personal problems to focus on learning and succeed in school.
- The number of students at risk of dropping out of school and the potential that high school might be too late to effectively intervene.

Figure 1.9
Critical problems and issues that plague the nation's schools.

EXERCISE 1.8
Interviewing a Teacher Candidate

Instructions: The purpose of this exercise is to identify why other teacher candidates have selected teaching as a career. Select a teacher candidate (preferably someone not in your class) and record that person's responses to the following questions. Share the answers with others of your class. (Note to instructor: This exercise could be used during the first week of class as an icebreaker.)

1. Name of interviewee: _____
_____

2. What motivated you to select secondary school teaching as a career? _____
_____
_____
_____
_____
_____

3. When did you decide on teaching as a career? _____
_____
_____

4. What major reasons prompted that decision? _____
_____
_____
_____
_____
_____
_____

5. Do you look forward to being free from teaching during the summer months? If so, what do you plan to do at that time? _____
_____
_____
_____
_____
_____
_____

6. Would you like to teach in a year-round school? Why or why not? _____

_____

_____

_____

_____

_____

_____

7. Do you plan a lifetime career as a classroom teacher? Why or why not? _____

_____

_____

_____

_____

_____

_____

_____

8. Are there any other teachers in your family? _____

_____

_____

_____

_____

_____

_____

_____

9. At this time, do you have a favorite grade level or subject, or both? _____

_____

_____

_____

_____

_____

_____

10. Do you plan a career as a classroom teacher, or do you eventually plan to move into a specialty
    or administrative position? _____

_____

_____

_____

_____

_____

11. How do you feel now about being a teacher? _____

_____

_____

_____

_____

_____

_____

12. What, specifically, are you most looking forward to during this program of teacher preparation?

_____

_____

_____

_____

_____

_____

13. Which of your personal and professional characteristics do you feel would make you an effective teacher? _____

_____

_____

_____

_____

_____

_____

14. What else would you like to say about you and your feelings about teaching? _____

_____

_____

_____

_____

_____

For Your Notes

SUMMARY

In beginning to plan for developing your teaching competencies, you have read an overview of today's schools, the trends and the challenge afforded by the diversity of students in those schools, and the problems and issues that plague our nation's schools. You have reviewed the characteristics of adolescents and learned some guidelines for working with specific students.

In addition, you have reflected upon your own school experiences; talked with teachers, students, and administrators; and attended a back-to-school night and a parent-teacher association meeting; and discussed these matters with your classmates. The knowledge from these experiences will be useful in your assimilation of the content explored in chapters that follow, beginning in the next chapter with the expectations, responsibilities, and facilitating behaviors of the classroom teacher.

QUESTIONS FOR CLASS DISCUSSION

1. Financial shortfalls have caused some school districts to decrease the number of counselors available to students. In California, for example, by 1993 the shortage had become a statewide crisis. In 1985, the California statewide ratio of students to counselors was 400 to 1; by 1990, the ratio had grown to 850 to 1; and by 1993, in some school districts that ratio had grown to 2,000 to 1. Students were no longer getting the individual attention they had once received from school counselors. One problem caused by such lack of attention is that many high school seniors are missing deadlines and requirements (such as letters from their counselors) for college admission. As a result, some colleges and universities have deleted counselor recommendations from their entrance requirements. Investigate the ratio of counselors to students in secondary schools in your area. Inquire about their responsibilities. How much time is devoted to college counseling, job counseling, crisis counseling, and school registration matters? If the ratio of counselors to students has decreased, have teachers been expected to assume some of the responsibilities formerly held by counselors? If not, who has?

2. It is estimated that approximately half a million children are being kept out of the public schools and taught at home, perhaps double the number that were home-schooled in 1990 and about 1 percent of all K–12 children. Why do you suppose so many parents are choosing to keep their children out of school? Should there be concerns about the quality of education and socialization for children schooled at home? Some school districts are reaching out to home-schooling parents and offering services such as textbooks, library privileges, and testing. What do you think about the trend toward home-schooling and its effects on children?

3. Confronted by serious problems in some of the nation's public schools and reflected in the growing number of children being taught at home or in private schools, some people advocate shifting financial support and authority for schools from the public to the private sector, which would mark a radical change in American education. Organize a class debate on this question: Is there still a need for public schools in this country? To partially support research on the question, we recommend the 1996 publications *Is There a Public for Public Schools?* by D. Mathews (Dayton, OH: Kettering Foundation Press), and *Do We Still Need Public Schools?*, prepared jointly by the Center on National Education Policy (1001 Connecticut Avenue, NW, Suite 310, Washington, DC 20036, phone 202-822-8065) and Phi Delta Kappa (408 North Union Street, PO Box 789, Bloomington, IN 47402-0789, phone 800-766-1156) and available from either address. See also the related articles in the October 1996 issue of *Educational Leadership.*

4. What concerns you most about teaching the diversity of students you are likely to have? Share those concerns with others in your class. Categorize your group's concerns. By accessing an Internet teacher bulletin board, see what kinds of problems secondary school teachers are currently concerned about. Are block scheduling, grading, group learning, and classroom management high in frequency of concern? Are the concerns of teachers as expressed on the Internet similar to yours? As a class, devise a plan and time line for attempting to ameliorate your concerns.

5. Compare and contrast your own school experiences with what you have recently observed in schools, especially related to the exercises of this chapter. Discuss your conclusions in small groups, then share your group's conclusions with the entire class.

6. Prepare a five-minute micro peer teaching demonstration and present it to your classmates. You may choose any topic and strategy, but have the micro peer teaching video recorded so that you can compare it with the final one that you do for this course.

7. How do high school graduation requirements and standards compare from one high school to another, from one region of the country to another? For instance, does a high school graduate's grade point average represent the same thing regardless of the high school? What do university and college admissions officers look for today when screening high school graduates' applications for admission? Is the SAT score of greater or lesser importance today than it was a decade ago?

8. Explain each of the following two concepts and why you agree or disagree with each. The teacher should (1) hold high expectations for all students and never waver from those expectations and (2) not be concerned about covering the contents of the textbook by the end of the school term.

9. From your current observations and field work as related to this teacher preparation program, clearly identify one specific example of educational practice that seems contradictory to exemplary practice or theory as presented in this chapter. Present your explanation for the discrepancy.

10. Do you have questions generated by the content of this chapter? If you do, list them along with ways answers might be found.

SUGGESTED READINGS

Adelman, N. E., and Walking-Eagle, K. P. "Teachers, Time, and School Reform." Chapter 5 in A. Hargreaves (ed.), *Rethinking Educational Change with Heart and Mind.* Alexandria, VA: ASCD 1997 Yearbook, Association for Supervision and Curriculum Development, 1997.

Arnold, J. "High Expectations for All: Perspective and Practice." *Middle School Journal* 28(3):51–53 (January 1997).

Baines, L. "Future Schlock: Using Fabricated Data and Politically Correct Platitudes in the Name of Education Reform." *Phi Delta Kappan* 78(7):492–498 (March 1997).

Berliner, D. C., and Biddle, B. J. *The Manufactured Crisis: Myth, Fraud, and the Attack on America's Public Schools.* New York: Addison-Wesley, 1995.

Boyer, E. *The Basic School: A Community for Learning.* Princeton, NJ: The Carnegie Foundation for the Advancement of Teaching, 1995.

Bracey, G. W. *Setting the Record Straight: A Practitioner's Guide to Refuting the Criticisms of American Public Education.* Alexandria, VA: Association for Supervision and Curriculum Development, 1997.

Bruckner, M. M. "One High School's Journey to Change." *Educational Forum* 60(3):272–282 (Spring 1996).

Budde, R. "The Evolution of the Charter Concept." *Phi Delta Kappan* 78(1):72–73 (September 1996).

Canady, R. L., and Rettig, M. D. *Block Scheduling: A Catalyst for Change in High Schools.* New York: Richard H. Adin Freelance Editorial Services, 1995.

Carnegie Council on Adolescent Development. *Great Transitions: Preparing Adolescents for a New Century.* Washington, DC: Carnegie Council on Adolescent Development, 1995.

Center on National Education Policy. *Do We Still Need Public Schools?* Washington, DC: Author, 1996.

Cochren, J. R. "Tracking: An Affront to American Idealism." *International Journal of Educational Reform* 5(2):179–185 (April 1996).

Colangelo, N., and Davis, G. A. *Handbook of Gifted Education.* 2d ed. Needham Heights, MA: Allyn & Bacon, 1997.

Cook, L., and Lodge, H. C., eds. *Voices in English Classrooms: Honoring Diversity and Change. Classroom Practices in Teaching English, Volume 28.* Urbana, IL: National Council of Teachers of English, 1996.

Corwin, S. "Tech Prep—An Education That Really Works. Indiana Programs Blaze a Trail." *Educational Horizons* 73(4):181–186 (Summer 1995).

Daniels, H. "The Best Practice Project: Building Parent Partnerships in Chicago." *Educational Leadership* 53(7):38–43 (April 1996).

deWijk, S. L. "Career and Technology Studies: Crossing the Curriculum." *Educational Leadership* 53(8):50–53 (May 1996).

Dixon, C., Mains, L., and Reeves, M. J. *Gifted and At Risk.* Bloomington, IN: Fastback 398, Phi Delta Kappa Educational Foundation, 1996.

Elam, S. *How America Views Its Schools: The PDK/Gallup Polls, 1969–1994.* Bloomington, IN: Phi Delta Kappa Educational Foundation, 1995.

Elkind, D. "School and Family in the Postmodern World." *Phi Delta Kappan* 77(1):8–14 (September 1995).

Fine, M. *Habits of Mind: Struggling Over Values in America's Classrooms.* San Francisco: Jossey-Bass, 1995.

French, M. P., and Andretti, A. P. *Attention Deficit and Reading Instruction.* Bloomington, IN: Fastback 382, Phi Delta Kappa Educational Foundation, 1995.

Gaddy, B. B., Hall, T. W., and Marzano, R. J. *School Wars: Resolving Our Conflicts over Religion and Values.* San Francisco: Jossey-Bass, 1996.

Gee, C. *2000 Voices: Young Adolescents' Perceptions and Curriculum Implications.* Columbus, OH: National Middle School Association, 1997.

Gersten, R. "The Double Demands of Teaching English Language Learners." *Educational Leadership* 53(5):18–22 (February 1996).

Glasser, W. *The Quality School.* New York: Harper & Row, 1990.

Goenner, J. N. "Charter Schools: The Revitalization of Public Education." *Phi Delta Kappan* 78(1):32, 34–36 (September 1996).

Graves, M. F., Graves, B. B., and Braaten, S. "Scaffolded Reading Experiences for Inclusive Classes." *Educational Leadership* 53(5):14–16 (February 1996).

Gray, K. "Vocationalism and the American High School: Past, Present, and Future?" *Journal of Industrial Teacher Education* 33(2):86–92 (Winter 1996).

Hackmann, D. G. "Ten Guidelines for Implementing Block Scheduling." *Educational Leadership* 53(3):24–27 (November 1995).

Johnson, D. W., and Johnson, R. T. *Reducing School Violence Through Conflict Resolution.* Alexandria, VA: Association for Supervision and Curriculum Development, 1995.

Jones, B. (comp.). *Promising Practices in Florida: Integrating Academic and Vocational Education.* Tallahassee: Division of Applied Technical and Adult Education, Florida State Department of Education, 1996.

Kellough, R. D., and Kellough, N. G. *Middle School Teaching: A Guide to Methods and Resources.* 2nd ed. Upper Saddle River, NJ: Prentice Hall, 1996.

Kelly, E. B. *Left-Handed Students: A Forgotten Minority.* Bloomington, IN: Fastback 399, Phi Delta Kappa Educational Foundation, 1996.

Kibby, M. W. *Student Literacy: Myths and Realities.* Bloomington, IN: Fastback 399, Phi Delta Kappa Educational Foundation, 1995.

Kuzmeskus, J., ed. *We Teach Them All.* York, ME: Stenhouse, 1996.

Langdon, C. A. "The Third Phi Delta Kappa Poll of Teachers' Attitudes Toward the Public Schools." *Phi Delta Kappan* 78(3):244–250 (November 1996).

Martin, J. R. "A Philosophy of Education for the Year 2000." *Phi Delta Kappan* 76(5):355–359 (January 1995).

Mehan, H., et al. *Constructing School Success. The Consequences of Untracking Low-Achieving Students.* New York: Cambridge University Press, 1996.

Meier, D. W. "The Big Benefits of Smallness." *Educational Leadership* 54(1):12–15 (September 1996).

Minicucci, C., et al. "School Reform and Student Diversity." *Phi Delta Kappan* 77(1):77–80 (September 1995).

Mizelle, N. B. "Enhancing Young Adolescents' Motivation for Literacy Learning." *Middle School Journal* 28(3):16–25 (January 1997).

National Commission on Excellence in Education. *A Nation at Risk: The Imperative for Educational Reform*. Washington, DC: Government Printing Office, 1983.

National Middle School Association. *This We Believe: Developmentally Responsive Middle Level Schools*. Columbus, OH: National Middle School Association, 1995.

O'Donnell, M. D. "Boston's Lewenberg Middle School Delivers Success." *Phi Delta Kappan* 78(7):508–512 (March 1997).

Penn, A. P., and Williams, D. *Integrating Academic and Vocational Education: A Model for Secondary Schools*. Alexandria, VA: Association for Supervision and Curriculum Development, 1997.

Rutherford, B., and Billig, S. H. "Eight Lessons of Parent, Family, and Community Involvement in the Middle Grades." *Educational Leadership* 77(1):64–66, 68 (September 1995).

Schmoker, M. *Results: The Key to Continuous School Improvement*. Alexandria, VA: Association for Supervision and Curriculum Improvement, 1996.

Secretary's Commission on Achieving Necessary Skills (SCANS). *SCANS Report*. Washington, DC: United States Department of Labor, 1992.

Sills-Briegel, T., Fisk, C., and Dunlop, V. "Graduation by Exhibition." *Educational Leadership* 54(4):66–71 (December 1996/January 1997).

Simonelli, R. "The Basic School: Recreating Community for Educational Development." *Winds of Change* 11(1):22–27 (Winter 1996).

Sizer, T. R. *Horace's School: Redesigning the American High School*. New York: Houghton Mifflin, 1992.

Smith, R., and Sherrell, S. "Mileposts on the Road to a Certificate of Initial Mastery." *Educational Leadership* 54(4):46–50 (December 1996/January 1997).

Spies, P. *Interdisciplinary Teams for High Schools*. Bloomington, IN: Fastback 416, Phi Delta Kappa Educational Foundation, 1997.

Vaugh, S., Bos, C. S., and Schumm, S. *Teaching Mainstreamed, Diverse, and At-Risk Students in the General Education Classroom*. Needham Heights, MA: Allyn & Bacon, 1997.

Walling, D. R., ed. *Hot Buttons: Unraveling 10 Controversial Issues in Education*. Bloomington, IN: Phi Delta Kappa International, 1997.

Winn, D. D., Menlove, R. R., and Zsiray, S., Jr. *Rethinking the Scheduling of School Time*. Bloomington, IN: Fastback 412, Phi Delta Kappa Educational Foundation, 1997.

Wolfe, D. "Three Approaches to Coping with School Violence." *English Journal* 84(5): 51–54 (September 1995).

Chapter

2

The Expectations, Responsibilities, and Facilitating Behaviors of a Classroom Teacher

The primary expectation of a classroom teacher is to help all students to learn. However, your professional responsibilities will extend well beyond the ability to work effectively in a classroom from approximately 8:00 A.M. until mid- or late afternoon. In this chapter, you will learn about the many responsibilities you will assume and the competencies and behaviors necessary for fulfilling them. Four categories of responsibilities and twenty-two competencies are identified.

The four categories are your (1) responsibility as a reflective decision maker, (2) commitment to children and to the profession, (3) noninstructional responsibilities, and (4) instructional responsibilities and fundamental teaching behaviors. As these categories and the twenty-two competencies are presented, you are guided through the reality of these expectations as they exist for today's secondary school teacher.

Specifically, upon completion of this chapter you should be able to

1. Describe the decision-making and thought-processing phases of instruction and the types of decisions a teacher must make during each.
2. Describe the importance of the concept of locus of control and its relationship to teacher responsibility.
3. Demonstrate your understanding of the concept of teacher as a competent professional.
4. Demonstrate your understanding of the depth and breadth of the instructional and noninstructional responsibilities of a secondary school classroom teacher.

5. Describe the importance of the concept of learning styles and its implications for developmentally appropriate practice.
6. Demonstrate an understanding of the concept of the three-phase learning cycle for student learning and types of learning activities that might occur in each phase.
7. Demonstrate an understanding of the concept of learning capacities (multiple intelligences) and its implications for developmentally appropriate practice.
8. Compare hands-on and minds-on learning.
9. Contrast teacher use of praise and of encouragement, and describe situations in which each is more appropriate.
10. Demonstrate how you would use the concept of multilevel instruction in your teaching.
11. Demonstrate awareness of and growth in your use of facilitating behaviors.

TEACHER AS A REFLECTIVE DECISION MAKER

During any single school day you will make hundreds, perhaps thousands, of decisions. It is said that a teacher makes 3,000 nontrivial decisions every day.[1] Some decisions will have been made prior to meeting your students for instruction, others will be made dur-

---

1. C. Danielson, *Enhancing Professional Practice: A Framework for Teaching* (Alexandria, VA: Association for Supervision and Curriculum Development, 1996), p. 2.

ing the instructional activities, and yet still others are made later as you reflect on the instruction for that day. Let's now consider further these decision-making and thought-processing phases of instruction.

Decision-Making Phases of Instruction

Instruction can be divided into four decision-making and thought-processing phases. These are (1) the planning, or *preactive,* phase, (2) the teaching, or *interactive,* phase, (3) the analyzing and evaluating, or *reflective,* phase, and (4) the application, or *projective,* phase.[2] The preactive phase consists of all those intellectual functions and decisions you will make prior to actual instruction. The interactive phase includes all the decisions made during the immediacy and spontaneity of the teaching act. Decisions made during this phase are likely to be more intuitive, unconscious, and routine than those made during the planning phase. The reflective phase is the time you will take to reflect on, analyze, and judge the decisions and behaviors that occurred during the interactive phase. As a result of this reflection, decisions are made to use what was learned in subsequent teaching actions. At this point, you are in the projective phase, abstracting from your reflection and projecting your analysis into subsequent teaching behaviors.

Reflection, Locus of Control, and Teacher Responsibility

During the reflective phase teachers can choose whether to assume full responsibility for the instructional outcomes or whether to assume responsibility for only the positive outcomes of the planned instruction while placing the blame for the negative outcomes on outside forces (e.g., parents and guardians or society in general, peers, other teachers, administrators, textbooks). Where the responsibility for outcomes is placed is referred to as locus of control.

Just because a teacher thinks that he is a competent teacher doesn't mean it is so. If many of a teacher's students are not learning, then that teacher is not competent. In the words of the late Madeline Hunter, "To say that I am an effective teacher, and acknowledge that my students may not be learning is the same as saying I am a great surgeon, but most of my patients die."[3] Teachers who are intrinsically motivated and competent tend to assume full responsibility for the instructional outcomes, regardless of whether the outcomes are as intended from the planning phase.

Now do Exercises 2.1 and 2.2 to further your understanding.

---

2. A. L. Costa, *The School as a Home for the Mind* (Palatine, IL: Skylight Publishing, 1991), pp. 97–106.

3. In R. A. Villa and J. S. Thousands, eds., *Creating an Inclusive School* (Alexandria, VA: Association for Supervision and Curriculum Development, 1995), p. 36.

EXERCISE 2.1

The Teacher as Reflective Decision Maker

Instructions: The purpose of this exercise is to learn more about the nature of the decisions and the decision-making process used by teachers. To accomplish this, you are to talk with and observe one middle school or secondary school teacher for one instructional period, tabulate the number of decisions the teacher makes for that period, and then share the results with your classmates. Obtain permission from a cooperating teacher by explaining the purpose of your observations. You will need to have a follow-up discussion with the cooperating teacher regarding your tabulations. A follow-up thank you note would be appropriate.

School, teacher, and class observed: _____

1. Use the following format for your tabulations. You may first want to make your tabulations on a separate blank sheet of paper and then organize and transfer those tabulations to this page. Tabulate and identify each decision. To tabulate the decisions made before and after instruction, confer with the teacher after class.

Decisions Made before Instruction

Examples:

- objectives of lessons
- amount of time to be devoted to particular activities
- classroom management procedures

_____

_____

_____

_____

_____

_____

Decisions Made during Instruction

Examples:

- called on Juanita to answer a question
- teacher remained silent until students in back row got quiet
- talked with tardy student

_____

_____

_____

_____

_____

_____

_____

Decisions Made after Instruction

Examples:

- to review a particular concept tomorrow
- to arrange a conference with Juanita to talk with her about her hostility during class
- to make a revision in tomorrow's homework assignment

_____

_____

_____

_____

_____

_____

2. What was the total number of decisions made by this teacher before instruction? _____
   During? _____ After? _____
   Compare your results with those of others in your class. _____

   _____

3. Did you see any evidence that this teacher assumed full responsibility for the learning outcomes of this class session? Describe the evidence.

   _____

   _____

   _____

4. What percentage of all decisions by this teacher were planned? _____ Spontaneous? _____

5. Did you share your results of this exercise with the cooperating teacher? What was her reaction?

   _____

   _____

6. What are your conclusions from this exercise? _____

   _____

   _____

   _____

   _____

   _____

   _____

   _____

   _____

   _____

   _____

EXERCISE 2.2
The Preactive Phase of Instruction

Instructions: Mentally rehearsing your actions before meeting your students is absolutely essential for effective teaching and learning. The purpose of this exercise is to stress the importance of thinking clearly and fully about what you will do and say in the classroom and to demonstrate how mental rehearsal of a lesson can identify possible problems. Follow these steps:

1. Select a middle school or secondary school grade level you are currently teaching or that you would like to teach.

_____

_____

_____

2. Objective of lesson: Students will design a name tag for their desks during a 20-minute time frame.

3. Without looking ahead at step 4, write a lesson plan for this activity. (Although you have not yet learned the details of lesson planning, outline the steps you would follow and things you would say to your students in order to accomplish the objective of step 2.)

_____

_____

_____

_____

_____

_____

_____

_____

_____

_____

_____

_____

4. To analyze the thoroughness of your preactive thinking, respond to the following questions.

   • Are materials listed in your plan? _____

   • Are those materials readily available in your classroom? _____

   • Will paper or tagboard need to be pre-cut? _____

   • How large can the name tags be? _____

   • How and where will they be attached to each desk? _____

   _____

   _____

- Should they be flat or three-dimensional? _____

- Do you have materials (markers, colored pencils, etc.) or are the students expected to have them?

  _____

  _____

  _____

  _____

  _____

- Will students need scissors? _____

- Do you have left-handed scissors available if needed? _____

- Should name tags have first name, last name or first name, last initial? _____

  _____

  _____

  _____

- Can other words or designs be added? _____

- When and how will materials be distributed? Collected? _____

  _____

  _____

  _____

  _____

  _____

- What plan do you have for absent or tardy students? _____

  _____

  _____

  _____

  _____

  _____

5. Share the results of steps 1–4 with others in your class. Did members of your class come up with other questions relevant to the preplanning of this instructional period? If so, share them with the rest of the class.

Conclusion: A teacher who practices thorough preactive planning should have planned answers for each of these questions.

CHARACTERISTICS OF THE COMPETENT TEACHER

The overall purpose of this resource guide is to assist you in identifying and building upon your instructional competencies. To do that, we need a starting place, and this section is it, beginning with what some teenagers have to say about what makes a teacher great, followed by our presentation of 22 specific competencies. You will continue to reflect on and to build upon these competencies through your study of the remaining chapters of this book and, indeed, throughout your professional career.

What Makes a Great Teacher: From the Viewpoint of Teenagers

Here are the replies of a few teenagers when asked the question "What makes a great teacher?"

APPROACHABLE AND INSPIRING. A 16-year-old female high school student said, "A great teacher is someone you can talk to about things. Someone who takes time out to help give you a better understanding with problems that seem impossible. Who will not allow you to settle for a C but inspires you to strive for an A."

RESPECTFUL AND COMMUNICATES WHAT IS NEEDED. A 13-year-old female middle school student said that a great teacher "respects students and appreciates them, and makes them learn a lot and tells us what we need to do to have a good job in life."

EDUCATED, ATTENTIVE, WILLING TO REACH OUT TO STUDENTS AND TO MAKE LEARNING FUN. A 17-year-old female high school student replied that great teachers are "educated, willing to teach and reach out to the students, patient and firm, and have discipline in the classroom. They establish trust and respect, thus receiving same from their students. They fill the classroom atmosphere with a sense of understanding. Perhaps most important, they shape the structure of the lesson around having fun, making learning easier."

A 17-year-old male high school student said that a great teacher is "one who reflects a bit of their personality into what they teach, allowing the material to be less boring and more attractive. No one ever said that learning couldn't be fun."

A 13-year-old female middle school student replied that a great teacher "has patience and treats everyone equally. She is attentive to what's going on in the classroom. In addition, she makes school fun and exciting."

Twenty-Two Characteristics of the Competent Teacher

We do not mean to overwhelm you with the following list; it may well be that no teacher expertly models all the characteristics that follow. The characteristics do, however, represent an ideal to strive for.[4]

1. *The teacher is knowledgeable about the subject matter content expected to be taught.* You should have both historical understanding and current knowledge of the structure of those subjects you are expected to teach and of the facts, principles, concepts, and skills needed for those subjects. This doesn't mean you need to know everything about the subject, but you should know more than you are likely to teach.

2. *The teacher is an active member of professional organizations, reads professional journals, has dialogues with colleagues, maintains currency in methodology and about the students and the subject matter content he is expected to teach.* While this resource guide offers valuable information about teaching and learning, you are much closer to the start of your professional career than you are to the end. As a teacher you are a learner among learners. As discussed in Chapter 12, through workshops, advanced course work, coaching, and training; through the acquisition of further knowledge by reading and study; and through collaboration with and role modeling of significant and more experienced colleagues, you will be in a perpetual learning mode.

3. *The teacher understands the processes of learning.* You will ensure that students understand the lesson objectives, your expectations, and the classroom procedures, that they feel welcomed to your classroom and involved in the learning activities, and that they have some control over the pacing of their own learning. Furthermore, when preparing your lessons, you will (a) consider the levels of development of each student; (b) present content in reasonably small doses—and in a logical and coherent sequence—while using visual, verbal, tactile, and kinesthetic learning activities, with opportunities for guided practice and reinforcement; and (c) frequently check comprehension to ensure the students are learning.

4. *The teacher is an "educational broker."* You will learn where and how to discover information about content you are expected to teach. You cannot know everything there is to know about each subject, but you should become knowledgeable about where and how to best research it and how to assist your students in developing some of those same skills. Among other things, this means that you should be computer literate, that is, have the ability to understand and use computers, paralleling reading and writing in verbal literacy.

---

4. See footnote 71 of Chapter 1.

5. *The teacher uses effective modeling behaviors.* Your own behaviors must be consistent with those expected of your students. If, for example, you want your students to demonstrate regular and punctual attendance, to have their work done on time, to have their materials each day for learning, to demonstrate cooperative behavior and respect for others, to maintain an open and inquisitive mind, to demonstrate critical thinking, and to use proper communication skills, then you will do likewise, modeling those same behaviors and attitudes for the students. Specific guidelines for effective modeling are presented later in this chapter.

6. *The teacher is open to change and willing to take risks and be held accountable.* If there were no difference between what is and what can be, then formal education would be of little value. A competent teacher knows not only of historical and traditional values and knowledge, but also of the value of change, and is willing to carefully plan and experiment, to move between that which is known and that which is not. Realizing that little of value is ever achieved without a certain amount of risk and possessing personal strength of convictions, the competent teacher stands ready to be held accountable, as the teacher undoubtedly will be, for assuming such risks.

7. *The teacher is nonprejudiced toward gender, sexual preference, ethnicity, skin color, religion, physical handicaps, socioeconomic status, learning disabilities, and national origin.* Among other things, this means no sexual innuendos, religious jokes, or racial slurs. It means being cognizant of how teachers, male and female, knowingly or unknowingly, historically have mistreated female students and of how to avoid those same errors in your own teaching. (Chapter 8 offers specific guidelines.) It means, as discussed in Chapter 1, learning about and attending to the needs of individual students in your classroom. It means having high, although not necessarily identical, expectations for *all* students.

8. *The teacher organizes the classroom and plans lessons carefully.* Long-range plans and daily lessons are prepared thoughtfully and well in advance, reflected on, revised, and competently implemented with creative, motivating, and effective strategies and skill. Much of this resource guide is devoted to assisting you in the development of this competency.

9. *The teacher is a capable communicator.* The competent teacher uses thoughtfully selected words, carefully planned questions, expressive voice inflections, useful pauses, meaningful gestures, and productive and nonconfusing body language, some of which were carefully and thoughtfully planned during the preactive phase of instruction and others of which have, through practice and reflection, become second-nature skills. Throughout this book you will find useful suggestions for your development of this competency.

10. *The teacher can function effectively as a decision maker.* The classroom is a complex place, busy with very fast-paced activities. As discussed at the beginning of this chapter, in a single day you may engage in a thousand or more interpersonal exchanges with students, to say nothing about the numerous exchanges possible with the many adults with whom you will be in contact. The competent teacher initiates rather than merely reacts and is proactive and in control of her interactions, having learned how to manage time to analyze and develop effective interpersonal behaviors. (For this purpose teachers have found it valuable to videotape a class period for later analysis of interactions.)

11. *The teacher is in a perpetual learning mode, striving to further develop a repertoire of teaching strategies.* As discussed in competency number 2, competent teachers are good students, continuing their own learning by reflecting on and assessing their work, attending workshops, studying the work of others, and talking with students, parents and guardians, and colleagues, sometimes over Internet bulletin boards. (The topic of ongoing professional development is the essence of Chapter 12.)

12. *The teacher demonstrates concern for the safety and health of the students.* The teacher strives to maintain a comfortable room temperature with adequate ventilation and to prevent safety hazards in the classroom. Students who are ill are encouraged to stay home and to get well. If a teacher suspects that a student may be ill or may be suffering from abuse at home (see Chapter 3), the teacher appropriately and promptly acts upon that suspicion by referring it to the school nurse or an appropriate administrator. Teachers consistently model safety procedures, ensuring precautions necessary to protect the health and psychological and physical safety of the students.

13. *The teacher demonstrates optimism for the learning of every student, while providing a constructive and positive environment for learning.* Much of this resource guide is devoted to the provision of specific guidelines and resources for developing this competency. Both common sense and research tell us clearly that students enjoy and learn better from a teacher who is positive and optimistic, encouraging, nurturing, and happy, rather than from a teacher who is negative and pessimistic, discouraging, uninterested, and grumpy.

14. *The teacher demonstrates confidence in each student's ability to learn.* For a student, nothing at school is more satisfying than a teacher who demonstrates confidence in that student's abilities. Unfortunately, for some students, a teacher's show of confidence may be the only positive indicator that student ever receives. Each of us can recall with admiration a

teacher (or other significant person) who demonstrated confidence in our ability to accomplish seemingly formidable tasks. A competent teacher demonstrates this confidence with each and every student. This doesn't mean that you must personally like every student with whom you will ever come into contact; it does mean that you accept each one as a person of dignity who is worthy of receiving your respect and professional competencies.

15. *The teacher is skillful and fair in the employment of strategies for the assessment of student learning.* The competent teacher is knowledgeable about the importance of providing immediate intensive intervention when learning problems become apparent, implementing appropriate learning assessment tools while avoiding the abuse of power afforded by the assessment process. Assessment is the central topic of Chapter 11.

16. *The teacher is skillful in working with parents and guardians, colleagues, administrators, and the classified staff and maintains and nurtures friendly and ethical professional relationships.* Teachers, parents and guardians, administrators, and classified staff all share one common purpose, and that is to serve the education of the students. It is done best when they do it cooperatively. An exemplary school and a skillful teacher ensure that parents and guardians are involved in their children's learning (as discussed in Chapter 1 and again in Chapter 11).

17. *The teacher demonstrates continuing interest in professional responsibilities and opportunities.* Knowing that ultimately each and every activity has an effect upon the classroom, the competent teacher assumes an active interest in total school life. The purpose of the school is to serve the education of the students, and the classroom is the primary, but not the only, place where this occurs. Every committee meeting, school event, faculty meeting, school board meeting, office, program, and any other planned function that is related to school life shares in the ultimate purpose of better serving the education of the students.

18. *The teacher exhibits a wide range of interests.* This includes interest in the activities of the students and the many aspects of the school and its surrounding community. The competent teacher is interesting because of his interests; a teacher with varied interests more often motivates and captures the attention of more students. A teacher with no interests outside her subject and the classroom is likely a dull teacher.

19. *The teacher shares a healthy sense of humor.* The positive effects of appropriate humor (i.e., humor that is not self-deprecating or disrespectful of others) on learning are well established: (a) a drop in pulse rate; (b) reduction of feelings of anxiety, tension, and stress; (c) secretion of endorphins; and (d) an increase

in blood oxygen. Because of these effects, humor encourages creativity and higher-level thinking. Students appreciate and learn more from a teacher who shares a sense of humor and laughs with the students.

20. *The teacher is quick to recognize a student who may be in need of special attention.* A competent teacher is alert to recognize any student who demonstrates behaviors indicating a need for special attention, guidance, or counseling. The teacher knows how and where to refer the student, doing so with minimal class disruption or embarrassment to the student. For example, a pattern of increasingly poor attendance or of steady negative attention-seeking behaviors is among the more obvious early signals of the student who is potentially at risk of dropping out of school.

21. *The teacher makes specific and frequent efforts to demonstrate how the subject content may be related to the lives of the students.* A potentially dry and dull topic is made significant and alive when taught by a competent teacher. Regardless of topic, somewhere there are competent teachers teaching that topic, and one of the significant characteristics of their effectiveness is that they make the topic relevant to their students, helping the students make meaningful connections. As stated by Schmoker, "numerous studies . . . point out what common sense should have already told us: Students don't learn much from dull, meaningless exercises and assignments. This situation may be one of the root causes of student disaffection, especially in secondary school where it is most pronounced."[5] Obtaining ideas from professional journals, attending workshops, and communicating with colleagues either personally or via electronic bulletin boards are ways of discovering how to make a potentially dry and boring topic interesting for students.

22. *The teacher is reliable.* The competent teacher can be relied on to fulfill professional responsibilities, promises, and commitments. A teacher who cannot be relied on is quick to lose credibility with the students (as well as with colleagues and administrators). An unreliable teacher is an incompetent teacher. For whatever reason, a teacher who is chronically absent from his teaching duties is an "at-risk teacher."

Specific teacher behaviors follow later in this chapter, and guidelines and resources to assist you in your development of these competencies permeate this resource guide. Let's next review the category of commitment and professionalism.

---

5. M. Schmoker, *Results: The Key to Continuous School Improvement* (Alexandria, VA: Association for Supervision and Curriculum Development, 1996), p. 99.

COMMITMENT AND PROFESSIONALISM

You are expected to show a commitment to the school's philosophy and mission and to the personal as well as the intellectual development of the students. Not only do effective teachers expect, demand, and receive positive results in learning from their students while in the classroom, they are also interested and involved in the activities of the students outside the classroom. They willingly sacrifice personal time to give them attention and guidance. In short, you are expected to be truly committed to the intellectual and personal development of your students.

1. Knowledge of activities of interest to the students.
2. Familiarity with the school campus and community.
3. Acquaintance with members of the faculty and the nonteaching staff.
4. Knowledge of school and district policies.
5. Familiarity with the backgrounds of the students.
6. Knowledge of procedures for such routine matters as planning and scheduling of before- and after-school activities; rest room regulations; distribution and collection of textbooks and other school materials; class dismissal; ordering of supplies; fire drills and severe weather; daily attendance records; school assemblies; sharing of instructional space with other teachers; arranging for and preparing displays for common areas of the school.
7. Understanding of your expected role in teaching common elements of the curriculum, such as writing.
8. Classroom duties such as maintaining a cheerful, pleasant, and safe environment; obtaining materials needed for each lesson; keeping supplies orderly; supervising students who are helpers.
9. Understanding of your expected role in the parent-teacher organization and other community participation meetings.
10. The many conferences that will be needed, such as those between teacher and teacher; teacher and student; teacher and parent or guardian; teacher, student, and parent; teacher and administrator; and teacher and community representative.
11. Professional meetings, such as those of the interdisciplinary teaching team, other school and district committees, parent-teacher and community groups, and local, regional, state, and national professional organizations.
12. Time to relax and enjoy family and hobbies.

Figure 2.1
Noninstructional responsibilities of the classroom teacher.

Noninstructional Responsibilities

The aspects of the teacher as a decision maker with professional commitments take on a very real dimension when you consider specific noninstruction-related and instruction-related responsibilities of the classroom teacher.

Figure 2.1 provides a dozen categories of items that should alert you to the many noninstructional matters with which you should become familiar, especially during your first year of teaching. Their importance and the amount of time they require are often underestimated by beginning teachers.

Instructional Responsibilities

The 14 items listed in Figure 2.2 introduce you to or remind you of the instructional responsibilities you will have as a classroom teacher; they are the primary focus of study of the remainder of this resource guide. After you have reviewed the lists of instructional and noninstructional responsibilities of the classroom teacher, do Exercise 2.3, which is a model of cooperative learning for a first-year teacher.

1. Planning long-range units and daily lessons.
2. Learning the interests of the students so that lessons will reflect those interests.
3. Incorporating the individual learning styles, capacities, and modalities of the students in lesson plans.
4. Reading student papers.
5. Assessing and recording student progress.
6. Preparing the classroom.
7. Providing classroom instruction.
8. Thinking about professional growth and development, which may include attending university courses, attending workshops and other presentations offered by the school district or professional organizations, and reading professional literature.
9. Developing a firm but fair classroom management system.
10. Reacquainting yourself with the developmental characteristics of the age level of the students.
11. Learning the backgrounds of students with special problems who might cause concerns in the learning environment.
12. Developing techniques and plans for cross-age tutoring, peer coaching, cooperative learning, and other teaching strategies.
13. Identifying resources such as those on the Internet.
14. Devoting time to team planning.

Figure 2.2
Instructional responsibilities of the classroom teacher.

EXERCISE 2.3

Reviewing the Professional Responsibilities of a First-Year Teacher

Instructions: The purpose of this exercise is to review the responsibilities of a first-year teacher. Have the class of teacher candidates divide into groups of four. Within each group, each member should play one of the following roles: (1) group facilitator; (2) recorder; (3) materials manager; and (4) reporter. The group is to choose one of these six categories of responsibilities:

1. Audiovisual/media.
2. Classroom environment.
3. Clerical.
4. Instructional.
5. Professional activities.
6. Supervision.

The group should then read the responsibilities for their selected category listed on the following cards and arrange them in prioritized order, beginning with the most important. The group facilitator will lead this discussion. Under the guidance of the materials manager, the group may cut the cards apart so that they can be physically manipulated as priorities are discussed. The recorder should take notes of the group's work, which can then be discussed in order to develop the report that will be made to the class.

After a prearranged discussion time, recall the entire class and ask each reporter to share the group's (1) prioritized order of responsibilities and (2) estimate of the amount of time that a beginning teacher might devote to these responsibilities each week.

As each group reports, all members of the class should enter its list of priorities and time estimate on the Recap Sheet.

After completion of this exercise, the class may wish to discuss the group dynamics of this model of cooperative learning (see Chapter 8). For discussion in either large or small groups, key questions might be:

1. Would you use this form of discussion in your own teaching?
2. How would you divide a class into groups of four?

Other questions may be generated by the group work.

For Your Notes

CARDS FOR EXERCISE 2.3
Audiovisual/Media Responsibilities

Selecting, ordering, and returning cassettes, films, videodiscs, and other materials.	
Preparing and operating equipment.	Reviewing selected materials.
Planning class introduction to the audiovisual materials.	Other audiovisual responsibilities as determined.

Estimated hours a beginning teacher will devote to audiovisual/media responsibilities each week = _____.

CARDS FOR EXERCISE 2.3
Classroom Environment Responsibilities

Planning and constructing displays.	Preparing bulletin boards.
Reading, announcing, and posting class notices.	Managing a classroom library.
Opening and closing windows, arranging furniture, cleaning the writing board.	Other classroom environment responsibilities as determined.

Estimated hours a beginning teacher will devote to classroom environment responsibilities each week = _____.

CARDS FOR EXERCISE 2.3
Clerical Responsibilities

Maintaining attendance and tardy records.	Entering grades, scores, or marks into a record book or onto the computer.
Preparing progress and grade reports.	Typing, drawing, and duplicating instructional materials.
Locating resource ideas and materials to support lessons.	Other clerical responsibilities as determined.

Estimated hours a beginning teacher will devote to clerical responsibilities each week = _____.

CARDS FOR EXERCISE 2.3
Instructional Responsibilities

Giving additional instruction (e.g., to students who need one-to-one attention, those who have been absent, or small review groups).	Correcting student work.
Preparing special learning materials.	Preparing, reading, and scoring tests; helping students self-evaluate.
Writing information on the board.	Preparing long-range and daily lesson plans.
Grouping for instruction.	Other instructional responsibilities as determined.

Estimated hours a beginning teacher will devote to clerical responsibilities each week = _____.

CARDS FOR EXERCISE 2.3
Professional Activities Responsibilities

Researching and writing teacher reports.	Attending teachers' and school district meetings.
Planning and attending parent-teacher meetings.	Attending local teachers' organization meetings.
Attending state, regional, and national professional organizations; taking university classes.	Other professional activities responsibilities as determined.

Estimated hours a beginning teacher will devote to clerical responsibilities each week = _____.

CARDS FOR EXERCISE 2.3
Supervision Responsibilities

Supervising before- or after-school activities.	Supervising hallways, lunchrooms, and bathrooms.
Supervising student assemblies.	Supervising field trips.
Supervising laboratory activities.	Settling students' disputes.

Other supervision responsibilities as determined.

Estimated hours a beginning teacher will devote to supervision responsibilities each week = _____.

EXERCISE 2.3
Recap Sheet

Audiovisual/Media Responsibilities

1. _____

2. _____

3. _____

4. _____

5. _____

    Estimated hours = _____

Classroom Environment Responsibilities

1. _____

2. _____

3. _____

4. _____

5. _____

6. _____

    Estimated hours = _____

Clerical Responsibilities

1. _____

2. _____

3. _____

4. _____

5. _____

6. _____

    Estimated hours = _____

Instructional Responsibilities

1. _____

2. _____

3. _____

4. _____

5. _____

6. _____

7. _____

8. _____

    Estimated hours = _____

Professional Activities Responsibilities

1. _____

2. _____

3. _____

4. _____

5. _____

6. _____

    Estimated hours = _____

Supervision Responsibilities

1. _____

2. _____

3. _____

4. _____

5. _____

6. _____

7. _____

    Estimated hours = _____

STYLES OF LEARNING AND TEACHING

Teachers who are most effective adapt their teaching styles and methods to their students, using approaches that interest the students, that are neither too easy nor too difficult, that match the students' learning styles and learning capacities, and that are relevant to the students' lives. This adaptation process is further complicated because, as implied in Chapter 1, each student is different from every other one. All do not have the same interests, abilities, backgrounds, or learning styles and capacities. As a matter of fact, not only do students differ from one another, but each student can change to some extent from one day to the next. What appeals to a student today may not have the same appeal tomorrow. Therefore, you need to consider both the nature of students in general (for example, methods appropriate for a particular seventh grade class are unlikely to be the same as those that work best for most classes composed of high school seniors) and each student in particular. What follows is a synopsis of knowledge about student learning.

Brain Laterality

How a person learns is, in part, related to differences in the left and right hemispheres of the brain. This theory is sometimes referred to as *brain laterality* or *brain hemisphericity.* Verbal learning, logical and convergent thinking, and the academic cognitive processes are dominated by the left cerebral hemisphere, while affective, intuitive, spatial, emotional, and divergent thinking and visual elements are dominated by the right cerebral hemisphere. Some students are oriented toward right cerebral hemisphere learning and others toward the left. This means that some students learn better through verbal interactions and others learn through visual, kinesthetic, and tactile involvement. However, "in a healthy person the two hemispheres are inextricably interactive, irrespective of whether a person is dealing with words, mathematics, music, or art."[6]

BRAIN LATERALITY AND ITS IMPLICATIONS FOR TEACHING. When integrating the disciplines, using a variety of teaching strategies to engage more of the sensory input channels and helping students connect what is being learned with real-life situations, the instruction is more likely to be directed to both hemispheres.

Learning Modalities

Learning modality refers to the *sensory portal means (or input channel) by which a student prefers to receive sensory reception (modality preference) or the actual way a student learns best (modality adeptness).* Some students prefer learning by seeing, a *visual modality;* others prefer learning through instruction from others (through talk), an *auditory modality;* still others prefer learning by doing and being physically involved, referred to as *kinesthetic modality,* and by touching objects, the *tactile modality.* Sometimes a student's modality preference is not that student's modality strength. Although primary modality strength can be determined by observing students, it can also be mixed and can change as the result of experience and intellectual maturity. As one might suspect, modality integration (i.e., engaging more of the sensory input channels, using several modalities at once or staggered) has been found to contribute to better achievement in student learning. We return to this concept in Planning and Selecting Learning Activities of Chapter 6.

LEARNING MODALITY AND ITS IMPLICATIONS FOR TEACHING. Because many secondary school students have neither a preference nor a strength for auditory reception, teachers of middle school grades in particular should severely limit their use of the lecture method of instruction, that is, too much reliance on teacher talk (informal lecture or discussion). Furthermore, instruction that uses a singular approach, such as auditory (e.g., talking to the students), cheats students who learn better another way. This difference can affect student achievement. A teacher, for example, who only lectures or uses discussions day after day is shortchanging the education of students who learn better another way, for example, kinesthetic learners.

Finally, if a teacher's verbal communication conflicts with her nonverbal messages, students can become confused, and this too can affect their learning. And when there is a discrepancy between what the teacher says and what that teacher does, the teacher's nonverbal signal will win every time. Actions do speak louder than words![7] A teacher, for example, who has just finished a lesson on the conservation of energy and does

---

6. R. Nummela Caine and G. Caine, "Understanding a Brain-Based Approach to Learning and Teaching," *Educational Leadership* 48(2):67 (October 1990). See also G. Salomon, "Of Mind and Media," *Phi Delta Kappan* 78(5):375–380 (January 1997); J. Abbott, "To Be Intelligent," and C. R. Pool, "Maximizing Learning: A Conversation with Renate Nummela Caine," *Educational Leadership* 54(6):6–10 and 11–15 (respectively) (March 1997).

---

7. P. W. Miller, *Nonverbal Communication* (Washington, DC: National Education Association, 1986), and T. L. Good and J. E. Brophy, *Looking in Classrooms* (New York: Longman, 1997), p. 131.

not turn off the room lights upon leaving the class-room for lunch has, by his inappropriate modeling behavior, created cognitive disequilibrium and sabotaged the purpose of the lesson.

As a general rule, many students prefer to learn by touching objects, by feeling shapes and textures, by interacting with each other, and by moving things around. In contrast, sitting and listening are difficult for many students. Learning-style traits are known that significantly discriminate between students who are at risk of dropping out of school and students who perform well. Students who are underachieving and at risk need (1) frequent opportunities for mobility, (2) options, (3) a variety of instructional resources, environments, and sociological groupings, rather than routines and patterns, (4) learning during late morning, afternoon, or evening hours, rather than in the early morning, (5) informal seating, rather than wooden, steel, or plastic chairs, (6) low illumination, because bright light contributes to hyperactivity, and (7) introductory tactile/visual resources reinforced by kinesthetic (i.e., direct experiencing and whole-body activities) and visual resources, or introductory kinesthetic/visual resources reinforced by tactile/visual resources.[8]

You are advised to use strategies that integrate the modalities. When well designed, thematic units and project-based learning incorporate modality integration. In conclusion, then, when teaching a group of students of mixed learning abilities, mixed modality strengths, mixed language proficiency, and mixed cultural backgrounds, you must integrate learning modalities for the most successful teaching.

Learning Styles

Related to learning modality is learning style, which can be defined as *independent forms of knowing and processing information.* Whereas some secondary school students may be comfortable with beginning their learning of a new idea in the abstract (e.g., visual or verbal symbolization), most need to begin with the concrete (e.g., learning by actually doing it). Some students prosper while working in groups, and others prefer to work alone. Some are quick in their studies, whereas others are slow and methodical and cautious and meticulous. Some can sustain attention on a single topic for a long time, becoming more absorbed in their study as time passes. Others are slower starters and more casual in their pursuits but are capable of shifting with ease from subject to subject. Some can study in the midst of music, noise, or movement, whereas others need quiet, solitude, and a desk or table. The point

is this: students vary not only in their skills and preferences in the way knowledge is received, but also in how they mentally process that information once it has been received. This mental processing is a person's style of learning. It is "a gestalt combining internal and external operations derived from the individual's neurobiology, personality, and development and reflected in learner behavior."[9] A technique for investigating directly your own students' learning-style preferences is presented in Providing a Supportive Learning Environment of Chapter 3.

CLASSIFICATIONS OF LEARNING STYLES.   It is important to note that *learning style is not an indicator of intelligence, but rather an indicator of how a person learns.* Although, as implied in the preceding paragraph, there are probably as many types of learning styles as there are individuals, David Kolb describes two major differences in how people learn: how they perceive situations and how they process information.[10] On the basis of perceiving and processing and the earlier work of Carl Jung,[11] Bernice McCarthy has described four major learning styles, presented in the following paragraphs.[12]

The *imaginative learner* perceives information concretely and processes it reflectively. Imaginative learners learn well by listening to and sharing with others, integrating the ideas of others with their own experiences. Imaginative learners often have difficulty adjusting to traditional teaching, which depends less on classroom interactions and students' sharing and connecting of their prior experiences. In a traditional classroom, the imaginative learner is likely to be an at-risk student.

The *analytic learner* perceives information abstractly and processes it reflectively. The analytic learner prefers sequential thinking, needs details, and values what experts have to offer. Analytic learners do well in traditional classrooms.

The *common sense learner* perceives information abstractly and processes it actively. The common sense learner is pragmatic and enjoys hands-on learning. Common sense learners sometimes find school frustrat-

8. R. Dunn, *Strategies for Educating Diverse Learners* (Bloomington, IN: Fastback 384, Phi Delta Kappa Educational Foundation, 1995), p. 9.

9. J. W. Keefe and B. G. Ferrell, "Developing a Defensible Learning Style Paradigm," *Educational Leadership* 48(2):59 (October 1990).
10. D. Kolb, *The Learning Style Inventory* (Boston, MA: McBer, 1985).
11. C. G. Jung, *Psychological Types* (New York: Harcourt Brace, 1923). See also A. Gregorc, *Gregorc Style Delineator* (Maynard, MA: Gabriel Systems, 1985), and R. Dunn and K. Dunn, *Teaching Students through Their Individual Learning Styles* (Reston, VA: Reston Publications, 1978).
12. B. McCarthy, "Using the 4MAT System to Bring Learning Styles to Schools," *Educational Leadership* 48(2):32 (October 1990). See also B. McCarthy, "A Tale of Four Learners: 4MAT's Learning Styles," *Educational Leadership* 54(6):47–51 (March 1997).

ing unless they can see immediate use to what is being learned. In the traditional classroom the common sense learner is likely to be a learner who is at risk of not completing school, of dropping out.

The *dynamic learner* perceives information concretely and processes it actively. The dynamic learner also prefer hands-on learning and is excited by anything new. Dynamic learners are risk takers and are frustrated by learning if they see it as being tedious and sequential. In a traditional classroom the dynamic learner also is likely to be an at-risk student.

Three-Phase Learning Cycle

To understand conceptual development and change, researchers in the 1960s developed a Piaget-based theory of learning in which students are guided from concrete, hands-on learning experiences to the abstract formulations of concepts and their applications. This theory became known as the three-phase learning cycle and was the basis for an elementary school science program developed in the 1960s by researcher Robert Karplus and his colleagues at the University of California at Berkeley. There have been more recent interpretations or modifications of the three-phase cycle, such as McCarthy's 4MAT.[13]

The three phases are (1) an *exploratory hands-on phase,* in which students can explore ideas that lead to their own questions and tentative answers; (2) a *concept development phase,* in which, under the guidance of the teacher, students invent concepts and principles that help them answer their questions and reorganize their ideas; and (3) a *concept application phase,* another hands-on phase in which the students try out their new ideas by applying them to situations that are relevant and meaningful to them. During application of a concept the learner may discover new information that causes a change in the learner's understanding of the concept being applied. Thus, as discussed further in Inquiry Teaching and Discovery Learning of Chapter 9, the process of learning is cyclical.

With the 4MAT system developed by McCarthy, teachers employ a learning cycle of instructional strategies to try to reach each student's learning style. As stated by McCarthy, in the cycle, learners "sense and feel, they experience, then they watch, they reflect, then they think, they develop theories, then they try out theories, they experiment. Finally, they evaluate and synthesize what they have learned in order to apply it to their next similar experience. They get smarter. They apply experi-

ence to experiences."[14] And, in this process, they are likely to be using all four learning modalities.

The three phases of the learning cycle are comparable to the three levels of questioning and thinking, described variously by others. For example, in Elliot Eisner's *The Educational Imagination* (Macmillan, 1979), the levels are referred to as "descriptive," "interpretive," and "evaluative." In Chapter 7, when discussing levels of questioning and thinking, we use the terms *input, processing,* and *application.*

To evince constructivist learning theory and to accentuate the importance of student self-assessment, some recent variations of the learning cycle include a fourth phase, an "assessment phase."[15] However, because we believe that assessment of what students know or think they know should be a continual process, permeating all three phases of the learning cycle, we reject any treatment of "assessment" as a self-standing phase.

Theory of Multiple Intelligences

In contrast to Jung's four learning styles, Gardner introduced what he calls "learning capacities" exhibited by individuals in differing ways.[16] Originally and sometimes still referred to as multiple intelligences, capacities thus far identified are:

- *Bodily/kinesthetic*: ability to use the body skillfully and to handle objects skillfully
- *Interpersonal*: ability to understand people and relationships
- *Intrapersonal*: ability to assess one's emotional life as a means to understand oneself and others
- *Logical/mathematical*: ability to handle chains of reasoning and to recognize patterns and orders
- *Musical*: sensitivity to pitch, melody, rhythm, and tone
- *Naturalist*: ability to draw on materials and features of the natural environment to solve problems or fashion products
- *Verbal/linguistic*: sensitivity to the meaning and order of words

---

13. For information about 4MAT, contact Excel, Inc., 23385 W. Old Barrington Road, Barrington, IL 60010 (847-382-7272), or 6322 Fenworth Court, Agoura Hills, CA 91301 (818-879-7442).

14. McCarthy, p. 33.

15. For further discussion of the use of the learning cycle model in a constructivist classroom, see J. G. Brooks and M. G. Brooks, *In Search of Understanding: The Case for Constructivist Classrooms* (Alexandria, VA: Association for Supervision and Curriculum Development, 1993), pp. 116–118.

16. For Gardner's distinction between learning style and the intelligences, see H. Gardner, "Reflections on Multiple Intelligences: Myths and Messages," *Phi Delta Kappan* 77(3):200–203, 206–209 (November 1995), or H. Gardner, "Multiple Intelligences: Myths and Messages," *International Schools Journal* 15(2):8–22 (April 1996), or V. Ramos-Ford and H. Gardner, "Giftedness from a Multiple Intelligences Perspective," Chapter 5, pp. 54–66, of N. Colangelo and G. A. Davis (eds.), *Handbook of Gifted Education,* 2d ed. (Needham Heights, MA: Allyn & Bacon, 1997).

CLASSROOM VIGNETTE
Using the Theory of Multiple Intelligences (and Multilevel Instruction)

In one seventh-grade classroom, during one week of a six-week thematic unit on weather, students were concentrating on learning about the water cycle. For this study of the water cycle, with the students' help the teacher divided the class into several groups of three to five students per group. While working on six projects simultaneously to learn about the water cycle: (1) one group of students designed, conducted, and repeated an experiment to discover the number of drops of water that can be held on one side of a new one-cent coin versus the number that can be held on the side of a worn one-cent coin; (2) working in part with the first group, a second group designed and prepared graphs to illustrate the results of the experiments of the first group; (3) a third group of students created and composed the words and music of a song about the water cycle; (4) a fourth group incorporated their combined interests in mathematics and art to design, collect the necessary materials for, and create a colorful and interactive bulletin board about the water cycle; (5) a fifth group read about the water cycle in materials they researched from the Internet and various libraries; and (6) a sixth group created a puppet show about the water cycle. On Friday, after each group had finished, the groups shared their projects with the whole class.

- *Visual/spatial*: ability to perceive the world accurately and to manipulate the nature of space, such as through architecture, mime, or sculpture[17]

As discussed earlier and as implied in the presentation of McCarthy's four types of learners, many educators believe that many students who are at risk of not completing school may be dominant in a cognitive learning style that is not in synch with traditional teaching methods. Traditional methods are largely of McCarthy's analytic style, where information is presented in a logical, linear, sequential fashion, and of three of the Gardner types: verbal/linguistic, logical/mathematical, and intrapersonal. Consequently, to better synchronize methods of instruction with learning styles, some teachers and schools have restructured the curriculum and instruction around Gardner's learning capacities.[18] See the sample classroom scenario in the Classroom Vignette.

LEARNING STYLE AND ITS IMPLICATIONS FOR TEACHING. The importance of the preceding information about learning styles is that you must realize at least two facts:

1. *Intelligence is not a fixed or static reality but can be learned, taught, and developed.*[19] This concept is important for students to understand, too. When students understand that intelligence is incremental, something that is developed through use over time, they tend to be more motivated to work at learning than when they believe intelligence is a fixed entity.[20]

2. *Not all students learn and respond to learning situations in the same way.* A student may learn differently according to the situation or according to the student's ethnicity, cultural background, or socioeconomic status.[21] A teacher who uses only one style of teaching for all students or who teaches to appeal to only one or a few styles of learning, day after day, is shortchanging those students who learn better another way. As emphasized by Rita Dunn, when students do not learn the way we teach them, then we must teach them the way they learn.[22]

17. See H. Gardner and T. Hatch, "Multiple Intelligences Go to School: Educational Implications of the Theory of Multiple Intelligence," *Educational Researcher* 18(8):4–9 (November 1989); T. Blythe and H. Gardner, "A School for All Intelligences," *Educational Leadership* 47(7):33–37 (April 1990); and H. Gardner, "The Theory of Multiple Intelligences," *Annals of Dyslexia* 37:19–35 (1987).
18. See, for example, L. Ellison, "Using Multiple Intelligences to Set Goals," *Educational Leadership* 50(2):69–72 (October 1992).

19. See G. W. Bracey, "Getting Smart(er) in School," *Phi Delta Kappan* 73(5):414–416 (January 1992), and R. J. Sternberg, "What Does It Mean to Be Smart?" *Educational Leadership* 54(6):20–24 (March 1997).
20. L. B. Resnick and L. E. Klopfer, *Toward the Thinking Curriculum: Current Cognitive Research* (Alexandria, VA: 1989 ASCD Yearbook, Association for Supervision and Curriculum Development, 1989), p. 8.
21. See P. Guild, "The Culture/Learning Style Connection," *Educational Leadership* 51(8):16–21 (May 1994).
22. R. Dunn, *Strategies for Educating Diverse Learners* (Bloomington, IN: Fastback 384, Phi Delta Kappa Educational Foundation, 1995), p. 30.

Table 2.1 A Contrast of Two Teaching Styles

	Traditional Style	*Facilitating Style*
Teacher	Autocratic	Democratic
	Curriculum-centered	Student-centered
	Direct	Indirect
	Dominative	Interactive
	Formal	Informal
	Informative	Inquiring
	Prescriptive	Reflective
Classroom	Teacher-centered	Student-centered
	Linear (seats facing front)	Grouped or circular
Instructional modes	Abstract learning	Concrete learning
	Teacher-centered discussion	Discussions
	Lectures	Peer and cross-age coaching
	Competitive learning	Cooperative learning
	Some problem solving	Problem solving
	Demonstrations by teacher	Student inquiries
	From simple to complex	Start with complex tasks and use instructional scaffolding and dialogue
	Transmission of information from teacher to students	Reciprocal teaching (using dialogue) between teacher and a small group of students, then among students

Teaching Styles

Teaching style is the way teachers teach, which includes their distinctive mannerisms complemented by their choices of teaching behaviors and strategies. A teacher's style affects the way that teacher presents information and interacts with the students. It clearly is the manner and pattern of those interactions with students that determine a teacher's effectiveness in promoting student learning, positive attitudes about learning, and self-esteem.

A teacher's style is determined by the teacher's personal characteristics (especially the teacher's own learning style), experiences, and knowledge of research findings about how children learn. Teaching style can be altered, intentionally or unintentionally, as a result of changes in any of these three areas.

Although there are other ways to label and describe teaching styles,[23] we shall consider two contrasting styles—the *traditional* and the *facilitating* styles (Table 2.1). We emphasize that although today's secondary school teacher must use aspects from each style (i.e., be eclectic in style choice), there must be a strong inclination toward the facilitating style.

Multilevel Instruction

As emphasized in the preceding discussion, students in your classroom have their own independent ways of knowing and learning and also may be at different stages (and substages) of cognitive development. It is important to try to attend to how each student best learns and to where each student is developmentally, that is, to individualize the instruction. To accomplish that, many teachers use multilevel instruction (known also as *multitasking*). *Multilevel instruction occurs when different students or groups of students are working at different tasks to accomplish the same objective or working at different tasks to accomplish different objectives.* An example is the classroom scenario on page 80.

In the integration of student learning, multitasking is an important and useful, perhaps even necessary, strategy. Project-centered teaching (discussed in Chapter 8) is an instructional method that easily allows for the provision of multilevel instruction. Multilevel teaching

---

23. For example, see D. M. Gollnick and P. C. Chinn, *Multicultural Education in a Pluralistic Society,* 3rd ed. (Upper Saddle River, NJ: Prentice Hall, 1990), pp. 286–287. Their descriptions of "field-independent" and "field-sensitive" teaching styles are similar to the traditional and facilitating teaching styles that are described here.

occurs when several levels of teaching and learning are going on simultaneously. When using multilevel instruction, individual students and small groups will be doing different activities at the same time to accomplish the same or different objectives. While some students may be working independently of the teacher—that is, within the facilitating mode—others may be receiving direct instruction—that is, more within the traditional mode.

The Theoretical Origins of Teaching Styles and Their Relation to Constructivism

Constructivism and the integration of curriculum are not new to education. The importance of the constructivist and curriculum integration approaches are found, for example, in the writings of John Dewey[24] and Arthur W. Combs.[25]

Teaching styles are deeply rooted in certain theoretical assumptions about learners and their development, and although it is beyond the scope of our intent to explore deeply into those assumptions, there are three major theoretical positions and research findings that may help you understand the basis of your own emerging teaching style. Each of the three positions is based on certain philosophical and psychological assumptions that suggest different ways of working with children.

1. The learner's mind is neutral-passive to good-active, and the main focus in teaching should be the addition of new ideas to a subconscious store of old ones (tied to the theoretical positions of *romanticism-maturationism*). Key persons include Jean J. Rousseau and Sigmund Freud. Key instructional strategies include classic lecturing with rote memorization.

2. The learner's mind is neutral-passive with innate reflexes and needs, and the main focus in teaching should be on the successive, systematic changes in the learner's environment to increase the possibilities of desired behavior responses (tied to the theoretical position of *behaviorism*). Key persons include John Locke, B. F. Skinner, A. H. Thorndike, Robert Gagné, and John Watson. Key instructional strategies include practice and reinforcement as epitomized in programmed instruction.

3. The learner is a neutral-interactive purposive individual in simultaneous interaction with physical and biological environments. The main focus in teaching should be on facilitating the learner's gain and constructing new perceptions that lead to desired behavioral changes and ultimately to a more fully functioning individual (tied to the theoretical position of *cognitive-experimentalism*). Key persons are John Dewey, Lev Vygotsky, Jerome Bruner, Jean Piaget, and A. W. Combs. Key instructional strategies include discovery, inquiry, project-centered teaching, and cooperative and social-interactive learning.

We believe that a competent teacher assumes a combination of thoughts from these three theoretical positions, which then makes that teacher's style an eclectic one. With a diversity of students, a teacher must be eclectic to be most effective, utilizing at appropriate times the best of strategies and knowledgeable instructor behaviors, regardless of whether individually they can be classified within any style of dichotomy, such as traditional or facilitating, direct or indirect, formal or informal, or didactic or progressive. While teaching and preparing this resource guide, we have tried to provide an eclectic approach with a strong emphasis on cognitive-experimentalism because of its divergence in learning and the importance given to learning as a change in perceptions.

Although there are several ways to determine the nature of your interactions with students and hence your own teaching style, these techniques essentially center on the collection and analysis of two types of data: (1) the amount of talking done by you and the students and (2) the quality of your interactions with students.

Now, to further your understandings of styles of learning and teaching, do Exercises 2.4 through 2.7.

24. J. Dewey, *How We Think* (Boston, MA: Heath, 1933).

25. A. W. Combs, ed., *Perceiving, Behaving, and Becoming: A New Focus for Education* (Alexandria, VA: 1962 ASCD Yearbook, Association for Supervision and Curriculum Development, 1962).

EXERCISE 2.4

My Perceptions of How I Learn: Sources of Motivation

Instructions: The purpose of this exercise is for you to explore your present understanding of what motivates you to learn. Answer the following questions and then share those answers with your colleagues. When answering these questions, don't concern yourself with whether your answers are "right" or "wrong."

1. How do you define learning? _____

_____

_____

_____

_____

_____

2. Do you think there is any difference in the way you personally learn for short-term retention as opposed to the way you learn for long-term retention? If so, explain that difference.

_____

_____

_____

_____

_____

_____

_____

_____

_____

_____

_____

_____

_____

_____

_____

_____

3. Identify and rank in order (from most important to least important) what you believe to be at least three sources of motivation for your own learning. For each, identify by writing either *I* or *E* in the blank whether you believe that source is Intrinsic (within yourself) or Extrinsic (e.g., grades, rewards, expectations of others).

_____ a. _____
_____
_____
_____

_____ b. _____
_____
_____
_____

_____ c. _____
_____
_____
_____

_____ d. _____
_____
_____
_____

_____ e. _____
_____
_____
_____

4. Did you ever learn something that you previously had thought you could never have learned? Explain, describing what motivated you and helped you to learn it.

_____
_____
_____
_____
_____
_____
_____
_____
_____

EXERCISE 2.5

My Perceptions of How I Learn: Techniques Used

Instructions: The purpose of this exercise is for you to explore your present understanding of how you learn best. Answer the following questions and then share those answers with your colleagues. When answering these questions, don't concern yourself with whether your answers are "right" or "wrong."

1. When in a class, how do you study for an examination? Check each of the following techniques you use, then elaborate with an example that will help you explain it to others. For each technique that you use, circle *S* or *L* to indicate that you believe you use this technique primarily for short-term (*S*) or long-term (*L*) retention.

_____ a. *Outline material?*   *S*   *L*

_____

_____

_____ b. Use *mnemonic* devices?   *S*   *L*

_____

_____

_____ c. Make *connections* (i.e., build bridges) of the new material with your prior knowledge, experiences, attitudes, beliefs, or values (known as elaboration)? *S*   *L*

_____

_____

_____ d. Write *summaries* of important ideas?   *S*   *L*

_____

_____

_____ e. Construct *visual (graphic) representations* (e.g., charts, graphs, maps, or networks) of verbal material to be learned?   *S*   *L*

_____

_____

_____ f. Participate in *cooperative study* groups?   *S*   *L*

_____

_____

_____ g. *Teach others* what you have learned or are learning?   *S*   *L*

_____

_____

_____   h. Other?   *S*   *L*

_____

_____

2. From your selections and descriptions in the first question, do you believe that there is any difference in how you learn, depending on whether you are learning for short-term or long-term retention? If so, in a paragraph describe this difference.

_____

_____

_____

_____

_____

_____

_____

_____

3. Now share your answers to questions 1 and 2 with your colleagues, and compare their results with your own. How do they compare?

_____

_____

_____

_____

_____

_____

_____

_____

4. From this exercise, what can you conclude? What have you learned about your own learning? About how others learn?

_____

_____

_____

_____

_____

_____

_____

EXERCISE 2.6

Using Observation of Classroom Interaction to Analyze One Teacher's Style*

Instructions: The purpose of this exercise is to visit a classroom to observe and identify the instructional style for that particular day. Be certain first to obtain permission and then to explain to the teacher that you are observing, not evaluating, for teaching style. The host teacher may be interested in discussing with you the results of your observation. A follow-up thank you letter is appropriate.

1. Class, grade level, and school visited: _____

2. Date of visit: _____

3. From the start of your classroom observation, observe at 1-minute intervals for a period of 10 minutes what the teacher is doing at that very moment, marking the appropriate traditional or facilitating teacher behavior on the chart below. Continue for the entire class meeting.

	Minutes										
Traditional teacher behaviors	*1*	*2*	*3*	*4*	*5*	*6*	*7*	*8*	*9*	*10*	*Totals*
Prescribing (giving advice or directions; being critical, evaluative; offering judgments)											
Informing (giving information; lecturing; interpreting)											
Confronting (directly challenging students)											

Traditional Behaviors Total _____

Facilitating teacher behaviors	*1*	*2*	*3*	*4*	*5*	*6*	*7*	*8*	*9*	*10*	*Totals*
Relaxing (releasing tension; using humor)											
Mediating (asking for information; being reflective; encouraging self-directed problem solving)											
Supporting (approving; confirming; validating; listening)											

Facilitating Behaviors Total _____

4. Total traditional (T) behaviors divided by total facilitating (F) behaviors = T/F Ratio.

   T/F ratio for this observation = _____

5. Conclusions about the host teacher's style on this day: _____

   _____

6. Did you discuss your observations with the host teacher? _____

*Adapted from J. Heron, *Six Category Intervention Analysis* (Guildford, England: Centre of Adult Education, University of Surrey, 1975).

For Your Notes

EXERCISE 2.7

Using a Questionnaire to Develop a Profile and a Statement about My Own Emerging Teaching Style*

Instructions: The purpose of this exercise is to help you clarify and articulate your own assumptions about teaching and learning. You will develop a profile of your emerging teaching style, and from that a statement representative of your current thinking about teaching and learning.

Step A. Read each of the 50 statements and rate your feelings about each, giving a *1* if you strongly agree, a *2* if you are neutral, and a *3* if you strongly disagree.

Remember: *1* = strongly agree; *2* = neutral; *3* = strongly disagree

_____ 1. Most of what students learn, they learn on their own.

_____ 2. Students should be concerned about other students' reactions to their work in the classroom.

_____ 3. An important part of schooling is learning to work with others.

_____ 4. Students learn more by working on their own than by working with others.

_____ 5. Students should be given opportunities to participate actively in class planning and implementation of lessons.

_____ 6. In an effective learning environment, grades are inappropriate.

_____ 7. Students enjoy working in a classroom that has clearly defined learning objectives and assessment criteria.

_____ 8. I favor teaching methods and classroom procedures that maximize students independence to learn from their own experiences.

_____ 9. Most of what students learn is learned from other students.

_____ 10. Students should be concerned with getting good grades.

_____ 11. An important part of teaching and learning is learning how to work independently.

_____ 12. The teacher should not be contradicted or challenged by a student.

_____ 13. Interchanges between students and a teacher can provide ideas about content better than those found in a textbook.

_____ 14. For students to get the most out of a class, they must be aware of the primary concerns and biases of the teacher.

_____ 15. Students should not be given high grades unless clearly earned.

_____ 16. Learning should help the student to become an independent thinker.

_____ 17. Most of what students learn is learned from their teachers.

_____ 18. A teacher who makes students do things they don't want to do is an ineffective teacher.

*Adapted from William H. Berquist and Steven R. Phillips, *A Handbook for Faculty Development* (Washington, DC: The Council for Independent Colleges, June 1975), pp. 25–27.

_____ 19. Learning takes place most effectively under conditions in which students are in competition with one another.

_____ 20. A teacher should try to persuade students that particular ideas are valid and exciting.

_____ 21. To do well in school, students must be assertive.

_____ 22. Facts in textbooks are usually accurate.

_____ 23. I favor the use of teaching methods and classroom procedures that maximize students and teacher interaction.

_____ 24. Most of what students learn is learned from books.

_____ 25. A teacher who lets students do whatever they want is incompetent.

_____ 26. Students can learn more by working with an enthusiastic teacher than by working alone.

_____ 27. I favor the use of teaching methods and classroom procedures that maximize students learning of basic subject matter content.

_____ 28. Ideas of other students are useful for helping a students understand the content of lessons.

_____ 29. A students should study what the teacher says is important and not necessarily what is important to that student.

_____ 30. A teacher who does not motivate students interest in subject content is incompetent.

_____ 31. An important part of education is learning how to perform under testing and evaluation conditions.

_____ 32. Students can learn more by sharing their ideas than by keeping their ideas to themselves.

_____ 33. Teachers tend to give students too many assignments that are trivial.

_____ 34. Ideas contained in the textbook should be the primary source of the content taught.

_____ 35. Students should be given high grades as a means of motivating them and increasing their self-esteem.

_____ 36. The ideas a students brings into a class are useful for helping the student to understand subject content.

_____ 37. Students should study what is important to them and not necessarily what the teacher claims is important.

_____ 38. Learning takes place most effectively under conditions in which students are working independently of one another.

_____ 39. Teachers often give students too much freedom of choice in content, methods, and procedures.

_____ 40. Teachers should clearly explain what it is they expect from students.

_____ 41. Students' ideas about content are often better than those ideas found in textbooks.

_____ 42. Classroom discussions are beneficial learning experiences.

_____ 43. A student's education should help the students to become a successful and contributing member of society.

_____ 44. Learning takes place most effectively under conditions in which students are working cooperatively with one another.

_____ 45. Teachers often are too personal with their students.

_____ 46. A teacher should encourage students to disagree with or challenge that teacher in the classroom.

_____ 47. Students have to be able to work effectively with other people to do well in school.

_____ 48. For students to get the most out of school, they must assume at least part of the responsibility for their learning.

_____ 49. Students seem to enjoy discussing their ideas about learning with the teacher and other students.

_____ 50. A student's education should help the student to become a sensitive human being.

Step B.   From the list of 50 items, write the items (by their number) in two columns, those with which you held strong agreement, and those with which you strongly disagreed, ignoring those items to which you gave a *2* (were neutral).

Strongly agreed   *Strongly disagreed*

Step C.   In groups of three or four, discuss your lists (in Step B) with your classmates. From the discussion, you may rerank any items you wish.

Step D.   You now have a finalized list of those items with which you were in agreement, and those with which you disagreed. On the basis of those two lists, write a paragraph that summarizes your philosophy about teaching and learning. It should be no longer than one-half page in length. That statement is a theoretical representation of your present teaching philosophy.

Step E.   Compare your philosophical statement with the three theoretical positions as discussed prior to this exercise. Can you clearly identify your position? Name it: _____

_____

_____

_____

Explain your rationale: _____

_____

_____

_____

_____

_____

_____

_____

_____

_____

_____

_____

_____

_____

_____

_____

_____

_____

_____

_____

_____

At the completion of this course, you may wish to revisit your philosophical statement, perhaps even to make revisions to it. It will be useful to have your educational philosophy firmly implanted in your memory for teaching job interviews at a later date (see Chapter 12).

TEACHER BEHAVIORS NECESSARY TO FACILITATE STUDENT LEARNING

Your ability to perform your instructional responsibilities effectively is directly dependent on your philosophy of learning and your knowledge of and the quality of your teaching skills. As we said at the beginning of this chapter, development of your strategy repertoire along with your skills in using specific strategies should be ongoing throughout your teaching career. To be most effective, you need a large repertoire from which to select a specific strategy for a particular goal with a distinctive group of students. In addition, you need skill in using that strategy. This section is designed to help you begin to build your strategy repertoire and to develop your skills in using specific teaching strategies. As with intelligences, teaching style is neither absolutely inherited nor fixed but continues to develop and emerge throughout one's career.

First, you must know why you have selected a particular strategy. An unknowing teacher is likely to use the teaching strategy most common in college classes—the lecture. However, the traditional lecture is seldom an effective way to instruct middle school students and even many high schoolers. As a rule, unlike many college and university students, not many secondary school students are strong auditory learners by preference and by adeptness. For most of them, learning by sitting and listening is difficult. Instead, they learn best when physically (hands-on) and intellectually (minds-on) active—that is, by using tactile and kinesthetic experiences, by touching objects, by feeling shapes and textures, by moving objects, and by talking about and sharing what they are learning. This subject is discussed further in Part III.

Second, there are basic teacher behaviors that create the conditions needed to enable students to think and to learn, whether the learning is a further understanding of concepts, the internalization of attitudes and values, the development of cognitive processes, or the actuating of the most complex psychomotor behaviors. The behaviors produce the following results: (1) students are physically and mentally engaged in the learning activities, (2) instructional time is efficiently used, and (3) classroom distractions and interruptions are minimal.

Third, the effectiveness with which a teacher carries out the basic behaviors can be measured by how well the students learn.

Basic teacher behaviors that facilitate student learning, discussed next, are: (1) structuring the learning environment; (2) accepting instructional accountability; (3) demonstrating withitness and overlapping; (4) providing a variety of motivating and challenging activities; (5) modeling appropriate behaviors; (6) facilitating student acquisition of data; (7) creating a psychologically safe environment; (8) clarifying whenever necessary; (9) using periods of silence; and (10) questioning thoughtfully. Clearly, at least some of the ten "behaviors" are also instructional "strategies"—questioning, for example. The difference is that while the behaviors must be in place for the most effective teaching to occur, strategies, discussed in Part III, are more or less discretionary—that is, they are pedagogical techniques from which the teacher may select but may not be obligated to use. For example, questioning and the use of silence are fundamental teaching behaviors, whereas lecturing and showing videos are not. Starting now and continuing throughout your teaching career, you will want to evaluate your developing competency for each of these behaviors and improve in areas where you need help. For now, we will identify and discuss each facilitating behavior and provide examples. To further your understanding of these behaviors, we suggest that the following ten behaviors and their examples be discussed in your class.

Structuring the Learning Environment

The teacher establishes an intellectual, psychological, and physical environment that enables all students to act and react productively. Specifically, the teacher:

- Attends to the organization of the classroom as a learning laboratory to establish a positive, safe, and efficient environment for student learning.
- Establishes and maintains clearly understood classroom procedures, definitions, instructions, and expectations. Helps students to clarify the learning expectations and to establish clearly understood learning objectives.
- Helps students assume tasks and responsibilities, thereby empowering them in their learning.
- Organizes the students, helping them to organize their learning. Helps students in identifying and understanding time and resource constraints. Provides instructional scaffolds, such as building bridges to student learning by helping students connect that which is being learned with what the students already know or think they know and have experienced.
- Plans and implements techniques for schema building, such as providing content and process outlines, visual diagrams, and opportunities for concept mapping.
- Plans and implements techniques for students' metacognitive development, such as *think-pair share,* in which students are asked to think about an idea, share thoughts about it with a partner, and then share the pair's thoughts with the entire class; *think-write-pair-share,* in which each student writes about his ideas and then shares in pairs before sharing with the entire class; and *jigsaw,* in which individuals or small

groups of students are given responsibilities for separate tasks, which lead to a bigger task or understanding, thereby putting together parts to make a whole (as done in this chapter with Exercise 2.3).

- Plans lessons that have clear and concise beginnings and endings with much of the planning done collaboratively with the students.
- Provides frequent summary reviews, often by using student self-assessment of what is being learned. Structures and facilitates ongoing formal and informal discussion based on a shared understanding of rules of discourse.

Accepting Instructional Accountability

While holding students accountable for their learning, the teacher is willing to be held accountable for the effectiveness of the learning process and outcomes (the locus of control discussed at the start of this chapter). Specifically, the teacher:

- Assumes responsibility for professional decision making and the risks associated with that responsibility. Shares some responsibility for decision making and risk taking with the students.
- Communicates clearly to parents, administrators, and colleagues.
- Communicates to the students that accomplishment of learning goals and objectives is a responsibility they share with the teacher.
- Plans exploratory activities that engage students in the learning.
- Provides continuous cues for desired learning behaviors and incentives contingent upon desired performance, such as grades, points, rewards, and privileges, and establishes a clearly understood and continuous program of assessment.
- Provides opportunities for the students to demonstrate their learning, to refine and explore their questions, and to share their thinking and results.

Demonstrating Withitness and Overlapping

Withitness and overlapping, first described by Kounin, are separate but closely related behaviors.[26] **Withitness** is the teacher's awareness of the whole group. **Overlapping** is the teacher's ability to attend to several matters simultaneously. (Further discussion of and guidelines for developing these two skills are presented in Chapter 3.) Specifically, the teacher:

- Attends to the entire class while working with one student or with a small group of students, communicat-

ing this awareness with eye contact, hand gestures, body language, and clear but rather quiet verbal cues.
- Continually and simultaneously monitors all classroom activities to keep students at their tasks and to provide students with assistance and resources.
- Continues monitoring the class during any distraction such as when a visitor enters the classroom or while the students are on a field trip.
- Demonstrates an understanding of when comprehension checks and instructional transitions are needed.
- Dwells on one topic only as long as necessary for the students' understandings.
- Quickly intervenes in and redirects potential undesirable student behavior.
- Refocuses or shifts activities for a student when the student's attention begins to fade.

Providing a Variety of Motivating and Challenging Activities

The teacher uses a variety of activities that motivate and challenge all students to work to the utmost of their abilities and that engage and challenge the preferred learning styles and learning capacities of more of the students more of the time. Specifically, the teacher:

- Demonstrates optimism toward each student's ability.
- Demonstrates an unwavering expectation that each student will work to the best of her ability.
- Shows pride, optimism, and enthusiasm in learning, thinking, and teaching.
- Views teaching and learning as an organic and reciprocal process that extends well beyond the two covers of the textbook, the four walls of the classroom, and the six hours of the school day.
- With the students, plans exciting and interesting learning activities, including those that take advantage of the students' natural interest in the mysterious and novel.

Modeling Appropriate Behaviors

Effective teachers model the behaviors expected of the students. Specifically, the teacher:

- Arrives promptly in the classroom and demonstrates on-task behaviors for the entire class meeting just as is expected of the students.
- Demonstrates respect for all students. Does not interrupt when a student is showing rational thinking, even though the teacher may disagree with the words used or the direction of the student's thinking.
- Demonstrates that making "errors" is a natural event in learning and during problem solving and readily admits and corrects a mistake made by himself.

---

26. J. S. Kounin, *Discipline and Group Management in Classrooms* (New York: Holt, Rinehart and Winston, 1970).

- Is prompt in returning student papers and offers comments that provide instructive and encouraging feedback to the student.
- Models (such as by thinking aloud when solving a problem or when reading aloud to the students) and emphasizes the skills, attitudes, and values of higher-order intellectual processes. Demonstrates rational problem-solving skills and explains to the students the processes being engaged while problem solving. Provides concrete evidence to support his tentative conclusions.
- Models professionalism by spelling correctly, using proper grammar, and writing clearly and legibly.
- Practices communication that is clear and to the point. Uses "I" when "I" is meant, "we" when "we" is meant.
- Practices moments of silence (see Using Periods of Silence), thus modeling thoughtfulness, reflectiveness, and restraint of impulsiveness.
- Reinforces appropriate student behaviors and intervenes when behaviors are not appropriate, realizing that adolescents are also models for other adolescents.

Facilitating Student Acquisition of Data

The teacher makes sure that data are accessible to students as input that they can process. Specifically, the teacher:

- Ensures that sources of information are readily available to students for their use. Selects books, media, and materials that facilitate student learning. Ensures that equipment and materials are readily available for students to use. Identifies and uses resources beyond the walls of the classroom and the boundaries of the school campus.
- Creates a responsive classroom environment with direct learning experiences.
- Emphasizes major ideas.
- Provides clear and specific instructions.
- Provides feedback and feedback mechanisms about each student's performance and progress. Encourages students to organize and maintain devices to self-monitor their progress in learning and thinking.
- Selects examples that help students bridge what is being learned with what they already know and have experienced.
- Serves as a resource person and uses cooperative learning, thus regarding students as resources.

Creating a Psychologically Safe Environment

To encourage the positive development of student self-esteem, to provide a psychologically safe learning environment, and to encourage the most creative thought and behavior, the teacher provides an attractive and stimulating classroom environment and appropriate nonevaluative and nonjudgmental responses. Specifically, the teacher:

- Avoids using criticism. Criticism is a negative value judgment, and "when a teacher responds to a student's ideas or actions with such negative words as 'poor,' 'incorrect,' or 'wrong,' the response tends to signal inadequacy or disapproval and ends the student's thinking about the task."[27]
- Frequently uses minimal reinforcement (i.e., nonjudgmental acceptance behaviors, such as nodding head, writing a student's response on the board, or saying "I understand"). Whereas elaborate praise is generally unrelated to student achievement, minimal reinforcement, using words like *right, okay, good, uh-huh,* and *thank you,* does correlate with achievement.
- Infrequently uses strong praise. By the time students are in secondary school, teacher praise, a positive value judgment and the opposite of criticism, has little or no value as a form of positive reinforcement. When praise is used, it should be mild, private, and for student accomplishment, rather than for effort, and for each student, the frequency in using praise should be gradually reduced. When praise is reduced, a more diffused sociometric pattern develops; that is, more of the students become directly and productively involved in the learning. As emphasized by Good and Brophy, praise should be simple and direct, delivered in a natural voice without dramatizing. Students see overly done theatrics as insincere.[28]

Let us consider this point. Probably no statement in this resource guide raises more eyebrows than the statement that praise for most secondary students has little or no value as a form of positive reinforcement. After all, praise may well motivate some people. However, at what cost? Praise and encouragement are often confused and considered to be the same (Figure 2.3), but they are not, and they do not have the same long-term results. This is explained as follows:

For many years there has been a great campaign for the virtues of praise in helping children gain a positive self-concept and improve their behavior. This is another time when we must "beware of what works." Praise may inspire some children to improve their behavior. The problem is that they become pleasers and approval "junkies." These children (and later these adults)

---

27. Costa, p. 54.
28. T. L. Good and J. E. Brophy, *Looking in Classrooms,* 7th ed. (New York: Longman, 1997), pp. 144–147.

Statement of Praise	**Statement of Encouragement**
1. Your painting is excellent.	1. It is obvious that you enjoy painting.
2. I am delighted that you behaved so well on our class field trip.	2. I am so delighted that we all enjoyed the class field trip.
3. You did a good job on those word problems.	3. I can tell that you have been working and are enjoying it more.
4. Your oral report on your project was well done.	4. I can tell that you got really interested in your topic for the oral report on your project.
5. Great answer, Louise!	5. Louise, your answer shows that you gave a lot of thought to the question.

Figure 2.3
Examples of statements of praise versus encouragement.

develop self-concepts that are totally dependent on the opinions of others. Other children resent and rebel against praise, either because they don't want to live up to the expectations of others or because they fear they can't compete with those who seem to get praise so easily. The alternative that considers long-range effects is encouragement. The long-range effect of encouragement is self-confidence. The long-range effect of praise is dependence on others.[29]

- Perceives her classroom as the place where she works and where students learn and makes that classroom, with its tools available, a place of pride—as stimulating and useful as possible.
- Plans within the lessons behaviors that show respect for the experiences and ideas of individual students.
- Provides positive individual student attention as often as possible. Writes sincere reinforcing personalized comments on student papers. Provides incentives and rewards for student accomplishments.
- Uses nonverbal cues to show awareness and acceptance of individual students. Uses paraphrasing and reflective listening. Uses empathic acceptance of a student's expression of feelings, that is, demonstrating by words and gestures that from the student position you can understand.

Clarifying Whenever Necessary

The teacher's responding behavior seeks further elaboration from a student about that student's idea or comprehension. Specifically, the teacher:

- Helps the students to connect new content to that previously learned. Helps students to relate content of a lesson to students' other school and nonschool experiences. Helps students make learning connections between disciplines.
- Politely invites a student to be more specific and the opportunity for a student to elaborate on or rephrase an idea or to provide a concrete illustration of an idea.
- Provides frequent opportunity for summary reviews.
- Repeats or paraphrases a student's response, allowing the student to correct any other person's misinterpretation of what the student said or implied.
- Selects instructional strategies that help students correct their prior notions.

Using Periods of Silence

The teacher effectively uses periods of silence in the classroom. Specifically, the teacher:

- Actively listens when a student is talking.
- Keeps silent when students are working quietly or are attending to a visual display and maintains classroom control by using nonverbal signals and indirect intervention strategies.
- Pauses while talking to allow for thinking and reflection.
- Uses teacher silence to stimulate group discussion.
- Waits longer than two seconds after asking a question or posing a problem.[30] (Wait-time is discussed further in Chapter 7.)

---

29. J. Nelsen, *Positive Discipline* (New York: Ballantine Books, 1987), p. 103. See also L. A. Froyen, *Classroom Management: The Reflective Teacher-Leader*, 2nd ed. (Upper Saddle River, NJ: Prentice Hall, 1993), pp. 294–298, and D. L. Silvernail, *Teaching Styles as Related to Student Achievement*, 2nd ed. (Washington, DC: National Education Association, 1987), pp. 17–21.

30. Studies in effective wait-time began with the classic study of M. B. Rowe, "Wait Time and Reward as Instructional Variables, Their Influence on Language, Logic and Fate Control: Part I. Wait Time," *Journal of Research in Science Teaching* 11(2):81–94 (1974). See also K. Tobin, "Effects of Extended Wait-Time on Discourse Characteristics in Achievement in Middle School Grades," *Journal of Research in Science Teaching* 21(8):61 (1987).

Questioning Thoughtfully

The teacher uses thoughtfully worded questions to induce learning and to stimulate thinking and the development of students' thinking skills. (Questioning is the topic of Chapter 7.) Specifically, the teacher:

- Encourages student questioning, without judging the quality or relevancy of a student's question. Attends to student questions and responds and encourages other students to respond, often by building upon the content of a student's questions and student responses.
- Helps students develop their own questioning skills and provides opportunities for students to explore their own ideas, to obtain data, and to find temporary answers to their own questions.
- Plans questioning sequences that elicit a variety of thinking skills and that maneuver students to higher levels of thinking and doing.
- Uses a variety of types of questions.
- Uses questions to help students to explore their knowledge, to develop new understandings, and to discover ways of applying their new understandings.

SUMMARY

You have reviewed the realities of the responsibilities of today's classroom teacher. Being a good teacher takes time, concentrated effort, and just plain hard work. Nobody truly knowledgeable about it ever said that good teaching was easy.

Your professional responsibilities as a teacher extend well beyond the four walls of the classroom, the six hours of the school day, the five days of the school week, and the 180 days of the school year. This chapter presented the many expectations of the classroom teacher: (1) to demonstrate effective decision making; (2) to be committed to the students, to the school's mission, and to the profession; (3) to offer effective instruction; and (4) to fulfill numerous noninstructional responsibilities. As you have read and discussed these responsibilities, you should have begun to comprehend the reality of being a competent secondary school classroom teacher. The next and final chapter of Part I presents ways of establishing an effective learning environment within which to carry out these responsibilities.

Teaching style is the way teachers teach, their distinctive mannerisms complemented by their choices of teaching behaviors and strategies. Style develops from tradition, from one's beliefs and experiences, and from one's knowledge of research findings. You analyzed your own beliefs, observed one teacher and that teacher's style for that lesson, and began the development of your philosophy about teaching and learning, a philosophical statement that should be useful to you during later job interviews (discussed in Chapter 12).

Exciting research findings continue to come from several, and related, areas: about student learning, conceptual development, thinking styles, and neurophysiology. The findings continue to support the hypothesis that a teacher's best choice of teaching style is eclectic with a bent toward the facilitating style, at least until the day arrives when students of certain thinking styles can be practically matched to teachers with particular teaching styles. Future research will undoubtedly shed additional light on the relationships between pedagogy, pedagogical styles, and student thinking and learning.

Today, there seems to be much agreement that the essence of the learning process is a combined self-awareness, self-monitoring, and active reflection. The most effective teaching and learning are an interactive process and involve both learning and learning how to learn.

QUESTIONS FOR CLASS DISCUSSION

1. A 1964 publication entitled *Six Areas of Teacher Competencies* (Burlingame, CA: California Teachers Association) identified six roles of the classroom teacher: director of learning, counselor and guidance worker, mediator of the culture, link with the community, member of the school staff, and member of the profession. Explain today's relevance, if any, of each of these six roles.
2. Identify a secondary school teacher whom you consider to be competent, and compare what you recall about that teacher's classroom with the characteristics of competent teachers as presented in this chapter. Share your comparison with others in the class.
3. Before studying this chapter, were you fully aware of the extent of a classroom teacher's responsibilities? Explain your response.
4. Explain why knowledge of learning styles, learning capacities, and teaching styles is or should be important to you.
5. In small groups, for a specific concept usually taught in a subject of your choice (grades 7 to 12), brainstorm, then demonstrate to the rest of the class specifically how you might help students bridge their learning of that concept with what is going on in their lives and with other disciplines.
6. Colleen, a social studies teacher, has a class of 33 eighth graders who, during her lecture, teacher-led discussion, and recitation lessons are restless and inattentive, creating for her a problem in classroom management. At Colleen's invitation, the school psychologist tests the students for learning modality and finds that of the 33 students, 29 are predominately kinesthetic learners. Of what value is this information to Colleen? Describe what, if anything, Colleen should try as a result of this information.

7. Compare the teacher use of praise and of encouragement for student work; describe specific classroom situations in which each is more appropriate.

8. Describe any prior concepts you held that changed as a result of your experiences with this chapter. Describe the changes.

9. From your current observations and field work as related to this teacher preparation program, clearly identify one specific example of educational practice that seems contradictory to practice or theory as presented in this chapter. Present your explanation for the discrepancy.

10. Do you have questions generated by the content of this chapter? If you do, list them along with ways answers might be found.

SUGGESTED READINGS

Airasian, P. W., and Walsh, M. E. "Constructivist Cautions." *Phi Delta Kappan* 78(6):444–449 (February 1997).

Armstrong, T. *Multiple Intelligences in the Classroom.* Alexandria, VA: Association for Supervision and Curriculum Development, 1994.

Beisenherz, P., and Dantonio, M. *Using the Learning Cycle to Teach Physical Science: A Hands-on Approach for the Middle Grades.* Portsmouth, NH: Heinemann, 1996.

Danielson, C. *Enhancing Professional Practice: A Framework for Teaching.* Alexandria, VA: Association for Supervision and Curriculum Development, 1996.

Dunn, R. *Strategies for Educating Diverse Learners.* Bloomington, IN: Fastback 384, Phi Delta Kappa Educational Foundation, 1995.

Dunn, R., and Dunn, K. *Teaching Secondary Students through Their Individual Learning Styles: Practical Approaches for Grades 7–12.* Boston: Allyn & Bacon, 1992.

Frymier, J. *Accountability in Education: Still an Evolving Concept.* Bloomington, IN: Fastback 395, Phi Delta Kappa Educational Foundation, 1996.

Gardner, H. *Creating Minds.* New York: Basic Books, 1993.

Gardner, H. "Multiple Intelligences: Myths and Messages." *International Schools Journal* 15(2):8–22 (April 1996).

Gardner, H. *Multiple Intelligences: The Theory in Practice.* New York: Basic Books, 1993.

Gredler, M. E. *Learning and Instruction: Theory into Practice.* Upper Saddle River, NJ: Prentice Hall, 1997.

Guild, P. "The Culture/Learning Style Connection." *Educational Leadership* 51(8):16–21 (May 1994).

Harris, K., and Graham, S. "Memo to Constructivists: Skills Count, Too." *Educational Leadership* 53(5):26–29 (February 1996).

Hoerr, T. R. *Implementing Multiple Intelligences: The New City School Experience.* Bloomington, IN: Fastback 407, Phi Delta Kappa Educational Foundation, 1996.

Kotulak, R. *Inside the Brain: Revolutionary Discoveries of How the Mind Works.* Kansas City, MO: Andrews and McMeel, 1996.

Kranz, B. *Identifying Talents among Multicultural Children.* Bloomington, IN: Fastback 364, Phi Delta Kappa Educational Foundation, 1994.

Mamchur, C. *A Teacher's Guide to Cognitive Type Theory and Learning Style.* Alexandria, VA: Association for Supervision and Curriculum Development, 1996.

Mansilla, V. B., and Gardner, H. "Of Kinds of Disciplines and Kinds of Understanding." *Phi Delta Kappan* 78(5):381–386 (January 1997).

Melton, L., and Pickett, W. *Using Multiple Intelligences in Middle School Reading.* Bloomington, IN: Fastback 411, Phi Delta Kappa International, 1997.

Mizelle, N. B. "Enhancing Young Adolescents' Motivation for Literacy Learning." *Middle School Journal* 28(3):16–25 (January 1997).

Parnell, D. "Cerebral Context." *Vocational Education Journal* 71(3):18–21, 50 (March 1996).

Rosenfeld, M., Freeberg, N. E., and Bukatko, P. *The Professional Functions of Secondary School Teachers.* Research Report 92-47. Princeton, NJ: Educational Testing Service, 1992.

Rosenfeld, M., Wilder, G., and Bukatko, P. *The Professional Functions of Middle School Teachers.* Research Report 92-46. Princeton, NJ: Educational Testing Service, 1992.

Salomon, G. "Of Mind and Media: How Culture's Symbolic Forms Affect Learning and Thinking." *Phi Delta Kappan* 78(5):375–380 (January 1997).

Sternberg, R. J. "Allowing for Thinking Styles." *Educational Leadership* 52(3):36–40 (November 1994).

Sternberg, R. J. "What Does It Mean to Be Smart?" *Educational Leadership* 54(6):20–24 (March 1997).

Strong, R., Silver, H. F., and Robinson, A. "What Do Students Want and What Really Motivates Them?" *Educational Leadership* 53(1):8–12 (September 1995).

Wagner, P. A. *Understanding Professional Ethics.* Bloomington, IN: Fastback 403, Phi Delta Kappa Educational Foundation, 1996.

Wubbels, T., Levy, J., and Brekelmans, M. "Paying Attention to Relationships." *Educational Leadership* 54(7):82–86 (April 1997).

Chapter

3

Establishing and Maintaining an Effective and Safe Classroom Learning Environment

To be an effective teacher and to have a minimum of distractions in the classroom, you must apply your knowledge of the characteristics of adolescents as outlined in Chapter 1 as well as your knowledge of learning and facilitating behaviors as discussed in Chapter 2. Effective techniques of classroom management derive from knowledge, careful thought, and planning and should not be left for the beginning teacher to learn on the job in a sink-or-swim situation.

You must establish a classroom environment that is conducive to student learning. It must be psychologically safe, help the students to perceive the importance of what is being taught, help them realize they can successfully learn, and be instructive in the procedures for doing it. Although it is important that they learn to control their impulses and delay their need for gratification, students are more willing to spend time on a learning task when they see a value or reward in doing so, when they have some ownership in planning and carrying out the task, and when they feel they can accomplish the task. Thoughtful and thorough planning of your procedures for classroom management is as important a part of your preactive phase of instruction (discussed at the beginning of Chapter 2) as is the preparation of units and lessons. Indeed, a recent analysis of 50 years of research studies concluded that classroom management is the single most important factor influencing student learning.[1]

This chapter presents guidelines and resources that will help you to establish and manage a classroom environment that is safe for the students and favorable to their learning. Specifically, upon completion of this chapter you should be able to

1. Describe perceptions that must be in place and why they must be in place for anticipated learning to occur.
2. Identify characteristics of a classroom environment that is both safe for students and favorable to their learning.
3. Prepare your written management system.
4. Explain how you will know if you have classroom control and are an effective classroom manager.
5. Explain the difference between direct and indirect intervention to refocus a student and describe situations in which you would be most likely to use each, thereby demonstrating that you have begun building your repertoire of understandings of a teacher's options for specific classroom situations.
6. Describe by examples how each of the following contributes to effective classroom control: a positive approach, well-planned lessons, a good start of the school term, classroom procedures and rules, consistency but with professional judgment in enforcing procedures and rules, correction of student misbehavior, and classroom management.
7. Demonstrate knowledge of basic legal guidelines for the classroom teacher.

---

1. M. C. Want, G. D. Haertel, and H. J. Walberg, "What Helps Students Learn?" *Educational Leadership* 51(4):74–79 (December 1993/January 1994).

THE IMPORTANCE OF PERCEPTIONS

Unless you believe that your students can learn, they will not. Unless you believe that you can teach them, you will not. Unless your students believe that they can learn and until they want to learn, they will not.

We all know of or have heard of teachers who get the very best from their students, even from those students whom many teachers find to be the most challenging to teach. Regardless of individual circumstances, the following characteristics are common to exemplary teachers. They (1) *know* that all students can learn, (2) *expect* the best from each student, (3) establish a classroom environment that is conducive to student learning and motivates students to do their best, and (4) effectively manage their classrooms so that class time is efficiently used with the least amount of distraction to the learning process. Regardless of how well you have planned the instruction (the focus of Part II), certain perceptions by students must be in place to support the successful implementation of those plans; students must perceive that (1) the classroom environment is supportive of their efforts, (2) you care about their learning and they are welcome in your classroom, (3) the expected learning is challenging but not impossible, and (4) the anticipated learning outcomes are worthy of their time and effort to try to achieve.

PROVIDING A SUPPORTIVE LEARNING ENVIRONMENT

It is probably no surprise to you to hear that teachers whose classrooms are pleasant, positive, and challenging places to be find that their students learn and behave better than do the students of teachers whose classroom atmospheres are harsh, negative, and unchallenging. What follows now are specific suggestions for making your classroom a pleasant, positive, and challenging place, that is, an environment that supports the development of meaningful understandings.

Create a Positive Classroom Atmosphere

All students should feel welcome in your classroom and accepted by you as individuals of dignity. Although these feelings and behaviors should be reciprocal, that is, expected of the students as well, they may have to begin with your frequent modeling of the behaviors expected of the students. You must help students know that any denial by you of a student's specific behavior is *not* a denial of that individual as a worthwhile person who is still welcomed to your class to learn as long as the student agrees to follow

expected procedures. Specific actions you can use to create a positive classroom environment, some of which are repeated from Chapter 2, are

- Admonish behavior, not persons.
- Ensure that no prejudice is ever displayed against any individual student.
- Attend to the classroom's physical appearance and comfort—it is your place of work; show pride in that fact.
- Be an interesting person and an optimistic and enthusiastic teacher.
- Encourage students to set high yet realistic goals for themselves, and then show them how to work in increments toward meeting their goals, letting each know that you are confident in her ability to achieve.
- Help students develop their skills in interactive and cooperative learning.
- Involve students in every aspect of their learning, including the planning of learning activities, thereby giving them part ownership and responsibility in their learning.
- Make the learning fun, at least to the extent possible and reasonable.
- Send positive messages home to parents or guardians, even if you have to get help and write the message in the language of the student's home.
- Recognize and reward truly positive behaviors and individual successes, no matter how meager they might seem to you.
- Use interesting and motivating learning activities. See, "Motivational Teaching Strategies and Ideas for Lessons," p. XXX; Chapter 8 for specific ideas.

Two items in the preceding list are statements about giving encouragement. When using encouragement to motivate student learning, *avoid* the following behaviors because they discourage learning: (1) comparing one student with another or one class of students with another, (2) encouraging competition among students, (3) giving up or appearing to give up on any student, (4) telling a student how much better he could be, and (5) using qualifying statements, such as "I like what you did, but . . ." or "It's about time."

Get to Know the Students So as to Build Intrinsic Motivation for Learning

For classes to move forward smoothly and efficiently, they should fit the students' learning styles, learning capacities, needs, interests, and goals. To make the learning meaningful and longest lasting, build curriculum around student interests, capacities, perceptions, and perspectives. Therefore, you need to know your students well enough to be able to provide learning experiences that they will find interesting, valuable, intrinsically motivating, challenging, and rewarding. The following paragraphs describe several ways you can get to know your students as people.

QUICKLY LEARNING AND USING STUDENT NAMES. Like everyone else, secondary school students appreciate being recognized and addressed by name. Quickly learning and using their names is an important motivating strategy. One technique for learning names quickly is to use a seating chart. Many teachers prefer to assign permanent seats and then make seating charts from which they can unobtrusively check the roll while students are doing seat work. It is usually best to get your students started on the lesson before taking roll and before doing other housekeeping chores.

One way to make seat assignments is as follows. On the first day of school tell students that they can sit wherever they want but by Friday of that first week they should be in a permanent seat, from which you will make a permanent seating chart. Other teachers prefer to assign permanent seats on the first or second day of school so they can begin learning student names even more quickly. Whichever way you proceed, a seating chart assists in your quickly learning names and in taking daily roll unobtrusively.

Addressing students by name every time you speak to them helps you to learn and remember their names. (Be sure to quickly learn to pronounce their names correctly; that helps in making a good impression.) Another helpful way to learn student names is to return papers yourself, calling student names and then handing the papers to them, paying careful attention to look at each student and make mental notes that may help you to associate names with faces.

CLASSROOM SHARING DURING THE FIRST WEEK OF SCHOOL. During the first week of school many teachers take some time each day to have students present information about themselves and/or about the day's assignment. For instance, perhaps five or six students are selected each day to answer questions such as "What name would you like to be called by?" "Where did you attend school last year?" "Tell us about your hobbies and other interests." "What interested you about last night's reading, or yesterday's lesson?" You might have your students share information of this sort with each other in groups of three or four while you visit each group in turn. Yet another approach is to include everyone in a game, having students answer the questions on paper and then, as you read their answers, asking them to guess which student wrote each. How the student answers such questions or participates in such activities can be as revealing about the student as is the information (or the lack thereof) that the student does share. From

what is revealed during this sharing, you sometimes get clues about additional information you would like to solicit from the student in private or to find out from school sources.

OBSERVATIONS OF STUDENTS IN THE CLASSROOM. During learning activities the effective teacher is constantly moving around the classroom and is alert to the individual behavior (nonverbal as well as verbal) of each student in the class, whether the student is on task or gazing off and perhaps thinking about other things. Be cautious, however; just because a student is gazing out the window does not mean that the student is not thinking about the learning task. During group work is a particularly good time to observe students and get to know more about each one's skills and interests.

OBSERVATIONS OF AND CONVERSATIONS WITH STUDENTS OUTSIDE THE CLASSROOM. Another way to learn more about students is by observing them outside class, for example, at ball games, dances, plays, art and music presentations, lunch time, intramural activities, and club meetings. Observations outside the classroom can give information about student personalities, friendships, interests, and potentialities. For instance, you may find that a student who seems phlegmatic, lackadaisical, or uninterested in your classroom is a real fireball on the playing field or at some other student gathering.

CONFERENCES AND INTERVIEWS WITH STUDENTS. Conferences with students, and sometimes with family members as well, afford yet another opportunity to show that you are genuinely interested in each student as a person as well as a student. Some teachers and teaching teams plan a series of conferences during the first few weeks in which, individually or in small groups of three or four, students are interviewed by the teacher or by the teaching team. Such conferences and interviews are managed by using open-ended questions. The teacher indicates by the questions, by listening, and by nonjudgmental and empathic responses (i.e., being able to put herself in the shoes of the student, thereby understanding from where the student is coming) a genuine interest in the students. Keep in mind, however, that students who feel they have been betrayed by prior adult associations may at first be distrustful of your sincerity. In such instances, don't force it. Be patient, but do not hesitate to take advantage of the opportunity afforded by talking with individual students outside of class time. Investing a few minutes of time in a positive conversation with a student, during which you indicate a genuine interest in that student, can pay real dividends when it comes to that student's learning in your classroom.

STUDENT WRITING.   Much can be learned about students by what they write (or draw). It is important to encourage writing in your classroom, to read everything that students write (except for personal journals), and to ask for clarification when needed. Useful for this are journals and portfolios, discussed in Chapters 7, 9, and 11.

QUESTIONNAIRES.   Some teachers find valuable the use of open-ended interest-discovering and autobiographical questionnaires. Student responses to questionnaires can provide ideas about how to tailor assignments for individual students. However, you must assure the students that their answers are optional, that you are not trying to invade their privacy.

In an interest-discovering questionnaire students are asked to answer questions such as "When at lunch with your friends, what do you usually talk about?" "When you read for fun or pleasure, what do you usually read?" "What are your favorite movies, videos, or TV shows?" "Who are your favorite music video performers?" "Athletes?" "Describe your favorite hobby or other non-school-related activity." "What are your favorite sport activities to participate in and as a spectator?"

In an autobiographical questionnaire students are asked to answer questions such as "Where were you born?" "What do you plan to do when you finish high school?" "Do you have a job?" "If so, what is it?" "Do you like it?" "How do you like to spend your leisure time?" "Do you like to read?" "What do you like to read?" "Do you have a favorite hobby; what is it?"

CUMULATIVE RECORD.   Held in the school office is the cumulative record for each student, containing information recorded from year to year by teachers and other school professionals. The information covers the student's academic background, standardized test scores, and extracurricular activities. Although you must use discretion before arriving at any conclusion about information contained in the file, the file may afford information for getting to know a particular student better. Remember, though, a student's past is history and should not be held against that student but used as a means for understanding a student's experiences and current perceptions.

DISCUSSIONS WITH OTHER PROFESSIONALS.   To better understand a student it is sometimes helpful to talk with that student's other teachers, adviser, or counselor, to learn of their perceptions and experiences with the student. As discussed in Chapter 1, one of the advantages of schools that use looping or are divided into "houses," or both, is that teachers and students get to know one another better. When you want to better know and understand a particular student, talking with

that student's other teachers can be enlightening (sometimes more so about the teachers).

LEARNING STYLES.   Learning style, discussed in Chapter 2, is included here as yet another important way of getting to know your students. Students who are different from you may prefer to learn in ways that differ from your own preferred way of learning. "Learning styles overlap somewhat with cultural background and gender. Although not all members of a cultural or gender group learn in the same way, patterns exist in how members of different groups tend to approach tasks." However, cautioning against stereotyping, experts suggest that "rather than generalizing about your own students based on the research on group differences, it is much more useful to investigate directly your own students' learning style preferences."[2] For doing that you can use Figure 3.1 for recording data. Here are descriptions of each of its five categories:[3]

1. *Working alone versus working with others.* While some students work best cooperatively with a partner or small group, others work better alone. A student's preference should be respected, although those who have not learned to work cooperatively may enjoy and benefit from the experience.

2. *Preferred learning modalities.* As discussed in Chapters 1 and 2, preferred learning modalities refer to the sensory channels or processes that students prefer to use for acquiring new information or ideas. Preferred modalities can be investigated by (a) giving students choices and recording which ones they choose most often, (b) recording the success with which students have learned under each condition, and (c) asking students which they prefer to use for gaining or expressing new ideas or information.

3. *Content about people versus content about things.* Students' interest in content can be investigated by offering students choices of people-centered content-related activities versus materials-centered content-related activities and observing which one they select more often. Students should not be forced to choose, however, because for some it makes no difference.

4. *Structured versus nonstructured tasks.* Some students prefer or work best when tasks are structured, whereas others prefer to create their own structure. The best way to investigate this preference is to give the student choices between highly structured work

---

2. C. A. Grant and C. E. Sleeter, *Turning on Learning* (Upper Saddle River, NJ: Prentice Hall, 1989), pp. 12–13. By permission of Prentice Hall.
3. Adapted from Grant and Sleeter, pp. 17–18. By permission of Prentice Hall.

Directions: For each student, record data you collect about the following items related to the student's preferred style of learning.

Student's name: _____

_____

_____

		Method of Data Collection	Findings
1. Style of working:	Alone		
	With others		
2. Learning modality:	Watching		
	Reading		
	Listening		
	Discussing		
	Touching		
	Moving		
	Writing		
3. Content:	People		
	Things		
4. Need for structure:	High		
	Low		
5. Details versus generalities:			

Figure 3.1
Learning styles record sheet. (From C. A. Grant and C. E. Sleeter, *Turning on Learning* [Upper Saddle River, NJ: Prentice Hall, 1989], pp. 17–18. By permission of Prentice Hall.)

and open-ended work and determine which is chosen more often. Sometimes the teacher may simply ask students which they prefer, although some students may not completely understand the question. Another clue is that students who seem lost or do poorly on open-ended assignments probably need structured work and those who seem bored with structured assignments probably need open-ended work.

5. *Detail versus the overall picture.* Some students do meticulous work well, are attentive to details, and can work through small steps to arrive at the larger idea; other students need to view the larger, more general picture first and may become bored or lost with details or small steps. For instance, when writing stories, some students use grammar and mechanics correctly, but their stories may not have much point; whereas other students may produce good overall story ideas but their first drafts are weak in grammar and mechanics. Students' preferences for details or generalities are best investigated through observation. Although all students eventually need to work on both details and generalities, some will have trouble learning these concepts if the teacher emphasizes one or the other solely or prematurely.

After analyzing data collected on your students you may notice certain learning-style patterns based on gender and ethnic background, but as said earlier, you should avoid stereotyping certain groups as learning a certain way. In research on cultures, one consistent finding is that, within a group, the variations among individuals are as great as their commonalities. Therefore, no one should automatically attribute a particular learning style to all individuals within a group.[4] Instead, use the patterns you discover in your students' learning-style preferences as guides for planning the lessons and selecting teaching strategies.

STUDENTS' EXPERIENTIAL BACKGROUND.   Another way of getting to know your students is to spend time in their neighborhoods. Observe and listen, finding and noting things that you can use as examples or as learning activities. Record your observations.

_____

4. P. Guild, "The Culture/Learning Style Connection," *Educational Leadership* 51(8):19 (May 1994).

CLASSROOM MANAGEMENT

Effective teaching requires a well-organized, businesslike classroom in which motivated students work diligently at their learning tasks, free from distractions and interruptions. Providing such a setting for learning is called effective classroom management. *Effective classroom management is the process of organizing and conducting a classroom so that it maximizes student learning.* There are at least two aspects to effective classroom management. (Classroom management and management systems are discussed in further detail in Classroom Control: Its Meaning—Past and Present later in this chapter.)

Establishing and Maintaining Classroom Control

Essential for effective classroom management is the establishment and maintenance of classroom control, that is, the process of controlling student behavior in the classroom. Classroom control involves both steps for preventing inappropriate student behavior (the establishment aspect) and ideas for responding to students whose behavior is inappropriate (the maintenance aspect). Both of these aspects are considered in detail later in this chapter.

Classroom control frequently is of the greatest concern to beginning teachers—and they have good cause to be concerned. Even experienced teachers sometimes find control difficult, particularly at the middle school level, where students are going through rapid physiological changes, and although to a somewhat lesser extent, in high school, where so many students come to school with psychological baggage and feelings of alienation as the result of negative experiences in their lives.

Effective Organization and Administration of Activities and Materials

In a well-managed classroom, students know what to do, have the materials needed to do it well, and stay on task while doing it; the classroom atmosphere is supportive, the assignments and procedures for doing them are clear, the materials of instruction are current, interesting, and readily available, and the classroom proceedings are businesslike. At all times, the teacher is in control, seeing that students are spending their time on appropriate tasks. For your teaching to be effective you must be skilled in managing the classroom.

To manage your classroom successfully, you need to (1) plan your lessons thoughtfully and thoroughly, (2) provide students with a pleasant, supportive atmosphere, (3) maintain or instill a desire and the confidence to learn and to achieve, (4) establish control procedures, (5) prevent distractions, interruptions, and disturbances, (6) deal quickly and unobtrusively with distractions and disturbances that are not preventable, and in general (7) promote effective student learning. If this sounds like a tall order, don't fret; if you adhere to the guidelines set forth throughout this resource guide and especially in this chapter you will be well on the road to success.

What is a well-managed, effectively controlled classroom? It is one where clearly the teacher is in charge and the students learn. In the sections that now follow we look at how it is achieved.

PREPARATION PROVIDES CONFIDENCE AND SUCCESS

For successful classroom management, beginning the school term well may make all the difference in the world. Remember that you have only one opportunity to make a first and lasting impression. Therefore, you should appear at the first class meeting (and every meeting thereafter) as well prepared and as confident as possible. Perhaps in the beginning you will feel nervous and apprehensive, but being ready and well prepared will help you at least to appear confident. It is likely that every beginning teacher is to some degree nervous and apprehensive; the secret is to not appear nervous to the students. Being well prepared provides the confidence necessary to cloud feelings of nervousness. Then, if you proceed in a businesslike, matter-of-fact way, the impetus of your well-prepared beginning will, most likely, cause the day, week, and year to proceed as desired.

CLASSROOM PROCEDURES AND RULES OF ACCEPTABLE BEHAVIOR

We cannot overemphasize the importance of getting the school year off to a good beginning, so we start this section by discussing further how that is done.

Starting the School Term Well

There are three keys to getting the school term off to a good beginning. First, be *prepared, fair,* and *consistent.* Remember—PFC! Preparation before the first day of school should include the determination of your classroom procedures and basic expectations for the behavior of the students while they are in your classroom. The procedures and rules must be consistent with school policy and seem reasonable to your students, and in enforcing them you must be consistent. However, as we repeat later in this chapter, being coldly consistent is not the same as being fair and professional. As a teacher, you are a professional who deals in matters of human relations and who must exercise professional judgment. You are not a robot, nor are your students. Human beings differ from one another, and seemingly similar situations can vary substantially because the people involved are different. Consequently, a teacher's response, or lack of response, to each of two separate but quite similar situations may differ. To be most effective, learning must be enjoyable for students; it cannot be enjoyable when a teacher consistently acts like a drill sergeant.

Second, in preparing your classroom management system, remember that too many rules and detailed procedures at the beginning can be a source of trouble. To avoid trouble, it is best at first to present only the minimum number of procedural expectations necessary to get an orderly start. By the time students are in high school, they already know the expected procedures—that is, the general rules of expected behavior, such as arriving in class promptly and prepared, listening attentively to others, showing mutual respect for the rights and property of others, allowing each student the right to learn, demonstrating appreciation for each individual in the classroom, and remaining in class until dismissed by the teacher. Some of their prior teachers may not always have been consistent or even fair about applying these expectations. However, by establishing and sticking to a few explained general expectations, and to those that may be specific to your subject field, you can leave yourself some room for judgments and maneuvering.

Third, consequences for not following established procedures must be reasonable, clearly understood, and consistently and fairly applied. The procedures should be quite specific so that students know exactly what is expected and what is not and what the consequences are for not following procedures.

To encourage a constructive and supportive classroom environment, throughout this resource guide we encourage you (and your students) to practice thinking in terms of procedures rather than rules and of consequences rather than punishment. Our reason is this: to many people, the term *rules* has a more negative connotation than does the term *procedures*. When you are working with a group of students, some rules are necessary, but we believe using the term *procedures* has a more positive ring to it. For example, a classroom rule might be that when one person is talking we do not interrupt that person until she is finished. When that rule is broken, rather than reminding students of the rule, you can change the emphasis to a procedure simply by asking, "What is our procedure (or expectation) when someone is talking?" Although some experts disagree with our reason, it is our contention that thinking in terms of and talking about procedures and consequences are more likely to contribute to a positive

classroom atmosphere than using the terms *rules* and *punishment*. Of course, some might argue that by the time students are in high school, you might as well tell it like it is. As always, after considering what the "experts" have to say, you make the final decision.

Once you have decided on your initial expectations, you are ready to explain them to your students and to begin rehearsing a few of the procedures on the very first day of class—more with young adolescents, fewer with seniors in high school. Whichever, you will want to do this in a positive way. Students work best in a positive atmosphere, when teacher expectations are clear to them, when procedures are clearly understood, are agreed upon, and have become routine, and when consequences for inappropriate behaviors are reasonable and also clearly understood.

The First Day of School

On the first day you will want to cover certain major points of common interest to you and the students. The following paragraphs provide guidelines for meeting your students the first time.

GREETING THE STUDENTS.   Welcome your students with a smile as they arrive and then the entire class with a friendly but businesslike demeanor. This means that you are not frowning or off in a corner doing something else as students arrive. As you greet the students, tell them to take a seat and start on the first assignment, which is located at their desk.

INITIAL ASSIGNMENT.   Begin the first meeting immediately with some sort of assignment, preferably a written assignment already on each student desk. This ensures that students have something to do immediately upon arriving in your classroom. That first assignment might be a questionnaire each student completes. This is a good time to instruct students on the procedure for heading their papers. Collect the first assignment.

STUDENT SEATING.   One option is to have student names on the first assignment paper, which is placed on student seats when students arrive that first class meeting. That allows you to have a seating chart ready on the first day, from which you can quickly take attendance and learn student names. Another option, not exclusive of the first, is to tell students that by the end of the week each should be in a permanent seat (either assigned by you or student selected). From this arrangement you will make a seating chart so that you can quickly learn their names and efficiently take attendance each day. Let them know, too, that you will redo the seating arrangement from time to time (if that is true).

INFORMATION ABOUT THE CLASS. After the first assignment has been completed, discussed, and collected (allowing rehearsal of the procedure for turning in papers), explain the course to students—what they will be learning and how they will learn it. Be sure to cover study habits and your expectations regarding quantity and quality of work. Many teachers make a list of expectations or put this information in a course syllabus (discussed in Chapter 5), give each student a copy, and review it with them, specifically discussing the teacher's expectations about how books will be used; about notebooks, portfolios, and assignments; about what students need to furnish; and about the location of resources in the classroom and elsewhere.

CLASSROOM PROCEDURES. Now, while you are on a roll, discuss in a positive way your expectations regarding classroom behavior, procedures, and routines (discussed in the next section). Most students work best when teacher expectations are well understood, with established routines. In the beginning it is important that there be no more procedures than necessary to get the class moving effectively for daily operation. Five or fewer expectations should be enough, such as arrive promptly and stay on task until excused, listen attentively, show mutual respect, use appropriate language, and appreciate the rights and property of others. Too many procedural expectations at first can be restricting and even confusing to students. High school students already know these things, so you shouldn't have to spend much time on the topic, except for those items specific to your course, such as dress and safety expectations for vocational courses, science laboratory courses, and physical education. Usually, middle school students need more control and reminding and rehearsing of procedures than do, say, high school seniors. Finding and applying the proper level of control for a given group of students is a skill that you develop from experience.

Although many schools traditionally have posted in the halls and in the classrooms a list of prohibited behaviors, more and more schools today are focusing on positive behaviors. For example, at the Constellation Community Middle School (Long Beach, CA), all students receive regular daily reminders when, after reciting the Pledge of Allegiance, they recite the school's five core principles: (1) Anything that hurts another person is wrong. (2) We are each other's keepers. (3) I am responsible for my own actions. (4) I take pride in myself. (5) Leave it better than when you found it.[5] And, at Boston's Lewenberg Middle School, classrooms display a list of five "agreements" that students and staff are expected to uphold: (1) Agree to create and participate in a group that is physically and emotionally safe. (2) Agree to work together to achieve individual and group goals. (3) Agree to give and receive honest feedback and to listen, to try, to care, to change, and to learn. (4) Agree not to devalue or discount yourself or others: no put-downs. (5) Agree to express negative thoughts and to learn and grow as a result.[6]

FIRST HOMEWORK ASSIGNMENT. End your first class meeting by saying something positive about being delighted to be working with the students, and then give the first homework assignment. Be sure you allow sufficient time to make assignment instructions clearly understood by every student, including a reminder of how you expect students to head their papers. We suggest you make this first homework assignment one that will not take too much student time and that each student can achieve a perfect score on with minimal effort.

Establishing Classroom Expectations, Procedures, and Consequences

When establishing classroom behavior expectations and procedures, remember this point: the learning time needs to run efficiently (i.e., with no "dead spots"), smoothly (i.e., routine procedures are established and transitions between activities are smooth), and with minimum distraction. As we implied in the previous section, when stating your expectations for student classroom behavior, try to do so in a positive manner, emphasizing procedures and desired behaviors, stressing what students should *do* rather than what they should *not* do. Displaying a list of *do nots* does not encourage a positive classroom atmosphere; a list of *dos* does. However, on this last point you need to know that people differ. For example, from Johns and Espinoza, "positive rules, such as 'raise your hand to speak,' do not communicate clearly. Does this mean that a child must ask permission to speak during a cooperative-group activity? This is like a city regulation saying, 'Please find a place other than here to put your car,' when the message is, 'No Parking.' A better way is to state the rule directly: 'No talking without permission,' permission being the operant word. Permission can then be communicated in a number of ways."[7] As we have said, after obtaining expert opinion, you will need to decide for yourself which works best for you

---

5. D. Harrington-Lueker, "Emotional Intelligence," *High Strides* 9(4):1 (March/April 1997).

6. M. D. O'Donnell, "Boston's Lewenberg Middle School Delivers Success," *Phi Delta Kappan* 78(7):508–512 (March 1997).

7. K. M. Johns and C. Espinoza, *Management Strategies for Culturally Diverse Classrooms* (Bloomington, IN: Fastback 396, Phi Delta Kappa Educational Foundation, 1996), p. 15.

with your own distinct group of students. It is, however, important that your expectations are communicated clearly to the students. Especially if your class of students is linguistically and culturally mixed you will need to be as direct and clear as possible to avoid sending confusing or mixed signals.

As you prepare your expectations for classroom behavior, you need to consider some of the specifics about what students need to understand from the start. These specific points, then, should be reviewed and rehearsed with the students, sometimes several times, during the first week of school and then followed consistently throughout the school term. Important and specific things that students need to know from the start will vary considerably depending on whether you are working with sixth graders, ninth graders, or seniors in high school and whether you are teaching ninth-grade English or high school students in electrical shop, but generally each of the following paragraphs describes matters that students need to understand from the beginning.

How a Student Is to Signal for Your Attention and Help. At least at the start of the school term, most teachers who are effective classroom managers expect their students to raise their hands for only as long as necessary, that is, until the teacher acknowledges (usually by a nod) that the student's hand has been seen. With that acknowledgment, the student should lower his hand. Then, to prevent the student from becoming bored and restless from waiting, you should attend to the student as quickly as possible. You want to avoid situations in which a student sits for long with his hand raised waiting for you to respond. Students should know that once their signal has been acknowledged by you they are expected to return to their work.

Expecting students to raise their hands before speaking allows you to control the noise and confusion level and to be proactive in deciding who speaks. The latter point is important if you are to manage a classroom with equality—that is, with equal attention to individuals regardless of their gender, ethnicity, proximity to the teacher, or another personal characteristic.

Another important reason for expecting students to raise their hands and be recognized before speaking is to discourage impulsive outbursts. One of the instructional responsibilities shared by all teachers is to help students develop intelligent behavior. Learning to control impulsivity is one of the 14 intelligent behaviors discussed in Chapter 9. In our opinion, teaching students to control their impulsivity is a highly important responsibility that is too often neglected by many teachers.

To avoid dependence on the teacher and having too many students raising their hands for the teacher's attention, and to encourage positive interaction among the students, some teachers employ the "three before me" procedure. That is, when a student has a question or needs help, the student must quietly ask up to three peers before seeking help from the teacher. This technique, however, may work better with upper-grade high school students than with many classes at the middle school. Again, as a beginning teacher, you need to try ideas and find what works best for you in your own unique situation.

How to Enter and Leave the Classroom. From the time that the class is scheduled to begin and until it officially ends, teachers who are effective classroom managers expect students to be in their assigned seats or at their assigned learning stations and to be attentive to the teacher or to the learning activity until excused by the teacher. This expectation works for college classes, for kindergarten, and for every level and class in between. For example, students should not be allowed to begin meandering toward the classroom exit in anticipation of the passing bell, otherwise their meandering toward the door will begin earlier and earlier each day and the teacher will increasingly lose control. Besides, it is a waste of valuable and limited instructional time.

How to Maintain, Obtain, and Use Materials for Learning and Items of Personal Use. Students need to know where, when, and how to store, retrieve, and care for items such as their coats, backpacks, books, pencils, and medicines; how to get papers, materials, and laboratory or shop items; and when to use the pencil sharpener and wastebasket. Classroom control is easiest to maintain when (1) items that students need for class activities and for their personal use are neatly arranged and located in places that require minimum foot traffic, (2) there are established procedures that students clearly expect and understand, (3) there is the least amount of student off-task time, and (4) students do not have to line up for anything. Therefore, you will want to plan the room arrangement, equipment and materials storage, preparation of equipment and materials, and transitions between activities to avoid needless delays and confusion. Problems in classroom control will most certainly occur whenever some or all students have nothing to do, even if only briefly.

How to Leave Class for a Personal Matter. Normally, students should be able to take care of the need for a drink of water or to go to the bathroom between classes; however, sometimes they do not or, for medical reasons or during long block classes, cannot. Reinforce the notion that they should do those things before coming into your classroom or during the scheduled times, but be flexible enough for the occasional student who has an immediate need. Follow established school procedures whenever you permit a student to leave class for a personal reason, which may, for reasons of personal security, mean that students can only leave the room in pairs and with a hall pass or accompanied by an adult.

How to React to a Visitor or an Intercom Announcement. Unfortunately, class interruptions do occur, and in some schools they occur far too often and for reasons that are not as important as interrupting a teacher and students' learning would imply (see Exercise 1.3). For an important reason the principal, vice-principal, or other office employee may interrupt the class to see the teacher or a student or to make an announcement to the entire class. Students need to understand what behavior is expected of them during those interruptions. When there is a visitor to the class, the expected procedure should be for students to continue their learning task unless directed otherwise by the teacher.

What to Do When a Student Is Late to Class or Will Be Leaving Early. You must understand and reinforce school policies on early dismissals and tardies. Routinize your own procedures so that students clearly understand what they are to do if they must leave your class early (e.g., for a medical appointment) or arrive late. Procedures should be such that late arriving and early dismissal students do not have to disturb you or the learning in progress.

What the Consequences Are for Inappropriate Behavior. Most teachers who are effective classroom managers have routinized their procedures for handling inappropriate behavior and ensure that the students understand the consequences for inappropriate behavior. The consequences are posted in the classroom and when not counter to school policy may be similar to the following five-step model.

First offense results in a direct but reasonably unobtrusive reminder (nonverbal warning) to the student.

Second offense results in a private but direct verbal warning.

Third offense results in the student's being given a time-out in an isolation area (but one that has adult supervision) followed by a private teacher-student conference. (The time-out is discussed in the next section.)

Fourth offense results in a suspension from class until there is a conference between the student, parent, and teacher (and perhaps the counselor).

Fifth offense results in the student's being referred to the vice-principal's, principal's, or counselor's office (depending on school policy), sometimes followed by a limited or permanent suspension from that class or from school.

Whether offenses subsequent to the first are those that occur on the same day or within a designated period of time, such as one week, is one of the many decisions that must be made by a teacher or by members of a teaching team, department, or the entire faculty.

Procedures to Follow during Emergency Drills, Real or Practice. Students need to clearly understand what to do, where to go, and how to behave in emergency conditions, such as those created by a fire, storm, earthquake, or disruptive campus intruder. Students are expected to behave well during these drills, whether for practice or for real.

A Time-out Procedure

When a time-out is used for a student's inappropriate behavior, the student should have something to do during the time-out. One suggestion is for the student to pick up a form (Figure 3.2) from a known place near the classroom exit and complete it while in the time-out area. This procedure is valuable because it (1) gives the student something constructive to do during the time-out, (2) causes the student to reflect on and assume ownership for her behavior that resulted in the time-out consequence, and (3) provides documentation that might be useful later in conferences with parents, team members, counselors, and school administrative personnel. A second time-out for the same student during the same school day might be cause for a follow-up, such as a conference between the student, members of that student's teaching team, and the school counselor. A third time-out during the same day may result in a trip to a school administrator and a parent conference before the student is allowed back in school.

Now do Exercises 3.1 and 3.2 to further your understanding of classroom management and to begin the development of your own management system.

Time-out

Your behavior failed to pass our classroom and house expectations and agreements. Those agreements are

- attentive listening,
- mutual respect for the rights and property of others,
- right of each student to learn, and
- appreciations of others with no put-downs.

Please reflect on your behavior today by answering the following questions.

1. Explain what you did in class that caused you to receive this time-out.

2. What agreement(s) did you fail to honor by your behavior?

3. Did your behavior cause another person to feel embarrassed, angry, or hurt?

4. Did your behavior jeapordize the safety of yourself or others?

5. Did your behavior keep you or other students from their learning tasks?

6. Did your behavior keep another student from being heard by the teacher and class?

7. Did your behavior help or hinder the class work? If yes, how?

8. Did your behavior break a school rule? If yes, which one?

9. Explain in your own words what positive behaviors your teacher and classmates will observe from you when you return to class.

When you are ready to honor our class and house agreements, do the following:

- Return to the classroom and place this completed and signed paper in the appropriate basket on my desk.
- Return to your assigned seat without disturbing anyone.
- Rejoin the classroom activity.

Student's signature _____ Date _____

Figure 3.2
Sample time-out form.

For Your Notes

EXERCISE 3.1
Teachers' Behavior Management Systems

Instructions: The purpose of this exercise is to interview two teachers, one from a middle or junior high school and the other from a high school, to find out how they manage their classrooms. Use the outline format that follows, conduct your interviews, and then share the results with your classmates, perhaps in small groups.

1. Teacher interviewed: _____

2. Date: _____

3. Grade level: _____

4. School: _____

5. Subject(s): _____

6. Please describe your classroom management system. Specifically, I would like to know your procedures for the following:

   a. How are students to signal that they want your attention and help? _____

   _____

   _____

   _____

   b. How do you call on students during question and discussion sessions? _____

   _____

   _____

   _____

   c. How and when are students to enter and exit the classroom? _____

   _____

   _____

   _____

   d. How are students to obtain the materials for instruction? _____

   _____

   _____

   _____

   e. How are students to store their personal items? _____

   _____

   _____

f. What are your procedures for students going to the drinking fountain or restroom?

_____

_____

_____

g. What are your procedures during class interruptions? _____

_____

_____

_____

h. What are your procedures for tardies or early dismissals? _____

_____

_____

_____

i. What are your procedures for turning in homework? _____

_____

_____

_____

7. Describe your expectations for classroom behavior and the consequences for misbehavior.

_____

_____

_____

_____

_____

_____

In discussion with your classmates following the interviews, consider the following. Many modern teachers advocate the use of a highly structured classroom; then, as appropriate over time during the school year, they share more of the responsibility with the students. Did you find this to be the case with the majority of teachers interviewed? Was it more or less the case in middle schools, junior highs, or high schools? Was it more or less the case with any particular subject area?

_____

_____

_____

_____

EXERCISE 3.2

Beginning the Development of My Classroom Management System

Instructions: The purpose of this exercise is to begin preparation of the management system that you will explain to your students during the first day or week of school. Answer the questions that follow, and share those answers with your peers for their feedback. Then make changes as appropriate. (Upon completion of this chapter, you may want to revisit this exercise to make adjustments to your management plan, as you will from time to time throughout your professional career.)

1. My teaching subject area and anticipated grade level: _____

2. Attention to procedures. Use a statement to explain your procedural expectation for each of the following:

   a. How are students to signal that they want your attention and help? _____

   _____

   _____

   b. How do you call on students during question and discussion sessions? _____

   _____

   _____

   c. How and when are students to enter and exit the classroom? _____

   _____

   _____

   d. How are students to obtain the materials for instruction? _____

   _____

   _____

   e. How are students to store their personal items? _____

   _____

   _____

   f. What are your procedures for students going to the drinking fountain or restroom?

   _____

   _____

   g. What are your procedures during class interruptions? _____

   _____

   _____

   h. What are your procedures for tardies or early dismissals? _____

   _____

i. What are your procedures for turning in homework? _____
_____

j. What are your procedures for turning in late homework? _____
_____

3. List of student behavior expectations that I will present to my class (no more than five):

Rule 1 _____
_____
_____

Rule 2 _____
_____
_____

Rule 3 _____
_____
_____

Rule 4 _____
_____
_____

Rule 5 _____
_____
_____

4. Explanation of consequences for broken rules: _____
_____
_____
_____
_____
_____

5. How my procedures, rules, or consequences may vary (if at all) according to the grade level taught, or according to any other criteria, such as in team teaching:
_____
_____
_____

EXTRINSIC AND INTRINSIC REINFORCERS (REWARDS) AS MOTIVATORS

Reinforcement theory contends that a person's gratification derived from receiving a reward strengthens the tendency for that person to continue to act in a certain way, and the lack of a reward (or the promise of a reward) weakens the tendency to act that way. For example, according to the theory, if students are promised a reward of "preferred activity time (PAT) on Friday" if they work well all week long, then the students are likely to work toward that reward, thus improving their standards of learning. Some educators argue that (1) once the extrinsic reinforcement (i.e., the reward from outside the learner) has been removed, the desired behavior tends to diminish; and that (2) rather than extrinsic sources of reinforcement, the focus should be on increasing the student's internal sense of accomplishment, an *intrinsic reward*. Perhaps, for the daily work of a teacher in a classroom of many diverse individuals, the practical reality is somewhere in between. After all, the reality of classroom teaching is less than ideal, and all activities cannot be intrinsically rewarding. Further, for many students intrinsic rewards are often too remote to be effective.[8]

The promise of extrinsic rewards is not always necessary or beneficial. Students generally will work harder to learn something because they want to learn it (i.e., it is intrinsically motivating) than they will merely to earn PAT, points, grades, candy, or some other form of extrinsic motivator.[9] In addition, regarding the promise of PAT on Friday, many teenagers are so preoccupied with "now" that for them the promise on Monday of preferred activity time on Friday probably will have little desired effect on their behavior on Monday. To them, Friday seems to be a long way off.

Activities that are interesting and intrinsically rewarding are not further served by the addition of external rewards. This is especially true when working with students who are already highly motivated to learn. Adding extrinsic incentives to learning activities that are already highly motivating tends to reduce student motivation. For most students, the use of extrinsic motivators should be minimal and is probably most helpful in drill and practice activities, where there is a lot of repetition and the potential for boredom. If students are working diligently on a highly motivating student-initiated project of study, extrinsic rewards are unnecessary and could even have negative effects.

Now, to explore your thoughts and expand your understanding about motivation, do Exercises 3.3 and 3.4.

---

8. P. Chance, "The Rewards of Learning," *Phi Delta Kappan* 74(3):206 (November 1992).

9. See E. L. Deci and R. M. Ryan, *Intrinsic Motivation and Self-Determination in Human Behavior* (New York: Plenum Press, 1985).

—— EXERCISE 3.3 ——
Reinforcing Positive Student Behavior

Instructions: The purpose of this exercise is for you to begin thinking about how you will use rewards as reinforcement for student behavior and learning. Your task is to arrive at tentative decisions about whether and how you will use extrinsic rewards (external motivators) for reinforcement of student learning. Several categories of extrinsic rewards are possible: (1) *activity and privilege rewards* (e.g., choice activity, free time); (2) *tangible rewards* (e.g., certificates, edibles); (3) *token or recognition rewards* (e.g., certification of achievement, progress report to parent); and (4) *social rewards* (e.g., peer coach, cross-age tutor, team leader, teacher assistant).

1. Do you believe that you will use extrinsic rewards as motivators and reinforcers for student learning? Explain why or why not.

_____

_____

_____

_____

_____

_____

_____

_____

_____

_____

_____

2. For the subject(s) and grade level that you intend to teach, list examples of student behaviors and consequent rewards in each category that you think would be appropriate.

Subject _____   Grade level _____

a. **ACTIVITY AND PRIVILEGE REWARDS**

Student Behavior   *Specific Reward*
(e.g., class worked well all week)   (e.g., preferred activity time for Friday)

_____   _____

_____   _____

_____   _____

_____   _____

_____   _____

_____   _____

b. TANGIBLE REWARDS

Student Behavior   *Specific Reward*

_____   _____

_____   _____

_____   _____

_____   _____

_____

c. TOKEN OR RECOGNITION REWARDS

Student Behavior   *Specific Reward*

_____   _____

_____   _____

_____   _____

_____   _____

_____   _____

d. SOCIAL REWARDS

Student Behavior   *Specific Reward*

_____   _____

_____   _____

_____   _____

_____   _____

_____   _____

3. Share your lists in each category with your colleagues for their feedback.

4. Now, observe several teachers to discover how they use extrinsic (and intrinsic) rewards for positive student behaviors. Record your observations, and share them with your classmates.

School, grade level, and classes observed: _____

Dates of observations: _____

a. Identify what student behaviors were rewarded and how they were rewarded.

Student Behavior   *Specific Reward*

_____   _____

_____   _____

_____   _____

_____   _____

b. What student behaviors were not rewarded?

_____

_____

_____

_____

_____

c. Were there examples of students being (inappropriately) rewarded for inappropriate behavior? If so, describe them.

_____

_____

_____

_____

_____

5. From your observations and discussions, do you want to make any changes in your answer to Question 1 and your lists of behaviors and rewards?

_____

_____

_____

_____

_____

_____

_____

_____

_____

_____

_____

_____

_____

_____

_____

_____

_____

_____

For Your Notes

EXERCISE 3.4
Sending a Positive Word Home

Instructions: For too many parents and guardians, the only communication ever received from teachers is negative messages about their child's academic or social behavior. Communication to a parent can convey a positive message as well. Practice writing one positive message, and then ask another teacher candidate to read and react to your message. Does your message convey what you intended?

1. Situation: _____

   _____

   _____

   _____

2. Note to parent or guardian: _____

   _____

   _____

   _____

   _____

   _____

   _____

   _____

3. Reaction comments from another teacher candidate: _____

   _____

   _____

   _____

   _____

4. Review your responses. What areas do you want to focus on for class discussion? Talk about them with others in your class. _____

   _____

   _____

   _____

   _____

For Your Notes

MANAGING DAILY CLASS MEETINGS

When it is time for the class period to begin, you should start the learning activities at once, with no delay. Although some schools do not use a bell system for the beginning and ending of class periods, many teachers still refer to the initial class activity as the *bell activity*. More frequently, perhaps, it is referred to as the *warm-up activity* or *opener*. At the beginning of each class, in order to take attendance and to attend to other routine administrative matters, most teachers expect the students to be in their assigned seats. Once administrative matters are completed (usually in a matter of a minute or two), the day's regular lesson should begin, which could mean that students will move to other stations within the classroom. Remember, though, movement of students (i.e., foot traffic) within the classroom should be purposeful and minimal.

When there are no announcements or other administrative matters to cover, you should try to begin the day's first lesson immediately. Then, within a few minutes after the students have begun their lesson activities, attend to attendance matters. Some teachers recommend beginning the day's lesson immediately while giving a reliable classroom aide or student assistant the responsibility of taking attendance and dealing with other routine administrative tasks. However, when another person performs the daily attendance routines, it is still your responsibility to check and sign the relevant attendance forms. Perhaps the best routine, one that requires your practice and overlapping skill, is to do both simultaneously—start a learning activity and take attendance. Whichever the case, once the class period has begun, routines and lesson activities should move forward briskly and steadily until the official end of the class period or, in the case of extended class periods or blocks, until the first break.

Warm-up Activity

As said, the effective teacher greets the students warmly and starts their learning immediately. (Unless you really want responses, we caution you against greeting students with a rhetorical question such as "How was your weekend?" See Purposes for Using Questioning at the start of Chapter 7.) If you are teaching in a school where you must attend to attendance matters at the beginning of each class meeting and are not yet comfortable with your overlapping skill, an effective management procedure is to have the overhead projector on each day when students arrive in class. The day's agenda and immediate assignment should be clearly written on a transparency and displayed on the screen, which then is referred to after your greeting.

Warm-up activities can include any variety of things, such as a specific topic or question each student responds to by writing in his journal or the same topic or question that pairs (dyads) of students discuss and write about in their journals (using the strategy referred to as think-write-pair-share). Other activities include a problem to be solved by each student or student pair, the exchange and discussion of a homework assignment, the completion of the write-up of a laboratory activity, and the writing of individual or student dyad responses to textbook questions.[10]

Now do Exercise 3.5 to learn further how teachers start their classes.

---

10. For class openers for math, history, and English, contact J. Weston Walch, 321 Valley Street, Portland, ME 04104-0658; (800) 341-6094.

EXERCISE 3.5
Observation and Analysis of How Teachers Open Class Meetings

Instructions: Select three teachers to observe, all of the same secondary school subject and grade level, for how they begin their class meetings. Observe only the first ten minutes of each class. After collecting these data, share, compile, and discuss the results as follows.

Grade level and subject discipline I observed: _____

1. Make a check for each of the following observations that you make, and for each teacher place a number, 1, 2, 3, and so on, for which of these things that teacher did first, second, third, and so on, during the initial ten minutes from time students begin entering the classroom until after the official clock start of class (i.e., when class is supposed to begin).

	√	*Teacher 1*	*Teacher 2*	*Teacher 3*
Greeting the students	_____	_____	_____	_____
Warm and friendly?	_____	_____	_____	_____
Giving an assignment (i.e., a warm-up activity)	_____	_____	_____	_____
Taking attendance	_____	_____	_____	_____
Talking with another adult	_____	_____	_____	_____
Talking with one or a few students	_____	_____	_____	_____
Readying teaching materials or equipment	_____	_____	_____	_____
Working at desk	_____	_____	_____	_____
Handing out student papers or materials	_____	_____	_____	_____
Other (specify)	_____	_____	_____	_____

2. For these three teachers, was there a common way in which they began class?

_____

_____

_____

_____

3. Compile your results with those of your classmates. Write the results here.

_____

_____

_____

_____

_____

_____

_____

_____

_____

_____

4. Compare the results of observations for all subjects and secondary school grade levels. What are the similarities and differences?

_____

_____

_____

_____

_____

_____

_____

_____

_____

5. Can you reach any conclusions as a class about teachers of particular grade levels and disciplines and how they spent the first ten minutes with their students?

_____

_____

_____

_____

_____

_____

_____

_____

_____

_____

Principles of Movement Management

Once class has begun, the pace of activities should be lively enough to keep students alert and busy, without dead time, but not so fast as to discourage or lose some students. The effective teacher runs a businesslike classroom—at no time does any student sit or stand around with nothing to do. To maintain a smooth and brisk pace and to lessen distractions and prevent dead time, consider the following three principles of movement management.[11]

First, by beginning your class without delay, you discourage the kind of fooling around and time wasting that might otherwise occur. To minimize problems with classroom control, you must practice this principle from the very first day of your teaching career.

Second, student movement about the classroom should be routinized, controlled, and purposeful to the learning activities. To minimize problems with classroom control, this principle too must be practiced from the very first day of your teaching career. As should be understood by your cooperating teacher and college or university supervisor during your student teaching, it will take some time for you to develop the skills necessary for the most successful application of this second principle. At the beginning of your student teaching, you may need to follow the movement procedures already established by your cooperating teacher, assuming, of course, that those procedures conform to this second principle. If your cooperating teacher's procedures for classroom management are ineffective or less than ideal, then you should talk with your supervisor about a different student teaching placement.

Third, lessons should move forward briskly and purposefully, with natural transitions from one lesson activity to the next and with each activity starting and ending conclusively, especially when using direct (teacher-centered) instruction. As a beginning teacher, it will take time to develop finesse in your application of this third principle; during your student teaching experience, your cooperating teacher and college or university supervisor will understand that it takes time and will help you develop and hone your skill in the application of this principle. Transitions (discussed subsequently), in particular, are a most troublesome time for many beginning teachers. Transitions are less troublesome when planned carefully during the preactive phase of instruction and written into the lesson plan.

---

11. The principles of movement management were adapted from J. S. Kounin, *Discipline and Group Management in the Classroom* (New York: Holt, Rinehart and Winston, 1977), pp. 102–108.

Smooth Application of the Principles of Movement Management

Teachers who are less effective in applying the principles of movement management are often those who themselves fail to adhere to the principles. To be sure that your movement management is effective, you will want to adhere to the guidelines described in the following paragraphs.

When giving verbal instructions to students, do so quickly and succinctly, without talking too long and giving so much detail that students begin to get restless and bored. Students are quickly bored with long-winded verbal instructions from a teacher.

Once students are busy at their learning tasks, avoid interrupting them with additional verbal instructions, statements, or announcements that get them off task and that could as easily be written on the board or overhead transparency; also avoid interventions that could be communicated to a student privately without disturbing the rest of the class. Some students, especially middle school students, are easily distracted; do not be the cause of their distractions.

With whole-class instruction, before starting a new activity, be sure that the present one is satisfactorily completed by most students. End each activity conclusively before beginning a new activity, and with a relevant and carefully prepared transition, bridge the new activity with the previous one, so students understand the connection.

With your skill in withitness, carefully and continuously monitor all students during the entire class session. If one or two students become inattentive and begin to behave inappropriately, quietly (i.e., using indirect intervention) redirect their attention without interrupting the rest of the class.

To help in the prevention of dead time and management problems, especially when using multiple learning tasks and indirect instruction, you will want to establish and rehearse the students in the use of transitional activities, which are ongoing, relevant tasks that students automatically move to whenever they have completed their individual or small group classroom learning activities.

Transitions: One of the Most Difficult Skills for Beginning Teachers

Transitions are the moments in lessons between activities or topics, times of change. It will probably take you a while to master the skill of smooth transitions. Planning and consistency are important to your mastering this important skill. With a dependable schedule and consistent routines, transitions usually occur efficiently and automatically, without disruption. Still, research suggests that the greatest number of discipline problems occur during times of transitions, especially when students must wait for the next activity. To avoid problems during transitions, eliminate wait times by thinking and planning ahead.

There are two types of transitions in lessons, and sometimes both are used in a transition. First is a lesson transition, the way that the teacher connects one activity to the next so that students understand the relationship between the two activities. The second type of transition occurs when some students have finished a learning activity but must wait for others to catch up before starting the next. As discussed in the previous section, we call this a transitional or anchor activity (see Sample 7 of the Appendix). The transitional activity is intended to keep all students academically occupied, allowing no time in which students have nothing to do but wait. A common example is when a test is given and some students finish while others have not. The effective teacher plans a transitional activity and gives instructions for that before students start the test.

Teachers who are most effective are those who during the preactive phase of instruction plan and rehearse nearly every move they and the students will make, thinking ahead to anticipate and avoid problems in classroom control. Transitions are planned, and students are prepared for them by clearly established transition routines. While in transition and waiting for the start of the next activity, students engage in these transitional activities. You can plan a variety of transitional activities relevant and appropriate to the topics being studied, although not necessarily related to the next activity of that particular day's lesson. Transitional activities may include any number of meaningful activities such as journal writing, worksheet activity, lab reports, portfolio work, homework, project work, and even work on an assignment for another class.

LEGAL GUIDELINES FOR THE CLASSROOM TEACHER

You must be knowledgeable about basic legal matters regarding teaching and supervising youth. This knowledge can minimize the possibility of making errors that abuse the rights of students, cause emotional or physical trauma to a student, and could result in litigation.

Among teachers and teacher candidates, the topic of teacher and student rights generates discussions and concerned questions, many of which rightfully belong in a methods text. You are, or will be, interested in teacher tenure laws, retirement laws, professional organizations, collective bargaining, legal requirements concerning student discipline, teacher liability and insurance, and teacher negligence, topics that this resource guide cannot pursue or cannot pursue in depth.

Most teacher candidates want to know about their legal status during the field experiences of their

teacher preparation program. Information on that should be available from your instructor or from your college or university office of field experience or student teacher placement.

The remainder of this section provides guidelines that will alert you as a classroom teacher to basic issues of law. It is not intended to be a definitive treatment of legal issues in education. Our intent is to provide a basic understanding necessary to teach students fairly, with minimum disruption and fear of litigation. In addition to federal laws, specific guidelines may be affected by state laws, local school board policies, and school site regulations. After reviewing the guidelines provided in the following paragraphs, you may want to study the suggested readings at the end of the chapter, as well as any documents available from local schools, to learn more about specific school-related legal matters.

Title IX

Federal law Title IX of the Education Act Amendments of 1972, P.L. 92-318, prohibits a teacher from discriminating among students on the basis of their gender. In all aspects of school, male and female students must be treated the same. This means, for example, that a teacher must not pit males against females in a subject content quiz game—or for any other activity or reason. Further, no teacher, student, administrator, or other school employee should make sexual advances toward a student (i.e., touching or speaking in a sexual manner).

Students should be informed by their schools of their rights under Title IX, and they should be encouraged to report any suspected violations of their rights to the school principal or other designated person. Each school or district should have a clearly delineated statement of steps to follow in the process of protecting students' rights.[12] More frequently now than ever before students are exercising their rights to be free from sexual harassment from peers, as well as from adults. Additional information and resources regarding sexual harassment in the schools are shown in Figure 3.3.

Teacher Liability and Insurance

Credentialed teachers and student teachers in public schools are usually protected by their districts against personal injury litigation (i.e., a negligence suit filed as the result of a student's being injured at school or at a school-sponsored activity). Student teachers and credentialed teachers should investigate carefully the extent of

12. To learn how schools are addressing the issue of sexual harassment, see the several articles on "Gender Equity" in the theme issue of *Educational Leadership* 53(8) (May 1996); see also the December 1997/January 1998 theme issue of *Educational Leadership*.

Figure 3.3
Resources on sexual harassment in schools.

- L. A. Brown, "Recent Developments in the Law of Sexual Harassment and Sexual Abuse," in N. Gittins (ed.), *School Law in Review in 1995* (Alexandria, VA: National School Boards Association, 1995), pp. 11–14.
- G. H. Gregory et al., *Sexual Harassment in the Schools: Preventing and Defending against Claims,* rev. ed., available from the National School Boards Association Council of School Attorneys Publication, 1680 Duke Street, Alexandria, VA 22314.
- D. L. Siegel, *Sexual Harassment: Research and Resources,* revised by M. Budhos, 1995, available from the National Council for Research on Women, 530 Broadway at Spring Street, New York, NY 10012-3920.
- N. Stein and L. Sjostrom, *Flirting or Hurting? A Teacher's Guide to Student-to-Student Sexual Harassment in Schools—Grades 6–12* (Washington, DC: NEA Professional Library, 1994).
- *Stopping Anti-Gay Abuse of Students in Public Schools: A Legal Perspective,* available from the Lambda Legal Defense and Education Fund, 666 Broadway, Suite 12, New York, NY 10012-2317; (212) 995-8585.
- D. H. Wishnietsky, *Establishing School Policies on Sexual Harassment* (Bloomington, IN: Fastback 370, Phi Delta Kappa Educational Foundation, 1994).
- E. Yaffe, "Expensive, Illegal, and Wrong: Sexual Harassment in Our Schools," *Phi Delta Kappan* 77(3):K1–K15 (November 1995).

their tort (i.e., any private or civil wrong for which a civil suit can be brought) liability coverage in districts where they work. You may decide that the coverage provided by the district is insufficient. Additional liability coverage can be obtained through private insurance agents and through national teachers' organizations.

Teachers sometimes find themselves in situations where they are tempted to transport students in their own private automobiles, such as for field trips and other off-campus activities. Before ever transporting students in your automobile—or in private automobiles driven by volunteer adults—you and other drivers should inquire from your insurance agents whether you have adequate automobile insurance liability coverage to do that and if any written permissions or release from liability is needed.

Inevitably, teachers take personal items to school—purses, cameras, compact disc players, and so on. It is unlikely that the school's insurance policy covers your personal items if stolen or damaged. A homeowner's or apartment renter's policy might. Our advice is to avoid taking valuable personal items to school.

Child Abuse and Neglect

Child abuse and neglect (e.g., physical abuse, incest, malnutrition, being improperly clothed, and inadequate dental care) have become a pressing national concern. *Teachers in all states are legally mandated to report any suspicion of child abuse.* It is a serious moral issue to not report such suspicion, and lawsuits have been brought against educators for negligence to report incidents. To report your suspicion of child abuse, you can

telephone toll free 1-800-4-A-CHILD. Proof of abuse is not necessary. If you do report your suspicion, you are probably immune from a libel suit. Check your own state or local school district for details about (1) what is designated as child abuse, (2) to whom to report your suspicion, (3) how to report, and (4) the immunity or protection provided to a teacher who does report suspected child abuse.

Although physical abuse is the easiest to spot, other types of abuse and neglect can be just as serious. Children who are abused or neglected have some general characteristics. They may

1. Have below-normal height and weight.
2. Exhibit destructive behaviors.
3. Exhibit hyperactive or aggressive behavior.
4. Exhibit short attention spans and lack of interest in school activities.
5. Exhibit sudden and dramatic changes in behavior.
6. Fear everyone and everything.
7. Fear going home after school.
8. Fear their parents and other adults.
9. Are frequently sick and absent from school.
10. Are frequently tired and often fall asleep in class.
11. Have a smell of alcohol.
12. Are unclean, smelling of body wastes.
13. Cry unexpectedly.
14. Have unexplained lacerations and bruises.
15. Exhibit withdrawal from adult contact.
16. Exhibit withdrawal from peer interaction.[13]

---

13. D. G. Gil, *Violence against Children: Physical Child Abuse in the United States* (Cambridge, MA: Rand McNally, 1970).

A student who comes to your classroom abused or neglected needs to feel welcome and secure while in the classroom. For additional guidance in working with such a student, contact experts from your local school district (e.g., the school psychologist) or obtain guidelines from your state department of education or the local Children's Protective Services (CPS) agency.

First Aid and Medication

Accidents and resulting injuries to students while at school do occur. While doing a laboratory experiment, a student is burned by an acid or a flame. In another class, a student is injured by glass from a falling windowpane when the teacher attempts to open a stuck window. Another student is injured in shop class. Do you know what you should do when a student is injured?

First, you should give first aid *only* when necessary to save a limb or life. When life or limb is not at risk, then you should follow school policy by referring the student immediately to professional care. When immediate professional care is unavailable and you believe that immediate first aid is necessary, then you can take prudent action, as if you were that student's parent or legal guardian. But you must always be cautious and knowledgeable about what you are doing, so you do not cause further injury.

Unless you are a licensed medical professional, you should *never* give medication to a minor, whether prescription or over-the-counter. Students who need to take personal medication should bring from home a written parental statement of permission and instructions. Under your supervision as the student's classroom teacher—or that of the school nurse (if there is one)—the student can then take the medicine. Most students will administer their personal medicine between classes and you will not be involved.

Teacher Contract and Tenure

What will it mean when you sign a teaching contract? Consider the following facts. The teaching contract is a legal agreement between you and the governing board of the school district. The contract guarantees you employment, a teaching assignment, a salary, and an expected length of service, *except* when there is a decline in enrollment and no longer a need for your service. Your length of service is identified in the contract, such as service for one year or continuing service to the district. You are legally obligated to perform your assigned duties as specified in your teaching contract.

Before a tenure contract is offered, there is a probationary period of continued employment within that district (varying from state to state, but usually one to three years). "Tenure is a creation of state statute designed to maintain adequate, permanent and qualified teaching staffs free from political and personal arbitrary interference. Tenure laws cannot be circumvented by local school board regulations or policies. Although there is not constitutional right to tenure, once tenure is granted a constitutional 'property' right arises and due process is required before dismissal."[14] Tenure is not a safeguard against reduction-in-force (RIF) policies or a protection against job loss. Tenure is not a guarantee that your job will continue regardless of events or financial situations that arise in the district. No reason need be given for nonrenewal of the contract of a probationary (nontenured) teacher.

Legal guidelines for the classroom teacher can vary from state to state. Because of those variations, we cannot tell you everything you might want or need to know about the subject. Exercise 3.6 is provided to help you obtain additional information you want or need. It will necessarily need to be supplemented with information from sources from your own state.

---

14. *Deskbook Encyclopedia of American School Law* (Rosemount, MN: Data Research, Inc., 1987), p. 390. For a discussion of cases where tenured teachers were fired, see P. A. Zirkel, "Academic Freedom: Professional or Legal Right?" *Educational Leadership* 50(6):42–43 (March 1993).

EXERCISE 3.6

An Analysis of What I Know about Legal Guidelines in My State

Instructions: Respond to each of the following questions with a yes or a no. Then research the correct answers according to the education code of your state. Compare those answers with the answer key that follows this exercise.

		Yes	*No*
1.	As a credentialed female teacher, can I expect less salary than a credentialed male teacher when we perform similar teaching services, have similar years' experience, and similar college degrees and credits?	_____	_____
2.	Has teacher tenure been abolished in my state?	_____	_____
3.	Will my substitute teaching and summer-school teaching experience be included in the computation toward my permanent teaching status?	_____	_____
4.	Can I be assigned supervision duties outside of my regular teaching assignment?	_____	_____
5.	Once tenured, can I be dismissed for not following the prescribed course of study?	_____	_____
6.	Must I maintain records of student attendance?	_____	_____
7.	Can I discipline a student who refuses to stand and salute the flag of the United States of America?	_____	_____
8.	May I require that my students purchase a weekly news supplement if I provide free copies to students who cannot afford to purchase it?	_____	_____
9.	Can I receive royalties for a state-adopted textbook of which I am coauthor?	_____	_____
10.	Can I administer a survey, a questionnaire, or a test asking about a student's sexual beliefs, practices, or preferences without parental (or legal guardian's) written permission?	_____	_____
11.	May I search a student or a student's locker at random?	_____	_____
12.	Can I be considered negligent if I am present in the classroom when a physical injury occurs to one of my students?	_____	_____
13.	Is a student guilty of a felony if the student places glue in the lock of a classroom door?	_____	_____
14.	Can I suspend a student from my class?	_____	_____
15.	Can I arrest a student?	_____	_____

	Yes	No

16. Can I arrest a student for taunting and challenging another student to fight? _____ _____

17. If I am attacked, assaulted, or menaced by a student, is someone in the administration obligated to report the incident to local law enforcement authorities? _____ _____

18. If a student resists my arrest with force, can the local authorities charge the student with assault and battery? _____ _____

19. Can one student arrest another? _____ _____

20. Do I have a professional obligation to break up a seemingly friendly altercation? _____ _____

21. Do I have the professional and legal obligation to administer consequences for misbehavior? _____ _____

22. Can I suspend a student from school for a week or longer? _____ _____

23. While in the faculty lounge and arguing over school policy, can I call the school principal or another teacher an abusive name? _____ _____

24. Am I obligated to give students the right to be heard as long as that process does not substantially disrupt the orderly operation of the school? _____ _____

25. Must I tolerate student statements or actions that degrade others? _____ _____

26. Can a student be expelled for selling or furnishing narcotics or other controlled substances? _____ _____

27. Can a student be expelled for causing or attempting to cause physical injury to me or to other school personnel? _____ _____

28. Can a student be expelled for the use of weapons, instruments, or substances intended to do or capable of doing bodily harm to me? _____ _____

29. Must I report a suspected instance of child abuse? _____ _____

30. Must a student be given a *Miranda* warning before being questioned by school authorities? _____ _____

31. Can I administer corporal punishment to a student for that student's misbehavior?* _____ _____

32. Can public school officials unilaterally expel students with exceptional needs when they are violent or disruptive? _____ _____

33. Do public school officials have the right to censor student newspapers? _____ _____

*Corporal punishment, forbidden in many school districts, as indeed it should be in all, "can be interpreted as other actions besides spanking, slapping, or paddling. Putting a student in a dark closet, making a student do an excessive number of pushups in a gym class for forgetting his gym clothes, or making a student stand on his tip-toes with his nose in a circle drawn on a blackboard could cause physical or emotional harm to a student and may be interpreted as forms of corporal punishment." From Robert L. Monks and Ernest I. Proulx, *Legal Basics for Teachers*, (Bloomington, IN: Fastback 235, Phi Delta Kappa Educational Foundation, 1986), p. 28.

	Yes	*No*

34. Should I administer first aid by putting burn ointment on a student who has burned a hand while in my classroom? _____ _____

35. If physically abused by a student, should I file legal charges against the student? _____ _____

36. Should a serious threat by a student upon a teacher be reported? _____ _____

37. Should I give aspirin to a student who is complaining of a headache? _____ _____

38. Should I give cough drops to a student who is coughing? _____ _____

39. While on a field trip off campus, should I allow a student to go to a public restroom unescorted? _____ _____

40. Can a school prohibit girls who are pregnant from attending school? _____ _____

41. Must vocational education courses be open to all students, regardless of student gender? _____ _____

42. Title IX prohibits discrimination against females. Does it also prohibit discrimination against males? _____ _____

43. In health classes, may boys and girls be taught separately? _____ _____

44. Can a school's physical education program specify that certain options are for boys (e.g., weight lifting) and others are only for girls (e.g., modern dance)? _____ _____

45. Can a school enforce a dress code? _____ _____

46. When a school district provides maternity leave or childbearing leave to its female teachers, must it also provide paternity leave to its male teachers? _____ _____

47. As a coach of a girls' basketball team, can I expect a lower salary than the coach of the boys' basketball team? _____ _____

48. As a classroom teacher, may I display rank scores of boys versus girls on an exam? _____ _____

49. When asking for help in moving tables in the classroom, may I ask for "some strong boys to help me"? _____ _____

50. May students in physical education classes be separated by sex when activities involve physical contact? _____ _____

Answer Key

Some of the answers in this key are based on Title IX and other legal decisions that have affected public schools in the United States. Some are based on common sense. Many others are based on the Education Code, the Health and Safety Code, and the Penal Code of the state of California. You are urged to become familiar with the laws of your own state and local district and, having done so, to compare the answers with those of this answer key.

Answer	*Source or Reasoning*
1. No	Title VII of the Civil Rights Act of 1964.
2. No	
3. No	California Education Code, sections 44913 and 44914.
4. No	California Education Code, section 44807.
5. Yes	California Education Code, section 44805.
6. Yes	California Education Code, section 46000.
7. No	*West Virginia State Board of Education* v. *Barnette* 319 U.S. 624.
8. No	California Education Code, section 60070.
9. Yes	California Education Code, section 60076.
10. No	California Education Code, section 60650.
11. No	This would probably violate the student's Fourth Amendment right against unreasonable search and seizure. You should leave this to school security and administrators. *In re Donaldson* 269 Cal. App. 2d 509.
12. Yes	*Biggers* v. *Sacramento City Unified School Dist.* 25 Cal App. 3d 269.
13. No	
14. Yes	California Education Code, sections 48900 and 48910.
15. Yes	California Penal Code, section 837.
16. Yes	California Penal Code, section 415.
17. Yes	California Education Code, section 44014.
18. Yes	*People* v. *Garcia* 274 Cal. App. 2d 100.
19. Yes	California Penal Code, section 837.
20. Yes	*Daily* v. *Los Angeles Unified School District* 2 Cal. 3d 741.
21. Yes	California Education Code, section 44807.
22. No	California Education Code, section 48910. A teacher may suspend a student from class for that day and the day following and must immediately report the suspension to the principal.
23. No	You should be careful. *Connick* v. *Myers* 461 U.S. 138 (1983) held that a public employee's critical or antagonistic speech is protected only if it addresses public concerns that outweigh the public employer's interest in workplace efficiency and discipline. See also *Watson* v. *Eagle County School District RE-50, 797 P.2d 768* (Colo. App. 1990).
24. Yes	California Education Code, section 48907.
25. No	California Education Code, section 32051.
26. Yes	California Education Code, section 48900; and California Health and Safety Code, sections 11351 through 11368.

Answer		*Source or Reasoning*
27.	Yes	California Education Code, section 48900.
28.	Yes	California Education Code, section 48909.
29.	Yes	California Penal Code, sections 1165.7, 11166, and 11172.
30.	No	*In re Christopher W.* 29 Cal. App. 3d 777.
31.	No	California Education Code, section 49001.
32.	No	Federal law requires that the states provide special procedural safeguards relating to the expulsion of students with exceptional needs. See, for example, California Education Code, section 48915.5.
33.	Yes	In 1988, the United States Supreme Court, in *Hazelwood School Dist.* v. *Kuhlmeier* 484 U.S. 260, gave broad powers to school officials to edit the style and content of student newspapers as long as their actions are related to legitimate pedagogical concerns. See also *Ingrum* v. *Nixa Reorganized School Dist. R-2, 966 F.2d 1232* (8th Cir. 1992). Each teacher should know her state's laws governing this subject. For example, California Education Code, section 48907, forbids educators from censoring student speech unless the material is obscene, libelous, or slanderous or incites others to create a clear and present danger, to commit unlawful acts on school premises, to violate lawful school regulation, or to substantially disrupt the orderly operation of the school.
34.	No	
35.	Yes	
36.	Yes	
37.	No	The student might be allergic to aspirin.
38.	No	
39.	No	
40.	No	This is a violation of Title IX.
41.	Yes	Title IX.
42.	Yes	Title IX.
43.	Yes	During the teaching of human sexuality.
44.	No	
45.	Yes	If the rules apply equally to both sexes.
46.	Yes	Title IX.
47.	No	At least not on the basis of gender.
48.	No	
49.	No	
50.	Yes	Title IX.

CLASSROOM CONTROL: ITS MEANING—PAST AND PRESENT

You have learned about the daily challenges of teaching and about certain legal rights and responsibilities. Now let us further consider the ever-important topic of classroom control, offering additional guidelines for maintaining a positive and psychologically safe classroom environment.

Classroom control has always been a topic of concern to teachers, especially to beginning teachers. They have good reasons for their concern. In one respect, being a classroom teacher is much like being a truck driver who must remain alert while going down a steep and winding grade; otherwise, the truck most assuredly will get out of control, veer off the highway, and crash. You will be happy to know that to help you with your concerns about control—and to help you avoid a crash—there are volumes of literature with sound advice. Some are listed in the suggested readings at the end of this chapter.

Historical Meaning of Classroom Control

To set the stage for your comprehension, compare what the term *classroom control* has meant historically with what it means today. In the 1800s, instead of "classroom control," educators spoke of "classroom discipline," and that meant "punishment." Such an interpretation was consistent with the then-popular learning theory that assumed children were innately bad and that inappropriate behavior could be prevented by strictness, or treated with punishment. Schools of the mid-1800s have been described as being "wild and unruly places" and "full of idleness and disorder."[15]

By the early 1900s, educators were asking, "Why are the children still misbehaving?" The accepted answer was that the children were misbehaving *because of* the rigid punitive system. On this point, the era of progressive education began, providing students more freedom to decide what they would learn. The teacher's job, then, became one of providing a rich classroom of resources and materials to stimulate the student's natural curiosity. And since the system no longer would be causing misbehavior, punishment would no longer be necessary. Classes that were highly permissive, however, turned out to cause more anxiety than the restrictive classes of the 1800s.

Today's Meaning of Classroom Control and the Concept of Classroom Management

Today, rather than classroom discipline, educators talk of classroom control, or the process of controlling student behavior in the classroom. Classroom control is an important aspect of the broader area of classroom management. Classroom control involves steps in preventing inappropriate student behaviors, procedures for dealing with inappropriate student behaviors, and steps in helping students develop self-control.

Although usually eclectic in their approaches to classroom control, today's teachers generally share a concern for selecting techniques that enhance student self-esteem and that help students learn how to assume control and ownership of their own learning. A teacher's classroom control procedures reflect the person's philosophy about how children learn and interpretation of and commitment to the school's stated mission. In sum, those procedures represent the teacher's concept of effective classroom management.

Although some schools subscribe heavily to one approach, such as the Jones Model, Gordon's Teacher Effectiveness Training (TET) model, or Canter's Assertive Discipline model, many other approaches, especially those of the high schools, are more eclectic, having evolved from the historical works of several leading authorities. Let's consider what some authorities have said. Table 3.1 illustrates the main ideas of each authority and compares their recommended approaches.

Contributions of Some Leading Authorities on Classroom Management

You are probably familiar with the term *behavior modification,* which describes several popular techniques for changing behavior in an observable and predictable way; with B. F. Skinner's (1902–1990) ideas about how students learn and how behavior can be modified by using reinforcement (rewards); and with how his principles of behavior shaping have been extended by others.[16]

Behavior modification begins with four steps: (1) identify the problem behavior to be modified; (2) record how often and under what conditions that behavior occurs; (3) cause a change by reinforcing a desired behavior with a positive reinforcer (a reward); (4) choose the type of positive reinforcers to award—*activity and privilege reinforcers* (choice of playing a game, pleasure reading, free art time, computer work);

15. I. A. Hyman and J. D'Allessandro, "Oversimplifying the Discipline Problem," *Education Week* 3(29):24 (April 11, 1984).

16. B. F. Skinner, *The Technology of Teaching* (New York: Appleton-Century-Crofts, 1968).

social reinforcers (attention, praise, proximity of teacher to student, nonverbal facial or bodily expressions); *tangible reinforcer* (certificates, edibles, posters); or *token reinforcers* (points, stars, or script or tickets that can be cashed in later for a tangible reinforcer, such as a trip to the pizza store or ice cream store with the teacher).

Lee Canter, a child guidance specialist, and Marlene Canter, who specializes in teaching people with learning disabilities, developed their popular *assertive discipline* model and lead workshops for teachers and administrators. Using a reinforcement approach, their model emphasizes four major points. First, as a teacher, you have professional rights in your classroom and should expect appropriate student behavior. Second, your students have rights to choose how to behave in your classroom, and you should plan limits for inappropriate behavior. Third, an assertive discipline approach means you clearly state your expectations in a firm voice and explain the boundaries for behavior. And fourth, you should plan a system of positive consequences (e.g., positive messages home; awards and rewards; special privileges) for appropriate behavior and establish consequences (e.g., time-out; withdrawal of privileges; parent conference) for inappropriate student misbehavior and follow through in a consistent way.[17] These four points are included in the guidelines presented earlier in this chapter.

With a *logical consequences* approach, Rudolf Dreikurs (1897–1972), a psychiatrist specializing in child and family counseling, emphasized six points. First, you should be fair, firm, and friendly and involve your students in developing and implementing class rules. Second, students need to clearly understand the rules and the logical consequences for misbehavior. For example, a logical consequence for a student who has painted graffiti on a school wall would be to either clean the wall or pay for a school custodian to do it. Third, you should allow the students to be responsible not only for their own actions but also for influencing others to maintain appropriate behavior in your classroom. Fourth, you should encourage students to show respect for themselves and for others, and you should provide each student with a sense of belonging to the class. Fifth, you should recognize and encourage student goals of belonging, gaining status, and gaining recognition. And sixth, you should recognize but not reinforce correlated student goals of getting attention, seeking power, and taking revenge.[18]

William Glasser, a psychiatrist, developed his concept of *reality therapy* (i.e., the condition of the present, rather than of the past, contributes to inappropriate behavior) for the classroom. Glasser emphasizes that students have a responsibility to learn at school and to maintain appropriate behavior while there. He stresses that with the teacher's help, students can make appropriate choices about their behavior in school.[19] Finally, he advises holding classroom meetings that are devoted to establishing class rules, student behavior, matters of misbehavior, and the consequences of misbehavior. Since the publication of his first book in 1965,[20] Glasser has expanded his message to include the student needs of belonging and love, control, freedom, and fun. If these needs are unattended to at school, children are bound to fail.[21]

Haim G. Ginott (1922–1973), a psychologist, emphasized ways for you and a student to communicate—a *communication model*. He advised a teacher's sending a clear message (or messages) about situations rather than about the child. And he stressed that teachers must model the behavior they expect from students.[22] These two points are emphasized throughout this resource guide. Ginott's suggested messages are those that express feelings appropriately, acknowledge students' feelings, give appropriate direction, and invite cooperation.

Thomas Gordon, a clinical psychologist, emphasizes influence over control and decries the use of reinforcement (i.e., rewards and punishment) as an ineffective tool for achieving a positive influence over a child's behavior.[23] Rather than using reinforcements for appropriate behavior and punishment for inappropriate behaviors, Gordon and his followers advocate encouragement and development of student self-control and self-regulated behavior. To have a positive influence and to encourage self-control, the teacher (and school) should provide a rich and positive learning environment, with rich and stimulating learning activities. Specific teacher behaviors include active listening, sending I-messages (rather than you-messages), shifting from I-messages to listening when there is student resistance to an I-message, clearly identifying ownership of problems to the student when

17. See L. Canter and M. Canter, *Assertive Discipline: Positive Behavior Management for Today's Schools,* rev. ed. (Santa Monica, CA: Lee Canter & Associates, 1992).
18. See R. Dreikurs and P. Cassel, *Discipline without Tears* (New York: Hawthorne Books, 1972), and R. Dreikurs, B. B. Grunwald, and F. C. Pepper, *Maintaining Sanity in the Classroom: Classroom Management Techniques,* 2nd ed. (New York: Harper & Row, 1982).

19. See, for example, W. Glasser, "A New Look at School Failure and School Success," *Phi Delta Kappan* 78(8):597–602 (April 1997).
20. W. Glasser, *Reality Therapy: A New Approach to Psychiatry* (New York: Harper & Row, 1965).
21. See W. Glasser, *Schools without Failure* (New York: Harper & Row, 1969), *Control Theory in the Classroom* (New York: Harper & Row, 1986), *The Quality School* (New York: Harper & Row, 1990), and *The Quality School Teacher* (New York: HarperPerennial, 1993).
22. See H. G. Ginott, *Teacher and Child* (Upper Saddle River, NJ: Prentice Hall, 1971).
23. See T. Gordon, *Discipline That Works: Promoting Self-Discipline in Children* (New York: Penguin, 1989).

Table 3.1 Comparing Approaches to Classroom Management

Authority	To Know What Is Going On	To Provide Smooth Transitions
Canter/Jones	Realize that the student has the right to choose how to behave in your class with the understanding of the consequences that will follow his choice.	Insist on decent, responsible behavior.
Dreikurs/Nelsen	Realize that the student wants status, recognition, and a feeling of belonging. Misbehavior is associated with mistaken goals of getting attention, seeking power, getting revenge, and wanting to be left alone.	Identify a mistaken student goal; act in ways that do not reinforce these goals.
Ginott	Communicate with the student to find out her feelings about a situation and about herself.	Invite student cooperation.
Glasser/Gordon	Realize that the student is a rational being; he can control his own behavior.	Help the student make good choices; good choices produce good behavior, and bad choices produce bad behavior.
Kounin	Develop withitness, a skill enabling you to see what is happening in all parts of the classroom at all times.	Avoid jerkiness, which consists of thrusts (giving directions before your group is ready), dangles (leaving one activity dangling in the verbal air, starting another one, and then returning to the first activity), flip-flops (terminating one activity, beginning another one, and then returning to the first activity you terminated).
Skinner	Realize value of nonverbal interaction (i.e., smiles, pats, and handshakes) to communicate to students that you know what is going on.	Realize that smooth transitions may be part of your procedures for awarding reinforcers (i.e., points and tokens) to reward appropriate behavior.

Source: Richard D. Kellough and Patricia L. Roberts, *A Resource Guide for Elementary School Teaching: Planning for Competence,* 4th ed. (Upper Saddle River, NJ: Prentice Hall, 1998), pp. 136–137. Reprinted by permission of Prentice-Hall, Inc.

To Maintain Group Alertness	*To Involve Students*	*To Attend to Misbehavior*
Set clear limits and consequences; follow through consistently; state what you expect; state the consequences and why the limits are needed.	Use firm tone of voice; keep eye contact; use nonverbal gestures as well as verbal statements; use hints, questions, and direct messages about requesting student behavior; give and receive compliments.	Follow through with your promises and the reasonable, previously stated consequences that have been established in your class.
Provide firm guidance and leadership.	Allow students to have a say in establishing rules and consequences in your class.	Make it clear that unpleasant consequences will follow inappropriate behavior.
Model the behavior you expect to see in your students.	Build student's self-esteem.	Give a message that addresses the situation and does not attack the student's character.
Understand that class rules are essential.	Realize that classroom meetings are effective means for attending to rules, behavior, and discipline.	Accept no excuses for inappropriate behavior; see that reasonable consequences always follow.
Avoid slowdowns (delays and time wasting) that can be caused by overdwelling (too much time spent on explanations) and by fragmentation (breaking down an activity into several unnecessary steps). Develop a group focus (active participation by all students in the group) through accountability (holding all students accountable for the concept of the lesson) and by attention (seeing all the students and using unison responses as well as individual responses).	Avoid boredom by providing a feeling of progress for the students, by offering challenges, by varying class activities, by changing the level of intellectual challenge, by varying lesson presentations, and by using many different learning materials and aids.	Understand that teacher correction influences behavior of other nearby students (the ripple effect).
Set rules, rewards, and consequences; emphasize that responsibility for good behavior rests with each student.	Involve students in "token economies," in contracts, and in charting own behavior performance.	Provide tangibles to students who follow the class rules; represent tangibles as "points" for the whole class to use to "purchase" a special activity.

such is the case (i.e., not assuming ownership if it is a student's problem), and encouraging collaborative problem solving. These points are made in the guidelines presented in this chapter and in other discussions throughout this resource guide.

Psychologist Fredric Jones also promotes the idea of helping students support their own self-control, essentially, however, by way of a negative reinforcement method—rewards follow good behavior.[24] Preferred activity time (PAT), for example, is an invention resulting from the Jones Model. The Jones Model makes four recommendations. First, you should properly structure your classroom so that students understand the rules and procedures. Second, you maintain control by selecting appropriate instructional strategies. Third, you build patterns of cooperative work. Finally, you develop appropriate backup methods for dealing with inappropriate student behavior. These four points are included in the guidelines presented earlier in this chapter and in the discussion later of the mistakes frequently made by beginning teachers.

Jacob Kounin is well known for his identification of the *ripple effect* (i.e., the effect of a teacher's response to one student's misbehavior on students whose behavior was appropriate) and, as discussed in Chapter 2, of *withitness* (i.e., the teacher's ability to remain alert in the classroom, to spot quickly and redirect potential student misbehavior, which is analogous to having "eyes in the back of your head").[25] In addition to being alert to everything that is going on in the classroom, there is another characteristic of a teacher who is "with it," and that is the teacher's ability to attend to the right student. Consider the following as guidelines for developing withitness.

- Avoid spending too much time with any one student or group; longer than 30 seconds may be approaching "too much time."
- Avoid turning your back to all or a portion of the students, such as when writing on the writing board.
- If two or more errant behaviors are occurring simultaneously in different locations, attend to the most serious first, while giving the other(s) a nonverbal gesture showing your awareness and displeasure.
- Involve all students in the act, not just any one student or group. Avoid concentrating on only those who appear most interested or responsive, sometimes referred to as the "chosen few."
- Keep students alert by calling on them randomly, asking questions and calling on an answerer, circu-

lating from group to group during team learning activities, and frequently checking on the progress of individual students.
- Maintain constant visual surveillance of the entire class, even when talking to or working with an individual or small group of students and when meeting a classroom visitor at the door.
- Move around the room. Be on top of potential misbehavior, and quietly redirect student attention before the misbehavior occurs or gets out of control.
- While giving direct instruction (e.g., a lecture or leading a class discussion), try to establish eye contact with each student about once every 60 seconds.

Overlapping Skill

A prerequisite to being with it is to have the skill to attend to more than one matter at a time. As discussed in the previous chapter, this is referred to as the overlapping ability. The teacher with overlapping skills uses body language, body position, and hand signals to communicate with students. Consider the following examples of overlapping ability:

- Rather than having students bring their papers and problems to his desk, the teacher expects them to remain seated and to raise their hands as he circulates in the room monitoring and attending to individual students.
- The teacher takes care of attendance while visually and/or verbally monitoring the students during their warm-up activity.
- While attending to a messenger who has walked into the room, the teacher demonstrates verbally or by gestures that he expects the students to continue their work.
- While working in a small group, a student raises his hand to get the teacher's attention. The teacher, while continuing to work with another group of students, signals with her hand to tell the student that she is aware that he wants her attention and will get to him quickly, which she does.
- Without missing a beat in her talk, the teacher aborts the potentially disruptive behavior of a student by gesturing, by making eye contact, or by moving closer to the student (proximity control).

Building upon the work of Dreikurs, psychotherapist Jane Nelsen provides guidelines for helping children developing positive feelings of self. Key points made by Nelsen and reflected throughout this resource guide are to (1) use natural and logical consequences as a means to inspire a positive classroom atmosphere, (2) understand that children have goals that drive them toward misbehavior (attention, power, revenge, and assumed adequacy), (3) use kindness (student retains

---

24. F. Jones, *Positive Classroom Discipline* (New York: McGraw-Hill, 1987), and *Positive Classroom Instruction* (New York: McGraw-Hill, 1987).

25. Kounin, 1977.

Figure 3.4
Resources for working with children affected by family breakup.

Banana Splits: A School-Based Program for the Survivors of the Divorce Wars. c/o Interact Publishers, Box 997, Lakeside, CA 92040; (800) 369-0961.

Rainbows for All God's Children, Inc. Contact: 1111 Tower Road, Schaumburg, IL 60173, (708) 310-1880.

Shapes, Families of Today: A Curriculum Guide on Today's Changing Families for Children Ages Eight to Eighteen. Contact: Families in Transition Education Project, Stepfamily Association of America, Santa Barbara Chapter, PO Box 91233, Santa Barbara, CA 93190-1233; (805) 687-4983.

Stepfamily Association of America, Inc., 215 Centennial Mall South, Suite 212, Lincoln, NE 68508; (402) 477-STEP.

The Pittsburgh Centre for Stepfamilies. Contact: Dr. Judith L. Bauersfeld, 4815 Liberty Avenue, Suite 422, Pittsburgh, PA 15224; (412) 362-7837.

dignity) and firmness when administering consequences for a student's misbehavior, (4) establish a climate of mutual respect, (5) use class meetings to give students ownership in problem solving, and (6) offer encouragement as a means of inspiring self-evaluation and focusing on the student's behaviors.[26]

Developing Your Own Consistent Approach

As you review these classic contributions to today's approaches to effective classroom management, the expert opinions as well as the research evidence will remind you of the importance of doing the following: (1) concentrating your attention on desirable student behaviors, (2) quickly attending to inappropriate behavior, (3) maintaining alertness to all that is happening in your classroom, (4) providing smooth transitions, keeping the entire class on task, preventing dead time, and (5) involving students by providing challenges, class meetings, ways of establishing rules and consequences, opportunities to receive and return compliments, and chances to build self-esteem.

Using the criteria of your own philosophy, feelings, values, knowledge, and perceptions, you are encouraged to construct a classroom environment and management system that is positive and effective for you and your students. Remember: you must have their attention before you can teach them.

Mood Swings and Interruption of Routine

As you plan and prepare to implement your management system, you must also be aware of your own moods and high-stress days and anticipate that your own tolerance levels may vary. Students, too, are susceptible to personal problems that can be the sources of high stress. As you come to know your students well, you will be able to ascertain when certain ones are under a lot of stress and anxiety. For many, one source of stress will be the breakup of the family. To learn more about how to help these students cope, teachers may consult resources such as those listed in Figure 3.4.

High-Energy Days and Disruption of Routine

You must understand that there are perfectly natural reasons why classroom routines are likely to be interrupted occasionally, especially on certain days and at certain times during the school year. Students will not have the same motivation and energy level on each and every day. Energy level also varies throughout the school day. Your anticipation of and thoughtful and careful planning for—during the preactive phase of instruction—periods of high and low energy levels will preserve your own mental health. Depending on a number of factors, including the age level and school, periods of high-energy level might include (1) the beginning of each school day; (2) before a field trip, holiday, or school event, such as a dance, picture day, homecoming pep rally, or school assembly; (3) day of a holiday (such as Halloween); (4) day following a holiday; (5) grade report day; (6) immediately before lunch and immediately after lunch; (7) a minimum day or the day a substitute teacher is present; (8) toward the end of each school day, toward the end of school each Friday afternoon, and toward the end of the school year, especially for seniors.

In addition, although there may be no hard evidence, many experienced teachers will tell you that particular troublesome days for classroom control are those days on which there is a strong north wind or a full moon. One teacher jokingly (we suspect) told us that on days when there are both a strong north wind and a full moon she calls in sick and asks for a substitute teacher.

---

26. J. Nelsen, *Positive Discipline,* 2nd ed. (New York: Ballantine Books, 1987), and J. Nelsen, L. Lott, and H. S. Glenn, *Positive Discipline in the Classroom: How to Effectively Use Class Meetings and Other Positive Discipline Strategies* (Rocklin, CA: Prima Publishing, 1993).

How should you prepare for these so-called high-energy days? There are probably no specific guidelines that will work for all teachers in all situations in each instance on the list. However, you should keep in mind that these are days on which you need to pay extra attention during your planning, days that students could possibly be restless and more difficult to control, and days when you might need to be especially forceful and consistent in your enforcement of procedures, or even compassionate and more tolerant than usual, and need to plan instructional activities that might be more readily accepted by the students. In no instance, however, do we mean to imply that learning ceases and play time takes over. What little instructional time is available to a teacher during a school year is too valuable for that to happen.

STUDENT MISBEHAVIOR

Inappropriate student behavior in the classroom can range from very serious acts to very minor ones. Sometimes student misbehavior is the result of problems that originated outside the classroom and spilled over into the classroom. Other misbehaviors are simply due to the fact that whenever a group of 30 or so teenagers are together for a period of time mischief is likely to ensue. Still others are the result of something the teacher did or did not do. Intelligent thinking and planning and implementation of those plans will prevent many of the incidents that otherwise can cause headaches for a classroom teacher. Read on attentively to the guidelines and hints that follow in the remainder of this chapter.

Types of Student Misbehavior

Described next are types of student misbehavior that teachers may have to contend with, listed in decreasing order of seriousness.[27]

AGGRESSIVE VIOLENCE. Occasionally teachers are confronted with major problems of misbehavior that have ramifications beyond the classroom or that begin elsewhere and spill over into the classroom. If this happens, you may need to ask for help and should not hesitate to do so. As a teacher, you must stay alert. In the words of Johnson and Johnson,

> Teaching is different from what it used to be. Fifty years ago, the main disciplinary problems were running in halls, talking out of turn, and chewing gum. Today's transgressions include physical and verbal violence, incivility, and in some schools, drug abuse, robbery, assault,

and murder. The result is that many teachers spend an inordinate amount of time and energy managing classroom conflicts. When students poorly manage their conflicts with each other and with faculty, aggression results. Such behavior is usually punished with detentions, suspensions, and expulsions. As violence increases, pressure for safe and orderly schools increases. Schools are struggling with what to do.[28]

Today's schools are adopting a variety of types of school-wide and classroom instructional programs designed to reduce or eliminate violent, aggressive student behaviors (see No Short-Term Solutions to Major Problems and There *Are* Success Stories that follow).

IMMORALITY. This includes cheating, lying, and stealing. A student who habitually exhibits any of these behaviors may need to be referred to a specialist. Whenever you have good reason to suspect immoral behavior, you should discuss your concerns with members of your teaching team and the student's counselor.

DEFIANCE OF AUTHORITY. When a student refuses, perhaps hostilely, to do what the teacher says, this defiance is worthy of temporary or permanent removal from the class, at least until there has been a conference about the situation, perhaps involving the teacher, members of your teaching team, the student, the student's parent or guardian, and a school official.

CLASS DISRUPTIONS. This includes talking out of turn, walking about the room without permission, clowning, and tossing objects, all of which every secondary school student knows are unacceptable in the classroom. In handling such misbehaviors, it is important that you have explained their consequences to students and then, following your stated rules, promptly and consistently deal with the violations. You must *not* ignore minor infractions of this type, for if you do, they most likely will escalate beyond your worst expectations. Without displaying anger (otherwise students are winning the battle for control), simply and quickly enforce your consequences and keep the focus on the lesson, not the inappropriate behavior. In other words, maintain your control of classroom events rather than become controlled by them.

GOOFING OFF. This least serious category includes fooling around, not doing assigned tasks, daydreaming, and just generally being off task. Fortunately, in most instances, this type of misbehavior is momentary, and sometimes it might even be best if you pretend for a

---

27. C. M. Charles, *Building Classroom Discipline,* 4th ed. (White Plains, NY: Longman, 1992), p. vi.

28. D. W. Johnson and R. T. Johnson, *Reducing School Violence through Conflict Resolution* (Alexandria, VA: Association for Supervision and Curriculum Development, 1995), p. 1.

moment or so to not be aware of it; if it persists, all it may take to get the student back on task is a quiet redirection (indirect or private intervention). It is important, however, to not make mountains out of molehills, or you could cause more problems than you would resolve. Keep students' focus on the lesson rather than the off-task behavior.

Examples of trivial misbehaviors that you need not worry about unless they become too disruptive are emotional excitement because the student is really "into the lesson"; brief whispering during a lesson; and short periods of inattentiveness, perhaps accompanied by visual wandering or daydreaming. Teacher responses to student behavior and enforcement of procedures such as raising hands and being recognized before speaking will naturally vary depending on the particular subject, lesson activity, and maturity of the students.

In addition, we caution you there is sometimes a tendency among beginning teachers, especially when they have a problem with students goofing off and being disruptive, to assume that the entire class is being unruly, when, in fact, more often it is only one, two, or maybe three students who are goofing off and being disruptive. When this is so, you want to avoid saying to the entire class anything that implies they all are being unruly. That false accusation will only alienate the majority of students, who are being attentive to the learning task.

No Short-Term Solutions to Major Problems

Most classroom problems will be prevented or resolved by following the guidelines that are presented in this resource guide. However, by the time students arrive in secondary school, peer pressure and resentment of authority by some students can result in classroom management becoming a major concern of their teachers. Major problems in classroom control may call for extra effort on the part of the teacher in understanding and in dealing with them. There are no short-term solutions for a teacher who is trying to resolve a conflict with a student who causes major problems. Although punishment (e.g., time-out, detention, suspension) may offer short-term relief, long-term counseling is often called for. Good and Brophy point to the lack of success in this area:

> There has been much debate, but little research and certainly no conclusive evidence, about how to handle the most serious behavioral problems: racial and other group tensions; severe withdrawal and refusal to communicate; hostile, antisocial acting out; truancy; refusal to work or obey; vandalism; and severe behavioral disorders or criminality. Psychotherapists have not achieved much success in dealing with behavior disorders, and neither they nor correctional institutions have achieved even modest success

in dealing with severe delinquency and criminality. Yet teachers must cope with such problems while at the same time instructing all their students in the curriculum.[29]

There *Are* Success Stories

There *are* success stories, examples of which are described in the following paragraphs.

ALTERNATIVE SCHEDULING. After instituting a 4×4 semester-block schedule (see Chapter 1) in the 1994–95 school year, Spring Valley High School (Columbia, SC) reported a more positive school climate with significantly fewer discipline problems.[30] And just three years after implementing a flexible-block schedule, North DeSoto High School (Louisiana) reports a significant decrease in discipline problems, improved student attendance, increased completion of homework, and a significantly lower rate of student failure.[31]

CAREER GUIDANCE INVOLVING PARENTS AND THE COMMUNITY. At Dorchester School District Two (Summerville, SC) teachers, counselors, students, parents, and community representatives joined in a career development program for all students of grades 9 through 12. As a result of an emphasis on the integration of academic and vocational studies, there have been increases in both the enrollment in vocational programs and the number of students entering postsecondary education.[32] Seven years after instituting a comprehensive career guidance and exploration program, Walhalla High School (South Carolina) reports a decline in the dropout rate, improved student attendance, a 90 percent decline in the number of students taking remedial courses, and an increase from 65 to 100 percent of students who are planning to pursue postsecondary studies.[33]

HIGHER EXPECTATIONS AND THE USE OF TECHNOLOGY TO LINK HOME AND SCHOOL. Just five years after raising graduation requirements, eliminating the lower curriculum track, and linking the school with parents (by phone or computer), Souderton Area High School (Pennsylvania) reports a drop in the student failure rate from 10 to 3 percent, a 60 percent decline in suspensions, and an average daily increase in attendance from 87 to 93 percent.[34]

29. T. L. Good and J. E. Brophy, *Looking in Classrooms,* 7th ed. (New York: Longman, 1997), pp. 178–179. By permission.
30. Southern Regional Education Board, *1995 Outstanding Practices* (Atlanta, GA: Author, 1995), p. 21. By permission.
31. Southern Regional Education Board, pp. 22–23. By permission.
32. Southern Regional Education Board, pp. 26–27. By permission.
33. Southern Regional Education Board, p. 30. By permission.
34. Southern Regional Education Board, p. 3. By permission.

MENTORING. A successful effort at helping students make a connection with the value and goals of school has been through school and business partnerships. A special form of partnership called mentoring has had success with at-risk students as they become more receptive to schooling. The mentoring component of the partnership movement is a one-on-one commitment by community volunteers to improve the self-esteem, attitudes, and attendance of youngsters, beginning as early as kindergarten. For example, in the Norwalk public schools (Connecticut), mentors and students are matched in a one-on-one relationship that may begin as early as kindergarten, where at-risk children are sometimes first identified, and continue through high school. Building self-esteem and preventing school dropout are the primary goals of the Norwalk program. Around the country there are a number of other successful mentoring programs, as many different forms are being established rapidly.[35]

PRINCIPALS MAKE A DIFFERENCE. In the 1980s, Lewenberg Middle School (Boston, MA) had become a run-down school in a run-down neighborhood, and the Boston School Committee considered closing the school. Thomas O'Neill became principal and in just 12 years turned the school around, making it an "exciting, effective, and attractive learning environment." In just 12 years Lewenberg Middle School went from the least chosen school in the city of Boston to one of the best, to "a school that is 'overchosen' by parents."[36]

PARTICIPATION. Yet another avenue for helping students make a positive connection with school is identifying students with particular difficulty in establishing a sense of connection with the purpose of schooling and counseling these students to take part in extracurricular activities. Schools have experienced success in establishing this connection by encouraging *all* students to participate in school activities, regardless of their skills or academic grades.[37]

Teacher Response to Student Misbehavior: Direct and Indirect Intervention

The purpose of responding to student misbehavior is to intervene and redirect the student's focus and to do so with the least amount of classroom disturbance as possible. Typically, teachers respond to student misbehaviors in one of three ways: hostilely, assertively, or nonassertively. Hostile and nonassertive responses should be avoided. Unlike a hostile response, an assertive response is not abusive or derogatory to the student. Unlike a nonassertive response, an assertive response is a timely and clear communication to the student of the teacher's want and an indication that the teacher is prepared to back that want with action.[38]

Too often, teachers intervene with verbal commands—direct intervention—when nonverbal gesturing such as eye contact, proximity, facial gesturing, and body language—indirect intervention—are less disruptive and often more effective in quieting a misbehaving student. Although the offense might be identical, the teacher's intervention for one student might have to be direct, while for another student indirect intervention is enough to stop the misbehavior.

Order of Behavior Intervention Strategies

To redirect a student's attention, your usual *first effort* should be indirect intervention (e.g., proximity, eye contact, gesturing, silence). Your *second effort* could be the simplest (i.e., the most private) direct intervention (e.g., "David, please follow procedures"). Your *third effort,* one that in time interval closely follows the second (i.e., within the same class period), should follow your rules and procedures as outlined in your management system, which might mean a time-out (as discussed earlier in this chapter) or detention and a private phone call to the student's parent or guardian. Normally, such a third effort is not necessary. A *fourth effort,* still rarer, is to suspend the student from class (and/or school) for some period of time until decisions about the future of that student in the school are made by school officials in consultation with the student, the parents or guardians, and other professionals such as the school psychologist.

Direct intervention should be reserved for repetitive and serious misbehavior. When using direct intervention, you should give a direct statement, either reminding the student of what he or she is supposed to be doing or telling the student what to do. You should avoid asking a rhetorical question, such as "David, why are you doing that?" When giving students directions about what they are supposed to be doing, you may be asked by a student, "Why do we have to do this?" To that question, you may give a brief academic answer, but do not become defensive or make threats. And rather than spend an inordinate amount of time on the misbehavior, try to focus the student's attention on a desired behavior.

35. S. G. Weinberger, *How to Start a Student Mentor Program* (Bloomington, IN: Fastback 333, Phi Delta Kappa Educational Foundation, 1992), p. 8.

36. M. D. O'Donnell, "Boston's Lewenberg Middle School Delivers Success," *Phi Delta Kappan* 78(7):509 (March 1997).

37. As an additional resource, especially for approaches to improving the academic achievement of students in low-performing educational settings, see J. A. Bell, A. Meza, and T. L. Williams, *Promising Practices and Programs for Improving Student Achievement* (Sacramento, CA: California Department of Education, 1995).

38. C. H. Edwards, *Classroom Discipline and Management,* 2nd ed. (Upper Saddle River, NJ: Prentice Hall, 1997), pp. 71–72.

One reason that direct intervention should be held in reserve is because by interrupting the lesson to verbally intervene you are doing exactly what the student who is being reprimanded was doing—interrupting the lesson. Not only is that improper modeling, but it can create a host of management problems beyond your wildest nightmares. Another reason for saving direct intervention is that, when used too often, direct intervention loses its effectiveness. In addition, its use can create a ripple effect that will cause the teacher an even greater loss of classroom control.

TEACHER-CAUSED STUDENT MISBEHAVIOR

As implied, some student misbehaviors and other problems in classroom control are caused by the teacher or the school. One of your major responsibilities is to model appropriate behavior and not to contribute to or be a cause of problems in the classroom.

Scenarios for Case Study Review

In addition to sometimes ignoring minor infractions of your behavior rules, you should avoid using negative methods of rule enforcement and ineffective forms of punishment, such as exemplified by the following scenarios. You and your classmates can treat these scenarios as case studies for small groups to consider and then discuss before the whole class.

EXTRA ASSIGNMENTS.   When students in Margaret Malopropros's seventh-grade reading class misbehave, she habitually assigns extra reading and written work as punishment, even for the most minor offenses. This behavior has simply reinforced the view of many of her students that school is drudgery, so they no longer look forward to her classes, and behavior problems in her class have steadily increased since the beginning of the school year.

EMBARRASSMENT.   When social studies teacher Denise Degradini was having difficulty controlling the behavior of one of her students, she got on the classroom phone and called the student's parent. While the entire class of 33 students could hear the conversation, she told the parent about her child's behavior in class and how she was going to have to give the student a referral if the student's behavior did not improve. From that one act, Ms. Degradini lost all respect of her students and class grades plummeted for the rest of the year.

GROUP PUNISHMENT.   Because Fred Flock has not developed his withitness and overlapping skills, he has developed the unfortunate habit of punishing the entire class for every instance of misbehavior. Yesterday, for example, because some students were noisy during a video presentation, he gave the entire class an unannounced quiz on the content of the film. He has lost the respect of the students, students are hostile toward him, and his problems with classroom control are steadily getting worse.

HARSH AND HUMILIATING PUNISHMENT.   Vince Van Pelt, a physical education teacher, has lost control of his classes and the respect of his students. His thrashing, whipping, tongue-lashing, and use of humiliation are ineffective and indicative of his loss of control. Parents have complained, and one is suing him. The district has given Mr. Van Pelt official notice of the nonrenewal of his contract.

INCONSISTENCY.   Because of her arbitrary and inconsistent enforcement of classroom rules, Fran Fickle has lost the respect and trust of her students as well as control of her classes. Students are constantly testing her to see what they can get away with.

LOUD TALK.   The noisiest person in Steve Shrill's English class is Mr. Shrill. His constant and mistaken efforts to talk over the classes have led to his own yelling and screaming, to complaints from neighboring teachers about the noise in his classes, and to a reprimand from the principal.

LOWERED MARKS.   Eunice Erudite, an eighth-grade language arts/social studies core teacher, has a policy of writing a student's name on the board each time the person is reprimanded for misbehavior. Then, when a student has accumulated five marks on the board, she lowers his academic grade by one letter. As a result of her not separating their academic and social behaviors, her students are not doing as well as they were at the start of the year. Parents and students have complained about this policy to the administration, arguing that the grades Ms. Erudite is giving do not reflect the students' academic progress or abilities.

NAGGING.   Paul Peck's continual and unnecessary scolding and criticizing of students upsets the recipient students and arouses resentment from their peers. His nagging resolves nothing and, like a snowball building in size as it rolls down the hill, causes Mr. Peck, a ninth-grade social studies teacher, more and more problems in the classroom.

NEGATIVE DIRECT INTERVENTION.   In senior government, Joshua swears more and more frequently and with graphic and startling language. Other students are beginning to behave similarly. Rather than giving

Joshua alternative ways of expressing his feelings, Polly Premio, the teacher, verbally reprimands Joshua each time this happens and threatens to call his parents about it. Ms. Premio doesn't realize that by giving her attention to Joshua's swearing she is rewarding, reinforcing, and causing the increase in Joshua's unacceptable behavior.

NEGATIVE TOUCH CONTROL. When Ezzard, an eighth-grade bully, pushes and shoves other students out of his way for no apparent reason other than to physically bully them, his teacher, Tony Trenchant, grabs Ezzard and yanks him into his seat. What "roughneck" Tony the teacher doesn't realize is that he is using the very behavior (physical force) that he is trying to stop Ezzard from using. This simply confuses students and teaches them (especially Ezzard) that the use of physical force is okay if you are bigger or older than the recipient of that force. In this situation, unfortunately, hostility begets hostility.

PHYSICAL PUNISHMENT. Mr. Fit, a ninth-grade geography teacher, punishes students by making them go outside and run around the school track when they misbehave in his class. Last week, Sebastian, a student whom he told to go out and run four laps for "mouthing off in class," collapsed and died while running. Mr. Fit has been placed on paid leave and is being sued for negligence by Sebastian's parents.

PREMATURE JUDGMENTS AND ACTIONS. Because of Kathy Kwik's impulsiveness, she does not think clearly before acting, and more than once she has reprimanded the wrong student. Because of her hasty and faulty judgments, students have lost respect for her. For them, her French class has become pure drudgery.

THREATS AND ULTIMATUMS. Threats and ultimatums from math teacher Bonnie Badger are known to be empty; because she does not follow through, her credibility with the students has been lost. Like wildfire, the word has spread around—"We can do whatever we want in old Badger's class."

TOO HESITANT. Because Tim Timideo is too hesitant and slow to intervene when students get off task, his classes have gotten increasingly out of his control, and it is still early in the school year. As a result, neighbor teachers are complaining about the noise from his classroom, and Tim has been writing more and more referrals.

WRITING PUNISHMENT. Because they were "too noisy," biology teacher Steve Scribe punished his class of 28 students by making each one hand-copy ten pages from encyclopedias. When they submitted this assignment, he tore up the pages in front of the class and said, "Now, I hope you have learned your lesson and from now on will be quiet." Upon hearing about this, all teachers of the school's English department signed and filed a complaint with the principal about Mr. Scribe's use of writing for punishment.

Fifty-one Mistakes Commonly Made by Beginning Teachers

Emphasizing that classroom behavior problems are often the result of inappropriate instruction, Alfie Kohn says that when students are off task, the teacher's first response should be to ask, "What's the task?"[39] In this section we do not mean to imply that beginning teachers are incompetent. Rather, we intend to further demonstrate that teaching is a highly skilled profession, with many things to be learned. As a beginning teacher you are doing just that, learning. The important thing is to be knowledgeable and to learn from your mistakes and from those of others. By sharing the following list of mistakes commonly made by beginning teachers, we hope to better prepare you with the skills necessary to be the most competent teacher you can be.

1. *Inadequately attending to long-range planning.* Long-range unit planning is important for reasons discussed in Part II that follows. A beginning teacher who inadequately plans ahead is heading for trouble.

2. *Using sketchy lesson plans.* Sketchy, inadequate daily lesson planning is a precursor to ineffective teaching and, eventually, to teaching failure. Many beginning teachers plan their lessons carefully at the beginning of the semester, and the students initially respond well. Then, after they have found a few strategies that seem to work, their lesson planning becomes increasingly sketchy, and they fall into a rut of doing pretty much the same thing day after day—lecture, discussion, videos, and worksheets are common in these instances. They fail to consider and plan for individual student differences. By mid-semester, they have stopped growing professionally, and they begin to experience an increasing number of problems, with students and with parents.

3. *Emphasizing the negative.* Too many warnings to students for their inappropriate behavior—and too little recognition for their positive behaviors—does not help to establish the positive climate needed for the most effective learning to take place. Reminding students of procedures is more positive than is reprimanding them when they do not follow procedures.

4. *Allowing students' hands to be raised too long.* When students have their hands raised for long periods before you recognize them and attend to their questions or

---

39. A. Kohn, *Beyond Discipline: From Compliance to Community* (Alexandria, VA: Association for Supervision and Curriculum Development, 1996), p. 19.

responses, you are providing them with time to fool around. Although you don't have to call on every student as soon as she raises a hand, you should acknowledge her quickly, such as with a nod or a wave of your hand, so the student can lower the hand and return to her work. Then you should get to the student as quickly as possible. Procedures for this should be clearly understood by the students and consistently followed by you.

5. *Spending too much time with one student or one group and not monitoring the entire class.* Spending too much time with any one student or a small group of students is, in effect, ignoring the rest of the class. For the best classroom management, you must continually monitor the entire classroom of students. How much time is too much? A rule of thumb is anything over 30 seconds is approaching too much time.

6. *Beginning a new activity before gaining the students' attention.* A teacher who consistently fails to insist that students follow procedures and who does not wait until all students are in compliance before starting a new activity is destined for major problems in classroom control. You must establish and maintain classroom procedures. Starting an activity before all students are in compliance is, in effect, telling the students that they don't have to follow expected procedures. You cannot afford to tell students one thing and then do another. A teacher's actions always speak louder than words.

7. *Pacing teacher talk and learning activities too fast.* Students need time to disengage mentally and physically from one activity before engaging in the next. You must remember that this takes more time for a classroom of 30 students than it does for just one person, you.

8. *Using a voice level that is always either too loud or too soft.* A teacher's voice that is too loud day after day can become irritating to some students, just as one that cannot be heard or understood can become frustrating.

9. *Assigning a journal entry without giving the topic careful thought.* If the question or topic about which students are supposed to write is ambiguous or obviously hurriedly prepared—without your having given thought to how students will interpret and respond to it—students will judge that the task is busywork (e.g., something for them to do while you take attendance). If they do it at all, it is with a great deal of commotion and much less enthusiasm than if they were writing on a topic that had meaning to them.

10. *Standing too long in one place.* In the classroom, you must be mobile in order to "work the crowd."

11. *Sitting while teaching.* As a beginning teacher, there is not time to sit while teaching. Unless a physical disability restricts your mobility, you cannot monitor the class while seated. You cannot afford to appear that casual.

12. *Being too serious and no fun.* No doubt, good teach-ing is serious business. But students respond best to teachers who obviously enjoy working with students and helping them learn.

13. *Falling into a rut by using the same teaching strategy or combination of strategies day after day.* This teacher's classroom becomes boring to students. Because of the multitude of differences, students respond best to a variety of well-planned and meaningful classroom activities.

14. *Inadequately using silence (wait time) after asking a content question.* When expected to think deeply about a question, students need time to do it.

15. *Poorly or inefficiently using the overhead projector and the writing board.* The ineffective use of the overhead projector and writing board (see Chapter 10) says to students that you are not a competent teacher. A competent teacher, like a competent surgeon or automobile mechanic, selects and effectively uses the best tools available for the job to be done.

16. *Ineffectively using facial expressions and body language.* Your gestures and body language say more to students than your words do. For example, one teacher didn't understand why his class of middle school students would not respond to his repeated expression of "I need your attention." In one class, he used that expression eight times in less than 15 minutes. Studying a videotape of his teaching helped him understand the problem. His dress was very casual, and he stood most of the time with his right hand in his pocket. At five feet, eight inches, with a slight build, a rather deadpan facial expression, and a nonexpressive voice, he was not a commanding presence in the classroom. Once he had seen himself on tape, he returned to the class wearing a tie, and he began using his hands, face, and voice more expressively. Rather than saying "I need your attention," he waited in silence for the students to become attentive. It worked.

17. *Relying too much on teacher talk for classroom control.* Beginning teachers have a tendency to rely too much on teacher talk. Too much teacher talk is deadly (see Chapter 9). Unable to discern between the important and the unimportant verbiage, students will quickly tune you out. In addition, useless verbalism, such as global praise and verbal fill-ins, causes students to pay less attention when you have something important to say.

18. *Inefficiently using teacher time.* Think carefully about what you are going to be doing every minute, and then plan for the most efficient and therefore the most effective use of your time in the classroom. Consider the following example. A teacher is recording student contributions on a large sheet of butcher paper taped to the writing board. She solicits student responses, acknowledges those responses, holds and manipulates the writing pen, and writes on the paper. Each of those actions requires decisions and movements that consume

valuable time and can distract her from her students. An effective alternative would be to have a reliable student helper do the writing while she handles the solicitation and acknowledgment of student responses. That way she has fewer decisions and fewer actions to distract her. And she does not lose eye contact and proximity with the classroom of students.

19. *Talking to and interacting with only half the class.* When leading a class discussion, too many beginning teachers favor (by their eye contact and verbal interaction) only 40 to 65 percent of the students, sometimes completely ignoring the others for an entire class period. Feeling ignored, those students will, in time, become uninterested and perhaps unruly. Remember to spread your interactions throughout the entire class. Try to establish eye contact with every student about once a minute.

20. *Not requiring students to raise their hands and be acknowledged before responding.* You cannot be in control of your interactions with students if you allow students to shout out responses and questions whenever they feel like it. In addition, indulging their natural impulsivity is not helping them to grow intellectually.

21. *Collecting and returning homework papers before assigning students something to do.* If, while turning in papers or waiting for their return, students have nothing else to do, they get restless and inattentive. Avoid any kind of dead time. Students should have something to do while papers are being collected or returned.

22. *Verbally or nonverbally interrupting students once they are on task.* Avoid doing or saying anything once students are working on a learning task. If there is an important point you must make, write it on the board. If you want to return some papers while they are working, do it in a way and when they are least likely to be interrupted from their learning task.

23. *Using "Shhh" to try to obtain student attention or to quiet them.* When doing that, you simply sound like a balloon with a slow leak. That sound and the overuse of verbal fill-ins, such as "okay," should be eliminated from your professional vocabulary.

24. *Overuse of verbal efforts to stop inappropriate student behavior.* Beginning teachers have a tendency to rely too much on verbal interaction and not enough on nonverbal intervention techniques. Verbally reprimanding a student for his interruptions of class activities is reinforcing that very behavior you are trying to stop. Develop your indirect, silent intervention techniques.

25. *Poor body positioning in the classroom.* Always position your body so that you can continue visually monitoring the entire class.

26. *Settling for less when you should be trying for more—not getting the most from student responses.* Don't hurry a discussion; "milk" student responses for all you can, especially when discussing a topic they are obviously inter-

ested in. Ask a student for clarification or reasons for his response. Ask for verification or data. Have another student paraphrase what a student said. Pump students for deeper thought and meaning. Too often, the teacher will ask a question, get an abbreviated (often one word) response from a student, and then move on to new content. Instead, follow up a student's response to your question with a sequence of questions, prompting and cueing to elevate the student's thinking to higher levels.

27. *Using threats.* One middle school teacher, for example, told her class that if they continued with their inappropriate talking they would lose their break time. She should have had that consequence as part of the understood procedures and then taken away the break time if student behavior warranted it. Avoid threats of any kind. In addition, be cautious about ever punishing the entire class for the misbehavior of some of the students. Although the rationale behind such action is clear (i.e., to get group pressure working for you), often the result is the opposite of that intended—students who have been behaving well become alienated from the teacher because they feel they have been punished unfairly for the misbehavior of others. Those students expect the teacher to be able to handle the misbehaving students without punishing those who are behaving well, and perhaps they are right.

28. *Global praise.* An instance would be: "Your rough drafts were really wonderful." This says nothing and is simply another instance of useless verbalism from the teacher. Be specific—tell what it was about their drafts that made them so wonderful.

29. *Meaningless use of color.* The use of color, such as varying color pens for overhead transparencies and colored chalkboard writing, can be nice but will lose its effectiveness over time unless the colors have meaning. If you color-code everything in the classroom so students understand the meaning of the colors, then use of color is helpful to their learning.

30. *Verbally reprimanding a student across the classroom.* This is needless interruption of all students. In addition, it simply increases the "you versus them" syndrome because of peer pressure. Reprimand, when necessary, but do it quietly and privately.

31. *Interacting with only a "chosen few" students rather than spreading interactions around to all students.* As a beginning teacher, it is easy to fall into a habit of interacting only with a few students, especially those who are vocal and who have "intelligent" contributions. Your job, however, is to teach all students. To do that, you must be proactive, not reactive, in your interactions.

32. *Not intervening quickly enough during inappropriate student behavior.* Inappropriate student behavior usually gets worse, not better, if allowed to continue. It won't go away by itself. It's best to nip it in the bud quickly

and resolutely. A teacher who ignores inappropriate behavior is, in effect, approving it. In turn, that approval reinforces the continuation of those inappropriate behaviors.

33. *Not learning and using student names.* A teacher who does not know or use names when addressing students is, in effect, seen by the students as being impersonal and uncaring. You want to quickly learn the names and then refer to students by their names when you call on them in class.

34. *Reading student papers only for correct answers and not for process and student thinking.* Reading student papers only for "correct" responses reinforces the notion that the process of arriving at answers or solutions is unimportant and that alternative solutions or answers are impossible.

35. *Not putting time plans on the board for students.* Yelling out how much time is left for an activity, such as a quiz or cooperative learning activity, interrupts student thinking. Rather, you should write on the board before the activity begins how much time is allowed for it. Write the time the activity is to end. If during the activity a decision is made to change that end time, then write the changed time on the board. Avoid interrupting students once they are on task.

36. *Asking global questions that nobody likely will answer.* Examples of this type of question are: "Does everyone understand how that was done?" "Are there any questions?" and "How do you all feel about . . . ?" If you want to check for student understanding or opinions, then do a spot check by asking specific questions, allow some time to think, and then call on students (the questioning strategy is discussed in Chapter 7).

37. *Failing to do frequent comprehension checks (every few minutes) to see if students are understanding.* Too often, teachers simply plow through their lesson, assuming students are understanding it.

38. *Using poorly worded, ambiguous questions.* Plan your questions. Write them out. Ask them to yourself, and try to predict how students will respond to a particular question.

39. *Failing to balance interactions with students according to student gender.* Many teachers (experienced as well as beginning) interact more often with male than with female students. Avoid that.

40. *Trying to talk over too much student noise.* This simply tells students that their making noise while you are talking is acceptable behavior. All that you will accomplish when trying to talk over a high student noise level is a sore throat by the end of the school day.

41. *Wanting to be liked by students.* Forget it. If you are a teacher, then teach. Respect will be earned as a result of your good teaching. Liking you may come later.

42. *Allowing students to be inattentive to an educationally useful video or movie.* This usually happens because the teacher has failed to give the students a written hand-out of questions or guidelines for what they should acquire from watching the audiovisual. Sometimes students need an additional focus. Furthermore, an audiovisual is exactly that—audio and visual. To reinforce the learning, add the kinesthetic, such as the writing aspect when questions are used. This provides the hands-on and minds-on learning that you want.

43. *Stutter starting.* A stutter start is when the teacher begins an activity, is distracted, begins again, is distracted again, tries again to start, and so on. During stutter starts, students become increasingly restless and inattentive, making the final start almost impossible for the teacher to achieve. Avoid stutter starts. Begin an activity clearly and decisively.

44. *Failing to give students a pleasant greeting on Monday or following a holiday or to remind them to have a pleasant weekend or holiday.* Students are likely to perceive such a teacher as uncaring or impersonal.

45. *Sounding egocentric.* Whether you are or are not egocentric, you want to avoid sounding so. Sometimes the distinction is subtle, such as when a teacher says, "What I am going to do now is . . ." rather than "What we are going to do now is . . ." If you want to strive for group cohesiveness—a sense of "we-ness"—then teach not as if you are the leader and your students are the followers, but rather in a manner that empowers your students in their learning.

46. *Taking too much time to give verbal directions for a new activity.* Students get impatient and restless during long verbal instructions from the teacher. It is better to give brief instructions (two or three minutes should do it) and get your students started on the task. For more complicated activities you can teach three or four students the instructions for the activity and then have those students do "workshops" with five or six students in each workshop group. This frees you to monitor the progress of each group.

47. *Taking too much time for an activity.* Whether lecturing or providing for group work, think carefully about how much time students can effectively attend to the activity. Here is a rule of thumb for most classes: When only one or two learning modalities are involved (e.g., auditory and visual), the activity should not extend beyond about 15 minutes; when more than two senses are involved (e.g., add tactile or kinesthetic), then the activity might extend longer, say for 20 or 30 minutes.

48. *Being uptight and anxious.* Students quickly, consciously or unconsciously, detect a teacher who is afraid that events in the classroom will probably not go well. And it's like a contagious disease—if you are uptight and anxious, your students will likely become the same. To prevent such emotions, at least to the extent that they damage your teaching and your students' learning, you must prepare lessons carefully, thoughtfully, and thoroughly. Unless there is something personal going on

in your life that is making you anxious, you are more likely to be in control and confident in the classroom when you have lessons that are well prepared. If you do have a personal problem, you need to concentrate on ensuring that your anger, hostility, fear, or other negative emotions do not negatively affect your teaching and your interactions with students. Regardless of your personal problems, your classes of students will face you each day expecting to be taught mathematics, history, science, physical education, or whatever it is you are supposed to be helping them learn.

49. *Overusing punishment for classroom misbehavior— jumping to the final step without trying alternatives.* Many beginning teachers mistakenly try either to ignore inappropriate student behavior or to skip steps, resorting too quickly to punishment. They immediately take away PAT (preferred activity time) or break time or quickly assign detention (an ineffective punishment). Inbetween steps that they should consider include the use of alternative activities in the classroom. By their instruction, too many teachers unrealistically seem to expect success having all 33 students doing the same thing at the same time rather than having several alternative activities simultaneously occurring in the classroom (multilevel teaching). For example, a student who is not responding well (i.e., being disruptive) to a class discussion might behave better if given the choice of moving to a quiet reading center in the classroom or to a learning center to work alone or with one other student. If, after trying an alternative activity, the student continues to be disruptive, then you may have to try another alternative activity. You may have to send the student to another supervised location (out of the classroom, to a place previously arranged by you) until you have time (after class or after school) to talk with her about the problem.

50. *Using negative language.* Too often, beginning teachers try to control their students with negative language, such as "There should be no talking," "No gum or candy in class or else you will get detention," and "No getting out of your seats without my permission." Negative language from the teacher does not help instill a positive classroom environment. As emphasized in this chapter, students need to know what is expected of them and to understand classroom procedures. Therefore, to encourage a positive classroom atmosphere, you should use concise, positive language. Tell students exactly what they are supposed to do rather than what they are not supposed to do.

51. *Introducing too many topics simultaneously.* Don't overload students' capacity to mentally engage by introducing different topics simultaneously. For example, during the first ten minutes of class a teacher started by introducing a bell activity, a writing activity with instructions for doing it clearly explained on the overhead. Although the instructions for the activity were clearly displayed on the screen, the teacher also verbally explained the activity. She could have simply pointed to the screen thereby nonverbally (without disrupting the thinking of students who had already begun) telling students to get started on the writing activity. One minute later the teacher was telling students about their quarter grades and how later in the period they would learn more about those grades. Then, the teacher went back to the overhead activity, explaining it again. Then she reminded students of the new tardy rules (introducing a third topic). At this time, however, most of the students were still thinking and talking about what she had said about quarter grades, few were working on the writing activity, and hardly any were listening to her talk about the tardy rules. There was a lot of commotion among the students. She had tried to focus student attention on too many topics at once, thus accomplishing little and losing control of the class in the process.

Now direct your attention to other specific instances of teacher behaviors, some of which reinforce or cause student misbehavior, by completing Exercises 3.7 to 3.9.

EXERCISE 3.7

Identifying Teacher Behaviors That Cause Student Misbehavior—A Self-check Exercise

Instructions: The purpose of this exercise is to practice your awareness of the kinds of teacher behaviors to avoid—namely, those that tend to reinforce or cause student misbehavior. Place a check next to each of the following situations you believe illustrate teacher behaviors that cause or reinforce student misbehavior. Then identify what the teacher should do instead. Share your responses with your classmates. An answer key follows.

_____ 1. Ms. Rodriquez is nearly always late in arriving to her eighth-grade English class that meets immediately after lunch, seldom beginning class until at least five minutes past the time it is supposed to start.

_____

_____

_____

_____

_____

_____

_____ 2. Mr. Pickering ignores brief whispering between two students during a quiet activity in his eleventh-grade history class.

_____

_____

_____

_____

_____

_____ 3. While lecturing to her biology class, Ms. Whyte ignores brief talking between two students.

_____

_____

_____

_____

_____ 4. During a class discussion in Mr. Stephen's social studies class, one student appears to be daydreaming and just staring out the window.

_____ 5. During quiet study time in Mr. Orey's seventh-grade reading class, Mr. Orey asks for everyone's attention, verbally reprimands two students for horsing around, and then writes out a referral for each of the two students.

_____ 6. Ms. Fueyo advises her students to pay attention during the viewing of a film or else she will give them a quiz over the film's content.

_____ 7. Ms. Lee tells a student that because of his behavior in class today he must come in after school and be detained with her for ten minutes, the same amount of time that he disturbed the class.

_____

8. When Mr. Murai sees a ninth-grade student cheating on a science test, he walks over to the student, picks up the student's test paper, and tears it up in front of the student and the rest of the class.

_____

_____

_____

_____

_____

9. While Ms. Wong is talking to her senior literature class, the school principal walks into the room. Ms. Wong stops her lecture and walks over to greet the principal and find out what the principal wants.

_____

_____

_____

_____

_____

10. While a student learning team is giving its oral report to the chemistry class, Mr. Edwards, the teacher, begins a conversation with several students in the back of the room.

_____

_____

_____

_____

_____

_____

Answer Key

You should have checked situations 1, 3, 5, 6, 7, 8, 9, and 10; these are teacher behaviors that reinforce or cause student misbehavior. For some situations, reasonable teachers will disagree. You should talk about these disagreements with your classmates and arrive at common understandings. Here are some thoughts on each of the ten situations:

1. Ms. Rodriquez's behavior is poor modeling for her students. She must model what she expects—as well as what the school expects—of students. In this instance, she should model arriving and starting on time.

2. Minor infractions, such as this, are often best ignored, as long as the whispering is brief and not disturbing.

3. This should not be ignored. Students are expected to give their attention to the teacher or whoever has the floor at the moment—a show of common courtesy. By not attending to these students (perhaps by eye contact, proximity, name dropping, or some other form of indirect intervention), Ms. Whyte is saying that it is okay for students to be discourteous and to talk during the teacher's lecture. In this instance, Ms. Whyte is not following through with classroom behavioral expectations. Her lack of follow-through will cause further and increasingly disturbing management problems.

4. Minor infractions are sometimes best ignored. Perhaps the student is really thinking about ideas presented in the discussion.

5. By his disruption of the class learning activity, Mr. Orey is reinforcing the very behavior he considers inappropriate from his students. This lack of consistency will cause continued problems in management for Mr. Orey.

6. Threats are unacceptable behaviors, from students or from teachers. And tests should never be administered as punishment. Ms. Fueyo could recommend that students take notes (mental or written) during the film and that these notes will serve as a focus for discussion after the film's showing. And she could advise them that there will be a follow-up quiz later.

7. By giving the student even more individual attention after school, Ms. Lee is reinforcing and rewarding the student's misbehavior that caused the student problem in the first place. Besides, this may not be safe for Ms. Lee to do. Detention, supervised by someone other than this teacher, is a better alternative.

8. Mr. Murai has taken no time to diagnose and to prescribe and thus is reacting too hastily and with hostility. This sort of teacher behavior reinforces the notion that the student is guilty until proven innocent and the notion that process is of greater importance than is the individual student. In addition, Mr. Murai violated this student's right to due process.

9. The error here is that by stopping her lesson, Ms. Wong and the principal are reinforcing the notion that classroom disruptions are acceptable—that the act of teaching is less important than other school business.

10. Mr. Edwards's behavior is both disrespectful and an example of poor modeling. Mr. Edwards and his class should be giving their full attention to the students' report. Mr. Edwards is not modeling the very behavior that he undoubtedly expects from his students when he is leading the class.

EXERCISE 3.8
Applying Measures of Control

Instructions: The purpose of this exercise is to provide practice in deciding your options when there is a behavior problem in your classroom. For each of the following, identify a situation (as specifically as possible) in which you *would* and a situation in which you *would not* use that measure. Share and discuss your responses with your classmates.

Your teaching field: _____

Intended grade level (considered for this exercise): _____

1. Give a verbal reminder of procedures.

   Would: _____

   _____

   _____

   _____

   Would not: _____

   _____

   _____

   _____

2. Give a prolonged stare.

   Would: _____

   _____

   _____

   _____

   Would not: _____

   _____

   _____

   _____

3. Use eye contact with and a hand signal to a student.

   Would: _____

   _____

   _____

   _____

Would not: _____

_____

_____

_____

4. Immediately send student to the principal's or vice-principal's office.

Would: _____

_____

_____

_____

Would not: _____

_____

_____

_____

5. Ignore the student's misbehavior.

Would: _____

_____

_____

_____

Would not: _____

_____

_____

_____

6. Assign the student to detention.

Would: _____

_____

_____

_____

Would not: _____

_____

_____

_____

7. Use immediate corporal punishment.

Would: _____

_____

_____

_____

Would not: _____

_____

_____

_____

8. Call or send a note home to the parent or guardian about the student's misbehavior.

Would: _____

_____

_____

_____

Would not: _____

_____

_____

_____

9. Touch the student gently on the shoulder.

Would: _____

_____

_____

_____

Would not: _____

_____

_____

_____

10. Provide a nonpunitive academic time-out.

Would: _____

_____

_____

Would not: _____

_____

_____

_____

11. Verbally redirect a student's attention.

Would: _____

_____

_____

_____

Would not: _____

_____

_____

_____

12. Use a strong verbal reprimand.

Would: _____

_____

_____

_____

Would not: _____

_____

_____

_____

EXERCISE 3.9
Selecting Measures of Control

Instructions: The purpose of this exercise is to provide situations to help you determine which measures of control you would apply in similar situations. For each of the following, describe the first thing you would do in that situation. Then share and discuss your responses with your colleagues.

1. While you are talking to the class, a student noisily and rhythmically taps a pencil on his desk.

   _____

   _____

   _____

   _____

2. While taking a test, one student pokes another, who loudly responds, "Stop it!"

   _____

   _____

   _____

   _____

3. Although you have asked a student to take her seat, she refuses.

   _____

   _____

   _____

   _____

4. While talking with a small group of eighth-grade students, you observe three students on the opposite side of the room combing their hair, putting on lipstick, and sharing a mirror back and forth.

   _____

   _____

   _____

   _____

5. During small-group work, one tenth grader shouts out, "This class sucks!"

   _____

   _____

   _____

   _____

6. Although chewing gum is not permitted at the school, at the start of class you observe a student chewing what you suspect to be gum.

_____

_____

_____

_____

_____

7. During band rehearsal, you (as band director) see a student about to stuff a scarf down the clarinet of another student.

_____

_____

_____

_____

8. During the presentation by a guest speaker, two boys in the back of the room are noisily talking to each other.

_____

_____

_____

_____

9. At the start of the class period, a boy pulls the chair from beneath a girl just as she is about to take her seat. She falls to the floor.

_____

_____

_____

_____

10. During an argument over a grade, a student pulls a gun and points it at you.

_____

_____

_____

_____

SITUATIONAL CASE STUDIES FOR ADDITIONAL REVIEW

To provide some insight about the day-to-day events that occur in teaching, as well as to let you think about what you might do in similar situations, ten case studies follow. These are teaching situations that have actually occurred. We recommend that they be analyzed and discussed in your class. For each case, you should think in terms of either a prevention or a remedy.

☐ CASE 1. THE BOY WHO HANGS AROUND

Background

Bill is male, age 13, in general science. He is tall and awkward and has poor skin. He is considered "crazy" by his classmates. He has minor police offenses and is apparently in conflict with his father. He has taken a liking to the general science teacher and spends many extra hours in the classroom. He is energetic and displays an inquisitive nature. He is quick to get interested in projects but almost as quick to lose interest. He likes to run the film projector for the teacher, but he does not like to participate in discussions with the rest of the class. He likes personal chats with the teacher but feels that the other students laugh at him.

The Situation

Bill's IQ is 95. The teacher attempted to work with Bill in improving his feelings of inadequacy. The teacher had frank talks with Bill about his gangliness and his acne. What follows is actual material as written by Bill during the first semester of school:

September: "I want to make the best out of the time I am on earth. I want to be somebody, not just exist either. . . . The members of this class influence me and what I think of doing. . . . They also make me feel real low. Their teasing me has changed me. . . . The teacher of my science class has helped me very much. . . . My greatest problem is in holding my head up and fighting for myself. . . ."

October: "I have made a lot of headway in the past weeks. . . . I think I have done a good choice in the subject I am studying. . . . I also thank my teacher's actions toward me, that we may get to be very good friends, and learn a lot to know that teachers are human too, that they also have problems to solve and goals to head for."

November: "I don't have to fear anybody or anything on the idea of getting up and saying what I feel I have accomplished in this class and I have learned to make my own dississions on what I will study or maybe do when I get out of school."

December: "I have learned that I have confidence in others only when I have confidence in myself."

January: "I have my report on the affect of geabriilic acid on plants. . . . I told (the class) about all my failures and they were quite interested. I told them that I had failed four times . . . that my science teacher told me I should not give up at this point and that a seintice [scientist] does not give up. I had no longer stated that fact and they all seemed like they could help in some way. I think the report went over well."

So the student developed courage to stand in front of his peers, holding his head high, and confidently reporting to the class how he kept at his plant experiment, even after four failures. He was proud of what he had learned about the work of the scientist. And he was even more proud that the students no longer teased and laughed at him.

Questions for Class Discussion

1. How did you feel after reading this case?
2. Did Bill learn anything that semester? What?
3. Did he learn science?
4. What did the teacher do to facilitate Bill's learning?
5. What is ahead for Bill in school?

☐ CASE 2. THE BULLY

Background

Tony is considered by his peers to be one of the "tough guys." He is 15 and in the tenth grade at Green High. Tony is prone to bullying, frequently quarreling with his fellow students and teachers, and is considered by his parents to be disobedient. He has a record of minor offenses that range from truancy to destructiveness of property to drunkenness and offensive behavior. In general, Tony gets his satisfactions in ways that are damaging and unfair to others.

It is obvious to school officials that Tony is beyond parental control. He is frequently beaten by his father. Tony's mother has no apparent ability to control Tony's behavior.

Tony is not a member of any school organization of an extracurricular nature. His midquarter progress shows that he is failing in three subjects.

The Situation

One of the subjects Tony is failing is tenth-grade English. Tony is a discipline problem in class, and although it makes the teacher feel guilty, she cannot help but be pleased when Tony is absent from class.

Questions for Class Discussion

1. Where is the problem?
2. Where is Tony heading?

3. What can and should be done, if anything? By whom?
4. What is the role for Tony? His teachers? His peers? The school administration? His parents? Society in general?
5. Is it too late for Tony?

☐ CASE 3. THE PROBLEM OF MARY

Background

Mary has been characterized by her peers and by her teachers as being lonely, indifferent, and generally unhappy. She avoids both students and teachers. She will lie and cheat to avoid attention. Her "close" friends describe her as thoughtless and unkind. She often uses damaging remarks about members of her class, calling them conceited, teacher's pets, and so on. She considers members of her class as thoughtless, unkind, and uninterested in her.

Mary will do what she has to do to achieve average success in her studies. Her association with adults, her parents, and her teachers would be described as one of "merely getting along," doing what "I have to do in order not to get too much attention."

The Situation

One of Mary's friends is another 15-year-old girl, Jane. Jane is an above-average student in school, seemingly well adjusted, and interested in people, and she has gotten to know Mary because they are neighbors and walk together to school. Because of Jane's interest in other people and her closeness to Mary, she has become interested in "trying to bring Mary out of her shell."

Mary has told Jane that she feels her teachers are unreasonably severe. Mary said, "The teachers are only interested in the popular kids." Jane disagreed. Mary said, "You only disagree because you are pretty and popular." At this point, the conversation was broken by a boy running up and saying, "Hey, Jane, you're late for the council meeting."

Questions for Class Discussion

1. Where is the problem?
2. What if you were Mary's teacher?
3. How did you feel after reading this case?

☐ CASE 4. THE STABBING VICTIM

Ron King, 16, who claims he was stabbed in the back during an English class, wants $100,000 in damages from North High School, Central Union High School District, and student Richard Decarlo.

According to the action, filed by King's mother, Lee, of 460 Bowman Avenue, the incident occurred last February. King says he was stabbed by Decarlo and lost his spleen as a result.

The suit says there was no teacher in the classroom when the stabbing took place and that the school was negligent in not providing supervision.

The action also contends that school officials knew that Decarlo secretly carried deadly weapons with him on the school grounds.

Question for Class Discussion

1. After reading this case, how did you feel and what were you thinking?

☐ CASE 5. FROM A DEADLY DARE

In an advanced biology class the students were just starting a lab involving the dissection of triple latex-injected formaldehyde-preserved bullfrogs. While the teacher was busy talking with a few students off to one side of the room—answering their questions and helping them get started on their work—she heard screaming and a commotion from the far side of the room. She looked up and immediately saw Robert, a junior, vomiting and convulsing. On a dare from other students, he had eaten his bullfrog, completely devouring it. Immediately the teacher sent a runner to the office (there was no phone in the classroom). Someone dialed 911, and an ambulance and paramedics soon arrived to take Robert to a nearby hospital, where his stomach was pumped and other treatment was administered. For the next 24 hours Robert was in very serious condition.

Question for Class Discussion

1. What were your thoughts after reading this case?

☐ CASE 6. BEGINNING THE CLASS

On the first day of school, two students arrived a half-minute late to Mr. Brown's class. On the second day, three students were a minute late, and Mr. Brown waited to begin class until they were in their seats. On the third day, four students were from one to three minutes late, and again Mr. Brown waited to begin class. By the end of the first week, Mr. Brown was delaying the start of the class for seven minutes after the bell because students continued to amble in throughout this time period.

Questions for Class Discussion

1. What do you predict will be the situation by the end of the second week? Why?
2. What alternatives are open to Mr. Brown for Monday of the second week?
3. Which of the alternatives are likely to lead to a worse situation? Why?
4. Which of the alternatives promise to lead to improvement? Why?

☐ CASE 7. STUDENT HAS A CRUSH ON TEACHER

During his first year of teaching it had become obvious that one of Mr. Kline's female ninth-grade students had developed a serious crush on him. One day, after class was over and all other students had left the room, she approached Mr. Kline and politely asked him if he had a photograph of himself that she could have.

Questions for Class Discussion

1. Is this a potentially serious situation?
2. How should Mr. Kline respond to the student's request?

☐ CASE 8. SERIOUS FELONIES AGAINST TEACHERS

The following three incidents of students committing felonies against teachers were reported in just one month, in 1996, in the state of California:

At a high school in Yolo County, at about 10:30 a.m., a drafting teacher began feeling sick and within four hours began to hallucinate with his whole body tingling. While he was trying to take roll in his sixth-period class, his students appeared to him to be floating around the classroom. A substitute teacher was called to finish the day for him. While walking to his home he could not step off curbs or climb stairs. He was found and taken to the hospital. The next day, after hearing of the teacher's problems, some students came forward and reported to the school administrators that the teacher's coffee had been spiked with LSD. A 17-year-old student from the teacher's second-period class, who had been bragging about putting a dose of LSD into her teacher's coffee, was arrested.

Four sixth graders in San Bernardino County spiked their teacher's Gatorade with rat poison.

In Sierra County a fourth grader allegedly put cleaning fluid in his teacher's water bottle.

Questions for Class Discussion

1. After reading of these incidents, how did you feel? What were you thinking?
2. Do you know of similar incidents?
3. What do you suppose causes students to commit such acts as these against teachers?
4. What precautions, if any, can teachers take to protect themselves and their students from such acts?

☐ CASE 9. SCIENCE TEACHER SOLICITS STUDENTS FOR MARIJUANA FOR EXPERIMENT

In 1997, a California high school teacher gave $30 to a 16-year-old student for a quantity of marijuana with the intention of putting the marijuana in a bowl with goldfish so students could study the effects on the fish. Before the experiment ever took place, other students reported the teacher's action to the school principal. The teacher was placed on administrative leave. Subsequently, after pleading guilty to charges of contributing to the delinquency of a minor, the teacher was sentenced to 45 days in jail and two years of probation. Apparently, the experiment was to be a repeat of one done earlier at the school by police officers, but with cutbacks and restraints the teacher decided to use her own money to repeat the experiment.

Questions for Class Discussion

1. After reading this, what were your thoughts?
2. What, if anything, did you learn from this situation that might be helpful to you during your own teaching career?

☐ CASE 10. STUDENT COMPLAINS TO A STUDENT TEACHER ABOUT CONTINUED SEXUAL HARASSMENT BY A PEER

During the first week after John began his student teaching in eighth-grade history, one of his female students came to him after class and complained that a boy in the class has continued to sexually harass her even after she had reported it to the school vice-principal. She says that the harassment is beyond just verbal abuse and she wants it stopped.

Questions for Class Discussion

1. After reading this case, what were your thoughts?
2. What, if anything, should John do?
3. What, if anything, did you learn from this situation that might be helpful to you during your own teaching career?

SUMMARY

In this chapter, you learned ways of coping with the daily challenges of teaching, guidelines for effectively managing students in the classroom, and the legal rights and responsibilities of students and teachers. Within that framework, your attention was then focused on specific approaches and additional guidelines for effective classroom management and control. You were offered advice for setting up and maintaining a classroom environment that is favorable to student learning and for establishing procedures for efficiently controlling student behavior.

This is the end of our overview of teaching and learning. You are now ready for Part II, planning for instruction.

QUESTIONS FOR CLASS DISCUSSION

1. Is it better to be very strict with students at first and then relax once your control has been established or to be relaxed at first and then tighten the reins later if students misbehave? Explain your answer.

2. Explain what your options would be if in your class (science or shop) students are provided with safety glasses but several students refuse to wear them.

3. Identify at least four guidelines for using praise for a student's appropriate behavior.

4. Explain why it is important to prevent behavior problems before they occur. Describe at least five preventive steps you can take to reduce the number of management problems that you will have.

5. Explain what you would do if two errant behaviors occurred simultaneously in different locations in your classroom.

6. Explain what you would do if a student from one of your classes came to you and reported that fellow students were harassing him by throwing objects at him, slapping him, pulling his chair out from under him, and pretending to rape him.

7. A historical review of disciplinary practices used in the nation's classrooms shows that corporal punishment has been a consistent and conspicuous part of schooling since the beginning. Many educators are concerned about the increased violence in schools, represented by possession of weapons, sexual or racial harassment, bullying, verbal intimidation, gang or cult activity, arson, and the continued use of corporal punishment of students (corporal punishment in public schools is legal in 26 states). They argue that schools are responsible for turning a child's behavior into an opportunity to teach character and self-control. When self-disciplined adults create a problem, they apologize, accept the consequences, make restitution, and learn from their mistakes. We have a responsibility for teaching children to do the same. What is your opinion about using corporal punishment? Organize a class debate on the issue. The following resources may be of use:

   - S. Black, "Throw Away the Hickory Stick," *Executive Editor* 16(4):44–47 (April 1994).
   - N. Block, "Paddling Strikes Out," *American School Board Journal* 181(9):40–41 (September 1994).
   - J. Dayton, "Corporal Punishment in Public Schools: The Legal and Political Battle Continues," *West's Educational Law Quarterly* 3(3):448–459 (July 1994).
   - I. A. Hyman, *Reading, Writing, and the Hickory Stick: The Appalling Story of Physical and Psychological Abuse in American Schools* (Lexington, MA: Lexington Books, 1990).
   - F. R. James, "Aversive Interventions for Combating School Violence: Profiles and Implications for Teachers and Directors of Special Education," *Preventing School Failure* 38(4):32–36 (Summer 1994).
   - S. Mulhern et al., *Preventing Youth Violence and Aggression and Promoting Safety in Schools* (Madison,

WI: Wisconsin State Department of Public Instruction, 1994).
   - Oklahoma State Department of Education, *A Handbook to Alternatives to Corporal Punishment,* 4th ed. (Oklahoma City, OK: Oklahoma State Department of Education, 1994).
   - R. Richardson et al., "Corporal Punishment in Schools: Initial Progress in the Bible Belt," *Journal of Humanistic Education and Development* 32(4):173–182 (June 1994).
   - F. J. Ryan, "From Rod to Reason: Historical Perspectives on Corporal Punishment in the Public School, 1642–1994," *Educational Horizons* 72(2):70–77 (Winter 1994).

8. Compare and contrast your own school experiences with what you have recently observed in secondary schools, especially related to the exercises of the three chapters of Part I of this resource guide. Discuss your conclusions in small groups, then share your group's conclusions with those of the entire class.

9. From your current observations and field work as related to this teacher preparation program, clearly identify one specific example of educational practice that seems contradictory to exemplary practice or theory as presented in this chapter. Present your explanation for the discrepancy.

10. Do you have questions generated by the content of this chapter? If you do, list them along with ways answers might be found.

SUGGESTED READINGS

Albert, L. "Discipline: Is It a Dirty Word?" *Learning* 24(2):43–46 (September 1995).

Blendinger, J., Devlin, S. D., and Elrod, G. F. *Controlling Aggressive Students.* Bloomington, IN: Fastback 387, Phi Delta Kappa Educational Foundation, 1995.

Curwin, R., and Mendler, A. *Discipline with Dignity.* Alexandria, VA: Association for Supervision and Curriculum Development, 1988.

Edwards, C. H. *Classroom Discipline and Management.* 2nd ed. Upper Saddle River, NJ: Prentice Hall, 1997.

Emmer, E. T., Evertson, C. M., Clements, B. S., and Worsham, M. E. *Classroom Management for Secondary Teachers.* 4th ed. Needham Heights, MA: Allyn & Bacon, 1997.

Fibkins, W. L. *Preventing Teacher Sexual Misconduct.* Bloomington, IN: Fastback 408, Phi Delta Kappa Educational Foundation, 1996.

Freiberg, J. "From Tourists to Citizens in the Classroom." *Educational Leadership* 54(1):32–36 (September 1996).

Glasser, W. "A New Look at School Failure and School Success." *Phi Delta Kappan* 78(8):597–602 (April 1997).

Glasser, W. *The Quality School Teacher.* New York: Harper-Perennial, 1993.

Good, T. L., and Brophy, J. E. *Looking in Classrooms.* 7th ed. New York: Longman, 1997.

Greenwood, G. E., and Fillmer, H. T. *Professional Core Cases for Teacher Decision-Making.* Upper Saddle River, NJ: Prentice Hall, 1997.

Hilke, E. V., and Conway-Gerhardt, C. *Gender Equity in Education*. Bloomington, IN: Fastback 372, Phi Delta Kappa Educational Foundation, 1994.

Johns, J. M., and Espinoza, C. *Management Strategies for Culturally Diverse Classrooms*. Bloomington, IN: Fastback 396, Phi Delta Kappa Educational Foundation, 1996.

Johnson, D. W., and Johnson, R. T. *Reducing School Violence through Conflict Resolution*. Alexandria, VA: Association for Supervision and Curriculum Development, 1995.

Knapczyk, D. R., and Rodes, P. *Teaching Social Competence: A Practical Approach for Improving Social Skills in Students At-Risk*. Pacific Grove, CA: Brooks/Cole, 1996.

Kohn, A. *Beyond Discipline: From Compliance to Community*. Alexandria, VA: Association for Supervision and Curriculum Development, 1996.

Murphy, C. "Managing Students: Building Positive Attitudes in the Classroom." *Schools in the Middle* 4(4):31–33 (May 1995).

Priest, L., and Summerfield, L. M. "Promoting Gender Equity in Middle Level and Secondary School Sports Programs." *NASSP (National Association of Secondary School Principals (Bulletin)* 79(575):52–56 (December 1995).

Prosise, R. *Beyond Rules and Consequences for Classroom Management*. Bloomington, IN: Fastback 401, Phi Delta Kappa Educational Foundation, 1996.

Reese, S. "Safety for Students." *High Strides* 9(4):6–7 (March/April 1997).

Sergiovanni, T. J. *Building Community in Schools*. San Francisco: Jossey-Bass, 1994.

Shakeshaft, C., and Cohan, A. "Sexual Abuse of Students by School Personnel." *Phi Delta Kappan* 76(7):512–520 (March 1995).

Sylwester, R. "The Neurobiology of Self-Esteem and Aggression." *Educational Leadership* 54(5):75–79 (February 1997).

Tiedt, P. L., and Tiedt, I. M. *Multicultural Teaching: A Handbook of Activities, Information, and Resources*. 4th ed. Boston: Allyn and Bacon, 1995.

Van Ness, R. *Raising Self-Esteem of Learners*. Bloomington, IN: Fastback 389, Phi Delta Kappa Educational Foundation, 1995.

Walker, J. E., and Shae, T. M. *Behavioral Management: A Practical Approach for Educators*. 6th ed. Upper Saddle River, NJ: Prentice Hall, 1995.

Willis, S. "Managing Today's Classroom: Finding Alternatives to Control and Compliance." *ASCD (Association for Supervision and Curriculum Development) Education Update* 38(6):1, 3–7 (September 1996).

Wiske, M. S. "How Teaching for Understanding Changes the Rules in the Classroom." *Educational Leadership* 51(5):19–21 (February 1994).

Wolfgang, C. H., and Glickman, C. D. *Solving Discipline Problems: Strategies for Classroom Teachers*. 3rd ed. Boston: Allyn & Bacon, 1995.

PART

II

PLANNING FOR INSTRUCTION

Part II responds to your needs concerning:

- Curriculum integration
- Dealing with content issues that may be controversial
- Preparing and using a course syllabus
- Preparing and using instructional objectives
- Preparing instructional units
- Preparing lesson plans

- Reasons for carefully planning your instruction
- Selecting and using textbooks
- Selecting content and planning the scope of a course
- Sources of guidance for instructional planning
- The different levels of instructional planning

Reflective Thoughts

You are responsible for planning at three levels—the semester or year, the units, and the lessons—with critical decisions to be made at each level.

To efficiently use precious instructional time, planning should be accomplished with two goals in mind—(1) to not waste anyone's time during the time allotted for instruction and (2) to select strategies that most effectively promote student learning.

Your challenge is to use performance-based criteria with a teaching style that encourages the development of intrinsic sources of student motivation and that provides for coincidental learning, which goes beyond what might be considered as predictable, immediately measurable, and minimal expectations.

Any effort to write all learning objectives in behavioral terms is, in effect, to neglect the individual learner for whom it purports to be concerned.

Teachers must be clear about what it is they want their students to learn and about the kinds of evidence needed to verify their learning, and they must communicate those things to the students so they are clearly understood.

Curriculum integration refers to both a way of teaching and a way of planning and organizing the instructional program so that the discrete disciplines of subject matter are related to one another in a design that (1) matches the developmental needs of the learners and (2) helps to connect their learning in ways that are meaningful to their current and past experiences.

Chapter

4

Preparing for the Levels of Planning, Selecting Content, and Setting Objectives

Effective teaching does not just happen; it is produced through carefully planning each phase of the learning process. Effective teachers begin their planning months before meeting students for the first time. Their daily lessons form parts of a larger scheme, which is developed to accomplish their long-range goals for the semester or year. A teacher who ignores this broader context—or who does not take into account where the students have been or where they are going—is doing a disservice to students. The students deserve better. Administrators, parents, and students expect more.

The two chapters in Part II are about the planning processes. Then, later, correlated with your plans, chapters of Part III guide you through the development of your strategy repertoire for implementing your plans.

The rationale for careful planning and the components of that planning are the topics of this chapter. Specifically, upon completion of this chapter you should be able to

1. Describe the relationship of planning to the preactive and reflective thought-processing phases of instruction.
2. Demonstrate an understanding of the rationale for planning for instruction, the levels of planning, and the components of a complete instructional plan.
3. Demonstrate knowledge of the value of various types of documents that can be resources for instructional planning.
4. Explain the value and limitations of student textbooks.

5. Demonstrate ability to plan the sequence of content for teaching a secondary school course in your subject field.
6. Prepare complete instructional objectives for each domain of learning and at various levels within each domain.
7. Explain both the value and the limitations afforded by using instructional objectives.
8. Explain the relationship between instructional objectives and assessment of student learning.

REASONS FOR PLANNING

Planning is done for a number of reasons, perhaps foremost of which is to ensure curriculum coherence. Periodic lesson plans are an integral part of a larger plan, represented by course goals and objectives, department goals, and the school-wide mission statement (discussed in Chapter 1) and goals. Students' learning experiences are thoughtfully planned in sequence and then orchestrated by a teacher who understands the rationale for their respective positions in the curriculum. Such plans do not preclude, of course, an occasional diversion from predetermined activities. Teachers plan for a number of reasons, as described in the following paragraphs.

TO PROVIDE A MECHANISM TO ENSURE THE SCOPE AND SEQUENCE OF THE COMPLETE CURRICULUM.   Unless your course stands alone, following nothing and leading to nothing (which is unlikely), there must be prerequisites for what you want the students to learn and learning objectives that follow and build upon this learning.

To Teach to Individual Differences.   The diversity of students demands that you give planning considerations to differences in such areas as cultural and ethnic experiences, learning capacities and styles, reading abilities, and special needs.

To Ensure Efficient and Effective Teaching with a Minimum of Classroom-Control Problems.   After deciding *what* to teach, you face the difficult and important task of deciding *how* best to teach it. To efficiently use precious instructional time, planning should be accomplished with two goals in mind—(1) to not waste anyone's time during the time allotted for instruction and (2) to select strategies that most effectively promote student learning.

To Ensure Program Continuation.   The program must continue even if you are absent and a substitute teacher is needed.

To Serve as a Criterion for Reflection and Self-Assessment.   After a learning activity and at the end of a school term, you can reflect on and assess what was done and how it affected student learning.

To Evaluate Your Teaching.   Your plans represent a criterion recognized and evaluated by administrators. With those experienced in such matters, it is clear that inadequate planning is usually a precursor to incompetent teaching.

LEVELS OF INSTRUCTIONAL PLANNING

As indicated, planning is a major part of your job. You will be responsible for planning at three levels—the school term (semester or year), the units, and the lessons—with critical decisions to be made at each level.

The heart of good planning is good decision making. For every plan and at each of the three levels, you must make decisions about the goals and objectives to be set, the subject to be introduced, the materials and equipment to be used, the methods to be adopted, and the assessments to be made. This decision-making process is complicated because so many options are available at each level. Decisions made at all three levels result in a total plan.

Although the planning process continues year after year, the task becomes somewhat easier after the first year as you learn to recycle plans. The process is also made easier by reviewing documents and sharing ideas and plans with other teachers.

COMPONENTS OF A COMPLETE INSTRUCTIONAL PLAN

A complete instructional plan has eight components, described as follows.

1. *Statement of Philosophy.* This is a general statement about why the plan is important and about how students will learn its content.
2. *Needs Assessment.* The statement of philosophy should demonstrate an appreciation for the cultural plurality of the nation and of the school, for the needs of the community and its learners, and for the functions of the school. The statement of philosophy and needs of the learners should be consistent with the school's mission statement and goals.
3. *Aims, Goals, and Objectives.* The plan's stated aims, goals, and objectives should be consistent with the statement of philosophy. (Aims, goals, and objectives are discussed later in this chapter.)
4. *Vertical Articulation.* The presentation of the vertical articulation shows the plan's relationship to the learning that preceded and the learning that will follow, from prekindergarten through 12th grade, and sometimes beyond in either the workplace or postsecondary education.
5. *Horizontal Articulation.* Horizontal articulation refers to the plan's integration with other curriculum and cocurriculum activities across a grade level. Vertical and horizontal articulation are usually represented in scope and sequence charting found in curriculum documents or in textbook programs.
6. *Sequentially Planned Learning Activities.* This is the presentation of organized and sequential units and lessons appropriate for the subject or grade level and for the age and diversity of the learners.
7. *Resources Needed.* This is a listing of resources, such as books, guest speakers, field trip locales, and media.
8. *Assessment Strategies.* This is the ongoing process of evaluating student learning.

PLANNING THE SCOPE OF THE COURSE

When planning the scope of a course for a semester or for a school year, you should decide what is to be accomplished in that period of time. To help in setting your goals, you should (1) examine school and other public resource documents for mandates and guidelines, (2) communicate with colleagues to learn of common expectations, and (3) probe, analyze, and translate your own convictions, knowledge, and skills into behaviors that foster the intellectual and psychological development of your students. Some may be found via the Internet.[1]

Documents That Provide Guidance for Content Selection

With the guidance of Exercises 4.1 and 4.2, you will now examine state department of education curriculum publications, school or district courses of study, and school-adopted printed or nonprinted materials. Many of the documents are generated through the process of

state accreditation. Your college or university library may be a source for the documents needed in these exercises. Others may be borrowed from cooperating teachers in your local schools.

To receive accreditation (which normally occurs every three to six years), a high school is reviewed by an outside accreditation team. Prior to the team's visit, the school prepares self-study reports for which each program area reviews and updates the curriculum guides that provide information about the goals, objectives, and content of each course and program offered. In some states, middle-level schools also are accredited by state or regional agencies. In other states, although it is not mandatory, those schools can volunteer to be reviewed for improvement. The accreditation process, which can be expensive, is paid for with school or district funds.

---

1. Content standards for the various disciplines may be accessed via the Internet at http://www.mcrel.org. An annotated list of Internet sites with educational standards and curriculum framework documents is available at http://www.putwest.boces.org/Standards.html.

EXERCISE 4.1
Examining State Curriculum Documents

Instructions: The purpose of this exercise is to become familiar with curriculum documents published by your state department of education. You must determine if that department publishes a curriculum framework for various subjects taught in schools. State frameworks provide valuable information about both content and process, and teachers need to be aware of these documents. You may want to duplicate this form so you can use it to evaluate several documents. After examining documents that interest you, use the following questions as a guideline for small- or large-group class discussions.

1. Are state curriculum documents available to teachers for your state? If so, describe them and explain how they can be obtained.

    Title of document: _____

    _____

    Source: _____

    _____

    Most recent year of publication: _____

    Other pertinent information: _____

    _____

2. Examine how closely the document follows the eight components presented in this chapter. Are any components omitted? Are there additional components? Specifically, check for these components:

	Yes	*No*
2.1. Statement of philosophy?	_____	_____
2.2. Evidence of a needs assessment?	_____	_____
2.3. Aims, goals, and objectives?	_____	_____
2.4. Schemes for vertical articulation?	_____	_____
2.5. Schemes for horizontal articulation?	_____	_____
2.6. Recommended instructional procedures?	_____	_____
2.7. Recommended resources?	_____	_____
2.8. Assessment strategies?	_____	_____

    Other:

    _____

    _____

3. Are the documents specific as to subject-matter content for each grade level? Describe evidence of both vertical and horizontal articulation schemes.

_____

_____

_____

_____

_____

_____

4. Do the documents offer specific strategies for instruction? If yes, describe.

_____

_____

_____

_____

_____

_____

5. Do the documents offer suggestions and resources for working with students who are culturally different, for students with special needs, and for students who are intellectually gifted and talented? Describe.

_____

_____

_____

_____

_____

_____

6. Do the documents offer suggestions or guidelines for dealing with controversial topics? If so, describe.

_____

_____

_____

_____

_____

_____

_____

7. Do the documents distinguish between what shall be taught (mandated) and what can be taught (permissible)?

_____

_____

_____

_____

_____

_____

8. Do the documents offer suggestions for specific resources?

_____

_____

_____

_____

_____

_____

9. Do the documents refer to assessment strategies? Describe.

_____

_____

_____

_____

_____

_____

10. Is there anything else about the documents you would like to discuss in your group?

_____

_____

_____

_____

_____

_____

For Your Notes

EXERCISE 4.2
Examining Local Curriculum Documents

Instructions: The purpose of this exercise is to become familiar with curriculum documents prepared by local school districts. A primary resource for what to teach is referred to as a *curriculum guide,* or *course of study,* which normally is developed by teachers of a school or district. Samples may be available in your university library or in a local school district resource center. Or perhaps you could borrow them from teachers you visit. Obtain samples from a variety of sources and then examine them using the format of this exercise. (You may duplicate this form for each document examined.) An analysis of several documents will give you a good picture of expectations. If possible, compare documents from several school districts and states.

Title of document: _____

_____

District or school: _____

Date of document: _____

1. Examine how closely the documents follow the eight components. Does the document contain the following components?

	Yes	No
1.1. Statement of philosophy?	_____	_____
1.2. Evidence of a needs assessment?	_____	_____
1.3. Aims, goals, and objectives?	_____	_____
1.4. Schemes for vertical articulation?	_____	_____
1.5. Schemes for horizontal articulation?	_____	_____
1.6. Recommended instructional procedures?	_____	_____
1.7. Recommended resources?	_____	_____
1.8. Assessment strategies?	_____	_____

2. Does the document list expected learning outcomes? If so, describe what they are.

_____

_____

_____

_____

_____

_____

_____

3. Does the document contain detailed unit plans? If so, describe them by answering the following questions:

   3.1. Do they contain initiating activities (how to begin a unit)? _____

   3.2. Do they contain specific learning activities? _____

   3.3. Do they contain suggested enrichment activities (as for gifted and talented students)?

   _____

   3.4. Do they contain culminating activities (activities that bring a unit to a climax)? _____

   3.5. Do they contain assessment procedures (for determining student achievement)? _____

   3.6. Do they contain activities for learners with special needs or for learners who are different in other respects? _____

4. Does it provide bibliographic entries for

   • The teacher? _____

   • The students? _____

5. Does it list audiovisual, media, and other materials needed?

   _____

   _____

   _____

   _____

6. Does the document clearly help you understand what the teacher is expected to teach?

   _____

   _____

   _____

   _____

7. Are there questions not answered by your examination of this document? If so, list them for class discussion.

   _____

   _____

   _____

   _____

   _____

   _____

   _____

   _____

National Curriculum Standards

Standards are a definition of what students should know (content) and be able to do (process and performance). At the national level, curriculum standards did not exist in the United States until the 1990s, except for those developed and released for mathematics education in 1989 (which are being revised at the time of preparation of this book).[2] In 1989, support for national goals in education was endorsed by the National Governors Association. Supporting that notion of national goals for education, President George Bush immediately formed the National Education Goals Panel. Shortly thereafter, the National Council on Education Standards and Testing recommended that national standards for subject matter content in K–12 education be developed for all core subjects—the arts, civics/social studies, English/language arts/reading, geography, history, mathematics, and science.

Initial funding for the development of standards was provided by the U.S. Department of Education. In 1994 the United States Congress passed the *Goals 2000: Educate America Act* (see Figure 4.1) (amended in 1996 with an Appropriations Act), encouraging states to set standards. Long before, however, national organizations devoted to various disciplines were defining standards.

What the National Standards Are

The national standards represent the best thinking by expert panels on responses from teachers in the field about what are the essential elements of a basic core of subject knowledge that all students should acquire. They serve not as national mandates but rather as voluntary guidelines to encourage curriculum development to promote higher student achievement. It is the discretion of state and local curriculum developers in deciding the extent to which the standards are used. Strongly influenced by the national standards, nearly all the 50 states are presently developing state standards, and many districts and schools are developing standards of their own.[3] You will want to become familiar with the standards in your area of curriculum interest.

By 1992, for example, more than 40 states, usually through state curriculum frameworks, were following the 1989 standards for mathematics education to

By the year 2000

- All children in America will start school ready to learn.
- The high school graduation rate will increase to at least 90 percent.
- All students will leave grades 4, 8, and 12 having demonstrated competency over challenging subject matter, including English, mathematics, science, foreign languages, civics and government, economics, the arts, history, and geography, and every school in America will ensure that all students learn to use their minds well, so they may be prepared for responsible citizenship, further learning, and productive employment in our nation's modern economy.
- U.S. students will be first in the world in mathematics and science achievement.
- Every adult American will be literate and will possess the knowledge and skills necessary to compete in a global economy and exercise the rights and responsibilities of citizenship.
- Every school in the United States will be free of drugs, violence, and the unauthorized presence of firearms and alcohol, and will offer a disciplined environment conducive to learning.
- The nation's teaching force will have access to programs for the continued improvement of their professional skills and the opportunity to acquire the knowledge and skills needed to instruct and prepare all American students for the next century.
- Every school will promote partnerships that will increase parental involvement and participation in promoting the social, emotional, and academic

Figure 4.1
Goals 2000: The national educational goals.

guide what and how mathematics is taught and how student progress is assessed. A summary of recommendations for secondary school mathematics instruction is shown in Figure 4.2. The essence of many of those recommendations—a hands-on, inquiry-oriented, performance-based approach to learning less but learning it better—can also be found in the standards that were subsequently developed for other disciplines. (See, for example, Figures 4.3 and 4.4.)

Standards by Discipline

The following paragraphs describe standards development for subject areas of the K–12 curriculum other than mathematics.

---

2. Contact NCTM, 1906 Association Drive, Reston, VA 22091. See also http://www.nctm.org.

3. S. Willis, "National Standards: Where Do They Stand?" *Education Update* 39(2):1, 6, 8 (March 1997).

Increased attention to

- The active involvement of students in constructing and applying mathematical ideas
- Problem solving as a means as well as a goal of instruction
- Effective questioning techniques that promote student interaction
- The use of a variety of instructional formats (e.g., small groups, individual explorations, peer interaction, whole-class discussions, project work)
- The use of calculators and computers as tools for learning and doing mathematics
- Student communication of mathematical ideas orally and in writing
- The establishment and application of the interrelatedness of mathematical topics

- The systematic maintenance of student learnings and embedding review in the content of new topics and problem situations
- The assessment of learning as an integral part of instruction.

Decreased attention to

- Teacher and text as exclusive sources of knowledge
- Rote memorization of facts and procedures
- Extended periods of individual seat work practicing routine tasks
- Instruction by teacher exposition
- Paper-and-pencil manipulative skill work
- The relegation of testing to an adjunct role with the sole purpose of assigning grades

Figure 4.2

Summary of recommendations for mathematics instruction. (*Source*: R.D. Kellough, et al., *Integrating Mathematics and Science for Intermediate and Middle School* [Upper Saddle River, NJ: Prentice Hall, 1996, p. 178]. Reprinted by permission of Prentice Hall.)

ARTS (VISUAL AND PERFORMING).   Developed jointly by the American Alliance for Theater and Education, the National Art Education Association, the National Dance Association, and the Music Educators National Conference, the National Standards for Arts Education were published in 1994.[4]

ECONOMICS.   Developed by the National Council on Economic Education, standards for the study of economics were published in early 1997.[5]

ENGLISH/LANGUAGE ARTS/READING.   Developed jointly by the International Reading Association, the National Council of Teachers of English, and the University of Illinois Center for the Study of Reading, standards for English education were published in 1996.[6]

FOREIGN LANGUAGES.   *Standards for Foreign Language Learning: Preparing for the 21st Century* was published by the American Council on the Teaching of Foreign Languages (ACTFL) in 1996.[7]

GEOGRAPHY.   Developed jointly by the Association of American Geographers, the National Council for Geographic Education, and the National Geographic Society, standards for geography education were published in 1994.[8]

HEALTH.   Developed by the Joint Committee for National School Health Education Standards, *National Health Education Standards: Achieving Health Literacy* was released in 1995.[9]

HISTORY/CIVICS/SOCIAL STUDIES.   The Center for Civic Education and the National Center for Social Studies developed standards for civics and government, and the National Center for History in the Schools developed the standards for history, all of which were published in 1994.[10]

---

8. Contact National Geographic Society, PO Box 1640, Washington, DC 20013-1640. See several articles about the standards in *Journal of Geography* 94(4) (July/August 1995).

9. Contact the American Alliance for Health, Physical Education, Recreation and Dance (AAHPERD), 1900 Association Drive, Reston, VA 20191. See also http://www.aahperd.org.

10. Contact the Center for Civic Education, 5146 Douglas Fir Road, Calabasas, CA 91302-1467, or the National Council for the Social Studies, 3501 Newark Street, NW, Washington, DC 20016-3167, or the National Center for History in the Schools, University of California at Los Angeles, 231 Moore Hall, 405 Hilgard Avenue, Los Angeles, CA 90024. The history standards are also printed in *OAH Magazine of History* 9(3):7–35 (Spring 1995). See also J. Appleby, "Controversy over the National History Standards," *OAH Magazine of History* 9(3):4 (Spring 1995); G. B. Nash and R. E. Dunn, "National History Standards: Controversy and Commentary," *Social Studies Review* 34(2):4–12 (Winter 1995); and G. B. Nash and R. E. Dunn, "History Standards and Culture Wars," *Social Education* 59(1):5–7 (January 1995). See also http://www.ncss.org.

---

4. Contact Music Educators National Conference (MENC), 1902 Association Drive, Reston, VA 22091. See also the several articles on the arts standards in *Arts and Education Policy Review* 96(2) (November/December 1994); T. L. Fallis, "National Standards: What's Next?" *Music Educators Journal* 81(3):26–28, 47 (November 1994); M. Greene, "The Arts and National Standards," *Educational Forum* 58(4):391–400 (Summer 1994); and *Teaching Theatre* 5(3) (Spring 1994). See also http://www.menc.org.

5. Contact NCEE, 1140 Avenue of the Americas, New York, NY 10036. See also http://oberon.calstatela.edu/centers/econeduc/eced.html.

6. Contact NCTE, 1111 Kenyon Road, Urbana, IL 61801. See also http://ncte.org.

7. Contact ACTFL, Six Executive Plaza, Yonkers, NY 10701-6801. See also http://www.actfl.org.

Increased emphasis on	Decreased emphasis on
• Understanding and responding to individual student's interests, strengths, experiences, and needs • Selecting and adapting curriculum • Focusing on student understanding and use of scientific knowledge, ideas, and inquiry processes • Guiding students in active and extended scientific inquiry • Providing opportunities for scientific discussion and debate among students • Continuously assessing student understanding • Sharing responsibility for learning with students • Supporting a classroom community with cooperation, shared responsibility, and respect • Working with other teachers to enhance the science program	• Treating all students alike and responding to the group as a whole • Rigidly following curriculum • Focusing on student acquisition of information • Presenting scientific knowledge through lecture, text, and demonstration • Asking for recitation of acquired knowledge • Testing students for factual information at the end of the unit or chapter • Maintaining responsibility and authority • Supporting competition • Working alone

Figure 4.3

Recommendations for science instruction. (*Source:* National Research Council, *National Science Education Standards* [Washington, DC: National Academy of Sciences, 1996], p. 52. Adapted by permission of the National Academy of Sciences.)

Increased emphasis on	Decreased emphasis on
• Understanding scientific concepts and developing abilities of inquiry • Learning subject matter disciplines in the context of inquiry, technology, science in personal and social perspectives, and history and nature of science • Integrating all aspects of science content • Studying a few fundamental science concepts • Implementing inquiry as instructional strategies, abilities, and ideas to be learned • Activities that investigate and analyze science questions • Investigations over extended periods of time • Process skills in content • Using evidence and strategies for developing or revising an explanation	• Knowing scientific facts and information • Studying subject matter disciplines (physical, life, earth sciences) for their sake • Separating science knowledge and science process • Covering many science topics • Implementing inquiry as a set of processes • Activities that demonstrate and verify science content • Investigations confined to one class period • Process skills out of context • Getting an answer

Figure 4.4

Sample recommendations for science learning. (*Source:* National Research Council, *National Science Education Standards* [Washington, DC: National Academy of Sciences, 1996], p. 113. Adapted by permission of the National Academy of Sciences.)

PHYSICAL EDUCATION. In 1995, the National Association of Sport and Physical Education (NASPE) published *Moving into the Future: National Standards for Physical Education*.[11]

SCIENCE. With input from the American Association for the Advancement of Science and the National Science Teachers Association, the National Research Council's National Committee on Science Education Standards and Assessment developed standards for science education, which were published in 1995.[12] (See Figures 4.3 and 4.4.)

11. Contact NASPE, 1900 Association Drive, Reston, VA 20191. See also http://www.aahperd.org.

12. Contact National Science Education Standards, 2101 Constitution Avenue, NW, Washington, DC 20418. See also N. J. Bodinar, "Staking a Claim with the Standards," *Science Teacher* 62(7):35–37 (October 1995), and R. W. Bybee and A. B. Champagne, "The National Science Education Standards," *Science Teacher* 62(1):40–45 (January 1995). See also http://www.nsta.org or http://www.nas.edu/nrc.

TECHNOLOGY. With initial funding from the National Science Foundation and the National Aeronautics and Space Administration, and in collaboration with the International Technology Education Association, standards for technology education are being developed with an anticipated release date of March 1999.[13]

Exercise 4.3 provides guidelines for your examination of national standards in curriculum areas of inter-

est to you. As with the math standards, the new standards will be used by state and local school districts for the revision of their curriculum documents. Guided by these standards and the content of state frameworks, especially those of the larger states, such as Texas and California, publishers of student textbooks and other instructional materials will then develop their new or revised printed and nonprinted instructional materials. Although there has been ongoing debate about their eventual value (see Suggested Readings at the end of this chapter), it is anticipated that by the dawn of the new millennium these standards will be in place and having a positive effect upon the academic achievement of students in the public schools of the United States.

---

13. Contact Technology for All Americans Project, 1997 South Main Street, Suite 701, Blacksburg, VA 24061-0353. See also http://www.scholar.lib.vt.edu/TAA/TAA.html.

EXERCISE 4.3
Examining National Curriculum Standards

Instructions: The purpose of this exercise is to become familiar with the national curriculum standards for various subjects of the K–12 curriculum. Using the addresses of sources provided in the preceding section, National Curriculum Standards, and other sources, such as professional journals, review the standards for your subject or subjects. Use the following questions as a guideline for small- or large-group class discussions. Following small subject-area group discussion, share the developments in each field with the rest of the class.

Subject area: _____

1. Name of the standards document reviewed: _____

    _____

2. Year of document publication: _____

3. Developed by: _____

4. Specific K–12 goals specified by the new standards:

    _____

    _____

    _____

    _____

    _____

    _____

5. Are the standards specific as to subject-matter content for each grade level? Explain.

    _____

    _____

    _____

    _____

    _____

    _____

6. Do the standards offer specific strategies for instruction? Describe.

    _____

    _____

    _____

    _____

    _____

7. Do the standards offer suggestions for teaching students who are different and for students with special needs? Describe.

_____

_____

_____

_____

8. Do the standards offer suggestions or guidelines for dealing with controversial topics?

_____

_____

_____

_____

9. Do the standards offer suggestions for specific resources? Describe.

_____

_____

_____

_____

10. Do the standards refer to assessment? Describe.

_____

_____

_____

_____

11. In summary, compared with what has been taught and how it has been taught in this field, what is new with the standards?

_____

_____

_____

_____

12. Is there anything else about the standards you would like to discuss in your group?

_____

_____

_____

_____

Student Textbooks

School districts periodically adopt new textbooks (usually every five or so years). If you are a student teacher or a first-year teacher, this will most likely mean that someone will tell you, "Here are the textbooks you will be using." You should become familiar with the textbooks that you will probably be using and how you might be using them.

Textbook appearance, content, and use have changed considerably in recent years for several reasons—the recognition of the diversity of learning styles, capacities, and modalities of students; the increasing cost of textbooks and the decreasing availability of funds; and the availability of nonprinted materials. Still, it is estimated that as much as 90 percent of all classroom activity is regulated by textbooks.[14]

VALUE OF STUDENT TEXTBOOKS.   We doubt anyone could rationally argue that textbooks are of no value to student learning. Textbooks can provide (1) an organization of basic or important content for the students, (2) a basis for deciding content emphasis, (3) previously tested activities and suggestions for learning, (4) information about other readings and resources to enhance student learning, and (5) a foundation for building higher-order thinking activities (e.g., inquiry discussions and student research) that help develop critical thinking skills. The textbook, however, should not be the "be all and end all" of the instructional experiences.

PROBLEMS WITH RELIANCE ON A SINGLE TEXTBOOK. The student textbook is only one of many teaching tools, and not the ultimate word. Of the many ways in which you may use textbooks for student learning, the *least* acceptable is to show a complete dependence on a single book and require students simply to memorize material from it. This is the lowest level of learning; furthermore, it implies that you are unaware of other significant printed and nonprinted resources and have nothing more to contribute to student learning.

Another potential problem brought about by reliance upon a single textbook is that because textbook publishers prepare books for use in a larger market—that is, for national or state-wide use—a state- and district-adopted book may not adequately address issues of special interest and importance to the community in which you teach.[15] That is one reason why some teachers and schools provide supplementary printed and nonprinted resources.

Still another problem brought about by reliance upon a single source is that the adopted textbook may not be at the appropriate reading level for many students. In today's heterogeneous classrooms, the level of student reading can vary by as much as two-thirds of the chronological age of the students. This means that if the chronological age is 15 years (typical for tenth graders), then the reading-level range would be ten years—that is, the class may have some students reading at only the fifth-grade level, and others have college-level reading ability.

TEXTBOOK READING LEVEL.   To determine a textbook's reading level, you can use any of several techniques, such as the Fry[16] or the Forecast[17] readability formulas. Since such formulas give only the technical reading level of a book, you have to interpret the results by subjectively estimating the conceptual reading level of the work. To do so, you must consider your students' experience in light of the content, the number of new ideas introduced, and the level of abstraction of the ideas.

To determine how well students can read a text, many teachers use the Cloze technique, which was first described by Bormuth in 1968 and has since appeared in a number of versions.[18] The technique is as follows. Select from the book several typical passages of a total of 400 to 415 words. Delete every eighth word except for those in the first and last sentences, proper names, numbers, and initial words in sentences. You will probably have deleted about 50 words. Replace the deleted words with blanks, duplicate the passages, and distribute them to the students. Ask them to fill in the blanks with the most appropriate words they can supply. Collect the papers. Score them by counting all the student-supplied words that are the same as those in the original text and dividing this number by the total number of blanks. Some educators recommend that you count only words that are exactly the same; others would allow synonyms. Perhaps you should not count synonyms or verbs of a different tense.[19]

$$\text{Score} = \frac{\text{Number of same words supplied}}{\text{Number of blanks}}$$

You can assume that students who score better than 50 percent can read the book quite well, that students

---

14. See, for example, R. Van Horn, "Teachers and Stuff," *Phi Delta Kappan* 76(10):744–750 (June 1995).

15. At least 24 states use state-wide textbook adoption committees to review books and to then provide local districts with lists of recommended titles from which to choose.

16. See E. Fry, "A Readability Formula That Saves Time," *Journal of Reading* 11:587 (April 1968).

17. See N. M. Ross, "Assessing Readability of Instructional Materials," *VocEd* 54:10–11 (February 1979).

18. See J. Bormuth, "The Cloze Readability Procedure," *Elementary English* 45:429–436 (April 1968).

19. See N. McKenna, "Synonymic versus Verbatim Scoring of the Cloze Procedure," *Journal of Reading* 20:141–143 (November 1976).

who score between 40 and 50 percent can read the book at the level of instruction, and that students who score below 40 percent will probably find the reading difficult and frustrating.

To conduct a silent and informal reading inventory of a book, you can have students read four or five pages of the text and then give them a ten-item quiz on the content. Consider the text as too difficult for a student who scores less than 70 percent on the quiz. Or you can conduct an oral and informal reading inventory by having a student read aloud to you a 100-word passage. The text may be too difficult if the student stumbles over or misses more than 5 percent of the words.[20]

GUIDELINES FOR TEXTBOOK USE. Generally speaking, students benefit by having their own copies of a textbook in the current edition. However, because of budget constraints, this may not always be possible. When that is the case, students may not be allowed to take the books home or perhaps may only occasionally do so. In other classrooms, there may be no textbook at all. Yet still, in some classrooms of schools that we recently have visited, there are *two* sets of the textbook, one set that remains in the classroom for use there and the other set that is assigned to students to take home and leave there for home studying. With that arrangement, students don't have to carry around heavy books in their backpacks, as heavy they often are for many subjects taught in high school today. History and biology books, for example, can be quite thick and heavy. The following general guidelines apply to using the textbook as a learning tool.

Progressing through a textbook from the front cover to the back in one school term is not necessarily an indicator of good teaching. The textbook is one resource; to enhance their learning, students should be encouraged to use a variety of resources. Encourage students to search additional sources to update the content of the textbook. This is especially important in certain disciplines such as science and social sciences, in which the amount of new information is growing rapidly and students may have textbooks that are several years old. The library and sources on the Internet should be researched by students for the latest information on certain subjects. Keep supplementary reading materials for student use in the classroom. School and community librarians and resource specialists usually are delighted to cooperate with teachers in the selection and provision of such resources.

Individualize the learning for students of various reading abilities. Consider differentiated reading and workbook assignments in the textbook and several supplementary sources (see multitext and multireadings approaches, a topic that follows). Except to make life simpler for the teacher, there is no advantage to having all students working out of the same book and exercises. Some students benefit from the drill, practice, and reinforcement afforded by workbooks that accompany textbooks, but this is not true for all students, nor do all benefit from the same activity. In fact, the traditional workbook, now nearly extinct at the high school level and in some disciplines, is being replaced by the modern technology afforded by computer software and laser videodiscs. As the cost of hardware and software programs becomes more realistic for schools, the use of computers by individual students is also becoming more common. Computers and other interactive media provide students with a psychologically safer learning environment in which they have greater control over the pace of the instruction, can repeat instruction if necessary, and can ask for clarification without the fear of having to do so publicly. More about computers for classroom learning is presented in Chapter 10.

Teach students how to study from their textbook, perhaps by using the **SQ4R** method: *survey* the chapter, ask *questions* about what was read, *read* to answer the questions, *recite* the answers, *record* important items from the chapter into notebooks, then *review* it all. Or use the **SQ3R** method: *survey* the chapter, ask *questions* about what was read, *read, recite,* and *review*. Or use the **PQRST** method: *preview, question, read, state* the main idea, and *test* yourself by answering the questions you posed earlier. Or use **reciprocal teaching,** in which students are taught and practice the reading skills of summarizing, questioning, clarifying, and predicting.[21]

Encourage students to be alert for errors in the textbook, both in content and printing—perhaps giving them some sort of credit reward, such as points, when they bring an error to your attention. This helps

20. See M. S. Johnson and R. A. Kress, *Informal Reading Inventories* (Newark, DE: International Reading Association, 1965). There is evidence that informal reading inventories and the Cloze procedure may provide inaccurate information and inhibit the progress of poor readers. See, for example, R. S. Pehrsson, "Challenging Frustration Level," *Reading and Writing Quarterly: Overcoming Learning Difficulties* 10(3):201–208 (July/September 1994).

21. Source of PQRST method: E. B. Kelly, *Memory Enhancement for Educators* (Bloomington, IN: Fastback 365, Phi Delta Kappa Educational Foundation, 1994), p. 18. The original sources of SQ4R and SQ3R are unknown. About reciprocal teaching, see C. J. Carter, "Why Reciprocal Teaching?" *Educational Leadership* 54(6):64–68 (March 1997), and T. L. Good and J. E. Brophy, *Looking in Classrooms* (New York: Longman, 1997), pp. 412–414.

them develop the skills of critical reading, critical thinking, and healthy skepticism. For example, a history book is reported to have stated that the first person to lead a group through the length of the Grand Canyon was John Wesley Powell. Critically thinking students quickly made the point that perhaps Powell was only the first white person to do this, that Native Americans had traveled the length of the Grand Canyon for centuries.[22]

Finally, encourage students to respect books by covering and protecting them and not marking in them. In many schools this is a rule; at the end of the term, students who have damaged or lost their books are charged a fee.

---

22. R. Reinhold, "Class Struggle," *The New York Times Magazine,* September 29, 1991, p. 46.

Multitext and Multireading Approaches

Expressing a dissatisfaction with the single-textbook approach to teaching, some teachers have substituted a multitext strategy, in which they use one set of books for one topic and another set for another topic. This strategy provides some flexibility, though it really is only a series of single texts.

Other teachers, especially those using an integrated thematic approach, use a strategy that incorporates many readings for a topic during the same unit. This multireading strategy gives students a certain amount of choice in what they read. The various readings allow for differences in reading ability and interest level. By using a study guide (see sample in Figure 4.5), all the students can be directed toward specific information and concepts, but they do not have to all read the same selections. Now, use Exercise 4.4 to examine student textbooks and accompanying teacher editions.

MULTITEXT TEACHER'S GUIDE: AMERICA'S REVOLUTIONARY TIMES IN 1776

- Purpose: To engage students in multitext reading, critical thinking, and problem solving related to America's Revolutionary Times in 1776.
- Activities:
    1. By reading and browsing through several books and by carefully observing several illustrations of people in this particular time period and geographical area, the students can engage in critical thinking and problem solving by working in small groups. The study guide bibliography that follows includes books suitable for a wide range of reading levels related to America's Revolutionary Times in 1776. Students can respond to the following questions after multitext reading.
        a. What features of the land (e.g., features of government, society) seem to be important to the people in this time period of 1776?
        b. What occupations seem to be most important? What inventions (tools, machines) appear to be most useful?
        c. What do the answers to these questions tell us about the way of life of the people who lived in this time period (geographical area)?
    2. Back with the whole group, have the students from each group report on the responses to the questions. Engage students in dictating or writing a paragraph summarizing the responses to the questions.
    3. Students can meet with response partners to read their individually written paragraphs aloud to one another and provide suggestions to each other for rewriting the paragraphs.
- Bibliography:

African American

Davis, B. *Black Heroes of the American Revolution.* (San Diego: HarBraceJ, 1976). Nonfictional account depicting the contributions of African Americans during the Revolutionary War. Includes drawings, etchings, bibliography, and an index.

Hanses, J. *The Captive.* (New York: Scholastic, 1994). Based on a journal written in the late 1700s, this is about Kofi, the 12-year-old son of an Ashanti chief. Kofi is sold and sent to America after his father is murdered by a family slave. Kofi and others escape from the Puritan farmer in Massachusetts and return to Africa by ship when the captain agrees to help them. The epilogue relates his good and orderly life when he returned to Africa.

Figure 4.5

Sample teacher-prepared guide and student bibliography to assist students in multitext reading about America's Revolutionary Times in 1776.

(continued)

Millender, D. H. *Crispus Attucks: Black Leader of Colonial Patriots.* (New York: Macmillan, 1986). Biographical portrayal of the life of a Colonial African American and his contribution to the American Revolution.

European

Wade, M. D. *Benedict Arnold.* (New York: Franklin Watts, 1995). Biographical story of Arnold's life from boyhood through his service as a general in the Revolutionary War, his heroic deeds, including his leadership at the battle of Saratoga, his later traitorous actions, and his death in London. Includes information about his wife, Peggy Shippen.

Female Image

DePaul, L. G. *Founding Mothers: Women in America in the Revolutionary Era.* (Boston: Houghton Mifflin, 1975). Nonfictional account of the contributions of women during the revolution.

McGovern, A. *Secret Soldier: The Story of Deborah Sampson.* (New York: Scholastic, 1991). Story of a young woman who disguised herself as a boy and joined the army to serve in America's War for Independence.

Latino/Hispanic

Anderson, J. *Spanish Pioneers of the Southwest.* Illustrated by G. Ancona. (New York: Dutton, 1989). Nonfictional account of the lives of the colonists on the East Coast contrasted with the lives of the members of a pioneer family in a Spanish community in New Mexico in the 1700s and the family's hard work, harsh living conditions, and their traditions.

Native American

Hudson, J. *Dawn Rider.* (New York: Putnam, 1990). Fictional account of 16-year-old Kit Fox, a Blackfoot, forbidden to ride horses. She disobeys, and her riding skills help her people when their camp is attacked.

Kinsey-Warock, N. *Wilderness Cat.* Illustrated by Mark Graham. (Minneapolis: Cobblehill, 1992). Lives of colonists on the East Coast are contrasted with the lives of Serena's family members when they move to Canada in the 1700s. Even though the family trades with the St. Francis Indians, they do not have enough to eat, so Papa and Serena's brother leave to find work.

Meyer, K. A. *Father Serra: Traveler on the Golden Chain.* (Huntington, IN: Our Sunday Visitor, 1990). Biographical account showing Father Serra's personality as well as the dangerous and challenging time in which he lived. Discusses the founding of the California Missions during 1769–1798.

Religious Minority

Faber, D. *The Perfect Life: The Shakers in America.* (New York: Farrar, Straus, & Giroux, 1974). Mother Ann escapes from Manchester, England, with several followers who voyage to America and set up the first settlement in upstate New York in 1776. Nonfictional account detailing the Shaker influence on furniture

Figure 4.5 (*continued*)

EXERCISE 4.4

Examining Student Textbooks and Teacher's Editions

Instructions: The purpose of this exercise is to become familiar with textbooks that you may be using in your teaching. Student textbooks are usually accompanied by a teacher's edition that contains specific objectives, teaching techniques, learning activities, assessment instruments, test items, and suggested resources. Your university library, local schools, and cooperating teachers are sources for locating and borrowing these enhanced textbooks. For your subject field of interest, select a textbook that is accompanied by a teacher's edition and examine the contents of both using the following format. If there are no standard textbooks available for your teaching field (such as might be the case for art, home economics, industrial arts, music, and physical education), then select a field in which there is a possibility you might teach. Beginning teachers are often assigned to teach in more than one field—sometimes, unfortunately, in fields for which they are untrained or have only minimal training. After completion of this exercise, share the book and your analysis of it with your colleagues.

Title of book: _____

Author(s): _____

Publisher: _____

Date of most recent publication: _____

	Yes	*No*
1. Analyze the teacher's edition for the following elements.		
a. Are its goals consistent with the goals of local and state curriculum documents?	_____	_____
b. Are there specific objectives for each lesson?	_____	_____
c. Does the book have scope and sequence charts for teacher reference?	_____	_____
d. Are the units and lessons sequentially developed, with suggested time allotments?	_____	_____
e. Are there any suggested provisions for individual differences?	_____	_____
for reading levels?	_____	_____
for students with special needs?	_____	_____
for students who are gifted and talented?	_____	_____
for students who have limited proficiency in English?	_____	_____
f. Does it recommend specific techniques and strategies?	_____	_____
g. Does it have listings of suggested aids, materials, and resources?	_____	_____

	Yes	No

h. Are there suggestions for extension activities (to extend the lessons beyond the usual topic or time)? _____ _____

i. Does the book have specific guidelines for assessment of student learning? _____ _____

2. Analyze the student textbook for the following elements.

a. Does it treat the content with adequate depth? _____ _____

b. Does it treat ethnic minorities and women fairly?* _____ _____

c. Is the format attractive? _____ _____

d. Does the book have good-quality binding with suitable type size? _____ _____

e. Are illustrations and visuals attractive and useful? _____ _____

f. Is the reading clear and understandable for the students? _____ _____

3. Would you like to use this textbook? Give reasons why or why not.

_____

_____

_____

_____

_____

_____

_____

_____

_____

_____

_____

_____

_____

_____

_____

_____

_____

*For a detailed procedure that is more specific to subject areas, see Carl A. Grant and Cristine E. Sleeter, *Turning on Learning: Five Approaches for Multicultural Teaching Plans for Race, Class, Gender, and Disability* (Upper Saddle River, NJ: Prentice Hall, 1989), pp. 104–109.

FUTURE OF STUDENT "TEXTBOOKS." Possibly, within the span of your teaching career, you will witness and even be a part of a revolution in the design of school textbooks. Already some school districts allow teachers in certain disciplines to choose between traditional textbooks and interactive videodisc programs. With the revolution in electronics and microcomputer chip technology, textbooks may take on a whole new appearance. With that will come dramatic changes in the importance and use of text as well as new problems for the teacher, some of which are predictable. Student "texts" may become credit card size, increasing the chance of students losing their "books." On the positive side, it is probable that the classroom teacher will have available a variety of "textbooks" to better address the reading levels, interests, and abilities of individual students. With these changes, the distribution and maintenance of reading materials could create a greater demand on the teacher's time. Regardless, dramatic and exciting events have begun to affect a teaching tool that had not changed much throughout the history of education in this country. The textbook of the twenty-first century may become a multimedia, interactive tool that encompasses text, sound, and video and allows for world-wide telecommunications.

Beginning to Think about the Sequencing of Content

As you have reviewed the rationale and components of instructional planning and examined state and local curriculum documents, national standards, and student reading materials, you have undoubtedly reflected on your own opinion regarding content that should be included in a subject at a particular grade level. Now it is time to obtain some practical experience in long-range planning. While some authors believe that the first step in preparing to teach is to write the objectives, it is our contention that a more logical starting point is to prepare a sequential topic outline—the next step in this chapter—from which you can then prepare the major instructional objectives.

The topic outlines and instructional objectives may be presented to most beginning teachers with the expectation that they will teach from them. For you this may be the case, but someone had to have written those outlines and objectives. As a teacher candidate, you must know how this is done, for someday it will be your task. To experience preparing a year-long (or semester-long) content outline for a subject or grade that you intend to teach, do Exercise 4.5 now.

EXERCISE 4.5
Preparing a Content Outline

Instructions: The purpose of this exercise is for you to organize your ideas about subject content and the sequencing of content. Unless instructed otherwise by your instructor, you should select the subject (e.g., algebra I, biology, English, U.S. history) and the grade level (7–12).

With *three levels of headings* (see example that follows and Unit and Daily Plan—Sample 5 in the Appendix), prepare a sequential topic outline (on a separate piece of paper as space is not provided here) for a subject and grade level you intend to teach. Identify the subject by title, and clearly state the grade level. This outline is of topic content only and does *not* need to include student activities associated with the learning of that content (i.e., do not include experiments, assignments, or assessment strategies).

For example, for the study of earth science, three levels of headings might include

I. The Earth's surface
    A. Violent changes in Earth's surface
        1. Earthquakes
        2. Volcanoes
    B. Earth's land surface
        1. Rocks
etc.

If the study of earth science was just one unit for a grade level's study of the broader area of "science," then three levels of headings for that study might include

I. Earth science
    A. The Earth's surface
        1. Violent changes in Earth's surface
etc.

Share your completed outline to obtain feedback from your colleagues and university instructor. Because content outlines are never to be "carved into stone," make adjustments to your outline when and as appropriate.

Content Outline Assessment Checklist

For the development of your own outline and for the assessment of outlines by others, here is a content outline assessment checklist:

• Does the outline follow a logical sequence, with each topic logically leading to the next?

Yes _____ No _____ Comment: _____

_____

_____

_____

_____

- Does the content assume prerequisite knowledge or skills that the students are likely to have?

  Yes _____ No _____ Comment: _____

  _____

  _____

  _____

- Is the content inclusive and to an appropriate depth?

  Yes _____ No _____ Comment: _____

  _____

  _____

  _____

- Does the content consider individual student differences?

  Yes _____ No _____ Comment: _____

  _____

  _____

  _____

- Does the content allow for interdisciplinary studies?

  Yes _____ No _____ Comment: _____

  _____

  _____

  _____

- Is the outline complete; are there serious content omissions?

  Yes _____ No _____ Comment: _____

  _____

  _____

  _____

- Is any content of questionable value for this level of instruction?

  Yes _____ No _____ Comment: _____

  _____

  _____

  _____

Save this completed exercise for later when you are working on Exercise 4.12.

Preparing to Deal with Controversial Content and Issues

Controversial content and issues, usually involving matters of religion, ethnicity, politics, gender, and sex, abound in certain disciplines, particularly in English (e.g., books—see Exercise 4.6B), social studies (e.g., values, moral issues), and science (e.g., biological evolution, use of animals in research). As a general rule, if you have concern that a particular topic or activity might create controversy, it probably will. During your teaching career, you undoubtedly will have to make decisions about how you will handle such matters. When selecting content that might be controversial, consider the paragraphs that follow as guidelines.

Maintain a perspective with respect to your own objective, which is at the moment to obtain your teaching credential and then a teaching job. Student teaching is not the time to "make waves," to get yourself involved in a situation that could lead to a lot of embitterment. If you communicate closely with your cooperating teacher and your college or university supervisor, you should be able to prevent major problems dealing with controversial issues. Sometimes, during normal discussion in the classroom, a controversial subject will emerge spontaneously, thereby catching the teacher off guard. When this happens, think before saying anything. You may wish to postpone further discussion until you have had a chance to talk over the issue with your supervisors. Controversial topics can seem to arise from nowhere for any teacher, and this is perfectly normal. Young people are in the process of developing their moral and value systems, and they need and want to know how adults feel about issues that are important to them, particularly those adults they hold in esteem—their teachers. Students, especially those in secondary schools, need to discuss issues that are important to society, and there is absolutely nothing wrong with dealing with those issues as long as the following guidelines are established.

First, students should learn about all sides of an issue. Controversial issues are open-ended and should be treated as such. They do not have "right" answers or "correct" solutions. If they did, there would be no controversy. (As used in this book, an "issue" differs from a "problem" in that a problem generally has a solution, whereas an issue has many opinions and several alternative solutions.) Therefore, the focus should be on process as well as on content. A major goal is to show students how to deal with controversy and to mediate wise decisions on the basis of carefully considered information. Another goal is to help students learn how to disagree without being disagreeable—how to resolve conflict. To that end students need to learn the difference between conflicts that are destructive and those that can be constructive, in other words, to see that conflict (disagreement) can be healthy, that

it can have value. A third goal, of course, is to help students learn about the content of an issue.

Second, as with all lesson plans, one dealing with a topic that could lead to controversy should be well thought out ahead of time. Potential problem areas and resources must be carefully considered and prepared for in advance. Problems for the teacher are most likely to occur when the plan has not been well thought out.

Third, at some point all persons directly involved in an issue have a right to input—students, parents and guardians, community representatives, and other faculty. This does not mean, for example, that people outside of the school have the right to censor a teacher's plan, but it does mean that parents or guardians and students should have the right *without penalty* to not participate and to select an alternate activity.

Fourth, there is nothing wrong with students knowing a teacher's opinion about an issue as long as it is clear that the students may disagree without reprisal or academic penalty. However, it is probably best for a teacher to wait and give her opinion only after the students have had full opportunity to study and report on facts and opinions from other sources. Sometimes it is helpful if you assist students in separating facts from opinions on a particular issue being studied by setting up on the overhead or writing board a fact-opinion table, with the issue stated at the top and then two parallel columns, one for facts, the other for related opinions.

A characteristic that has made this nation so great is the freedom of all its people to speak out on issues. This freedom should not be excluded from classrooms. Teachers and students should be encouraged to express their opinions about the great issues of today, to study the issues, to suspend judgment while collecting data, and then to form and accept each other's reasoned opinions. We must understand the difference between teaching truth, values, and morals and teaching *about* truth, values, and morals. (Character education is discussed later in this chapter.)

As a college or university student, it is not unusual to encounter a professor who pontificates on a certain issue, but as a public school teacher you will not necessarily have the same academic freedom. You must understand the difference. The students with whom you will be working are not yet adults; they must be protected from dogma and allowed the freedom to learn and to develop their values and opinions, free from coercion from those who have power and control over their learning.

Now that we have expressed our opinion and have offered suggested guidelines, what do you think about this topic, which should be important to you as a teacher? For the development and expression of your opinion, please do Exercises 4.6A and 4.6B.

EXERCISE 4.6A
Dealing with Controversial Content and Issues

Instructions: The purpose of this exercise is for you to discover controversial content and issues that you may face as a teacher and to consider what you can and will do about them. After completing this exercise, share it with members of your class.

1. After studying current periodicals and talking with colleagues in the schools you visit, list two potentially controversial topics that you are likely to encounter as a teacher. (Two examples are given for you.)

Issue	*Source*
Use of chimpanzees for medical research	*National Geographic, March 1992*
Human cloning	*Time, March 1997*

2. Take one of these issues, and identify opposing arguments and current resources.

_____

_____

_____

_____

3. Identify your own positions on this issue.

_____

_____

_____

_____

4. How well can you accept students (and parents or guardians) who assume the opposite position?

_____

_____

_____

_____

5. Share the preceding with other teacher candidates. Note comments that you find helpful or enlightening.

_____

_____

_____

_____

EXERCISE 4.6B

Censorship: Books That Are Sometimes Challenged

Instructions: Continuing with the topic introduced in Exercise 4.6A, this exercise concentrates on certain books that, although frequently used in middle and secondary school teaching, are sometimes challenged by members of some communities. Book censorship becomes a concern when literature is the base for integrated teaching since there may be attempts to censor books and curricular materials in the schools. Books that have been challenged include

The Adventures of Huckleberry Finn (Mark Twain)

Annie on My Mind (Nancy Garden)

The Arizona Kid (Ron Koertge)

The Catcher in the Rye (J. D. Salinger)

The Chocolate War (Robert Cormier)

Christine (Stephen King)

The Clan of the Cave Bear (Jean Auel)

The Color Purple (Alice Walker)

A Day No Pigs Would Die (Robert Newton Peck)

Diary of a Young Girl (Anne Frank)

Fallen Angels (Walter Dean Myers)

Flowers in the Attic (V. C. Andrews)

Forever (Judy Blume)

Go Ask Alice (Anonymous)

The Great Santini (Pat Conroy)

Grendel (John Gardner)

The Handmaid's Tale (Margaret Atwood)

I Am the Cheese (Robert Cormier)

I Know Why the Caged Bird Sings (Maya Angelou)

Lord of the Flies (William Golding)

Of Mice and Men (John Steinbeck)

The Outsiders (S. E. Hinton)

Romeo and Juliet (William Shakespeare)

Running Loose (Chris Crutcher)

Scary Stories to Tell in the Dark (Alvin Schwartz)

Tarzan of the Apes (Edgar Rice Burroughs)

Review one of these books and explain how it might be challenged for censorship and how you would respond to the challenge. We leave the organization of this exercise for your class to decide; we recommend that you assign small groups to review certain books, then report to the entire class so that all the books on the list have been addressed.

_____

_____

_____

_____

_____

_____

_____

_____

_____

_____

_____

_____

AIMS, GOALS, AND OBJECTIVES: CLARIFICATION OF TERMS

Now that you have examined content typical of the school curriculum and have prepared a tentative content outline for a subject that you intend to teach, you are ready to write specific instructional objectives, known also as *behavioral, performance,* or *terminal objectives.* ("Terminal objective" is sometimes used to distinguish between instructional objectives that are intermediate and those that are final, or "terminal," to an area of learning.) *Instructional objectives are statements describing what the student will be able to do upon completion of the instructional experience.*

As a teacher, you frequently will encounter the compound structure that reads "goals and objectives," as you likely found in the curriculum documents that you reviewed (Exercises 4.1 through 4.3). A distinction needs to be understood. The easiest way to understand the difference between the two words, *goals* and *objectives,* is to look at your *intent.*

Goals are ideals that you intend to reach, that is, ideals that you would like to have accomplished. Goals may be stated as teacher goals, as student goals, or, collaboratively, as course goals. Ideally, in all three, the goal is the same. If, for example, the goal is to improve students' reading skills, it could be stated as follows:

"To help students develop their reading skills" or	*Teacher or course goal*
"To improve my reading skills"	*Student goal*

Educational goals are general statements of intent and are prepared early in course planning. (Some writers use the phrase *general goals and objectives,* but that is incorrect usage. Goals *are* general; objectives are specific.) Goals are useful when planned cooperatively with students and/or when shared with students as advance mental organizers to establish a mind-set. The students then know what to expect and will begin to prepare mentally to learn the material. From the goals, specific objectives are prepared and written in behavioral terms. The value of stating learning objectives in behavioral terms and in providing advance organizers is well documented by research.[23] Objectives are *not* intentions. They are the actual behaviors teachers intend to cause students to display. In short, objectives are what students *do.*

The most general educational objectives are often called *aims;* the general objectives of schools, curricula, and courses are called *goals;* the objectives of units and lessons are called *instructional objectives.* Aims are more general than goals, goals are more general than objectives. Instructional objectives are quite specific. (Whereas some authors distinguish between "instructional objectives," hence referring to objectives that are *not* behavior specific, and "behavioral or performance objectives," objectives that *are* behavior specific, the terms are used here as if they are synonymous to emphasize the importance of writing instructional objectives in terms that are measurable).

As implied in the preceding paragraphs, goals guide the instructional methods; objectives drive student performance. Assessment of student achievement in learning should be an assessment of that performance. When the assessment procedure does match the instructional objectives, that is sometimes referred to as assessment that is *aligned* or *authentic* (discussed in Chapter 11). When objectives, instruction, and assessment match the stated goals, we have what is referred to as an *aligned curriculum.*

Goals are general statements, usually not even complete sentences, often beginning with the infinitive *to,* which identify what the teacher intends the students to learn. Objectives, stated in performance (behavioral) terms, are specific actions and should be written as complete sentences that include the verb *will* to indicate what each student is expected to be able to do as a result of the instructional experience.

Whereas instructional goals may not always be quantifiable (i.e., readily measurable), instructional objectives should be measurable. Furthermore, those objectives then become the essence of what is measured in instruments designed to assess student learning. Consider the examples shown in Figure 4.6.

INSTRUCTIONAL OBJECTIVES AND THEIR RELATIONSHIP TO INSTRUCTION AND ASSESSMENT

One purpose for writing objectives in behavioral terms is to be able to assess with precision whether the instruction has resulted in the desired behavior. In many school districts the educational goals are established as competencies that the students are expected to achieve. These goals are then divided into specific performance objectives, sometimes referred to as *goal indicators.* Instruction is designed to teach toward those objectives. When students perform the competencies called for by these objectives, their education is considered successful. This is known variously as *criterion-referenced, competency-based, performance-based,* or *outcome-based education.* Expecting students to achieve one set of competencies before moving on

---

23. T. L. Good and J. E. Brophy, *Looking in Classrooms,* 7th ed. (New York: Longman, 1997), p. 240.

Figure 4.6
Examples of goals and objectives.

Goals

1. To acquire knowledge about the physical geography of North America.
2. To develop an appreciation for music.
3. To develop an enjoyment for reading.

Objectives

1. On a map the student will identify specific mountain ranges of North America.
2. The student will identify ten different musical instruments by listening to a tape recording of the Boston Pops Symphony Orchestra and identify which instrument is being played at specified times as determined by the teacher.
3. The student will read two books, three short stories, and five newspaper articles at home, within a two-month period. The student will maintain a daily written log of these activities.

---

to the next set is called **mastery learning** (discussed further in Chapter 8). The success of the school, teacher performance, and student achievement may each be assessed according to these criteria.

Assessment is not difficult to accomplish when the desired performance is *overt* behavior, that is, when it can be observed directly. Each of the sample objectives of the preceding section is an example of an objective that is overt. Assessment is more difficult to accomplish when the desired behavior is *covert,* that is, when it is not directly observable. Although certainly no less important, behaviors that call for "appreciation," "discovery," or "understanding," for example, are not directly observable because they occur within a person and so are covert behaviors. Since covert behavior cannot be observed directly, the only way to tell whether the objective has been achieved is to observe behavior that may be indicative of that achievement. The objective, then, is written in overt language, and evaluators can only assume or trust that the observed behavior is, in fact, reasonably close to being indicative of the expected learning outcome.

Furthermore, when assessing whether an objective has been achieved, that learning has occurred, the assessment device must be consistent with the desired learning outcome; otherwise the assessment is invalid. As said earlier, when the measuring device and the learning objective are compatible, we say that the assessment is authentic. For example, a person's competency to teach specific skills in physical education to high school juniors is best (i.e., with highest reliability) measured by directly observing that person *doing* that very thing—teaching specific skills in physical education to high school juniors. Using a standardized paper-and-pencil test of multiple-choice items to determine a person's ability to teach specific physical education skills to high school juniors is not authentic assessment.

Balance of Behaviorism and Constructivism

Whereas behaviorists (behaviorism) assume a definition of learning that deals only with changes in observable (overt) behavior, constructivists (constructivism or cognitivism) hold that learning entails the construction or reshaping of mental schemata and that mental processes mediate learning, and so they are concerned with both overt and covert behaviors.[24] Does this mean that you must be one or the other, a behaviorist or a constructivist? Probably not. For now, the point is that when writing instructional objectives, you should write most or all of your basic expectations (minimal competency expectations) in overt terms (the topic of the next section), but on the other hand, you cannot be expected to foresee all learning that occurs or to translate all that is learned into behavioral terms—most certainly not before it occurs.

Any effort to write all learning objectives in behavioral terms is, in effect, to neglect the individual learner for whom they purport to be concerned; such an approach does not allow for diversity among learners. Learning that is most meaningful to children is not so neatly or easily predicted or isolated. Rather than teaching one objective at a time, much of the time you should direct your teaching toward the simultaneous learning of multiple objectives, understandings, and appreciations. However, when you assess for learning, assessment is cleaner when objectives are assessed one at a time.

More on this matter of objectives and their use in teaching and learning follows in "Using the Taxonomies," later in this chapter.

---

24. See D. Perkins and T. Blythe, "Putting Understanding Up Front," *Educational Leadership* 51(5):4–7 (February 1994), and J. A. Zahorik, *Constructivist Teaching* (Bloomington, IN: Fastback 390, Phi Delta Kappa Educational Foundation, 1995).

Figure 4.7
Verbs to avoid when writing
objectives.

Appreciate	Familiarize	Learn
Believe	Grasp	Like
Comprehend	Indicate	Realize
Enjoy	Know	Understand

WRITING INSTRUCTIONAL OBJECTIVES

When writing instructional objectives, you must ask yourself, "How is the student to demonstrate that the objective has been reached?" The objective must include an action that demonstrates that the objective has been achieved. Inherited from behaviorism, this portion of the objective is sometimes called the terminal behavior or the *anticipated measurable performance.*

Four Key Components to Writing Objectives

When completely written in behavioral terms, an instructional objective has four key components. To aid your understanding and remembering, you can refer to these as the ABCDs of writing behavioral objectives.

One of the components is the *audience*—the *A* of the ABCDs, that is, the student for whom the objective is intended. To address this, sometimes teachers begin their objectives with the phrase, "The student will be able to . . . ," or, to personalize the objective, "You will be able to . . . ." (To conserve space and to eliminate useless language, in examples that follow we eliminate use of "be able to," and write simply "The student will . . . ." For brevity, writers of objectives sometimes use the abbreviation "TSWBAT" for "The student will be able to . . . .")

The second key component is the expected *behavior*—the *B* of the ABCDs. The expected behavior (or performance) should be written with verbs that are measurable—that is, with action verbs—so that it is directly observable that an objective has been reached. As discussed in the preceding section, some verbs are too vague, ambiguous, and not clearly measurable. When writing objectives, you should avoid verbs that are not clearly measurable, verbs that are covert, such as *appreciate, comprehend,* and *understand* (see Figure 4.7). For the three examples given in Figure 4.6, for objectives 1 and 2 the behaviors (action or overt verbs) are "will *identify,*" and for objective 3 the behaviors are "will *read* and *maintain.*"

Now do Exercise 4.7 to assess and to further your understanding.

The third ingredient is the *conditions*—the *C* of the ABCDs—the setting in which the behavior will be demonstrated by the student and observed by the teacher. For the first sample objective in Figure 4.5, the conditions are "on a map." For the second sample objective, the conditions are "by listening to a tape recording of the Boston Pops Symphony Orchestra" and "specified times as determined by the teacher." For the third sample, the conditions are "at home, within a two-month period."

The fourth ingredient, but not always included in objectives written by teachers, is the *degree* (or *level*) *of expected performance*—the *D* of the ABCDs. This ingredient allows for the assessment of student learning. When mastery learning is expected (achievement of 85 to 100 percent), the level of expected performance is usually omitted (because it is understood). In teaching for mastery learning, the performance-level expectation is 100 percent. In reality, however, the performance level will most likely be between 85 and 95 percent, particularly when working with a group of students rather than with an individual student. The 5 to 15 percent difference allows for human error, as can occur when using written and oral communication.

Now, to reinforce your comprehension, do Exercise 4.8.

Performance level is used to assess student achievement, and sometimes it is used to evaluate the effectiveness of the teaching. Student grades might be based on performance levels; evaluation of teacher effectiveness might be based on the level of student performance.

Now, with Exercise 4.9, try your skill at recognizing objectives that are measurable.

CLASSIFYING INSTRUCTIONAL OBJECTIVES

When planning instructional objectives, it is useful to consider the three domains of learning objectives: **cognitive domain,** which involves mental operations from the lowest level of the simple recall of information to complex, high-level evaluative processes; **affective domain,** which involves feelings, attitudes, and values and ranges from the lower levels of acquisition to the highest level of internalization and action; and **psychomotor domain,** which originally dealt with gross to fine motor control but, as used in this resource guide, ranges from the simple manipulation of materials to the

---

EXERCISE 4.7

Recognizing Verbs That Are
Acceptable for Overt Objectives—
A Self-Check Exercise

Instructions: The purpose of this exercise is to check your recognition of verbs that are suitable for use in overt behavioral objectives. From the list of verbs below, circle those that *should not* be used in overt objectives—that is, those verbs that describe covert behaviors that are not directly observable and measurable. Check your answers against the answer key that follows. Discuss any problems with the exercise with your classmates and instructor.

1. apply	11. design	21. know
2. appreciate	12. diagram	22. learn
3. believe	13. enjoy	23. name
4. combine	14. explain	24. outline
5. comprehend	15. familiarize	25. predict
6. compute	16. grasp	26. realize
7. create	17. identify	27. select
8. define	18. illustrate	28. solve
9. demonstrate	19. indicate	29. state
10. describe	20. infer	30. understand

Answer Key for Exercise 4.7: The following verbs should be circled: 2, 3, 5, 13, 15, 16*, 19, 21, 22, 26, 30. If you missed more than a couple, then you need to read the previous sections again and discuss your errors with your classmates and instructor.
*If used meaning to grip, then the verb would not be circled. If grasp is used as a synonym for "understand," then it is covert.

---

communication of ideas and finally to the highest level of creative performance.

The Domains of Learning and the Developmental Needs of Students

Educators attempt to design learning experiences to meet the five areas of developmental needs of the total child that were discussed in Chapter 1: intellectual, physical, psychological, social, and moral and ethical. As a teacher, you must include objectives that address learning within each of these categories of needs. The intellectual needs are primarily within the cognitive domain, the physical are within the psychomotor, and the other needs mostly are within the affective domain.

Too frequently, teachers focus on the cognitive domain while only assuming that the psychomotor and affective domains will take care of themselves. Many

experts argue that teachers should do just the opposite: When the affective domain is directly attended to, the psychomotor and cognitive domains naturally develop. In any case, you should plan your teaching so that your students are guided from the lowest to highest levels of operation within each of the domains, separately or simultaneously.

The three developmental hierarchies are discussed next to guide your understanding of each of the five areas of needs. Notice the illustrative verbs within each hierarchy. These verbs help you fashion objectives When you are developing unit plans and lesson plans. Caution must be urged, however, for there can be considerable overlap among the levels at which some action verbs may be used appropriately. For example, the verb *identifies* is appropriate in each of the following objectives at different levels (noted in parentheses) within the cognitive domain:

EXERCISE 4.8
Recognizing the Parts of Criterion-Referenced Behavioral Objectives— A Self-Check Exercise

---

Instructions: The purpose of this exercise is to practice your skill in recognizing the four components of a behavioral objective. In the following two objectives, identify the parts of the objectives by underlining

once the *audience,*

twice the *behavior,*

three times the *conditions,* and

four times the *performance level* (that is, the degree or standard of performance).

Check your answers against the answer key that follows, and discuss any problems with this exercise with your classmates and instructor.

1. Given a metropolitan transit bus schedule, at the end of the lesson the student will be able to read the schedule well enough to determine at what times buses are scheduled to leave randomly selected locations, with at least 90-percent accuracy.

2. Given five rectangular figures, you will correctly compute the area in square centimeters of at least four, by measuring the length and width with a ruler and computing the product using an appropriate calculation method.

Answer Key for Exercise 4.8

	Objective 1	*Objective 2*
Audience	the student	you
Behavior	will be able to read the schedule	will compute
Conditions	given a metropolitan transit bus schedule	given five rectangular figures
Performance level	well enough to determine (and) with at least 90 percent accuracy	correctly compute the area in square centimeters of at least four (80 percent accuracy)

The student will identify the correct definition of the term *osmosis.* (knowledge)

The student will identify examples of the principle of osmosis. (comprehension)

The student will identify the osmotic effect when a cell is immersed into a hypotonic solution. (application)

The student will identify the osmotic effect on turgor pressure when the cell is placed in a hypotonic solution. (analysis)

Cognitive Domain Hierarchies

In a widely accepted taxonomy of objectives, Bloom and his associates arranged cognitive objectives into classifications according to the complexity of the skills and abilities they embodied.[25] The result was a ladder

---

25. B. S. Bloom, ed., *Taxonomy of Educational Objectives, Book 1, Cognitive Domain* (White Plains, NY: Longman, 1984).

EXERCISE 4.9
Recognizing Measurable Objectives— A Self-Check Exercise

Instructions: The purpose of this exercise is to assess your ability to recognize objectives that are measurable. Place an *X* before each of the following that is an overt, student-centered behavioral objective, that is, a learning objective that is clearly measurable. Although audience, conditions, or performance levels may be absent, ask yourself, "As stated, is this a student-centered and measurable objective?" If it is, place an *X* in the blank. A self-checking answer key follows. After checking your answers, discuss any problems with the exercise with your classmates and instructor.

_____ 1. To develop an appreciation for literature.

_____ 2. To identify those celestial bodies that are known as planets.

_____ 3. To provide meaningful experiences for the students.

_____ 4. To recognize antonym pairs.

_____ 5. To boot up the program on the computer.

_____ 6. To analyze and compare patterns of data or specific quartile maps.

_____ 7. To develop skills in inquiry.

_____ 8. To identify which of the four causes is most relevant to the major events leading up to the Civil War.

_____ 9. To use maps and graphs to identify the major areas of world petroleum production and consumption.

_____ 10. To know the causes for the diminishing ozone concentration.

Answer Key

You should have marked items 2, 4, 5, 6, 8, and 9.

Items 1, 3, 7, and 10 are inadequate because of their ambiguity. Item 3 is not even a student learning objective; it is a teacher goal. "To develop" and "to know" can have too many interpretations.

Although the conditions are not given, items 2, 4, 5, 6, 8, and 9 are clearly measurable. The teacher would have no difficulty recognizing when a learner had reached those objectives. Discuss any problem you had with this exercise with your classmates and instructor.

---

ranging from the simplest to the most complex intellectual processes. *(Within each domain, prerequisite to a student's ability to function at one particular level of the hierarchy is the ability to function at the preceding level or levels. In other words, when a student is functioning at the third level of the cognitive domain, that student is* *automatically also functioning at the first and second levels.)* Rather than an orderly progression from simple to complex mental operations as illustrated by Bloom's taxonomy, other researchers prefer an organization of cognitive abilities that ranges from simple information storage and retrieval, through a higher level of discrimination and concept attainment, to the highest cognitive ability to recognize and solve problems.[26]

The six major categories (or levels) in Bloom's taxonomy of cognitive objectives are (1) *knowledge* (recognizing and recalling information), (2) *comprehension* (understanding the meaning of information), (3) *application* (using information), (4) *analysis* (dissecting information into its component parts to comprehend their relationships), (5) *synthesis* (putting components together to generate new ideas), and (6) *evaluation* (judging the worth of an idea, notion, theory, thesis, proposition, information, or opinion). Although space does not allow elaboration here, Bloom's taxonomy includes various subcategories within each of these six major categories. It is our opinion that it is less important that an objective be absolutely classified than it is to be cognizant of hierarchies of thinking and doing and to understand the importance of attending to student intellectual behavior from lower to higher levels of operation in all three domains. Discussion of each of Bloom's six categories follows.

KNOWLEDGE.   The basic element in Bloom's taxonomy concerns the acquisition of knowledge—that is, the ability to recognize and recall information. (As discussed in Chapter 7, this is similar to the input level of thinking and questioning.) Although knowledge is the lowest of the six categories, the information to be learned may not itself be of a low level. In fact, it may be of an extremely high level. Bloom includes here knowledge of principles, generalizations, theories, structures, and methodology, as well as knowledge of facts and ways of dealing with facts.

Action verbs appropriate for this category include *choose, complete, define, describe, identify, indicate, list, locate, match, name, outline, recall, recognize, select,* and *state.*

The following are examples of objectives at the knowledge level. Note especially the verb (in italics) used in each example:

- From memory, the student *will recall* the letters in the English alphabet that are vowels.
- The student *will list* the organelles found in animal cell cytoplasm.
- The student *will identify* the major parts of speech in the sentence.
- The student *will name* the positions of players on a soccer team.

The remaining five categories of Bloom's taxonomy of the cognitive domain deal with the *use* of knowledge. They encompass the educational objectives aimed at developing cognitive skills and abilities, including comprehension, application, analysis, synthesis, and evaluation of knowledge. The last four—application, analysis, synthesis, and evaluation—are referred to as *higher-order thinking skills,* as are, too, the higher categories of the affective and psychomotor domains.[27]

COMPREHENSION.   Comprehension includes the ability to translate, explain, or interpret knowledge and to extrapolate from it to address new situations. Action verbs appropriate for this category include *change, classify, convert, defend, describe, estimate, expand, explain, generalize, infer, interpret, paraphrase, predict, recognize, summarize,* and *translate.* Examples of objectives in this category are

- From a sentence, the student *will recognize* the letters that are vowels in the English alphabet.
- The student *will describe* each of the organelles found in animal cell cytoplasm.
- The student *will recognize* the major parts of speech in the sentence.
- The student *will recognize* the positions of players on a soccer team.

APPLICATION.   Once learners understand information, they should be able to apply it. Action verbs in this category of operation include *apply, compute, demonstrate, develop, discover, modify, operate, participate, perform, plan, predict, relate, show,* and *use.* Examples of objectives in this category are

- The student *will use* in a sentence a word that contains at least two vowels.
- The student *will predict* the organelles found in plant cell cytoplasm.
- The student *will demonstrate* in a complete sentence each of the major parts of speech.
- The student *will relate* how the positions of players on a soccer team depend upon each other.

26. See R. M. Gagné, L. J. Briggs, and W. W. Wager, *Principles of Instructional Design*, 4th ed. (New York: Holt, Rinehart and Winston, 1994).

27. Compare Bloom's higher-order thinking skills with R. H. Ennis's, "A Taxonomy of Critical Thinking Dispositions and Abilities," and Qellmalz's "Developing Reasoning Skills," both in J. B. Barron and R. J. Sternberg (eds.), *Teaching Thinking Skills: Theory and Practice* (New York: W. H. Freeman, 1987), and with Marzano's "complex thinking strategies" in R. J. Marzano, *A Different Kind of Classroom: Teaching With Dimensions of Learning* (Alexandria, VA: Association for Supervision and Curriculum Development, 1992).

ANALYSIS. This category includes objectives that require learners to use the skills of analysis. Action verbs appropriate for this category include *analyze, break down, categorize, classify, compare, contrast, debate, deduce, diagram, differentiate, discriminate, identify, illustrate, infer, outline, relate, separate,* and *subdivide.* Examples of objectives in this category include

- From a list of words, the student *will differentiate* those that contain vowels from those that do not.
- Under the microscope, the student *will identify* the organelles found in animal cell cytoplasm.
- The student *will analyze* a paragraph for misuse of major parts of speech.
- The student *will illustrate* on the writing board the different positions of players on a soccer team.

SYNTHESIS. This category includes objectives that involve such skills as designing a plan, proposing a set of operations, and deriving a series of abstract relations. Action verbs appropriate for this category include *arrange, categorize, classify, combine, compile, constitute, create, design, develop, devise, document, explain, formulate, generate, modify, organize, originate, plan, produce, rearrange, reconstruct, revise, rewrite, summarize, synthesize, tell, transmit,* and *write.* Examples of objectives in this category are

- From a list of words, the student *will rearrange* them into several lists according to the vowels contained in each.
- The student *will devise* a classification scheme of the organelles found in animal cell and plant cell cytoplasm according to their functions.
- The student *will write* a paragraph that correctly uses each of the major parts of speech.
- The student *will illustrate* on the chalkboard an offensive plan that uses the different positions of players on a soccer team.

EVALUATION. This, the highest category of Bloom's cognitive taxonomy, includes offering opinions and making value judgments. Action verbs appropriate for this category include *appraise, argue, assess, compare, conclude, consider, contrast, criticize, decide, discriminate, evaluate, explain, interpret, judge, justify, rank, rate, relate, standardize, support,* and *validate.* Examples of objectives in this category are

- The student *will listen to and evaluate* other students' identifications of vowels from sentences written on the board.
- While observing living cytoplasm under the microscope, the student *will justify* his interpretation that certain structures are specific organelles of a plant or animal cell.

- The student *will evaluate* a paragraph written by another student for the proper use of major parts of speech.
- The student *will interpret* the reasons for an opposing team's offensive use of the different positions of players on a soccer team.

Now use Exercise 4.10 to assess your understanding of the level of objectives within the cognitive domain.

Affective Domain Hierarchies

Krathwohl, Bloom, and Masia developed a useful taxonomy of the affective domain.[28] The following are their major levels (or categories), from least internalized to most internalized: (1) *receiving* (being aware of the affective stimulus and beginning to have favorable feelings toward it); (2) *responding* (taking an interest in the stimulus and viewing it favorably); (3) *valuing* (showing a tentative belief in the value of the affective stimulus and becoming committed to it); (4) *organizing* (placing values into a system of dominant and supporting values); (5) *internalizing* (demonstrating consistent beliefs and behavior that have become a way of life). Although there is considerable overlap from one category to another within the affective domain, these categories do give a basis by which to judge the quality of objectives and the nature of learning within this area. A discussion of each of the five categories follows.

RECEIVING. At this level, which is the least internalized, the learner exhibits willingness to give attention to particular phenomena or stimuli, and the teacher is able to arouse, sustain, and direct that attention. Action verbs appropriate for this category include *ask, choose, describe, differentiate, distinguish, hold, identify, locate, name, point to, recall, recognize, reply, select,* and *use.* Examples of objectives in this category are

- The student *pays attention* to the directions for enrichment activities.
- The student *listens attentively* to the ideas of others.
- The student *demonstrates sensitivity* to the property, beliefs, and concerns of others.

RESPONDING. At this level, learners respond to the stimulus they have received. They may do so because of some external pressure, because they find the stimulus interesting, or because responding gives them satis-

---

28. D. R. Krathwohl, B. S. Bloom, and B. B. Masia, *Taxonomy of Educational Goals, Handbook 2, Affective Domain* (New York: David McKay, 1964).

EXERCISE 4.10

Classifying Cognitive Objectives— A Self-Check Exercise

Instructions: The purpose of this exercise is to assess your ability to recognize the level of cognitive objectives. For each of the following cognitive objectives, identify by appropriate letter the *highest* level of operation that is called for. Check your answers with the answer key, and then discuss the results with your classmates and instructor. Your understanding of the concept involved is more important than whether you score 100 percent against the answer key.

Use the following codes for your answers: 1 = knowledge; 2 = comprehension; 3 = application; 4 = analysis; 5 = synthesis; 6 = evaluation.

_____ 1. The student will be able to detect faulty logic in advertising propaganda.

_____ 2. The student will be able to differentiate fact and opinion in news stories.

_____ 3. Given the facts of the political situation, the student will be able to draw reasonable hypotheses concerning the causes of the Persian Gulf War.

_____ 4. The student will be able to devise a workable plan for investigating a social phenomenon.

_____ 5. The student will write an original short story.

_____ 6. At the end of the lesson, the students will perceive the moods of melancholy and retreat in Byron's *The Ocean*.

_____ 7. You will be able to define *corporation* in your own words.

_____ 8. Given the requisite tools and materials—electric drill and bit, knife, screwdriver, ruler, soldering gun, wire strippers, solder, and flux—the student will construct a portable testing device for repair of motors and sealed-in units.

_____ 9. Given a list of five solids, five liquids, and five gases, students will be able to describe the physical and chemical properties of each.

_____ 10. You will be able to devise a method to prove a ray to be the bisector of an angle.

Answer Key

1. level 6	3. level 4	5. level 5	7. level 2	9. level 1
2. level 4	4. level 5	6. level 2	8. level 3	10. level 5

faction. Action verbs appropriate for this category include *answer, applaud, approve, assist, command, comply, discuss, greet, help, label, perform, play, practice, present, read, recite, report, select, tell,* and *write.* Examples of objectives at this level are

• The student *reads* for enrichment.
• The student *discusses* what others have said.

• The student *cooperates* with others during group activities.

VALUING. Objectives at the valuing level deal with learner's beliefs, attitudes, and appreciations. The simplest objectives concern the acceptance of beliefs and values; the higher ones involve learning to prefer certain values and finally becoming committed to them. Action verbs appropriate for this level include *argue, assist, complete, describe, differentiate, explain, follow, form, initiate, invite, join, justify, propose, protest, read, report, select, share, study, support,* and *work.* Examples of objectives in this category include

- The student *protests* against racial or ethnic discrimination.
- The student *synthesizes* a position on biological evolution.
- The student *argues* a position on pro-choice for women.

ORGANIZING. This fourth level in the affective domain concerns the building of a personal value system. Here the learner is conceptualizing and arranging values into a system that recognizes their relative importance. Action verbs appropriate for this level include *adhere, alter, arrange, balance, combine, compare, defend, define, discuss, explain, form, generalize, identify, integrate, modify, order, organize, prepare, relate,* and *synthesize.* Examples of objectives in this category are

- The student *forms judgments* concerning proper behavior in the classroom, school, and community.
- The student *integrates* personal values into his work ethic.
- The student *defends* the important values of particular subculture.

INTERNALIZING. This is the last and highest category within the affective domain, at which the learner's behaviors have become consistent with her beliefs. Action verbs appropriate for this level include *act, complete, display, influence, listen, modify, perform, practice, propose, qualify, question, revise, serve, solve,* and *verify.* Examples of objectives in this category are

- The student's behavior *displays* a well-defined and ethical code of conduct.
- The student *practices* accurate verbal and nonverbal communication.
- The student *performs* independently.

Psychomotor Domain Hierarchies

Whereas identification and classification within the cognitive and affective domains are generally agreed upon, there is less agreement on the classification within the psychomotor domain. Originally, the goal of this domain was simply to develop and categorize proficiency in skills, particularly those dealing with gross and fine muscle control. The classification of the domain presented here follows this lead but includes at its highest level the most creative and inventive behaviors, thus coordinating skills and knowledge from all three domains. Consequently, the objectives are in a hierarchy ranging from simple gross locomotor control to the most creative and complex, requiring originality and fine locomotor control—for example, from simply turning on a computer to designing a software program. From Harrow we offer the following taxonomy of the psychomotor domain: (1) *moving,* (2) *manipulating,* (3) *communicating,* and (4) *creating.*[29]

MOVING. This level involves gross motor coordination. Action verbs appropriate for this level include *adjust, carry, clean, grasp, jump, locate, obtain,* and *walk.* Sample objectives for this category are

- The student *will jump* a rope ten times without missing.
- The student *will correctly grasp* the putter.
- The student *will carry* the microscope to the desk correctly.

MANIPULATING. This level involves fine motor coordination. Action verbs appropriate for this level include *assemble, build, calibrate, connect, play, thread,* and *turn.* Sample objectives for this category are

- The student *will assemble* a kite.
- The student *will play* the C-scale on the clarinet.
- The student *will turn* the fine adjustment until the microscope is in focus.

COMMUNICATING. This level involves the communication of ideas and feelings. Action verbs appropriate for this level include *analyze, ask, describe, draw, explain,* and *write.* Sample objectives for this category are

- By *asking* appropriate questions, the student will demonstrate active listening skills.
- The student *will draw* what he observes on a slide through the microscope.
- The student *will describe* her feelings about the cloning of humans.

CREATING. Creating is the highest level of this domain and of all domains and represents the student's coordination of thinking, learning, and behaving in all three domains. Action verbs appropriate for this level

---

29. A. J. Harrow, *Taxonomy of the Psychomotor Domain* (New York: Longman, 1977). A similar taxonomy for the psychomotor domain is that of E. J. Simpson, *The Classification of Educational Objectives in the Psychomotor Domain. The Psychomotor Domain: Volume 3* (Washington, DC: Gryphon House, 1972).

include *create, design,* and *invent.* Sample objectives for this category are

- The student *will design* a mural.
- The student *will create, choreograph, and perform* a dance pattern.
- The student *will invent* and build a kite pattern.

Now, use Exercise 4.11 to assess your recognition of performance objectives according to which domain they belong. Then, with Exercise 4.12, begin writing your own objectives for use in your teaching. You may want to correlate your work on Exercise 4.12 with Exercises 5.6A and 5.7.

EXERCISE 4.11

Recognition of Cognitive, Affective, and Psychomotor Objectives—A Self-Check Exercise

---

Instructions: The purpose of this exercise is to assess your ability to recognize objectives according to their domains. Classify each of the following instructional objectives by writing in the blank space the appropriate letter according to its domain: *C*—cognitive, *A*—affective, *P*—psychomotor. Check your answers with the key at the end; then discuss the results with your classmates and instructor.

_____ 1. The student will continue shooting free throws until the student can successfully complete 80 percent of the attempts.

_____ 2. The student will identify on a map the mountain ranges of eastern United States.

_____ 3. The student will summarize the historical development of the Democratic party of the United States.

_____ 4. The student will demonstrate a continuing desire to learn more about using the classroom computer for word processing by volunteering to work at it during free time.

_____ 5. The student will volunteer to tidy up the storage room.

_____ 6. After listening to several recordings, the student will identify the respective composers.

_____ 7. The student will translate a favorite Cambodian poem into English.

_____ 8. The student will accurately calculate the length of the hypotenuse.

_____ 9. The student will indicate an interest in the subject by voluntarily reading additional library books about earthquakes.

_____ 10. The student will write and perform a piano concerto.

2. C	4. A	6. C	8. C	10. P
1. P	3. C	5. A	7. C	9. A

Answer Key

EXERCISE 4.12
Preparing My Own Behavioral Objectives

Instructions: The purpose of this exercise is to begin construction of objectives for your own teaching. For a subject-content area and grade level of your choice (perhaps from the content outline you developed in Exercise 4.5), prepare ten specific behavioral objectives. (Audience, conditions, and performance level are not necessary unless requested by your course instructor.) Exchange completed exercises with your classmates; discuss and make changes where necessary.

Subject field: _____   Grade Level: _____

1. Cognitive knowledge:

   _____

   _____

   _____

   _____

   _____

2. Cognitive comprehension:

   _____

   _____

   _____

   _____

   _____

3. Cognitive application:

   _____

   _____

   _____

   _____

   _____

4. Cognitive analysis:

   _____

   _____

   _____

   _____

   _____

5. Cognitive synthesis:

   _____

_____

_____

_____

_____

6. Cognitive evaluation:

_____

_____

_____

_____

_____

7. Affective (low level):

_____

_____

_____

_____

_____

8. Affective (highest level):

_____

_____

_____

_____

_____

9. Psychomotor (low level):

_____

_____

_____

_____

_____

10. Psychomotor (highest level):

_____

_____

_____

_____

_____

Outcome-based education helps produce people who are life-long learners, are effective communicators, have high self-esteem, and are

Problem Solvers

- Are able to solve problems in their academic and personal lives
- Demonstrate higher-level analytical thinking skills when they evaluate or make decisions
- Are able to set personal and career goals
- Can use knowledge, not just display it
- Are innovative thinkers

Self-Directed Learners

- Are independent workers
- Can read, comprehend, and interact with text
- Have self-respect with an accurate view of themselves and their abilities

Quality Producers

- Can communicate effectively in a variety of situations (oral, aesthetic/artistic, nonverbal)
- Are able to use their knowledge to create intelligent, artistic products that reflect originality
- Have high standards

Collaborative Workers

- Are able to work interdependently
- Show respect for others and their points of view
- Have their own values and moral conduct
- Have an appreciation of cultural diversity

Community Contributors

- Have an awareness of civic, individual, national, and international responsibilities
- Have an understanding of basic health issues
- Have an appreciation of diversity

Figure 4.8
Sample learning outcome standards expected by a school district.

USING THE TAXONOMIES

Theoretically, the taxonomies are so constructed that students achieve each lower level before being ready to move to the higher levels. But, because categories and behaviors overlap, as they should, this theory does not always hold in practice. "Thoughts and feelings are inextricably interconnected—we 'think' with our feelings and 'feel' with our thoughts."[30]

The taxonomies are important in that they emphasize the various levels to which instruction must aspire. For learning to be worthwhile, you must formulate and teach to objectives from the higher levels of the taxonomies as well as from the lower ones. Student thinking and behaving must be moved from the lowest to the highest levels of thinking and behavior. When it is all said and done, it is, perhaps, the highest level of the psychomotor domain (creating) to which we aspire.

In using the taxonomies, remember that the point is to formulate the best objectives for the job to be done. In schools that use outcome-based education models, those models describe levels of mastery standards (*rubrics*) for each outcome. The taxonomies provide the mechanism for ensuring that you do not spend a disproportionate amount of time on facts and other low-level learning that is relatively trivial, and they can be of tremendous help where teachers are expected to correlate learning activities to one of the school's or district's outcome standards (see Figure 4.8).

Preparing objectives is essential to the preparation of good items for the assessment of student learning. Clearly communicating your behavioral expectations to students and then specifically assessing student learning against those expectations makes the teaching most efficient and effective, and it makes the assessment of the learning closer to being authentic. This does not mean to imply that you will always write behavioral objectives for everything taught, nor will you always be able to accurately measure what students have

---

30. G. Caine and R. N. Caine, "The Critical Need for a Mental Model of Meaningful Learning," *California Catalyst* (Fall 1992), p. 19.

learned. Learning that is meaningful to students is not as easily compartmentalized as the taxonomies of educational objectives would imply.

Observing for Connected (Meaningful) Learning

In learning that is most important and that has the most meaning to students, the domains are inextricably interconnected. Consequently, when assessing for student learning you must look for those connections. One way of doing that is to have students maintain a response journal, in which they reflect on and respond to their learning (student journals are discussed further in Chapter 8), using five categories described as follows[31]:

1. "I never knew that." In this category, student responses are primarily to factual information, to their new knowledge, to the bits and pieces of raw information often expected to be memorized regardless of how meaningful to students it might be. However, because this is only fragmented knowledge, and merely scratches the surface of meaningful learning, it must not be the end-all of student learning. Learning that is truly meaningful goes beyond the "I never knew that" category, expands upon the bits and pieces, connects them, allowing the learner to make sense out of what he is learning. Learning that does not extend beyond the "I never knew that" category is dysfunctional.
2. "I never thought of that." Here, student responses reveal an additional way of perceiving. Their responses may include elements of "I never knew that" but also contain higher-level thinking as a result of their reflection on that knowledge.
3. "I never felt that." In this category, student responses are connected to the affective, eliciting more of an emotional response than a cognitive one. Learning that is truly meaningful is much more than intellectual understanding; it includes a "felt" meaning.[32]
4. "I never appreciated that." Responses in this category reflect a sense of recognition that one's own life can be enriched by what others have created or done or that something already known can be valued from an additional perspective.
5. "I never realized that." In this category, student responses indicate an awareness of overall patterns and dynamic ways in which behavior is holistic, establishing meaningful and potentially useful connections among knowledge, values, and purposes.

Character Education

Related especially to the affective domain, although not exclusive of the cognitive and psychomotor domains, is interest in the development of students' values, especially those of honesty, kindness, respect, and responsibility, an interest in what is sometimes called character education.[33] Wynne and Ryan state that "transmitting character, academics, and discipline—essentially, 'traditional' moral values—to pupils is a vital educational responsibility."[34] Thus, if one agrees with that interpretation, then the teaching of moral values is the transmission of character, academics, and discipline and clearly implies learning that transcends the three domains of learning presented in this chapter. Whether defined as ethics, citizenship, moral values, or personal development, character education has long been part of public education in this country.[35] Today, stimulated by a perceived need to reduce student antisocial behaviors (such as drug abuse and violence) and to produce more dignified, respectful, and responsible citizens, with a primary focus on the affective domain, many schools are developing curricula in character education and instruction in conflict resolution, with the ultimate goal of developing in students values that lead to responsible community and national citizenship and moral action. Techniques include (1) sensitizing students to value issues through role play and creative drama, (2) having students take opposing points of view in discussions, (3) promoting higher-order thinking about value issues through appropriate questioning techniques, (4) action-oriented community-based service projects, using parents and community members to assist in the projects, highlighting anchor examples of class and individual cooperation in serving the school and community, and making student service projects visible in the school and community.[36] Resources on character education are listed in Figure 4.9.

---

31. Adapted from S. Fersh, *Integrating the Trans-National/Cultural Dimension* (Bloomington, IN: Fastback 361, Phi Delta Kappa Educational Foundation, 1993), pp. 23–24.
32. Caine and Caine, p. 19.
33. M. Massey, "Interest in Character Education Seen Growing," *ASCD Update* 35(4):1, 4–5 (May 1993).
34. E. A. Wynne and K. Ryan, *Reclaiming Our Schools: A Handbook on Teaching Character, Academics, and Discipline* (Upper Saddle River, NJ: Prentice Hall, 1993), p. 3.
35. K. Burrett and T. Rusnak, *Integrated Character Education* (Bloomington, IN: Fastback 351, Phi Delta Kappa Educational Foundation, 1993), p. 10.
36. See, for example, the articles in the theme issues "Youth and Caring," *Phi Delta Kappan* 76(9) (May 1995), and "Education for a Democratic Society," *Educational Leadership* 54(5) (February 1997).

Figure 4.9
Resources on character education.

- Character Education Institute, 8918 Tesoro Drive, San Antonio, TX 78217 (800-284-0499).
- Developmental Studies Center, Child Development Project, 111 Deerwood Place, Suite 165, San Ramon, CA 94583 (415-838-7633).
- Ethics Resource Center, 1120 G Street NW, Suite 200, Washington, DC 20005 (202-434-8465).
- Jefferson Center for Character Education, 202 S. Lake Avenue, Suite 240, Pasadena, CA 91101 (818-792-8130).
- Josephson Institute of Ethics, 310 Washington Boulevard, Suite 104, Marina Del Rey, CA 90292 (310-306-1868).

LEARNING THAT IS NOT IMMEDIATELY OBSERVABLE

Unlike behaviorists, constructivists do not limit the definition of learning to that which is observable behavior, nor should you. Bits and pieces of new information are stored in short-term memory, where the new information is "rehearsed" until ready to be stored in long-term memory. If the information is not rehearsed, it eventually fades from short-term memory. If it is rehearsed and made meaningful through connections with other stored knowledge, then this new knowledge is transferred to and stored in long-term memory, either by building existing schemata or by forming new schemata. As a teacher, you must provide learning experiences that will result in the creation of new schemata as well as the modification of existing schemata.

To be an effective teacher, you are challenged to use performance-based criteria, but simultaneously with a teaching style that encourages the development of intrinsic sources of student motivation and allows, provides, and encourages coincidental learning—learning that goes beyond what might be considered predictable, immediately measurable, and representative of minimal expectations.

SUMMARY

As you reviewed curriculum documents and student textbooks, you undoubtedly found most of them well organized and useful. In your comparison and analysis of courses of study and teacher's editions of student textbooks, you probably discovered that many are accompanied by sequentially designed resource units from which the teacher can select and build specific teaching units. A resource unit usually consists of an extensive list of objectives, a large number and variety of activities, suggested materials, and extensive bibliographies for teacher and students.

As you may have also found, some courses of study contain actual teaching units that have been prepared by teachers of the school district. Beginning teachers and student teachers often ask, "How closely must I follow the school's curriculum guide or course of study?" To obtain an answer, you must talk with teachers and administrators of the school before you begin teaching.

In conclusion, your final decisions about what content to teach are guided by (1) discussions with other teachers, (2) review of state curriculum documents, local courses of study, and articles in professional journals, (3) your personal convictions, knowledge, and skills, and (4) the unique characteristics of your students.

In this chapter we explained the differences between the terms *aims, goals,* and *objectives.* Regardless of how these terms are defined, the important point is this: *teachers must be clear about what they want their students to learn and about the kinds of evidence needed to verify their learning, and they must communicate those things to the students so they are clearly understood.*

Many teachers do not bother to write specific objectives for all the learning activities in their teaching plans. However, when teachers do prepare specific objectives (by writing them themselves or by borrowing them from textbooks and other curriculum documents), teach toward them, and assess students' progress against them, student learning is enhanced; this is called **performance-based instruction** and **criterion-referenced measurement.** It is also known as an *aligned curriculum.* In schools that use outcome-based education mastery learning models, those models describe levels of mastery standards (rubrics) for each outcome. The taxonomies are of tremendous help in schools where teachers are expected to correlate learning activities to the school's outcome standards.

As a teacher, you will be expected to (1) plan your lessons well, (2) convey specific expectations to your students, and (3) assess their learning against that specificity. However, because it tends toward high objectivity, there is the danger that such performance-based teaching could become too objective, which can have negative consequences. If students are treated as objects, then the relationship between teacher and student becomes impersonal and counterproductive to real learning. Highly specific and impersonal teaching can be discouraging to serendipity, creativity, and the excitement of discovery, to say nothing of its possibly negative impact on the development of students' self-esteem.

Performance-based instruction works well when teaching toward mastery of basic skills, but the concept of mastery learning is inclined to imply that there is some foreseeable end to learning, an assumption that is obviously erroneous. With performance-based instruction, the source of student motivation tends to be extrinsic. Teacher expectations, marks and grades, society, and peer pressures are examples of extrinsic sources that drive student performance. To be a most effective teacher, you are challenged to use performance-based criteria together with a teaching style that encourages the development of intrinsic sources of student motivation and that allows for, provides for, and encourages coincidental learning—learning that goes beyond what might be considered as predictable, immediately measurable, and representative of minimal expectations. Part III of this book is designed to assist you in meeting that challenge. With a knowledge of the content of the school curriculum and the value of instructional objectives, you are now ready to prepare detailed instructional plans with daily lessons, the subject of the next chapter.

QUESTIONS FOR CLASS DISCUSSION

1. Have you observed or been a student of any classes using nonprint material as a substitution for student textbooks? If so, describe your observations for others in your class.
2. It is sometimes said that teaching less is better.[37] Explain the meaning and significance of that statement. Explain why you agree or disagree with the concept.
3. Recall your own schooling. What do you really remember? Most likely you remember projects, your presentations, the lengthy research you did, and your extra effort doing artwork to accompany your presentations. Maybe you remember a compliment by a teacher or a pat on the back by peers. Most likely you do *not* remember the massive amount of factual content that was covered. Discuss this and your feelings about it with your classmates.

4. Identify and describe observable behaviors that would enable you to tell whether a student is learning to think critically.
5. Some people say that it is easier to write behavioral objectives after a lesson has been taught. What is the significance of that notion?
6. Should a teacher encourage serendipitous (coincidental) learning? If no, why not? If so, describe ways that a teacher in your subject field can do it.
7. Describe the relationship between goals and objectives. Describe the relationship between scope and sequence and instructional goals and objectives. At any time during your teaching, should you ignore the planned scope and sequence, goals and objectives? If so, explain why, when, and to what extent. If not, explain why not.
8. Some people believe—and some fear—that the national curriculum standards are a first step toward national assessment of student learning. Explain how you feel about this and any concerns that you have.
9. From your current observations and fieldwork as related to this teacher preparation program, clearly identify one specific example of educational practice that seems contradictory to exemplary practice or theory as presented in this chapter. Present your explanation for the discrepancy.
10. Do you have questions generated by the content of this chapter? If you do, list them along with ways that answers might be found.

SUGGESTED READINGS

Airasian, P. W., and Walsh, M. E. "Constructivist Cautions." *Phi Delta Kappan* 78(6):444–449 (February 1997).

Alper, L., et al. "Problem-Based Mathematics—Not Just for the College Bound." *Educational Leadership* 53(8):18–21 (May 1996).

American Library Association. *Intellectual Freedom Manual.* 5th ed. Chicago: American Library Association, 1996.

American Textbook Council. *History Textbooks: A Standard and Guide.* 1994–95 edition. New York: American Textbook Council, 1994.

Arries, J. F. "Decoding the Social Studies Production of Chicano History." *Equity and Excellence in Education* 27(1):37–44 (April 1994).

Association for Supervision and Curriculum Development. *Curriculum Materials Directory.* Alexandria, VA: Association for Supervision and Curriculum Development, 1996.

Betts, F. "Only the Best: Hot Links to Good Resources." *Educational Leadership* 53(8):38–39 (May 1996).

Binko, J. B., and Neubert, G. A. *Teaching Geography in the Disciplines.* Bloomington, IN: Fastback 400, Phi Delta Kappa Educational Foundation, 1996.

Chapel, D. "Putting Science Back into Social Science." *Social Studies Review* 34(3):54–57 (Spring 1996).

Checkley, K. "Geography's Renaissance." *ASCD Curriculum Update* (Spring 1996).

Cohen, D. "What Standards for National Standards?" *Phi Delta Kappan* 76(10):751–757 (June 1995).

---

37. See, for example, F. N. Dempster, "Exposing Our Students to Less Should Help Them Learn More," *Phi Delta Kappan* 74(6):433–437 (February 1993).

Coxford, A. F., and Hirsch, C. R. "A Common Core of Math for All." *Educational Leadership* 53(8):22–25 (May 1996).

Eisner, E. W. "Standards for American Schools: Help or Hindrance?" *Phi Delta Kappan* 76(10):758–764 (June 1995).

Farivar, S. "Citizenship Education: What Is It?" *Social Studies Review* 34(3):58–64 (Spring 1996).

Gaddy, B. B., Hall, T. W., and Marzano, R. J. *School Wars: Resolving Our Conflicts over Religion and Values.* San Francisco: Jossey-Bass, 1996.

Glatthorn, A. A. *Content of the Curriculum.* 2nd ed. Alexandria, VA: Association for Supervision and Curriculum Development, 1995.

Gronlund, N. E. *How to Write and Use Instructional Objectives.* 5th ed. Upper Saddle River, NJ: Prentice Hall, 1995.

Haynes, C. *Religion in American History: What to Teach and How.* Alexandria, VA: Association for Supervision and Curriculum Development, 1990.

Johnson, D. W., and Johnson, R. T. *Reducing School Violence through Conflict Resolution.* Alexandria, VA: Association for Supervision and Curriculum Development, 1995.

Koba, S. B. "Narrowing the Achievement Gap in Science." *Educational Leadership* 53(8):14–17 (May 1996).

Kohn, A. "How Not to Teach Values: A Critical Look at Character Education." *Phi Delta Kappan* 78(6):429–439 (February 1997).

Lewis, A. C. "An Overview of the Standards Movement." *Phi Delta Kappan* 76(10):744–750 (June 1995).

Manno, B. V. "The New School Wars: Battles over Outcome-Based Education." *Phi Delta Kappan* 76(9):720–726 (May 1995).

Martin, B. L., and Briggs, L. J. *The Affective and Cognitive Domains.* Englewood Cliffs, NJ: Educational Technology Publications, 1986.

Martin, R. "African-American Women in History." *School Library Media Activities Monthly* 10(6):44–47 (February 1994).

McMillan, J. H. *Classroom Assessment: Principles and Practice for Effective Instruction.* Chapter 2. Needham Heights, MA: Allyn & Bacon, 1997.

McTighe, J. "What Happens between Assessments?" *Educational Leadership* 54(4):6–12 (December 1996/January 1997).

Monks, M. M., and Pistolis, D. R. *Hit List: Frequently Challenged Books for Young Adults.* Chicago, IL: Young Adult Library Services Association, 1996.

Phelan, P., ed. *High Interest—Easy Reading: An Annotated Booklist for Middle School and Senior High School.* 7th ed. Urbana, IL: National Council of Teachers of English, 1996.

Rogers, S., and Dana, B. *Outcome-Based Education: Concerns and Responses.* Bloomington, IN: Fastback 388, Phi Delta Kappa Educational Foundation, 1995.

Roucher, N., and Jovano-Kerr, J. "Can the Arts Maintain Integrity in Interdisciplinary Learning?" *Arts Education Policy Review* 96(4):20–25 (March/April 1995).

Samuels, B. G., and Beers, G. K., eds. *Your Reading: An Annotated Booklist for Middle School and Junior High, 1995–96 Edition.* NCTE Bibliography Series. Urbana, IL: National Council of Teachers of English, 1996.

Schmoker, M. "Setting Goals in Turbulent Times." In A. Hargreaves (ed.), *Rethinking Educational Change with Heart and Mind* (Alexandria, VA: ASCD 1997 Yearbook, Association for Supervision and Curriculum Development, 1997).

Shannon, P. "Can Standards Really Help?" *Clearing House* 68(4):229–232 (March/April 1995).

Staples, S. F. "What Johnny Can't Read: Censorship in American Libraries." *ALAN Review* 23(2):49–50 (Winter 1996).

Sternberg, R. J. "What Does It Mean to Be Smart?" *Educational Leadership* 54(6):20–24 (March 1997).

Sternberg, R. J., and Williams, W. M. *How to Develop Student Creativity.* Alexandria, VA: Association for Supervision and Curriculum Development, 1996.

Swiderek, B. "Censorship." *Journal of Adolescent & Adult Literacy* 39(7):592–594 (April 1996).

Vossler, J. M. "Beyond Stereotypes: Books about Other Cultures for Middle School Readers." *Middle School Journal* 28(3):54–57 (January 1997).

Zabaluk, B. L., and Samuels, S. J. *Readability: Its Past, Present, and Future.* Newark, DE: International Reading Association, 1988.

Zahorik, J. A. *Constructivist Teaching.* Bloomington, IN: Fastback 390, Phi Delta Kappa Educational Foundation, 1995.

Chapter

5

Preparing an Instructional Plan

The teacher's edition of the student textbook and other resource materials will expedite your planning but should not substitute for it. You must know how to create a good instructional plan. In this chapter you will learn how it is done. With that knowledge you will develop an instructional plan with daily lessons (see Exercises 5.6 and 5.7). Specifically, upon completion of this chapter you should be able to

1. Demonstrate an understanding of the value and components of a course syllabus.
2. Demonstrate an understanding of the similarities and differences between various types of instructional units.
3. Demonstrate an understanding of the difference between procedural knowledge and conceptual knowledge and the place for each in learning.
4. Demonstrate an understanding of the purpose and process of curriculum integration.
5. Have created one complete unit of instruction with sequential lesson plans.
6. Differentiate among preassessment, formative assessment, and summative assessment, and describe how and when each is used.
7. Explain the concept of planning as a continual process.
8. Demonstrate an understanding of the place and role of each of the four decision-making and thought-processing phases in unit planning and implementation.

PLANNING FOR INSTRUCTION: A THREE-LEVEL AND SEVEN-STEP PROCESS

As you learned from Chapter 4, complete planning for instruction occurs at three levels—the semester or year, the units, and the daily lessons. There are seven steps in

the process. This section identifies and describes each step. Some planning guidelines have previously been addressed and are included here to illustrate where they fit into the following seven-step planning procedure.

1. COURSE, GRADE LEVEL, AND SCHOOL GOALS. Consider and understand your curriculum goals and their relationship to the goals and the mission of the school. Your course is not isolated on Jupiter but is an integral part of the total school curriculum.

2. EXPECTATIONS. Consider topics and skills that you are expected to teach, such as those found in the course of study (Chapter 4).

3. ACADEMIC YEAR, SEMESTER, OR TRIMESTER PLAN. Think about the goals you want the students to reach months from now. Working from your tentative topic outline (see Exercise 4.5) and with the school calendar in hand, you will begin by deciding how much time should be devoted to each topic (or unit), penciling those times onto the outline. (Unless you are doing your planning at a computer, we suggest pencil because you will probably modify these times often.)

4. COURSE SCHEDULE. This schedule becomes a part of the course syllabus that is presented to students at the beginning (discussed in the next section). However, the schedule *must* remain flexible to allow for the unexpected, such as the cancellation or interruption of a class meeting or an extended study of a particular topic.

5. PLANS FOR EACH CLASS MEETING. Working from the calendar plan or the course schedule, you are ready to prepare plans for each class meeting, keeping in mind the abilities and interests of your students while making

decisions about appropriate strategies and learning experiences (the focus of Part III). The preparation of daily plans takes considerable time and continues throughout the year as you prepare instructional notes, demonstrations, discussion topics and questions, and classroom exercises and arrange for guest speakers, audiovisual materials, media equipment, field trips, and tools for the assessment of student learning. Because the content of each class meeting is often determined by the accomplishments of and your reflections upon the preceding one, your lessons are never "set in concrete" but need continual revisiting and assessment by you.

6. INSTRUCTIONAL OBJECTIVES.   Once you have the finalized schedule and as you prepare the daily plans, you will complete your preparation of the instructional objectives (begun in Exercise 4.12). Those objectives are critical for proper development of the next and final step.

7. ASSESSMENT.   The final step is to decide how to assess student achievement. Included in this component are your decisions about how you will accomplish **preassessment** (i.e., the assessment of what students know or think they know at the start of a new unit of study), **formative assessment** (the ongoing assessment during a unit of study, that is, what the students are learning), and **summative assessment** (the assessment of learning at the conclusion of a unit of study, that is, what the students have learned). Also included in the assessment component are your decisions about assignments and grading procedures (discussed in Chapter 11).

You will proceed through these steps as you develop your first instructional plan. However, first, let's consider the course syllabus.

THE COURSE SYLLABUS

A course syllabus is a written statement of information about the workings of a particular class. As a student in postsecondary education, you have seen a variety of syllabi written by professors, each with their individual ideas about what general and specific logistical information is most important for students to have about a course. Some instructors, however, err in thinking that a course outline constitutes a course syllabus; a course outline is only one component of a syllabus.

Although it may be true that some teachers do not use a course syllabus, at least as is described here, we believe they should. Related to that belief are several questions that we shall try to answer next, such as "Why should teachers use a syllabus?" "Of what value is it?" "What use can be made of it?" "What purpose does it fulfill?" "How do I develop one?" "Where do I start?" "What information

should be included?" "When should it be distributed to students?" and "How rigidly should it be followed?"

Reasons for a Syllabus

The course syllabus is printed information about the course that is usually presented to students on the first day or during the first week of school. As you will soon learn, the syllabus may be developed collaboratively with students. It should be designed so that it helps establish a rapport between students, parents or guardians, and the teacher, helps students feel at ease by providing an understanding of what is expected of them, and helps them to organize, conceptualize, and synthesize their learning experiences.

The syllabus should provide a reference, helping to eliminate misunderstandings and misconceptions about the nature of the class—its rules, expectations, procedures, requirements, and other policies. It should provide students with a sense of connectedness (often by allowing students to work collaboratively in groups and actually participate in fashioning *their* course syllabus).

The syllabus should also serve as a plan to be followed by the teacher and the students, and it should be a resource for substitute teachers and (when relevant) members of a teaching team. Each team member should have a copy of every other member's syllabus. In essence, the syllabus stands as documentation for what is taking place in the classroom for those outside the classroom (i.e., parents or guardians, administrators, other teachers and students).

Development of a Syllabus

Usually the syllabus, or at least portions of it, is prepared by the classroom teacher long before the first class meeting. If you maintain a syllabus template on your computer, then it is a simple task to customize it for each group of students that you teach. You may find it more useful if students participate in the development of the syllabus, thereby having an ownership of it and a commitment to its contents. By having input into the workings of a course and knowing that their opinions count, students will take more interest in what they are doing and learning. This empowerment of students has been demonstrated, for example, at East Paulding High School (Dallas, GA), where students in applied communications participate in developing the course syllabus by choosing literature selections, preparing study guides, creating project assignments, and devising assessment criteria.[1] Figure 5.1 shows steps you can use for a collaborative learning experience in which

---

1. Southern Regional Education Board, *1995 Outstanding Practices* (Atlanta: Southern Regional Education Board, 1995), p. 8. By permission.

Step 1

Sometime during the first few days of the course, arrange students in heterogeneous groups (mixed abilities) of three or four members to brainstorm the development of their syllabus.

Step 2

Instruct each group to spend five minutes listing everything they can think of that they would like to know about the course. Tell the class that a group *recorder* must be chosen to write their list of ideas on paper and then, when directed to do so, to transfer the list to the writing board or to sheets of butcher paper to be hung in the classroom for all to see (or on an overhead transparency—a transparency sheet and pen are made available to each group). Tell them to select a group *spokesperson* who will address the class, explaining the group's list. Each group could also appoint a *materials manager,* whose job is to see that the group has the necessary materials (e.g., pen, paper, transparency, chalk), and a *task master,* whose job is to keep the group on task and to report to the teacher when each task is completed.

Step 3

After five minutes, have the recorders prepare their lists. When a transparency or butcher paper is used, the lists can be prepared simultaneously while recorders remain with their groups. If using the writing board, then recorders, one at a time, write their lists on areas of the board that you have designated for each group's list.

Step 4

Have the spokesperson of each group explain the group's list. As this is being done, you should make a master list. If transparencies or butcher paper is being used rather than the writing board, you can ask for either as backup to the master list you have made.

Step 5

After all spokespersons have explained their lists, you ask the class collectively for additional input. "Can anyone think of anything else that should be added?"

Step 6

You now take the master list and design a course syllabus, being careful to address each question and to include items of importance that students may have omitted. However, your guidance during the preceding five steps should ensure that all bases have been covered.

Step 7

At the next class meeting, give each student a copy of the final syllabus. Discuss its content. (Duplicate copies to distribute to colleagues, especially those on your teaching team, interested administrators, and to parents and guardians at back-to-school night.)

Figure 5.1
Steps for involving students in the development of their course syllabus.

students spend approximately 30 minutes during the first (or an early) class meeting brainstorming the content of their syllabus.

Content of a Syllabus

The syllabus should be concise, matter-of-fact, uncomplicated, and brief—perhaps no more than two pages—and include the following information:

DESCRIPTIVE INFORMATION ABOUT THE COURSE.   This includes the teacher's name, course title, class period, days of class meetings, beginning and ending times, and room number.

EXPLANATION OF THE IMPORTANCE OF THE COURSE. This information should describe the course, cite how students will profit from it, tell whether the course is a required course and, if relevant, from which program in the curriculum—for example, a core curriculum course, a cocurriculum course, an elective, a vocational-technical course, an advanced placement course, or some other arrangement.

MATERIALS REQUIRED.   Explain what materials are needed—such as a textbook, notebook, binder, calculator, supplementary readings, apron, safety goggles—and state which are supplied by the school and which must be supplied by each student. Also, specify what materials must be brought to class each day.

COURSE GOALS AND OBJECTIVES.   This should include the major goals and a few major objectives.

TYPES OF ASSIGNMENTS THAT WILL BE GIVEN.   These should be clearly explained in as much detail as possible this early in the course, including your policy regarding late work (discussed in Chapter 8). There should also be a statement about where daily assignments will be posted in the classroom (a regular place each day) and about the procedures for completing and turning in assignments and, if relevant, for making corrections to assignments already turned in. Also, parents will need to know your expectations of them regarding helping with assignments.

ATTENDANCE EXPECTATIONS.   Explain how attendance is related to grades and the procedure for making up work. Typical school policy allows that, for an excused absence, missed work can be completed without penalty if done within a reasonable period of time after the student returns to school.

ASSESSMENT AND GRADING PROCEDURES.   Explain the assessment procedures and the procedures for deter-

mining grades. Will there be quizzes, tests, homework, projects, and group work? What will be their formats, coverage, and weights in the procedure for determining grades? For group work, how will the contributions and learning of individual students be evaluated? (For these topics, you may need to refer to Chapter 11.)

OTHER INFORMATION SPECIFIC TO THE COURSE.   Field trips? Special privileges? Computer work? Homework hot line? Classroom procedures and rules for expected behavior (discussed in Chapter 3) should be included here.

Now do Exercises 5.1 and 5.2.

EXERCISE 5.1

Collaborating on the Content of a Syllabus

Instructions: The purpose of this exercise is to begin your thinking about preparing a syllabus for use in your teaching. From the following list of items that might appear on a syllabus, identify (by circling) all those you would include in your own syllabus. And, for each, explain why you would or would not include that item. Then share the syllabus with your classmates. After sharing, you might want to make revisions in your own list.

1. Name of teacher (my name): _____

2. Course title (and/or grade level): _____

3. Room number: _____

4. Beginning and ending times: _____

5. Time when students could schedule a conference with teacher:

   _____

   _____

6. Course description:

   _____

   _____

   _____

   _____

7. Course philosophy or rationale (underline which):

   _____

   _____

   _____

   _____

8. Instructional format (such as lecture-discussion, student-centered learning groups, or laboratory-centered):

   _____

   _____

9. Absence policy:

   _____

   _____

10. Tardy policy:

   _____

   _____

11. Classroom procedures and rules for behavior:

_____

_____

_____

_____

_____

12. Goals of course:

_____

_____

_____

_____

_____

13. Objectives of course:

_____

_____

_____

_____

_____

14. Policy about plagiarism:

_____

_____

_____

_____

_____

15. Name of textbook and other supplementary materials:

_____

_____

_____

_____

_____

16. Policy about use and care of textbook and other reading materials:

_____

_____

_____

_____

_____

_____

17. Materials to be supplied by student:

_____

_____

_____

_____

18. Assignments:

_____

_____

_____

_____

_____

_____

19. Policy about homework assignments (due dates, format, late assignments, weights for grades):

_____

_____

_____

_____

_____

_____

20. Course relationship to adviser-advisee program, core, cocurricular, exploratories, or some other aspect of the school curriculum:

_____

_____

_____

_____

_____

_____

21. Grading procedure:

_____

_____

_____

_____

_____

22. Study skills:

_____

_____

_____

_____

_____

23. Themes to be studied:

_____

_____

_____

_____

_____

24. Field trips and other special activities:

_____

_____

_____

_____

_____

25. Group work policies and types:

_____

_____

_____

_____

_____

26. Other members of the teaching team and their roles:

_____

_____

_____

_____

_____

27. Tentative daily schedule:

_____

_____

_____

_____

28. Other (specify):

_____

_____

_____

_____

_____

29. Other (specify):

_____

_____

_____

_____

_____

30. Other (specify):

_____

_____

_____

_____

_____

EXERCISE 5.2

Preparing a Course Syllabus—An Exercise in Collaborative Thinking

Instructions: The purpose of this exercise is to prepare (in a group) a syllabus for a course that you intend to teach. Using your results from Exercise 5.1, work in groups of three or four members to develop one syllabus for a course you and other group members may some day teach. Each group should produce one course syllabus that represents that group's collaborative thinking; the finished product should be duplicated and shared with the entire class. Discuss within your group the pros and cons of having student input into the course syllabus (see Figure 5.1). Share the results of that discussion with the entire class.

THE INSTRUCTIONAL UNIT

The instructional unit is a major subdivision of a course (for one course there are several to many units of instruction) and consists of instruction planned around a central theme, topic, issue, or problem. Organizing the content of the semester or year into units makes the teaching process more manageable than when no plan or only random choices are made by a teacher.

Whether an interdisciplinary thematic unit (known also as an integrated unit), or a stand-alone standard subject unit, the instructional unit is not unlike a chapter in a book, an act or scene in a play, or a phase of work when undertaking a project such as building a house or an airplane. Breaking down information or actions into component parts and then grouping the related parts makes sense out of learning and doing. The unit brings a sense of cohesiveness and structure to student learning and avoids the piecemeal approach that might otherwise unfold. You can learn to articulate lessons within, between, and among unit plans and focus on important elements while not ignoring tangential information of importance. Students remember "chunks" of information, especially when those chunks are related to specific units.

Types of Instructional Units

Although the steps for developing any type of instructional unit are essentially the same, units can be organized in a number of ways, basically differentiated and described as follows.

CONVENTIONAL UNIT. A conventional unit (known also as a standard unit) consists of a series of lessons centered on a topic, theme, major concept, or block of subject matter. Each lesson builds on the previous lesson by contributing additional subject matter, providing further illustrations, and supplying more practice or other added instruction, all of which are aimed at bringing about mastery of the knowledge and skills on which the standard unit is centered.

INTEGRATED UNIT. When a conventional unit is centered on a theme, such as transportation, then the unit may be referred to as a **thematic unit.** When, by design, the thematic unit integrates disciplines, such as one that combines the learning of science and mathematics or social studies and English/language arts or all four of these core disciplines, then it is called an *integrated* (or *interdisciplinary*) *thematic unit.*

SELF-INSTRUCTIONAL UNIT. A self-instructional unit (known also as a modular unit) is a unit of instruction that is designed for individualized or modularized self-instruction. Such a unit is designed for independent,

individual study; because it covers much less content than the units previously described, it can generally be completed in a much shorter time, usually an hour or less. The unit consists of instruction, references, self-check exercises, problems, and all other information and materials that a student needs to independently carry out the unit of work. Consequently, students can work on the units individually at their own speed, and different students can be working on different units at the same time—yet another example of using multi-level instruction. Students who successfully finish a modular unit can move on to another unit of work without waiting for the other students to catch up. Such units are essential ingredients of continuous-progress (multiage or nongraded) programs. Whether for purposes of remediation, enrichment, or make-up, self-instructional units work especially well when done at and in conjunction with a learning activity center (both of which are discussed further in Chapter 8).

CONTRACT UNIT. A contract unit is an individualized unit of instruction for which a student agrees (contracts with the teacher) to carry out certain activities. Some contract units have a variable-letter-grade agreement built into them. For example, specified on the contract may be information such as the following:

> For an A grade, you must complete activities 1–5, satisfactorily complete six of the optional activities, and receive a score of no less than 85 percent on the unit test.
>
> For a grade of B, you must complete activities 1–5, satisfactorily complete four of the optional related activities, and receive a score of no less than 80 percent on the unit test.
>
> For a grade of C, you must complete activities 1–5, satisfactorily complete two of the optional related activities, and receive a score of no less than 70 percent on the unit test.
>
> To pass with a D grade, you must complete activities 1–5 and receive a score of no less than 60 percent on the unit test.

Six Steps for Planning and Developing Any Unit of Instruction

For the several types of unit plans, the steps in planning and developing the unit are the same and are detailed in the following paragraphs.

1. *Select a suitable theme, topic, issue, or problem.* These may be already laid out in your course of study or textbook or may already have been agreed to by members of the teaching team.

2. *Select the goals of the unit.* The goals are written as an overview or rationale, covering what the unit is about and what the students are to learn. In planning the goals, you should (a) become as familiar as possible with the topic and materials used, (b) consult curriculum documents, such as courses of study, state frameworks, and resource units for ideas, (c) decide

the content and procedures (i.e., what the students should learn about the topic and how), (d) write the rationale or overview, where you summarize what you expect the students will learn about the topic, and (e) be sure your goals are congruent with those of the course or grade-level program.

3. *Select suitable specific learning objectives.* In doing this, you should (a) include understandings, skills, attitudes, appreciations, and ideals; (b) be specific, avoiding vagueness and generalizations; (c) write the objectives in behavioral (performance) terms; and (d) be as certain as possible that the objectives will contribute to the major learning described in the overview.

4. *Detail the instructional procedures.* These procedures include the subject content and the learning activities, established as a series of lessons. Proceed with the following steps in your initial planning of the instructional procedures.

  a. By referring to curriculum documents, resource units, and colleagues as resources, gather ideas for learning activities that might be suitable for the unit.

  b. Check the learning activities to make sure that they will actually contribute to the learning designated in your objectives, discarding ideas that do not.

  c. Make sure that the learning activities are feasible. Can you afford the time, effort, or expense? Do you have the necessary materials and equipment? If not, can they be obtained? Are the activities suited to the intellectual and maturity levels of your students?

  d. Check resources available to be certain that they support the content and learning activities.

  e. Decide how to introduce the unit. Provide introductory activities that will arouse student interest; inform students of what the unit is about; help you learn about your students— their interests, abilities, experiences, and present knowledge of the topic; provide transitions that bridge this topic with that which students have already learned; and involve the students in the planning.

  f. Plan developmental activities that will sustain student interest, provide for individual student differences, promote the learning as cited in the specific objectives, and promote a project.

  g. Plan culminating activities that will summarize what has been learned, bring together loose ends, apply what has been learned to new situations, and provide transfer to the unit that follows.

5. *Plan for preassessment and assessment of student learning.* Preassess what students already know or think they know. Assessment of student progress in achievement of the learning objectives (formative evaluation) should permeate the entire unit (that is, as often as possible, assessment should be a component of daily lessons). Plan to gather information in several ways, including informal observations, checklist observations of student performance and their portfolios, and paper-and-pencil tests. Assessment must be congruent with the specific learning objectives.

6. *Provide for the materials and tools of instruction.* The unit cannot function without materials. Therefore, long before the unit begins you must plan for media equipment and materials, references, reading materials, reproduced materials, and community resources. Librarians and media center personnel are usually more than willing to assist in finding appropriate materials to support a unit of instruction. Material that is not available to the students is of no help to them.

Follow those six steps to develop any type of unit. In addition to the six steps, there are two general points that should be made. First, there is no single best format for a teaching unit. Particular formats may be best for specific disciplines, topics, and types of activities. (Samples units from various disciplines are provided in the Appendix, each with one sample lesson; see also Figure 5.8.) During your student teaching, your college or university program for teacher preparation and/or your cooperating teacher(s) may have a format that you will be expected to follow. Regardless of the format, the unit plan should include the seven items as presented in Team 1 of Exercise 5.7.

Second, there is no set time period that a unit plan should cover, although, for specific units, curriculum guides will recommend certain time spans. Units may extend for a minimum of several days or, as in the case of interdisciplinary thematic units, for several weeks. However, be aware that when conventional units last more than two or three weeks they tend to lose the character of clearly identifiable units. For any unit of instruction, the exact time duration will be dictated by several factors, including the topic, problem, or theme, the grade level, and the interests and abilities of the students.

CURRICULUM INTEGRATION

Many teachers realize that much of the learning in each discipline can be made more effective and longer lasting when it is integrated with the whole curriculum, and made meaningful to the lives of the students, rather than when a subject is simply taught as an unrelated and separate discipline at the same time each day.

CLASSROOM VIGNETTE
Advice to Beginning Teachers: A Precious Moment in Teaching

Aside from the preceding discussion of teaching units, we share with you this teaching vignette that we think is not only very humorous but also indicative of creative thinking. While teaching an 11th-grade English class, the teacher began a lesson with the question, "What comes to your mind when you hear the words *Puritan* and *Pilgrim?*" Without hesitation, one young man replied, "Cooking oil and John Wayne." To us, that represented a rare and precious moment in teaching and reaffirmed our belief that every beginning teacher should maintain throughout his teaching career a journal in which such intrinsically rewarding events are recorded so they can be reviewed and enjoyed years later.

Procedural and Conceptual Knowledge

If learning is defined only as being the accumulation of bits and pieces of information, then we already know how that is acquired and how to teach it. However, the accumulation of pieces of information is at the lowest end of a spectrum of types of learning and leads to what is sometimes referred to as *procedural knowledge.* For higher levels of thinking and for learning that is most meaningful and longest lasting, referred to as *conceptual knowledge,* the results of research support using a curriculum in which disciplines are integrated and instructional techniques that involve the learners in social-interactive learning, such as cooperative learning, peer tutoring, and cross-age teaching.[2] (Procedural knowledge and conceptual knowledge as related to *authentic learning* are discussed further in the next chapter.)

The Spectrum of Integrated Curriculum

When learning about integrated curriculum, it is easy to be confused by the plethora of terms that are used, such as *integrated studies, thematic instruction, multidisciplinary teaching, integrated curriculum, interdisciplinary curriculum,* and *interdisciplinary thematic instruction.* In essence, regardless of which of these terms is being used, the reference is to the same thing.

Because it is not always easy to tell where the term *curriculum* leaves off and the term *instruction* begins, let's assume for now that, for the sake of better understanding the meaning of integrated curriculum, there is no difference between curriculum and instruction. In other words, for the intent of this discussion, whether we use the term *integrated curriculum* or *integrated instruction,* we will be referring to the same thing.

DEFINITION OF INTEGRATED CURRICULUM. **Integrated curriculum** (or any of its aforementioned synonyms) refers to *both a way of teaching and a way of planning and organizing the instructional program so that the discrete disciplines of subject matter are related to one another in a design that (1) matches the developmental needs of the learners and (2) helps to connect their learning in ways that are meaningful to their current and past experiences.* In that respect, integrated curriculum is the antithesis of traditional disparate subject-matter-oriented teaching and curriculum designations.

INTEGRATED CURRICULA PAST AND PRESENT. The reason for the various terms is, in part, because the concept of integrated curriculum is not new. In fact, it has had a roller-coaster ride throughout most of the history of education in this country. Over time those efforts to integrate student learning have had varying labels.

The most recent popularity stems from the late 1950s, with some of the discovery-oriented, student-centered projects supported by the National Science Foundation. Some of these are *Elementary School Science* (ESS), a hands-on and integrated science program for grades K–6; *Man: A Course of Study* (MACOS), a hands-on, anthropology-based program for fifth graders; and *Environmental Studies* (later called *ESSENCTIA*), an interdisciplinary program for use at all grades, K–12, regardless of subject-matter orientation. The popularity of integrated curriculum also stems from the middle school movement that began in the 1960s and from the whole-language movement in language arts that started in the 1980s.

Current interest in the development and implementation of integrated curriculum and instruction has risen from at least three sources: (1) the success of curriculum integration that has been enjoyed by many schools, (2) the literature-based movement in reading and language arts, and (3) research in cognitive science and neuroscience about how people learn.

---

2. See, for example, articles in the theme issue of *Educational Leadership* 49(2) (October 1994).

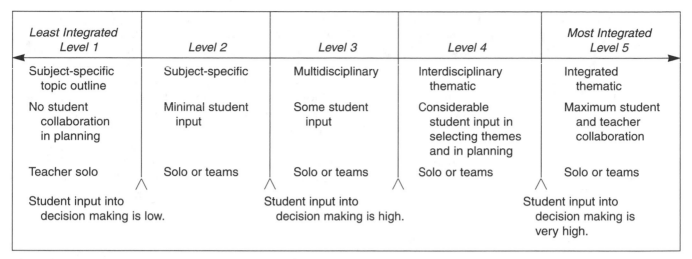

Figure 5.2
Levels of curriculum integration.

An integrated curriculum approach may not necessarily be the best approach for every school, or the best for all learning for every student, nor is it necessarily the manner by which every teacher should or must always plan and teach. As evidenced by practice, the truth of this statement becomes obvious. And, as you should be well aware of now, we, the authors of this resource guide, strongly believe that a teacher's best choice of an approach to instruction—and to classroom management—is an eclectic one.

Levels of Curriculum Integration

In attempts to connect students' learning with their experiences, efforts fall at various places on a spectrum or continuum, from the least integrated instruction (level 1) to the most integrated (level 5), as illustrated in Figure 5.2. It is not our intent that this illustration be interpreted as going from "worst-case scenario" (far left) to "best-case scenario" (far right), although some people may interpret it in exactly that way. It is meant solely to show how efforts to integrate fall on a continuum of sophistication and complexity. We now describe each level of the continuum.

Level 1

Level 1 is the traditional organization of curriculum and classroom instruction, in which teachers plan and arrange the subject-specific scope and sequence in the format of topic outlines, much as you did for Exercise 4.5. If there is an attempt to help students connect their learning and their experiences, then it is up to individual classroom teachers to do it. A student who moves during the school day from classroom to classroom, teacher to teacher, subject to subject, and one topic to another is likely learning in a level 1 instruc-

tional environment. A topic in science, for example, might be earthquakes. A related topic in social studies might be the social consequences of natural disasters. These two topics may or may not be studied by a student at the same time.

Level 2

If the same students are learning English/language arts, social studies/history, mathematics, or science using a thematic approach rather than a topic outline, then they are learning at level 2. At this level, themes for one discipline are not necessarily planned and coordinated to correspond to or integrate with themes of another or to be taught simultaneously. The difference between what is a topic and what is a theme is not always clear. But, for example, whereas earthquakes and social consequences of natural disasters are topics, natural disasters could be the theme or umbrella under which these two topics could fall. At this level, the students may have minimal input into the decision making involved in planning themes and content.

Level 3

When the same students are learning two or more of their core subjects (English/language arts, social studies/history, mathematics, or science) around a common theme, such as natural disasters, from one or more teachers, they are learning at level 3 integration. At this level, teachers agree on a common theme, then they *separately* deal with that theme in their individual subject areas, usually at the same time during the school year. So what the student is learning from a teacher in one class is related to and coordinated with what the student is concurrently learning in another or several others. Some authors may refer to levels 2 and

3 as *coordinated curriculum*. At level 3, students may have some input into the decision making involved in selecting and planning themes and content.

Level 4

When teachers and students do collaborate on a common theme and its content and when discipline boundaries begin to disappear as teachers teach about this common theme, either solo or as an interdisciplinary teaching team (as discussed in Chapter 1), level 4 integration is achieved. This is the level at which many exemplary middle schools function.

Level 5

When teachers and their students have collaborated on a common theme and its content, discipline boundaries are truly blurred during instruction, and teachers of several grade levels and various subjects teach toward student understanding of aspects of the common theme, this is level 5, an integrated thematic approach.[3]

Procedure for Planning and Developing an Interdisciplinary Thematic Unit

The six unit planning and development steps outlined previously are essential for planning any type of teaching unit, including the interdisciplinary unit.

The primary responsibility for the development of interdisciplinary thematic units can depend on a single teacher or on the cooperation of several teachers, who, in the case of secondary schools, represent several disciplines. Remember, as discussed in Chapter 1, this interdisciplinary team may meet daily during a common planning time. Flexible scheduling allows for instructional blocks so that team members can have such common time, and unit lessons can likewise be less constrained by time.

A teaching team may develop from one to four interdisciplinary thematic units a year. Over time, then, a team will have several units that are available for implementation. However, the most effective units are often those that are the most current or the most meaningful to students. This means that ever-changing global, national, and local topics provide a veritable smorgasbord from which to choose, and teaching teams must constantly update old units and develop new and exciting ones.

One teaching team's unit should not conflict with another's at the same or another grade level. If a school has two or more teams at the same grade level

that involve the same disciplines, for example, the teams may want to develop units on different themes and share their products. For example, a ninth-grade team must guard against developing a unit quite similar to one that the students had or will have at another grade level. Open lines of communication within, between, and among teams and schools are critical to the success of thematic teaching.

Because developing interdisciplinary thematic units is an essential task for many of today's teachers, teacher candidates should learn this process now. One other point needs to be made: An interdisciplinary thematic unit can be prepared and taught by one teacher, but more often it is prepared and taught by a team of teachers. When the latter is the case, the instructional strategy is referred to as interdisciplinary thematic team teaching. Most often, the team is composed of teachers from at least four areas: social studies or history, language arts or English, mathematics, and science. However, a thematic unit and a teaching team might also consist of fewer than four, for example, just math and science, English and history, an academic discipline and a vocational class, or some other combination of subjects. Here are a few examples:

- *Elk Grove High School* (Elk Grove, CA). Teachers from the English and history departments worked together with all sophomore students on a project that had an Elizabethan theme.
- *Manatee High School* (Bradenton, FL). Students from mathematics and vocational business studies worked together on a backyard swimming pool project; students from a computer-assisted drafting class and an honors geometry class designed and built a nine-hole miniature golf course; and students from marketing classes and foreign language classes worked together in an examination of international laws and customs.
- *North Penn High School* (Lansdale, PA). Students in classes in child development, mathematics, and manufacturing combined efforts to design and produce equipment for the school's child development program playground, including a 40-foot-long simulated train consisting of a locomotive and four cars. All students submitted papers for their English classes about the project.
- *Tolsia High School* (Fort Gay, WV). Students from English and from vocational classes in horticulture worked together to design and build a scale-model medieval town complete with castles.[4]

---

3. For detailed accounts of teaching at this level of integration, see C. Stevenson and J. F. Carr, eds., *Integrated Studies in the Middle Grades* (New York: Teachers College Press, 1993).

4. The Florida, West Virginia, and Pennsylvania examples are from Southern Regional Education Board, pp. 11, 25, and 26, respectively. By permission of the Southern Regional Education Board.

Steps in Developing an Interdisciplinary Thematic Unit[5]

The steps in developing an ITU are as follows:

1. *Agree on the nature or source of the unit.* Team members should view the interdisciplinary approach as a collective effort in which all members (and other faculty) can participate if appropriate. Write what you want the students to receive from interdisciplinary instruction. Troubleshoot possible stumbling blocks.

2. *Discuss subject-specific frameworks, goals, and objectives as well as curriculum guidelines, textbooks, supplemental materials, and units already in place for the school year.* Focus on what you must teach, and explain the scope and sequence of the teaching so that all team members understand the constraints.

3. *Choose a topic and develop a time line.* From the information provided by each subject-specialist teacher in step 2, start listing possible topics that can be drawn from within the existing course outlines. Give-and-take is essential here, as some topics will fit certain subjects better than others. The chief goal is to find a topic that can be adapted to each subject without detracting from the educational plan already in place. This may require choosing and merging content from two or more other units previously planned. The theme is then drawn from the topic. When considering a theme, you should ask these questions:

- Is the theme within the realm of understanding and experience of the teacher involved?
- Will the theme interest all members of the team?
- Do we have sufficient materials and resources to supply information we might need?
- Does the theme lend itself to active learning experiences?
- Can this theme lead to a unit that is of the proper duration, not too short and not too long?
- Is the theme helpful, worthwhile, and pertinent to the course objectives?
- Will the theme be of interest to students, and will it motivate them to do their best?
- Is the theme sufficiently unfamiliar to teachers so that they can share in the excitement of the learning?
- Will this theme be of interest to students, and will it motivate them to do their best?

4. *Establish two time lines.* The first is for the team only and is to ensure that each member will meet the deadlines for specific work required in developing the unit. The second time line is for both students and teachers and shows how long the unit will be, when it will start, and in which classes it will be taught.

5. *Develop the scope and sequence for content and instruction.* To develop the unit, follow the six steps for planning and developing a unit of instruction outlined earlier in this chapter. This should be done by each team member as well as by the group during common planning time so that members can coordinate dates and activities in logical sequence and depth. This is an organic process and will generate both ideas and anxiety. Under the guidance of the team leader, members should strive to keep this anxiety at a level conducive to learning, experimenting, and arriving at group consensus.

6. *Share goals and objectives.* Each team member should have a copy of the goals and objectives of every other team member. This helps to refine the unit and lesson plans and to prevent unnecessary overlap and confusion.

7. *Give the unit a name.* The unit has been fashioned and is held together by the theme you have chosen. Giving the theme a name and using that name tell the students that this unit of study is integrated, important, and meaningful to school and to life.

8. *Share subject-specific units, lesson plans, and printed and nonprinted materials.* Exchange the finalized unit to obtain one another's comments and suggestions. Keep a copy of each teacher's unit(s) as a resource, and see if you could present a lesson using it as your basis (some modification may be necessary).

9. *Field-test the unit.* Beginning at the scheduled time and date, present the lessons. Team members may trade classes from time to time. Team teaching may take place when two or more classes can be combined for instruction (if a classroom space large enough is available), such as is possible with block scheduling.

10. *Evaluate and perhaps adjust and revise the unit.* Team members should discuss their successes and failures during their common planning time and determine what needs to be changed and how and when that should be done to make the unit successful. Adjustments can be made along the way (formative assessments), and revisions for future use can be made after the unit is taught (summative assessment).

The preceding ten steps are not absolutes and should be viewed only as guides. Differing teaching teams and levels of teacher experience and knowledge make the strict adherence to any plan less productive than would be the use of group-generated plans. For instance, some teachers have found that the next to last point under step 3 could state exactly the opposite; they recommend that the topic for an interdisciplinary unit should be one that a teacher or a teaching team already knows well. In practice, the process that works well—one that results in meaningful learning for the students and in positive feelings about themselves, about learning, and about school—is the appropriate process.

Now do Exercises 5.3 and 5.4.

---

5. See also P. L. Roberts and R. D. Kellough, *A Guide for Developing an Interdisciplinary Thematic Unit* (Upper Saddle River, NJ: Prentice Hall, 1996).

EXERCISE 5.3
Generating Ideas for Interdisciplinary Units

Instructions: The purpose of this exercise is to use brainstorming to generate a list of potential topics suitable as interdisciplinary units. Divide your class into groups of three to seven. Each group is to decide the grade or age level for which its unit ideas will be generated. If the group chooses, cooperative learning can be used; group members are then assigned roles such as facilitator, recorder, reporter, monitor of thinking processes, on-task monitor, and so on. Each group is to generate as many topics as possible. One member of each group should record all ideas. Reserve discussion of ideas until no further topics are generated. Lists can be shared in the large group.

Grade-level interest of the group: _____

1. Existing subject-area content units (as the group knows them to be or as they are predicted to exist): _____

   _____

   _____

2. Current topics of

   a. Global interest: _____

   _____

   _____

   b. National interest: _____

   _____

   _____

   c. State-wide interest: _____

   _____

   _____

   d. Local interest: _____

   _____

   _____

   e. Interest to the school: _____

   _____

   _____

   f. Interest to students of this age: _____

   _____

   _____

For Your Notes

EXERCISE 5.4
Integrating the Topic

Instructions: The purpose of this exercise is to practice weaving interdisciplinary themes into curricula. In groups of three or four, choose one idea that was generated during Exercise 5.3, and derive a list of suggestions about how that theme could be woven into the curricula of various classes, programs, and activities, as indicated below. It is possible that not all areas listed are relevant to the grade level to which your group is addressing its work. Cooperative learning can be used, with appropriate roles assigned to group members. One person in the group should be the recorder. Upon completion, share your group's work (the process and product of which will be much like that of an actual interdisciplinary teaching team) with the class. Copies should be made available to those who want them.

Unit theme: _____

1. In core classes

   a. English: _____

   _____

   _____

   b. Social studies: _____

   _____

   _____

   c. Mathematics: _____

   _____

   _____

   d. Science: _____

   _____

   _____

   e. Reading: _____

   _____

   _____

   f. Physical education: _____

   _____

   _____

   g. Art: _____

   _____

   _____

h. Music: _____

_____

_____

2. In cocurricular programs and activities

a. Electives: _____

_____

_____

b. Clubs: _____

_____

_____

c. School functions: _____

_____

_____

d. Assemblies: _____

_____

_____

e. Intramurals: _____

_____

_____

f. Study skills: _____

_____

_____

3. In exploratories: _____

_____

_____

4. In homerooms: _____

_____

5. Explain how multicultural components could be incorporated into the unit. _____

_____

_____

6. As individuals and as a group, how productive was this exercise? _____

_____

WRITING LESSON PLANS: RATIONALE, ASSUMPTIONS, AND VALUE

As described at the beginning of this chapter, step 5 of the seven steps of instructional planning is the preparation for class meetings. The process of designing a lesson is important in getting you to plan a lesson that provides the most effective learning for the students. We next present a rationale for, description of, and guidelines for detailed lesson planning.

Rationale for Writing Lesson Plans

This section discusses written plans used by the classroom teacher as tools in the teaching and learning process. Therefore, consider the following reasons why beginning teachers must write detailed lesson plans.

Written and detailed lesson plans provide a sense of security, which is especially useful to a beginning teacher. Like the rudder of a ship, a written lesson plan helps keep you on course. Without it, you are likely to drift aimlessly. Sometimes a disturbance in the classroom can distract from the lesson, causing the teacher to get off track or forget a part of the lesson. A written and detailed lesson plan helps the teacher get back on track.

Written lesson plans cause teachers to be or become reflective decision makers. Without a written plan, it is difficult or impossible to analyze how something might have been planned or implemented differently after the lesson has been taught.

Written lesson plans help you organize material and search for loopholes, loose ends, or incomplete content. Careful and thorough planning during the preactive phase of instruction includes anticipation of how the lesson activities will develop as the lesson is being taught. You will actually visualize yourself in the classroom setting teaching your students, using that visualization to anticipate possible problems.

Written lesson plans serve as resources for the next time you teach the same or a similar lesson and are useful for teacher self-evaluation and for the evaluation of student learning and the curriculum.

Written lesson plans provide substitute teachers and members of a teaching team with a guide to follow if you are absent. Written plans also help other members of the teaching team understand what you are doing and how you are doing it. This is especially important when implementing an interdisciplinary thematic unit.

Carefully preparing and writing lesson plans shows everyone—your students, your colleagues, your administrator, and, if you are a student teacher, your college or university supervisor—that you are a committed professional.

The preceding reasons clearly express the need to write detailed lesson plans. The list is not exhaustive, however, and you may discover additional reasons why written lesson plans are crucial to effective teaching. Master teachers are experts in the art of lesson planning. They can construct exemplary lesson plans that are workable and validated in applied research. Two points must be made: (1) lesson planning is an ongoing process, even for competent veteran teachers; and (2) teachers must take time to plan, reflect on, write, test, evaluate, and rewrite their plans to reach optimal performance. In short, writing lesson plans is important work.

The Written Lesson Plan

Notice that we have not titled this section the Daily Lesson Plan. That's because when you prepare a lesson plan, it may or may not be a daily plan. In some instances, a single lesson plan may run for more than one class period, perhaps two or three. In other instances, the lesson plan is, in fact, a daily plan and may run for an entire class period or, in instances of block scheduling, for less than an entire two-hour block of time. In the latter case, more than one lesson plan may be used during that block of time. See The Problem of Time later in this chapter.

Effective teachers are always planning for their classes. For the long range, they plan the scope and sequence and develop content. Within this long-range planning, they develop units, and within units, they design the activities to be used and the assessments of learning to be done. They familiarize themselves with books, materials, media, and innovations in their fields of interest. Yet, despite all this planning activity, the lesson plan remains pivotal to the planning process.

Assumptions about Lesson Planning

Not all teachers need elaborate written plans for every lesson. Sometimes effective and skilled teachers need only a sketchy outline. Sometimes they may not need written plans at all. Experienced teachers who have taught the topic many times in the past may need only the presence of a class of students to stimulate a pattern of presentation that has often been successful. Frequent use of old patterns, however, may lead one into the rut of unimaginative teaching. In addition, researchers of educational practices have substantiated repeatedly the obsolescence of many past classroom practices.

Considering the diversity among teachers, their instructional styles, their students, and research findings, certain assumptions can be made about lesson planning. Ten assumptions are

1. Not all teachers need elaborate written plans for all lessons.
2. Beginning teachers need to prepare detailed written lesson plans.

3. Some subject-matter fields, topics, or learning activities require more detailed planning than others do.

4. Some experienced teachers have clearly defined goals and objectives in mind even though they have not written them into lesson plans.

5. The depth of knowledge a teacher has about a subject or topic influences the amount of planning necessary for the lessons.

6. The skill a teacher has in remaining calm and in following a trend of thought in the presence of distraction will influence the amount of detail necessary when planning activities and writing the lesson plan.

7. A plan is more likely to be carefully plotted when it is written out.

8. The diversity of students within today's classroom necessitates careful and thoughtful consideration about individualizing the instruction; these considerations are best implemented when they have been thoughtfully written into lesson plans.

9. Although we will share with you what we refer to as a preferred format, there is no particular pattern or format that all teachers need to follow when writing out plans. (Some teacher-preparation programs have agreed on certain lesson plan formats for their teacher candidates; you need to know if this is the case for your program.) Obviously, we believe that, initially, beginning teachers should follow our preferred format as closely as possible.

10. Competent teachers have a planned pattern of instruction for every lesson, whether that plan is written out or not.

The Value of Written Lesson Plans

Well-written lesson plans have many uses. They give a teacher an agenda or outline to follow in teaching a lesson. They give a substitute teacher a basis for presenting appropriate lessons to a class. They are certainly useful when a teacher is planning to use the same lesson in the future. They provide the teacher with something to fall back on in case of a memory lapse, an interruption, or a distraction such as a call from the office or a fire drill. Using a written plan demonstrates to students that you care and are working for them. Above all, written plans provide beginners with security, because with a carefully prepared plan a beginning teacher can walk into a classroom with a confidence gained from having developed a sensible framework for that day's instruction.

Thus, as a beginning teacher, you should make considerably detailed lesson plans. Naturally, this will require a great deal of work for at least the first year or two, but the reward of knowing that you have prepared and presented effective lessons will compensate for that effort. You can expect a busy first year of teaching.

Some beginning teachers are concerned with being seen using a written plan in class, thinking it may suggest they have not mastered the material. On the contrary, a lesson plan is a visible sign of preparation on the part of the teacher. It demonstrates that you are working at your job and respect the students. A written lesson plan shows that thinking and planning have taken place and that the teacher has a road map to work through the lesson no matter what the distractions. There is absolutely no excuse for appearing before a class without evidence of being thoroughly prepared.

A Continual Process

Lesson planning is a continual process even for experienced teachers, for there is always a need to keep materials and plans current and relevant. Because no two classes of students are ever identical, today's lesson plan will probably need to be tailored to the peculiar needs of each classroom of students. Also, because the content of a course will change as a result of each distinct group of students and the input given by their needs and interests and as new developments occur or new theories are introduced, your objectives and those of the students, school, and teaching faculty will change.

For these reasons, lesson plans should be in a constant state of revision, never "set in concrete." Once the basic framework is developed, however, the task of updating and modifying becomes minimal. If you maintain your plans on a computer, making changes from time to time is even easier.

Well Planned But Open to Last-Minute Change

The lesson plan should provide a tentative outline of the class or time period given for the lesson but should always remain flexible. A carefully worked out plan may have to be set aside because of the unpredictable, serendipitous effect of a "teachable moment" or because of unforeseen circumstances, such as a delayed school bus, an impromptu school assembly program, an emergency drill, or the cancellation of school due to inclement weather. A daily lesson planned to cover six aspects of a given topic may end with only three of the points having been considered. These occurrences are natural in a school setting, and the teacher and the plans must be flexible enough to accommodate this reality.

IMPLEMENTATION OF TODAY'S LESSON MAY NECESSITATE CHANGES IN TOMORROW'S PLAN. Although you may have your lesson plans completed for several consecutive lessons, what actually transpires during the implementation of today's lesson may necessitate last-minute adjustments to the lesson plan you had completed for tomorrow. Consequently, during student teaching in particular, it is not uncommon or unwanted to have last-minute changes penciled in your lesson plan. If, however, modifications are substantial and might be confusing to you during implementation of the lesson, then you probably should rewrite the lesson plan.

The Problem of Time

A lesson plan should provide enough materials and activities to consume the entire class period or time allotted. (As mentioned earlier, it should be well understood that in your planning for teaching, you need to plan for every minute of every class period. The lesson plan, then, is more than a plan for a lesson to be taught; it is a plan that accounts for the entire class period or time that the students are in the classroom.) Since planning is a skill that takes years of experience to master, especially when teaching a block of time that may extend for 90 minutes or more and that involves more than one discipline and perhaps more than one teacher, a beginning teacher should overplan rather than run the risk of having too few activities to occupy the time the students are in the classroom. One way of ensuring that you overplan is to include alternate activities in your lesson plan, as shown in the lesson plan in Figure 5.3.

When a lesson plan does not provide enough activity to occupy the entire class period or time that the students are available for the lesson, a beginning teacher often loses control of the class as behavior problems develop. Thus, it is best to prepare more than you likely can accomplish in a given period of time. Students are very perceptive when it comes to a teacher who has finished the plan and is attempting to bluff through the minutes that remain before dismissal. If you ever do get caught short, as most teachers do at one time or another, ways to avoid embarrassment are to spend the remaining time in a review of material that has been covered that day or in the past several days and to allow students the time to work on a homework assignment or project. Regardless of how you handle time remaining, however, it works best when you plan for it and write that aspect into your lesson plan.

LESSON PLAN

Descriptive Course Data

Instructor: Michelle Yendrey   *Course:* Western Civilizations   *Period:* 1
Grade level: 9   *Unit:* History of Religion   *Topic:* Persecution of Christians

Objectives

Upon completion of this lesson students will be able to

1. Make connections between persecutions today and persecutions that occurred approximately 2,000 years ago.
2. Describe the main teachings of Christianity and how the position of Christianity within the Roman Empire changed over time.
3. Share ideas in a positive and productive manner.

Instructional Components

Activity 1 (Anticipatory Set—10 minutes) Write on overhead: You have until 8:40 (5 minutes) to write a defense to one of the following statements. (Remember, there are no right or wrong answers. Support your position to the best of your ability.)

- The recent hate crimes in our city can be related to our current unit on the history of religion.
- The recent hate crimes in our city cannot be related to our current unit on the history of religion.

Activity 2 (3–5 minutes) Students will be asked, by a show of hands, how many chose statement A and how many chose statement B. Some reasons for each will be shared orally and then all papers collected.

Activity 3 (3–5 minutes) Return papers of previous assignment. Give students new seat assignments for the activity that follows, and have them assume their new seats.

Activity 4 (15 minutes) The students are now arranged into seven groups. Each group will write a paragraph using the concepts from certain assigned words (for their definition sheets of Section 3 of Chapter 7, "Christianity spread through the empire") to answer the essay question(s) at the end of the definition sheet.

   Each group will select a

Task master to keep members of the group on task.
Recorder to write things down.
Spokesperson to present the results.
Timekeeper to keep group alert so task is completed on time.

In addition, some groups will have a

Source master to look up or ask about any questions that arise.

Activity 5 (15–20 minutes) Each group's spokesperson will come to the front of the classroom and present the group's result for activity 4.

Alternate Activity (Plan B: 5–10 minutes) Should the activities run more quickly than anticipated, the students will take out their "Religion Comparison Sheets." Using Chapter 2, Section 2, "Jews worshipped a single God," and Chapter 7, Section 3 definition sheets, with the teacher's direction, the students will fill in the boxes for "similar" and "different" with regard to Christianity and Judaism.

Second Alternate Activity (Plan C: 25–30 minutes) In the unlikely event that timing is really off, each student will be given a blank grid and assigned ten vocabulary words from the definition sheets. Students will be directed to create a crossword puzzle using the definitions as clues, and the words as answers. After 15–20 minutes, the crosswords will be collected and distributed to different students to solve. If not completed in class, students will finish and hand them in later along with their essays, for a few points of extra credit. Students will be required to write their names in the appropriate spaces marked, "Created By" and "Solved By."

Activity 6 (7–10 minutes) Collect the overhead sheets and pens. Hand out the take-home essay test. Explain and take questions about exactly what is expected from the essay (this is their first take-home test).

Figure 5.3
Lesson plan sample with alternative activities. (*Source:* Courtesy of Michelle Yendrey.)

(continued)

Materials and Equipment Needed

Overhead projector and transparency sheets (7) and transparency markers (7); 36 copies of the essay question plus directions; 36 copies of the blank grid sheets.

Assessment, Reflection, and Plans for Revision

_____

_____

_____

_____

_____

_____

_____

_____

_____

_____

_____

_____

_____

_____

_____

_____

_____

_____

_____

_____

_____

_____

_____

_____

_____

_____

Figure 5.3 *(continued)*

DAILY PLANNING BOOK

Grade _____ Lesson _____ Teacher _____

Date	Content	Materials	Procedure	Evaluation
Monday				
Tuesday				
Wednesday				
Thursday				
Friday				

Figure 5.4
An example of a daily planning book.

A Caution about the "The Daily Planning Book"

A distinction needs to be made between actual lesson plans and the book for daily planning that many schools require teachers to maintain and even submit to their supervisors a week in advance. A daily planning book (see Figure 5.4) is most assuredly not a lesson plan; rather, it is a layout sheet on which the teacher shows what lessons will be taught during the day, week, month, or term. Usually the book provides only a small lined box for time periods for each day of the week. These books are useful for outlining the topics, activities, and assignments projected for the week or term, and supervisors sometimes use them to check the adequacy of teachers' course plans. But they are not lesson plans. Teachers who believe that the notations in the daily planning book are actual lesson plans are fooling themselves. Student teachers should not use these in place of authentic lesson plans.

CONSTRUCTING A LESSON PLAN: FORMAT, COMPONENTS, AND SAMPLES

Each teacher develops a personal system of lesson planning—the system that works best for that teacher. But a beginning teacher needs a more substantial framework from which to work. For that reason, this section provides a preferred lesson plan format (Figure 5.5). In addition, you will find alternative formats in Figures 5.6 and 5.7 as well as other samples in the Appendix. Nothing is sacred about any of these formats, however. Each has worked for some teachers in the past. As you review the preferred for-

mat and the others, determine which appeals to your style of presentation and use it with your own modifications until you find or develop a better model. All else being equal, we encourage you, however, to begin your teaching following our preferred format as closely as possible.

All plans should be written out in an intelligible style. There is good reason to question teachers who say they have no need for a written plan because they have their lessons planned "in their heads." The periods in a school day range from several to many, as do the numbers of students in each class. When multiplied by the number of school days in a week, a semester, or a year, the task of keeping so many things in one's head becomes mind-boggling. Few persons could effectively do that. Until you have considerable experience, you will need to write and keep detailed daily plans for guidance and reference.

Basic Elements of a Lesson Plan

A written lesson plan should contain the following basic elements: (1) descriptive course data, (2) goals and objectives, (3) rationale, (4) procedure, (5) assignments and assignment reminders, (6) materials and equipment, and (7) a section for assessment, reflection, and revision. These components need not be present in every written lesson plan, nor must they be presented in any particular format. Nor are they inclusive or exclusive. You might choose to include additional components or subsections. You may not want to spend time developing a formal rationale, although you probably should. Figure 5.5 illustrates a format that includes the seven components and sample subsections of those components. (If you choose, you may make copies of this format for use in teaching.) Additionally, Figure 5.6 illustrates a completed multiple-day, project-centered, interdisciplinary, and transcultural lesson using world-wide communication via the Internet.

Following are descriptions of the seven major components, explanations of why each is important, and examples.

Descriptive Data

This is demographic and logistical information that identifies details about the class. Anyone reading this information should be able to identify when and where the class meets, who is teaching it, and what is being taught. Although as the teacher you know this information, someone else may not. Members of the teaching team, administrators, and substitute teachers (and, if you are the student teacher, your university supervisor and cooperating teacher) appreciate this information, especially when asked to fill in for you, even if only for a few minutes during a class session. Most teachers find out which items of descriptive data are most beneficial in their situation and then develop their own identifiers. Remember this: The mark of a well-prepared, clearly written lesson plan is the ease with which someone else (such as another member of your teaching team or a substitute teacher) could implement it.

For the sample lesson plans of Figures 5.3 (Western Civilizations, grade 9), 5.6 (English/Science, grades 10–12), and 5.7 (Physical Science, grade 9), descriptive data include

1. *Name of course or class and grade level.* These serve as headings for the plan and facilitate orderly filing of plans.

   Western Civilizations
      Grade 9

   English/Science (integrated block course)
      Grades 10–12

   Physical Science
      Grade 9

2. *Name of unit.* Inclusion of the unit name facilitates the orderly control of the hundreds of lesson plans a teacher constructs. For example:

   Western Civilizations
      Grade 9
      Unit: History of Religion

   English/Science
      Grades 10–12
      Unit: Investigative Research and Generative Writing

   Physical Science
      Grade 9
      Unit: What's the Matter?

3. *Topic to be considered within the unit.* This is also useful for control and identification. For example:

   Western Civilizations
      Grade 9
      Unit: History of Religion
      Topic: Persecution of Christians

   English/Science
      Grades 10–12
      Unit: Investigative Research and Generative Writing
      Topic: Writing Response and Peer Assessment via the Internet

   Physical Science
      Grade 9
      Unit: What's the Matter?
      Topic: Density of Solids

ANTICIPATED CLASSROOM NOISE LEVEL. Although it is not included in any of the sample lesson plans in this resource guide, the teacher might include in the descriptive data the category of anticipated classroom noise level, such as high, moderate, or low. Its inclusion is useful to you during the planning phase of instruction to determine how active and noisy the students might become during the lesson, how you might prepare for that, and whether you should warn an administrator and teachers of neighboring classrooms. Cooperating teachers and university supervisors sometimes request inclusion of this item.

Goals and Objectives

The instructional goals are general statements of intended accomplishments from that lesson. Teachers and students need to know what the lesson is designed to accomplish. In clear, understandable language, the general goal statement provides that information. In Figure 5.6, the goals are

- To collaborate and prepare response papers to peers from around the world who have shared the results of their own experimental research findings and research paper about ozone concentrations in the atmosphere.
- For students around the world to prepare and publish for world-wide dissemination a final paper about global ozone levels in the atmosphere.

And, from the sample unit of Figure 5.7, some goals are to

- Understand that all matter is made of atoms.
- Develop a positive attitude about physical science.

Because the goals are also included in the unit plan, sometimes a teacher may include only the objectives in the daily lesson plan (as done in Figure 5.3). For a beginning teacher, it is a good idea to include both.

1. **Descriptive Data**

   Teacher _____ Class _____ Date _____ Grade level _____

   Room number _____ Period _____ Unit _____

   Lesson number _____ Topic _____

   Anticipated noise level (high, moderate, low)

2. **Goals and Objectives**

   Instructional goals: _____

   _____

   _____

   Specific objectives:

      Cognitive: _____

   _____

   _____

      Affective: _____

   _____

   _____

      Psychomotor: _____

   _____

   _____

3. **Rationale** _____

   _____

   _____

4. **Procedure** (procedure with modeling examples, transitions, coached practice, and so on)

   Content: _____

   _____

   _____

   _____ minutes. Activity 1: Set (introduction) _____

   _____

   _____

   _____ minutes. Activity 2: _____

   _____

(continued)

Figure 5.5
Sample of a preferred lesson plan format with seven components. (This sample lesson plan format is placed alone, so if you choose, you may remove it from the book and make copies for use in your teaching.)

_____ minutes. Activity 3 (the exact number of activities in the procedures will vary.): _____

_____

_____

_____ minutes. Final activity (lesson conclusion or closure): _____

_____

_____

If time remains: _____

_____

_____

5. Assignments and Reminders of Assignments

_____

_____

_____

Special notes and reminders to myself: _____

_____

_____

_____

6. Materials and Equipment Needed

Audiovisual: _____

_____

Other: _____

_____

7. Assessment, Reflection, and Revision

Assessment of student learning: _____

_____

_____

Reflective thoughts about the lesson: _____

_____

_____

Suggestions for revision: _____

_____

_____

Figure 5.5 *(continued)*

LESSON PLAN

1. Descriptive Data

Teacher _____ Class _English/Science_ Date _____ Grade level _10–12_

Unit _Investigative Research and Generative Writing_ _____

Lesson Topic _Writing Response and Peer Assessment via the Internet_ _____

Time duration: _several days_ _____

2. Goals and Objectives of Unit

Instructional Goals:

2.1. One goal for this lesson is for the students to collaborate and prepare response papers to peers from around the world who have shared the results of their own experimental research findings and research paper about ozone concentrations in the atmosphere.

2.2. The ultimate goal of this unit is for students around the world to prepare and publish for world-wide dissemination a final paper about global ozone levels in the atmosphere.

Objectives:

Cognitive:

a. Through cooperative group action students will conduct experimental research to collect data about the ozone level of air in their environment. (application)

b. In cooperative groups, students will analyze the results of their experiments. (analysis)

c. Students will compile data and infer from their experimental data. (synthesis and evaluation)

d. Through collaborative writing groups, the students will prepare a final paper that summarizes their research study of local atmospheric ozone levels. (evaluation)

e. Through sharing via the Internet, students will write response papers to their peers from other locations in the world. (evaluation)

f. From their own collaborative research and world-wide communications with their peers, the students will draw conclusions about global atmospheric ozone levels. (evaluation)

Affective:

a. Students will respond attentively to the response papers of their peers. (attending)

b. Students will willingly cooperate with others during the group activities. (responding)

c. Students will offer opinions about the atmospheric level of ozone. (valuing)

d. Students will form judgments about local, regional, and world-wide ozone levels. (organizing)

e. Students communicate accurately their findings and attend diligently to the work of their world-wide peers. (internalizing)

Psychomotor:

a. Students will manipulate the computer so that their e-mail communications are transmitted accurately. (manipulating)

b. In a summary to the study, students will describe their feelings about atmospheric ozone concentrations and what might be done. (communicating)

c. Students will ultimately create a proposal for world-wide dissemination. (creating)

3. Rationale

3.1. Important to improvement in one's writing and communication skills are the processes of selecting a topic, decision making, arranging, drafting, proofing, peer review, communicating, revising, editing, rewriting, and publishing the results—processes that are focused on in the writing aspect of this unit.

3.2. Student writers need many readers to respond to their work. Through world-wide communication with peers and dissemination of their final product, this need can be satisfied.

3.3. Students learn best when they are actively pursuing a topic of interest and meaning to them. Resulting from brainstorming potential problems and arriving at their own topic, this unit provides that.

3.4. Real-world problems are interdisciplinary and transcultural; involving writing (English), science, mathematics (e.g., data collecting, graphing), and intercultural communication, this unit is an interdisciplinary transcultural unit.

(continued)

Figure 5.6
Lesson plan sample: multiple-day, project-centered, interdisciplinary, and transcultural lesson using world-wide communication via the Internet.

4. Procedure

Content:

At the start of this unit, collaborative groups were established via Intercultural E-mail Classroom Connections (IECC) (http://www.stolaf.edu/network/iecc) with other classes from schools around the world. These groups of students from around the world conducted several scientific research experiments on the ozone level of their local atmospheric air. To obtain relative measurements of ozone concentrations in the air, students set up experiments that involved stretching rubber bands on a board, then observing the number of days until the bands broke. Students maintained daily journal logs of the temperature, barometric pressure, wind speed/direction, and the number of days that it took for the bands to break.* After compiling their data and preparing single-page summaries of their results via the Internet, students exchanged data with others groups. From data collected world-wide, students wrote a one-page summary as to what conditions may account for the difference in levels of ozone. Following the exchange of students' written responses and their subsequent revisions based on feedback from the world-wide peers, students are now preparing a final summary report about the world's atmospheric ozone level. The intention is to disseminate world-wide (to newspapers and via Internet) this final report.

Activity 1: Introduction (10 minutes)

Today, in think-share-pairs, you will prepare initial responses to the e-mail responses we have received from other groups from around the world. (Teacher shares the list of places from which e-mail has been received.) Any questions before we get started?

As we discussed earlier, here are the instructions: In your think-share-pairs (each pair is given one response received via e-mail), prepare written responses according to the following outline: (1) note points or information you would like to incorporate in the final paper to be forwarded via the Internet; (2) comment on one aspect of the written response you like best; and (3) provide questions to the sender to seek clarification or elaboration. I think you should be able to finish this in about 30 minutes, so let's try for that.

Activity 2: (30 minutes, if needed)

Preparation of dyad responses

Activity 3: (open)

Let's now hear from each response pair.

Dyad responses are shared with whole class for discussion of inclusion in response paper to be sent via the Internet.

Activity 4: (open)

Discussion, conclusion, and preparation of final drafts to be sent to each e-mail correspondent to be done by cooperative groups (the number of groups needed to be decided by the number of e-mail correspondents at this time).

Activity 5: (open)

Later, as students receive e-mail responses from other groups, the responses will be printed and reviewed. The class then responds to each using the same criteria as before and returns this response to the e-mail sender.

Closure:

The process continues until all groups (from around the world) have agreed upon and prepared the final report for dissemination.

5. Materials and Equipment Needed

School computers with Internet access; printers; copies of e-mail responses.

6. Assessment, Reflection, and Revision

Assessment of student learning for this lesson is formative: journals; daily checklist of student participation in groups; writing drafts.

Reflective thoughts about lesson and suggestions for revision:

_____

_____

*The information about the science experiment is from R. J. Ryder and T. Hughes, *Internet for Educators* (Upper Saddle River, NJ: Prentice Hall, 1997), p. 98, as is the Internet address for IECC (p. 96).

Figure 5.6 *(continued)*

UNIT PLAN SAMPLE WITH A DAILY LESSON

Course *Ninth-Grade Physical Science*

Teacher _____ **Duration of Unit** *Ten days*

Unit Title *What's the Matter?*

Purpose of the Unit

This unit is designed to develop students' understanding of the concept of matter. At the completion of the unit, students should have a clearer understanding of matter and its properties, of the basic units of matter, and of the source of matter.

Rationale of the Unit

This unit topic is important for building a foundation of knowledge for subsequent courses in science. This can increase students' chances of success in those courses, and thereby improve their self-confidence and self-esteem. A basic understanding of matter and its properties is important because of daily decisions that affect the manipulation of matter. It is more likely that students will make correct and safe decisions when they understand what matter is, how it changes form, and how its properties determine its use.

Goals of the Unit

The goals of this unit are for students to

1. Understand that all matter is made of atoms.
2. Understand that matter stays constant and that it is neither created nor destroyed.
3. Develop certain basic physical science laboratory skills.
4. Develop a positive attitude about physical science.
5. Look forward to taking other science courses.
6. Understand how science is relevant to their daily lives.

Instructional Objectives of the Unit

Upon completion of this unit of study, students should be able to

1. List at least ten examples of matter.
2. List the four states of matter, with one example of each.
3. Calculate the density of an object when given its mass and volume.
4. Describe the properties of solids, liquids, and gases.
5. Demonstrate an understanding that matter is made of elements and that elements are made of atoms.
6. Identify and explain one way that knowledge of matter is important to their daily lives.
7. Demonstrate increased self-confidence in pursuing laboratory investigations in physical science.
8. Demonstrate skill in communicating within the cooperative learning group.
9. Demonstrate skill in working with the triple-beam balance.

Unit Overview

Throughout this unit, students will be developing a concept map of matter. Information for the map will be derived from laboratory work, class discussions, lectures, student readings, and research. The overall instructional model is that of concept attainment. Important to this is an assessment of students' concepts about matter at the beginning of the unit. The preassessment and the continuing assessment of their concepts will center on the following:

1. What is matter and what are its properties? Students will develop the concept of matter by discovering the properties that all matter contains (that is, it has mass and takes up space).
2. Students will continue to build upon their understanding of the concept of matter by organizing matter into its four major states (that is, solid, liquid, gas, plasma). The concept development will be used to define the attributes of each state of matter, and students will gather information by participating in laboratory activities and class discussions.
3. What are some of the physical properties of matter that make certain kinds of matter unique? Students will experiment with properties of matter such as elasticity, brittleness, and density. Laboratory activities will allow students to contribute their observations and information to the further development of their concept of matter. Density activities enable students to practice their lab and math skills.

(continued)

Figure 5.7
Sample of a unit plan with one daily lesson for lab science. (*Source:* Courtesy of Will Hightower.)

4. What are the basic units of matter, and where did matter come from? Students will continue to develop their concept of matter by working on this understanding of mixtures, compounds, elements, and atoms.

Assessment of Student Achievement

For this unit, assessment of student achievement will be both formative and summative. Formative evaluation will be done daily by checklists of student behavior, knowledge, and skills. Summative evaluation will be based on the following criteria:

1. Student participation as evidenced by completion of daily homework, class work, laboratory activities, and class discussions and by the information on the student behavior checklists.
2. Weekly quizzes on content.
3. Unit test.

Lesson Number _____   **Duration of Lesson** 1–2 hours _____

Unit Title What's the Matter? _____   **Teacher** _____

Lesson Title Mission Impossible _____   **Lesson Topic** Density of Solids _____

Objectives of the Lesson

Upon completion of this lesson, students should be able to

1. Determine the density of a solid cube.
2. Based on data gathered in class, develop their own definition of density.
3. Prepare and interpret graphs of data.
4. Communicate the results of their experiments to others in the class.

Materials Needed

1. Two large boxes of cereal and two snack-size boxes of the same cereal.
2. Four brownies (two whole and two cut in halves).
3. Four sandboxes (two large plastic boxes and two small boxes, each filled with sand).
4. Two triple-beam balances.
5. Several rulers.
6. Six hand-held calculators.
7. Eighteen colored pencils (six sets with three different colors per set).
8. Copies of lab instructions (one copy for each student).

Instructional Procedure with Approximate Time Line

ANTICIPATORY SET (10–15 MINUTES)
Begin class by brainstorming to find what students already know about density. Place the word on the board or overhead, and ask students if they have heard of it. Write down their definitions and examples. Hold up a large box of cereal in one hand and the snack-size box in the other. Ask students which is more dense. Allow them time to explain their responses. Then tell them that by the end of this lesson they will know the answer to the question and that they will develop their own definition of density.

LABORATORY INVESTIGATION (30–60 MINUTES)
Students are divided into teams of four students of mixed abilities. Each member has a role:

1. *Measure master:* In charge of the group's ruler and ruler measurements.
2. *Mass master:* In charge of the group's weighings.
3. *Engineer:* In charge of the group's calculator and calculations.
4. *Graph master:* In charge of plotting the group's data on the graph paper.

Each team has eight minutes before switching stations. Each team completes three stations and then meets to make their graphs and to discuss results.

Station 1: **Cereal Box Density.** Students calculate the density of a large and a small box of cereal to determine if a larger and heavier object is more dense. The masses versus the volumes of the two boxes are plotted on graph paper using one of the pencil colors.

Figure 5.7 *(continued)*

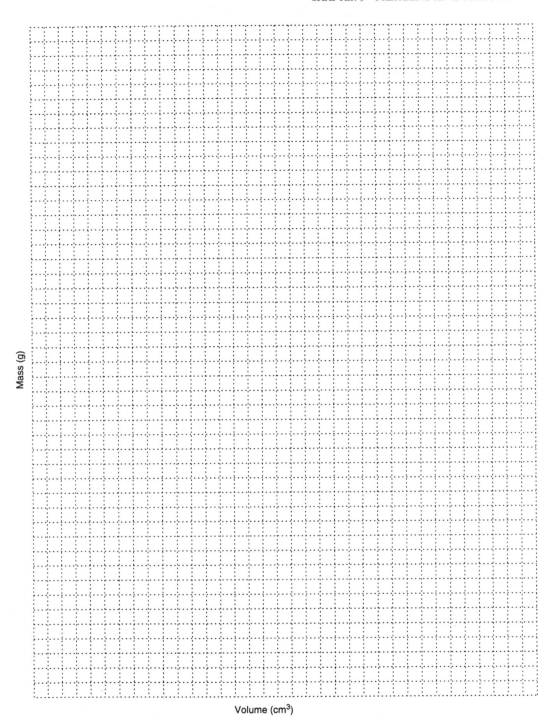

Mass (g)

Volume (cm³)

INSTRUCTIONS

1. The density of any object is determined by dividing its mass by its volume. Density in grams is divided by volume in cubic centimeters. Example: 20 g/10 cm^3 = 2 g/cm^3.

2. Measure the volume of the small cereal box (length × width × height), and use the balance to determine its mass in grams. The engineer can do the calculations on the calculator. The graph master should graph the results of each trial and connect two points with a straight line.

3. Repeat the procedure using the large box of cereal.

4. The engineer computes the density of both cereal boxes with the calculator and records the results on the proper blank below the graph.

Figure 5.7 *(continued)*

(continued)

   a. Density of large box of cereal _____

   b. Density of small box of cereal _____

   c. Density of large brownie _____

   d. Density of small brownie _____

   e. Density of large sandbox _____

   f. Density of small sandbox _____

Station 2: Brownie Density. Students calculate the density of a full-size brownie and a half-size brownie. Results are plotted on the same graph as in Station 1, but with the second color.

INSTRUCTIONS

1. The density of any object is determined by dividing its mass by its volume. Density in grams is divided by volume in cubic centimeters. Example: 20 g/10 cm^3 = 2 g/cm^3.
2. Measure the volume of a small brownie (length × width × height), and use the balance to determine its mass in grams. The engineer can do the calculations on the calculator. The graph master should graph the results of each trial and connect two points with a straight line.
3. Repeat the procedure using the large brownie.
4. The engineer computes the density of both brownies and records the result on the proper blank.

Station 3: Sandbox Density. Students calculate the density of a large and a small box filled with sand. Results are plotted on the graph, but with the third color.

INSTRUCTIONS

1. The density of any object is determined by dividing its mass by its volume. Density in grams is divided by volume in cubic centimeters. Example: 20 g/10 cm^3 = 2 g/cm^3.
2. Measure the volume of the small sandbox (length × width × height), and use the balance to determine its mass in grams. The engineer can do the calculations on the calculator. The graph master should graph the results of each trial and connect two points with a straight line.
3. Repeat the procedure using the large sandbox.
4. The engineer computes the density of both boxes and records the results on the proper blank.

Lab Worksheet. Teams return to their seats to do the graphing, analyze the results, and answer the following questions from their lab sheets:

1. Is a larger, heavier object more dense than its smaller counterpart? Explain your evidence.
2. What is your definition of density?
3. Which is more dense, a pound of feathers or a pound of gold? Explain your answer.

LESSON CLOSURE (10 MINUTES OR MORE)
When all teams are finished, teams should display their graphs and share and discuss the results.

Concepts
1. Density is one of the properties of matter.
2. Mass and volume are related.
3. Density is determined by dividing mass by volume.

Extension Activities
1. Use a density graph to calculate the mass and volume of a smaller brownie.
2. Explore the story of Archimedes and the king's crown.

Evaluation, Reflection, and Revision of Lesson
Upon completion of this lesson and of the unit, revision in this lesson may be made on the basis of teacher observations and student achievement.

Figure 5.7 *(continued)*

Objectives of the lesson are included as specific statements detailing precisely what students will be able to do as a result of the instructional activities. Teachers and students need to know that. Behavioral objectives provide clear statements of what learning is to occur. In addition, from clearly written behavioral objectives, assessment items can be written to measure whether students have accomplished the objectives. The type of assessment item used (discussed in Chapter 11) not only should measure *for* the instructional objective but also should be compatible *with* the objective being assessed. As discussed earlier, your specific objectives might be covert, overt, or a combination of both. From the lesson plan shown in Figure 5.6, sample objectives are

- Through cooperative group action students will conduct experimental research to collect data about the ozone level of air in their environment. (cognitive, application)
- Through sharing via the Internet, students will write response papers to their peers from other locations in the world. (cognitive, evaluation)
- Students will form judgments about local, regional, and world-wide ozone levels. (affective, organizing)
- Students will ultimately create a proposal for world-wide dissemination. (psychomotor, creating)

And, from the lesson illustrated in Figure 5.7, sample objectives are

- Determine the density of a solid cube. (overt, cognitive)
- Communicate the results of their experiments to others in the class. (overt, psychomotor)

Setting specific objectives is a crucial step in the development of any lesson plan. It is at this point that many lessons go wrong. In writing specific objectives, teachers sometimes mistakenly list what *they* intend to do, such as "cover the next five pages" or "do the next ten problems." In so doing, they fail to focus on just what the learning objective in these activities truly is— that is, what the children will be able to do (performance) as a result of the instruction. When you approach this step in your lesson planning, ask yourself, "What do I want my students to learn as a result of this lesson?" Your answer to that question is your objective!

Rationale

The rationale is an explanation of why the lesson is important and why the instructional methods chosen will achieve the objectives. Parents, students, teachers, administrators, and others have the right to know why specific content is being taught and why the methods employed are being used. Teachers become reflective decision makers when they challenge themselves to think about *what*

they are teaching, *how* they are teaching it, and *why* it must be taught. Sometimes teachers include the rationale statement in the beginning of the unit plan, but not in each daily lesson. As illustrated in Figure 5.7, sometimes the rationale is included within the unit introduction and goals. Beginning teachers should include a rationale for each new lesson (see the rationale in Figure 5.6) and be sure it covers why the lesson is important and why the instructional methods chosen will achieve the objectives.

Procedure

The procedure consists of the instructional activities for a scheduled period of time. The substance of the lesson— the information to be presented, obtained, and learned— is the *content*. Appropriate information is selected to meet the learning objectives, the level of competence of the students, and the requirements of the course. To be sure your lesson actually covers what it should, you should write down exactly what content you intend to cover. This material may be placed in a separate section or combined with the procedure section. The important thing is to write down your information so that you can refer to it quickly and easily when you need to. If, for instance, you intend to conduct the lesson using discussion, you should write out the key discussion questions. For example:

- Why do you think Longfellow sees the sky as troubled in "Snowflakes"?
- Why do you think Dickinson wanted to remain a nobody?

Or, if you are going to introduce new material using a 12-minute lecture, then you need to outline the content of that lecture. The word *outline* is not used casually; you need not have pages of notes to sift through, nor should you ever read declarative statements to your students. You should be familiar enough with the content so that an outline (in as much detail as you believe necessary) will be sufficient to carry on the lesson as in the following example:

Causes of Civil War
   A. Primary causes
      1. Economics
      2. Abolitionist pressure
      3. Slavery
      4. etc.
   B. Secondary causes
      1. North-South friction
      2. Southern economic dependence
      3. etc.

The procedure or procedures to be used, sometimes referred to as the *instructional components,* constitute the *procedure* component of the lesson plan. Appropriate instructional activities are chosen to meet the objectives, to match the students' learning styles and special needs, and to ensure that all students have an equal opportunity to learn. The procedure is the section in which you establish what you and your students will do during the lesson. Ordinarily, you should plan this section of your lesson as an organized entity having a beginning (an introduction or set), a middle, and an end (called the closure) to be completed during the lesson. This structure is not always needed, because some lessons are simply parts of units or long-term plans and merely carry on activities spelled out in those long-term plans. Still, most lessons need to include the following in the procedure:

1. An *introduction,* the process used to prepare the students mentally for the lesson, sometimes referred to as the *set, initiating activity,* or *stimulus.*
2. *Lesson development,* the detailing of *activities* that occur between the beginning and end of the lesson, including the transitions that connect activities (see discussion in Chapter 3 and transitions in Unit and Daily Plan—Sample 5 of the Appendix).
3. Plans for *coached practice,* sometimes referred to as the *follow-up.* This includes ways that you intend to have students interact in the classroom, such as practicing individually, in dyads, or in small groups, receiving guidance or coaching from each other and from you.
4. The *lesson conclusion* (or *closure*). This is the planned process of bringing the lesson to an end, thereby providing students with a sense of completeness and, with effective teaching, accomplishment and comprehension by helping students to synthesize the information learned from the lesson.
5. A *timetable,* which serves simply as a planning and implementation guide.
6. A plan for what to do if you finish the lesson and time remains.
7. *Assignments,* that is, what students are instructed to do as follow-up to the lesson, either as homework or as in-class work. Assignments provide students an opportunity to practice and enhance what is being learned.

Let's now consider some of these elements in further detail.

INTRODUCTION TO THE LESSON.   Like any good performance, a lesson needs an effective beginning. In many respects the introduction sets the tone for the rest of the lesson by alerting the students that the business of learning is to begin. The introduction should be an attention-getter. If it is exciting, interesting, or innovative, it can create a favorable mood for the lesson. In any case, a thoughtful introduction serves as a solid indicator that you are well prepared. Although it is difficult to develop

an exciting introduction to every lesson taught each day, a variety of options is always available to spice up the launching of a lesson. You might, for instance, begin the lesson by briefly reviewing the previous lesson, thereby helping students connect the learning. Another possibility is to review vocabulary words from previous lessons and to introduce new ones. Still another possibility is to use the key point of the day's lesson as an introduction and then again as the conclusion. Sometimes teachers begin a lesson by demonstrating a discrepant event (i.e., an event that is contrary to what one might expect), sometimes referred to as a hook. Yet another possibility is to begin the lesson with a writing activity on some controversial aspect of the ensuing lesson. Samples follow.

For high school English, study of interpretations:

• As students enter the classroom, the state song, "I Love You, California," is playing softly in the background. The teacher begins class by showing on the overhead the state seal and asks students to discuss in dyads and write down what they believe it is.

For U.S. history, study of westward expansion:

• The teacher asks, "Who has lived somewhere else other than (*name of your state*)?" After students show hands and answer, the teacher asks individuals why they moved to (*name of your state*). The teacher then asks students to recall why the first European settlers came to the United States, then moves into the next activity.

For U.S. history, study of the Constitution:

• Teacher tells the students, "We are going to take the first two or three days of this unit for you to write a classroom bill of rights." Then, with no other direction, the teacher charges the class of students with that task.

For science, study of diffusion of gas in a gas:

• Asking the students to raise their hands as soon as they smell it, the teacher sprays perfume in one corner of the classroom.

For science, study of adhesion or the process of predicting:

• The teacher takes a glass filled to the brim with colored water and asks students to discuss and predict (in dyads) how many pennies can be added to the glass before any water spills over the edge of the glass.

In short, you can use the introduction of the lesson to review past learning, tie the new lesson to the previous lesson, introduce new material, point out the objectives of the new lesson, help students connect their learning with other disciplines or with real life, or, by showing what will be learned and why the learning is important, induce in students motivation and a mind-set favorable to the new lesson.

LESSON DEVELOPMENT.   The developmental activities form the bulk of the plan and are the specifics by which you intend to achieve your lesson objectives. They include activities that present information, demonstrate skills, provide reinforcement of previously learned material, and provide other opportunities to develop understanding and skill. Furthermore, by actions and words, during lesson development the teacher models the behaviors expected of the students. Students need such modeling. By effective modeling, the teacher can exemplify the anticipated learning outcomes. Activities of this section of the lesson plan should be described in some detail so that you will know exactly what you plan to do and, during the stress of the class meeting, you do not forget important details and content. For this reason you should consider, for example, noting answers (if known) to questions you intend to ask and solutions to problems you intend to have students solve.

LESSON CONCLUSION.   Having a clear-cut closure to the lesson is as important as having a strong introduction. The closure complements the introduction. The concluding activity should summarize and bind together what has ensued in the developmental stage and should reinforce the principal points of the lesson. One way to accomplish these ends is to restate the key points of the lesson. Another is to briefly outline the major points. Still another is to repeat the major concept. Sometimes the closure is not only a review of what was learned but also the summarizing of a question left unanswered that signals a change in your plan of activities for the next day. No matter how it is done, the concluding activity is usually brief and to the point.

TIMETABLE.   To estimate the time factors in any lesson can be very difficult. A good procedure is to gauge the amount of time needed for each learning activity and note that alongside the activity and strategy in your plan, as shown in Figure 5.5. Placing too much faith in your time estimate may be foolish—an estimate is more for your guidance during the preactive phase of instruction than for anything else. Beginning teachers frequently find that their discussions and presentations do not last as long as was expected. To avoid being embarrassed by running out of material, try to make sure you have planned enough meaningful work to consume the entire class period. Another important reason for including a time plan in your lesson is to give information to students about how much time they have for a particular activity, such as a quiz or a group activity.

Assignment

When an assignment is to be given, it should be noted in your lesson plan. When to present an assignment to the students is optional, but it should never be yelled as an afterthought as the students are exiting the classroom at the end of the period. Whether assignments are to be begun and completed during class time or done out of school, it is best to write them on the writing board, in a special place on the bulletin board, or on a handout, taking extra care to be sure that assignment specifications are clear to the students.

It is also important that you understand the difference between assignments and procedures. An assignment tells students *what* is to be done, while procedures explain *how* to do it. Although an assignment may include specific procedures, spelling out procedures alone is not the same thing as an academic assignment. When students are given an assignment, they need to understand the reasons for doing it as well as have some notion of ways the assignment might be done.

Many teachers give assignments to their students on a weekly basis, requiring that the students maintain an assignment schedule in their portfolios. When given periodically, rather than daily, assignments should still show in your daily lesson plans so that you can remind students of them. Once assignment specifications are given it is a good idea to not make major modifications to them, and it is especially important to not change assignment specifications several days after an assignment has been given. Last-minute changes in assignment specifications can be very frustrating to students who have already begun or completed the assignment; it shows little respect for those students.

BENEFITS OF COACHED PRACTICE.   Allowing time in class for students to begin work on homework assignments and long-term projects is highly recommended; it provides an opportunity for the teacher to provide individual attention to students. Being able to coach students is the reason for in-class time to begin assignments. The benefits of *coached practice* include being able to (1) monitor student work so a student doesn't go too far in a wrong direction, (2) help students to reflect on their thinking, (3) assess the progress of individual students, (4) provide for peer tutoring, and (5) discover or create a "teachable moment." Regarding the last item, for example, while observing and monitoring student practice, the teacher might discover a commonly shared student misconception. The teacher then stops and discusses that and attempts to clarify the misconception or collaboratively with students plans a subsequent lesson centered on the common misconception.

Date   Reflection

May 9   Yesterday was interesting in that I didn't notice the absence of the VCR until it was too late. I had known it was going away and that I would have to get one from the school, but had totally forgotten. Fortunately, I had overplanned for that day and there was no lack of activity. I got everyone in their groups and found, as usual, mostly off-task behavior taking place, even with the advent of my brilliant student accountability form. I am still trying desperately for ways to get these sixth graders to stay on task in small groups. Better do more research.

May 10   Yesterday we mainly watched the film, and so of course the kids were pretty well behaved. Most are making progress on their stories, and today I held an optional afterschool workshop for students who wanted some help. I was surprised at the number of students who showed up. It was a good day.

May 11   I'm still having trouble with small-group management, but at least I got them all to remain seated and stay with their groups. They're just so loud, and when there are five groups all talking in one room, the volume keeps rising. They did pretty much stay on task though; my constant circulating and sitting in on groups help, I think.

May 12   Yesterday the students vociferously demanded that I show more of *Star Wars* since I seemingly promised I would. I told them they had to earn it, though, and write silently for 20 minutes on their stories. It worked! Score one for teacher (and the students).

May 15   We broke into groups to read "My Journey," but I'm afraid they thought it was boring. Oh well. My bizarre life holds no fascination for them whatsoever. You definitely leave your ego home in this job. It's good for you.

May 16   It's taking too long to show *Star Wars*, and I'm losing some of the girls. They are not all that interested, and I can't say I blame them. When I teach this unit again, I will be more mindful of showing, reading myths, reading stories that have broad appeal across gender, ethnicity, etc. Although the film does have a female hero as well as a male hero, some of the girls in the class just aren't interested in science fiction.

Figure 5.8
Reflective thoughts as recorded by a middle school language arts teacher on six consecutive lesson plans after teaching each lesson.

Special Notes and Reminders

Many teachers provide a place in their lesson plan format for special notes and reminders. Most of the time you will not need such reminders, but when you do, it helps to have them in a regular location in your lesson plan so that you can refer to them quickly. Reminders might concern such matters as announcements to be made, school programs, and make-up work for certain students.

Materials and Equipment to Be Used

Materials of instruction include the textbook, supplementary readings, media, and other supplies necessary to accomplish the lesson objectives. Teachers must be certain that the proper and necessary materials and equipment are available for the lesson, and to be certain takes planning.

Assessment, Reflection, and Revision

You must include in your lesson plan details of how you will assess how well students *are learning* (**formative assessment**) and how well they *have learned* (**summative assessment**). Comprehension checks for formative assessment can be in the form of questions both you and the students ask during the lesson, as well as informal checklists. Questions you intend to ask (and possible answers) should be built into the developmental section.

For summative assessment, teachers typically use review questions at the end of a lesson (as a closure)

or the beginning of the next lesson (as a review or transfer introduction), independent practice or summary activities at the completion of a lesson, and tests. Again, major questions for checking for comprehension should be detailed in your lesson plan.

In most lesson plan formats, a section is reserved for the teacher to make notes or reflective comments about the lesson. Sample reflective questions you might ask yourself are

- How did I feel about my teaching today?
- If I feel successful, what did I see the students saying and doing that made me feel that way?
- Would I do anything differently next time? If so, what and why?
- What changes to tomorrow's lesson need to be made as a result of today's?

As shown in Figure 5.8, both writing and later reading your reflections not only may be useful if you plan to use the lesson again at some later date, but also offer catharsis, easing the stress from teaching. To continue working effectively at a challenging task (that is, to prevent downshifting as discussed in Chapter 1) requires significant reflection.

If you have reviewed the sample lesson plan formats, proceed now to Exercise 5.5, in which you will analyze a lesson that failed; then, as instructed by your course instructor, do Exercises 5.6A and B and 5.7.

EXERCISE 5.5
Analysis of a Lesson That Failed

Instructions: The planning and structure of a lesson are often predictors of the success of its implementation. First, read the synopsis of implementation of a specific lesson. Then answer the discussion questions individually. Finally, use your responses as a basis for class discussion (in small groups) about the lesson. Questions for discussion follow the synopsis.

The setting: tenth-grade life science class; 1:12–2:07 P.M.; spring semester.

Synopsis of Events

1:12	Bell rings.
1:12–1:21	Teacher directs students to read from their text while he takes attendance.
1:21–1:31	Teacher distributes to each student a handout; students are now to "label the parts of a flower" shown on the handout.
1:31–1:37	Students reading handout and labeling the flower parts.
1:37–1:39	Teacher verbally gives instructions for working on a real flower—"Compare with the flower drawing on the ditto handout"; students can use the microscopes if they want.
1:39–1:45	Teacher walks around room distributing to each student a real flower.
1:45–2:07	Chaos erupts. Much confusion, students wandering around room, throwing flower parts at each other. Teacher begins writing referrals and then sends two students to the office for their misbehavior. Teacher, flustered, directs students to spend remainder of period quietly reading from their texts. Two more referrals are written.
2:05–2:07	A few students begin meandering toward the exit.
2:07	End of period (much to the delight of the teacher).

Questions for Class Discussion

1. Do you think the teacher had a lesson plan? If so, what (if any) were its good points? Its problems?

_____

_____

_____

_____

_____

_____

2. If you believed that the teacher had a lesson plan, do you believe the teacher had a written and detailed lesson plan? Explain. What is your evidence?

_____

_____

_____

_____

_____

3. Explain how the lesson might have been prepared and implemented to avoid the chaos.

_____

_____

_____

_____

_____

_____

4. Was the format of the lesson "traditional"? Explain.

_____

_____

_____

_____

_____

_____

5. Have you experienced a class such as this? Explain.

_____

_____

_____

_____

_____

_____

6. What were this teacher's behaviors that were probable causes of much of the chaos?

_____

_____

_____

_____

_____

_____

7. What teacher behaviors could have prevented the chaos and made the lesson more effective?

_____

_____

_____

_____

_____

8. Within the 55-minute class period, students of this class were expected to operate rather high on the Learning Experiences Ladder (see Figure 6.5). Consider this analysis: 9 minutes of silent reading, 10 minutes of listening, 6 minutes of silent reading and labeling, 2 minutes of listening, 6 minutes of action (the only direct experience), and an additional 22 minutes of silent reading. In all, approximately 49 minutes (89 percent of the class time) were given to abstract verbal and visual symbolization. Is that a problem?

_____

_____

_____

_____

_____

9. Identify what you have learned from this exercise.

_____

_____

_____

_____

_____

_____

_____

_____

_____

_____

_____

_____

For Your Notes

─── **EXERCISE 5.6A** ───

Preparing a Lesson Plan

────────

Instructions: Use the model lesson format or an alternative format that is approved by your instructor to prepare a _____-minute lesson plan (length to be decided in your class) for a grade and course of your choice. After completing your lesson plan, evaluate it yourself, modify it, and then have your modified version evaluated by at least three peers, using Exercise 5.6B for the evaluation, before turning it in for your instructor's evaluation. This exercise may be connected with Exercise 5.7.

─── **EXERCISE 5.6B** ───

Evaluating a Lesson Plan

────────

Instructions: You may duplicate blank copies of this form for evaluation of the lesson you developed for Exercise 5.6A. Have your lesson plan evaluated by at least three of your peers and instructor. For each of the items below, evaluators should check either yes or no and write instructive comments. Compare the results of your self-evaluation with the evaluations of the others.

	No	*Yes*	*Comments*
1. Are descriptive data adequately provided?	____	____	_____ _____ _____ _____
2. Are the goals clearly stated?	____	____	_____ _____ _____ _____ _____
3. Are the objectives specific and measurable?	____	____	_____ _____ _____ _____

	No	*Yes*	*Comments*
4. Are objectives correctly classified?	____	____	
5. Are objectives only low-order, or is higher-order thinking expected?	____	____	
6. Is the rationale clear and justifiable?	____	____	
7. Is the plan's content appropriate?	____	____	
8. Is the content likely to contribute to achievement of the objectives?	____	____	

	No	*Yes*	*Comments*

9. Given the time frame and
other logistical considerations,
is the plan workable?

10. Will the opening (set) likely
engage the students?

11. Is there a preassessment
strategy?

12. Is there a proper mix of
learning activities for the
time frame of the lesson?

13. Are the activities
developmentally appropriate
for the intended students?

14. Are transitions planned?

	No	*Yes*	*Comments*

15. If relevant, are key
    questions written out and
    key ideas noted in the plan?

16. Does the plan indicate how
    coached practice will be
    provided for each student?

17. Is adequate closure provided
    in the plan?

18. Are needed materials and
    equipment identified, and
    are they appropriate?

19. Is there a planned formative
    assessment, and is it formal
    or informal?

20. Is there a planned summative
    assessment?

	No	*Yes*	*Comments*

21. Is the lesson coordinated in any way with other aspects of the curriculum?

22. Is the lesson likely to provide a sense of meaning for the students by helping to bridge their learning?

23. Is an adequate amount of time allotted to address the information presented?

24. Is a thoughtfully prepared and relevant student assignment planned?

25. Could a substitute who is knowledgeable follow the plan?

Additional comments:

For Your Notes

EXERCISE 5.7

Preparing a Teaching Unit

Instructions: The purpose of this exercise is threefold: (1) to give you experience in preparing an instructional unit, (2) to assist you in preparing an instructional unit that you can use in your teaching, and (3) to start your collection of instructional units that you may be able to use in your teaching. This assignment will take several hours to complete, and you will need to read ahead in this resource guide. Our advice, therefore, is to start the assignment early, with a due date much later in the course. Your course instructor may have specific guidelines for your completion of this exercise; what follows is the essence of what you are to do.

First, your course instructor will divide your class into three teams, each with a different assignment pertaining to this exercise. The units completed by these teams are to be shared with all members of the class for feedback and possible use later.

Team 1

Members of this team, individually or in dyads, will develop standard teaching units, perhaps with different grade levels in mind. (You will need to review the content of Chapters 6–13.) Using a format that is practical, each member or pair of this team will develop a minimum two-week (10-day) unit for a particular subject and grade level. Regardless of format chosen, each unit plan should include the following elements:

1. Identification of (a) grade level, (b) subject, (c) topic, and (d) time duration.

2. Statement of rationale and general goals.

3. Separate listing of instructional objectives for each daily lesson. Wherever possible, the unit should include objectives from all three domains—cognitive, affective, and psychomotor.

4. List of materials and resources needed and where they can be obtained (if you have that information). These should also be listed for each daily lesson.

5. Ten consecutive daily lesson plans (see Exercise 5.6).

6. List of all items that will be used to assess student learning *during* and *at completion of* the unit of study.

7. Statement of how the unit will attend to variations in students' reading levels, socioethnic backgrounds, and special needs.

Team 2

Following the steps of Exercise 8.1, *each member* of this team will develop a self-instructional module.

Team 3

In collaboration, members of this team will develop interdisciplinary thematic units.* Depending upon the number of students in your class, Team 3 may actually comprise several teams, with each team developing an interdisciplinary thematic unit. Each team should have no less than two members (e.g., a math specialist and a science specialist) and no more than four (e.g., social studies, language arts/reading, mathematics, and science).

---

* Sample interdisciplinary thematic units can be seen in the 1996 publications by Kellough, by Roberts and Kellough, and by Schurr, listed in the Suggested Readings at the end of this chapter.

Summary

With this chapter you continued building your knowledge base about why planning is important and how units with lessons are useful pedagogical tools. Developing units of instruction that integrate student learning and provide a sense of meaning for the students requires coordination throughout the curriculum. Hence, for students, learning is a process of discovering how information, knowledge, and ideas are interrelated so that they can make sense out of self, school, and life. Preparing chunks of information into units and units into lessons helps students to process and understand knowledge. You have developed your first unit of instruction and are well on your way to becoming a competent planner of instruction.

In Part II, you have been guided through the processes necessary to prepare yourself to teach in a classroom. Later, after you have studied Part III on specific instructional strategies, aids, media, and resources to supplement your instruction, you may choose to revisit this chapter and make revisions to your completed unit and lessons.

Questions for Class Discussion

1. Explain the value of organizing instruction into units. For a specific grade level, identify and describe criteria for selecting a topic for a unit of study. Describe the types of activities that could be used in the introductory phase of a unit and in the culminating phase.
2. Describe the concept of integrated curriculum.
3. Explain the importance of the notion that all teachers are teachers of reading, writing, studying, and thinking. Do you agree or disagree with the notion? Why?
4. Describe how the teacher can attend to student learning styles, learning capacities, and modality strengths in unit and lesson planning.
5. Give several reasons why both a student teacher and a first-year teacher need to prepare detailed lesson plans. Explain why you need to know how to prepare detailed unit and lesson plans even if the textbook program you are using provides them.
6. In subject-field discussion groups, list and describe specific considerations you should give to student safety when preparing unit and lesson plans. Share your lists with other groups.
7. Collaborating with several classmates from the same teaching field as you, identify two or three units of instruction that are common for a certain grade level in your subject. Brainstorm creative and motivating ways of introducing those units to students. Share your results with the rest of your class.
8. Describe any prior concepts you held that changed as a result of your experiences with this chapter. Describe the changes.
9. From your current observations and fieldwork as related to this teacher preparation program, clearly identify one specific example of educational practice that seems contradictory to exemplary practice or theory as presented in this chapter. Present your explanation for the discrepancy.
10. Do you have questions generated by the content of this chapter? If you do, list them along with ways answers might be found.

Suggested Readings

Barab, S. A., and Landa, A. "Designing Effective Interdisciplinary Anchors." *Educational Leadership* 54(6):52–55 (March 1997).

Beane, J. A. "Curriculum Integration and the Disciplines of Knowledge." *Phi Delta Kappan* 76(8):616–622 (April 1995).

Burns, R. C., and Sattes, B. D. *Dissolving the Boundaries: Planning for Curriculum Integration in Middle and Secondary Schools.* Charleston, WV: Appalachia Educational Laboratory, 1995.

Clarke, J. H., and Agne, R. M. *Interdisciplinary High School Teaching: Strategies for Integrated Learning.* Boston: Allyn & Bacon, 1997.

Coate, J., and White, N. "History/English Core." *Social Studies Review* 34(3):12–15 (Spring 1996).

Fogarty, R., and Stoehr, J. *Integrating Curricula with Multiple Intelligences.* Palatine, IL: Skylight Publishing, 1995.

House, P. A., and Coxford, A. F., eds. *Connecting Mathematics across the Curriculum. 1995 Yearbook.* Reston, VA: National Council of Teachers of Mathematics, 1995.

Huebel-Drake, M., et al. "Planning a Course for Success: Using an Integrated Curriculum to Prepare Students for the Twenty-First Century." *Science Teacher* 62(7):18–21 (October 1995).

Impson, P. D., et al. "Interdisciplinary Education—You Bet It Can Work!" *NASSP Bulletin* 79(569):32–37 (March 1995).

Irvin, J. L. "Building Sound Literacy Learning Programs for Young Adolescents." *Middle School Journal* 28(3):4–9 (January 1997).

Kellough, R. D. *Integrating Language Arts and Social Studies for Intermediate and Middle School Students.* Upper Saddle River, NJ: Prentice Hall, 1996.

Kellough, R. D. *Integrating Mathematics and Science for Intermediate and Middle School Students.* Upper Saddle River, NJ: Prentice Hall, 1996.

Korithoski, T. "Finding Quadratic Equations for Real-Life Situations." *Mathematics Teacher* 89(2):154–157 (February 1996).

Light, C. "Illuminated Medieval Newspaper: Cross Curriculum Research for World History." *Social Studies Review* 34(3):36–39 (Spring 1996).

Lindquist, T. *Seeing the Whole through Social Studies.* Portsmouth, NH: Heinemann, 1995.

Loewen, J. W. *Lies My Teacher Told Me: Everything Your American History Textbook Got Wrong.* New York: Touchstone Books, 1996.

Martin-Kniep, G. O., et al. "Curriculum Integration: An Expanded View of an Abused Idea." *Journal of Curriculum and Supervision* 10(3):227–249 (Spring 1995).

McFaden, D., et al. "Redesigning the Model: A Successfully Integrated Approach to Teaching and Learning." *NASSP (National Association of Secondary School Principals) Bulletin* 80(577):1–6 (February 1996).

Monroe, B. "Teaching Extended Class Periods." *Social Education* 60(2):77–79 (February 1996).

Nagel, N. G. *Learning through Real-World Problem Solving: The Power of Integrative Teaching.* Thousand Oaks, CA: Corwin Press, 1996.

North Carolina State Department of Public Instruction. *A Guide for Curriculum Integration of Academic and Vocational/Technical Education: Why? How?* Raleigh, NC: North Carolina State Department of Public Instruction, 1995.

Nowicki, J. J., and Meehan, K. F. *Interdisciplinary Strategies for English and Social Studies Classrooms: Toward Collaborative Middle and Secondary School Teaching.* Boston: Allyn & Bacon, 1997.

Panaritis, P. "Beyond Brainstorming: Planning a Successful Interdisciplinary Program." *Phi Delta Kappan* 76(8):623–628 (April 1995).

Peters, T., Schubeck, K., and Hopkins, K. "A Thematic Approach: Theory and Practice at the Aleknagik School." *Phi Delta Kappan* 76(8):633–636 (April 1995).

Post, T. R., et al. *Interdisciplinary Approaches to Curriculum: Themes for Teaching.* Upper Saddle River, NJ: Prentice Hall, 1997.

Roberts, P. L., and Kellough, R. D. *A Guide for Developing an Interdisciplinary Thematic Unit.* Upper Saddle River, NJ: Prentice Hall, 1996.

Rosen, C., and Bartels, D. "Trade and Exploration: A Representation." *Social Studies Review* 34(3):30–34 (Spring 1996).

Sadowski, M. "Moving beyond Traditional Subjects Requires Teachers to Abandon Their 'Comfort Zones.'" *The Harvard Education Letter* 11(5):1–5 (September/October 1995).

Schurr, S., et al. *Signaling Student Success: Thematic Learning Stations and Integrated Units for Middle Level Classrooms.* Columbus, OH: National Middle School Association, 1996.

Seely, A. E. *Integrated Thematic Units.* Westminster, CA: Teacher Created Materials, 1995.

Shabbas, A. "Living History with a Medieval Banquet in the Alhambra Palace." *Social Studies Review* 34(3):22–29 (Spring 1996).

Tomlinson, C. A. *How to Differentiate Instruction in Mixed-Ability Classrooms.* Alexandria, VA: Association for Supervision and Curriculum Development, 1995.

PART

III

CHOOSING AND IMPLEMENTING INSTRUCTIONAL STRATEGIES, AIDS, MEDIA, AND RESOURCES

Part III helps you to develop an instructional strategy repertoire by

- Developing your understanding about when and how to use direct and indirect instruction.

- Providing guidelines and resources for
  —establishing a resource file.
  —helping students to develop their thinking skills.
  —using media.

- Providing guidelines and skill development for using (1) questioning and (2) formal and informal teacher talk.
- Providing guidelines for
  —developing a self-instructional module.
  —individualizing the instruction.
  —maintaining equality in the classroom.
  —planning and selecting appropriate learning activities.
- Providing guidelines for using
  —assignments.
  —homework.
  —discussions.
  —the community.
  —field trips.
  —learning activity centers.
  —cooperative learning.
  —copyrighted materials.
  —demonstrations and educational games.

  —independent study, projects, papers, and oral reports.
  —inquiry and discovery learning activities.
  —the overhead projector and other equipment.
  —the writing board and other visual displays.
  —various ways of grouping students for the most effective learning.
- Providing information about (1) the ERIC information network and (2) teaching toward mastery learning.
- Providing information and resources for
  —an on-line classroom.
  —use of television.
  —writing across the curriculum.
- Providing resources for computer software, CD-ROMs, and videodiscs.
- Providing sources for free and inexpensive materials.

Reflective Thoughts

Your goals should include helping students to learn how to solve problems, to make decisions, to think creatively and critically, and to feel good about themselves and their learning. To do this, you will

1. *Involve students in direct experiences, both hands-on and minds-on, so they use more of their sensory modalities and develop their learning capacities.*

When all the senses are engaged, learning is the most effective and longest lasting.

2. *Use questioning in a way designed to guide students to higher levels of thinking and doing.*

3. *Share in the responsibility for teaching reading, writing, thinking, and study skills.*

Chapter

6

Theoretical Considerations for the Selection of Instructional Strategies

In Chapter 2, you learned about specific teacher behaviors that must be in place for students to learn. These fundamental nondiscretionary behaviors are structuring the learning environment; accepting instructional accountability; demonstrating withitness and overlapping; providing a variety of motivating and challenging activities; modeling appropriate behaviors; facilitating students' acquisition of data; creating a psychologically safe environment; clarifying whenever necessary; using periods of silence; and questioning thoughtfully. In this part of the book, you will learn more not only about how to implement some of those fundamental behaviors, but also about the large repertoire of other strategies, aids, media, and resources available (see Figure 6.1). You will learn how to select from and implement this repertoire.

You must make myriad decisions to select and implement a particular teaching strategy effectively. The selection of a strategy depends in part upon your decision either to deliver information directly (direct, expository, or didactic teaching) or to provide students with the access to information (indirect or facilitative teaching). Direct teaching tends to be teacher-centered, while indirect teaching is more student-centered. To assist in your selection of strategies, it is important that you understand basic principles of learning. That is the purpose of this brief but fundamentally important first chapter of Part III. Specifically, upon completion of this chapter you should be able to

1. Demonstrate an understanding of the differences between and the advantages and disadvantages of direct and indirect instructional strategies.
2. Describe at least three important principles of teaching and learning.

3. Explain the difference and the relationship between hands-on and minds-on learning.
4. Give examples in your subject field of learning experiences from each of these categories and when and why you would use each one: verbal, visual, vicarious, simulated, and direct. Give examples of how, why, and when they could be combined.
5. Demonstrate your understanding of the meaning of the term *authentic learning*.

DIRECT AND INDIRECT INSTRUCTION: A CLARIFICATION OF TERMS

You are probably well aware that professional education is replete with its own special jargon, which can be confusing to the beginner. The term *direct teaching* (or its synonym, *direct instruction*) and its antonym, *direct experience*, are examples of how confusing the jargon can be. Direct teaching (or direct instruction, expository teaching, or teacher-centered instruction) has a variety of definitions, depending on who is doing the defining. For now, you should keep this distinction in mind—do not confuse direct teaching with direct experience. The two terms indicate two separate (though not incompatible) instructional modes. The dichotomy of pedagogical opposites shown in Figure 6.2 provides a useful visual distinction of the opposites. While terms in one column are similar if not synonymous, they are near or exact opposites of those across in the other column.

Rather than focus attention on the selection of a particular model of teaching, we prefer to emphasize the importance of an eclectic model, selecting the best from various models or approaches (see Figure 6.3). For example,

Figure 6.1
A list of instructional strategies.

Assignment	Laser videodisc or compact disc
Autotutorial	Lecture
Brainstorming	Library/resource center
Coaching	Metacognition
Collaborative learning	Mock-up
Cooperative learning	Multimedia
Debate	Panel discussion
Demonstration	Problem solving
Discovery	Project
Drama	Questioning
Drill	Review and practice
Expository	Role play
Field trip	Self-instructional module
Game	Simulation
Group work	Study guide
Guest speaker	Symposium
Homework	Telecommunication
Individualized instruction	Term paper
Inquiry	Textbook
Interactive media	Think-pair-share
Laboratory investigation	Tutorial

Figure 6.2
Pedagogical opposites.

Delivery mode of instruction versus Access mode of instruction
Didactic instruction versus Facilitative teaching
Direct instruction versus Indirect instruction
Direct teaching versus Direct experiencing
Expository teaching versus Discovery learning
Teacher-centered instruction versus Student-centered instruction

there will be times when you want to use a direct, teacher-centered approach, perhaps with a minilecture or a demonstration. And then there are many more times when you will want to use an indirect, student-centered or social-interactive approach, such as the use of cooperative learning and other small-group activities. And perhaps there are even more times when you will be doing both at the same time, for example, working with a teacher-centered approach with one small group of students, perhaps giving them direct instruction, while another group or several groups of students, in another area of the classroom, are working on their project study (a student-centered approach). This chapter and those that follow in Part III will help you make decisions about when each approach is most appropriate and provide guidelines for their use.

Principles of Instruction and Learning

To decide which mode of instruction to use, you must bear in mind certain principles of instruction and learning that have evolved from studies of recent years. Six important principles are as follows:

1. To a great degree, it is the mode of instruction that determines what is learned.
2. Students must be actively involved in their own learning and in the assessment of their learning.
3. You must hold high expectations for the learning of each student (although not necessarily identical expectations for every student) and not waiver from those expectations.
4. Students need constant, steady, understandable, and reliable feedback about their learning.
5. Students should be engaged in independent study and cooperative learning and give and receive tutorial instruction.
6. Most important, you are a teacher of reading, writing, thinking, and study skills.

A student does not learn to write by learning to recognize grammatical constructions of sentences. Neither does a person learn to play soccer solely by listening to a lecture on soccer. School learning is superficial unless the instructional methods and learning activities are developmentally appropriate for the age level of the learn-

Figure 6.3
Families of instructional models.
(*Source:* B. R. Joyce and E. F.
Calhoun, *Creating Learning
Experiences: The Role of
Instructional Theory and
Research* [Alexandria, VA:
Association for Supervision and
Curriculum Development,
1996].)

Information-processing models
- Advance organizer
- Concept attainment
- Inductive thinking
- Scientific inquiry
- Mnemonics
- Synectics

Personal models
- Nondirective teaching
- Classroom meeting
- Self-actualization

Social models
- Group investigation
- Laboratory method
- Role-play
- Social inquiry

Behavioral systems models
- Direct teaching
- Mastery learning
- Programmed learning
- Simulation
- Social learning

ers and intellectually appropriate for the understanding, skills, and attitudes desired. Memorizing, for instance, is not the same as understanding. Yet far too often, memorization seems all that is expected of students in school. The result is low-level learning, a mere verbalism or mouthing of poorly understood words and sentences. That is not teaching, but just the orchestration of short-term memory exercises. A mental model of learning that assumes a brain is capable of doing only one thing at a time is invidiously incorrect.[1]

Authentic Learning: Conceptual versus Procedural Knowledge

As discussed in Chapter 5, researchers have distinguished between conceptual knowledge and procedural knowledge. Conceptual knowledge refers to the knowledge of relationships, whereas procedural knowledge entails the recording in memory of the meanings of symbols and rules and procedures needed to accomplish tasks. Unless it is connected in meaningful ways for the formation of conceptual knowledge, the accumulation of memorized procedural knowledge is fragmented and ill-fated and will be maintained in the brain for only a brief time.

To help students establish conceptual knowledge, the learning for students must be real. To make learning real to students, you should use direct and real experiences as often as possible. Vicarious experiences are sometimes necessary to provide students with otherwise unattainable knowledge; however, direct experiences that en-

gage all the students' senses and all their learning modalities are more powerful. Students learn to write by writing and by receiving coaching and feedback about their progress in writing. They learn to play soccer by experiencing playing soccer and by receiving coaching and feedback about their developing skills and knowledge in playing the game. They learn these things best when they are actively (hands-on) and mentally (minds-on) engaged in doing them. This is real learning, learning that is meaningful, or as known today, *authentic learning*.

Direct versus Indirect Instructional Modes: Strengths and Weaknesses of Each

When selecting an instructional strategy (see the comparison of pedagogical opposites in Figure 6.2), you must make a decision based on two distinct choices: should you deliver information to students (expository teaching), or should you provide students with access to information? The purpose of the *delivery mode* (known also as the didactic style) is to deliver information. Knowledge is passed on from those who know (the teachers, with the aid of textbooks) to those who do not (the students). Within the delivery mode, traditional and time-honored strategies are textbook reading, the lecture (formal teacher talk), questioning, and teacher-centered or teacher-planned discussions. For the classroom teacher, teacher talk (discussed in Chapter 9) is an important and nearly unavoidable teaching tool, and it can be valuable when used judiciously.

With the *access mode,* instead of direct delivery of information and direct control over what is learned, you provide access to information by working *with* the students. Together, you and the students design experiences that facilitate their building of their existing schemata and their obtaining new knowledge and skills. Learning is often better when students are taught by the

---

1. See, for example, R. Sylwester, *A Celebration of Neurons: An Educator's Guide to the Human Brain* (Alexandria, VA: Association for Supervision and Curriculum Development, 1995), and R. N. Caine and G. Caine, *Making Connections: Teaching and the Human Brain* (Alexandria, VA: Association for Supervision and Curriculum Development, 1991).

DELIVERY MODE

Strengths

- Much content can be covered within a short span of time, usually by formal teacher talk, which then may be followed by an experiential activity.
- The teacher is in control of what content is covered.
- The teacher is in control of time allotted to specific content coverage.
- Strategies within the delivery mode are consistent with competency-based instruction.
- Student achievement of specific content is predictable and manageable.

Potential Weaknesses

- The sources of student motivation are mostly extrinsic.
- Students have little control over the pacing of their learning.
- Students make few important decisions about their learning.
- There may be little opportunity for divergent or creative thinking.
- Student self-esteem may be inadequately served.

Figure 6.4
Delivery mode: its strengths and weaknesses.

ACCESS MODE

Strengths

- Students learn content and in more depth.
- The sources of student motivation are more likely intrinsic.
- Students make important decisions about their own learning.
- Students have more control over the pacing of their learning.
- Students develop a sense of personal self-worth.

Potential Weaknesses

- Content coverage may be more limited.
- Strategies are time-consuming.
- The teacher has less control over content and time.
- The specific results of student learning are less predictable.
- The teacher may have less control over class procedures.

Figure 6.5
Access mode: its strengths and weaknesses.

access mode, especially learning at the higher levels of the learning domains. Within the access mode, two important instructional strategies are cooperative learning and inquiry, which most certainly will use questioning, although the questions will come from the students more frequently than from you or the textbook. Discussions and lectures on particular topics also may be involved, but when used in the access mode, they follow or occur during (rather than precede) direct, hands-on learning by the students.

You are probably more experienced with the delivery mode. To be most effective as a teacher, however, you must become knowledgeable of and skillful in using access strategies. Strategies within the access mode clearly facilitate the positive learning and acquisition of conceptual knowledge by students and help build student self-esteem.

To be most effective as a teacher, you should be eclectic in selecting strategies—that is, you should appropriately select and effectively use strategies from both modes, but with a strong favor toward access strategies. Thus, from your study of the chapters that follow in this part, you will become knowledgeable about using techniques within each mode so that you can make intelligent decisions for choosing the best strategy for particular goals and objectives for your own discipline and unique group of students. The information in Figures 6.4 and 6.5 provides

an overview of the specific strengths and weaknesses of each mode. By comparing those figures, you can see that the strengths and weaknesses of one mode are nearly mirror opposites of the other. As noted earlier, although you should be skillful in the use of strategies from both modes, you should concentrate more on using strategies from the access mode to be most effective in teaching the diversity of learners in today's classrooms. Strategies within that mode are more student-centered, hands-on, and concrete; students interact with one another and are actually or closer to doing what they are learning to do. Learning that occurs from the use of that mode is longer lasting (fixes into long-term memory). And, as the students interact with one another and with their learning, they develop a sense of "can do," which enhances their self-esteem.[2]

PLANNING AND SELECTING LEARNING ACTIVITIES

Can you imagine a soccer coach teaching students the skills and knowledge needed to play soccer without ever letting them experience playing the game? Can you imagine a science teacher instructing students on how to read a thermometer without ever letting them actually read an authentic thermometer? Can you imagine a geography teacher teaching students how to read a map

---

2. See, for example, R. V. Ness, *Raising Self-Esteem of Learners* (Bloomington, IN: Fastback 389, Phi Delta Kappa Educational Foundation, 1995).

Figure 6.6

The Learning Experiences Ladder. (*Source:* Earlier versions of this concept are found in Charles F. Hoban, Sr., et al., *Visualizing the Curriculum* [New York: Dryden, 1937], p. 39; Jerome S. Bruner, *Toward a Theory of Instruction* [Cambridge: Harvard University Press, 1966], p. 49; Edgar Dale, *Audio-Visual Methods in Teaching* [New York: Holt, Rinehart & Winston, 1969], p. 108; and Eugene C. Kim and Richard D. Kellough, *A Resource Guide for Secondary School Teaching*, 2nd ed. [Upper Saddle River, NJ: Prentice Hall, 1978], p. 136.)

Verbal Experiences

Teacher talk, written words; engaging only one sense; using the most abstract symbolization; students physically inactive. *Examples:* (1) Listening to the teacher talk about tidal pools. (2) Listening to a student report about the Grand Canyon. (3) Listening to a guest speaker talk about how the state legislature functions.

Visual Experiences

Still pictures, diagrams, charts; engaging only one sense; typically symbolic; students physically inactive. *Examples:* (1) Viewing slide photographs of tidal pools. (2) Viewing drawings and photographs of the Grand Canyon. (3) Listening to a guest speaker talk about the state legislature and show slides of it in action.

Vicarious Experiences

Laser videodisc programs; computer programs; video programs; engaging more than one sense; learner indirectly "doing"; may be some limited physical activity. *Examples:* (1) Interacting with a computer program about wave action and life in tidal pools. (2) Viewing and listening to a video program about the Grand Canyon. (3) Taking a field trip to observe the state legislature in action.

Simulated Experiences

Role-playing; experimenting; simulations; mock-up; working models; all or nearly all senses engaged; activity often integrating disciplines; closest to the real thing. *Examples:* (1) Building a classroom working model of a tidal pool. (2) Building a classroom working model of the Grand Canyon. (3) Designing a classroom role-play simulation patterned after the operating procedure of the state legislature.

Direct Experiences

Learner actually doing what is being learned; true inquiry; all senses engaged; usually integrates disciplines; the real thing. *Examples:* (1) Visiting and experiencing a tidal pool. (2) Visiting and experiencing the Grand Canyon. (3) Designing an elected representative body to oversee the operation of the school-within-the-school program and pattern after the state legislative assembly.

ABSTRACT

CONCRETE

without ever letting them put their eyes and hands on a real map? Can you imagine trying to teach a child to play the piano without ever letting the child put her hands on a keyboard? Unfortunately, too many teachers do almost those exact things—they try to teach students to do something without letting the students practice doing it.

In planning and selecting learning activities, an important rule to remember is to select activities that are as direct as possible. When students are involved in direct experiences, they are using more of their sensory input channels, their learning modalities (i.e., auditory, visual, tactile, kinesthetic). And when all the senses are engaged, learning is most effective, most meaningful, and longest lasting. This "learning by doing" is authentic learning or, as it is sometimes referred to, *hands-on/minds-on learning.*

The Learning Experiences Ladder

Figure 6.6 depicts a range of experiences known as the Learning Experiences Ladder. Hands-on/minds-on learning is at the bottom of the ladder. At the top are abstract experiences, where the learner is exposed only to symbolization (i.e., words and numbers) and uses only one or two senses (auditory or visual). The teacher lectures while the students sit and watch and hear. Visual and verbal symbolic experiences, although impossible to avoid when teaching, are less effective in ensuring that planned and meaningful learning occurs. This is especially so with learners who have special needs, learners with ethnic and cultural differences, and students who have only a limited English-language proficiency. Thus, when planning learning experiences and selecting instructional materials, you are advised to select activities that engage the students in the most direct experiences possible and that are developmentally and intellectually appropriate for your specific group of students.

As can be inferred from the Learning Experiences Ladder, when you are teaching about tidal pools (the first example for each step), the most effective mode is to take the students to a tidal pool (direct experience), where they can see, hear, touch, smell, and perhaps even taste (if not toxic) it. The least effective mode is for the teacher to merely talk about the tidal pool (verbal experience, the most abstract and symbolic experience), engaging only one sense—auditory.

Of course, for various reasons, such as matters of safety, lack of resources, or geographical location of your school, you may not be able to take your students to a tidal pool. You cannot always use the most direct experience, so sometimes you must select an experience higher on the ladder. Self-discovery teaching is not always appropriate. Sometimes it is more appropriate to build upon what others have discovered and learned. Although learners do not need to "reinvent the wheel," the most effective and longest-lasting learning is that which engages most or all of their senses. On the Learning Experiences Ladder, those are the experiences that fall within the bottom three categories—direct, simulated, and vicarious. This is true with adult learners or with primary grade children or students of any age group in between.

Another value of direct, simulated, and vicarious experiences is that they tend to be interdisciplinary; that is, they blur or cross subject-content boundaries. That makes those experiences especially useful for teachers who want to help students connect the learning of one discipline with that of others and to bridge what is being learned with their own life experiences. Direct, simulated, and vicarious experiences are more like real life. That means that the learning is authentic.

Now do Exercises 6.1 and 6.2.

EXERCISE 6.1

Recalling My Own Learning Experiences in School

Instructions: The purpose of this exercise is to recall and share learning experiences from your own school days. You should reflect upon those with respect to their relationship to the Learning Experiences Ladder and the discussion of the access and delivery modes of instruction.

1. Recall one vivid learning experience from each level of your schooling and identify its position on the learning experiences ladder.

   a. Elementary school

   Experience: _____

   _____

   _____

   _____

   _____

   _____

   Position on ladder: _____

   _____

   _____

   _____

   _____

   b. Middle grades

   Experience: _____

   _____

   _____

   _____

   _____

   _____

   Position on ladder: _____

   _____

   _____

   _____

   _____

c. High school

Experience: _____

_____

_____

_____

_____

_____

Position on ladder: _____

_____

_____

_____

d. College

Experience: _____

_____

_____

_____

_____

_____

Position on ladder: _____

_____

_____

_____

2. Share your information with small groups of classmates. What conclusions, if any, can your group reach? Write them here, and share them with the entire class. _____

_____

_____

_____

_____

_____

_____

EXERCISE 6.2
Conversion of an Abstract Learning Experience to a Direct One

Instructions: This exercise is to tax your creative imagination. Its purpose is for you to select from your course outline a topic that is typically taught by the use of symbolization (at or near the top of the Learning Experiences Ladder), then devise a technique by which, with limited resources, that same content would be taught more directly (at or close to the bottom of the ladder). Upon completion of this exercise, share your proposal with your colleagues for their feedback.

1. Grade level: _____

2. Topic: _____

   _____

3. Traditional way of teaching this topic: _____

   _____

   _____

   _____

   _____

4. Detailed description of how to teach this topic using direct learning experiences: _____

   _____

   _____

   _____

   _____

   _____

5. Statement about why you believe a direct way of teaching this topic is uncommon: _____

   _____

   _____

   _____

   _____

   _____

6. Ideas resulting from sharing your proposal with others in your class: _____

   _____

   _____

   _____

   _____

SUMMARY

You have learned of the importance of learning modalities and instructional modes. You have learned about adolescents, their needs, and the importance of providing an accepting and supportive learning environment, as well as about teacher behaviors that are necessary to facilitate student learning beyond that of procedural knowledge. In this chapter in particular, you learned about the importance of selecting strategies that enhance authentic learning. And, in connection with those things, you have reflected on your own experiences as a student.

In the remaining chapters of Part III, your attention is directed to the selection and implementation of specific strategies, aids, and resources to facilitate students learning of particular skills and content, beginning in the next chapter with the use of questioning.

QUESTIONS FOR CLASS DISCUSSION

1. Working in groups of three, make two lists, one of direct instructional strategies and one of indirect instructional strategies. Next to each item on each list, describe a specific teaching situation in which you would most likely use that strategy.
2. Divide your class into subject groups. Have each group devise two separate lesson plans to teach the same topic to the same group of students (identified), with one plan using direct instruction and the other using indirect. Have groups share the outcomes of this activity with one another.
3. Compare and contrast the words in the following sets of terms: direct and indirect instruction; access and delivery modes of instruction; didactic and facilitating teaching styles. Within which mode is project-centered thematic teaching? Why?
4. Explain why, when taught by access strategies, students learn less content but learn it more effectively? Which mode, access or delivery, do you believe better encourages student thinking? Explain. Can you find research evidence to support your conclusion? Do you believe use of either mode, access or delivery, does more to enhance the development of student self-esteem? Explain. Can you find research evidence to support your conclusion?
5. Regarding the significance of the Learning Experiences Ladder, explain why activities at the bottom of the ladder are less abstract than those at the top.
6. In your subject field, do female students learn any differently from male students? Is it even fair to ask this question? Explain.
7. Which mode, access or delivery, better encourages student thinking? Explain your reasons why.
8. Describe any prior concepts you held that changed as a result of your experiences with this chapter. Describe the changes.
9. From your current observations and field work as related to this teacher preparation program, clearly identify one specific example of educational practice that seems contradictory to exemplary practice or theory as presented in this chapter. Present your explanation for the discrepancy.
10. Do you have questions generated by the content of this chapter? If you do, list them along with ways answers might be found.

SUGGESTED READINGS

Brooks, J. G., and Brooks, M. G. *In Search of Understanding: The Case for Constructivist Classrooms.* Alexandria, VA: Association for Supervision and Curriculum Development, 1993.

Caine, R. N., and Caine, G. *Making Connections: Teaching and the Human Brain.* Alexandria, VA: Association for Supervision and Curriculum Development, 1991.

Cronin, J. F. "Four Misconceptions about Authentic Learning." *Educational Leadership* 50(7):78–80 (April 1993).

Dunn, R. *Strategies for Educating Diverse Learners.* Bloomington, IN: Fastback 384, Phi Delta Kappa Educational Foundation, 1995.

Dunn, R., and Dunn, K. *Teaching Secondary Students through Their Individual Learning Styles: Practical Approaches for Grades 7–12.* Boston: Allyn & Bacon, 1992.

McTighe, J. "What Happens between Assessments?" *Educational Leadership* 54(4):6–12 (December 1996/January 1997).

Perkins, D., and Blythe, T. "Putting Understanding Up Front." *Educational Leadership* 51(5):4–7 (February 1994).

Rafoth, M. A., et al. *Strategies for Learning and Remembering.* Washington, DC: National Education Association, 1993.

Sadowski, M. "Moving beyond Traditional Subjects Requires Teachers to Abandon Their 'Comfort Zones.'" *The Harvard Education Letter* 11(5):1–5 (September/October 1995).

Slavin, R. E. *Educational Psychology: Theory into Practice.* 4th ed. Boston: Allyn & Bacon, 1994.

Sylwester, R. *A Celebration of Neurons: An Educator's Guide to the Human Brain.* Alexandria, VA: Association for Supervision and Curriculum Development, 1995.

Wlodkowski, R. J., and Ginsberg, M. B. "A Framework for Responsive Teaching." *Educational Leadership* 53(1):17–21 (September 1995).

Wlodkowski, R. J., and Ginsberg, M. B. *Diversity and Motivation: Culturally Responsive Teaching.* San Francisco: Jossey-Bass, 1995.

Zahorik, J. A. *Constructivist Teaching.* Bloomington, IN: Fastback 390, Phi Delta Kappa Educational Foundation, 1995.

Chapter

7

Questioning for Teaching and Learning

A strategy of fundamental importance to any mode of instruction is, as introduced in Chapter 2, questioning. You will use questioning for so many purposes that you must be skilled in its use to teach effectively. Because it is so important, and because it is so frequently used and abused, this entire chapter is devoted to assisting you in the development of your skills in using questioning. Specifically, upon completion of this chapter you should be able to

1. Identify five categories of purposes for which questioning can be used as an instructional strategy.
2. Demonstrate an understanding of the types of cognitive questions.
3. Develop ways of helping students to develop their metacognitive skills.
4. Contrast the three levels of questioning and compare those with levels of thinking.
5. Demonstrate skill in the use of questioning as an instructional strategy.
6. Explain the value and use of students' questions.

PURPOSES FOR USING QUESTIONING

You will adapt the type and form of each question to the purpose for which it is asked. The purposes that questions can serve can be separated into five categories, as follows.

1. *To politely give instructions.* An example, "Alexandria, would you please turn out the lights so we can show the slides?" Although they probably should avoid doing so, teachers sometimes also use rhetorical questions for the purpose of regaining student

attention and maintaining classroom control, for example, "Josephine, would you please attend to your work?" Rhetorical questions can sometimes backfire on the teacher. In this case, for example, Josephine might say no; then the teacher would have a problem that could perhaps have been avoided had he simply told Josephine to attend to her work rather than asked her to.
2. *To review and remind students of classroom procedures.* For example, if students continue to talk when they shouldn't, you can stop the lesson and ask, "Class, I think we need to review the procedure for listening when someone else is talking. What is the procedure that we agreed upon?"
3. *To gather information.* An example is, "How many of you have finished the exercise?" Or, to find out whether a student knows something, "Charlie, can you please tell us what the difference is between a synonym and an antonym?"
4. *To discover student knowledge, interests, or experiences.* Examples are, "How many of you think you know the process by which water in our city is made potable?" or "How many of you have visited the local water treatment plant?"
5. *To guide student thinking and learning.* This category of questioning is the focus of our attention in this chapter. Questions in this category are used to (a) clarify a student response, (b) develop appreciation, (c) develop student thinking and metacognition, (d) diagnose learning difficulty, (e) emphasize major points, (f) encourage students, (g) establish rapport, (h) assess learning, (i) provide practice in expression, (j) help students to organize and interpret materials, (k) probe more deeply into a student's thinking,

(l) provide drill and practice, (m) provide review, (n) show agreement or disagreement, and (o) show relationships, such as cause and effect or comparisons.

Questions to Avoid Asking

Before going further, we must emphasize that while it is important to avoid asking rhetorical questions, that is, questions for which you do not want a response, you should also avoid asking questions that call for little or no student thinking, such as those that can be answered with a simple yes or no or some other alternative response. Such questions have little or no diagnostic value; they encourage guessing and inappropriate student responses that can cause classroom control problems for the teacher.

It is even more important to avoid using questions that embarrass a student, punish a student, or in any way deny the student's dignity. Questions that embarrass or punish tend to damage the student's developing self-esteem and serve no meaningful academic or instructional purpose. Questioning is an important instructional tool that should be used by the teacher only for academic reasons. Although it is not always possible to predict when a student might be embarrassed by a question, a teacher should *never* deliberately ask questions for the purpose of embarrassment or punishment. When done deliberately, that teacher's action borders on abuse!

Here are some ways that teachers have used questions to punish or embarrass students.[1] Following each example is a suggestion for handling the problem without punishing or embarrassing the student:

- A student who forgot to do the homework assignment is deliberately asked a question from that assignment.
  Instead, make a list of the students who didn't do the homework.
- A student who never volunteers is asked a question.
  Instead, give students who never volunteer a list of sample questions beforehand and tell them that you will be calling on them.
- A student gives a wrong response and then is asked an even more difficult question.
  Instead, give the student another try, and provide prompts, hints, and clues.
- A student who disrupts the class is purposely asked a question for which the answer cannot possibly be known.
  Instead, use a disciplinary sanction for disrupting the class, such as a time-out (discussed in Chapter 3).

TYPES OF COGNITIVE QUESTIONS: A GLOSSARY

In this section we define, describe, and provide examples for each of the *types* of cognitive questions that you will use in teaching. Although we refer to these as cognitive questions, any question type could relate to any of the three domains of learning (cognitive, affective, or psychomotor). In the section that follows, your attention is focused on the *levels* of cognitive questions.

CLARIFYING QUESTION.   The clarifying question is used to gain more information from a student to help the teacher better understand a student's ideas, feelings, and thought processes. Often, asking a student to elaborate on an initial response will lead her to think more deeply, restructure her thinking, and while doing so, discover a fallacy in the original response. Examples of clarifying questions are "What I hear you saying is that you would rather work alone than in your group. Is that correct?" "So, Patrick, you think the poem is a sad one, is that right?" Research has shown a strong positive correlation between student learning and development of metacognitive skills and the teacher's use of questions that ask for clarification.[2] In addition, by seeking clarification, the teacher is likely to be demonstrating an interest in the student and his thinking.

CONVERGENT-THINKING QUESTION.   Convergent-thinking questions, also called narrow questions, are low-order thinking questions that have a single correct answer (such as recall questions, discussed and exemplified in the next section). Examples of convergent-thinking questions are "How would you classify the word spelled *c-l-o-s-e*, as a homophone or homograph?" "If the radius of a circle is 20 meters, what is the circle's circumference?" "What is the name of the first battle of the Civil War?"

CUEING QUESTION.   If you ask a question to which, after sufficient **wait-time** (longer than two seconds and as long as nine), no students respond or to which their inadequate responses indicate they need more information, then you can ask a question that cues the answer or response you are seeking.* In essence, you are going backward in your questioning sequence to cue the students. For example, as an introduction to a lesson on the study of prefixes, a teacher asks her students, "How many legs do crayfish, lobsters, and shrimp have?," and there is no accurate response. She might then cue the

---

1. Adapted from G. D. Borich, *Effective Teaching Methods,* 2nd ed. (Upper Saddle River, NJ: Prentice Hall, 1992), p. 278.

---

*Studies in wait-time began with the classic study of M. B. Rowe, "Wait Time And Reward As Instructional Variables, Their Influence On Language, Logic And Fate Control: Part I. Wait Time," *Journal of Research in Science Teaching* 11(2):81–94 (1974).

2. A. L. Costa, *The School as a Home for the Mind* (Palatine, IL: Skylight Publishing, 1991), p. 63.

answer with the following information and question, "The class to which those animals belong is class Decapoda. Does that give you a clue about the number of legs they have?" If that clue is not enough, then she might ask, "What is a decathlon?" and so on.

DIVERGENT-THINKING QUESTION.   Divergent-thinking questions (also known as broad, reflective, or thought questions) are *open-ended* (i.e., usually having no singularly correct answer), high-order thinking questions (requiring analysis, synthesis, or evaluation). These questions require students to think creatively by leaving the comfortable confines of the known and reaching out into the unknown. Examples of questions that require divergent thinking are "What measures could be taken to improve the effectiveness of crime prevention in our city?" and "What measures could be taken to improve the trash problem after lunch on our school grounds?"

EVALUATIVE QUESTION.   Some questions, whether convergent or divergent, require students to place a value on something; these are referred to as evaluative questions. If the teacher and the students all agree on certain premises, then the evaluative question would also be a convergent question. If original assumptions differ, then the response to the evaluative question would be more subjective, and therefore that evaluative question would be divergent. Examples of evaluative questions are "Should the United States allow clear-cutting in its national forests?" and "Should women be allowed to choose to have abortions?"

FOCUS QUESTION.   This is any question that is designed to focus student thinking. For example, the first question of the preceding paragraph is a focus question when the teacher asking it is attempting to focus student attention on the economic issues involved in clear-cutting.

PROBING QUESTION.   Similar to a clarifying question, the probing question requires student thinking to go beyond superficial first-answer or single-word responses. Examples of probing questions are "Why, Siobhan, do you think it to be the case that every citizen has the right to have a gun?" and "Could you give us an example?"

Socratic Questioning[3]

In the fifth century B.C., the great Athenian teacher Socrates used the art of questioning so successfully that to this day we still hear of the Socratic method.[4] What, exactly, is the Socratic method? Socrates' strategy was to ask his students a series of leading questions that gradually snarled them up to the point where they had to look carefully at their own ideas and to think rigorously for themselves. Socratic discussions were informal dialogues taking place in a natural, pleasant environment. Although Socrates sometimes had to go to considerable lengths to ignite his students' intrinsic interest, their response was natural and spontaneous. In his dialogues, Socrates tried to aid students in developing ideas. He did not impose his own notions on the students. Rather, he encouraged them to develop their own conclusions and draw their own inferences. Of course, Socrates may have had preconceived notions about what the final learning should be and carefully aimed his questions so that the students would arrive at the desired conclusions. Still, his questions were open-ended, causing divergent rather than convergent thinking. The students were free to go wherever the facts and their thinking led them.

Throughout history, teachers have tried to adapt the methods of Socrates to the classroom. In some situations, they have been quite successful. Indeed, at Atheneum Middle School, an independent school for grades 6–9 in Anchorage, Alaska, Socratic seminars are a major mode of instruction.* However, we must remember that Socrates used this method in the context of a one-to-one relationship between the student and himself. Some teachers have adapted it for whole-class direct instruction by asking questions first of one student and then of another, moving slowly about the class. This technique may work, but it is difficult because the essence of the Socratic technique is to build question on question in a logical fashion so that each question leads the student a step further toward the understanding sought. When you spread the questions around the classroom, you may find it difficult to build up the desired sequence and to keep all the students involved in the discussion. Sometimes you may be able to use the Socratic method by directing all the questions at one student, at least for several minutes, while the other students look on and listen in. This is the way Socrates did it. When the topic is interesting enough, this technique can be quite successful and even exciting, but in the

---

3. The section on Socratic questioning is adapted from L. H. Clark and I. S. Starr, *Secondary and Middle School Teaching Methods,* 7th ed. (Upper Saddle River, NJ: Prentice Hall, 1996), pp. 239–240. By permission of Prentice Hall.

*See the Atheneum Middle School home page at <http://www.customcpu.com/atheneum/home.html>.

4. For an original dialogue of Socrates' method, see "The Classic Socratic Method," *Physics* Teacher 32(3):138–141 (March 1994). To read how Socratic questioning is used at Lookout Valley Middle School (Chattanooga, TN), see V. C. Polite and A. H. Adams, *Improving Critical Thinking through Socratic Seminars, Spotlight on Student Success,* No. 110 (Philadelphia, PA: Mid-Atlantic Laboratory for Student Success, 1996).

long run, the Socratic method works best when the teacher is working in one-on-one coaching situations or with small groups of students, such as those who may be working on a group inquiry, rather than in whole-class direct instruction.

When Socratic questioning is being used, the focus is on the questions, not answers, and thinking is valued as the quintessential activity.[5] In essence, to conduct Socratic questioning, identify a problem (either student- or teacher-posed) and then ask the students a series of probing questions designed to cause them to examine critically the problem and potential solutions to it. The main thrust of the questioning and the key questions must be planned in advance so that the questioning will proceed logically. To think of quality probing questions on the spur of the moment is too difficult. It is the Socratic method that you will be using in micro peer teaching one later in this chapter (Exercise 7.6).

LEVELS OF COGNITIVE QUESTIONS AND STUDENT THINKING

Questions you pose are cues to your students to the level of thinking expected of them, ranging from the lowest level of mental operation, requiring simple recall of knowledge (convergent thinking), to the highest, requiring divergent thought and application of that thought. It is important that you are aware of the levels of thinking, understand the importance of attending to student thinking from low to higher levels of operation, and realize that what for one student may be a matter of simple recall of information may for another require a higher-order mental activity, such as figuring something out by deduction.

You should structure and sequence your questions (and assist students in developing their own skill in structuring and sequencing their questions) in a way that is designed to guide students to higher levels of thinking. To help your understanding, three levels of questioning and thinking are described as follows.[6] You should recognize the similarity between these three levels of questions and the six levels of thinking from Bloom's taxonomy of cognitive objectives (see Chapter 4). For your daily use of questioning it is just as useful but more practical to think and behave in terms of these three levels, rather than of six.

1. *Lowest level (data input phase): Gathering and recalling information.* At this level questions are designed to solicit from students concepts, information, feelings, or experiences that were gained in the past and stored in memory. Sample key words and desired behaviors are *complete, count, define, describe, identify, list, match, name, observe, recall, recite,* and *select.*
2. *Intermediate level (data processing phase): Processing information.* At this level questions are designed to draw relationships of cause and effect, to synthesize, analyze, summarize, compare, contrast, or classify data. Sample key words and desired behaviors are *analyze, classify, compare, contrast, distinguish, explain, group, infer, make an analogy, organize, plan,* and *synthesize.*
3. *Highest level (data output phase): Applying and evaluating in new situations.* Questions at this level encourage students to think intuitively, creatively, and hypothetically; to use their imaginations; to expose a value system; or to make a judgment. Sample key words and desired behaviors are *apply a principle, build a model, evaluate, extrapolate, forecast, generalize, hypothesize, imagine, judge, predict,* and *speculate.*

You should use the type of question that is best suited for your purpose and a variety of levels of questions. You must structure questions in a way intended to move student thinking to higher levels. When teachers use higher-level questions, their students tend to score higher on tests of critical thinking and on standardized tests of achievement.[7]

Developing your skill in using questioning requires attention to detail and practice. The following guidelines will provide that detail and some practice, but first, to check your understanding of the cognitive levels of questions, do Exercise 7.1.

5. B. R. Brogan and W. A. Brogan, "The Socratic Questioner: Teaching and Learning in the Dialogical Classroom," *Educational Forum* 59(3):288–296 (Spring 1995).

6. This three-tiered model of thinking has been described variously by others. For example, in E. Eisner's *The Educational Imagination* (Upper Saddle River, NJ: Prentice Hall, 1979), the levels are referred to as "descriptive," "interpretive," and "evaluative." For a comparison of thinking models, see Costa, p. 44.

7. See, for example, B. Newton, "Theoretical Basis for Higher Cognitive Questioning—An Avenue to Critical Thinking," *Education* 98(3):286–290 (March–April 1978), and D. Redfield and E. Rousseau, "A Meta-analysis of Experimental Research on Teacher Questioning Behavior," *Review of Educational Research* 51(2):237–245 (Summer 1981).

EXERCISE 7.1
Identifying the Cognitive Levels of Questions—
A Self-Check Exercise

Instructions: The purpose of this exercise is to test your understanding and recognition of the levels of questions. Mark each of the following questions with:

- *1,* if it is at the lowest level—gathering and recalling data.

- *2,* if it requires the student to process data.

- *3,* if it is at the highest level of mental operation, requiring the student to apply or to evaluate data in a new situation.

Check your answers against the key that follows. Resolve problems by discussing them with your classmates and instructor.

_____   1. Do you recall the differences between an Asian elephant and an African elephant?

_____   2. How are the natural habitats of the two elephants similar and how are they different?

_____   3. Which of the elephants do you think is more interesting?

_____   4. For what do you think the elephant uses its tusks?

_____   5. Do all elephants have tusks?

_____   6. Did the trick ending make the story more interesting for you?

_____   7. How might these evergreen needles be grouped?

_____   8. Could you explain how these two types of pine needles differ?

_____   9. For how many years was the Soviet Union a communist nation?

_____ 10. How many countries do you believe there will be in the African continent in the year 2010?

_____ 11. What do you think caused the city to move the location of its zoo?

_____ 12. How would the park be different today had the zoo been left there?

_____ 13. How do zoos today differ from those of the mid-nineteenth century?

_____ 14. Should a teacher be entitled to unemployment benefits during the summer months or when school is not in session?

_____ 15. If $4x + 40 = 44$, what does x equal?

_____ 16. Tell me, what happens when I spin this egg?

_____ 17. How does this poem make you feel?

_____ 18. What do you think will happen when we mix equal amounts of the two solutions, the red solution with the yellow solution?

_____ 19. What is the capital of Florida?

_____ 20. What do you think will be the long-term global effects if the trees of world rain forests continue to be removed at the present rate?

Answer Key

1. *1* (recall)	11. *2* (explain cause and effect)
2. *2* (compare)	12. *3* (speculate)
3. *3* (judge)	13. *2* (contrast)
4. *3* (imagine)	14. *3* (judge)
5. *3* (extrapolate)	15. *1* (recall of how to work the problem)
6. *3* (evaluate)	16. *1* (observe)
7. *2* (classify)	17. *1* (describe)
8. *2* (contrast)	18. *3* (hypothesize)
9. *1* (recall)	19. *1* (recall)
10. *3* (predict)	20. *3* (speculate or generalize)

Figure 7.1
Examples of questions that
use appropriate cognitive
terminology.

Instead of	*Say*
How else might it be done?	How could you *apply* . . . ?
Are you going to get quiet?	if we are going to hear what Joan has to say, what do you need to do?
How do you know that is so?	What evidence do you have?

GUIDELINES FOR USING QUESTIONING

As emphasized in several ways throughout this resource guide, your goals are to help your students learn how to solve problems, to make decisions and value judgments, to think creatively and critically, and to feel good about themselves and their learning, rather than simply to fill their minds with bits and pieces of information that will probably last for only a brief time in the students' short-term memory. How you construe your questions and how you carry out your questioning strategy are important to the realization of these goals.

Preparing Questions

When preparing questions, consider the following guidelines.

Cognitive questions should be planned, thoughtfully worded, and written into your lesson plan. Thoughtful preparation of questions helps to ensure that they are clear and specific, not ambiguous, that the vocabulary is appropriate, and that each question matches its purpose. Incorporate questions into your lessons as instructional devices, welcomed pauses, attention grabbers, and checks for student comprehension. Thoughtful teachers even plan questions that they intend to ask specific students, targeting questions to the readiness level, interest, or learning profile of a student.

Match questions with their purposes. Carefully planned questions are sequenced and worded to match the levels of cognitive thinking expected of students. To help students in developing their thinking skills, you need to demonstrate how to do this. To demonstrate, you must use terminology that is specific and that provides students with examples of experiences consonant with the meanings of the cognitive words. You should demonstrate this every day so students learn the cognitive terminology. As stated by Brooks and Brooks, "framing tasks around cognitive activities such as analysis, interpretation, and prediction—and explicitly using those terms with students—

fosters the construction of new understandings."[8] See the three examples in Figure 7.1.

Implementing Questions

Careful preparation of questions is one part of the skill in questioning. Implementation is the other part. Here are guidelines for effective implementation.

*Ask your well-worded question **before** calling on a student for a response.* A common error is for the teacher to first call on a student and then ask the question, such as "Sean, would you please tell us what you believe the author meant by the title 'We Are One'?" Although probably not intended by the teacher, as soon as she called on Sean, that signaled to the rest of the class that they were released from having to think about the question. The preferred strategy is to phrase the question, allow time for all students to think, and then call on Sean and other students for their interpretations of the author's meaning by the title.

Avoid bombarding students with teacher talk. Sometimes teachers talk too much. This could be especially true for teachers who are nervous, as might be the case for many during the initial weeks of their student teaching. Knowing the guidelines presented here will help you avoid that syndrome. Remind yourself to be quiet after you ask a question that you have carefully formulated. Sometimes, due to lack of confidence and especially poor planning of a question, the teacher asks the question and then, with a slight change in wording, asks it again. Or she may ask several questions, one after another. That is verbiage. "Shotgun" questioning only confuses students, while allowing too little time for them to think.

After asking a question, provide students with adequate time to think. The pause after asking a question is called wait-time (or think-time). Knowing the subject better than the students know it and having given prior thought to the subject, too many teachers fail to allow students sufficient time to think after asking a question. In addition, by

---

8. J. G. Brooks and M. G. Brooks, *In Search of Understanding: The Case for Constructivist Classrooms* (Alexandria, VA: Association for Supervision and Curriculum Development, 1993), p. 105.

the time they have reached high school (or sooner), students have learned pretty well how to play the "game"—that is, they know that if they remain silent long enough the teacher will probably answer her own question. After asking a well-worded question you should remain quiet for a while, allowing students time to think and to respond. If you wait long enough, they usually will. You may need to rehearse your students on this procedure.

After asking a question, how long should you wait before you do something? You should wait at least two seconds and as long as nine. Stop reading now and look at your watch or a clock to get a feeling for how long two seconds is. Then, observe how long nine seconds is. Did nine seconds seem a long time? Because most of us are not used to silence in the classroom, two seconds of silence can seem quite long, while nine seconds may seem eternal. If, for some reason, students have not responded after two to nine seconds of wait time, then you can ask the question again. However, don't reword an already carefully worded question, or else students are likely to think it is a new question. Pause for several seconds; then if you still haven't received a response, you can call on a student, then another, if necessary, after sufficient wait time. Soon you will get a response that can be built upon. Avoid answering your own question!

Practice calling on all students, not just the bright or the slow, not just the boys or the girls, not only those in the front or middle of the room, but all of them. To do these things takes concentrated effort on your part, but it is important. To ensure that students are called on equally, some teachers have in hand laminated copies of their seating charts, perhaps on bright neon-colored clipboards, and, with a wax pencil or water-soluble marker, make a mark next to the name of the student each time he is called on. Using a laminated seating chart and erasable markers, the teacher can erase the marks at the end of the day and reuse the seating chart. Additional suggestions for ensuring equity in the classroom are presented in Chapter 8.

Give the same minimum amount of wait time (think time) to all students. This, too, will require concentrated effort on your part but is important to do. A teacher who waits for less time when calling on a slow student or students of one gender is showing a prejudice toward or lack of confidence in certain students, both of which are detrimental when a teacher is striving to establish for all students a positive, equal, and safe environment for classroom learning. Show confidence in all students, and never discriminate by expecting less or more from some than from others. Although some students may take longer to respond, it is not necessarily because they are not thinking or have less ability. There may be cultural differences to consider; for example, some cultures simply allow more wait time

than others. The important point is to individualize to allow students who need more time to have it. Variation in wait time allowed should be used not to single out some students and to lead to lower expectations but rather to allow for higher expectations.

When asking questions, instead of allowing students to randomly shout out their answers, require them to raise their hands and be called on before they respond. Establish that procedure and stick with it. This helps to ensure both that you call on all students equally, fairly distributing your interactions with the students, and that girls are not interacted with less because boys tend to be more obstreperous (see Exercise 8.5). Even in college classrooms, male students tend to be more vocal than female students and, when allowed by the instructor, tend to outtalk and to interrupt their female peers. Every teacher has the responsibility to guarantee a nonbiased classroom and an equal distribution of interaction time in the classroom.

Another important reason for this advice is to help students to control their impulsivity. Controlling one's impulsivity is one of the 14 characteristics of intelligent behavior discussed in Chapter 9. One of your many instructional responsibilities is to help students develop this skill.

To keep all students mentally engaged, you will want to call on students who are sitting quietly and have not raised their hands, but avoid badgering or humiliating an unwilling participant. When a student has no response, you might suggest he think about it and you will come back to ensure he eventually understands or has an answer to the original question.

Use strong praise sparingly. A teacher's use of strong praise is sometimes okay. But when you want students to think divergently and creatively, you should be stingy with use of strong praise to student responses. Strong praise from a teacher tends to terminate divergent and creative thinking. Strong praise can also cause students to become dependent on external praise—to become "praise junkies."

One of your goals is to help students find intrinsic sources of motivation, that is, an inner drive of intent or desire that causes them to want to learn. Use of strong praise tends to build conformity, causing students to depend on outside forces—that is, the giver of praise—for their worth rather than on themselves. An example of a strong praise response is "That's right! Very good." On the other hand, passive acceptance responses, such as "Okay, that seems to be one possibility," keep the door open for further thinking, particularly for higher-level, divergent thinking.

Another example of a passive acceptance response is one used in brainstorming sessions, when the teacher says, "After asking the question and giving you time to think about it, I will hear your ideas and record them on the board." Only after all student responses have been heard and recorded does the class begin its consideration of each. That kind of nonjudgmental acceptance of all ideas in the classroom will generate a great deal of expression of high-level thought.[9] Also, as discussed in Chapter 2, whenever you are interacting with students, you want to ensure that your nonverbal behavior is consistent with your verbal behavior. When those two behaviors are consistent, you are modeling expected behavior and are less likely to confuse students.

Avoid bluffing an answer to a question for which you do not have an answer. Nothing will cause you to lose credibility with students any faster than faking an answer. There is nothing wrong with admitting that you do not know. It helps students realize that you are human. It helps them maintain an adequate self-esteem, realizing that they are okay. What *is* important is that you know where and how to find possible answers and that you help students develop that same knowledge and those same skills.

Encourage students to ask questions about content and process. From students, there is no such thing as a dumb question. Sometimes students, like everyone else, ask questions that could just as easily have been looked up. Those questions can consume precious class time. For a teacher, they can be frustrating. A teacher's initial reaction might be to quickly and mistakenly brush off that type of question with sarcasm, while assuming that the student is too lazy to look up an answer. In such instances, you are advised to think before responding and to respond kindly and professionally, although in the busy life of a classroom teacher, that may not always be so easy to do. However, be assured, there is a reason for a student's question. Perhaps the student is signaling a need for recognition or simply demanding attention.

In large comprehensive high schools in particular, it is sometimes easy for a student to feel alone and insignificant.[10] (This seems less the case, however, in schools that use a school-within-a-school plan and where teachers and students work together in interdisciplinary teams or, as in looping—or banding, where one cadre of teachers remains with the same group of students for two or more years.) When a student makes an effort to interact with you, that can be a pos-

itive sign, so gauge carefully your responses to those efforts. If a student's question is really off-track, off-the-wall, out of order, and out of context with the content of the lesson, consider this as a possible response: "That is an interesting question (or comment), and I would very much like to talk with you more about it. Could we meet at lunchtime or before or after school or at some other time that is mutually convenient?"

QUESTIONS FROM STUDENTS

Student questions can and should be used as springboards for further questions, discussion, and investigations. Indeed, in a constructivist classroom, student questions often drive content. Students should be encouraged to ask questions that challenge the textbook, the process, or other persons' statements, and they should be encouraged to seek the facts or evidence behind a statement.

Being able to ask questions may be more important than having right answers. Knowledge is derived from asking questions. Being able to recognize problems and to formulate questions is a skill and the key to developing ability in problem solving and critical thinking. You have a responsibility to encourage students to formulate questions and to help them word their questions in such a way that tentative answers can be sought. That is the process necessary to build a base of knowledge that can be called upon over and over as a way to link, interpret, and explain new information in new situations.[11]

Questioning: The Cornerstone of Critical Thinking, Real-World Problem Solving, and Meaningful Learning

With real-world problem solving, there are usually no absolute right answers. Rather than "correct" answers, some are better than others. The student with a problem needs to learn how to (1) recognize the problem, (2) formulate a question about that problem (e.g., "Should I abstain from sex or not?" "Should I date this person or not?" "Should I take this after-school job or not?" "Should I abuse drugs or not?" "To which colleges should I apply?"), (3) collect data, and (4) arrive at a temporarily acceptable answer to the problem, while realizing that at some later time, new data may dictate a review of the former conclusion. For example, if an astronomer believes she has discovered a

9. For further discussion of the use of praise and rewards in teaching, see C. H. Edwards, *Classroom Discipline and Management,* 2nd ed. (Upper Saddle River, NJ: Prentice Hall, 1997).
10. For interesting and informative articles about school size, see T. J. Seriovanni, "Small Schools, Great Expectations," and E. A. Wynne and H. J. Walberg, "The Virtues of Intimacy in Education," *Educational Leadership* 53(3):48–52 and 53–54 (respectively) (November 1995). See also J. McPartland et al., "Finding Safety in Small Numbers," *Educational Leadership* 55(2):14–17 (October 1997).

11. L. B. Resnick and L. E. Klopfer, eds., *Toward the Thinking Curriculum: Current Cognitive Research* (Alexandria, VA: 1989 ASCD Yearbook, Association for Supervision and Curriculum Development, 1989), p. 5.

planet, there is no textbook, teacher, or other outside authoritative source to which she may refer to find out if she is correct. Rather, on the basis of her self-confidence in identifying the problem, asking questions, collecting sufficient data, and arriving at a tentative conclusion based on those data, she assumes that for now her conclusion is safe.

THE LEVEL OF QUESTIONS IN COURSE MATERIALS

One study found that "of more than 61,000 questions found in teacher guides, student workbooks, and tests for nine history textbooks, more than 95 percent were devoted to factual recall."[12] Similar results have been found time and again. Using the questions in Exercise 7.2, examine course materials used by a school where you might soon be teaching, and analyze the results according to the level of thinking implied by the questions found.

---

12. California State Department of Education, *Caught in the Middle* (Sacramento, CA: California State Department of Education, 1987), p. 13.

EXERCISE 7.2

Examining Course Materials for the Levels of Questions

Instructions: The purpose of this exercise is to examine course materials for the levels of questions presented to students. Examine a student textbook (or other written or software program material) for a subject and grade level you intend to teach, specifically examining questions posed for the students, perhaps found at the ends of chapters. Also examine workbooks, tests, instructional packages, and any other printed or electronic materials used by students. Share your findings with other members of your class.

1. Materials examined (include date of publication and target students): _____

_____

_____

_____

_____

_____

_____

2. Questions at the recall (lowest) level, Level 1: _____

_____

_____

_____

_____

_____

_____

_____

3. Questions at the processing (intermediate) level, Level 2: _____

_____

_____

_____

_____

_____

_____

_____

4. Questions at the application (highest) level, Level 3: _____

_____

_____

_____

_____

_____

_____

_____

_____

5. Approximate percentages of questions at each level:

   Level 1 = _____ %   Level 2 = _____ %   Level 3 = _____ %

6. Did you find evidence of question-level sequencing? If so, describe it. _____

_____

_____

_____

_____

_____

_____

_____

7. From your analysis, what can you conclude about the level of thinking expected of students using the materials analyzed? For example, was there any difference in the nature and quality of questions depending on the type of material analyzed (e.g., textbooks versus software programs)?

_____

_____

_____

_____

_____

_____

_____

_____

_____

_____

_____

Raising the Level of Student Textbook Questions

When using a textbook that you believe has a disproportionately high percentage of its questions at the input, or recall, level, consider the following suggestions to incorporate higher-order questions and hence higher-order thinking:[13]

1. Develop and present higher-level cognitive questions to students before textbook reading, thus requiring them to link prior textual information and experiences with current textual information.
2. Develop and present higher-level cognitive statements that require students to prove or disprove the statements through the application of the textual information.

---

13. E. L. Pizzini et al., "The Questioning Level of Select Middle School Science Textbooks," *School Science and Mathematics* 92(2):78 (February 1992).

3. Have students scan chapter subheadings and develop higher-level cognitive questions based on the subheadings, which they may answer through reading.
4. Progressively increase the number of higher-level cognitive questions inserted into the text from the first chapter to the last chapter. This enables students to become more experienced in responding to such questions.
5. Where appropriate, have students develop higher-level cognitive questions from prior textual information that relates to the current textual information.
6. Integrate higher-level cognitive questions into chapter activities that require students to think about the information derived from the activity.
7. Require students to defend their answers to low-level cognitive chapter review and end-of-chapter questions with textual information and experience.

Now, to reinforce your understanding, do Exercises 7.3 through 7.6.

EXERCISE 7.3
Observing the Cognitive Levels of Classroom Verbal Interaction

Instructions: The purpose of this exercise is to develop your skill in recognizing the levels of classroom questions. Arrange to visit a secondary school classroom. On the lines provided here, tally each time you hear a question (or statement) from the teacher that causes students to gather or recall information, to process information, or to apply or evaluate data. In the left column, you may want to write in additional key words to assist your memory. After your observation, compare and discuss the results of this exercise with your colleagues.

School and class visited: _____

Date of observation: _____

Level	*Tallies of Level of Question or Statement*
1. Recall level (key words: *complete, count, define, describe,* and so on)	1. _____
2. Processing level (key words: *analyze, classify, compare,* and so on)	2. _____
3. Application level (key words: *apply, build evaluate,* and so on)	3. _____

For Your Notes

EXERCISE 7.4
Raising Questions to Higher Levels

Instructions: The purpose of this exercise is to further develop your skill in raising questions from one level to the next higher level. Complete the blank lines with questions at the appropriate levels (for the last series, create your own recall question and then vary it for the higher levels). Share and discuss your responses with your classmates.

Recall Level	*Processing Level*	*Application Level*
1. How many of you read a newspaper today?	1. Why did you read a newspaper today?	1. What do you think would happen if nobody ever read a newspaper again?
2. What was today's newspaper headline?	2. Why was that so important to be a headline?	2. Do you think that news items will be in tomorrow's paper?
3. Who is the vice-president of the United States today?	3. How does the work he has done compare with that done by the previous vice-president?	3. _____
4. How many presidents has the United States had?	4. _____	4. _____
5. _____	5. _____	5. _____

For Your Notes

EXERCISE 7.5
Creating Cognitive Questions

Instructions: The purpose of this exercise is to provide practice in writing cognitive questions. Read the following example of verse. Then, from that verse, compose three questions about it that would cause students to identify, list, and recall; three that would cause students to analyze, compare, and explain; and three that would cause students predict, apply, and hypothesize. Share and check questions with your peers.

We Are One

Truth, love, peace, and beauty,
We have sought apart
    but will find within, as our
Moods—explored, shared,
    questioned, and accepted—
Together become one and all.

Through life my friends
We can travel together,
for we now know
each could go it alone.

To assimilate our efforts into one,
While growing in accepting,
and trusting, and sharing the
    individuality of the other,
Is truly to enjoy God's greatest gift—
Feeling—knowing love and compassion.

Through life my friends
We are together,
for we must know
we are one.

—R. D. Kellough

Recall Questions

1. (to *identify*) _____

_____

_____

2. (to *list*) _____

_____

_____

3. (to *recall*) _____

_____

_____

Processing Questions

1. (to *analyze*) _____

_____

_____

_____

2. (to *compare*) _____

_____

_____

_____

3. (to *explain*) _____

_____

_____

_____

Application Questions

1. (to *predict*) _____

_____

_____

_____

2. (to *apply*) _____

_____

_____

_____

3. (to *hypothesize*) _____

_____

_____

_____

_____

EXERCISE 7.6

A Cooperative Learning and Micro Peer Teaching Exercise in the Use of Questioning—Micro Peer Teaching I

Instructions: The purpose of this exercise is to practice preparing and asking questions that are designed to lead student thinking from the lowest level to the highest. Before class, prepare a five-minute lesson for posing questions that will guide the learner from lowest to highest levels of thinking. Teaching will be one-on-one, in groups of four, with each member of the group assuming a particular role—teacher, student, judge, or recorder. Each of the four members of your group will assume each of those roles once for five minutes. (If there are only three members in a group, the roles of judge and recorder can be combined during each five-minute lesson; or, if there are five members in the group, one member can sit out each round, or two can work together as judge.) Each member of the group should have his own tally sheet.

Suggested Lesson Topics

- Teaching styles
- Characteristics of youngsters of a particular age
- Learning styles of students
- Evaluation of learning achievement
- A skill or hobby
- Teaching competencies
- A particular teaching strategy
- Student teaching and what it will really be like

Each of your group members should keep the following role descriptions in mind:

- *Teacher (sender).* Pose recall (input), processing, and application (output) questions related to one of the topics above or to any topic you choose.
- *Student (receiver).* Respond to the questions of the teacher.
- *Judge.* Identify the level of each question or statement used by the teacher *and* the level of the student's response.
- *Recorder.* Tally the number of each level of question or statement used by the teacher (S = sender) as indicated by the judge; also tally the level of student responses (R = receiver). Record any problems encountered by your group.

TALLY SHEET

Sender _____

Receiver _____

Minute	Input	Processing	Output
1 S			
R			
2 S			
R			
3 S			
R			
4 S			
R			
5 S			
R			

TALLY SHEET

Sender _____

Receiver _____

Minute	Input	Processing	Output
1 S			
R			
2 S			
R			
3 S			
R			
4 S			
R			
5 S			
R			

SUMMARY

This chapter presented a great deal of information about one teaching strategy, which is perhaps the most important in your teaching repertoire. Questioning is the cornerstone of meaningful learning, thinking, communication, and real-world problem solving. The art of its use is something you will continue to develop throughout your teaching career.

In the next two chapters, your attention is directed to the selection and implementation of specific strategies to facilitate students' learning of particular skills and content.

QUESTIONS FOR CLASS DISCUSSION

1. Have you ever noticed that some teachers seem to anticipate a lower-level response to their questions from particular students? Discuss your answer with your peers.
2. Should a teacher verbally respond to every student's verbal comment or inquiry? Explain why or why not. If not, on what basis does the teacher decide when and how to respond?
3. When questioning students, does a teacher need to be concerned about how students from different cultures might respond to certain types of questions or to the teacher's questioning technique? Explain why or why not.
4. Describe when, if ever, and how strong praise could be used by a teacher. Explain the difference, if any, between strong praise and positive reinforcement.
5. Explain why it is important to wait after asking students a content question. How long should you wait? What should you do if after waiting a certain amount of time there is no student response?
6. To what extent should (or can) a classroom teacher allow student questions to determine content studied? To what extent should students' initial interest, or lack of interest, in a topic determine whether the topic gets taught?
7. Explain the meaning of the following statement: We should look not for what students can reiterate but for what they can demonstrate and produce. Explain why you agree or disagree with the concept.
8. Describe any prior concepts you held that changed as a result of your experiences with this chapter. Describe the changes.
9. From your current observations and fieldwork as related to this teacher preparation program, clearly identify one specific example of educational practice that seems contradictory to exemplary practice or theory as presented in this chapter. Present your explanation for the discrepancy.
10. Do you have questions generated by the content of this chapter? If you do, list them along with ways answers might be found.

SUGGESTED READINGS

Baloche, L. "Breaking Down the Walls: Integrating Creative Questioning and Cooperative Learning into the Social Studies." *Social Studies* 85(1):25–30 (January/February 1994).

Barnette, J. J., et al. *Wait Time: Effective and Trainable.* Charleston, WV: Appalachia Educational Laboratory, 1995.

Benito, Y. M., et al. "The Effect of Instruction in Question-Answer Relationships and Metacognition in Social Studies Comprehension." *Journal of Research in Reading* 16(1):20–29 (February 1993).

Busching, B. A., and Slesinger, B. A. "Authentic Questions: What Do They Look Like? Where Do They Lead?" *Language Arts* 72(5):341–351 (September 1995).

Cardellichio, T., and Field, W. "Seven Strategies That Encourage Neural Branching." *Educational Leadership* 54(6):33–36 (March 1997).

Chuska, K. R. *Improving Classroom Questions: A Teacher's Guide to Increasing Student Motivation, Participation, and Higher-Level Thinking.* Bloomington, IN: Phi Delta Kappa Educational Foundation, 1995.

Clarke, J. H., and Agne, R. M. *Interdisciplinary High School Teaching: Strategies for Integrated Learning.* Chapter 2. Needham Heights, MA: Allyn & Bacon, 1997.

Commeyras, M., and Sumner, G. *Student-Posed Questions for Literature-Based Discussion.* Instructional Resource Number 6. Athens, GA: National Reading Research Center, 1995.

Deal, D., and Sterling, D. "Kids Ask the Best Questions." *Educational Leadership* 54(6):61–63 (March 1997).

Elkind, D. H., and Sweet, F. "The Socratic Approach to Character Education." *Educational Leadership* 54(8):56–59 (May 1997).

Good, T. L., and Brophy, J. E. *Looking in Classrooms.* 7th ed. Chapter 9. New York: Longman, 1997.

Hancock, C. L. "Implementing the Assessment Standards for School Mathematics: Enhancing Mathematics with Open-Ended Questions." *Mathematics Teacher* 88(6):496–499 (September 1995).

Hunkins, F. P. *Teaching Thinking through Effective Questioning.* Norwood, MA: Christopher-Gordon, 1995.

King, A. "Inquiring Minds Really Do Want to Know: Using Questioning to Teach Critical Thinking." *Teaching of Psychology* 22(1):13–17 (February 1995).

Latham, A. "Asking Students the Right Questions." *Educational Leadership* 54(6):84–85 (March 1997).

Penick, J. E., et al. "Questions Are the Answers." *Science Teacher* 63(1):26–29 (January 1996).

Richards, M. "Planning for Successful Teaching: Questioning in the Language Classroom." *Mosaic* 2(3):21–22 (Spring 1995).

Sampson, M. B., et al. "Circle of Questions." *Reading Teacher* 48(4):364–365 (December/January 1994–1995).

Wassermann, S. *Asking the Right Question: The Essence of Teaching.* Bloomington, IN: Fastback 343, Phi Delta Kappa Educational Foundation, 1992.

Whitmore, K. F. "What Makes a Question Good Is . . ." *New Advocate* 7(1):45–57 (Winter 1994).

Chapter

8

Instructional Strategies for Positive Interaction and Quality Learning

The focus of this chapter and the next one is a variety of instructional strategies from which you may select to teach toward particular goals. Regardless of strategies and the subject, all teachers share in the responsibility for teaching reading, writing, thinking, and study skills. This responsibility is reflected throughout.

An important strategy for effective instruction is to group students in ways that enhance positive interaction and quality learning. During any given week of school, a student might experience a succession of group settings. Ways of grouping students for instruction is the initial topic of this chapter, from individualized instruction to working with dyads, small groups, and large groups. You also will learn how to ensure equality in the classroom, how to use assignments and homework, and how to coordinate various forms of independent and small-group project-based study. Specifically, upon completion of this chapter you should be able to

1. Describe the meaning of mastery learning and its implications for secondary school teaching.
2. Explain the advantages and disadvantages of various ways of grouping students for learning.
3. Develop a self-instructional module and describe other practical ways to individualize the instruction.
4. Demonstrate an understanding of the meaning and importance of classroom equity.
5. Demonstrate a theoretical and practical understanding of how to use each of these instructional strategies: assignments, homework, written and oral reports, cooperative learning, learning activity centers, and projects.

MASTERY LEARNING AND INDIVIDUALIZED INSTRUCTION

Learning is an individual experience. Yet the teacher is expected to work effectively with students on other than an individual basis—often 35 to 1 or even higher. Much has been written of the importance of individualizing the instruction for students. Virtually all the research concerning better instructional practice emphasizes greater individualization of instruction.[1]

We also know that while some students are primarily verbal learners, others are primarily visual, tactile, or kinesthetic learners. As the teacher, though, you find yourself in the difficult position of simultaneously "treating" many individual learners with individual learning styles and preferences. To individualize instruction in such circumstances seems an impossible expectation, yet occasionally teachers do succeed. Our desire is that the resources and guidelines presented in this book will help you to maximize your efforts and minimize your failures.

Common sense tells us that student achievement in learning is related to both the quality of attention and the length of time given to learning tasks. In 1968, Benjamin Bloom, building upon a model developed earlier by John Carroll, developed the concept of individualized instruction called **mastery learning**, saying that students need sufficient time on task (i.e., engaged

---

1. J. M. Carroll, "The Copernican Plan Evaluated," *Phi Delta Kappan* 76(2):105–113 (October 1994).

time) to master content before moving on to new content.[2] From that concept Fred Keller developed an instructional plan called the Personalized System of Instruction (PSI), or the Keller Plan, which by the early 1970s enjoyed popularity and success, especially at many two-year colleges. PSI involves the student's learning from printed modules of instruction (which, today, would likely be presented as computer software programs), which allow the student greater control over the learning pace. The instruction is mastery oriented; that is, the student demonstrates mastery of the content of one module before proceeding to the next.

Emphasis today is on mastery of content, or *quality learning,* rather than on coverage of content or quantity of learning.[3] Because of that emphasis, the importance of the concept of mastery learning has resurfaced. For example, in today's efforts to restructure schools, two approaches—Outcome-Based Education (OBE) and the Coalition of Essential Skills Schools (CESS)—are both built on the premise that each student can learn and focus on the construction of individual knowledge through mastery.[4] In some instances, however, attention may only be on the mastery of minimum competencies; thus, students are not encouraged to work and learn to the maximum of their talents and abilities.

By mastery of content, we mean that the student demonstrates his use of what has been learned. As explained by Horton:

> Mastery learning may be broadly defined as the attainment of adequate levels of performance on tests that measure specific learning tasks. Mastery learning also describes an instructional model whose underlying assumption is that nearly every student can learn everything in the school curriculum at a specified level of competence if the learner's previous knowledge and attitudes about the subject are accounted for, if the instruction is of good quality, and if adequate time is allowed to permit mastery.[5]

Assumptions about Mastery, or Quality, Learning

Mastery, or quality, learning is based on the following six assumptions. (1) Mastery of content, or quality learning, is possible for all students. (2) For quality learning to occur,

it is the instruction that must be modified and adapted, not the students. Tracking and ability grouping do not fit with the concept of mastery learning. (3) Although all students can achieve mastery, to master a particular content some students may require more time than others. The teacher and the school must provide for this difference in time needed to complete a task successfully. (4) Most learning outcomes can be specified in terms of observable and measurable performance. (5) Most learning is sequential and logical. (6) Mastery learning can ensure that students experience success at each level of the instructional process. Experiencing success at each level provides incentive and motivation for further learning.[6]

Components of Any Mastery Learning Model

Any instructional model designed to teach toward mastery will contain the following four components: (1) objectives that are stated in specific behavioral terms, (2) a preassessment of the learner's present knowledge, (3) an instructional component, with practice, reinforcement, frequent comprehension checks (diagnostic or formative assessment), and corrective instruction at each step to keep the learner on track, and (4) a postassessment to determine the extent of student mastery of the objectives.

LEARNING ALONE

While some students learn well in pairs (dyads), others learn well with their peers in groups (either cooperatively or competitively) or collaboratively with adults, and others learn well in combinations of these patterns, at least 13 percent of students learn best alone. "Learning-alone youngsters often are gifted, nonconforming, able to work at their own pace successfully, comfortable using media, or seemingly underachieving but potentially able students for whom unconventional instructional strategies, such as structured contract activity packages or multisensory instructional packages, encourage academic success."[7]

The Self-Instructional Module

One technique that can be used to ensure mastery of learning is the self-instructional module (SIM), which is a learning package (written, on audio- or videotape, or on computer) specifically designed for an individual student. It uses small sequential steps, with frequent

2. See B. Bloom, *Human Characteristics and School Learning* (New York: McGraw-Hill, 1987), and J. Carroll, "A Model of School Learning," *Teachers College Record* 64(8):723–733 (May 1963).

3. See, for example, F. N. Dempster, "Exposing Our Students to Less Should Help Them Learn More," *Phi Delta Kappan* 74(6):433–437 (February 1993).

4. C. T. Desmond, "A Comparison of the Assessment of Mastery in an Outcome-Based and a Coalition of Essential Skills School," paper presented at the annual meeting of the American Educational Research Association, San Francisco, April 20–24, 1992.

5. L. Horton, *Mastery Learning* (Bloomington, IN: Fastback 154, Phi Delta Kappa Educational Foundation, 1981), p. 9.

6. Adapted from Horton, *Mastery Learning,* pp. 15–18.

7. R. Dunn, *Strategies for Diverse Learners* (Bloomington, IN: Fastback 384, Phi Delta Kappa Educational Foundation, 1995), p. 15.

practice and immediate learning feedback to the student. It is designed to teach a relatively small amount of material, at the mastery level, requiring a relatively brief amount of learning time (about 30 minutes for middle school students; up to an hour for high school students). The SIM can be designed to teach any topic, at any grade level, in any subject, for any domain or combination of domains of learning. Exercise 8.1 is a self-instructional module designed to guide you through completion of your first SIM.

As instructed by your course instructor, do Exercises 8.1 and 8.2.

EXERCISE 8.1
*Preparing a Self-Instructional Module**

Instructions: The purpose of this exercise is to guide you through the process of preparing a self-instructional module for use in your own teaching. The exercise continues for several pages; it is important that you follow it step-by-step, beginning with the following boxed-in "cover page."

Self-Instructional Module Number: 1
Instructor's Name: Professor Richard D. Kellough
School: California State University, Sacramento
Course: Methods of Teaching
Intended Students: Students in Teacher Preparation
Topic: How to Write a Self-Instructional Module
Estimated Working Time: 10 hours

For the challenge of today's classroom . . .

The Self-Instructional Module

You are about to embark upon creating and writing a perfect lesson plan. The result of your hard work will be an instructional module in which you will take a lot of pride. More important, you will have learned a technique of teaching that ensures learning takes place. For what more could you ask?

---

*Copyright 1991 by Richard D. Kellough.

Let us get to the essence of what this self-instructional module (SIM) is: This SIM is about how to write an SIM. The general objective is to guide you gently through the process of preparing and writing your first SIM. Let's begin the experience with background about the history of the SIM.

A History

Research evidence indicates that student achievement in learning is related to time and to the *quality of attention* being given to the learning task. You knew that already! In 1968, Benjamin Bloom developed a concept of individualized instruction called mastery learning, based on the idea that students need sufficient time on task to master content before moving on to new content. Did you know that? _____. (Please read along with a pencil, and fill in the blanks as you go.)

Although Bloom is usually given credit for the concept of mastery learning, the idea did not originate with him. He reinforced and made popular a model developed earlier by John Carroll. In 1968, Fred Keller developed a similar model called the Keller Plan, or the Personalized System of Instruction (PSI). The PSI quickly became a popular teaching technique in the community and four-year colleges. In about 1972, enter Johnson and Johnson (not of the Band-Aid family, but Rita and Stuart Johnson), who developed their model of mastery learning and called it the Self-Instructional Package (SIP). Since 1972, I (Richard D. Kellough) have been developing my version, the Self-Instructional Module, which you are now experiencing. As you will learn, *frequent comprehension checks and corrective instructions* are important to the effectiveness of the SIM.

One other thing. There are several devices available to individualize instruction, but the SIM has the flexibility to be adaptable for use at all grade levels, from kindergarten through college. I believe the following to be the reasons for the popularity of this strategy:

- The SIM allows the teacher to *create an experience that ensures learning*. Creating makes you feel good; when your students learn, you feel good—two reasons for the SIM's popularity.
- The SIM is truly *individualized*, because it is a package written for an individual student, with that student in mind as it is being written.
- Although it takes time to prepare, the SIM *requires little financial expenditure*, a fact important to today's teacher.
- Once you have prepared your first SIM, it is possible that you will see that you have begun a series. Subsequent packages are easier to do, and you may see the value in having a series available.
- With today's emphasis on the *basics*, the SIM is particularly helpful for use in remediation.
- When you finish your SIM, you will have collected the content that could be used for a computer program.
- With today's *large and mixed-ability classes*, teachers need help! Here is time- and cost-effective help!
- With emphasis today on competency-based instruction, the SIM makes sense.

How are we doing so far? _____ Are your interests and curiosity aroused?

_____ Do you have questions? _____ If so, write them down, then continue.

Questions: _____

_____

_____

_____

What Is the Self-Instructional Module and Why Use It?

The SIM is a learning package designed for an individual student; it is self-instructional (i.e., if you, the teacher, drop dead—heaven forbid—the student can continue to learn), and *it requires about 15 to 50 minutes of learning time.* The final package can be recorded on tape, video, or computer disc, or it can be written in booklet form, or it can exist in any combination of these.

Here are ways that teachers have found the SIM to be useful:

- As an *enrichment* activity for an accelerated student.
- As a strategy for make-up for a student who has been absent.
- As a strategy for a student in need of *remediation*.
- As a strategy for introducing basic information to an entire class, freeing the teacher to work with individual students, making the act of teaching more *time-efficient,* a particularly significant value of the SIM.
- As a learning experience especially coordinated with manipulatives, perhaps in connection with a science experiment, library work, a computer, a tape recording, a videotape, a videodisc, or hands-on materials for an activity, or any combination of these.

One other point before we stop and check your comprehension: *The single most important characteristic of the SIM is that it uses small sequential steps followed by immediate and corrective feedback to the learner.* In that respect, the SIM resembles programmed instruction.

 Stop the action!

Let's check your learning with the review questions and instructions that follow.

Comprehension Check 1

Answer the following three questions, then check your responses by reviewing Feedback Check 1. If you answer all three questions correctly, continue the package; otherwise, back up and review.

---

1. How would you define a SIM? _____

_____

_____

2. What is the single most important characteristic of the SIM? _____

_____

3. What is one way that the SIM could be used in your own teaching, a way that currently

stands out in your thinking? _____

_____

_____

Feedback Check 1

1. Although we will continue development of the definition, at this point it should resemble this: The SIM is an individualization of learning—teaching strategy that teaches toward mastery learning of one relatively small bit of content by building upon small, sequential steps and providing corrective feedback throughout.
2. Referring to the small, sequential steps, followed by immediate and corrective feedback.
3. Your answer is probably related to one of those listed earlier but it could differ.

How Does the SIM Differ from Other Kinds of Learning Packages?

Another characteristic of the SIM is the *amount of learning contained in one package.* Each SIM is designed to teach a relatively small amount of material, but to do it well. *This is a major difference in the SIM from other types of learning activity packages.*

And, in case you have been wondering about what the SIM can be designed to teach, I want to emphasize that it *can be designed:*

- For any topic,
  - At any grade level,
    - In any discipline,
      - For cognitive understanding,
        - For psychomotor development, and
          - For affective learning.

That probably brings to your mind all sorts of thoughts and questions. Hold them for a moment, and let's do another comprehension check.

 Stop the action and check your learning.

Comprehension Check 2

Answer the following two questions, then check your responses in the feedback box that follows.

1. How does the SIM differ from other self-contained learning packages?

_____

_____

_____

2. Although teachers frequently emphasize learning that falls within the cognitive domain, is it possible for the SIM to be written to include learning in the psychomotor and affective domains? Yes or no? _____

Feedback Check 2

1. Length of learning time is shorter for the SIM, and it is written with an individual student in mind. It is written to teach one thing well, to one student.
2. The SIM *can* be written for any domain, although evaluation is trickier for the affective and for the highest-level psychomotor.

Perhaps we should now say a word about what we mean when we use the expression *teach one thing well*—that is, to explain what is meant by mastery learning. Theoretically, if the package is being used by an individual student, performance level expectation is 100%. In reality, performance level will most likely be between 85 and 95%, particularly if you are using the SIM for a group of students rather than an individual. That 5–15% difference allows for human errors that can occur in writing and in reading.

Now that you have learned what the SIM is—and how this learning strategy differs from other learning activity packages—it is time to concentrate on development of your SIM. Please continue.

SIM Development

How Do I Develop a SIM?

As with any good lesson plan, it takes time to develop an effective SIM. Indeed, preparation of your first SIM will test your imagination and writing skills! Nevertheless, it will be time well spent; you will be proud of your product. *It is important that you continue following this package, step-by-step; do not skip parts, or I will assume no responsibility for your final product! Understand?* _____ Development of your SIM emphasizes the importance of

- Writing the learning objectives clearly, precisely, and in behavioral terms.
- Planning the learning activities in small, sequential steps.
- Providing frequent practice and learning comprehension checks.
- Providing immediate feedback, corrective instruction, and assurance to the learner.
- Preparing evaluative questions that measure against the learning objectives.

As you embark on preparing what may be the perfect lesson plan, keep in mind the following two points:

1. Prepare your first SIM so it will take no more than

---

30 minutes for middle school students
50 to 60 minutes for high school students

---

2. Use a *conversational tone* in your writing. Write in the first person, as though you are talking directly to the student for whom it is intended. For example, when speaking of the learning objectives, use *You will be able to* rather than *The student will be able to*. Keep in mind that you are communicating with one person rather than with an entire class (even though you may be preparing your package for entire class use). It helps to pretend that you are in a one-on-one situation tutoring the student at the writing board.

 Stop the action, and again check your learning.

Comprehension Check 3

Answer the following two questions; then check your responses in Feedback Check 3.

1. What maximum learning-time duration is recommended? _____

2. What major item of importance has been recommended for you to keep in mind as you

write your SIM? _____

_____

Feedback Check 3

1. Approximately 30 to 60 minutes, depending upon the grade and achievement level.
2. Write in the first person, as if you are speaking directly with the student.

Now that we have emphasized the *length of learning time* and *the personalization of your writing*, here are other important reminders.

1. Make your SIM attractive and stimulating. Consider using cartoons, puns, graphics, scratch-and-sniff stickers, and interesting manipulatives. Use your creative imagination! Use both cerebral hemispheres!

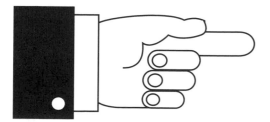 *Add sketches, diagrams, modules, pictures, magazine clippings, humor, and a conversational tone, as students appreciate a departure from the usual textbooks and worksheets.*

2. Use colleagues as resource persons, brainstorming ideas as you proceed through each step of package production.

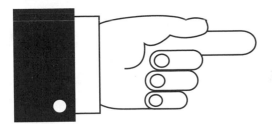

During production, use your best cooperative learning skills.

3. The package should not be read (or heard) like a lecture. It <u>must</u> involve small sequential steps with frequent practice and corrective feedback instruction (as modeled in this package).

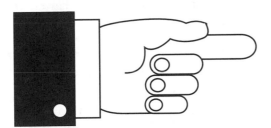

". . . and with the course material broken down into small self-instructional units, students can move through at individual rates."

4. The package should contain a variety of activities, preferably involving all four learning modalities—<u>visual, auditory, tactile, and kinesthetic.</u>

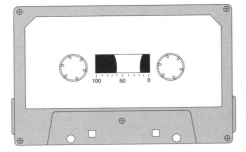

5. Vary margins, indentations, and fonts

so the final package does not have the usual textbook or worksheet appearance with which students are so familiar. Build into your package the "Hawthorne Effect."

Note about the cosmetics of your SIM: My own prejudice about the SIM is that it should be spread out more than the usual textbook page or worksheet. Use double-spaced lines, varied margins, and so on. Make cosmetic improvements after finishing your final draft. Write, review, sleep on it, write more, revise, add that final touch. This package that you are using has been "toned down" and modified for practical inclusion in this textbook.

6. Your SIM does not have to fit the common 8 1/2″ × 11″ size. You are encouraged to be creative in the design of your SIM's shape, size, and format.
7. Like all lesson plans, the SIM is subject to revision and improvement after use. *Write, review, sleep on it, write more, revise, test, revise. . . .*

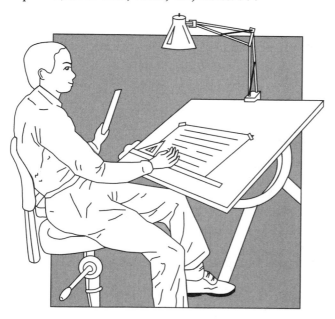

Perhaps before proceeding, it would be useful to review the preceding points. Remember, too, the well-written package *will ensure learning*. Your first SIM will take several hours to produce, but it will be worth it!

Proceed with the steps that follow.

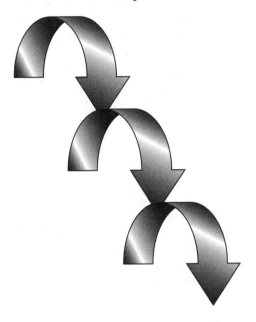

STEPS FOR DEVELOPING YOUR SIM

Instructions: It is important that you proceed through the following package development step-by-step.

One thing you will notice is that immediately after writing your learning objectives you prepare the evaluative test items; both steps precede the preparation of the learning activities. That is not the usual order followed by a teacher when preparing lessons, but it does help to ensure that test items match objectives. Now, here we go! *Step-by-step*, please.

Note: From here on, write on separate paper for draft planning.

Step 1. Prepare the cover page. It should include the following items:

- Instructor's name (that is you)
  - School (yours)
    - Class or intended students (whom it's for)
      - Topic (specific but not wordy)
        - Estimated working time

For a sample, refer to the beginning of this package. You can vary the design of the cover page according to your needs.

Step 2. Prepare the instructional objectives. For now, these should be written in specific behavioral terms. Later, when writing these into your package introduction, you can phrase them in more general terms.

> Recommended is the inclusion of at least one attitudinal (affective) objective, such as "Upon completion of this package, you will tell me your feelings about this kind of learning."

Step 3. **Comprehension Check 4**

Share with your colleagues what you have accomplished (with steps 1 and 2) to solicit their valuable feedback and input.

Step 4. Depending on feedback (from step 3), *modify items 1 and 2,* if necessary. For example, after listing the learning instructions, you may find that you really have more than one package in preparation, and within the list of objectives you may find a natural cut-off between packages 1 and 2. You may discover that you have a *series* of modules begun.

Step 5. Prepare the pretest. If the learner does well on the pretest, there may be no need for the student to continue the package. Some packages (like this one) may not include a pretest, though most will. And if this is your first SIM writing experience, I think you *should* include a pretest.

> *Suggestion:* The pretest need not be as long as the posttest but should include a limited sample of questions to determine whether the student already knows the material and need not continue with the package. A pretest also serves to set the student mentally for the SIM.

Step 6. Prepare the posttest. The pretest and posttest could be identical, but usually the pretest is shorter. It is important that both pretest and posttest items actually test against the objectives (of step 2). Try to keep the items objective (e.g., multiple-choice type), avoiding as much as possible the use of subjective test items (e.g., essay type), but do include at least one item measuring an affective objective (see boxed item in step 2).

Important reminder: If your package is well written, the student <u>should</u> achieve 85–100% on the posttest.

Step 7. **Comprehension Check 5**

Share with colleagues your pretest and posttest items (providing a copy of your objectives) for suggested improvement changes before continuing to the next step.

Use the following space to write notes to yourself about ideas you are having and regarding any materials you may need to complete your package.

Dear Self—

| |
| |
| |
| |
| |
| |
| |

Good work so far! Before continuing, take a break.

It is time to stop working for a while . . .   . . . and go play!

Step 8. Okay, enough play, it is time to prepare the text of your SIM. This is the "meat" of your package, what goes between the pretest and the posttest. It is the INSTRUCTION. *Reminder:* For the SIM to be self-instructional, the learner should be able to work through the package with little or no help from you.

An important ingredient in your package is the <u>directions</u>. The package should be self-directed and self-paced. Therefore, each step of the package should be clear to the learner, making you, the instructor, literally unnecessary. *Everything needed by the learner to complete the package should be provided with the package.*

Use small, sequential steps with frequent practice cycles, followed by comprehension checks and corrective feedback. Make it fun and interesting with a variety of activities for the student, activities that provide for learning in several ways, from writing to reading, from viewing a video-tape to drawing, from listening to a tape recording to doing a hands-on activity. And be certain the activities correlate with the learning objectives. The learning cycles should lead to satisfaction of the stated objectives, and the posttest items *must* measure against those objectives.

Step 9. **Comprehension Check 6**

    Test your package. Try it out on your colleagues as they look for content errors, spelling and grammar errors, clarity, as well as offer suggestions for improvement. Duplicate and use the SIM Assessment Form provided at the end of this exercise.

Stop the Action!
Congratulations on the development of your first SIM!
However, two additional steps need your consideration.

Step 10. Revise if necessary. Make appropriate changes to your SIM as a result of the feedback from your colleagues. Then you are ready to give your SIM its first real test—try it out on the student for whom it is intended.

Step 11. Further revisions. This comes later, after you have used it with the student for whom it was originally intended. Like any other well-prepared lesson or unit plan, it should always be subject to revision and to improvement, never "set in concrete."

SIM ASSESSMENT FORM

1. Packet identification

   Author: _____

   _____

   _____

   Title of SIM: _____

   _____

   _____

2. Packet Objectives: Do they tell the student

   a. What the student will be able to do? _____

   _____

   _____

   _____

   _____

   b. How the student will demonstrate this new knowledge or skill? _____

   _____

   _____

   _____

   _____

   Is there a clear statement (overview or introduction) of the importance, telling the learner
   what will be learned by completing the packet?

   _____

   _____

   _____

   _____

3. Pretest

   _____

   _____

   _____

   _____

   _____

   _____

4. Activities (practice cycles)

Are small sequential steps used? _____

_____

_____

_____

_____

Are there frequent practice cycles, with comprehension checks and corrective feedback to

the learner? _____

_____

_____

_____

_____

5. Posttest: Does it test against the objectives? _____

_____

_____

_____

_____

6. Clarity and continuity of expression: _____

_____

_____

_____

_____

7. Is the packet informative, attractive, and enjoyable? _____

_____

_____

_____

_____

8. Additional comments useful to the author of this packet: _____

_____

_____

_____

_____

_____

EXERCISE 8.2

Practical Ways for Individualizing the Instruction

Instructions: The purpose of this exercise is for you to become familiar with the many practical ways that instruction can be individualized for students in the secondary school classroom.

1. Divide your class into groups of about four members per group.
2. Each group should focus on one particular subject for a particular grade level and one special group of children, such as children with special needs, children who are gifted and talented, children with cultural or ethnic differences, and children who have limited proficiency or no proficiency in English.
3. Each group is to research in the literature techniques and strategies successfully used in teaching that particular group of students at that particular grade level. Sources of information should include library research, especially current journals, and observations and discussions with experienced teachers.
4. Each group then prepares and presents an oral report to the entire class about its findings. The oral reports are often best received when accompanied by visuals and realia.

LEARNING IN PAIRS

Sometimes it is advantageous to pair students (dyads) for studying and learning. Four types of dyads are described as follows.

CROSS-AGE COACHING. In cross-age coaching one student is coached by another from a different, and usually higher, grade level. It is similar to peer tutoring except that the coach is a different age than the student being coached.[8]

PEER TUTORING. In peer tutoring one classmate tutors another. It is useful, for example, when one student helps another who has limited proficiency in English or when a student skilled in math helps another who is less skilled. For many years, it has been demonstrated repeatedly that peer tutoring is a significant strategy for promoting active learning.

TEAM LEARNING. With team learning students study and learn in teams of two. Students identified as gifted work and learn especially well when paired. Specific uses for paired team learning include drill partners, reading buddies, book report pairs, summary pairs, project assignment pairs, and elaborating and relating pairs.

THINK-PAIR-SHARE. With think-pair-share students, in pairs, examine a new concept or topic about to be studied. After the students of each dyad discuss what they already know or think they know about the concept, they present their perceptions to the whole group. This is an excellent technique for discovering student's misconceptions (also called naïve theories) about a topic. Introducing a writing step, the modification called *think-write-pair-share* involves having the dyad think and write their ideas or conclusions before sharing with the larger group.

The Learning Activity Center

Another significantly beneficial way of pairing students for instruction (as well as of individualizing the instruction and learning alone) is by using the learning activity center (LAC), a special technique for both integrating disciplines and individualizing the learning. A LAC is a special station located in the classroom where one student (or two, if student interaction is necessary or preferred at the center) can quietly work and at her own pace learn more about a special topic or improve specific skills. All materials needed are provided at that station, including clear instructions for operation of the center. Whereas the LAC used to be thought of as belonging to the domain of elementary school teachers with self-contained classrooms, now, with block scheduling and longer class periods, the LAC has even more relevance for middle and secondary school teachers. The LAC can be an effective and developmentally appropriate instructional device for

---

8. For a report of successful use of cross-age tutoring, see A. J. Gartner and F. Reissman, "Tutoring Helps Those Who Give, Those Who Receive," *Educational Leadership* 52(3):58–60 (November 1994).

use at any grade level, including college. A familiar example is the personal computer station.

The value of learning centers as instructional devices undoubtedly lies in the following facts. LACs can provide instructional diversity. While working at a center, the student is giving time and quality attention to the learning task (learning toward mastery) and is likely to be engaging her most effective learning modality or integrating several modalities or all of them. To adapt instruction to students' individual needs and preferences, it is possible to design a learning environment that includes several learning centers, each of which uses a different medium and modality or focuses on a special aspect of the curriculum. Students then rotate through the various learning centers according to their needs and preferences.[9]

TYPES OF LEARNING ACTIVITY CENTERS. LACs are of three types. In the *direct-learning center,* performance expectations for cognitive learning are specific and the focus is on mastery of content. In the *open-learning center,* the goal is to provide opportunity for exploration, enrichment, motivation, and creative discovery. In the *skill center,* as in a direct-learning center, performance expectations are quite specific but the focus is on the development of a particular skill or process.

PURPOSES OF A LEARNING ACTIVITY CENTER. Although in all instances the primary reason for using a learning center is to individualize the learning, there are additional reasons. These are to provide (1) a mechanism for learning that crosses discipline boundaries, (2) a special place for a student with special needs, (3) opportunities for creative work, enrichment experiences, multisensory experiences, and (4) opportunity to learn from learning packages that utilize special equipment or media, of which only one or a limited supply may be available for use in your classroom (e.g., science materials, a microscope, a computer, or a laser videodisc player, or some combination of these).

GUIDELINES FOR CONSTRUCTING A LEARNING ACTIVITY CENTER. To construct a LAC, you can be as elaborate and as creative as your time, imagination, and resources allow. Students can even help you plan and set up learning centers, which will relieve some of the burden from your busy schedule. The following paragraphs present guidelines for setting up and using this valuable instructional tool.

The center should be designed with a theme in mind, preferably one that integrates the student's learning by providing activities that cross discipline boundaries. Decide the purpose of the center and give the center a name, such as the center for the study of wetlands, or traveling to New York City, or structure and function, or patterns in nature, or the United Nations, or photosynthesis, or how to use a triple beam balance, or discrimination, and so on. The purpose of the center should be clearly understood by the students. Centers should always be used for educational purposes and *never* for punishment.

The center should be attractive, purposeful, and uncluttered and should be identified with an attractive sign. LACs should be activity-oriented (i.e., dependent on the student's manipulation of materials, not just paper-and-pencil tasks).

Topics for the center should be related to the instructional program—for review and reinforcement, remediation, or enrichment. The center should be self-directing (i.e., specific instructional objectives and procedures for using the center should be clearly posted and understandable to the student user). An audio- or videocassette or a computer program is sometimes used for this purpose. The center should also be self-correcting (i.e., student users should be able to tell by the way they have completed the task whether they have done it correctly and have learned).

The center should contain a variety of activities geared to the varying abilities and interest levels of the students. A choice of two or more activities at a center is one way to provide for this.

Materials to be used at the center should be maintained at the center, with descriptions for use provided to the students. Materials should be safe for student use, and the center should be easily supervised by you or another adult.

LEARNING IN SMALL GROUPS

Small groups consist of three to eight students, in either a teacher- or student-directed setting. Using small groups for instruction, including the cooperative learning group (CLG), enhances the opportunities for students to assume greater control over their own learning, sometimes referred to as *empowerment.*

Purposes for Using Small Groups

Small groups can be formed to serve a number of purposes. They might be useful for a specific learning activity (e.g., reciprocal reading groups, where students take turns asking questions, summarizing, making predictions about, and clarifying a story). Or they might be formed to complete an activity that requires materials that are of short supply or to complete a science experiment or a project, only lasting as long as the project does. Teachers have various rationales for

---

9. A. A. Glatthorn, *Developing a Quality Curriculum* (Alexandria, VA: Association for Supervision and Curriculum Development, 1994), p. 105.

assigning students to groups. Students can be grouped according to (1) personality type (e.g., sometimes a teacher may want to team less assertive students together to give them the opportunity for greater management of their own learning), (2) social pattern (e.g., sometimes it may be necessary to break up a group of rowdy friends, or it may be desirable to broaden the association among students), (3) common interest, (4) learning styles (e.g., forming groups of either mixed styles or styles in common), or (5) according to their abilities in a particular skill or their knowledge in a particular area. One specific type of small-group instruction is the cooperative learning group.

The Cooperative Learning Group

A contemporary of Piaget, psychologist Lev Vygotsky (1896–1934) studied the importance of a learner's social interactions in learning situations. Vygotsky argued that learning is most effective when learners cooperate with one another in a supportive learning environment under the careful guidance of a teacher. Cooperative learning, group problem solving, and cross-age tutoring are instructional strategies used today that have grown in popularity as a result of research evolving from the work of Vygotsky.

The cooperative learning group is a heterogeneous group (i.e., mixed according to one or more criteria, such as ability or skill level, ethnicity, learning style, learning capacity, gender, and language proficiency) of three to six students who work together in a teacher- or student-directed setting, emphasizing support for one another. Often, a CLG consists of four students of mixed ability, learning styles, gender, and ethnicity, with each member of the group assuming a particular role. Teachers usually change the membership of each group a few to many times during the year.

The Theory and Use of Cooperative Learning

Well supported by many research studies, the theory of cooperative learning is that when small groups of students of mixed backgrounds and capabilities work together toward a common goal, members of the group increase their friendship and respect for one another. As a consequence, each individual's self-esteem is enhanced, and academic achievement is accomplished.[10]

There are several techniques for using cooperative learning.[11] Yet the primary purpose of each is for the groups to learn, which means, of course, that individuals within a group must learn. Group achievement in learning, then, is dependent upon the learning of individuals within the group. Rather than competing for rewards for achievement, members of the group cooperate with one another by helping one another learn, so that the group reward will be a good one. Normally, the group is rewarded on the basis of group achievement, though individual members within the group can later be rewarded for individual contributions. Because of peer pressure, when using CLGs you must be cautious about using group grading. For grading purposes, bonus points can be given to all members of a group; individuals can add to their own scores when everyone in the group has reached preset standards. The preset standards must be appropriate for all members of a group. Lower standards or improvement criteria could be set for students with lower ability so that everyone feels rewarded and successful. To determine each student's term grades, measure individual student achievement later through individual student results on tests and other criteria, as well as through each student's performance in the group work.

Roles within the Cooperative Learning Group

When CLGs are used, it is advisable to assign roles (specific functions) to each member of the group; the lesson plan shown in the unit plan of Figure 5.7 shows the use of a CLG activity using assigned roles for a lesson in lab science. These roles should be rotated, either during the activity or from one time to the next. Although titles may vary, typical roles are

- *Group facilitator.* Role is to keep the group on task.
- *Materials manager.* Role is to obtain, maintain, and return materials needed for the group to function.
- *Recorder.* Role is to record all group activities and processes and perhaps to periodically assess how the group is doing.

---

10. Social studies teachers in particular will be interested in the articles in the "Cooperative Learning" theme issue of *Social Science Record* 31(1) (Spring 1994); see also B. Avery et al., "You Are There: Cooperative Teaching Makes History Come Alive," *Social Education* 58(5):271–276 (September 1994).

11. Of special interest to teachers are general methods of cooperative learning, such as (1) student team—achievement division (STAD), in which the teacher presents a lesson, students work together in teams to help each other learn the material, individuals take quizzes, and team rewards are earned based on the individual scores on the quizzes, (2) teams-games-tournaments (TGT), in which students compete against others of similar academic achievements in tournaments (rather than quizzes) and winners contribute toward their team's score, and (3) group investigations. See R. E. Slavin, *Student Team Learning: A Practical Guide for Cooperative Learning,* 3rd ed. (Washington, DC: National Education Association, 1991); E. Coelho, *Learning Together in the Multicultural Classroom* (Portsmouth, NH: Heinemann, 1994); and Y. Sharan and S. Sharan, *Expanding Cooperative Learning through Group Investigation* (New York: Teachers College Press, 1992).

- *Reporter.* Role is to report group processes and accomplishments to the teacher and/or to the entire class. For groups of four members, the roles of recorder and reporter can easily be combined.
- *Thinking monitor.* Role is to identify and record the sequence and processes of the group's thinking. This role encourages metacognition and the development of thinking skills.

It is important that students understand and perform their individual roles, that each member of the CLG performs her tasks as expected. No student should be allowed to ride on the coattails of the group. To give significance to and reinforce the importance of each role and to be able to readily recognize the role any student is playing during CLG activity, one teacher we know had an office supplier make permanent badges for the various CLG roles. During CLGs, then, each student pins the appropriate badge to his clothing.

What Students and the Teacher Do When Using Cooperative Learning Groups

Actually, for learning by CLGs to work, each member of the CLG must understand and assume two roles or responsibilities—the role he or she is assigned as a member of the group and the job of seeing that all others in the group are performing their roles. Sometimes this requires interpersonal skills that students have yet to learn or to learn well. This is where the teacher must assume some responsibility, too. Simply placing students into CLGs and expecting each member and each group to function and to learn the expected outcomes may not work. In other words, skills of cooperation must be taught, and if all your students have not yet learned those skills, then you will have to teach them. This doesn't mean that if a group is not functioning you immediately break up the group and reassign members to new groups. Part of group learning is learning the process of how to work out conflict. For a group to work out a conflict may require your assistance. With your guidance the group should be able to discover what problem is causing the conflict, then identify some options and mediate at least a temporary solution. If a particular skill is needed, then with your guidance students identify and learn that skill.

When to Use Cooperative Learning Groups

CLGs can be used for problem solving, investigations, experiments, review, project work, test making, or almost any other instructional purpose. Just as you would for small-group work in general, you can use CLGs for most any purpose at any time, but as with any other type of instructional strategy, it should not be overused.

Outcomes of Using Cooperative Learning Groups

When the process is well planned and managed, the outcomes of cooperative learning include (1) improved communication and relationships of acceptance among students of differences, (2) quality learning with fewer off-task behaviors, and (3) increased academic achievement. For example, regarding the last outcome, students who practice in cooperative groups demonstrate greater long-term memory of problem-solving strategies in mathematics.[12] In the words of Good and Brophy,

> Effects on outcomes other than achievement are . . . impressive. Cooperative learning arrangements promote friendships and prosocial interaction among students who differ in achievement, sex, race, or ethnicity, and they promote the acceptance of mainstreamed handicapped students by their nonhandicapped classmates. Cooperative methods also frequently have positive effects, and rarely have negative effects, on affective outcomes such as self-esteem, academic self-confidence, liking for the class, liking and feeling liked by classmates, and various measures of empathy and social cooperation.[13]

Why Some Teachers Have Difficulty Using Cooperative Learning Groups

Sometimes, when they think they are using CLGs, teachers have difficulty and either give up trying to use the strategy or simply tell students to divide into groups for an activity and call it cooperative learning. As emphasized earlier, for the strategy to work, each student must be given training in and have acquired basic skills in interaction and group processing and must realize that individual achievement rests with the achievement of their group. And, as true for any other strategy, the use of CLGs must not be overused—teachers must vary their strategies.

For CLGs to work well, planning and effective management are a must. Students must be instructed in the necessary skills for group learning. Each student must be assigned a responsible role within the group and be held accountable for fulfilling that responsibility. And, when a CLG activity is in process, groups must be continually monitored by the teacher for possible breakdown of this process within a group. In other words, while students are working in groups, the teacher must exercise his skills of withitness. When a potential breakdown is noticed, the teacher quickly intervenes to help the group get back on track.

---

12. See, for example, P. E. Duren and A. Cherrington, "The Effects of Cooperative Group Work versus Independent Practice on the Learning of Some Problem-Solving Strategies," *School Science and Mathematics* 92(2):80–83 (February 1992).

13. T. L. Good and J. E. Brophy, *Looking in Classrooms* (New York: Longman, 1997), p. 278.

Figure 8.1
Sample scoring rubric for group or individual presentation

PRESENTATION SCORING RUBRIC

5. Presentation was excellent. Project clearly understood and delivery organized.
    - Made eye contact throughout presentation.
    - Spoke loud enough for all to hear.
    - Spoke clearly.
    - Spoke for time allotted.
    - Stood straight and confidently.
    - Covered at least five pieces of important information.
    - Introduced project.
    - All members spoke.

4. Presentation was well thought out and planned.
    - Made eye contact throughout most of presentation.
    - Spoke loud enough and clearly most of the time.
    - Spoke nearly for time allotted.
    - Covered at least four pieces of important information.
    - Introduced project.
    - All members spoke.

3. Adequate presentation. Mostly organized.
    - Made eye contact at times.
    - Some of audience could hear the presentation.
    - Audience could understand most of what was said.
    - Spoke for about half of time allotted.
    - At least half of team spoke.
    - Covered at least three pieces of important information.
    - Project was vaguely introduced.

2–1. Underprepared presentation. Disorganized and incomplete information.
    - No eye contact during presentation.
    - Most of audience were unable to hear presentation.
    - Information presented was unclear.
    - Spoke for only brief time.
    - Covered less than three pieces of information.
    - Project was not introduced or only vaguely introduced.

LARGE-GROUP OR WHOLE-CLASS LEARNING

Large groups involve more than eight students, usually the entire class. Most often, they are teacher-directed. Student presentations and whole-class discussions are two techniques that involve the use of large groups.

Student Presentations

Students should be encouraged to be presenters for discussion of the ideas, opinions, and knowledge obtained from their own independent and small-group study. Several techniques encourage the development of certain skills, such as studying and organizing material, discovery, discussion, rebuttal, listening, analysis, suspending judgment, and critical thinking. Possible forms of discussion involving student presentations are described in the following paragraphs.

DEBATE. The debate is an arrangement in which formal speeches are made by members of two opposing teams, on topics preassigned and researched. The speeches are followed by rebuttals from each team.

JURY TRIAL. The jury trial is a discussion approach in which the class simulates a courtroom, with class members playing various roles of judge, attorneys, jury members, bailiff, and court recorder.

PANEL. The panel is a setting in which four to six students, with one designated as the chairperson or moderator, discuss a topic they have studied, followed by a question-and-answer period involving the entire class. The panel usually begins with each panel member giving a brief opening statement.

RESEARCH REPORT. One or two students or a small group of students gives a report on a topic that they investigated, followed by questions and discussions by the entire class.

ROUNDTABLE. The roundtable is a small group of three to five students, who sit around a table and discuss among themselves (and perhaps with the rest of the class listening and perhaps later asking questions) a problem or issue that they have studied. One member of the panel may serve as moderator.

SYMPOSIUM. Similar to a roundtable discussion but more formal, the symposium is an arrangement in which each student participant presents an explanation of her position on a preassigned topic she researched. Again, one student should serve as moderator. After the presentations, questions are accepted from the rest of the class.

To use these techniques effectively, students may need to be coached by you—individually, in small groups, or in whole-class sessions—on how and where to gather information; how to listen, take notes, select major points, organize material, and present a position succinctly and convincingly (see Figure 8.1 for sample scoring rubric for student presentation); how to play roles; and how to engage in dialogue and debate with one another. Exercise 8.3, which you should do now, will further your understanding about student presentations.

EXERCISE 8.3

Investigation of Student Presentation Techniques

Instructions: The purpose of this exercise is for you and your classmates, in groups of four, to use your university library to research in detail the distinctive characteristics of using the following for teaching: (1) student reports; (2) debates; (3) forums; (4) round tables; (5) symposiums; and (6) any other technique that you find.

Following your research, compile your findings within your group. Then, through your small-group discussions, derive examples of appropriate uses for each type of activity, relative to teaching specific content in your subject field and grade-level interest. Functioning as a panel of experts, share your findings and examples with the entire class.

Whole-Class Discussion

Direct whole-class discussion is a teaching technique used frequently by most or all teachers. On this topic, you should consider yourself an expert. Having been a student in formal learning for at least 15 years, you are undoubtedly knowledgeable about the advantages and disadvantages of whole-class discussions. So, explore your knowledge and experiences by responding to Exercise 8.4A. Then do Exercise 8.4B, where guidelines for using whole-class discussion will be generated.

EXERCISE 8.4A

Whole-Class Discussion as a Teaching Strategy: What Do I Already Know?

Instructions: Answer the following questions, and then share your responses with your class, perhaps in discussion groups organized by subject field or grade level.

1. Your grade-level interest or subject field: _____

2. For what reasons would you hold a whole-class discussion? _____

   _____

   _____

   _____

   _____

3. Assuming that your classroom has movable seats, how would you arrange them? _____

   _____

   _____

   _____

4. What would you do if the seats were not movable? _____

   _____

   _____

   _____

5. What rules would you establish before starting the discussion? _____

   _____

   _____

   _____

   _____

6. Should student participation be forced? Why or why not? If so, how? _____

   _____

   _____

   _____

   _____

7. How would you discourage a few students from dominating the discussion? _____

   _____

   _____

8. What preparation should be expected of the students and teacher before beginning the discussion? _____

_____

_____

_____

_____

_____

9. How would you handle digression from the topic? _____

_____

_____

_____

_____

10. Should students be discussion leaders? Why or why not? If so, what training, if any, should they receive, and how? _____

_____

_____

_____

_____

11. What teacher roles are options during a class discussion? _____

_____

_____

_____

_____

_____

12. When is each of these roles most appropriate? _____

_____

_____

_____

_____

_____

13. When, if ever, is it appropriate to hold a class meeting for discussing class procedures, not subject matter? _____

_____

_____

_____

_____

_____

_____

14. Can brainstorming be a form of whole-class discussion? Why or why not? _____

_____

_____

_____

_____

_____

15. What follow-up activities would be appropriate after a whole-class discussion? On what basis would you decide to use each? _____

_____

_____

_____

_____

_____

16. What sorts of activities should precede a class discussion? _____

_____

_____

_____

_____

_____

_____

17. Should a discussion be given a set length? Why or why not? If so, how long? How is the length to be decided? _____

_____

_____

_____

_____

_____

_____

18. Should students be graded for their participation in class discussion? Why or why not? If so, how? On what basis? By whom? _____

_____

_____

_____

_____

_____

_____

19. For effective discussions, 10 to 12 feet is the maximum recommended distance between participants. During a teacher-led discussion, what can a teacher do to keep within this limit? _____

_____

_____

_____

_____

_____

20. Are there any pitfalls or other points of importance that a teacher should be aware of when planning and implementing a whole-class discussion? If so, explain them and how to guard against them. _____

_____

_____

_____

_____

_____

_____

EXERCISE 8.4B
Generating Guidelines for Using Whole-class Discussions

Instructions: Share your responses to Exercise 8.4A with your colleagues. Then individually answer the first two questions below. Next, as a group, use all three questions to guide you as you generate a list of five general guidelines for the use of whole-class discussion as a strategy in teaching. Share your group's guidelines with the entire class. Then, as a class, derive a final list of general guidelines.

1. How effective was your small-group discussion in sharing Exercise 8.4A? _____

_____

_____

_____

_____

_____

_____

_____

2. What allowed for or inhibited the effectiveness of that small-group discussion? _____

_____

_____

_____

_____

_____

_____

_____

3. How effective is this small-group discussion? Why? _____

_____

_____

_____

_____

_____

_____

_____

General Guidelines Generated from Small-Group Discussion

1. _____
_____

2. _____
_____

3. _____
_____

4. _____
_____

5. _____
_____

General Guidelines: Final List Derived from Whole Class Discussion

_____
_____
_____
_____
_____
_____
_____
_____
_____
_____
_____
_____
_____
_____
_____
_____
_____
_____
_____
_____

EQUALITY IN THE CLASSROOM

Especially when conducting direct whole-group discussions, it is easy for a teacher to fall into the trap of interacting with only "the stars," or only those in the front of the room or on one side, or only the most vocal and assertive. You must exercise caution and avoid falling into that trap. To ensure a psychologically safe and effective environment for learning for every person in your classroom, you must attend to all students and try to involve them equally in all class activities. You must avoid biased expectations about certain students, and you must avoid discriminating against students according to their personal characteristics.

You must avoid the unintentional tendency of teachers of *both* sexes at all grade levels to discriminate on the basis of gender. For example, teachers, along with the rest of society, tend to have lower expectations for girls than for boys in mathematics and science. They tend to call on and encourage boys more than girls. They often let boys interrupt girls but praise girls for being polite and waiting their turn.[14] To avoid such discrimination may take special effort on your part, no matter how aware of the problem you may be.

To guarantee equity in interaction with students, many teachers have found it helpful to ask someone secretly to tally classroom interactions between the teacher and students during a class discussion. After an analysis of the results, the teacher arrives at decisions about her own attending and facilitating behaviors. Such an analysis is the purpose of Exercise 8.5. You are welcome to make blank copies and share them with your teaching colleagues.

In addition to the variables mentioned at the beginning of Exercise 8.5, modifications to the exercise can include responses and their frequencies according to

other teacher-student interactions, such as your calling on all students equally for responses to your questions, or your calling on students equally to assist you with classroom helping jobs, or your chastising students for their inappropriate behavior, or your asking questions to assume classroom leadership roles.

Ensuring Equity

There are many ways of ensuring that students are treated fairly in the classroom, including the following:

- Encourage students to demonstrate an appreciation for one another by applauding all individual and group presentations.
- Have and maintain high expectations, although not necessarily identical expectations, for all students.
- Insist on politeness in the classroom. For example, for his contribution to the learning process a student can be shown appreciation with a sincere "thank you" or "I appreciate your contribution," or with a whole-class applause, or with a genuine smile.
- Insist that students be allowed to finish what they are saying, without being interrupted by others. Be certain that you model this behavior yourself.
- During whole-class instruction, insist that students raise their hands and be called on by you before they are allowed to speak.
- Keep a stopwatch handy to unobtrusively control the wait-time given for each student. Although at first this idea may sound impractical, it works.
- Use a seating chart attached to a clipboard; next to each student's name, make a tally of each interaction you have with a student. This also is a good way to maintain records to reward students for their contributions to class discussion. Again, it is workable at any grade level. The seating chart can be laminated so that it can be used day after day simply by erasing the marks of the previous day.

Now, do Exercise 8.5, through which you will examine a teacher's behavior with students according to gender.

---

14. B. Vetter, "Ferment: Yes; Progress, Maybe; Change: Slow," *Mosaic* 23(3):34 (Fall 1992).

EXERCISE 8.5

Teacher Interaction with Students according to Student Gender

Instructions: The purpose of this exercise is to provide a tool for your analysis of your own interactions with students according to gender. To become accustomed to the exercise, you should do a trial run in one of your university classes, then use it during your student teaching, and again during your first years of teaching. The exercise can be modified to include (1) the amount of time given for each interaction; (2) the response time given by the teacher according to student gender; and (3) other student characteristics, such as ethnicity.

Prior to class, select a student (this will be you during the trial run recommended above) or an outside observer, such as a colleague, to do the tallying and calculations as follows. Ask the person to tally secretly the interactions between you and the students by placing a mark after the name of each student (or on the student's position on a seating chart) with whom you have verbal interaction. If a student does the tallying, she should not be counted in any of the calculations.

Exact time at start _____

Exact time at end _____

Total time in minutes _____

Total in class today = _____	Girls = _____	Boys = _____
	% Girls = _____	% Boys = _____

Tally of Interactions

With girls	With boys

Total Interactions = _____

% with girls = _____   % with boys = _____

Teacher Reflections and Conclusions: _____

_____

_____

_____

_____

For Your Notes

LEARNING FROM ASSIGNMENTS AND HOMEWORK

An assignment is a statement of *what* the student is to accomplish or do and is tied to a specific instructional objective. Assignments, whether completed at home or at school, can ease student learning in many ways, but when poorly planned they can be discouraging.

Purposes for Assignments

Purposes for giving homework assignments can be any of the following: to constructively extend the time that students are engaged in learning; to help students develop personal learning; to help students develop their research skills; to help students develop their study skills; to help students organize their learning; to individualize the learning; to involve parents and guardians in their children's learning; to provide a mechanism by which students receive constructive feedback; to provide students with an opportunity to review and practice what has been learned; to reinforce classroom experiences; and to teach new content.

Guidelines for Using Assignments

To use assignments, consider the guidelines in the following paragraphs.

As said earlier, an assignment is a statement of *what* the student is to accomplish. Procedures, in contrast, are statements of *how* to do something. Although students may need some procedural guidelines, especially with respect to your expectations for an assignment, generally you will want to avoid supplying too much detail on how to accomplish an assignment.

Plan early the types of assignments you will give (e.g., daily and long-range; minor and major; in class or at home, or both), and prepare assignment specifications. Assignments must correlate with specific instructional objectives and should *never* be given as busywork or as punishment. For each assignment, let students know what the objectives are.

Use caution about giving assignments that could be controversial or that could pose a hazard to the safety of students. In such cases (especially if you are new to the community), before giving the assignment it is probably a good idea to talk it over with members of your teaching team, the departmental chair, or an administrator. Also, for a particular assignment, you may need to have parental or guardian permission for students to do it or be prepared to give an alternate assignment for some students.

Provide differentiated or optional assignments—assignment variations given to students or selected by them on the basis of their interests and learning capacities. Students can select or be assigned different activities to accomplish the same objective, such as read and discuss, or they can participate with others in a more direct learning experience. After their study, as a portion of the assignment, students share what they have learned. This is an example of using multilevel teaching.

The time a student needs to complete assignments beyond school time will vary according to school policy and grade level. Generally, middle school students may be expected to complete all their school assignments on an average of an hour or two per school day, while high school students may be expected to spend several hours on assignments each day.

Teachers have found it beneficial to prepare individualized study guides with questions to be answered and activities to be done by the student while reading textbook chapters as homework. One advantage of a study guide is that it can make the reading more than a visual experience. A study guide can help to organize student learning by accenting instructional objectives, emphasizing important points to be learned, providing a guide for studying for tests, and encouraging the student to read the homework assignment.

As a general rule, homework assignments should stimulate thinking by arousing a student's curiosity, raising questions for further study, and encouraging and supporting the self-discipline required for independent study.

Determine the resources that students will need to complete assignments, and check the availability of these resources. This is important; students can't be expected to use that which is unavailable to them. Many will not use that which is not readily available.

Avoid yelling out assignments as students are leaving your classroom. When giving assignments in class, you should write them on a special place on the writing board, give a copy to each student, or require that each student write the assignment into her assignment folder. Another idea is to include assignments in the course syllabus. Take extra care to ensure that assignment specifications are clear to students, and allow time for students to ask questions about an assignment. Be prepared if a parent complains that you never assign homework. To keep that from happening, the written syllabus with assignments, as well as the use of student portfolios, is helpful. It's important that your procedure for giving and collecting assignments be consistent throughout the school year.

Students should be given sufficient time to complete their assignments. In other words, avoid announcing an assignment that is due the very next day. As a general rule, all assignments should be given far in advance of the day they are due. Try to avoid changing assignment specifications after they are given. Especially avoid changing them at the last minute. Changing specifications at the last minute can be very frustrating to students

TEACHING VIGNETTE
Late Homework Paper and an At-Risk Student

Consider this case: An 11th-grade student turned in an English class assignment several days late and the paper was accepted by the teacher without penalty, although the teacher's policy was that late papers would be severely penalized. During the week that the assignment was due, the student had suffered a miscarriage. In this instance, her teacher accepted the paper late sans penalty because the student carried a great deal of psychological baggage and the teacher felt that turning in the paper at all was a positive act. If the paper had not been accepted, or had been accepted only with severe penalty to her grade, then, in the teacher's professional opinion, the student would have simply quit trying and probably dropped out of school altogether.

who have already completed the assignment, and it shows little respect for those students.

After due dates for assignments have been negotiated or set, you should strictly adhere to them and give no credit or reduced credit (such as one letter grade for each day late) for work that is turned in late. You may think this is harsh and rigid, but experience has shown it to be a good policy to which students can and should adjust. It is much like the world of work (and of college) to which they must become accustomed, and it is sensible for a teacher who deals with many papers each day. Of course, for this policy to work well, students must be given their assignments not at the last minute but long before the work is due.

Sometimes, however, students have legitimate reasons for not completing an assignment by the due date, and we believe the teacher should listen and exercise professional judgment in each instance. As someone once said, there is nothing democratic about treating unequals as equals. Consider the above teaching vignette.

Although it is important that teachers have rules and procedures—and that they consistently apply them—the teacher is a professional who must consider all aspects of an individual student's situation and, after doing so, show compassion, caring, and understanding of the human situation. A teacher must exercise intelligent judgment and decision making.

Allow time in class for students to begin work on homework assignments, so that you can give them individual attention (guided or coached practice). Your ability to coach students is the *reason* for in-class time to begin work on assignments. As you have learned, many secondary schools have extended the length of class periods to allow more in-class time for teacher guidance on assignments. The benefits of coached practice include being able to (1) monitor student work so that a student does not go too far in a wrong direction, (2) help students reflect on their thinking,

(3) assess the progress of individual students, and (4) discover or create a "teachable moment." For example, while monitoring students doing their work, the teacher might discover a commonly shared student misconception. The teacher, taking advantage of this teachable moment, stops and talks about that and attempts to clarify that misconception.

Timely, constructive, and corrective feedback from the teacher on the homework—and grading of homework—increases the positive contributions of homework dramatically.[15] If the assignment is important for students to do, then you must give your full and immediate attention to the product of their efforts. Read almost everything that students write. Students are much more willing to do homework when they believe it is useful, when teachers treat it as an integral part of instruction, when it is read and evaluated by the teacher, and when it counts as part of the grade.[16]

Provide feedback about each student's work, and be positive and constructive in your comments. Always think about the written comments that you make, to be relatively certain they will convey your intended meaning to the student. When writing comments on student papers, consider using a color other than red. To many people, red brings with it a host of negative connotations (e.g., blood, hurt, danger, stop).

Rather than grading (i.e., giving a percentage or numerical grade), with its negative connotations, teachers sometimes prefer to score assignments with constructive and reinforcing comments.

Regardless of grade level or subject taught, each teacher must give attention to the development of students' reading, listening, speaking, and writing skills. Attention to these skills must also be obvious in your

---

15. H. J. Walberg, "Productive Teaching and Instruction: Assessing the Knowledge Base," *Phi Delta Kappan* 71(6):472 (February 1990).
16. *What Works: Research about Teaching and Learning* (Washington, DC: United States Department of Education, 1986), p. 42.

assignment specifications and your assignment grading policy. Reading is crucial to the development of a person's ability to write. For example, to foster high-order thinking, students in any subject can and should be encouraged to write (in their journals, as discussed in Chapter 5) their thoughts and feelings about the material they have read.

Although resubmission of a graded paper increases the amount of paperwork, many teachers report that it is worthwhile to give students a day or so to make corrections and resubmit the assignment for an improved score. However, out of regard for students who do well from the start, we advise against allowing a resubmitted paper to receive an A grade (unless, of course, it was an A paper for the first grading).

How to Avoid Having So Many Papers to Grade That Time for Effective Planning Is Restricted

A downfall for some student teachers and beginning teachers is being buried under mounds of homework to be read and graded, leaving less and less time for effective planning. To keep this from happening to you, we offer the following suggestions. Although we adhere to our earlier statement—that you should read almost everything that students write—you will read student papers with varying degrees of intensity and scrutiny, depending on the purpose of the assignment. For assignments that are designed for learning, understanding, and practice, you can allow students to check them themselves using either self-checking or peer-checking. During the self- or peer-checking, you can walk around the room, monitor the activity, and record whether a student did the assignment or not, or after the checking, you can collect the papers and do your recording. Besides reducing the amount of paperwork for you, self- or peer-checking provides other advantages: it allows students to see and understand their errors, and it helps them develop self-evaluation techniques and standards. If the purpose of the assignment is to assess mastery competence, then the papers should be read, marked, and graded only by the teacher.

LEARNING FROM STUDENT-CENTERED PROJECTS, INDEPENDENT AND GROUP STUDY, PAPERS, AND ORAL REPORTS

For the most meaningful student learning to occur, independent study, individual writing, student-centered projects, and oral reports should be major features of your instruction. There will be times when the students are interested in an in-depth inquiry of a topic and will want to pursue a particular topic for study. This undertaking can be flexible—the investigation can be done by an individual student, a team of two, a small group, or the entire class. *The project is a form of study in which students produce something, such as a paper, an investigation, a model, a skit, a report, or a combination of these.*

In collaboration with the teacher, students select a topic for the project. Sometimes a teacher will write the general problem or topic in the center of a graphic web and ask the students to brainstorm some questions. The questions will lead to ways for students to investigate, draw sketches, construct models, record findings, predict items, compare and contrast, and discuss understandings.

You can keep track of the students' progress by reviewing weekly updates of their work. Set deadlines with the groups. Meet with groups daily to discuss their questions or problems. Based on their investigations, the students will prepare and present their findings in reports and include a hands-on item (e.g., a display, play or skit, book, song or poem, video or slide show, 3-D model, maps, charts). If necessary, have a "grand finale" class meeting prior to the day or days the final reports are given so that students can clarify the specific details of their final reports and hands-on participation. Make an agenda of the reports for the grand finale so that all is clear to the students.

At William Diamond Middle School (Lexington, MA), for example, one day each week of the school year students spend all four instructional periods with one teacher or adviser as they pursue intensive, independent learning projects, one each quarter in science, math, social studies, and English. Independent study affords the opportunity students need to explore their own interests; small-group project work can help satisfy their need to have worthwhile experiences with their peers; and the opportunity to share a project with the rest of the class can help contribute to their feelings of self-worth and competence. At William Diamond Middle School, the intent is to (1) foster student engagement, independent learning and thinking skills, (2) allow for different learning styles, (3) incorporate multiple intelligences, and (4) provide an opportunity for students to make decisions about their own learning and manage time and materials effectively.[17] And, as has been demonstrated time and again, when students choose their own projects, integrating knowledge as the need arises, motivation and learning follow naturally.[18]

17. L. A. Murdock et al., "Horace's Fridays," *Educational Leadership* 53(3):38 (November 1995).
18. S. Volk, "Project-Based Learning: Pursuits with a Purpose," *Educational Leadership* 53(3):42 (November 1994).

Purposes for Using Student-Centered Project Study

Purposes for using project-centered student learning include the following. (1) A student can become especially knowledgeable and experienced in one area of subject content or in one process skill, thus adding to the student's knowledge and experience base and sense of importance and self-worth. (2) A student can exercise his preferred learning modality or special learning capacity; consideration and accommodation of individual interests, learning styles, intelligences, and life experiences can optimize personal meaning to the student. (3) Under the teacher's guidance, a student develops skill in communication through sharing this special knowledge and experience with the teacher and with peers. (4) Students become intrinsically motivated to learn when working on topics of personal meaning, with outcomes and even time lines that are relatively open ended. (5) Students can practice and develop independent learning skills; students learn to work independently, or work somewhat independently of the teacher in small groups. (6) With proper guidance and coaching by the teacher, students develop skills in writing, communication, and higher-level thinking and doing.

Developing a Sense of Connectedness through Community Service Project Learning

Increasingly, schools are providing students with the opportunity to learn by serving in the community. From soup kitchens and playground equipment projects to volunteer activities in government and business, these hands-on opportunities are especially powerful when linked to the school curriculum and classroom learning. In some cases in which student skills have been linked to employee needs, not only have employers expanded opportunities for student learning, but their companies have also benefited. Through these programs, employers are able to complete important projects, while students benefit from new learning experiences in real-world work settings.[19] Several sample community service learning projects are presented in the last section of this chapter.

Guiding Students in Project Work

Without careful planning, and unless students are given guidance, project-based teaching can be a frustrating experience, for both the teacher and the students, and especially for a beginning teacher who is inexperienced in such an undertaking. Students should do projects because they want to and because the project seems meaningful. Therefore, students should, under guidance

from the teacher, decide *what* project to do and *how* to do it. The teacher's role is to advise and guide students so that they experience success. If a project is laid out in too much detail by the teacher, that project is a procedure rather than a project assignment. There must be a balance between structure and opportunities for student choices and decision making. Without frequent progress reporting by the student and guidance and reinforcement from the teacher, a student can get frustrated and quickly lose interest in the project.

Guidelines for Using Project-Centered Learning

With the provision of structure and proper guidance by the teacher, the results can be well worth the effort. For these types of instructional strategies to be educationally beneficial, the teacher should follow the guidelines discussed in the paragraphs that follow.

Stimulate ideas and provide anchor studies. You can stimulate ideas by providing lists of things students might do; by mentioning each time an idea comes up in class that this would be good for an independent, small-group, or class project; by having former students tell about their projects; by showing the results of other students' projects (anchor studies); by suggesting readings that are likely to give students ideas; and by using class discussions to brainstorm ideas.

Allow students to individually choose whether they will work alone or in small groups. If they choose to work in groups, then help them delineate job descriptions for each member of the group. For project work, groups of four or fewer students usually work better than groups of more than four. Even if the project is one the whole class is pursuing, the project should be broken down into parts, with individuals or small groups of students undertaking independent study of these parts.

Provide options but insist that writing be a part of each student's work. Allow students individually to choose whether to do a project, a paper, or an oral report, or a combination of these three types of assignments. Regardless of whether a student selects a project, paper, or oral report, insist that writing be a part of the student's work. In many schools that use project-centered teaching, a paper and an oral presentation are automatically required of all students. It is recommended that you use the *I-Search* paper instead of the traditional research paper. Under your careful guidance, the student (1) lists things that she would like to know, and from the list selects one item that becomes the research topic, (2) conducts the study while maintaining a log of activities and findings, which, in fact, becomes a process journal, (3) prepares a booklet that presents

---

19. National PTA, *National Standards for Parent/Family Involvement Programs* (Chicago, IL: National PTA, 1997), p. 21.

her findings and consists of paragraphs and visual representations, (4) prepares a summary of the findings, including the significance of the study and her personal feelings, and (5) shares the project as a final oral report with the teacher and classmates. Research examining the links among writing, thinking, and learning has helped emphasize the importance of writing. Writing is a complex intellectual behavior and process that helps the learner create and record his understanding—that is, to construct meaning. See the next section.

Provide coaching and guidance. Work with each student or student team in topic selection, as well as in the processes of written and oral reporting. Allow students to develop their own procedures, but guide their preparation of work outlines and preliminary drafts, giving them constructive feedback and encouragement along the way. Aid students in their identification of potential resources and in the techniques of research. Your coordination with the library and other resource centers is central to the success of project-centered learning. Frequent drafts and progress reports from the students are a must. With each of these stages, provide students with constructive feedback and encouragement. Provide written guidelines, and negotiate time lines for the outlines, drafts, and completed project.

Promote sharing. Insist that students share both the progress and the results of their study with the rest of the class. The amount of time allowed for this sharing will, of course, depend upon many variables. The value of this type of instructional strategy comes not only from individual contributions but also from the learning that results from the experience and the communication of that experience to others.

Assess the product. The final product of the project, including papers and oral reports, should be graded. The method of determining the grade should be clear to students from the beginning, as well as the weight of the project grade toward the term grade. Provide students with clear descriptions (rubrics) of how evaluation and grading will be done. Evaluation should include whether deadlines for drafts and progress reports were met. The final grade for the study should be based on four criteria: (1) how well it was organized, including meeting draft deadlines; (2) the quality and quantity of knowledge gained from the experience; (3) the quality of the student's sharing of that learning experience with the rest of the class; and (4) the quality of the student's final written or oral report. Sample assessment rubrics for oral presentations are shown in Figures 8.1 and 11.3, and for papers and other aspects of project study see Figures 11.2, 11.4, 11.8, 11.9, and Table 11.2.

WRITING ACROSS THE CURRICULUM

Research examining the links among writing, thinking, and learning has helped emphasize the importance of writing across the curriculum. In exemplary schools, student writing is encouraged in all subjects (i.e., across the curriculum). For example, at Elk Grove High School (Elk Grove, CA), a history-English writing project is required of all sophomores; at Polytech High School (Woodside, DE), a writing project combining academic and vocational studies is required of all seniors.

Kinds of Writing

A student should experience various kinds of writing rather than the same form, class after class, year after year. Perhaps most important is that writing should be emphasized as a process that illustrates one's thinking, rather than solely as a product completed as an assignment. Writing and thinking develop best when a student experiences various kinds and forms of writing during any school day. From Tiedt and Tiedt, here are eight forms of writing that students can use to express their ideas:[20]

- Report of information. The writer collects data from observation and research and chooses material that best represents a phenomenon or concept.
- Eyewitness account. The writer tells about a person, group, or event that was objectively observed from the outside.
- Autobiographical incident. The writer narrates a specific event in his life and states or implies the significance of the event.
- Firsthand biographical sketch. Through incident and description, the writer characterizes a person she knows well.
- Story. Using dialogue and description, the writer shows conflict between characters or between a character and the environment.
- Analysis—speculation about effects. The writer conjectures about the causes and effects of a specific event.
- Problem solving. The writer describes and analyzes a specific problem and then proposes and argues for a solution.
- Evaluation. The writer presents a judgment on the worth of an item—book, movie, artwork, consumer product—and supports this with reasons and evidence.

---

20. P. L. Tiedt and I. M. Tiedt, *Multicultural Teaching: A Handbook of Activities, Information, and Resources,* 4th ed. (Boston: Allyn and Bacon, 1995), p. 208.

Figure 8.2
Resources for writing across the curriculum.

- International Reading Association, 800 Barksdale Road, Newark, DE 19711.
- National Center for the Study of Writing and Literature, School of Education, University of California–Berkeley, Berkeley, CA 94720. (Having completed its mission, the NCSWL no longer functions as an independent entity. Its publications, however, may be obtained from the NWP headquarters.)
- National Council of Teachers of English, 1111 Kenyon Road, Urbana, IL 61801.
- National Writing Project, 5627 Tolman Hall, University of California–Berkeley, Berkeley, CA 94720.
- Whole Language Umbrella, Unit 6-846, Marion Street, Winnipeg, Manitoba, Canada R2JOK4.
- Writing to Learn, Council for Basic Education, 725 15th Street, NW, Washington, DC 20005.

Student Journals

Many teachers across the curriculum have their students maintain journals in which the students keep a log of their activities, findings, and thoughts (i.e., *process journals,* as discussed previously) and write their thoughts about what they are studying (*response journals,* as discussed in Chapter 4). Actually, commonly used are two types of response journals: dialogue journals and reading-response journals. In *dialogue journals* students write anything that is on their minds, usually on the right side of a page, while peers, teachers, and parents or guardians respond on left side of a page, thereby "talking with" the journal writer. In *reading-response journals* students write their reactions to what is being studied.

Purpose and Assessment of Student Journal Writing

Normally, academic journals are not the personal diaries of the writer's recollection of and thoughts about daily events. Rather, the purpose of journal writing is to encourage students to write, to think about their writing, to record their creative thoughts about *what they are learning,* and to share their written thoughts with an audience—all of which help in the development of their thinking skills, in their learning, and in their development as writers. Students are encouraged to write about experiences, both in school and out, that are related to the topics being studied. They should be encouraged to record their feelings about what and how they are learning.

Journal writing provides practice in expression and should not be graded by the teacher. Negative comments and evaluations from the teacher will discourage creative and spontaneous expression by students. Teachers should read the journal writing and then offer constructive and positive feedback. For grading purposes, most teachers simply record whether a student does, in fact, maintain the required journal.

The National Council of Teachers of English (NCTE) has developed guidelines for journal writing. Your school English department will likely have a copy of these guidelines, or you can contact NCTE directly (address above). Resources on writing across the curriculum are shown in Figure 8.2.

A COLLECTION OF MORE THAN 100 ANNOTATED MOTIVATIONAL TEACHING STRATEGIES AND IDEAS FOR LESSONS, INTERDISCIPLINARY TEACHING, TRANSCULTURAL STUDIES, AND STUDENT PROJECTS

Students today are used to multimillion-dollar productions on television, videodiscs, arcade games, and the movie screen. When they come into a classroom and are subjected each day to something short of a high-budget production, it is little wonder that they sometimes react in a less than highly motivated fashion. No doubt, today's youth are growing up in a highly stimulated instant-action society, a society that has learned to expect instant headache relief, instant meals, instant gratification, and perhaps, in the minds of many youth, instant high-paying employment. In light of this cultural phenomenon, we are on the side of you, the teacher, who is on the firing line each day and who is expected to perform, perhaps instantly and entertainingly but most certainly in a highly competent and professional manner and in situations not even close to ideal. In any case, and as we said in Chapter 3, you must gain your students' attention before you can teach them.

In this final section of the chapter, we present an annotated list of ideas, many of which have been offered over the years by classroom teachers (see also Figure 8.3). Although the ideas are organized according to subject fields, we suggest that you read all entries for each field, for although one entry might be identified as specific to one field, it might also be useful in other areas. (Many of them can be used in inter-

Figure 8.3
Web sites for teaching ideas.

- *All subjects, lessons, units, and project ideas*
  eDscape, at <http://www.edscape.com>.
  National Service Learning Cooperative Web site
  <http://www.nicsl.coled.umn.edu> to review middle school learning projects.
  Teachers Net Lesson Exchange at <http://www.teachers.net/lessons/posts.html>.

- *Arts*
  Incredible Art Department at <http://www.in.net/~kenroar>, lessons and student art work.
  World Wide Arts Resources at <http://www.wwar.com>.

- *English/language arts/reading*
  The Encyclopedia Mythica at <http://www.pantheon.org/mythica>.
  Mandel's Internet site at <http://www.pacificnet.net/~mandel/LanguageArts.html>.

- *History/social studies*
  Historical Text Archive at <http://www.msstate.edu/Archives/History/index.html>.
  History/social studies resources at <http://www.execpc.com/~dboals/boals.html>.
  Links to literally thousands of lesson plans, unit plans, thematic units, and resources at <http://www.csun.edu/~hcedu013/index.html>.
  Native American resources at <http://hanksville.phast.umass.edu/misc/NAresources.html>.
  Social Science Resources Home Page at <http://www.nde.state.ne.us/SS/ss.html>.
  Women's history at <http://frank.mtsu.edu/~kmiddlet/history/women.html>.

- *Mathematics*
  Math resources at <http://www-personal.umd.umich.edu/~jobrown/math.html>.
  PBS Mathline at <http://www.pbs.org/learn/mathline/>.
  Plane Math at <http://www.planemath.com/>.

- *Music*
  Music Educator's Home Page at <http://www.athenet.net/~wslow/>.
  Music, the Universal Language at <http://www.jumpoint/com/bluesman/>.
  Music lesson plans and other resource links at <http://www.csun.edu/~vceed009/music.html>.

- *Science*
  Cody's Science Education Zone at <http://www.ousd.k12.ca.us/~codypren/CSEZ_Home>.
  Mandel's Web site at <http://www.pacificnet.net/~mandel/Science.html>.
  Science and Mathematics Education Resources at <http://www.hpec.astro.washington.edu/scied/science.html>.
  Weather Underground at <http://groundhog.sprl.umich.edu/>.

disciplinary teaching—for example, number one can clearly be combined with mathematics and science as well as art.) Or an entry might stimulate a creative thought for your own stock of motivational techniques, such as an idea for a way to utilize the theory of multiple learning capacities or to emphasize the multicultural aspect of a lesson in math, or social studies, or whatever the central discipline or theme of a lesson or unit of instruction.

The Visual and Performing Arts

1. As part of a unit on design or creativity, have students construct, design, and decorate their own kites. When the projects are complete, designate a time to fly them.

2. Use lyrics from popular music to influence class work, such as by putting the lyrics into pictures.

3. Bring in examples of your own pieces of art, those that are both current and from when you first began working in the medium.

4. Utilize the outdoors or another environment for a free-drawing experience.

5. Invite a local artist who has created a community mural to speak to the class about his mural. Plan and create a class mural, perhaps on a large sheet of plywood or some other location approved by the school administration.

6. Use a mandala to demonstrate the importance of individual experience, as in interpreting paintings and poetry.

7. Arrange a field trip for the class to dig up natural clay. In class, sift and refine, soak in water, and work it into usable clay. Follow with a hand-built clay project.

8. Collect books, magazines, posters, films, videos, computer software programs, and so forth that show different kinds of masks people around the world wear. Ask students to identify the similarities and differences between the masks. Have students research to find out the significance of mask characters in various cultures. Have students design and create their own masks to illustrate their own personalities, cultures, and so forth.

9. As part of a unit on the creative process, have each student draw or sketch on a piece of paper, then pass it on to the next person, who will make additions to the drawing. Instructions could include "improve the drawing," "make the drawing ugly," and "add what you think would be necessary to complete the composition."

10. Listen to a musical recording and try to illustrate it.

11. Imagine that you're a bird flying over the largest city you have visited. What do you see, hear, smell, feel, and taste? Draw a "sensory" map.

12. Assign a different color to each student. Have them arrange themselves into warm and cool colors and explain their decisions (e.g., why blue is cool). Discuss emotional responses to each color.

13. Watch videos of dances from various countries and cultures. Have students identify similarities and differences. Have students research meanings and occasions of particular dances.

14. Have students find ways in which music, art, and dance are used around them.

15. Periodically during the school year, after the students have memorized or can perfectly play a certain piece, switch the band or orchestra around by not putting any two of the same instruments together. For example, put no flutes next to each other, put a cello by a trumpet, a violin beside a drummer, or a saxophone next to a viola and bass. This ensures that each person knows her own part and can carry her own weight in terms of performance. This can also be done in chorus, mixing sopranos with altos, tenors, basses, and so on.

16. Find a popular song that students like. Transpose the melody into unfamiliar keys for each instrument. This makes the student want to learn the song, but in the process the student will have to become more familiar with his instrument.

17. Set aside one weekend morning a month and hold small informal recitals (workshops) allowing students to participate in or observe the performances among their peers and themselves. (Students might be told previously about these special days and encouraged to prepare a selection of their own choosing.)

18. Play a group-activity rhythm game, one such as the "Dutch Shoe Game," to get students to cooperate, work together, and enjoy themselves using rhythm. Participants sit in a circle, and as the song is sung, each person passes one of her shoes to the person on the right in rhythm to the music. Shoes continue to be passed as long as verses are sung. Those with poor rhythm will end up with a pile of shoes in front of them!

19. Choose a rhythmical, humorous poem or verse to conduct. The students read the poem in chorus, while the teacher stands before them and conducts the poem as if it were a musical work. Students must be sensitive to the intonation, speed, inflection, mood, and dynamics that the teacher wants them to convey in their reading.

20. Plan a series of studies of non-Western music. As a break from studying just Western music, once a week or once every two weeks prepare a program to expose students to the music of a different country, for example, Japan, India, or the Polynesian Islands. Tapes or CDs can be used to introduce the sound of the music, slides can be used to view the country and its people, and instruments can be found from different countries. Guest speakers may be available to lecture or perform.

21. Start a Retired Senior Citizens Volunteer Program. Senior citizens present folk art workshops with students and together create artworks for the school.

Family and Consumer Economics, Foods, and Textiles

22. Often the foods we like originated from another part of our country or the world. Have students identify such foods and from where they came, foods such as spaghetti, enchiladas, fajitas, wontons, tacos, quiches, croissants, teriyaki, and fried rice. Have students list the names and origins and place pictures of the food on a large world map.

23. Take still photos of class members at special events such as dinners, fashion shows, field trips, and special projects. Build a scrapbook or bulletin board with these, and display it on campus or at an open house.

24. As a class or group project, collect cartoons related to food costs, consumer problems, and family relationships.

25. Plan a unit on cultural foods, using the traditions, costumes, and music of a particular culture. Have the students decorate the room. Invite the principal for a meal and visit.

26. Students at Agassiz Middle School (Fargo, ND) worked on a project about culture and how culture affects the way we live. They learned that cultural dif-

ferences can effect how an individual dresses, eats, worships, celebrates, and communicates.

27. At Discovery Middle School (Vancouver, WA), students provided child care, cross-age tutoring, and companionship to approximately 700 preschool and elementary students and elderly clients at fifteen off-campus locations.

28. Have students research from where each of these foods originated: pizza, hot dog, hamburger, noodle, tomato, chocolate, potato, hoagie, chop suey, ice cream cone, submarine, poor boy.

29. Have students plan and create a bulletin board displaying pictures of 100-calorie portions of basic nutritional foods and popular fad foods that contain only empty calories. The display can motivate a discussion on foods with calories and nutrients versus foods with empty calories.

30. Pin the names of different garments on the backs of students. The students are then to sort themselves into different wash loads.

31. For a clothing unit hold an "idea day." Ask each student to bring in an idea of something that can be done to give clothes a new look, a fun touch, or an extended wearing life. Ideas they may come up with include appliqués, embroidery, tie-dye, batik, colorful patches, and restyling of old clothes into current or creative fashions.

32. Have the students write, practice, and present skits, perhaps for videotape presentation, on consumer fraud.

33. Once a month have students plan a menu, prepare the food, and serve it to invited senior citizens from the community.

34. Organize a program with senior citizens and students working together on a community garden.

35. Plan a program at a senior citizens center whereby students and seniors work together on planning activities and decorating the center for special occasions and holidays.

English, Languages, and the Language Arts

36. Organize a letter-writing activity between senior citizens in the community and your students.

37. For a unit such as Elizabethan English, creation of a wall-to-wall mural depicting a village of the times may be a total class project. Students can research customs, costumes, and architecture. Others may paint or draw.

38. On a U.S. road map, have students find the names of places that sound "foreign" and categorize the names according to nationality or culture.

39. For the holidays, students can design their own holiday cards, perhaps using a computer program such as *Print Shop Deluxe*™, creating their own poems for their cards.

40. To enhance understanding of parts of speech, set up this problem: Provide several boxes containing different parts of speech. Each student is to form one sentence from the fragments chosen from each box, being allowed to discard only at a penalty. The students then nonverbally make trades with other students to make coherent and perhaps meaningfully amusing sentences. A student may trade a noun for a verb but will have to keep in mind what parts of speech are essential for a sentence. Results may be read aloud as a culmination to this activity.

41. Have students match American English and British English words (or any other combination of languages), such as cookies and biscuits; hood and bonnet; canned meat and tinned meat; elevator and lift; flashlight and torch; subway and tube; garbage collector and dustman; undershirt and vest; sweater and jumper; gasoline and petrol. Or, have students compare pronunciations and spellings.

42. English words derive from many other languages. Have students list some, such as ketchup (Malay), alcohol (Arabic), kindergarten (German), menu (French), shampoo (Hindi), bonanza (Spanish), piano (Italian), kosher (Yiddish), and smorgasbord (Swedish).

43. Try this for an exercise in objective versus subjective writing: After a lesson on descriptive writing, bring to the class a nondescript object, such as a potato, and place it before the class. Ask them to write a paragraph either describing the potato in detail, that is, its color, size, markings, and other characteristics, or describing how the potato feels about them.

44. Read to the class a story but without an ending, then ask the students (as individuals or in dyads) to create and write their own endings or conclusions.

45. Ask students to create an advertisement using a propaganda device of their choice.

46. Ask students to (individually or in dyads) create and design an invention and then to write a "patent description" for the invention.

47. Using think-pair-write-share, have students write a physical description of some well-known public figure, such as a movie star, politician, athlete, or musician. Other class members may enjoy trying to identify the "mystery" personality from the written description.

48. A bulletin board may be designated for current events and news in the world of writers. Included may be new books and record releases as well as reviews. News of poets and authors (student authors and poets, too) may also be displayed.

49. Everyone has heard of or experienced stereotyping. For example: Girls are not as athletic as boys, boys are insensitive, women are better cooks than men, men are more mechanical. Ask students to list

some stereotypes they have heard and examples they find in newspapers, magazines, movies, and television. Have students discuss these questions: How do you suppose these stereotypes came to be? Does stereotyping have any useful value? Is it sometimes harmful?

50. Remove the text from a Sunday newspaper comic strip and have the students create the story line.

51. Use popular recordings to introduce vocabulary words. Use them for analysis of antonyms, synonyms, listening, writing, comprehension, and other skill development.

52. Use newspaper want ads to locate jobs as a base for completing job application forms and creating letters of inquiry. Use videotape equipment to record employer-employee role-play situations, interviews for jobs, or child-parent situations to develop language and listening skills.

53. Have students choose a short story from a text and write it into a play.

54. When beginning a poetry unit, ask students to bring in the words to their favorite songs. Show how these fit into the genre of poetry.

55. Have students look for commercial examples of advertisements that might be classed as "eco-pornographic," that is, ads that push a product that is potentially damaging to our environment, or have students analyze advertisements for the emotions they appeal to, techniques used, and their integrity. Try the same thing with radio, teen magazines, and other media.

56. Change the environment and ask students to write poetry to see if the change in surroundings stimulates or discourages their creativeness. For example, take your class to write at a large supermarket, a lake, or a forest, or the school athletic stadium.

57. To introduce the concept of interpretations, use your state's seal to start the study. Have students analyze the seal for its history and the meaning of its various symbols.

58. Provide puppets in native costume for students to use in practicing dialogue.

59. Using the Internet, establish communication with students from another area of the country or world.

60. Use rap to have students compare the traditional elements of music and poetry.

61. Use advertisements to enhance students' consciousness of the power of visual and verbal imagery to evoke a place, person, situation, or idea.

Mathematics

62. Collaboratively plan with students to have them role-play the solar system. Students calculate their weights, set up a proportion system, find a large field, and on the final day actually simulate the solar system, using their own bodies to represent the sun, planets, and moons. Arrange to have the event photographed.

63. Encourage students to look for evidence of Fibonacci number series (e.g., 1, 1, 2, 3, 5, 8, 13, 21), outside of mathematics, such as in nature and in manufactured objects. Here are examples of where evidence may be found: piano keyboard, petals on flowers, and spermatogenesis and oogenesis. Perhaps your students might like to organize a Fibonacci Club and through the Internet establish communication with other clubs around the world.

64. Divide the class into a metric team and a nonmetric team. Have each team solve a series of measurement conversion problems. One team would convert nonmetric to metric, the other would convert metric to nonmetric.

65. Give students the history of the cost of a first-class U.S. postage stamp and ask the students to devise ways of predicting its cost by the year they graduate, the year they become grandparents, or some other target year.

66. Give students a list of the frequencies of each of the 88 keys and strings of a piano (a local music store can provide the information). Challenge students to derive an equation to express the relation between key position and frequency. After they have done this, research and tell them about the Bösendorfer piano (Germany) with its nine extra keys at the lower end of the keyboard. See if students can predict the frequencies of those extra keys.

67. Using a light sensor to measure the intensity of a light source from various distances, have students graph the data points and then, with their scientific calculators, find the relevant equation.

68. Have students locate and design large posters to hang on the classroom walls that show the meaning of special grammatical constructions used in mathematics that are not typical of everyday language usage.

Physical Education

69. Have students choose individually (or in dyads) a famous athlete they most (or least) admire. A short report will be written about the athlete. The students will then discuss the attributes and/or characteristics that they admire (or dislike) in the athlete and how they feel they can emulate (or avoid) those qualities.

70. Have students in cooperative learning groups make up an exercise routine to their favorite music recording and share it with the class, and discuss how they arrived at decisions along the way.

71. Have the class divide into groups. Given the basic nonlocomotive skills, have each group come up with a "people machine." Each student within the group is hooked up to another demonstrating a nonlo-

comotive skill and adding some sort of noise to it. Have a contest for the most creative people machine.

72. Give students a chance to design a balance-beam routine that has two passes on the beam and that must include front support mount, forward roll, leap, low or high turn, visit, chassé, and cross support dismount. These routines will be posted to show the variety of ways the different maneuvers can be put together.

73. Divide the class into groups. Have them create a new game or activity for the class, using only the equipment they are given. Let the class play their newly created games.

74. Organize exercises done to popular music. Let students take turns bringing in music and leading the exercises. The teacher will furnish a general outline to follow.

Science

75. Have students create and test their own microscopes using bamboo rods with a drop of water in each end.

76. Have students create and test litmus indicators using the petals of flowers.

77. Use Polaroid or video cameras for students to record and immediately share their experiments and observations.

78. Use cassette-tape recorders to record sounds of the environment. Compare and write about day and night sounds.

79. If you are a life science teacher, make sure your classroom looks like a place for studying life rather than death.

80. Use landlord-tenant situations to simulate predator-prey relationships.

81. Have students create their own cosmetics.

82. With each student playing the role of a cell part, have students set up and perform a role-play of cells.

83. Divide your class into groups and ask each group to create an environment for an imaginary animal, using discarded items from the environment. By asking questions, each group will try to learn about other groups' "mystery" animals.

84. Let each student "adopt" a chemical element. The student then researches that element and becomes the class expert whenever that particular substance comes up in discussion. There could be a special bulletin board for putting up questions on interesting or little-known facts about the elements.

85. Milk can be precipitated, separated, and the solid product dried to form a very hard substance that was, in the days before plastic, used to make buttons. Let students make their own buttons from milk.

86. Spray-paint molecular models gold. Give the "golden molecule" award for exceptional lab work.

87. Have your students build a model of a molecule using gumdrops and toothpicks. Different-colored gumdrops are to represent different elemental atoms. When students show the teacher that they have correctly named and constructed their models, they can eat the gumdrops.

88. As a class or school project, obtain proper permission to "adopt" a wetlands area near the school.

89. Have students research the composition and development of familiar objects. For example, the ordinary pencil is made of cedar wood from the forests of the Pacific Northwest. The graphite is often from Montana or Mexico and is reinforced with clays from Georgia and Kentucky. The eraser is made from soybean oil and latex from trees in South America and is reinforced with pumice from California or New Mexico and sulfur, calcium, and barium. The metal band is aluminum or brass, made from copper and zinc, mined in no fewer than 13 states and nine provinces of Canada. The paint to color the wood and the lacquer to make it shine are made from a variety of minerals and metals, as is the glue that holds the wood together.

90. Have students locate and design large posters to hang on the classroom walls that show the meaning of words used in science that are not typical of their meaning in everyday language usage.

91. To bridge cross-cultural differences, have students design large posters to hang on the classroom walls showing potential differences in perceptions or views according to ethnoscience and formal science.

Social Sciences

92. Organize an intergenerational advocacy program, in which students and senior citizens work together to make a better society for both groups.[21]

93. Let your class plan how they would improve their living environment, beginning with the classroom, then moving out to the school, home, and community.

94. Start a pictorial essay on the development and/or changes of a given area in your community, such as a major corner or block adjacent to the school. This is a study project that could continue for years and that has many social, political, and economic implications.

95. Start a folk hero study. Each year ask, "What prominent human being who has lived during (a particular period of time) do you most (and/or least) admire?" Collect individual responses to the question, tally, and discuss. After you have done this for several

21. See, for example, D. E. MacBain, *Intergenerational Education Programs* (Bloomington, IN: Fastback 402, Phi Delta Kappa Educational Foundation, 1996).

years, you may wish to share with your class for discussion purposes the results of your surveys of previous years.

96. Start a sister school program. Establish a class relationship with another similar class from another school from around the country or the world, perhaps by using the Internet.

97. Role-play a simulated family movement to the West in the 1800s. What items would they take? What would they throw out of the wagon to lighten the load?

98. Have students collect music, art, or athletic records from a particular period of history. Have them compare those with items of today and predict the future.

99. Using play money, establish a capitalistic economic system within your classroom. Salaries may be paid for attendance and bonus income for work well done, taxes may be collected for poor work, and a welfare section established in a corner of the room.

100. Divide your class into small groups and ask that each group make predictions as to what world governments, world geography, world social issues, or some other related topic will be like some time in the future. Let each group give its report, followed by debate and discussion. Plant the predictions in some secret location on the school grounds for a future discovery.

101. Play the game Alphabet Geography: A place is given by the teacher, such as a state, city, or river. The next person must name a place starting with the same letter as the last in that name previously mentioned. Students are eliminated or given points. This game can be used as a drill to acquaint students with place names and where these places are. The class can be divided into groups, or students can stand individually.

102. Have students use a mandala to demonstrate the importance of individual experiences, as in interpreting current events.

103. Have students locate and design large posters to hang on the classroom walls that illustrate the meaning of words used in social science that are unique to social studies or that are atypical of their meaning in everyday language usage.

104. As an opener to a unit on the U.S. Constitution, have students design their own classroom "bill of rights."

105. Initiate a full-time service learning project, where for an extended period of time students work directly with community organizations.[22]

106. Using *Legos*™ as construction blocks, have your students simulate and role-play the building of the Great Wall of China.

Vocational-Career Education[23]

107. At Bell County High School (Pineville, KY), students of a banking and finance class operate an on-campus bank where the high school students can actually make deposits, earn interest, and borrow money.

108. At Northern Wayne Vocational-Technical School (WV), students study castles and build model castles that are shared with students at Wayne High School who are in an interdisciplinary thematic study (history and literature of the medieval period).

109. At Gloucester High School (Gloucester, VA), students designed and built an electric-powered automobile.

110. At Manatee High School (Bradenton, FL), students of applied mathematics and business studies worked together on a backyard swimming pool project.

111. At North Penn High School (Lansdale, PA), students from several classes (child development, advanced manufacturing, mathematics) worked together to design and create equipment for the school's child development playground.

SUMMARY

This chapter has continued the development of your repertoire of teaching strategies necessary to become an effective teacher. As you know, secondary school students can be quite peer-conscious, have relatively short attention spans, and prefer active experiences that engage many or all of their senses. Most are intensely curious about things of interest to them. Cooperative learning, student-centered projects, and teaching strategies that emphasize shared discovery and inquiry (discussed in the next chapter) within a psychologically safe environment encourage the most positive aspects of thinking and learning. Central to your strategy selection should be those strategies that encourage students to become independent thinkers and skilled learners who can help in the planning, structuring, regulating, and assessing of their own learning and learning activities.

QUESTIONS FOR CLASS DISCUSSION

1. Describe research that you can find on the use of cooperation (cooperative learning groups) versus competition (competitive learning groups) in teaching. Explain why you would or would not use cooperative learning groups as they were discussed in this chapter.

---

22. See, for example, J. Van Til, "Facing Inequality and the End of Work," *Educational Leadership* 54(6):78–81 (March 1997).

23. Source for items in this section: Southern Regional Education Board, *1995 Outstanding Practices* (Atlanta, GA: Southern Regional Education Board, 1995), pp. 6, 8, 24, 25, and 26. By permission.

2. Do you have concerns about using project-centered teaching and not covering all the content you believe you should be covering? Think back to your own schooling. What do you really remember? Most likely you remember projects, yours and other students' presentations, the lengthy research you did, and your extra effort for the artwork to accompany your presentation. Maybe you remember a compliment by a teacher or a pat on the back by peers. Most likely you do not remember the massive amount of content that was covered. Discuss your feelings about this with your classmates. Share common experiences and concerns.

3. It is an aphorism that to learn something well students need time to practice it. There is a difference, however, between solitary practice and coached practice. Describe the difference and which type of practice is better for learning in your subject field and grade-level interest.

4. Divide into teams of four, and have each team develop one interdisciplinary thematic learning activity center. Set up and share the LACs in your classroom.

5. Explain how a teacher can tell when he is truly using cooperative learning groups for instruction as opposed to traditional small-group learning.

6. Do you have special techniques and ideas to add to the list of motivational teaching strategies and ideas given in this chapter? Share them with your classmates, and if you want, mail them to the authors of this book for consideration of inclusion in the next edition.

7. When a student is said to be on task, does that necessarily imply that the student is mentally engaged? Explain your answer. Is it possible for a student to be mentally engaged although not on task? Explain your answer.

8. Describe any prior concepts you held that changed as a result of your experiences with this chapter. Describe the changes.

9. From your current observations and fieldwork as related to this teacher preparation program, clearly identify one specific example of educational practice that seems contradictory to exemplary practice or theory as presented in this chapter. Present your explanation for the discrepancy.

10. Do you have questions generated by the content of this chapter? If you do, list them along with ways answers might be found.

Suggested Readings

Artzt, A. F. "Integrating Writing and Cooperative Learning in the Mathematics Class." *Mathematics Teacher* 87(2):80–85 (February 1994).

Artzt, A. F., and Newman, C. M. *How to Use Cooperative Learning in the Mathematics Class*. Reston, VA: National Council of Teachers of Mathematics, 1990.

Baloche, L. "Breaking Down the Walls: Integrating Creative Questioning and Cooperative Learning into the Social Studies." *Social Studies* 85(1):25–30 (January/February 1994).

Boers, D., and Caspary, P. "Real-Life Homework." *The Executive Educator* 17(3):37–38 (March 1995).

Clarke, J. H., and Agne, R. M. *Interdisciplinary High School Teaching: Strategies for Integrated Learning*. Chapters 6 and 8. Needham Heights, MA: Allyn & Bacon, 1997.

Farivar, S. H., and Webb, N. M. "Are Your Students Prepared for Group Work?" *Middle School Journal* 25(3):51–54 (January 1994).

Flynn, V., and Chambers, R. D. "Promoting Gender Equity: What You Can Do." *Learning* 22(5):58–59 (January 1994).

Graves, N., and Graves, T. *Cooperative Learning: A Book*. Santa Cruz, CA: The International Association for the Study of Cooperation in Education, 1990.

Gussin, L. "Constructive Lessons: Building and Playing Simulation Games." *CD-ROM Professional* 8(5):40–42, 44, 46, 48, 50 (May 1995).

Guzetti, B. J., and Williams, W. O. "Gender, Text, and Discussion: Examining Intellectual Safety in the Science Classroom." *Journal of Science Teaching* 33(1):5–20 (January 1996).

Harmin, M. *Inspiring Active Learning: A Handbook for Teachers*. Alexandria, VA: Association for Supervision and Curriculum Development, 1994.

Johnson, D. W., and Johnson, F. P. *Joining Together: Group Theory and Group Skills*. 6th ed. Boston: Allyn & Bacon, 1997.

Kaplan, J., and Aronson, D. "The Numbers Gap." *Teaching Tolerance* 3(1):21–27 (Spring 1994).

Kaszyca, M., and Krueger, A. M. "Collaborative Voices: Reflections on the I-Search Project." *English Journal* 83(1):62–65 (January 1994).

Kudlas, J. M. "Implications of OBE: What You Should Know about Outcome-Based Education." *The Science Teacher* 61(5):32–35 (May 1994).

Langer, J. A. *A Response-Based Approach to Reading Literature*. Albany, NY: Report Series 6.7, National Research Center on Literature Teaching and Learning, 1994.

Lord, T. R. "Using Cooperative Learning in the Teaching of High School Biology." *American Biology Teacher* 56(5):280–284 (May 1994).

MacBain, D. E. *Intergenerational Education Programs*. Bloomington, IN: Fastback 402, Phi Delta Kappa Educational Foundation, 1996.

McFaden, D., et al. "Redesigning the Model: A Successfully Integrated Approach to Teaching and Learning." *NASSP Bulletin* 80(577):1–6 (February 1996).

McTighe, J. "What Happens between Assessments?" *Educational Leadership* 54(4):6–12 (December 1996/January 1997).

Mizelle, N. B. "Enhancing Young Adolescents' Motivation for Literacy Learning." *Middle School Journal* 28(3):16–25 (January 1997).

Nagel, N. G. *Learning through Real-World Problem Solving: The Power of Integrative Teaching*. Thousand Oaks, CA: Corwin Press, 1996.

Nelson, B. "Cooperative Learning." *Science Teacher* 63(5):22–25 (May 1996).

Nichols, J. E., and Miller, R. B. "Cooperative Learning and Student Motivation." *Contemporary Educational Psychology* 19(2):167–178 (April 1994).

Parson, L. *Expanding Response Journals in All Subject Areas*. Portsmouth, NH: Heinemann, 1994.

Reid, L., et al. "Making Small Groups Work." *English Journal* 83(3):59–63 (March 1994).

Rothermel, D. *Starting Points: How to Set Up and Run a Writing Workshop—and Much More*. Columbus, OH: National Middle Schools Association, 1996.

Sadker, M., et al. "Gender Equity in the Classroom: The Unfinished Agenda." *College Review Board* 170:14–21 (1993–1994).

Schlafly, P. "What's Wrong with Outcome-Based Education?" *School Administrator* 51(8):26–27 (September 1994).

Schmuck, P. A., and Schmuck, R. A. "Gender Equity: A Critical Democratic Component of America's High Schools." *NASSP Bulletin* 78(558):22–31 (January 1994).

Schmurak, C. B., and Ratliff, T. M. "Gender Equity and Gender Bias: Issues for the Middle School Teacher." *Middle School Journal* 25(5):63–66 (May 1994).

Slavin, R. E. "Cooperative Learning in Middle and Secondary Schools," *Clearing House* 69(4):200–204 (March/April 1996).

Slavin, R. E., et al. "Research on Cooperative Learning and Achievement: What We Know, What We Need to Know." *Contemporary Educational Psychology* 21(1):43–69 (January 1996).

Smagorinsky, P., and Fly, P. A. "A New Perspective on Why Small Groups Do and Don't Work." *English Journal* 83(3):54–58 (March 1994).

Spies, P. "High School Learning Teams. Engaging and Empowering Students and Teachers through Interpersonal and Interdisciplinary Connections." *New Schools, New Communities* 12(2):45–51 (Winter 1996).

Tassinari, M. "Hands-On Projects Take Students Beyond the Book." *Social Studies Review* 34(3):16–20 (Spring 1996).

Thousand, J., Villa, R., and Nevin, A. *Creativity and Collaborative Learning: A Practical Guide to Empowering Students and Teachers*. Baltimore: Paul H. Brookes, 1994.

Tomlinson, C. A. *How to Differentiate Instruction in Mixed-Ability Classrooms*. Alexandria, VA: Association for Supervision and Curriculum Development, 1995.

Wenning, C. J., and Muehsler, H. "Nondirected Research Projects in Physics Coursework." *Physics Teacher* 34(3):158–161 (March 1996).

Wolk, S. "Project-Based Learning: Pursuits with a Purpose." *Educational Leadership* 52(3):42–45 (November 1994).

Wood, K. D., et al. "Improving Young Adolescent Literacy through Collaborative Learning." *Middle School Journal* 28(3):26–34 (January 1997).

Wynne, E. A. *Cooperation-Competition: An Instructional Strategy*. Bloomington, IN: Fastback 378, Phi Delta Kappa Educational Foundation, 1995.

Using Teacher Talk, Demonstrations, Thinking, Inquiry, and Games

Perhaps no other strategy is used more by teachers than is teacher talk, both formal and informal, so this chapter begins with a presentation of guidelines for use of that vital and significant instructional strategy. A strategy related to teacher talk is the demonstration, which is addressed later in the chapter, followed by guidelines for other important strategies, namely, for the use of thinking, inquiry and discovery, and educational games.

Specifically, upon completion of this chapter you should be able to demonstrate your understanding of

- When and how to use teacher talk in the classroom.
- The characteristics of an effective demonstration.
- The relationship between thinking, problem solving, discovery, and inquiry.
- The concept of integrating strategies for integrated learning.

and demonstrate your knowledge of

- How to teach students to think.
- How and when to use student inquiry.
- Advantages and disadvantages of various categories of educational games for learning.

TEACHER TALK: FORMAL AND INFORMAL

Teacher talk encompasses both lecturing *to* students and discussions *with* students. A lecture is considered formal teacher talk, whereas a teacher-led discussion is considered informal teacher talk.

Cautions in Using Teacher Talk

Whether your teacher talk is formal or informal, there are certain cautions that you need to be mindful of. Perhaps the most important is not to *talk too much*. If a teacher talks too much, the significance of her words may be lost because some students will tune her out.

Another caution is to avoid *talking too fast*. Students can hear faster than they can understand what is heard. It is a good idea to remind yourself to talk slowly and to check frequently for student comprehension of what you are talking about. It is also important to remember that your one brain is communicating with many student brains, each of which responds to sensory input (auditory in this instance) at different rates. Because of this, you will need to pause to let words sink in and you will need to pause during transitions from one point or activity to the next.

A third caution is to be sure you are being *heard and understood*. Sometimes teachers talk in too low a pitch, use words that are not understood by many of the students, or do both. You should vary the pitch of your voice, and you should stop and help students with their understanding of vocabulary that may be new to them. Remember, as discussed in Chapter 1, if some students in your class are recent immigrants and have only limited English-language proficiency, then you need to help those students learn what is essentially two languages—the English language and the language unique to your subject.

A fourth caution is to remember that just *because students have heard something before does not necessarily mean that they understand it or learned it*. From our earlier discussion of learning experiences (the Learning Experiences Ladder in Chapter 6), remember that although verbal communication is an important form of communication, it is not a very reliable form of communication because of its reliance on abstract symbolization. Teacher talk relies on words and on listening, a skill that is not mastered by many middle schools students and even many high school students. For that and other reasons, to ensure student understanding, reinforce your teacher talk with the use of direct and simulated learning experiences.

Related to that is yet another caution—*to resist believing that students have attained a skill or have learned something that was taught previously by you or by another teacher.* During any discussion (formal or informal), rather than assuming that your students know something, you should *ensure* they know it. For example, if the discussion and a student activity involve a particular thinking skill, then you will want to make sure that students know how to use that skill (see The Teaching of Thinking later in this chapter).

Still another problem is *talking in a humdrum monotone*. Students need teachers whose voices exude enthusiasm and excitement (although not to be overdone) about the subject and about teaching and learning. Such enthusiasm and excitement for learning are contagious. A voice that demonstrates enthusiasm for teaching and learning is more likely to motivate students to learn. Some teacher candidates benefit from taking a course designed to help improve their voice and delivery.

Keep those cautions in mind as you study the general principles of and specific guidelines for the productive and effective use of teacher talk.

General Guidelines

Certain general guidelines should be followed whether your talk is formal or informal. First, *begin the talk with an advance organizer.* Advance organizers are introductions that mentally prepare students for a study by helping them make connections with material already learned or experienced—a *comparative organizer*—or by providing students with a conceptual arrangement of what is to be learned—an *expository organizer*.[1] An advance organizer can be a brief introduction or statement about the main idea you intend to convey and how it is related to other aspects of the students' learning (an expository organizer), or it can be a presentation of a discrepancy to arouse curiosity (a comparative organizer, in this instance causing students to compare what they have observed with what they already know or thought they knew). Preparing an organizer helps you plan and organize the

sequence of ideas, and its presentation helps students organize their own learning and become motivated about it. An advance organizer can also make their learning meaningful by providing important connections between what they already know and what is being learned.

Second, *your talk should be planned so that it has a beginning and an end, with a logical order between.* During your talk, you should reinforce your words with visuals (discussed in the specific guidelines that follow). These visuals may include writing unfamiliar terms on the board (helping students learn new vocabulary) and using prepared graphs, charts, photographs, and various audiovisuals.

Third, *pacing is important.* Your talk should move briskly but not too fast. The ability to pace the instruction is difficult for many beginning teachers because many tend to talk too fast and too much. However, pacing will improve with experience. Until you have developed your skill in pacing, you probably will need to constantly remind yourself during lessons to slow down and provide silent pauses (allowing for think time) and frequent checks for student comprehension. Specifically, your talk should

- Be brisk, though not too fast, but with occasional slowdowns to change the pace and to check for student comprehension.
- Be adequately paced to allow students time to think, ask questions, and make notes.
- Have a time plan. A talk planned for ten minutes, if interesting to students, will probably take longer. If not interesting to them, it will probably take less time. When the latter is the case, problems in classroom control can be expected.

Fourth, *encourage student participation.* Active participation enhances student learning. This encouragement can be planned as questions that you ask, as time allowed for students to comment and ask questions, or as a conceptual outline that students complete during the talk.

Fifth, *plan a clear ending (closure).* Be sure your talk has a clear ending, followed by another activity (during the same or next class period) that will help secure the learning. As for all lessons, you want to strive for planning a clear and mesmerizing beginning, an involving lesson body, and a firm and meaningful closure.

Specific Guidelines

Understand the various purposes for using teacher talk. Teacher talk, formal or informal, can be useful to discuss the progress of a unit of study, explain an inquiry, introduce a unit of study, present a problem, promote student inquiry or critical thinking, provide a transition from one unit of study to the next, provide information

---

1. D. P. Ausubel, *The Psychology of Meaningful Learning* (New York: Grune & Stratton, 1963).

otherwise unobtainable to students, share the teacher's experiences, share the teacher's thinking, summarize a problem, summarize a unit of study, and teach a thinking skill by modeling that skill.

Clarify the objectives of the talk. Your talk should center on one idea. The learning objectives, which should not be too numerous for one talk, should be clearly understood by the students.

Choose informal and formal talk. Although an occasional formal "cutting-edge" lecture may be appropriate for some high school classes, spontaneous interactive informal talks of 5 to 12 minutes are preferred for most classes. A teacher should *never* give long lectures with no teacher-student interaction. Remember also, today's students are of the "media, or light, generation," and are used to video interactions as well as "commercial breaks." For many lessons, especially those that are teacher-centered, student attention is likely to begin to stray after about ten minutes. When that happens, you need to have elements planned that will recapture their attention. These planned elements can include analogies to help connect the topic to students' experiences; verbal cues, such as voice inflections; pauses to allow information to sink in; humor; visual cues, such as the use of slides, overhead transparencies, charts, board drawings, excerpts from videodiscs, real objects (realia), or body gestures; and sensory cues, such as eye contact and proximity (as in moving around the room or casually and gently touching a student on the shoulder without interrupting your talk).

Vary strategies and activities frequently. Perhaps most useful for recapturing student attention is to change to an entirely different strategy or learning modality. For example, from teacher talk (a teacher-centered strategy) you would change to a student activity (a student-centered strategy). Notice that changing from a lecture (mostly teacher talk) to a teacher-led discussion (mostly more teacher talk) would not be changing to an entirely different modality. Figure 9.1 provides a comparison of four changes.

As a generalization, when using teacher-centered direct instruction, with most classes you will want to change the learning activities about every 10 to 15 minutes. (That is why in our sample lesson plan format of Chapter 5, we include space for at least four activities, including the introduction and closure.) This means that in a 60-minute time block, for example, you should probably plan three or four *sequenced* learning activities, with some that are teacher-centered and many others that are more student-centered. And, in a 90-minute block, plan five or six learning activities. In exemplary classrooms, teachers often have several activities *concurrently* being performed by individuals, dyads, and small groups of students (i.e., multitasking or multilevel instruction).

Prepare and use notes as a guide for your talk. Planning your talk and preparing notes to be used during formal and informal teacher talk is important—just as important as implementing the talk with visuals. There is absolutely nothing wrong with using notes during your teaching. You can carry them on a clipboard, perhaps a brightly colored one, as you move around the room. Your notes for a formal talk can first be prepared in narrative form; for class use, though, they should be reduced to an outline form. *Talks to students should always be from an outline, never read from prose.* (The teacher's reading aloud from prose to students is appropriate only when reading a brief published article [science or social studies] or portions of a story or a poem [reading, English, language arts]).

In your outline, use color coding with abbreviated visual cues to yourself. You will eventually develop your own coding system, though keep it simple lest you forget what the codes are for. Consider these examples of coding: where transition of ideas occurs and you want to allow silent moments for ideas to sink in, mark *P* for *pause,* *T* for a *transition,* and *S* for moments of *silence;* where a slide or other visual aid will be used, mark *AV* for *audiovisual;* where you intend to stop and ask a question, mark *TQ* for *teacher question,* and mark *SQ* or *?* where you want to stop and allow time for *student questions;* where you plan to have a discussion, mark *D;* where you plan *small-group work,* mark *SG,* and where you plan to switch to a *laboratory* investigation, mark *L;* for *reviews* and *comprehension checks,* mark *R* and *CC.*

Rehearse your talk. Rehearsing your planned talk is important. Using your lesson plan as your guide, rehearse your talk using a camcorder or an audiorecorder, or rehearse it while talking into a mirror or to a roommate. Remember to allow more time for implementation than it takes for rehearsal. You may want to include a time plan for each subtopic to allow you to gauge your timing during implementation of the talk.

Avoid racing through the talk solely to complete it by class dismissal time. It is more important that students understand some of what you say than none of it because you try to cover all the material. If you do not finish, continue the talk later.

Augment your talk with multisensory stimulation. Your presentation should not overly rely on verbal communication. When using visuals, such as videodisc excerpts or overhead transparencies, do not think that you must be constantly talking; after clearly explaining the purpose of a visual, give students sufficient time to look at it, to think about it, and to ask questions about it. The visual is new to the students, so give them time to take it in.

Carefully plan the content of your talk. The content of your talk should supplement and enhance that found in the student textbook rather than simply rehash content

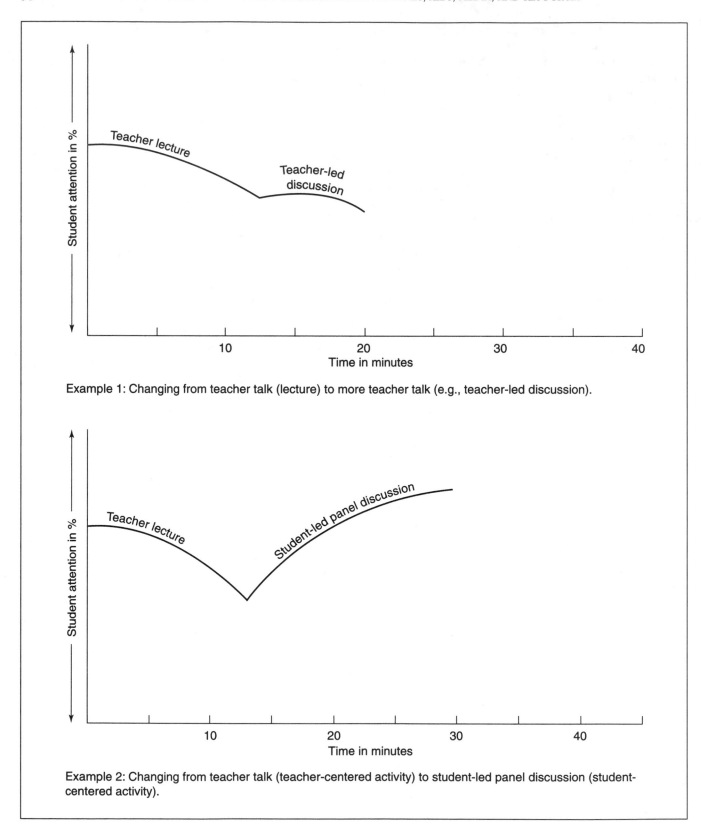

Example 1: Changing from teacher talk (lecture) to more teacher talk (e.g., teacher-led discussion).

Example 2: Changing from teacher talk (teacher-centered activity) to student-led panel discussion (student-centered activity).

Figure 9.1
Comparison of recapturing student attention by changing the instructional strategy.

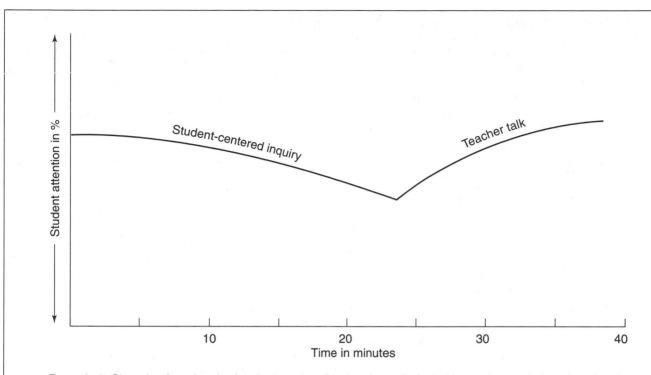

Example 3: Changing from inquiry (student-centered) to teacher talk, fueled by student questions from inquiry.

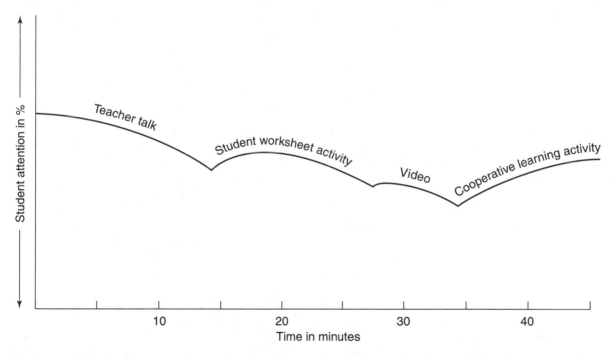

Example 4: Changing from teacher talk (teacher-centered activity) to cooperative learning activity (student-centered activity).

Figure 9.1 *(continued)*

from the textbook. Students may never read their books if you tell them in an interesting and condensed fashion everything that they need to know from them.

Monitor your voice. Your voice should be pleasant and interesting to listen to rather than monotonous or shrieking and irritating. On the other hand, it is good to show enthusiasm for what you are talking about. Occasionally use dramatic voice inflections to emphasize important points and meaningful body language to give students a visual focus.

As is always the case when teaching and lecturing, avoid standing in the same spot for long periods of time. Even while lecturing, you need to monitor student behavior and to use proximity as one way of preventing unwanted student behavior.

View the vocabulary of the talk as an opportunity to help students with their word morphology. Words you use should be easily understood by the students, though you should still model professionalism and help students develop their vocabulary—both the vocabulary of your discipline and the more general vocabulary of the English language. During your lesson planning, predict when you are likely to use a word that is new to most students, and plan to ask a student to help explain its meaning and perhaps demonstrate its derivation. Help students with word meaning. This aids students in remembering. Keep in mind that regardless of subject or grade level, *all teachers are language arts teachers.* Knowledge of word morphology is an important component of skilled reading and includes the ability to generate new words from prefixes, roots, and suffixes. For some students, every subject in the school schedule is like a foreign language. That is certainly true for students who have limited or no proficiency in English. For them, teacher talk, especially formal teacher talk, should be used sparingly, if at all. General biology, for example, is said to contain more new words for students than does beginning French. Every teacher has the responsibility of helping students learn how to learn, and that includes helping students develop their word comprehension skills, reading skills, thinking and memory skills, and motivation for learning.

For example, when introducing the word *hermaphrodite,* the science teacher has the opportunity to teach a bit of Greek mythology in the process of helping the students understand an important biological term. The teacher could show students the origin of the word's two roots (Hermes, or Mercury, the messenger of the gods, and Aphrodite, or Venus, goddess of love and beauty). Taking time to teach a bit of Greek mythology affords the science teacher an opportunity to cross disciplines and capture the interest of a few more students.

Lecture only when appropriate. You may not need to lecture—sometimes a handout will do. Some students can read and understand faster than they can listen and understand. For other students, however, talking to them may better reinforce the information than a handout can. Remember, though, a formal period-long noninteractive lecture, common in some college teaching, is inappropriate when teaching most secondary school students. (Some experts believe that its appropriateness is questionable for most learning, even at the college level.) On the other hand, to arouse student interest and provide new information in relatively small and intellectually digestible chunks, the lecture may be appropriate. If during your student teaching you have doubt or questions about your selection and use of a particular instructional strategy, discuss it with your cooperating teacher or your university supervisor, or both. When you doubt the appropriateness of a particular strategy, trust your intuition. Without some modification, the strategy probably is inappropriate.

Provide students with a conceptual outline or a study guide. An outline of major ideas of the talk, with lines connecting them, or a study guide (an expository organizer) can facilitate students' understanding and organization of the content of your talk. Note that the outline should be a skeletal one, not a complete copy of the talk. Giving students something to do besides listening during your talk is a good idea, because it not only helps students understand what is being said but also engages their visual and kinesthetic senses in addition to their auditory sense.

Use familiar examples and analogies to help students make relevant connections (bridges). Although this sometimes takes a great deal of creative thinking during the preactive planning phase, it is important that you attempt to connect the talk with ideas and events with which the students are already familiar. The most effective talk is one that makes frequent and meaningful connections between what students already know and what they are learning, which bridges what they are learning with what they have experienced in their lives.

Consider student diversity. While preparing your talk (during the preactive phase of planning), consider students who are culturally and linguistically different and those who have special needs. Personalize the talk for them by planning meaningful analogies and examples and relevant audio and visual displays.

Establish eye contact frequently. We cannot overemphasize the importance of this point: your primary eye contact should be with your students—always! Only momentarily should you look at your notes, your visuals, the projection screen, the writing board, and other adults or objects in the classroom. With practice, you can learn to scan a classroom of 30 students, establishing eye contact with each student about once a minute. To "establish" eye contact means that the student is aware that you are looking at her. Frequent eye contact can have two major benefits. First, as you "read" a student's body posture and facial expressions, you obtain clues about that student's attentiveness and comprehension. Second, eye contact helps to establish rapport between you and a student. Be alert, though, for students who are from cultures where eye contact is infrequent or unwanted and could have negative consequences.

Frequent eye contact is easier when using an overhead projector than when using the writing board. When using a writing board, you have to turn at least partially away from your audience, and you may have to pace back and forth from the board to the students to retain that important proximity to them.

Remember our earlier discussions of overlapping being an important teaching skill? Well, this is one of those times when its importance really comes into play. While lecturing on a topic in your subject field, you must remain aware of and attentive to everything that is happening in the classroom (i.e., to student behavior as well as to the content of your lecture). Good teaching isn't easy. But don't be dismayed; with the knowledge of the preceding guidelines and with practice, experience, and reflection, you will develop the necessary skills.

Now, to reinforce your learning about this important instructional strategy, do Exercise 9.1.

EXERCISE 9.1

A Cooperative Learning and Micro Peer Teaching Exercise in the Use of the Lecture—Micro Peer Teaching II

Instructions: The purpose of this exercise is to provide a summary review and developmental exercise to check your comprehension of and learning about using formal teacher talk as an instructional strategy. In groups of four, first discuss and answer questions 1 through 6; then do items 7 and 8, much in the manner of Exercise 7.6.

1. Describe how the lecture differs from informal teacher talk. _____

_____

_____

_____

2. Although sometimes a useful technique, lecturing should be used only sparingly in high school teaching and even less at the middle school level. Why is this so recommended?

_____

_____

_____

_____

3. Specifically, when in your teaching might you use the lecture? _____

_____

_____

_____

4. Describe how a secondary school teacher can arouse and sustain student interest during the lecture. _____

_____

_____

_____

_____

5. What are some main principles you must keep in mind while preparing a lecture? Identify at least five things representing these principles that you can do to make a lecture successful.

_____

_____

_____

_____

_____

_____

_____

_____

6. Reflecting on your recent college or university experiences, recall a good lecturer and the behaviors of that professor that made his lectures better than average. _____

_____

_____

_____

_____

_____

_____

7. Prepare one behavioral objective for a topic in your field. Identify the major points that you would like to make and how you would try to get those points across in a lecture designed to support your objective. This lesson can be designed specifically for your peer-students *or* as if your students were of a specific secondary school grade level.

   Field: _____ Grade level: _____

   Topic: _____ Behavioral objective: _____

   Major points: _____

   _____

   _____

   Method of achieving: _____

   _____

   _____

   _____

   _____

8. Now, with the information you provided in question 7, prepare a five-minute lecture-centered lesson plan and implement the lecture to a small group of three or four class-mates. Upon completion of your lecture, obtain peer feedback using criteria presented in the guidelines earlier in this chapter. If possible, have your lecture videotaped so that you can review it yourself. Finally, prepare a self-assessment to share with your course instructor.

DEMONSTRATIONS

Students like demonstrations because the demonstrator is actively engaged in a learning activity rather than merely verbalizing about it. Demonstrations can be used in teaching any subject and for a variety of purposes. A role-playing demonstration can be used in a social studies class. A mathematics teacher demonstrates the steps in solving a problem. An English/language arts teacher demonstrates clustering to students ready for a creative writing assignment. A science teacher demonstrates the combining of a weak acid and a weak base.

Purposes of Demonstrations

A demonstration can be designed to serve any of the following purposes: to assist in recognizing a solution to an existing problem; to bring an unusual closure to a lesson or unit of study; to demonstrate a thinking skill; to establish problem recognition; to give students opportunity for vicarious participation in active learning; to illustrate a particular point of content; to introduce a lesson or unit of study in a way that grabs the students' attention; to reduce potential safety hazards (where the teacher demonstrates with materials that are too dangerous for students to handle); to review; to save time and resources (as opposed to the entire class doing the activity being demonstrated); and to set up a discrepancy recognition.

Guidelines for Using Demonstrations

When planning a demonstration, you should consider the following paragraphs as guidelines.

Decide what is the most effective way to conduct the demonstration (e.g., as a verbal or a silent demonstration; by a student or by the teacher; by the teacher with a student helper; to the entire class or to small groups).

Be sure that the demonstration is visible to all students. For this purpose, some high schools have overhead mirrors or, where demonstrations are frequent and where financial resources have been available, classrooms with overhead video cameras that are connected to computers and to large-screen television monitors.

Practice with the materials and procedure before demonstrating to the students. During your practice, try to prepare for anything that could go wrong during the real demonstration; if you don't, as Murphy's Law says, if anything can go wrong, it probably will. Then, if something does go wrong during the live demonstration, use that as an opportunity for a teachable moment—engage the students in working with you to try to figure out what went wrong.

Consider your pacing of the demonstration, allowing for enough student wait-see and think time. At the start of the demonstration, explain its purpose and the learning objectives. Remember this adage: tell them what you are going to do, show them, and then tell them what they saw. As with any lesson, plan your closure and allow time for questions and discussion. During the demonstration, as in other types of teacher talk, use frequent stops to check for student understanding.

Consider the use of special lighting to highlight the demonstration. For example, a slide projector can be set up and used as a spotlight.

Be sure that the demonstration table and area are free of unnecessary objects that could distract, be in the way, or pose a safety hazard. With potentially hazardous demonstrations, such as might occur in physical education, science, or shop classes, you should *model* proper safety precautions: wear safety goggles, have fire-safety equipment at hand, and place a protective shield between the demonstration table and nearby students.

THE TEACHING OF THINKING

Pulling together findings about learning and brain functioning, teachers are encouraged to integrate explicit thinking instruction into daily lessons. In other words, teachers should help students develop their thinking skills.

> In teaching for thinking, we are interested not only in what students know but also in how students behave when they don't know. . . . Gathering evidence of the performance and growth of intelligent behavior is difficult through standardized testing. It really requires 'kid-watching': observing students as they try to solve the day-to-day academic and real-life problems they encounter. . . . By collecting anecdotes and examples of written, oral, and visual expressions, we can see students' increasingly voluntary and spontaneous performance of these intelligent behaviors.[2]

Characteristics of Intelligent Behavior

Characteristics of intelligent behavior that teachers should model, teach for, and observe developing in students are described in the following paragraphs.[3]

PERSISTENCE.   Persistence is sticking to a task until it is completed. Consider the following examples.

- In 1882, nearly single-handedly and against formidable odds, Clara Barton persevered to form the American Red Cross.
- In 1963, Rachel Carson was not intimidated by the chemical industry, powerful politicians, and the

---

2. A. L. Costa, *The School as a Home for the Mind* (Palatine, IL: Skylight Publishing, 1991), p. 19.

3. Costa, pp. 20–31.

media in her persistent and relentless pursuit to educate society about the ill effects of pesticides on humans and the natural world and refused to accept the premise that damage to nature was the inevitable cost of technological and scientific progress. Her book *Silent Spring* was the seed for the beginning of the development of today's more responsible ecological attitude.

- Born in 1898, Amelia Earhart demonstrated from the time she was a young girl that she was creative, curious, and persistent. She learned to fly in 1920 and eight years later became the first woman to fly the Atlantic Ocean, thereby paving the way for other women to become active in aviation.
- Babe Ruth for years held not only the home run record in professional baseball but also the record for the most strike-outs.
- At the age of ten, Wilma Rudolf could not walk without the aid of leg braces, the result of diseases during her childhood. Just ten years later, at the age of 20, she was declared the fastest-running woman in the world, having won three gold medals in the 1960 World Olympics.

DECREASING IMPULSIVITY.   When students develop impulse control, they think before acting. Students can be taught to think before shouting out an answer, before beginning a project or task, and before arriving at conclusions with only limited data. One of the several reasons that teachers should usually insist on a show of student hands before a student is acknowledged to respond or question is to discourage students from impulsively shouting out in class.[4]

LISTENING TO OTHERS WITH UNDERSTANDING AND EMPATHY.   Some psychologists believe that the ability to listen to others, empathizing with and understanding their point of view, is one of the highest forms of intelligent behavior. Piaget refers to this behavior as *overcoming egocentrism*. In class meetings, brainstorming sessions, think tanks, town meetings, and legislative bodies, people from various walks of life convene to share their thinking, to explore their ideas, and to broaden their perspectives by listening to the ideas and reactions of others.

COOPERATIVE THINKING AND SOCIAL INTELLIGENCE. Humans are social beings. Real-world problem solving has become so complex that seldom can any person

go it alone. Not all students come to school knowing how to work effectively in groups. They may exhibit competitiveness, narrow-mindedness, egocentrism, ethnocentrism, or criticism of others' values, emotions, and beliefs. Listening, consensus seeking, giving up an idea to work on someone else's, empathy, compassion, group leadership, cooperative learning, knowing how to support group efforts, and altruism are behaviors indicative of intelligent human beings, and they can be learned at school and in the classroom.

FLEXIBILITY IN THINKING.   Approaching a problem from a new angle, using a novel approach, is an intelligent behavior.   This is referred to as *lateral thinking*.[5] Students can learn to consider alternative points of view and to deal with several sources of information simultaneously.

METACOGNITION.   Learning to plan, monitor, assess, and reflect on one's own thinking is another characteristic of intelligent behavior.

STRIVING FOR ACCURACY AND PRECISION.   Teachers can observe students' growth in this behavior when students take time to check over their work, review the procedures, refuse to draw conclusions until they have obtained sufficient data, and use concise and descriptive language.

SENSE OF HUMOR.   The positive effects of humor on the body's physiological functions are well established: a drop in the pulse rate, the secretion of endorphins, and increased oxygen in the blood. Humor liberates creativity and provides high-level thinking skills, such as anticipation, finding novel relationships, and visual imagery. The acquisition of a sense of humor follows a developmental sequence similar to that described by Piaget[6] and Kohlberg.[7] Initially, children may find humor in all the wrong things—human frailty, ethnic humor, sacrilegious riddles, ribald profanities. Later, creative children thrive on finding incongruity and will demonstrate a whimsical frame of mind during problem solving.

QUESTIONING AND PROBLEM POSING.   As said before, young people are full of questions, and they ask them. We want students to be alert to, and recognize, discrepancies and phenomena in their environment and to freely inquire about their causes. In exemplary edu-

---

4. For further reading about the relation of impulse control to intelligence, see D. Goleman, *Emotional Intelligence: Why It Can Matter More Than IQ* (New York: Bantam Books, 1995), and D. Harrington-Lueker, "Emotional Intelligence," *High Strides* 9(4):1, 4–5 (March/April 1997).

5. E. de Bono, *Lateral Thinking: Creativity Step by Step* (New York: Harper and Row, 1970).

6. J. Piaget, *The Psychology of Intelligence* (Totowa, NJ: Littlefield Adams, 1972).

7. I. Kohlberg, *The Meaning and Measurement of Moral Development* (Worcester, MA: Clark University Press, 1981).

cational programs, students are encouraged to ask questions (discussed in Chapter 7) and then from those questions to develop a problem-solving strategy to investigate their questions.

DRAWING ON KNOWLEDGE AND APPLYING IT TO NEW SITUATIONS.   A major goal of education is for students to apply school-learned knowledge to real-life situations. To develop skills in drawing on past knowledge and applying that knowledge to new situations, students must be given opportunity to practice doing that very thing.

TAKING RISKS.   Students should be encouraged to venture forth and explore their ideas. Teachers can provide this opportunity with techniques such as brainstorming, exploratory investigations, experimentation, and cooperative learning.

USING ALL THE SENSES.   As often as is appropriate and feasible, students should be encouraged to learn to use all their sensory input channels to learn (i.e., verbal, visual, tactile, and kinesthetic).

INGENUITY, ORIGINALITY, INSIGHTFULNESS: CREATIVITY.   All students must be encouraged to do and be discouraged from saying "I can't." Students must be taught in such a way as to encourage intrinsic motivation rather than reliance on extrinsic sources. Teachers must be able to offer criticism so that the student understands it is not a criticism of self. In exemplary educational programs, students learn the value of feedback. They learn the value of their own intuition, of guessing.

WONDERMENT, INQUISITIVENESS, CURIOSITY, AND THE ENJOYMENT OF PROBLEM SOLVING: A SENSE OF EFFICACY AS A THINKER.   Young children express wonderment, an expression that should never be stifled. Through effective teaching, all students can recapture that sense of wonderment as they are guided by an effective teacher into a feeling of "I can" and express a feeling of "I enjoy."

We should strive to help our own students develop these 14 characteristics of intelligent behavior. In Chapter 2 you learned of specific teacher behaviors that facilitate this development. Now, let's review additional research findings that offer important considerations in the facilitation of student learning and intelligent behaving.

Direct Teaching for Thinking

The curriculum of any school includes the development of skills that are used in thinking. Because the academic achievement of students increases when they are taught thinking skills directly, many researchers

and educators concur that direct instruction should be given to students on how to think.[8] They also concur that learning to think is as valid an educational goal for students who are special, at risk, disadvantaged, or limited in speaking English as it is for those who are recognized as being gifted.

Research Imperatives for the Teaching of Thinking

The direct teaching of thinking has been influenced by four research perspectives. The *cognitive view of intelligence* asserts that intellectual ability is not fixed but can be developed. The *constructivist approach to learning* maintains that learners actively and independently construct knowledge by creating and coordinating relationships in their mental repertoire. The *social psychology view of classroom experience* focuses on the learner as an individual who is a member of various peer groups and a society. The *perspective of information processing* deals with the acquisition, elaboration, and management of information.[9]

Direct Teaching of Skills Used in Thinking

Rather than assuming students have developed thinking skills (such as *classifying, comparing, concluding, generalizing, inferring,* and others—see Figure 9.3), teachers should devote classroom time to teaching them directly. When a thinking skill is taught directly, the subject content becomes the vehicle for thinking. For example, a social studies lesson can teach students how to distinguish fact from opinion; an English teacher's lesson instructs students how to compare and analyze; a science lesson can teach students how to set up a problem for their inquiry.

Inquiry teaching and discovery learning are both useful tools for teaching and learning thinking skills. For further insight and additional strategies, as well as for the many programs concerned with teaching thinking, see the resources in this chapter's suggested readings at the end of the chapter.[10]

---

8. See, for example, A. Whimbey, "Test Results from Teaching Thinking," in A. L. Costa (ed.), *Developing Minds: A Resource Book for Teaching Thinking* (Alexandria, VA: Association for Supervision and Curriculum Development, 1985), pp. 269–271. See also Carnegie Council for Adolescent Development, *Turning Points: Preparing American Youth for the 21st Century* (Washington, DC: Carnegie Council for Adolescent Development, 1989).

9. B. Z. Presseisen, *Implementing Thinking in the School's Curriculum,* unpublished paper presented at the third annual meeting of the International Association for Cognitive Education, Riverside, CA, on February 9, 1992.

10. For a catalog of products for teaching thinking, contact Critical Thinking Press & Software, PO Box 448, Pacific Grove, CA 93950. Phone (800) 458-4849.

Table 9.1. Levels of Inquiry

	Level I (not true inquiry)	*Level II*	*Level III*
Problem Identification	By teacher or textbook	By teacher or textbook	By student
Process of Solving the Problem	Decided by teacher or text	Decided by student	Decided by student
Identification of Tentative Solution	Resolved by student	Resolved by student	Resolved by student

INQUIRY TEACHING AND DISCOVERY LEARNING

Intrinsic to the effectiveness of both inquiry and discovery is the assumption that students would rather actively seek knowledge than receive it through expository (i.e., information delivery) methods such as lectures, demonstrations, and textbook reading. Although inquiry and discovery are important teaching tools, there is sometimes confusion about exactly what inquiry teaching is and how it differs from discovery learning. The distinction should become clear as you study the following descriptions of these two important tools for teaching and learning.

Problem Solving

Perhaps a major reason why inquiry and discovery are sometimes confused is that in both, students are actively engaged in problem solving. Problem solving is *the ability to define or describe a problem, determine the desired outcome, select possible solutions, choose strategies, test trial solutions, evaluate outcomes, and revise these steps where necessary.*[11]

Inquiry versus Discovery

Problem solving is *not* a teaching strategy but a high-order intellectual behavior that facilitates learning. What a teacher can and should do is provide opportunities for students to identify and tentatively solve problems. Experiences in inquiry and discovery can provide those opportunities. With the processes involved in inquiry and discovery, teachers can help students develop the skills necessary for effective problem solving. Two major differences between discovery and inquiry are (1) who identifies the problem and (2) the percentage of decisions that are made by the students. Table 9.1 shows three levels of inquiry, each level defined according to what the student does and decides.

It should be evident from Table 9.1 that what is called *Level I inquiry* is actually traditional, didactic, "cookbook" teaching, where both the problem and the process for resolving it are defined for the student. The

student then works through the process to its inevitable resolution. If the process is well designed, the result is inevitable, because the student "discovers" what was intended by the writers of the program. This level is also called *guided inquiry* or *discovery,* because the students are carefully guided through the investigation to (the predictable) "discovery."

Level I is in reality a strategy within the *delivery mode,* the advantages of which were described in Chapter 6. Because Level I "inquiry" is highly manageable and the learning outcome is predictable, it is probably best for teaching basic concepts and principles. Students who never experience learning beyond Level I are missing an opportunity to engage their highest mental operations, and they seldom (or never) get to experience more motivating, real-life problem solving. Furthermore, those students may come away with the false notion that problem solving is a linear process, which it is not. As illustrated in Figure 9.2, true inquiry is cyclical rather than linear. For that reason, Level I is *not* true inquiry, because it is a linear process. Real-world problem solving is a cyclical rather than linear process. One enters the cycle whenever a discrepancy or problem is observed and recognized, and that can occur at any point in the cycle.

True Inquiry

Students should be provided experiences for true inquiry, which begins with *Level II,* where students actually decide and design processes for their inquiry. In true inquiry there is an emphasis on the tentative nature of conclusions, which makes the activity more like real-life problem solving, where decisions are always subject to revision if and when new data so prescribe.

At *Level III* inquiry students recognize and identify the problem as well as decide the processes and reach a conclusion. In *project-centered teaching,* as has been discussed and described throughout this resource guide, students are usually engaged at this level of inquiry. By the time students are in middle school, Level III inquiry should be a major strategy for instruction, which is often the case in schools that use cross-age teaching and interdisciplinary thematic instruction. But, it is not easy; like most good teaching practices it is a lot of work. But also like good teaching, the intrinsic rewards make the effort worthwhile. As exclaimed by one teacher using

11. A. L. Costa, ed., *Developing Minds: A Resource for Teaching Thinking* (Alexandria, VA: Association for Supervision and Curriculum Development, 1985), p. 312.

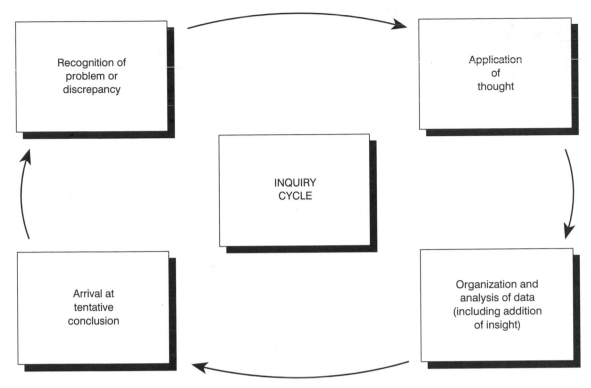

Figure 9.2
The inquiry cycle.

interdisciplinary thematic instruction with student-centered inquiry, "I've never worked harder in my life, but I've never had this much fun, either."

The Critical Thinking Skills of Discovery and Inquiry

In true inquiry, students generate ideas and then design ways to test those ideas. The various processes used represent the many critical thinking skills. Some of those skills are concerned with generating and organizing data; others are concerned with building and using ideas. Figure 9.3 provides four main categories of these thinking processes and illustrates the place of each within the inquiry cycle.

Some processes in the cycle are discovery processes, and others are inquiry processes. Inquiry processes include the more complex mental operations (including all of those in the idea-using category). Project-centered teaching provides an avenue for doing that, as does problem-centered teaching.

Inquiry learning is a higher-level mental operation that introduces the concept of the discrepant event, something that establishes cognitive disequilibrium (using the element of surprise to challenge their prior notions) to help students develop skills in observing and being alert for discrepancies. Such a strategy provides opportunities for students to investigate their own ideas about explanations. Inquiry, like discovery, depends upon skill in problem solving; the difference between the two is in the amount of decision-making responsibility given to students. Experiences afforded by inquiry help students understand the importance of suspending judgment and also the tentativeness of answers and solutions. With those understandings, students eventually are better able to deal with life's ambiguities. When students are not provided these important educational experiences, their education is incomplete.

One of the most effective ways of stimulating inquiry is to use materials that provoke students' interest. These materials should be presented in a nonthreatening, noncompetitive context so that students think and hypothesize freely. The teacher's role is to encourage students to form as many hypotheses as possible and then support their hypotheses with reasons. After the students suggest several ideas, the teacher should begin to move on to higher-order, more abstract questions that involve the development of generalizations and evaluations. True inquiry problems have a special advantage in that they can be used with almost any group of students. Members of a group approach the problem as an adventure in thinking and apply it to whatever background they can muster. Background experience may enrich a student's

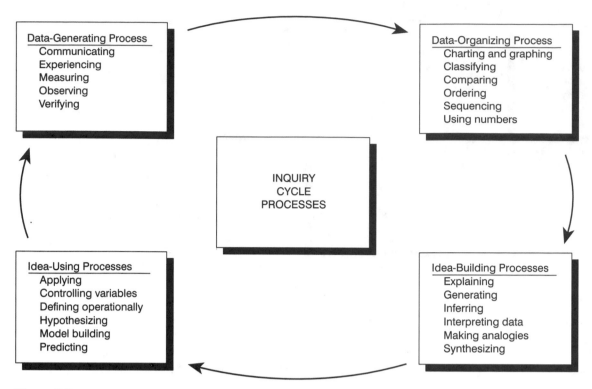

Figure 9.3
Inquiry cycle processes.

approach to the problem, but it is not crucial to the use or understanding of the evidence presented to him. Locating a Colony, in Figure 9.4, is a Level II inquiry. As a class, do the inquiry now.

Integrating Strategies for Integrated Learning

In today's exemplary classrooms, teaching strategies are often combined to establish the most effective teaching-learning experience. For example, in an integrated language arts program, teachers are interested in their students' speaking, reading, listening, thinking, study, and writing skills. These skills (and not textbooks) form a holistic process that is the primary aspect of integrated language arts.

In the area of speaking skills, oral discourse (discussion) in the classroom has a growing research base that promotes methods of teaching and learning through oral language. These methods include cooperative learning, instructional scaffolding, and inquiry teaching.

In cooperative learning groups, students discuss and use language for learning that benefits both their content learning and skills in social interaction. Working in heterogeneous groups, students participate in their own learning and can extend their knowledge base and cul-

tural awareness with students of different backgrounds. When students share information and ideas, they are completing difficult learning tasks, using divergent thinking and decision making, and developing their understanding of concepts. As issues are presented and responses are challenged, student thinking is clarified. Students assume the responsibility for planning within the group and for carrying out their assignments. When needed, the teacher models an activity with one group in front of the class, and when integrated with student questions, the modeling can become inquiry teaching. Activities can include the following.

BRAINSTORMING.   Members generate ideas related to a key word and record them. Clustering or chunking, mapping, and the Venn diagram (all discussed subsequently) are variations of brainstorming.

THINK-PAIR-SHARE.   As discussed in Chapter 8, a concept is presented by the teacher, and students are paired to discuss the concept. They share what they already know or have experienced about that concept and then share that information with the rest of the class. This strategy is an excellent technique for preassessing and discovering students' prior notions.

Presentation of the Problem. In groups of three or four, students receive the following information.

Background. You (your group is considered as one person) are one of 120 passengers on the ship, the *Prince Charles.* You left England 12 weeks ago. You have experienced many hardships, including a stormy passage, limited rations, sickness, cold and damp weather, and hot, foul air below deck. Ten of your fellow immigrants to the New World, including three children, have died and been buried at sea. You are now anchored at an uncertain place, off the coast of the New World, which your captain believes to be somewhere north of the Virginia Grants. Seas are so rough and food so scarce that you and your fellow passengers have decided to settle here. A landing party has returned with a map they made of the area. You, as one of the elders, must decide at once where the settlement is to be located. The tradesmen want to settle along the river, which is deep, even though this seems to be the season of low water levels. Within ten months they expect deep-water ships from England with more colonists and merchants. Those within your group who are farmers say they must have fertile, workable land. The officer in charge of the landing party reported seeing a group of armed natives who fled when approached. He feels the settlement must be located so that it can be defended from the natives and from the sea.

Directions, step one: You (your group) are to select a site on the attached map that you feel is best suited for a colony. Your site must satisfy the different factions aboard the ship. A number of possible sites are already marked on the map (letters *A–G*). You may select one of these locations or use them as reference points to show the location of your colony. When your group has selected its site, list and explain the reasons for your choice. When each group has arrived at its tentative decision, these will be shared with the whole class.

Directions, step two: After each group has made its presentation and argument, a class debate is held about where the colony should be located.

Notes to teacher: For the debate, have a large map drawn on the writing board or on an overhead transparency, where each group's mark can be made for all to see and discuss. After each group has presented its argument for its location and against the others, we suggest that you then mark on the large

map the two, three, or more hypothetical locations (assuming that, as a class, there is no single favorite location yet). Then take a straw vote of the students, allowing each to vote on her own, independently rather than as members of groups. At this time you can terminate the activity by saying that if the majority of students favor one location, then that, in fact, is the solution to the problem—that is, the colony is located wherever the majority of class members believe it should be. No sooner will that statement be made by you than someone will ask, "Are we correct?" or "What is the right answer?" They will ask such questions because, as students in school, they are used to solving problems that have right answers (Level I inquiry teaching). In real-world problems, however, there are no "right" answers, though some answers may seem better than others. It is the process of problem solving that is important. You want your students to develop confidence in their ability to solve problems and understand the tentativeness of "answers" to real-life problems.

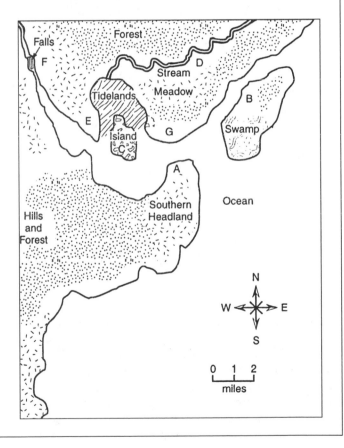

Figure 9.4
Locating a Colony: a level II inquiry. (*Source:* Adapted by permission from unpublished material provided by Jennifer Devine and Dennis Devine.)

CHUNKING OR CLUSTERING. Groups of students apply mental organizers by clustering information into chunks for easier manipulation and remembering.

MEMORY STRATEGIES. The teacher and students model the use of acronyms, mnemonics, rhymes, or clustering of information into categories to promote learning. Sometimes, such as in memorizing the social security number, one must learn by rote information that is not connected to any prior knowledge. To do that it is helpful to break the information to be learned into smaller chunks, such as dividing the nine-digit social security number into smaller chunks of information (with, in this instance, each chunk separated by a hyphen). Learning by rote is also easier if one can connect that which is to be memorized to some prior knowledge. Strategies such as these are used to bridge the gap between rote learning and meaningful learning and are known as mnemonics. Sample mnemonics are

- The notes on a treble staff are FACE for the space notes and *Empty Garbage Before Dad Flips* (EGBDF) for the line notes. The notes on the bass staff are *Grizzly Bears Don't Fly Airplanes* (GBDFA).
- The order of the planets from the Sun are *My Very Educated Mother Just Served Us Nine Pizzas* (Mercury, Venus, Earth, Mars, Jupiter, Saturn, Uranus, Neptune, and Pluto—although, in reality, Pluto and Neptune alternate in this order because of their elliptical orbits).
- The names of the Great Lakes: HOMES for *H*uron, *O*ntario, *M*ichigan, *E*rie, and *S*uperior.
- Visual mnemonics are useful too, such as remembering that Italy is shaped like a boot.

COMPARING AND CONTRASTING. Similarities and differences between items are found and recorded.

CONCEPT MAPPING. Concept mapping has been useful for helping students organize their learning and change their misconceptions. Simply put, concepts can be thought of as classifications that attempt to organize the world of objects and events into a smaller number of categories. In everyday usage, the term *concept* means idea, as when someone says, "My concept of love is not the same as yours." Concepts embody a meaning that develops in complexity with experience and learning over time. For example, the concept of love held by a second grader is unlikely to be as complex as that held by a high school senior.

A variety of terms for the visual tools useful for learning have been invented—some of which are synonymous—such as *brainstorming web, mind-mapping web, spider map, cluster, concept map, cognitive map, semantic map, Venn diagram, visual scaffold, and graphic organizer.* Clark[12] and Hyerle[13] separate these visual tools into three categories, according to purpose: (1) *brainstorming tools* (such as mind mapping, webbing, and clustering) for the purpose of developing one's knowledge and creativity; (2) *task-specific organizers* (such as life cycle diagrams used in biology, decision trees used in mathematics, and text structures in reading); and (3) *thinking process maps* (such as concept mapping) for encouraging cognitive development across disciplines.[14] It is the last one about which we are interested here.

Based on Ausubel's theory of meaningful learning, concept mapping has been found useful for helping students in changing prior notions—their misconceptions. Concept mapping can help students in their ability to organize and to represent their thoughts, as well as to connect new knowledge to their past experiences and precepts.[15] A concept map typically refers to a visual or graphic representation of concepts with bridges (connections) that show relationships. Figure 9.5 shows a partially complete concept map in social studies, in which students have made connections between concepts related to fruit farming and marketing.

The general procedure for concept mapping is to have the students (1) identify important concepts in materials being studied, often by circling those concepts, (2) rank order the concepts from the most general to the most specific, and (3) arrange the concepts on a sheet of paper, connect related ideas with lines, and define the connections between the related ideas.

INFERRING. Students can assume the roles of people (real or fictional) and infer their motives, personalities, and thoughts.

MAKING TESTS. Each group creates a test, and members of another group take it.

OUTLINING. Each group completes an outline that contains some of the main ideas but with subtopics omitted.

12. J. H. Clark, *Patterns of Thinking* (Needham Heights, MA: Allyn & Bacon, 1991).
13. D. Hyerle, *Visual Tools for Constructing Knowledge* (Alexandria, VA: Association for Supervision and Curriculum Development, 1996).
14. For an informative presentation on the use of visual tools in all three categories, see Hyerle, ibid.
15. For further information about concept mapping, see J. D. Novak, "Concept Maps and Vee Diagrams: Two Metacognitive Tools to Facilitate Meaningful Learning," *Instructional Science* 19(1):29–52 (1990).

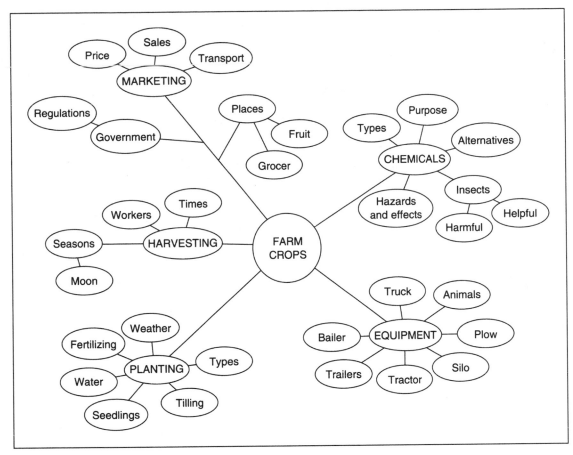

Figure 9.5
Sample partially completed concept map.

PARAPHRASING.   In a brief summary, each student restates a short selection of what was read or heard.

RECIPROCAL TEACHING.   In classroom dialogue, students take turns at generating questions, summarizing, clarifying, and predicting.[16]

TEXTBOOK STUDY STRATEGIES.   Students use the SQ4R or related study strategies (see section on the textbooks in Chapter 4).

VEE MAPPING.   This is a kind of road map completed by students, as they learn, showing the route they follow from prior knowledge to new and future knowledge.

VENN DIAGRAMMING.   This is a technique for comparing two concepts or, for example, two stories to show similarities and differences. Using stories as an example, a student is asked to draw two circles that intersect and to mark the circles one and two and the area where they intersect three. In circle one, the student lists the characteristics of one story, and in circle two she lists the characteristics of the second story. In the area of the intersection, marked three, the student lists characteristics common to both stories.

Now, to further explore inquiry teaching and integrated learning, do Exercise 9.2.

---

16. See C. J. Carter, "Why Reciprocal Teaching?" *Educational Leadership* 54(6):64–68 (March 1997).

EXERCISE 9.2
A Study of Inquiry and Strategy Integration

Instructions: The purpose of this exercise is to experience a Level II inquiry (Figure 9.4), to analyze the Locating a Colony inquiry and the discussion in the text about integrating strategies, and to synthesize that information for use in your own teaching. We suggest that you first answer the questions of this exercise and then share your answers with others in your discipline (in groups of about four). Finally, share your group's collective responses with the entire class.

1. My subject field: _____

2. a. How could I use the Locating a Colony inquiry in my subject field (for what purpose, goals, or objectives)? _____

   _____

   _____

   _____

   b. What content in my subject field might students be expected to learn from doing the Locating a Colony inquiry? _____

   _____

   _____

   _____

3. How could I involve my students in cooperative learning while doing the Locating a Colony inquiry? _____

   _____

   _____

   _____

4. How could brainstorming be used while doing the Locating a Colony inquiry? _____

   _____

   _____

   _____

   _____

5. How could clustering be used while doing the Locating a Colony inquiry? _____

   _____

   _____

   _____

6. How could concept mapping be used while doing the Locating a Colony inquiry? _____

_____

_____

_____

7. How could comparing and contrasting be used while doing the Locating a Colony inquiry?

_____

_____

_____

8. How could outlining be used while doing the Locating a Colony inquiry? _____

_____

_____

_____

9. How could paraphrasing be used while doing the Locating a Colony inquiry? _____

_____

_____

_____

10. How could summarizing be used while doing the Locating a Colony inquiry? _____

_____

_____

_____

11. How could memory strategies be used while doing the Locating a Colony inquiry? _____

_____

_____

_____

12. How could inferring be used while doing the Locating a Colony inquiry? _____

_____

_____

_____

13. What other skills could be taught while doing the Locating a Colony inquiry? For each, briefly describe how. _____

_____

_____

_____

Table 9.2. Classification of Educational Games

Type	Characteristics	Examples
1. Pure game*	Promotes laughter; fun	*Ungame, Cooperation Square Game*
2. Pure contest	Stimulates competition; built-in inefficiency[†]	Political contests (e.g., U.S. presidential race)
3. Pure simulation*	Models reality	Toddler play
4. Contest/game	Stimulates competition; fun; built-in inefficiency	Golf, bowling, *Trivial Pursuit*
5. Simulation/game*	Models reality; fun	*Redwood Controversy*[‡]
6. Contest/simulation	Stimulates competition; models reality; built-in inefficiency	Boxcar Derby of Akron, OH
7. Simulation/game/contest	Models reality; fun; stimulates competition; built-in inefficiency	*Careers, Life, Monopoly*

*These game types do not emphasize competition and thus are particularly recommended for use in the classroom.

[†]This means that rules for accomplishing the game objective make accomplishment of that objective less than efficient. For example, in golf the objective is to get the ball into the hole with the least amount of effort; but to do that, one has to take a peculiarly shaped stick (the club) and hit the ball, find it, and hit it again, continuing that sequence until the ball is in the hole. Yet, common sense tells us that the best way to get the ball into the hole with the least amount of effort would be to simply pick up the ball and place it by hand into the hole.

[‡]*Redwood Controversy* is a powerful simulation role-play game patterned after congressional hearings during President Lyndon Johnson's administration that considered enlarging the Redwood National Parks. The game is interdisciplinary, and teachers have found it excellent for use in grades 6 and up, especially for social studies, English, science, debate, and classes that are interdisciplinary. Although published several years ago, the game remains relevant to events today, is inexpensive, includes rules for play, role cards, a transparency, and a wall map, and can be played in approximately two hours (or could be extended over many days or weeks). One high school social studies teacher had his class playing the game for a period of about six weeks. Available from Houghton Mifflin.

LEARNING BY EDUCATIONAL GAMES

Devices classified as educational games include a wide variety of learning activities, such as simulations, role-play and sociodrama activities, mind games, board games, computer games, and sporting games, all of which provide valuable learning experiences. That is, they are experiences that tend to involve several senses and several learning modalities, engage higher-order thinking skills, and be quite effective as learning tools.

Simulations, for example, serve many of the developmental needs of students. They provide for interaction with peers and allow students of different ability to work together on a common project. They engage students in physical activity and give them an opportunity to try out different roles, which help them to better understand themselves. Simulations, like the *Redwood Controversy,* for example, can provide concrete experiences that help students to understand complex concepts and issues, and they provide opportunities for exploring values and decision making.

Educational games can play an integral role in interdisciplinary teaching and serve as valuable resources for enriching the effectiveness of students' learning. As with any other instructional strategy, the use of games should follow a clear educational purpose, have a careful plan, and be congruent with the instructional objectives.

Classification of Educational Games

What are educational games? Seven types of games fall under the general heading of educational games. Table 9.2 shows the seven types, with characteristics and examples of each. Certain types have greater educational value than do others. Games that do not emphasize the element of competition—that are not "contests"—are particularly recommended for use in the academic classroom (types 1, 3, and 5 in Table 9.2).

Purposes of Educational Games

Games can be powerful tools for teaching and learning. A game can have one to several of the following purposes: (1) add variety and change of pace, (2) assess student learning, (3) enhance student self-esteem, (4) motivate students, (5) offer a break from the usual rigors of learning, (6) provide learning about real-life issues through simulation and role-playing, (7) provide learning through tactile and kinesthetic modalities, (8) provide problem-solving situations and experiences, (9) provide skill development and

Figure 9.6
Sources of educational games.

- Aristoplay, Ltd., PO Box 7028, Ann Arbor, MI 48107.
- Broderbund Software, Inc., 500 Redwood Boulevard, Novato, CA 94948-6121.
- Carolina Biological Supply Company, 2700 York Road, Burlington, NC 27215.
- Delta Educational, PO Box 3000, Nashua, NH 03061-3000.
- Denoyer Geppert Co., 5215 North Ravenswood Avenue, Chicago, IL 60640.
- Houghton Mifflin Co., One Wayside Road, Burlington, MA 08103-9842.
- Interact Company, PO Box 997-Y92, Lakeside, CA 92040.
- Lingo Fun, Inc., PO Box 486, Westerville, OH 43086.
- Modern School Supplies, PO Box 958, Hartford, CT 06143.
- National Geographic Society Education Services Division, 1145 17th Street, NW, Washington, DC 20036-4688.
- New York Zoological Society, Education Department, Bronx, NY 10460.
- Other Worlds Educational Enterprises, PO Box 6193, Woodland Park, CO 80866-6193.
- Social Studies School Service, 10000 Culver Boulevard, Culver City, CA 90230.
- Teaching Aids Company, 925 South 300 West, Salt Lake City, UT 84101.
- Wiff 'N Proof, 1490-TZ South Boulevard, Ann Arbor, MI 48104.

motivation through computer usage, (10) provide skill development in inductive thinking, (11) provide skill development in verbal communication and debate, (12) reinforce convergent thinking, (13) review and reinforce subject-matter learning, (14) encourage learning through peer interaction, (15) stimulate critical thinking, (16) stimulate deductive thinking, (17) stimulate divergent and creative thinking, and (18) teach both content and process.

Sources of Educational Games

There are many sources of commercially available educational games for use in teaching; many have come and gone so quickly that it is impossible to maintain a current list of sources and prices. Figure 9.6 shows sources with a successful history of marketing useful educational games.

Now, as requested by your course instructor, do Exercise 9.3.

EXERCISE 9.3

Developing a Lesson Using Level II Inquiry, Thinking Skill Development, a Demonstration, or an Interactive Lecture—Micro Peer Teaching III

Instructions: The purpose of this exercise is to provide the opportunity for you to create a brief lesson (about twenty minutes of instructional time but to be specified by your instructor) designed for a specific grade level and subject and to try it out on your peers for their feedback in an informal (i.e., nongraded) micro peer teaching demonstration.

Divide your class into four groups. The task of members of each group is to prepare lessons (individually) that fall into one of the four categories: Level II inquiry; thinking level; demonstration; or interactive lecture. Schedule class presentations so that each class member has the opportunity to present his lesson and to obtain feedback from class members about it. For feedback, class members who are the "teacher's" audience can complete the assessment rubric shown after this exercise (by circling one of the three choices for each of the ten categories) and give their completed form to the teacher for use in analysis and self-assessment. Before your class starts this exercise, you may want to review the scoring rubric and make modifications to it that the class agrees on.

To structure your lesson plan, use one of the sample lesson plan formats presented in Chapter 5; however, each lesson should be centered on one major theme or concept and be planned for about 20 minutes of instructional time.

Group 1: Develop a Level II inquiry lesson.

Group 2: Develop a lesson designed to raise the level of student thinking.

Group 3: Develop a lesson that involves a demonstration.

Group 4: Develop a lesson that is an interactive lecture.

PEER AND SELF-ASSESSMENT RUBRIC FOR USE WITH EXERCISE 9.3

For: _____ Group: _____

	1	0.5	0
1. Lesson beginning Comment:	effective	less effective	not effective
2. Sequencing Comment:	effective	less effective	rambling
3. Pacing of lesson Comment:	effective	less effective	too slow or too fast
4. Audience involvement Comment:	effective	less effective	none
5. Motivators (e.g., analogies, verbal cues, humor, visual cues, sensory cues) Comment:	effective	less effective	not apparent
6. Content of lesson Comment:	well chosen	interesting	boring or inappropriate
7. Voice of teacher Comment:	stimulating	minor problem	major problems
8. Vocabulary used Comment:	well chosen	appropriate	inappropriate
9. Eye contact Comment:	excellent	average	problems
10. Closure Comment:	effective	less effective	unclear or none

Other Comments:

SUMMARY

This marks the completion of our effort to provide for the development of your repertoire of teaching strategies necessary to becoming an effective secondary school teacher. Central to your strategy selection should be those strategies that encourage students to become independent thinkers and skilled learners who can help plan, structure, regulate, and assess their own learning and learning activities.

Important to helping students construct their understandings are the cognitive tools that are available for their use. There is a large variety of useful and effective aids, media, and resources from which to draw as you plan your instructional experiences—the topic of the next and final chapter of Part III.

QUESTIONS FOR CLASS DISCUSSION

1. Many cognitive researchers believe that students should spend more time actively using knowledge to solve problems and less time reading introductory material and listening to teachers. Describe the meaning of this statement and how you feel about it with respect to your decision to become a teacher.

2. Explain how you will decide when to use direct instruction and when to use indirect instruction.

3. Explain why you would or would not like to teach by inquiry (Level II or III).

4. About strategy choice, how eclectic in strategy choice can or should a teacher be? Explain the meaning of integrating strategies for integrated learning.

5. Are there any cautions teachers need to be aware of when using games for teaching? If there are, describe them.

6. Explain some specific ways you can help students develop their skills in thinking and learning.

7. Select one of the 14 characteristics of intelligent behavior and write a lesson plan (for a grade level of your choice and time limit as decided by your class) for helping students develop that behavior. Share or teach your lesson to others in your class for their analysis and suggestions.

8. Describe any prior concepts you held that changed as a result of your experiences with this chapter. Describe the changes.

9. From your current observations and fieldwork as related to this teacher preparation program, clearly identify one specific example of educational practice that seems contradictory to exemplary practice or theory as presented in this chapter. Present your explanation for the discrepancy.

10. Do you have questions generated by the content of this chapter? If you do, list them along with ways answers might be found.

SUGGESTED READINGS

Arico, A. "Blood Type Compatibility: A Simulation of Medical Transfusion Reactions." *American Biology Teacher* 57(2):108–110 (February 1995).

Barrell, J. *Teaching for Thoughtfulness*. White Plains, NY: Longman, 1995.

Beyer, B. K. *Critical Thinking*. Bloomington, IN: Fastback 385, Phi Delta Kappa Educational Foundation, 1995.

Cardellichio, T., and Field, W. "Seven Strategies That Encourage Neural Branching." *Educational Leadership* 54(6):33–36 (March 1997).

Chalupa, M. R., and Sormunen, C. "Strategies for Developing Critical Thinking: You Make the Difference in the Classroom." *Business Education Forum* 49(3):41–43 (February 1995).

Finkel, E. A. "Making Sense of Genetics: Students' Knowledge Use during Problem Solving in a High School Genetics Class." *Journal of Research in Science Teaching* 33(4):345–368 (April 1996).

Geocaris, C. "Increasing Student Engagement: A Mystery Solved." *Educational Leadership* 54(4):72–75 (December 1996/January 1997).

Goleman, D. *Emotional Intelligence: Why It Can Matter More Than IQ*. New York: Bantam Books, 1995.

Gussin, L. "Constructive Lessons: Building and Playing Simulation Games." *CD-ROM Professional* 8(5):40–42, 44, 46, 48, 50 (May 1995).

Klein, P. "Using Inquiry to Enhance the Learning and Appreciation of Geography." *Journal of Geography* 94(2):358–367 (March/April 1995).

Klies, C. "The Humor in Horror." *Voice of Youth Advocates* 18(3):143–144 (August 1995).

Lacy, C. "Entrepreneurial Earth Science." *Science Teacher* 64(1):54–58 (January 1997).

Levy, T. "The Amistad Incident: A Classroom Reenactment." *Social Education* 59(5):303–308 (September 1995).

Lewis, P. "Why Humor?" *Voices from the Middle* 2(3):10–16 (September 1995).

Maceri, D. "Reducing Stress in the Foreign Language Classroom: Teaching Descriptive Adjectives through Humor." *Mosaic* 2(4):21–22 (Summer 1995).

McCann, T. M. "A Pioneer Simulation for Writing and for the Study of Literature." *English Journal* 85(3):62–67 (March 1996).

O'Neil, J. "On Emotional Intelligence: A Conversation with Daniel Goleman." *Educational Leadership* 54(1):6–11 (September 1996).

Owens, K. D. et al. "Playing to Learn: Science Games in the Classroom." *Science Scope* 20(5):31–33 (February 1997).

Pan, W. L. "Role Playing and Mind Mapping Issues on Nitrate Contamination." *Journal of Natural Resources and Life Science Education* 25(1):37–42 (Spring 1996).

Paul, R. *Critical Thinking: How to Prepare Students for a Rapidly Changing World*. Santa Rosa, CA: Foundation for Critical Thinking, 1995.

Potthoff, D. et al. "Responding to Industry's Call: Using Discrepant Events to Promote Team Problem-Solving Skill." *Clearing House* 69(3):180–182 (January/February 1996).

Rice, G. H. "AIDS in Sub-Saharan Africa: A Diffusion Simulation." *Journal of Geography* 94(1):317–322 (January/February 1995).

Rode, G. A. "Teaching Protein Synthesis Using a Simulation." *American Biology Teacher* 57(1):50–52 (January 1995).

Rothermel, D. "What's So Funny in 303?" *Voices from the Middle* 2(3):20–25 (September 1995).

Sadowski, M. "Moving beyond Traditional Subjects Requires Teachers to Abandon Their 'Comfort Zones.' " *The Harvard Education Letter* 11(5):1–5 (September/October 1995).

Sternberg, R. J. "What Does It Mean to Be Smart?" *Educational Leadership* 54(6):20–24 (March 1997).

Sternberg, R. J., and Spear-Swerling, L. *Teaching for Thinking*. Washington, D.C.: American Psychological Association, 1996.

Sternberg, R. J., and Williams, W. M. *How to Develop Student Creativity*. Alexandria, VA: Association for Supervision and Curriculum Development, 1996.

Teague, M., and Teague, G. "Planning with Computers—A Social Studies Simulation." *Learning and Leading with Technology* 23(1):20, 22 (September 1995).

Tishman, S., Perkins, D. N., and Jay, E. *The Thinking Classroom: Learning and Teaching in a Culture of Thinking*. Boston: Allyn & Bacon, 1995.

Vogt, K. D. "Demonstrating Biological Classification Using a Simulation of Natural Taxa." *American Biology Teacher* 57(5):282–283 (May 1995).

Wright, E. L., and Govindarajan, G. "Discrepant Event Demonstrations." *Science Teacher* 62(1):24–28 (January 1995).

Chapter

10

Using Media and Other Instructional Aids and Resources

Important to helping students construct their understandings are the cognitive tools that are available for their use. You will be pleased to know that there is a large variety of useful and effective media, aids, and resources from which to draw as you plan your instructional experiences. On the other hand, you could also become overwhelmed by the sheer quantity of materials available—textbooks, supplementary texts, pamphlets, anthologies, paperbacks, encyclopedias, tests, programmed instructional systems, dictionaries, reference books, classroom periodicals, newspapers, films, records and cassettes, computer software, transparencies, realia, games, filmstrips, audio- and videotapes, slides, globes, manipulatives, CD-ROMs, digital videodiscs and videodiscs, and graphics. You could spend a great deal of time reviewing, sorting, selecting, and practicing with the materials and tools for your use. Although nobody can make the job easier for you, information in this chapter will expedite the process.

Specifically, upon completion of this chapter you should be able to

1. Demonstrate an understanding of the virtues of and guidelines for using audiovisual aids, media, and other resources in teaching and learning.

2. Begin your personal resources file.

3. Demonstrate an awareness of media available for teaching your subject field, how they can be used, and how and where they can be obtained.

4. Demonstrate an understanding of the limitations in using copyrighted materials other than your own.

5. Demonstrate competency in using the classroom writing board and the overhead projector.

PRINTED MATERIALS

Historically, of all the materials available for instruction, the printed textbook has had, and still has, the most influence on teaching and learning. We discussed the textbook in Chapter 4; it is referred to here only with respect to its combined use with other reading materials.

When selecting reading materials, teachers should be concerned about the readability level of the material. Sometimes the reading level is supplied by the textbook publisher. If not, you can apply selections to a readability formula (see Chapter 4) or use a simpler method of merely having students read selections from the book aloud. If they can read the selections without stumbling over many of the words and can tell you the gist of what has been said, you can feel confident that the textbook is not too difficult.

Beginning a Resources File

Besides the student textbook and perhaps an accompanying workbook, a vast array of other printed materials is available for use in teaching, many of them free. (See sources of free and inexpensive materials that follow.) It is a good idea to immediately begin a file of printed materials and other resources that you can use in your teaching. Exercise 10.1 is offered to help you begin that process.

EXERCISE 10.1
Beginning My Professional Materials Resource File

Instructions: The purpose of this exercise is to get you started on building your personal file of aids and resources for teaching, a project that you should continue throughout your career. Begin your file either on a computer database program or on three-by-five-inch color-coded file cards that list

1. Name of resource
2. How and when to obtain the resource
3. How to use the resource
4. Evaluative comments

Organize the file in whatever way that makes the most sense to you. Cross-reference or color-code your system to accommodate the following categories of aids and resources:

1. Articles from magazines, newspapers, journals, and periodicals
2. Compact disc and videodisc titles and sources
3. Computer software titles and sources
4. Examination questions
5. Games and game sources
6. Guest speakers and other community resources
7. Internet sources
8. Media catalogs
9. Motivational ideas
10. Multimedia programs
11. Pictures, posters, and other stills
12. Resources to order
13. Sources of free and inexpensive items
14. Student worksheets
15. Supply catalogs
16. Thematic units
17. Unit and lesson plan ideas
18. Completed unit and lesson plans
19. Videocassette titles and sources
20. Miscellaneous

Figure 10.1
Resources for free and
inexpensive printed materials.

- Civil Aeronautics Administration, *Sources of Free and Low-Cost Materials.* Washington, DC: U.S. Department of Commerce.
- Educators Progress Service, Inc., *Educator's Guide to Free Materials; Educator's Guide to Free Teaching Aids.* 214 Center Street, Randolph, WI 53956, phone (414) 326-3126.
- *Freebies: The Magazine with Something for Nothing.* PO Box 5025, Carpinteria, CA 93014-5025.
- Freebies editors. *Freebies for Teachers.* Los Angeles: Lowell House, 1994.
- *A Guide to Print and Nonprint Materials Available from Organizations, Industry, Governmental Agencies and Specialized Publishers.* New York: Neal Schuman.
- *Video Placement Worldwide (VPW).* Source of free sponsored educational videos and print material on the Internet <http://www.vpw.com>.

Printed materials include books, workbooks, pamphlets, magazines, brochures, newspapers, professional journals, periodicals, and duplicated materials. When reviewing these materials, you should be alert for (1) appropriateness of the material in both content and reading level; (2) articles in newspapers, magazines, and periodicals, related to the content that your students will be studying or to the skills they will be learning; (3) assorted workbooks available from trade book publishers that emphasize thinking and problem solving rather than rote memorization; (With an assortment of workbooks you can have students working on similar but different assignments depending upon their interests and abilities—an example of multilevel teaching.) (4) pamphlets, brochures, and other duplicated materials that students can read for specific information and viewpoints about particular topics; and (5) inexpensive paperback books that would provide multiple book readings for your class and that make it possible for students to read primary sources.

Sources of Free and Inexpensive Printed Materials

For free and inexpensive printed materials look for sources in your college or university, public library, or the resource center at a local school district. Sample sources are listed in Figure 10.1. Additionally, many teachers obtain free and inexpensive teaching materials through connections with electronic bulletin boards on the Internet. When considering using materials that you have obtained free or inexpensively, you will want to ensure that the materials are appropriate for use with the age group with whom you work and are free of bias or an unwanted mes-

sage. The National Education Association (NEA) has published guidelines for teachers to consider before purchasing or using commercial materials; for a free copy of the guidelines, contact NEA Communications, 1201 16th Street, NW, Washington, DC 20036; phone (202) 822-7200.

The Internet

Originating from a Department of Defense project in 1969 (called ARPANET) to establish a computer network of military researchers, its successor, the federally funded Internet, has become an enormous, steadily expanding, worldwide system of connected computer networks. The Internet provides literally millions of resources to explore, with thousands more added nearly every day. Only a few years ago it was difficult to find any published information about the Internet. Today you can surf the Internet and find many sources about it, on how to use it, and you can walk into many bookstores and find hundreds of recent titles, most of which give their authors' favorite web sites. However, because new technologies are steadily emerging and because the Internet changes every day, with some sites and resources disappearing or not kept current, with others having changed their location and undergone reconstruction, and new ones appearing, it would be superfluous for us to make too much of sites that we have found and can recommend as teacher resources. Nevertheless, shown in Figure 10.2 are Internet resources available that we have recently surfed and do recommend. Perhaps you have found others that you can share with your classmates (and with us). To that end, do Exercise 10.2.

- *Beyond the MLA Handbook: Documenting Electronic Sources on the Internet* (http://falcon.eku.edu/honors/beyond-mla); *Citing Internet Addresses* (http://www.classroom.net/classroom/CitingNetResources.htm); and J. Walker's *MLA-Style Citations of Electronic Sources* (http://www.cas.usf.edu/english/walker/mla.html). Useful references for teachers and students.
- *Electronic Emissary* (http://www.tapr.org/emissary). A Web site for teachers with experts in science, mathematics, and engineering.
- *ERIC Documents Online* (http://ericir.syr.edu). A Web site for searching ERIC documents.
- *Global Schoolnet Foundation* (http://www.gsn.org/). A Web site with resources and links for parents, teachers, and students from around the world.
- *Kathy Schrock's Guide for Educators* (http://www.capecod.net/schrockguide/). A Web site with resources and information on education.
- *MainFunction Sources for Education* (http://www.mainfunction.com). Microsoft's Web site for distance learning and computer programming.
- *Map Resources* (http://www.gsn.org/cf/maps.html) for maps.
- *MidLink Magazine* (http://longwood.cs.ucf.edu/~MidLink/). Electronic magazine for young adolescents.
- *NASA Spacelink: An Aeronautics & Space Resource for Educators* (http://spacelink.nasa/gov/.index.html).
- *National Education Association Resources for Teachers* (http://www.nea.org/resources/refs.html). Resources and links to sources.
- *National Science Teachers Association* (http://www.nsta.org). Information about science education; discussions with other teachers.
- *National Service Learning Cooperative Clearinghouse* (http://www.nicsl.coled.umn.edu). Information about federally funded service learning projects.
- *Newspapers in Education* (http://ole.net/ole/). Detroit News supported site for information about education.
- *School Match* (http://schoolmatch.com). Directory of U.S. schools.
- *School Page* (http://www.eyesoftime.com/teacher/index.html). A teacher's resource exchange.
- *Science Stuff* (http://www.sciencestuff.com). Products and some free materials for science teaching.
- *Teachers Network* (http://www.teachnet.org). A teacher's exchange.
- *The 21st Century Teachers Network* (http://www.21ct.org). Network of teachers helping their colleagues in education technology.
- *United States Copyright Office* (http://lcweb.loc.gov/copyright). Information and forms for copyrighting material.
- *Windows to the Universe Project* (http://www.windows.umich.edu). Provides information on recent space research and discoveries.
- *WWW4Teachers* (http://4teachers.org). A source about using modern technology.

Figure 10.2
Sample Internet sites.

EXERCISE 10.2

Internet Sites of Use to Secondary School Teachers

Instructions: The purpose of this exercise is to search the Internet for sites that you find interesting and useful, or useless, for secondary school teaching and to share those sites with your classmates (and, if you want, with the authors of this resource guide). Make copies of this page for each site visited; then share your results with your classmates.

Web site I investigated: http://_____

I consider the site   *highly useful*   *moderately useful*   *of no use*

Sponsor of site: _____

Features of interest and usefulness to secondary school teachers: _____

_____

_____

_____

_____

_____

_____

_____

_____

_____

_____

_____

_____

_____

_____

_____

_____

_____

_____

_____

_____

Cautions and Guidelines for Using the Internet

If you have not yet learned to use the Internet, we shall leave the mechanics of that to the many resources available to you, including the experts that can be found among your peers, on your college or university staff, and members of any school faculty. In the remaining pages of this section, we address the "how" of using the Internet from an academic perspective. We do it with the following fictitious, although feasible, scenario.

Let us suppose that ninth grade students from your "house" have been working nearly all year on an interdisciplinary thematic unit titled "surviving natural disasters" (returning to our example in Chapter 5 regarding ITU themes). As culmination to their study they "published" a document titled "Natural Disaster Preparation and Survival Guide for _____ (name of their community)" and proudly distributed the guide to their parents, guardians, and other members of the community.

Long before preparing the guide, however, the students had to do a large volume of research. To learn about the history of various kinds of natural disasters that had occurred or might occur locally and about the sorts of preparations a community should take for each kind of disaster, students searched sources on the Internet, such as federal documents, scientific articles, and articles from newspapers from around the world where natural disasters had occurred. They also searched in the local library and the local newspaper's archives to learn of floods, tornadoes, and fires that had occurred during the past 200 years. Much to their surprise, they learned that their community is located near the New Madrid Fault and did, in fact, experience a serious earthquake in 1811, although none since. As a result of that earthquake, two nearby towns completely disappeared and the Mississippi River flowed in reverse and caused the formation of a new lake in Tennessee.

From published and copyrighted sources, including Web sites, the students found many useful photographs, graphics, and articles and they included those in whole or in part in their "Natural Disaster Preparation and Survival Guide." They did so without obtaining permission from the original copyright holders or even citing those sources.

You and the other members of the teaching team and others were so impressed with the student's work that students were encouraged to offer the document for publishing on the school's Web site. In addition, the document was received with so much acclaim that the students decided to sell the document in local stores. This would help defray the original cost of duplication and enable them to continue the supply of guides.

There is an up side and a down side to this scenario. The up side is that the students used a useful technological tool (the Internet) to research a variety of sources, including many primary ones. The down side is that

when they published their document on the Internet and when they made copies of their guide to be sold, they did so without the permission from original copyright holders. They were infringing copyright law. Although we are not attorneys, with this fictitious scenario it is probable that the students, you, the school, and the school district would be liable. As is true for other documents (such as published photos, graphics, and text), unless there is a *clear statement* that materials taken from the Internet are "public domain," it is best to assume that they are copyrighted and should not be republished for profit or on another Web site.[1]

There is such a proliferation of information today, from both printed materials and the Internet, except for the obvious reliable sites such as the *New York Times* or the Library of Congress, how can a person determine the legitimacy of a particular piece of information? How can one be protected from wasting time sifting through all the information when searching for useful and reliable information on a particular topic. Children need to know that just because information is found on a printed page or is published on the Internet doesn't necessarily mean that the information is accurate. With a checklist such as that of Figure 10.3, you can teach students how to assess materials and information found on the Internet, showing them examples of materials that meet and do not meet the criteria. Once students have acquired a basic understanding of the checklist, you might select material and post a message on a student discussion group, such as <http://k12.chat.>, requesting others to examine that material and evaluate it using the same criteria.

Teaching all students how to assess Web sites adds to their repertoire of skills for lifelong learning. Consider allowing each student or teams of students to become experts on specific sites during particular units of study. It might be useful to start a chronicle of student-recorded log entries about particular Web sites to provide comprehensive long-term data about sites.

When students use information from the Internet, require that they print copies of sources of citations and materials so you can check for accuracy. These copies may be maintained in their portfolios.

Student work published on the Internet should be considered as intellectual material and protected from plagiarism by others. Many school districts now post a copyright notice on their home page. Also, to protect students from unwanted solicitations, full names of students probably should not be used on Web sites. See

---

1. J. McKenzie, "Keeping It Legal: Questions Arising Out of Web Site Management," *From Now On* 5(7):5 (June 1996). <http:www. pacificrim.net/~mckenzie/jun96/legal.html> (August 13, 1997).

Figure 10.3
Checklist for evaluating Internet information. (*Source:* R. J. Ryder and T. Hughes, *Internet for Teachers* [Upper Saddle River, NJ: Merrill/ Prentice Hall, 1997], pp. 185–186. By permission of Prentice Hall Publishing Company.)

Purpose and audience: Consider the intent of this information and why it is being communicated.

- Is this material designed for your student audience?
- What is the goal of the site?
- Who supports this site and what is their goal in presenting this information?

Authority: Consider the credentials of the individual(s) or groups presenting this information. If not provided, send them an e-mail message and request information on their credentials.

- Does the individual or group who constructed this information have the knowledge or experience to be considered reliable?
- Does the author cite other authorities?
- Are you confident that the individual or group that constructed this information is well qualified?

Scope: Consider the breadth and detail of the information provided.

- Skim the headings, table of contents, pictorial/graphic information. Does the content appear to be useful for your purpose?
- Does the site provide links to other sites that would allow for greater breadth or detail? Do you need to conduct a search to find additional information?

Format: Consider how the information is presented, how easily it can be interpreted, and whether it can be readily acquired or reproduced.

- Is the material clearly presented? Look for a table of contents, index, or preview that describes the site's content.
- Is the information presented in a format that is easily understood?
- Is there a statement as to whether you can reproduce this information for educational purposes?

Acceptance of materials: Consider the opinion others have of this material.

- Have you contacted others on the Net to determine if the material is useful?
- Does this material come from a source that is widely recognized?
- Does the site provide information as to how many individuals access the site?

---

sample school rules in Figure 10.4. Someone in your school should be assigned in charge of supervision of the school Web site to see that district and school policy and legal requirements are observed.

For additional current and specific information on using the Internet, we refer you to the many sources available, such as reliable sources on the Internet, professional journals, and periodicals (see Figure 10.5), and books, some of which are listed at the end of this chapter.

For a home computer, connecting to the Internet is easy if you have a modem (preferably a fast one); just contact one of the providers[2] and purchase one of the

- Do not give your home phone number to anyone.
- Do not give your home address to anyone.
- Do not join unmoderated chat lines.
- Do not play games on the Internet and waste valuable data lines we need for educational use.
- Report any harassment you receive on the Internet to the technology coordinator or your teacher.
- Do not download large files to your workstation (over 100k).
- Report inappropriate mail to your teacher or the technology coordinator.
- Avoid giving personal information to people you do *not* know.

Figure 10.4
Sample rules for safe use of the Internet. (*Source:* Nathan Hale High School [Seattle, WA] home page. Available <http://hale.ssd.k12.wa.us/> [August 22, 1997].)

---

2. Such as America Online (800-827-6364), CompuServe (800-848-8199), or Prodigy (800-776-3449).

The American Biology Teacher	*Language Learning*
American Educational Research Quarterly	*Learning*
American Journal of Physics	*The Mathematics Teacher*
The American Music Teacher	*Mathematics Teaching in the Middle School*
American Teacher	*The Middle School Journal*
The Art Teacher	*Modern Language Journal*
The Computing Teacher	*Music Educator's Journal*
Creative Classroom	*NEA Today*
The Earth Scientist	*The Negro Educational Review*
Educational Horizons	*The New Advocate*
Educational Leadership	*Phi Delta Kappan*
English Journal	*Physical Education*
English Language Teaching Journal	*The Physics Teacher*
The Good Apple Newspaper	*The Reading Teacher*
Hispania	*Reading Today*
The History Teacher	*School Arts*
The Horn Book	*School Library Journal*
Instructor	*The School Musician*
Journal of Business Education	*School Science and Mathematics*
Journal of Chemical Education	*School Shop*
Journal of Economic Education	*Science*
Journal of Geography	*Science Scope*
Journal of Home Economics	*Social Education*
Journal of Learning Disabilities	*The Social Studies*
Journal of the National Association of Bilingual	*Teacher Magazine*
Educators	*TESOL Quarterly*
Journal of Physical Education and Recreation	*Theory and Research in Social Education*
Journal of Reading	*Voices from the Middle*
Journal of Teaching in Physical Education	*Writing Teacher*
Language Arts	

Figure 10.5
Professional journals and periodicals for secondary school teachers: sample listing.

software programs that provides connection to the Internet.[3] For more specific and the most current information on connecting to the Internet, services, and related questions, we refer you to the many sources available, such as professional journals and periodicals and books.[4]

Professional Journals and Periodicals

Figure 10.3 lists examples of the many professional periodicals and journals that can provide useful teaching ideas and Web site information and that carry information about instructional materials and how to get them. Some of these may be in your university or college library. Check there for these and other titles of interest to you.

The ERIC Information Network

The Educational Resources Information Center (ERIC) system, established by the United States Office of Education, is a widely used network providing access to information and research in education. Selected clearinghouses and their addresses are shown in Figure 10.6.

Copying Printed Materials

You must be familiar with the laws about the use of copyrighted materials, printed and nonprinted, including those obtained from sources on the Internet. Although space here prohibits full inclusion of United States legal guidelines, your local school district should be able to provide a copy of current district policies for compliance with copyright laws. If not, when using printed materials, adhere to the guidelines shown in Figure 10.7.

When preparing to make a copy, you must find out whether the copying is permitted by law under the category of permitted use. If copying is not allowed

---

3. Such as *Netscape Navigator* or *Microsoft Explorer.*
4. See, for example, R. J. Ryder and T. Hughes, p. 389, Figure 10.8.

- *Assessment and Evaluation.* The Catholic University of America, 210 O'Boyle Hall, Washington, DC 20064-4035. <http://ericae2.educ.cua.edu>
- *Counseling and Student Services.* School of Education, 201 Ferguson Building, University of North Carolina at Greensboro, Greensboro, NC 27412-5001. <http://www.unicg.edu/~ericcas2>
- *Elementary and Early Childhood Education.* University of Illinois at Urbana-Champaign, Children's Research Center, 51 Gerty Drive, Champaign, IL 61820-7469. <http://ericps.crc.uiuc.edu/ericecee.html>
- *Handicapped and Gifted Children.* Council for Exceptional Children, 1920 Association Drive, Reston, VA 22191-1589. <http://www.cec.sped.org/ericed.htm>
- *Information and Technology.* Center for Science and Technology, Syracuse University, Syracuse, NY 13244-4100. <http://eric.r.syr.edu/ithame>
- *Languages and Linguistics.* Center for Applied Linguistics, 1118 22nd Street, NW, Washington, DC 20037-1214. <http://www.cal.org/ericcll>
- *Reading, English, and Communication Skills.* Indiana University, 2805 East 10th Street, Smith Research Center, Suite 150, Bloomington, IN 47408-2698. <http://www.indiana.edu/~eric_rec>
- *Rural Education and Small Schools.* Appalachia Educational Laboratory, 1031 Quarrier Street, PO Box 1348, Charleston, WV 25325-1348. <http://aelvira.ael.org/erichp.htm>
- *Science, Mathematics, and Environmental Education.* Ohio State University, 1929 Kenny Road, Columbus, OH 43210-1080. <http://www.ericse.org.>
- *Service Learning.* University of Minnesota, College of Education and Human Development, 1954 Bufford Ave., VoTech Building, St. Paul, MN 55108. <http://www.nicsl.coled.um.educ>
- *Social Studies/Social Science Education.* Indiana University, Social Studies Development Center, 2805 East 10th St., Bloomington, IN 47408-2698. <http://www.indiana.edu/~ssac/eric_chess.html>
- *Urban Education.* Teachers College, Columbia University, Institute for Urban and Minority Education, Main Hall, Rm. 303, Box 40, New York, NY 10027-6696. <http://eric_web.tc.columbia.edu>

Figure 10.6
Selected ERIC addresses.

Permitted Uses—You May Make

1. Single copies of
   - A chapter of a book.
   - An article from a periodical, magazine, or newspaper.
   - A short story, short essay, or short poem whether or not from a collected work.
   - A chart, graph, diagram, drawing, or cartoon.
   - An illustration from a book, magazine, or newspaper.
2. Multiple copies for classroom use (not to exceed one copy per student in a course) of
   - A complete poem if less than 250 words.
   - An excerpt from a longer poem, but not to exceed 250 words.
   - A complete article, story, or essay of less than 2,500 words.
   - An excerpt from a larger printed work not to exceed 10 percent of the whole or 1,000 words.
   - One chart, graph, diagram, cartoon, or picture per book or magazine issue.

***Prohibited Uses—You May* Not**

1. Copy more than one work or two excerpts form a single author during one class term (semester or year).
2. Copy more than three works from a collective work or periodical volume during one class term.
3. Reproduce more than nine sets of multiple copies for distribution to students in one class term.
4. Copy to create, replace, or substitute for anthologies or collective works.
5. Copy "consumable" works, (e.g., workbooks, standardized tests, or answer sheets).
6. Copy the same work year after year.

Figure 10.7
Guidelines for copying printed materials that are copyrighted. (From section 107 of the 1976 Federal Omnibus Copyright Revision Act.)

under permitted use, then you must get written permission to reproduce the material from the holder of the copyright. If the address of the source is not given on the material, addresses may be obtained from various references, such as *Literary Market Place, Audio-Visual Market Place,* and *Ulrich's International Periodical's Directory.*

VISUAL DISPLAYS

Visual display materials include the classroom writing board, bulletin boards, charts, graphs, flip charts, magnetic boards, realia (real objects), pictures, and posters. As a new or visiting member of a faculty, you must as one of your first tasks find out what visual display materials are available for your use and where they are kept. The following subsections cover guidelines for their use.

The Writing Board

Can you imagine a classroom without a writing board? They used to be, and in some schools still are, slate blackboards. In today's classroom, however, the writing board is more likely to be either a painted plywood board (chalkboard); a magnetic chalkboard (plywood with a magnetic backing); or a white or colored (light green and light blue are common) **multipurpose board** on which you write with special marking pens. In addition to providing a surface upon which you can write and draw, the multipurpose board can be used as a projection screen and as a surface to which figures cut from colored transparency film will stick. It may also have a magnetic backing.

Extending the purposes of the multipurpose board and correlated with modern technology is an *electronic whiteboard.* It can transfer information that is written on it to a connected computer monitor, which in turn can save the material as a computer file. The electronic whiteboard uses dry-erase markers and special erasers that have optically encoded sleeves that enable the device to track their position on the board. The data are then converted into a display for the computer monitor and may then be printed, cut and pasted into other applications, sent as an e-mail or fax message, or networked to other sites.[5]

Each day, each class, and even each new idea should begin with a clean board, except for announcements that have been placed there by you or another teacher. At the end of each class, it is simple professional courtesy to clean the board, especially if another teacher follows you in that room.

Use colored chalk or marking pens to highlight your "board talk." This is especially helpful for students with learning difficulties. Beginning at the top left of the board, print or write neatly and clearly, with the writing intentionally positioned to indicate content relationships (e.g., "causal, oppositional, numerical, comparative, categorical, and so on").[6]

Use the writing board to acknowledge acceptance of and to record student contributions. Print instructions for an activity on the board, in addition to giving them orally. At the top of the board frame, you may find clips for hanging posters, maps, and charts.

Learn to use the board without having to turn your back entirely on students and without blocking their view of the board. When you have a lot of material to put on the board, do it before class and then cover it or, better yet, put the material on transparencies and use the overhead projector rather than the board, or use both. Be careful not to write too much information. When using the writing board to complement your lesson and teacher talk, write only key words and simple diagrams, thereby making it possible for the student's right brain hemisphere to process what is seen, while the left hemisphere processes the elaboration provided by your words.[7]

The Classroom Bulletin Board

Bulletin boards are found in nearly every classroom, and although sometimes poorly used or not used at all, they can be relatively inexpensively transformed into attractive and valuable instructional tools. Among other uses, the bulletin board is an excellent place to post reminders, assignments, and schedules and to celebrate and display model student work and anchor papers.

To plan, design, and prepare bulletin board displays, some teachers use student assistants or committees, giving those students responsibility for planning, preparing, and maintaining bulletin board displays. When preparing a bulletin board display, keep these guidelines in mind: the display should be simple, emphasizing one main idea, concept, topic, or theme, and captions should be short and concise; illustrations can accent learning topics; verbs can vitalize the captions; phrases can punctuate a student's thoughts; and alliteration can announce anything you wish on the board. Finally, remember to ensure that the board display reflects gender and ethnic equity.

---

5. Sources of electronic whiteboards include MicroTouch, Tewksbury, MA (800-642-7686); Numonics, Montgomeryville, PA (215-362-2766); Smart Technologies, Calgary, AB, Canada (403-245-0333); SoftBoard, Portland, OR (888-763-8262); and TEGRITY, San Jose, CA (408-369-5150).

6. M. Hunter, *Enhancing Teaching* (Upper Saddle River, NJ: Prentice Hall, 1994), p. 135.

7. Hunter, p. 133.

Airport	Highway patrol station
Apiary	Historical sites and monuments
Aquarium	Industrial plant
Archeological site	Legislature session
Art gallery	Levee and water reservoir
Assembly plant	Library and archive
Bakery	Mass transit authority
Bird and wildlife sanctuary	Military installation
Book publisher	Mine
Bookstore	Museum
Broadcasting and TV station	Native American Indian reservation
Building being razed	Newspaper plant
Building under construction	Observatory
Canal lock	Oil refinery
Cemetery	Park
Chemical plant	Poetry reading
City or county planning commission	Police station
Courthouse	Post office and package delivery company
Dairy	Recycling center
Dam and floodplain	Retail store
Dock and harbor	Sanitation department
Factory	Sawmill or lumber company
Farm	Shopping mall
Fire department	Shoreline (stream, lake, wetland, ocean)
Fish hatchery	Telecommunications center
Flea market	Town meeting
Foreign embassy	Universities and colleges
Forest and forest preserve	Utility company
Freeway under construction	Warehouse
Gas company	Water reservoir and treatment plant
Geological site	Weather bureau and storm center
Health department and hospital	Wildlife park and preserve
Highway construction site	Zoo

Figure 10.8
Community resources for speakers and field trips.

THE COMMUNITY AS A RESOURCE

One of the richest resources for learning is the local community and the people and places in it. You will want to build your own file of community resources—speakers, sources for free materials, and field trip locations. Your school may already have a community resource file available for your use. However, it may need updating. A community resource file (see Figure 10.8) should contain information about (1) possible field trip locations, (2) community resource people who could serve as guest speakers or mentors, and (3) local agencies that can provide information and instructional materials. There are many ways of utilizing community resources, and quite a variety have been demonstrated by the schools specifically mentioned throughout this resource guide. We limit the discussion here to the use of guest speakers and the out-of-classroom excursion commonly called the field trip.

Guest Speaker

Bringing outside speakers into your classroom can be for students a valuable educational experience, but not automatically so. In essence, guest speakers are on a spectrum of four types, two of which should be avoided. (1) Ideally, a speaker is both informative and inspiring. (2) A speaker might be inspiring but with nothing substantive to offer and, except for the diversion he might offer from the usual rigors of classroom work, makes the experience a waste of valuable instructional time. (3) A speaker might be informative but boring to students. (4) At the worst end of this spectrum is the guest speaker who is both boring and uninformative. So, as for any other instructional experience, the bottom line is to make the experience most effective takes careful planning on your part. To make the experience most beneficial for student learning, consider the following guidelines:

- If at all possible, meet and talk with the guest speaker in advance to inform the speaker about your students and your expectations for the presentation and to gauge how motivational and informative the speaker might be. If you believe the speaker might be informative but boring, then perhaps you can help structure the presentation in some way to make it a bit more inspiring. For example, stop the speaker every few minutes and involve the students in questioning and discussions of points made.
- Prepare your students with key points of information that you expect students to obtain.
- Prepare students with questions to ask the speaker, things the students want to find out, and information you want them to inquire about.
- Follow up the presentation with a thank you letter to the guest speaker, and perhaps further questions that developed into class discussions subsequent to the speaker's presentation.

Field Trip

To prepare for and implement a successful field trip, there are three important stages of planning—before, during, and after—and critical decisions to be made about each stage. Consider the following guidelines.

BEFORE THE FIELD TRIP. Today's schools often have very limited funds for the transportation and liability costs for field trips. In some cases, schools have no field trip funds at all. At times, parent-teacher groups and civic organizations help by providing financial resources so that students get the valuable first-hand experiences that field trips so often can offer. When planning a field trip, adhere to the steps as presented in the following paragraphs.

When the field trip is your idea (and not the students), discuss the idea with your principal, teaching team, or department or division chair, especially when transportation will be needed. Do this *before* mentioning the idea to your students. There is no cause served by getting students excited about a trip before you know if it is feasible.

Once you have obtained the necessary but tentative approval from school officials, take the trip yourself, if possible. A previsit allows you to determine how to make the field trip most productive and what arrangements will be necessary. For this previsit you might want to consider taking a couple of your students

along for their ideas and help. If a previsit is not possible, you still will need to arrange for travel directions, arrival and departure times, parking, briefing by the host, if there is one, storage of students' personal items, such as coats and lunches, provisions for eating and rest rooms, and fees, if any.

If there are fees, you need to talk with your administration about who will pay them. If the trip is worth taking, the school should cover the costs. If that is not possible, perhaps financial assistance can be obtained from some other source, such as the parent-teacher organization or the special parent club that supports your department in particular. If this does not work, you might consider an alternative that does not involve costs. No student should ever be left out of a field trip because of the student's lack of money or because of the student's race, religion, or ethnicity.

Arrange for official permission from the school administration. This probably requires a form for requesting, planning, and reporting field trips.

After permission has been obtained, you can discuss the field trip with your students and arrange for permissions from their parents or guardians. You need to realize that although parents or guardians sign official permission forms allowing their children to participate in the trip, these only show that the parents or guardians are aware of what will take place and give their permission for that. Although the permission form should include a statement that the parent or guardian absolves the teacher and the school from liability should an accident occur, it *does not* lessen the teacher's and the school's responsibilities should there be negligence by a teacher, driver, or chaperone.

Arrange for students to be excused from their other classes while on the field trip. Using an information form prepared and signed by you and perhaps by the principal, the students should then assume responsibility for notifying their other teachers of the planned absence from classes and assure them that they will make up whatever work is missed. In addition, you will need to make arrangements for your own teaching duties to be covered. In some schools, teachers cooperate by taking over the classes of those who will be gone. In other schools, substitute teachers are hired. Occasionally, teachers have to hire their own substitutes.

Arrange for whatever transportation is needed. Your principal, or the principal's designee, will help you with the details. In many schools, this detail is done by someone else. In any case, the use of private automobiles is ill advised, because you and the school could be liable for the acts of the drivers.

Arrange for the collection of money that is needed for fees. If there are out-of-pocket costs to be paid by students, this information needs to be included on the permission form. As said earlier, no students should ever be left out of the field trip because of a lack of money. This can be a tricky issue, because there may be some students who would rather steal the money for a field trip than say they don't have it. Try to anticipate problems; hopefully the school or some organization can pay for the trip so that student fees need not be collected and therefore potential problems of this sort are avoided.

Plan details for student safety and the monitoring of their safety from departure to return. Included should be a first-aid kit and a system of student control, such as a "buddy system," whereby students must remain paired throughout the trip. The pairs sometimes are given numbers that are recorded and kept by the teacher and the chaperones and then checked at departure time, periodically during the trip, at the time of return, and again upon return.

Use adult chaperones. As a very general rule, there should be one adult chaperone for every ten students. Some districts have a policy regarding this.

Plan the complete route and schedule, including stops along the way. If transportation is being provided, you will need to discuss the plans with the provider.

Establish and discuss rules of behavior with your students to the extent you believe necessary. Included in this might be details of the trip, its purpose, directions, what they should wear and bring, academic expectations of them (consider, for example, giving each student a study guide), and follow-up activities. Also included should be information about what to do if anything should go awry, for example, if a student is late for the departure or return, loses a personal possession along the way, gets lost, is injured, becomes sick, or misbehaves. For the last case, *never* send a misbehaving student back to school alone. While on a field trip, all students should be under the direct supervision of an adult at all times. Involve the adult chaperones in the previsit discussion. All this information should also be included on the parental permission form.

If a field trip is supposed to promote some kind of learning, as is probably the case, then to avoid leaving the learning to happen by chance, the learning expectations need to be clearly defined and the students given an explanation of how and where they may encounter the learning experience. Before the field trip, students should be pretested with, "What do we know about _____ ? What do we want to find out about _____ ? How can we find out?" An appropriate guide can then be prepared for the students to use during the field trip.

Plan the follow-up activities. As with any other lesson plan, the field trip lesson is complete only when there is both a proper introduction and a well-planned closure.

DURING THE FIELD TRIP. If your field trip has been carefully planned according to the preceding guidelines, then it should be a valuable and safe experience for all. While at the trip location, you and your adult chaperones should monitor student behavior and learning just as you do in the classroom. While on the trip, your students may take notes and follow the prepared study guide. You may want to take recorders and cameras so that the experience can be relived and shared in class upon return.

AFTER THE FIELD TRIP. All sorts of follow-up activities can be planned as an educational wrap-up to this valuable and exciting first-hand experience. For example, a bulletin board committee can plan and prepare an attractive display summarizing the trip. Students can write about their experiences, in their journals or as papers. Small groups can give oral reports to the class about what they did and learned. Their reports can then serve as springboards for further class discussion. Finally, for future planning, all who were involved should contribute to an assessment of the experience.

AUDIOVISUAL MEDIA TOOLS

We now direct your attention to teaching tools that depend upon electricity to project light and sound and to focus images on screens. Included are projectors of various sorts, computers, CD-ROMs, sound recorders, video recorders, and laser videodisc players. The aim here is *not* to provide instruction on how to operate modern equipment but to help you develop a philosophy for using it and to provide strategies for using these instructional tools in your teaching. Consequently, to conserve space in this book, we devote no attention to traditional audiovisual equipment, such as 16-mm film, opaque, and slide projectors. There are staff members on any school faculty who gladly will assist you in locating and using those tools.

These instructional tools are aids to your teaching. It is important to remember that their role is to aid student learning, not to teach for you. You must still select the objectives, orchestrate the instructional plan, assess the results, and follow up the lessons, just as you have learned to do for various other instructional strategies. If you use media tools prudently, your teaching and students' learning will benefit.

General Guidelines for Using Audiovisual Media Tools

Like any other boon to progress, audiovisual media tools must be worked with if they are to yield what is expected. The mediocre teacher who is content to get by without expending additional effort will in all likelihood remain just that, a mediocre teacher, despite the excellent quality of whatever tools she chances to use. Because the mediocre teacher fails to rise to the occasion and hence presents poorly, that teacher's lesson is less effective and less impressive that it could have been. The effective teacher inquires about available tools and expends the effort needed to implement them well for the benefit of the students. The effective teacher capitalizes on the drama made possible by the shift in interaction strategy and enhances the quest for knowledge by using vivid material. Such teaching involves four steps—selecting the proper audiovisual material, preparing for using the material, guiding the activity, and following up the activity.

Selecting the Proper Audiovisual Tools

Care must be exercised in the selection of an audiovisual tool for use in the classroom. Selecting inappropriate material can turn an excellent lesson plan into a disappointing fiasco. An audiovisual aid that projects garbled sound, outdated pictures, or obscure or shaky images will not be met with delighted response from the students. Material that is too difficult or boring, takes too long to set up, or is not suitable for students at a particular school age or maturity will dampen the enthusiasm of students.

In your selection of audiovisual materials, you should follow an inquiry routine similar to this: (1) Is the contemplated material appropriate? Will it help to achieve the objective of the intended lesson? Will it present an accurate understanding of the facts in the case? Will it highlight the important points? Will it work with the equipment available at the school? (2) Is the material within the level of understanding of the students? Is it too mature? Too embarrassing? Too dated? (3) Is the material lucid in its presentation? Is it clear in its images and sounds? (4) Is the material readily available? Will it be available when needed?

You can best answer most of these questions after carefully previewing the material. Sometimes this dry run is not possible. However, the best way to discover how inadequate the catalog descriptions are of films, filmstrips, videotapes, videodiscs, computer software, and compact discs—or the condition in which the products have been left by previous users—is to try them out yourself under practice conditions.

Preparing for Using the Material

To use audiovisual material with maximum effectiveness will usually require preparation of two types: psychological and physical. From the psychological standpoint, students have to be prepared for the utilization of the material and coached on how best to profit from its presentation. You will need to set the scene, make clear the purpose of the activity, suggest points to look for, present problems to solve, and, in general, clue your students in about potential dangers that may mislead them.

From the physical standpoint, preparation pertaining to the machine to be used, the equipment involved, and the arrangement of the classroom furniture will have to be attended to. Sometimes, as with the use of the writing board, the preparation is minimal. Other than making sure you have enough chalk and erasers, all that may be necessary may be to identify the aid and briefly explain the use you intend to make of it. At other times, however, as when the morning or afternoon sun affects classroom visibility, you will need to check the classroom as well as the focusing dials of the apparatus for appropriate sharpness of images and the amplitude dials for clarity of sound. In the absence of preparation, bedlam can ensue. The missing chalk, the borrowing and lending of board erasers among the students, or the absence of an extension cord can spell defeat for even the best audiovisual material. Double-checking of action-readiness of the equipment to be used is vital to success.

Guiding the Activity

The purpose of using audiovisual media is not to replace instruction but to make learning more effective. Therefore, you cannot always expect the tool to do all the work. You should, however, make it work for your purposes. Ways to do this are to highlight in advance those things that you want remembered most completely; enumerate the concepts that are developed or illustrate relationships or conclusions that you wish the students to draw; prepare and distribute a study guide or a list of questions for students to respond to; and stop the presentation periodically for hints or questions, or maybe even repeat the entire performance to ensure a more thorough grasp of particulars. You can enhance student learning by providing coached guidance before, during, and after viewing or using the materials.

Following Up the Activity

Audiovisual presentations that have no follow-up after completion squander valuable learning opportunities. Some activity and/or discussion should ensue that is pointed and directed toward closure. Scheduling the time for such postmortems should be a vital part of your preactive planning and preparation. After the presentation, students should be permitted and indeed expected to respond to the questions proposed in the preview activity. Points that were fuzzily made should be clarified. Questions that were not answered should be pursued in depth. Deeper responses that go beyond the present scope of the inquiry should be noted and earmarked for further probing at some later date. Quizzes, reviews, practice, and discussions all can be used to tie loose ends together, to highlight the major concepts, and to connect and clinch the essential learnings. The planned, efficient use of the aid helps create the atmosphere that audiovisual presentations are learning opportunities rather than recreational time-outs.

WHEN EQUIPMENT MALFUNCTIONS

When you are using audiovisual equipment, it is nearly always best to set up the equipment and have it ready to go before students arrive. That helps avoid problems in classroom management that can occur when there is a delay because the equipment is not ready. After all, if you were a surgeon ready to begin an operation and your tools and equipment weren't ready, your patient's life would likely be placed in extra danger. Like any other professional, a competent teacher is ready when work is to begin.

Of course, delays may be unavoidable when equipment breaks down or a videotape breaks. Remember Murphy's Law, which says if anything can go wrong it will. It is particularly relevant when using equipment discussed in this section. The professional teacher is prepared for such emergencies. Effectively planning for and responding to this eventuality is a part of your system of movement management and takes place during the preactive stage of your planning. That preparation includes consideration of the following.

When equipment malfunctions, three principles should be kept in mind: (1) you want to avoid dead time in the classroom; (2) you want to avoid causing permanent damage to the equipment; (3) you want to avoid losing content continuity of a lesson. So, what do you do when equipment breaks down? The answer is: Be prepared for the eventuality.

If a projector bulb goes out, quickly insert another. That means that you should have an extra bulb on hand. If a tape breaks, you can do a quick temporary splice with cellophane tape. That means that tape should be readily available. If you must do a temporary splice, do it on the film or videotape that has already run through the machine rather than on the end yet to go through, so as not to ruin the machine or the film. Then, after class or after school, be sure to notify the person in charge of the tape that a temporary splice was made so that the tape can be permanently repaired before its next use.

If a computer program freezes or aborts on the screen, your computer stops working, a fuse blows or for some other reason you lose power, or you see that there is going to be too much dead time before the equipment is working again, that is the time to go to an alternate lesson plan. You have probably heard the expression "go to Plan B." It is a useful phrase; what it means is that without missing a beat in the lesson, to accomplish the same or another instructional objective, you immediately and smoothly switch to an alternate learning activity. For you, the beginning teacher, it doesn't mean that you must plan *two* lessons for every one, but when planning a lesson that utilizes audiovisual equipment, you should plan in your lesson an alternative activity, just in case. Then, you move your students into the planned alternate activity quickly and smoothly.

PROJECTORS

Projection machines today are lighter, more energy efficient, and easier to operate than they were a few years ago; they have been almost "defanged." Among the most common and useful to the classroom teacher are the VCR, the overhead projector, the slide projector, the filmstrip projector, and, of course, the 16-mm film projector. Because limited space in this textbook does not allow presenting the operating procedures for every model and type of projector that you may come across in classrooms, this presentation is limited to the overhead projector. At any school there are teachers who will gladly answer questions you may have about a specific projector.

The Overhead Projector

The overhead projector is a versatile, effective, and reliable teaching tool. Except for the bulb burning out, not much else can go wrong with an overhead projector. There is no film to break or program to crash. Along with a bulletin board and a writing board, nearly every classroom has one.

The overhead projector transmits light through transparent objects (see Figure 10.9). A properly functioning overhead projector usually works quite well in a fully lit room. Truly portable overhead projectors are available that can be carried easily from place to place in their compact cases.

Other types of overhead projectors include rear-projection systems, which allow the teacher to stand off to the side rather than between students and the screen, and overhead video projectors, which use video cameras to send images that are projected by television monitors. Some schools use overhead video camera technology that focuses on an object, pages of a book, or a demonstration, while sending a clear image to a video monitor with a screen large enough for an entire class to clearly see.

In some respects, the overhead projector is more practical than the writing board, particularly for a beginning teacher who is nervous. Using the overhead

Figure 10.9
Overhead projector, cutaway
view.

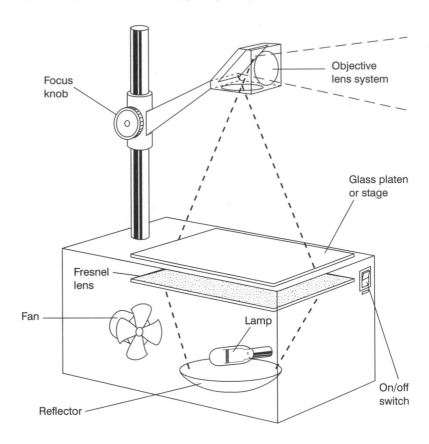

projector rather than the writing board can help avoid tension by decreasing the need to pace back and forth to the board. And while using an overhead projector, you can maintain both eye contact and physical proximity with students, both of which are important for maintaining classroom control.

Guidelines for Using the Overhead Projector

As with any projector, find the best location in your classroom for it. If there is no classroom projection screen, you can hang white paper or a sheet or use a white multipurpose board or a white or near-white wall.

Have you ever attended a presentation by someone who was not using an overhead projector properly? It can be frustrating to members of an audience when the image is too small, out of focus, partially off the screen, or partially blocked from view by the presenter. To use this teaching tool in a professional manner, turn on the projector (the switch is probably on the front), place the projector so that the projected white light covers the entire screen and hits the screen at a 90-degree angle, and focus the image to be projected. Face the students while using the projector. The fact that you do not lose eye contact with your students is a major advantage of the overhead projector, over the writing board. What you write, as you face your students, will show up perfectly (unless out of focus or off the screen). Rather than using

your finger to point to detail, or pointing to the screen (thereby turning away from your students), use a pencil. Lay the pencil directly on the transparency with the tip of the pencil pointing to the detail being emphasized. To lessen distraction, you might turn the overhead projector off when you want the students' attention to shift back to you or when changing transparencies.

To preserve the life of the projector's bulb, it is best not to move the projector until the bulb has cooled. In addition, bulbs will last longer if you avoid touching them with your fingers.

For writing on overhead transparencies, ordinary felt-tip pens are not satisfactory. Select a transparency-marking pen available at an office supply store. The ink of these pens is water soluble, so keep the palm of your hand from resting on the transparency or you will have ink smudges on your transparency and on your hand. Non-water-soluble pens—permanent markers—can be used, but the transparency must be cleaned with an alcohol solvent or a plastic eraser. (Ditto fluid works, but for safety, be sure there is proper ventilation.) When using a cleaning solvent, you can clean and dry with paper toweling or a soft rag. To highlight the writing on a transparency and to organize student learning, use pens in a variety of colors. Transparency pens tend to dry out quickly, and they are relatively expensive, so the caps must be taken on and off frequently, which

- **Adventures Co.,** 435 Main St., Johnson City, NY 13790; (800) 477-6512.
- **Boreal Laboratories, Ltd.,** 399 Vansickle Rd., St. Catharines, ON, Canada L2S 3T4; (800) 387-9393.
- **Connecticut Valley Biological Supply Co.,** 82 Valley Rd., PO Box 326, Southampton, MA 01073; (800) 628-7748.
- **Instructional Video,** PO Box 21, Maumee, OH 43537; (419) 865-7670.
- **Learning Alternatives,** 2370 W. 89A, Suite 5, Sedona, AZ 86336; (800) 426-3766.
- **Milliken Publishing Co.,** 1100 Research Blvd., PO Box 21579, St. Louis, MO 63132; (800) 325-4136.
- **Mosby,** 11830 Westline Industrial Dr., St. Louis, MO 63146; (800) 325-4177.
- **The Naidus Group,** 77 Arkay Dr., Haupopauge, NY 11788; (516) 436-7490.
- **Nasco,** 901 Janesville Ave., PO Box 901, Fort Atkinson, WI 53538-0901; (800) 550-9595.
- **National Geographic Society,** Educational Services, 1145 17th St., NW, Washington, DC 20036; (800) 368-2728.
- **National School Products,** 101 E. Broadway, Maryville, TN 37804; (800) 627-9393.
- **Planetary Arts & Sciences,** 15 Catherwood Rd., #8-130, Ithaca, NY 14850; (800) 272-1154.
- **Prentice Hall,** 1 Lake St., Upper Saddle River, NJ 07458; (800) 848-9500.
- **Schoolmasters Science,** 745 State Circle, PO Box 1941, Ann Arbor, MI 48106; (800) 521-2832.
- **Science Kit and Boreal Laboratories,** 777 E. Park Dr., Tonawanda, NY 14150; (800) 828-7777.

Figure 10.10
Selected sources of prepared overhead transparencies.

can be a nuisance when working with several colors. Practice writing on a transparency and making overlays. You can use an acetate transparency roll or single sheets of flat transparencies. Flat sheets of transparency come in different colors—clear, red, blue, yellow, and green—which can be useful in making overlays.

Some teachers in advance prepare lesson outlines on transparencies. This allows more careful preparation of the transparencies and makes them ready for reuse at another time. Some teachers use an opaque material, such as a 3 × 5 note card, to block out prewritten material and then uncover it at the moment it is being discussed. For preparation of permanent transparencies you will probably want to use permanent markers, rather than water-soluble pens that smudge easily. Heavy paper frames are available for permanent transparencies; marginal notes can be written on the frames. Personal computers with laser printers and thermal processing (copy) machines, probably located in the teacher's workroom or the school's main office, can be used to make permanent transparencies.

Other transparent objects can be shown on an overhead projector, such as transparent rulers, protractors, and Petri dishes; and even opaque objects can be used if you want simply to show a silhouette, as you might in math and art activities. Calculators, too, are available specifically for use on the overhead projector, as is a screen that fits onto the platform and is circuited to a computer so that whatever is displayed on the computer monitor is also projected onto the classroom screen.

Commercial transparencies are available from a variety of school supply houses. For sources, check the catalogs available in your school office or at the media or curriculum resource centers in your school district. See Figure 10.10 for sources.

The overhead projector can also be used for tracing transparent charts or drawings into larger drawings on paper or on the writing board. The image projected on the screen can be made smaller or larger by moving the projector closer or farther away, respectively, and then traced when you have the size you want. Also, an overhead projector (or a filmstrip projector) can be used as a light source (spotlight) to highlight demonstrations by you or students.

MULTIMEDIA PROGRAM

A multimedia program is a collection of teaching and learning materials involving more than one type of medium and organized around a single theme or topic. The types of media involved vary from rather simple kits—perhaps a videotape, a game, activity cards, student worksheets, and a manual of instructions for the teacher—to very sophisticated packages involving site-licensed computer software, student handbooks, reproducible activity worksheets, classroom wall hangings, and an on-line subscription to a telecommunications network. Some kits are designed for teacher's use, others for individual or small groups of students, and yet many more for the collaborative use of students and teachers. Teachers sometimes use multimedia programs at learning activity centers.

Many multimedia programs are available on CD-ROM and are designed principally as reference resources for students and teachers but include other aspects as well. One example is National Geographic's *Mammals: A Multimedia Encyclopedia*, which provides a lesson planning guide, facts on more than 200 animals, 700 still color photos, range

Table 10.1 Selected Multimedia Programs

Title	Source*	Phone
Age of Discovery	Society for Visual Education (M,W)	(800) 829-1900
The American Journals CD	K-12 Micromedia Publishing (M)	(800) 292-1997
Atlas of the Ancient World	Maris Multimedia (M,W)	(415) 492-2819
The Balkan Odyssey	Chelsea House Publishers (M,W)	(800) 848-2665
Battles of the World	SoftKey Multimedia (M,W)	(510) 792-2101
Chronicle of the 20th Century	DK Multimedia (M,W)	(212) 213-4800
Civilization II	Spectrum HoloByte, Inc. (W)	(510) 522-3584
Civil War II	Entrex Software (M,W)	(800) 667-0007
Culture & Technology	The Learning Team (M)	(800) 793-8326
Decisions, Decisions 5.0	Tom Snyder Productions (M,W)	(800) 342-0236
Discovering America	Lawrence Productions (M,W)	(800) 421-4157
Exploring Ancient Cities	Sumeria, Inc. (M,W)	(415) 904-0800
Go West!	Steck-Vaughn (M,W)	(800) 531-5015
Greatest Moments of Our Time	E.M.M.E. Interactive (M,W)	(800) 424-3663
History CD-ROMs	CLEARVUE/eav (M,W)	(800) 253-2788
Ideas That Changed the World	Integrated Communications & Entertainment	(416) 868-6423
IDIOM History	Chadwyck-Healey (W)	(800) 752-0515
Klondike Gold	DNA Multimedia (W)	(800) 797-3303
Multicultural CD	UXL (D,M)	(800) 877-4253
The Native Americans	Philips Media Software (M,W)	(800) 883-3767
Oregon Trail II	The Learning Co. (M,W)	(800) 227-5609
Paths to Freedom	Encyclopaedia Britannica (M)	(800) 554-9862
Robert E. Lee: Civil War General	Sierra On-Line (W)	(800) 853-7788
Social Science 2000	Decision Development Corp. (M,W)	(800) 835-4332
Time Travel to the 18th Century	Folkus Atlantic (M,W)	(800) 780-8266
Vital Links	Davidson & Associates (M,W)	(800) 545-7677
The Voyages of the Mimi	Sunburst Communications (M,W)	(800) 321-7511
Who Built America?	Voyager (M)	(800) 446-2001
World History Interactive Library	Thynx (M,W)	(609) 514-1600
World War II	FlagTower Multimedia (W)	(617) 338-8720

*Computer: D = DOS; M = Macintosh; W = Windows.

maps, animal vocalizations, full-motion movie clips, an animal classification game, glossary, and printing capability. Additional sample multimedia programs are shown in Table 10.1.

TELEVISION, VIDEOS, AND VIDEODISCS

Everyone knows that television, videos, and videodiscs represent a powerful medium. Their use as teaching aids, however, may present scheduling, curriculum, and physical problems that some school systems have not been able to handle adequately.

Television

For purposes of professional discussion, television programming can be divided into three categories: instructional television, educational television, and general commercial television. Instructional television refers to programs specifically designed as classroom instruction. Educational television refers to programs of cable television and of public broadcasting designed to educate in general but not aimed at classroom instruction. Commercial television programs include the entertainment and public service programs of the television networks and local stations.

Watch for announcements of special educational programs in professional journals. And, of course, television program listings can be obtained from your local television station or cable companies or by writing directly to network stations. Addresses for national networks are listed in Figure 10.11.

Videos and Videodiscs

Combined with a television monitor, the VCR (videocassette recorder) is one of the most popular and frequently used pieces of audiovisual equipment in today's classroom. Videotaped programs can do nearly

- **American Broadcasting Company, Inc. (ABC),** 77 West 66th Street, New York, NY 10019; (212) 456-7777.
- **American Movie Classics, Bravo (AMC, BRV), Rainbow Programming Holdings, Inc.,** 150 Crossways Pk. W, Woodbury, NY 11797, (516) 364-2222.
- **Arts & Entertainment Network (A&E),** 235 E. 45th Street, New York, NY 10017; (212) 661-4500.
- **Black Entertainment Television,** 1899 Ninth Street, NE, Washington, DC 20007; (202) 636-2400.
- **Cable News Network—WTBS, (CNN),** One CNN Center, Box 105366, Atlanta, GA 30348-5366; (404) 827-1500.
- **Cable-Satellite Public Affairs Network (C-Span),** 400 North Capitol Street, NW, Suite 650, Washington, DC 20001; (202) 737-3220.
- **Columbia Broadcasting System, Inc. (CBS-TV),** 51 West 52nd Street, New York, NY 10019; (212) 975-4321.
- **Consumer News and Business Channel (CNBC),** 2200 Fletcher Avenue, Fort Lee, NJ 07024; (201) 585-2622.
- **The Discovery Channel,** 7700 Wisconsin Ave., Bethesda, MD 20814-3522; (301) 986-0444.
- **The Disney Channel,** 3800 West Alameda Ave., Burbank, CA 91505; (818) 569-7500.
- **ESPN,** ESPN Plaza, 935 Middle Street, Bristol, CN 06010-9454; (860) 585-2000.
- **Fox Television,** 205 East 67th Street, New York, NY 10021, (212) 452-5555.
- **The Learning Channel,** 7700 Wisconsin Ave., Bethesda, MD 20815-3579; (301) 986-0444.
- **Lifetime,** 309 West 49th Street, New York, NY 10019, (212) 424-7000.
- **National Broadcasting Company (NBC),** 30 Rockefeller Plaza, New York, NY 10112; (212) 664-4444.
- **Public Broadcasting Service (PBS),** 1320 Braddock Place, Alexandria, VA 22314-1698; (703) 739-5068.
- **Turner Broadcasting (TBS),** One CNN Center, Atlanta, GA 30348-5366; (404) 827-1647.
- **United Paramount Network,** 5555 Melrose Ave., MOB 1200, Los Angeles, CA 90038; (213) 956-5000.
- **USA Network,** 1230 Avenue of the Americas, New York, NY 10020; (212) 408-9100.
- **Warner Brothers Television Network,** 4000 Warner Blvd., Bldg. 34R, Burbank, CA 91522; (818) 954-6000.

Figure 10.11
Addresses for national television networks.

everything that the former 16-mm films could do. In addition, the VCR, combined with a video camera, makes it possible to record student activities, practice, projects, and demonstrations as well as your own teaching. It gives students a marvelous opportunity to self-assess as they see and hear themselves in action.

Entire course packages, as well as supplements, are now available on videocassettes or on computer software programs. The schools where you student teach and where you eventually are employed may have a collection of such programs. Some teachers make their own.

Laser videodiscs and players for classroom use are reasonably priced, and there is a large variety of disc topics for classroom use. There are two formats of laser videodisc: freeze-frame format (CAV—Constant Angular Velocity, or Standard Play) and non-freeze-frame format (CLV—Constant Linear Velocity, or Extended Play). Both will play on all laser disc players. Laser videodisc players are quite similar to VCRs and just as easy to operate. The discs are visual archives or visual databases that contain large amounts of information that can be easily retrieved, reorganized, filed, and controlled by the user with the remote control that accompanies the player. Each side of a double-sided disc stores 54,000 separate frames of information—whether pictures, printed text, diagrams, films, or any combination of these. Visuals, both still and motion sequences, can be stored and then selected for show-

ing on a television monitor or programmed onto a computer disc for a special presentation. Several thousand videodisc titles are available for educational use. (See Table 10.2 for a few sample titles.) Your school or district media or curriculum resource center probably has many titles; for additional titles, refer to the latest annual edition of *Videodisc Compendium*.[8]

Carefully selected programs, tapes, discs, films, and slides enhance student learning. For example, laser videodiscs and CD-ROMs offer quick and efficient access to thousands of visuals, thus providing an appreciated boost to teachers of students with limited language proficiency. With the use of frame control, students can observe phenomena and detail, that previous students could only read about.

Resources for Videodisc Titles

Check school supply catalogs and www.pioneerusa. com/whatondisc.html for additional titles and sources for videodiscs. Generally, companies that sell computer software and CD-ROMs also sell videodiscs. Figure 10.12 provides addresses from which you may obtain catalogs of information.

---

8. Published and sold by Emerging Technology Consultants, Inc., 2819 Hamline Avenue North, St. Paul, MN 55113; phone (612) 639-3973, fax (612) 639-0110.

Table 10.2 Selected Videodisc Titles and Sources

Subject	Title	Source
Art	*The Louvre*	Voyager (800) 446-2001
Earth science	*Restless Earth*	National Geographic Society*
English	*Treasure Island*	Pioneer Laserdisc Corporation (800) 527-3766
Environmental science	*Global Warning: Hot Times Ahead?*	Churchill Media*
Foreign languages	*Basic French by Video*	Pioneer Laserdisc Corporation
Health	*AIDS—What Everyone Needs to Know*	Churchill Media*
History	*Time Detectives for Hire*	Rand McNally Educational Publishing (800) 678-7263
Life science	*Rain Forest*	National Geographic Society*
Physical science	*Principles of Physical Science*	Optical Data School Media (800) 201-7103
Social studies	*Visual Experiences: Social Studies*	Optical Data School Media (800) 201-7103

*See Figure 10.12 for telephone numbers.

- **A.D.A.M. Software, Inc.,** 1600 River Edge Pkwy., Ste. 800, Atlanta, GA 30328; (800) 755-2326 ext. 3018.
- **Broderbund Software,** 500 Redwood Blvd., Novato, CA 94948; (800) 474-8840.
- **Churchill Media,** 6677 N. Northwest Hwy., Chicago, IL 60631; (800) 829-1900.
- **Coronet/MTI Film & Video,** 108 Wilmot Rd., Deerfield, IL 60015; (800) 777-8100.
- **CyberEd,** PO Box 3037, Paradise, CA 95767-3037; (916) 872-2432.
- **Emerging Technology Consultants,** 2819 Hamline Ave. N, St. Paul, MN 55113; (612) 639-3973.
- **Encyclopaedia Britannica Educational Corp.,** 310 S. Michigan Ave., Chicago, IL 60604-9839; (800) 554-9862.
- **Environmental Media Corp.,** PO Box 99, Beaufort, SC 29901-0099; (800) 368-3382.
- **Glencoe,** PO Box 544, Blacklick, OH 43004-0544; (800) 848-1567.
- **GPN,** PO Box 80669, Lincoln, NE 68501-0669; (800) 228-4630.
- **Harcourt Brace School Publishers,** 6277 Sea Harbor Dr., Orlando, FL 32887; (800) 346-8648.
- **Instructional Video,** PO Box 21, Maumee, OH 43537; (419) 865-7670.
- **Intellimation,** 130 Cremona Dr., PO Box 1922, Santa Barbara, CA 93116-1922; (800) 346-8355.
- **MECC,** 6160 Summit Drive North, Minneapolis, MN 55430-4003; (800) 685-6322 ext. 529.
- **National Geographic Society,** Education Services, 1145 17th St., NW, Washington, DC 20036; (800) 368-2728.
- **National School Products,** 101 E. Broadway, Maryville, TN 37804; (800) 627-9393.
- **Optical Data School Media,** 512 Means St. NW, Atlanta, GA 30318; (800) 201-7103.
- **Optilearn, Inc.,** PO Box 997, Stevens Point, WI 54481; (800) 850-9480.
- **Sunburst Communications,** 101 Castleton Street, PO Box 100, Pleasantville, NY 10570-0100; (800) 321-7511.
- **Tangent Scientific,** 10-261 Martindale Rd., St. Catharines, ON, Canada L2E 1A2; (800) 363-2908.
- **Tom Snyder Productions, Inc.,** 80 Coolidge Hill Road, Watertown, MA 02172-2817; (800) 342-0236.
- **Videodiscovery, Inc.,** 1700 Westlake Ave. N, Suite 600, Seattle, WA 98109-3012; (800) 548-3472.
- **WeatherDisc Associates,** 4584 NE 89th, Seattle, WA 98115; (206) 524-4314.
- **Ztek Co.,** PO Box 1055, Louisville, KY 40201-1055; (800) 247-1063.

Figure 10.12
Selected resources for videodiscs, videotapes, computer software, CD-ROMs, and interactive multimedia.

COMPUTERS AND COMPUTER-BASED INSTRUCTIONAL TOOLS

As a teacher of the twenty-first century, you must be **computer literate,** that is, understand and be able to use computers as well as you can read and write. As a matter of fact, some K–12 public school districts have added computer literacy as a requirement for student matriculation as have programs for teacher certification.

The computer can be valuable to a classroom teacher in several ways. For example, the computer can help you manage the instruction by obtaining information, storing and preparing test materials, maintaining attendance and grade records, and preparing programs to aid in the academic development of individual students. This category of uses of the computer is referred to as **computer-managed instruction (CMI).** The computer can also be used for instruction by employing various instructional software programs. In their analysis of research studies, Hancock and Betts report that "in some schools, *computer-assisted instruction* (CAI) using integrated learning systems (individualized academic tutorials) has shown impressive gains, especially in the early years and among under-achieving urban populations."[9] The computer can be used to teach about computers and to help students develop their skills in computer use. And, with the help of software programs about thinking, the computer can be used to teach about thinking and to help students develop their thinking skills.

The Placement and Use of Computers in Schools

The way that you use the computer for instruction is determined by your knowledge of and skills in its use, the number of computers that you have available, where computers are placed in the school, and the software that is available. Despite tight budgets, schools continue to purchase computers and to upgrade their telecommunications capabilities.[10] Because of the tremendous expense involved in giving a school the advantage of leading-edge technology, some districts are exploring the leasing of computers and equipment rather than purchasing them outright. Leasing might protect a district from becoming stuck in a very short time with expensive but obsolete equipment.

Regarding computer placement, here are some possible scenarios and how classroom teachers work within each.

SCENARIO 1.   Many schools have one or more computer labs. A teacher may schedule time to take an entire class or send a small group of students there for computer work. For example, at Skowhegan Area Middle School (Maine), computers have been integrated into the whole curriculum. In collaboration with members of interdisciplinary teaching teams, the manager of the school's computer lab assists students in using computers as a tool to build their knowledge, to write stories with word processors, to illustrate diagrams with paint utilities, to create interactive reports with hypermedia, and to graph data they have gathered using spreadsheets.[11] In many schools with computer labs, student computers are networked to the teacher's computer in the lab so that the teacher can control and monitor the work of each student.

SCENARIO 2.   In some schools, students can take a computer course as an elective. To students in your classes who are simultaneously enrolled in the computer course, you may give special computer assignments that they can then share with the rest of the class.

SCENARIO 3.   Some classrooms have a computer connected to a large-screen video monitor. The teacher or a student works the computer, and the monitor screen can be seen by the entire class. As they view the screen, students can verbally respond to and interact with what is happening on the computer.

SCENARIO 4.   You may be fortunate to have one or more computers in your classroom, computers with CD-ROM playing capabilities, a videodisc player, an overhead projector, and an LCD (liquid crystal display) projection system. Coupled with the overhead projector, the LCD projection system allows you to project onto your large wall screen and TV monitor any image from computer software or a videodisc. With this system, all students can see and verbally interact with the multimedia instruction.[12]

SCENARIO 5.   Many classrooms have at least one computer, and some have many. When this is the case, you most likely will have one or two students working at the computer while others are doing other learning activities (an example of multilevel teaching). Computers can be an integral part of a learning activity center and an important aid in your overall effort to individualize the instruction within your classroom. Unfortunately, however, many schools have old computers, for which software is no longer made and multimedia software and computer networks are not available.

Selecting Computer Software

You and your colleagues need to choose software programs that are compatible with your brand of computer(s) and with your instructional objectives.

Programs are continually being developed and enhanced for the new and more powerful computers being made available. (Videodiscs, computer software, and CD-ROMs are usually available from the same companies, addresses of which are listed in Figure 10.12.) For evaluating computer software programs and testing them for their compatibility with your instructional objectives, many forms are available, from either the local school district, the state department of education, or professional associations. A sample form for evaluating instructional courseware is shown in Figure 10.13.

9. V. Hancock and F. Betts, "From the Lagging to the Leading Edge," *Educational Leadership* 51(7):25 (April 1994).

10. U.S. Department of Education, National Center for Education Statistics, *Advanced Telecommunications in U.S. Public Schools, K–12* (Washington, DC: Office of Educational Research and Improvement, 1995), p. 3.

11. M. Muir, "Putting Computer Projects at the Heart of the Curriculum," *Educational Leadership* 51(7):30–32 (April 1994).

12. Available from Chisholm, 910 Campisi Way, Campbell, CA 95008-2340.

Title _____   Publisher _____

Content Area _____   Hardware Required _____

Courseware Functions

_____ Drill and practice   _____ Instructional gaming   _____ Problem solving

_____ Simulation   _____ Tutorial   _____ Other _____

Many characteristics should be considered when selecting courseware for use in one's classroom or lab, but the following should be considered *essential qualities* for any instructional product on the computer. If courseware does not meet these criteria, it should not be considered for purchase. For each item, indicate *Y* for yes if it meets the criterion or *N* for no if it does not.

I. Instructional Design and Pedagogical Soundness

_____ Teaching strategy appropriate for student level and based on best-known methods.

_____ Presentation on screen contains nothing that misleads or confuses students.

_____ Readability and difficulty at an appropriate level for students who will use it.

_____ Comments to students not abusive or insulting.

_____ Graphics fulfill important purpose (motivation, information) and are not distracting to learners.

Criteria specific to drill and practice functions

_____ High degree of control over presentation rate (unless the method is timed review).

_____ Appropriate feedback for correct answers (none, if timed; not elaborate or time-consuming).

_____ Feedback more reinforcing for correct than for incorrect responses.

Criteria specific to tutorials

_____ High degree of interactivity (not just reading information).

_____ High degree of user control (forward and backward movement, branching upon request).

_____ Comprehensive teaching sequence so instruction is self-contained and stand-alone.

_____ Adequate answer-judging capabilities for student-constructed answers to questions.

Criteria specific to simulations

_____ Appropriate degree of fidelity (accurate depiction of system being modeled).

_____ Good documentation available on how program works.

Criteria specific to instructional games:

_____ Low quotient of violence or combat-type activities.

_____ Amount of physical dexterity required appropriate to students who will use it.

II. Content

_____ No grammar, spelling, or punctuation errors on screen.

_____ All content accurate and current.

_____ No racial ethnic, or gender stereotypes.

_____ Sensitive treatment of moral and/or social issues (e.g., perspectives on war or capital punishment).

III. User Flexibility

_____ User normally has some control of movement within the program (e.g., can go from screen to screen at desired rate; can read text at desired rate; can exit program when desired).

_____ Can turn off sound, if desired.

IV. Technical Soundness

_____ Program loads consistently, without error.

_____ Program does not break, no matter what the student enters.

_____ Program does what the screen says it should do.

Decision

_____ Is recommended for urchase.

_____ Is not recommended.

Figure 10.13

Minimum criteria checklist for evaluating instructional courseware. (*Source:* M. D. Roblyer, J. Edwards, and M. A. Havriluk, *Integrating Educational Technology into Teaching* [Upper Saddle River, NJ: Prentice Hall, 1997], p. 122. By permission of Prentice Hall.)

- *CD-ROM Finder,* 5th ed., J. Shelton, ed. (Medford, NJ: Learned Information, 1993).
- *CD-ROM for Librarians and Educators: A Book of Over 300 Instructional Programs,* by B. H. Sorrow and B. S. Lumpkin (Jefferson, NC: McFarland, 1993).
- *CD-ROMs in Print,* Meckler Publishing, 11 Ferry Lane West, Westport, CT 06880.
- *The Directory of Video, Computer, and Audio-Visual Products,* published annually by the International Communications Industries Association, Fairfax, VA.
- Educational Software Institute catalog, 4213 South 94th Street, Omaha, NE 68127, (800) 955-5570.

Figure 10.14
Resources for information about CD-ROM titles.

- Best freeware and shareware at <http://wwwl.zdnet.com/pccomp/1001dl/html/1001.html>.
- Professional periodicals and journals.
- *Catalog of Audiovisual Materials: A Guide to Government Sources* (ED 198 822). Arlington, VA: ERIC Documents Reproduction Service.
- *Educator's Guide to Free Audio and Video Materials; Educator's Guide to Free Films; Educator's Guide to Free Filmstrips; Guide to Free Computer Materials; Educator's Guide to Free Science Materials,* Educator's Progress Service, Inc., 214 Center Street, Randolph, WI 53956 (414) 326-3126.
- *Video Placement Worldwide (VPW).* Source of free sponsored educational videos on the Internet at

---

Figure 10.15
Resources for free and inexpensive audiovisual materials.

The CD-ROM

For computers there are three types of storage discs—the floppy disc, the hard disc, and the CD-ROM, which is an abbreviation for *c*ompact *d*isc-*r*ead *o*nly *m*emory. Use of a CD-ROM requires a computer and a CD-ROM drive. Newer computers may have built-in CD-ROM drives, while others may be connected to one. As with floppy and hard discs, CD-ROMs are used for storing characters in a digital format, whereas images on a videodisc are stored in an analog format. The CD-ROM is capable of storing some 20,000 images or the equivalent of approximately 250,000 pages of text. This capacity is the same as that of 1,520 360K floppy discs or eight 70MB hard discs. Therefore, the CD-ROM is ideal for storing large amounts of information such as dictionaries, encyclopedias, and general reference works full of graphic images that you can copy and modify.

The same material is used for both CD-ROMs and videodiscs, but the videodisc platter is 12 inches across and the CD-ROM just 4.5 inches across. Newer CD-ROMs include video segments, just like those of videodiscs. Any information stored on a CD-ROM or a videodisc can be found and retrieved within a few seconds. CD-ROMs are available from the distributors of videodiscs and ultimately will likely replace videodiscs, or both the CD-ROM and videodisc may be replaced

by even more advanced technology, such as the DVD (digital videodisc).

With superior sound and visual performance, the DVD may replace compact discs, VCR tapes, videodiscs, and computer CD-ROMs. Although it looks like the CD-ROM, the DVD can store nearly 17 gigabytes of information, provide a faster retrieval of data, and can be made interactive. Computers with DVD drives, that can still play the old CD-ROMs, are expected to be available by the time this book is published.

Information about CD-ROM titles available for education can be found in the sources listed in Figure 10.14.

Sources of Free and Inexpensive Audiovisual Materials

For free and inexpensive audiovisual materials, check your college or university library for the sources listed in Figure 10.15.

Using Copyrighted Video, Computer, and Multimedia Programs

You must be knowledgeable about the laws on the use of copyrighted videos and computer software materials. Although space here prohibits full inclusion of United States legal guidelines, your local school district

PERMITTED USES—YOU MAY

1. Request your media center or audiovisual coordinator to record a program for you if you cannot or if you lack the equipment.
2. Keep a videotaped copy of a broadcast (including cable transmission) for 45 calendar days, after which the program must be erased.
3. Use the program in class once during the first 10 school days of the 45 calendar days and a second time if instruction needs to be reinforced.
4. Have professional staff view the program several times for evaluation purposes during the full 45-day period.
5. Make a few copies to meet legitimate needs, but these copies must be erased when the original videotape is erased.
6. Use only a part of the program if instructional needs warrant (but see the next list).
7. Enter into a licensing agreement with the copyright holder to continue use of the program.

PROHIBITED USES—YOU MAY *NOT*

1. Videotape premium cable services such as HBO without expressed permission.
2. Alter the original content of the program.
3. Exclude the copyright notice on the program.
4. Videotape before a request for use is granted. The request to record must come from an instructor.
5. Keep the program, and any copies, after 45 days.

Figure 10.16
Copyright law for off-air videotaping. (*Source:* R. Heinich, M. Molenda, J. D. Russell, and S. E. Smaldino, *Instructional Media and Technologies for Learning,* 5th ed. [Upper Saddle River, NJ: Prentice Hall, 1996], p. 387. By permission of Prentice Hall.)

PERMITTED USES—YOU MAY

1. Make a single backup or archival copy of the computer program.
2. Adapt the computer program to another language if the program is unavailable in the target language.
3. Add features to make better use of the computer program.

PROHIBITED USES—YOU MAY *NOT*

1. Make multiple copies.
2. Make replacement copies from an archival or backup copy.
3. Make copies of copyrighted programs to be sold, leased, loaned, transmitted, or given away.

Figure 10.17
Copyright law for use of computer software. (*Source:* Congressional amendment to the 1976 Copyright Act, December 1980.)

undoubtedly can provide a copy of current district policies to ensure compliance with all copyright laws. As said earlier about the use of printed materials that are copyrighted, when preparing to make any copy you must find out whether the copying is permitted by law under the category of permitted use. If copying is not allowed under permitted use, then you must get written permission to reproduce the material from the holder of the copyright. Figures 10.16 and 10.17 present guidelines for the copying of videotapes and computer software.

Usually, when purchasing CD-ROMs and other multimedia software packages intended for use by schools,

you are also paying for a license to modify and use their contents for instructional purposes. However, not all CD-ROMs include copyright permission, so always check the copyright notice on any disc you purchase and use. When in doubt, don't use it until you have asked your district media specialists about copyrights or have obtained necessary permissions from the original source.

As yet, there are no guidelines for fair use of films, filmstrips, slides, and multimedia programs. A general rule of thumb for using any copyrighted material is to treat the work of others as you would want your own material treated were it protected by a copyright (see Figure 10.18).

1. For portions of copyrighted works used in your own multimedia production for teaching, follow normal copyright guidelines (e.g., the limitations on the amount of material used, whether it be motion media, text, music, illustrations, photographs, or computer software).
2. You may show your own multimedia work using copyrighted works to other teachers, such as in workshops. However, you may *not* make copies to give to colleagues without obtaining permission from copyright holders.
3. You may use your own multimedia production for instruction over an electronic network (e.g., distance learning) provided there are limits to access and to the number of students enrolled. You may *not* distribute such work over any electronic network without express permission from copyright holders.
4. You must obtain permissions from copyright holders before using any copyrighted materials in educational multimedia productions for commercial reproduction and distribution or before replicating more than one copy, before distributing copies to others, or for use beyond your own classroom.

Figure 10.18
Fair-use guidelines for using multimedia programs.

THE ON-LINE CLASSROOM

Teachers looking to make their classrooms more student-centered, collaborative, and interactive are increasingly turning to telecommunications networks.[13] Ranging in scale from local bulletin board systems to the Internet, these webs of connected computers allow teachers and students from around the world to reach each other directly and gain access to quantities of information previously unimaginable. Students using networks learn new inquiry and analytical skills in a stimulating environment, and as many people believe, they also gain an increased awareness of their role as world citizens.[14]

Now, to further your understanding of how some teachers use and procure media and materials, do Exercises 10.3 and 10.4.

---

13. See, for example, J. A. Levin and C. Thurston, "Research Summary: Electronic Networks," *Educational Leadership* 54(3):46–50 (November 1996), and other articles in that theme issue titled "Networking."

14. P. Cohen, "The Online Classroom," *Association for Supervision and Curriculum Development Update* 36(10):1, 5–6 (December 1994).

—— EXERCISE 10.3 ——

*Observation of Teacher's Use
of Audiovisual Materials*

————

Instructions: The purpose of this exercise is for you to observe the actual use of audiovisual materials in a classroom. At a school of your choice, arrange to visit one classroom for five consecutive days (Monday through Friday). Observe and record the materials that are used by the teacher, how they are used, and to what extent students are involved in their use. Share the results of this exercise with your classmates.

School and class visited: _____

Dates: _____

Materials and Equipment Used	*How Used*	*Student Involvement*
M		
T		
W		

T

_____

_____

_____

_____

_____

_____

F

_____

_____

_____

_____

_____

_____

1. Which materials were most effective and why? _____

_____

_____

_____

_____

_____

2. Which materials were least effective and why? _____

_____

_____

_____

_____

_____

3. After discussing this exercise with your classmates, describe any conclusions that you have drawn as a group or as an individual. _____

_____

_____

_____

_____

_____

EXERCISE 10.4

The Classroom Teacher and the Purchase of Materials for Teaching

Instructions: The purpose of this exercise is for you to obtain practical information about how materials and equipment for teaching are procured and the role of the classroom teacher in the process. To complete this exercise, you are to visit a school and talk with the teachers, using the following questions as a guideline. After completion of the exercise, share results with your classmates.

School and class visited: _____

Date: _____

Person(s) interviewed and their functions: _____

_____

_____

1. In your department (or school), how is it decided what specific equipment and instructional materials will be purchased for classroom use? _____

_____

_____

_____

_____

2. Is money allotted to the classroom teacher for the purchase of materials during the school year? If so, how much? How is the money obtained and spent by the teacher? _____

_____

_____

_____

_____

_____

_____

3. What else can you tell about the process of obtaining teaching materials? _____

_____

_____

_____

_____

SUMMARY

You have learned of the variety of tools available to supplement your instruction. When used wisely, these tools will help you to reach more of your students more of the time. As you know, teachers must meet the needs of a diversity of students, many of whom are linguistically and culturally different. The material selected and presented in this chapter should be of help in doing that. The future will undoubtedly continue bringing technological innovations that will be even more helpful; compact discs, computers, and telecommunications equipment have marked only the beginning of a revolution for teaching. As we enter the next millennium, new instructional delivery systems made possible by microcomputers and multimedia workstations will likely fundamentally alter what had become the traditional role of the classroom teacher during the twentieth century.

You should remain alert to developing technologies for your teaching. Laser videodiscs, digital videodiscs, CD-ROMs interfaced with computers (i.e., the use of multimedia), and telecommunications offer exciting technologies for learning. New instructional technologies are advancing at an increasingly rapid rate. You and your colleagues must maintain vigilance over new developments, constantly looking for those that not only will help make student learning meaningful and interesting, and your teaching effective, but also are cost-effective.

QUESTIONS FOR CLASS DISCUSSION

1. Explain how your effective use of the writing board can help students see relationships among verbal concepts or information.
2. Describe what you should look for when deciding whether material that you have obtained free or inexpensively is appropriate for use in your teaching.
3. Meet with a peer and tell one another how you would respond to a parent who questioned you about the benefit of using CD-ROM material in teaching. Note that researchers have found that students who read selections on interactive CD-ROMs scored higher on longer and more difficult comprehension passages on tests than their peers who read the same selections in print.[15] The researchers suggest the reason is that the CD-ROMs provide instant help for students confronting new vocabulary. Students can click on a word and hear it pronounced, defined, and used in context. Additionally, students enjoy the music, special effects, and interactive approach.
4. Share with others in your class your knowledge, observations, and feelings about the use of multimedia and telecommunications for teaching. From your discussion, what more would you like to know about the use of multimedia and telecommunications for teaching? How might you learn more about these things?
5. In 1922, Thomas Edison predicted that "the motion picture is destined to revolutionize our educational system and . . . in a few years it will supplant largely, if not entirely, the use of textbooks." In 1945, William Levenson of the Cleveland public schools' radio station claimed that "the time may come when a portable radio receiver will be as common in the classroom as is the blackboard." In the early 1960s, B. F. Skinner believed that with the help of the new teaching machines and programmed instruction, students could learn twice as much in the same time and with the same effort as in a standard classroom. Did motion pictures, radio, programmed instruction, and television revolutionize education? Will computers become as much a part of the classroom as chalkboards? What do you predict the public school classroom of the year 2050 will be like? Will the role of a teacher be different in any way from what it is today?
6. Select and identify one instructional tool that is *not* discussed in this chapter and explain to your classmates its advantages and disadvantages for use in teaching your subject.
7. Has the purchase of new textbooks and library books become stagnated as schools increase their spending on leading-edge technology? Have traditional shop classes given way to technology education programs? Have music and art programs suffered as a result of increased expenditures on technology? How are school districts finding funds necessary for the cost of technology, such as for the cost of wiring classrooms for networking and for updated computers, for the planning, installation, and maintenance of complex computer networks? Or are districts not finding the necessary funds? In this respect, are some districts worse off or better off than others? Is this an issue? Is this an issue for which every classroom teacher need be concerned?
8. Describe any prior concepts you held that changed as a result of your experiences with this chapter. Describe the changes.
9. From your current observations and fieldwork as related to this teacher preparation program, clearly identify one specific example of educational practice that seems contradictory to exemplary practice or theory as presented in this chapter. Present your explanation for the discrepancy.
10. Do you have questions generated by the content of this chapter? If you do, list them along with ways answers might be found.

SUGGESTED READINGS

Association for Supervision and Curriculum Development. *Only the Best: The Annual Guide to the Highest-Rated Educational Software and Multimedia.* Alexandria, VA: Association for Supervision and Curriculum Development, 1996.

Botterbusch, H. R. *Copyright in the Age of New Technology.* Bloomington, IN: Fastback 405, Phi Delta Kappa Educational Foundation, 1996.

Bruwelheide, J. *The Copyright Primer for Librarians and Educators.* 2nd ed. Chicago: American Library Association, 1995.

---

15. R. Olson and R. Meyer, "News: Survey Says CD-ROMs Boost Reading Scores," *School Library Journal* 41(9):108 (September 1995).

Cafolla, R., Kauffman, D., and Knee, R. H. *World Wide Web for Teachers: An Interactive Guide*. Needham Heights, MA: Allyn & Bacon, 1997.

Cooper, G. and Cooper, G. *Gopher It! An Internet Resource Guide for K–12 Educators*. Englewood, CO: Libraries Unlimited, 1997.

Cotton, E. G. *The Online Classroom: Teaching with the Internet*. 2d ed. Bloomington, IN: EDINOFO Press, 1997.

National Association of Secondary School Principals. *Breaking Ranks: Changing an American Institution*. Reston, VA: National Association of Secondary School Principals, 1996.

Olszewski, W. E., and Maury, K. " 'If It Helps the Kids': What Teachers Spend on Their Students." *Phi Delta Kappan* 78(7):570–571 (March 1997).

O'Neill, D. K., et al. "Online Mentors: Experimenting in Science Class." *Educational Leadership* 54(3):39–42 (November 1996).

Roblyer, M. D., Edwards, J., and Havriluk, M. A. *Integrating Educational Technology into Teaching*. Upper Saddle River, NJ: Prentice Hall, 1997.

Ryder, R. J., and Hughes, T. *Internet for Educators*. Upper Saddle River, NJ: Prentice Hall, 1997.

Schrum, L., and Berenfeld, B. *Teaching and Learning in the Information Age: A Guide to Educational Telecommunications*. Needham Heights, MA: Allyn & Bacon, 1997.

Tarquin, P. and Walker, S. *Creating Success in the Classroom! Visual Organizers and How to Use Them*. Englewood, CO: Teacher Ideas Press/Libraries Unlimited, 1997.

Virginia Space Grant Consortium. *The Educator's Guide to the Internet: A Handbook with Resources and Activities*. 3d ed. Palo Alto, CA: Dale Seymour Publications, 1997.

Williams, C. D. *The Internet for Newbies: An Easy Access Guide*. Englewood, CO: Libraries Unlimited, 1997.

Woody, R. H., III, and Woody, R. H., II. *Music Copyright Law in Education*. Fastback 368. Bloomington, IN: Phi Delta Kappa Educational Foundation, 1994.

Zimmerman, L. W. "Guidelines for Using Videos in the Classroom." *School Library Media Activities Monthly* 13(5):32–33 (January 1997).

PART

IV

ASSESSMENT AND CONTINUING PROFESSIONAL DEVELOPMENT

The two chapters of Part IV assist you with

- Guidelines for meeting with parents and guardians.
- Guidelines for obtaining a teaching job.
- Guidelines for remaining an alert and effective teacher.
- Knowledge about the student teaching experience.
- Means of preparing and administering instruments for assessment.

- Methods of assessing teacher performance.
- Methods of grading student achievement.
- Methods of reporting student achievement.
- Sample scoring rubrics for use in assessment.
- Self-assessment through micro peer teaching.
- Tools for assessing student achievement.

Reflective Thoughts

When assessing for student achievement, it is important to use procedures that are compatible with the instructional objectives.

Performance-based assessment procedures require students to produce rather than to select responses.

That which separates the professional teacher from "anyone off the street" is the teacher's ability to go beyond mere description of a student's behavior.

For students' continued intellectual and emotional development, your comments about their work should be useful, productive, analytical, diagnostic, and prescriptive.

You must provide opportunities for students to think about what they are learning, how they are learning it, and how far they have progressed in learning it.

Grades for student achievement should be tied to performance levels and determined on the basis of each student's achievement toward preset standards.

It is unprofessional to place a student teacher into a "sink-or-swim" situation.

Teaching is such an electrifying profession that it is not easy to remain energetic and to stay abreast of changes and trends in research and practice.

Chapter

11

Assessing and Reporting Student Achievement

While preceding parts of this resource guide addressed the *why* (Part I), *what* (Part II), and *how* (Part III) of teaching, Part IV focuses on the fourth and final component—the *how well,* or assessment, component. Together, these four components are the essentials of effective instruction.

Teaching and learning are reciprocal processes that depend on and affect one another. Thus, the assessment component deals with how well the students are learning and how well the teacher is teaching. This chapter addresses the first.

Assessment is an integral part of and an ongoing process in the educational scene. Curricula, buildings, materials, specific courses, teachers, supervisors, administrators, and equipment must all be periodically assessed in relation to student learning, the purpose of the school. When gaps between anticipated results and student achievement exist, efforts are made to eliminate those factors that seem to be limiting the educational output or to improve the situation in some other way. Thus, educational progress occurs.

To learn effectively, students need to know how they are doing. Similarly, to be an effective teacher, you must be informed about what the student knows, feels, and can do so that you can help the student build on her skills, knowledge, and attitudes. Therefore, you and your students need continuous feedback on their progress and problems in order to plan appropriate learning activities and to make adjustments to those already planned. If this feedback says that progress is slow, you can provide alternative activities; if it indicates that some or all of the students have already mastered the desired learning, you can eliminate unnecessary activities and practice for some or all

of the students. In short, assessment provides a key for both effective teaching and learning.

The importance of continuous assessment mandates that you know various principles and techniques of assessment. This chapter explains some of those and shows you how to construct and use assessment instruments and to make sense from data obtained. We define terms related to assessment, consider what makes a good assessment instrument, suggest procedures to use in the construction of assessment items, point out the advantages and disadvantages of different types of assessment items procedures, and explain the construction and use of alternative assessment devices.

Also in this chapter we discuss grading and reporting of student achievement, two responsibilities that can consume much of a teacher's valuable time. Grading is time-consuming and frustrating for many teachers. What should be graded? Should grades represent student growth, level of achievement in a group, effort, attitude, general behavior, or a combination of these? What should determine grades—homework, tests, projects, class participation and group work, or all of these? And what should be their relative weights? These are just a few of the questions that plague teachers, parents, and indeed the profession.

The development of the student encompasses growth in the cognitive, affective, and psychomotor domains. Traditional objective paper-and-pencil tests provide only a portion of the data needed to indicate student progress in those domains. Many experts today question the traditional sources of data and encourage the search for, development of, and use of alternative means to more authentically assess the students' development of thinking and higher-level learning.[1] Although many things are not yet clear, one thing that is clear is that various techniques of assessment must be used to determine how the student works, what the student is learning, and what the student can produce as a result of that learning. As a teacher, you must develop a repertoire of means of assessing learner behavior and academic progress.

Grades have been a part of school for about 100 years, yet it is clear to many experts that the conventional report card with marks or grades falls short of being a developmentally appropriate procedure for reporting the academic performance or progress of students. As a result, some schools are experimenting with other ways of reporting student achievement in learning. Still, letter grades for secondary school seem firmly entrenched. Parents, students, colleges, and employers have come to expect grades as evaluations. Some critics suggest that the emphasis in schools is on getting a high grade rather than on learning, arguing that, as traditionally measured, the two do not necessarily go hand in hand. Today's interest is more on what the student can do (performance testing) as a result of learning than merely on what the student can recall (memory testing) from the experience.

In addition, there have been complaints about subjectivity and unfair practices. As a result of these concerns, a variety of systems of assessment and reporting has evolved, is still evolving, and will likely continue to evolve throughout your professional career. When educators are aware of alternative systems, they may be able to develop assessment and reporting processes that are fair and effective for particular situations. So, after beginning with assessment, the final focus of this chapter considers today's principles and practices in grading and reporting student achievement.

Specifically, upon completion of this chapter you should be able to

1. Demonstrate an understanding of the importance of assessment in teaching and learning.
2. Explain the concept of authentic assessment.
3. Explain the value of and give an example of a performance assessment that could be used in your subject.
4. Explain why criterion-referenced grading is preferred over norm-referenced grading.
5. Explain how rubrics, checklists, portfolios, and journals are used in the assessment of student learning.

6. Differentiate between diagnostic assessment, summative assessment, and formative assessment, with examples of when and how each can be used in teaching your subject.
7. Describe the importance of parental involvement in the education of their children and the manner by which it can be achieved.

SEVEN PURPOSES OF ASSESSMENT

Assessment of achievement in student learning is designed to serve the following seven purposes:

1. *To assist in student learning.* This is the purpose usually first thought of when speaking of assessment, and it is the principal topic of this chapter. For the classroom teacher it is (or should be) the most important purpose.

2. *To identify students' strengths and weaknesses.* Identification and assessment of students' strengths and weaknesses are necessary for two purposes: to structure and restructure the learning activities and to restructure the curriculum. Concerning the first purpose, for example, data on student strengths and weaknesses in content and process skills are important in planning activities appropriate for both skill development and intellectual development. This is **diagnostic assessment** (known also as **preassessment**). For the second purpose, data on student strengths and weaknesses in content and skills are useful for making appropriate modifications to the curriculum.

3. *To assess the effectiveness of a particular instructional strategy.* It is important for you to know how well a particular strategy helped accomplish a particular goal or objective. Competent teachers continually reflect on and evaluate their strategy choices, using a number of sources: student achievement as measured by assessment instruments, their own intuition, informal feedback given by the students, and, sometimes, informal feedback given by colleagues, such as members of a teaching team or mentor teachers. (Mentor teachers are discussed in Chapter 12.)

4. *To assess and improve the effectiveness of curriculum programs.* Components of the curriculum are continually assessed by committees of teachers and administrators. The assessment is done while students are learning (i.e., formative assessment) and afterward (summative assessment).

5. *To assess and improve teaching effectiveness.* To improve student learning, teachers are periodically evaluated on the basis of (1) their commitment to working with students at a particular level, (2) their ability to cope with students at a particular age or grade level, and (3) their ability to show mastery of appropriate instructional techniques—techniques that are articulated throughout this book.

---

1. See, for example the theme issue "Reporting What Students Are Learning" in *Educational Leadership* 52(2):4–55 (October 1994), and J. Bailey and J. McTighe, "Reporting Achievement at the Secondary Level: What and How," pp. 119–140 in T. R. Guskey (ed.), *Communicating Student Learning* (Alexandria, VA: 1996 Yearbook, Association for Supervision and Curriculum Development, 1996).

6. To provide data that assist in decision making about a student's future, such as program placement and postsecondary options. Assessment of student achievement is important in guiding decision making about course and program placement, promotion, school transfer, class standing, eligibility for honors and scholarships, and career planning and in selecting postsecondary options.

7. To communicate with and involve parents and guardians in their children's learning. Parents, communities, and school boards all share in an accountability for the effectiveness of the learning of the children. Today's schools are reaching out and engaging parents, guardians, and the community in their children's education. All teachers play an important role in the process of communicating with, reaching out to, and involving parents.

EIGHT PRINCIPLES THAT GUIDE THE ASSESSMENT PROGRAM

Because the welfare and, indeed, the future of so many people depend on the outcomes of assessment, it is impossible to overemphasize its importance. For a learning endeavor to be successful, the learner must have answers to basic questions: Where am I going? Where am I now? How do I get where I am going? How will I know when I get there? Am I on the right track for getting there? These questions are integral to a good program of assessment. Of course, in the process of teaching and learning, the answers may be ever-changing, and the teacher and students continue to assess and adjust plans as appropriate and necessary.

Based on the preceding questions are the following eight principles that guide the assessment program and that are reflected in the discussions in this chapter.

1. Teachers need to know how well they are doing.
2. Students need to know how well they are doing.
3. Assessment is a reciprocal process that includes assessment of teacher performance as well as student achievement.
4. The program of assessment should aid teaching effectiveness and contribute to the intellectual and psychological growth of children.
5. Evidence and input data for knowing how well the teacher and students are doing should come from a variety of sources and types of data-collecting devices.
6. Assessment is an ongoing process. The selection and implementation of plans and activities require continuing monitoring and assessment to check on progress and to change or adopt strategies to promote desired behavior.
7. Reflection and self-assessment are important components of any successful assessment program. Reflection and self-assessment are important if students are to develop the skills necessary for them to assume increasingly greater ownership of their own learning.
8. A teacher's responsibility is to facilitate student learning and to assess student progress in that learning, and for that, the teacher is, or should be, held accountable.

TERMS USED IN ASSESSMENT: A CLARIFICATION

When discussing the assessment component of teaching and learning it is easy to be confused by the terminology. The following clarification of terms is offered to aid your reading and comprehension.

Assessment and Evaluation

Although some authors distinguish between the terms **assessment** (the process of finding out what students are learning, a relatively neutral process) and **evaluation** (making sense of what was found out, a subjective process), in this text we do not. We consider the difference too slight to matter; we consider the terms to be synonymous.

Measurement and Assessment

Measurement refers to quantifiable data about specific behaviors. Tests and the statistical procedures used to analyze the results are examples. Measurement is a descriptive and objective process; that is, it is relatively free from human value judgments.

Assessment includes objective data from measurement but also other types of information, some of which are more subjective, such as information from anecdotal records and teacher observations and ratings of student performance. In addition to the use of objective data (data from measurement), assessment includes arriving at value judgments made on the basis of subjective information.

An example of the use of these terms is as follows. A teacher may share the information that Penny Brown received a score in the 90th percentile on the eighth-grade state-wide achievement test in reading (a statement of measurement) but may add that "according to my assessment of her work in my language arts class, she has not been an outstanding student" (a statement of assessment).

Validity and Reliability

The degree to which a measuring instrument actually measures that which it is intended to measure is the instrument's **validity**. For example, when we ask if an instrument (such as a performance assessment instrument) has validity, key questions concerning that instrument are: Does the instrument adequately sample the intended content? Does it measure the cognitive, affective, and psychomotor knowledge and skills that are important to the unit of content being tested? Does it sample all the instructional objectives of that unit?

The accuracy with which a technique consistently measures that which it does measure is its **reliability**. If, for example, you know that you weigh 114 pounds, and a scale consistently records 114 pounds when you stand on it, then that scale has reliability. However, if the same scale consistently records 100 pounds when you stand on it, we can still say the scale has reliability. By this example, then, it should be clear to you that an instrument could be reliable (it produces similar results when used again and again) although not necessarily valid. In this second instance, the scale is not measuring what it is supposed to measure, so although it is reliable, it is not valid. Although a technique might be reliable but not valid, a technique must have reliability before it can have validity. The greater the number of test items or situations on a particular content objective, the higher the reliability. The higher the reliability, the more consistency there will be in students' scores measuring their understanding of that particular objective.

Authentic Assessment: Advantages and Disadvantages

When assessing for student achievement, it is important that you use procedures that are compatible with the instructional objectives. This is referred to as authentic assessment. Other terms used for *authentic* assessment are *accurate, active, aligned, alternative,* and *direct*. Although *performance* assessment is sometimes used, performance assessment refers to the type of student response being assessed, whereas authentic assessment refers to the assessment situation. Although not all performance assessments are authentic, assessments that are authentic are most assuredly performance assessments.

In English/language arts, for example, although it may seem fairly easy to develop a criterion-referenced test, administer it, and grade it, tests often measure language *skills* rather than language use. It is extremely difficult to measure students' communicative competence with a test. Tests do not measure listening and talking very well, and a test on punctuation marks, for example, does not indicate students' ability to use punctuation marks correctly in their own writing. Instead, tests typically evaluate students' ability to add punctuation marks to a set of sentences created by someone else or to proofread and spot punctuation

errors in someone else's writing. An alternative and far better approach is to examine how students use punctuation marks in their own writing.[2] An authentic assessment of punctuation, then, would be an assessment of a performance item that involves students in writing and punctuating their own writing. For the authentic assessment of the student's understanding of that which the student has been learning, you would use a performance-based assessment procedure, that is, a procedure that requires students to produce rather than to select a response.

In another example, "if students have been actively involved in classifying objects using multiple characteristics, it sends them a confusing message if they are then required to take a paper-and-pencil test that asks them to 'define classification' or recite a memorized list of characteristics of good classifications schemes."[3] An authentic assessment technique would be a performance item that actually involves the students in classifying objects. In other words, to obtain an accurate assessment of a student's learning, the teacher uses a performance-based assessment procedure.

Advantages claimed for the use of authentic assessment include (1) the direct (also known as performance-based, criterion-referenced, outcome-based) measurement of what students should know and can do and (2) an emphasis on higher order thinking. On the other hand, disadvantages of authentic assessment include a higher cost, difficulty in making results consistent and usable, and problems with validity, reliability, and comparability.

Unfortunately, for the teacher who may never see a student again after a given school semester or year is over, the effects that teacher has had on a student's values and attitudes may never be observed by that teacher at all. In schools where groups or teams of teachers remain with the same cohort of students—as in the house concept programs and looping or banding—those teachers often do have an opportunity to observe the positive changes in their students' values and attitudes.[4]

Assessing Student Achievement: Diagnostic, Formative, and Summative

Assessing a student's achievement is a three-stage process. These three stages are (1) **diagnostic assessment** (sometimes called preassessment), the assessment

---

2. G. E. Tompkins and K. Hoskisson, *Language Arts: Content and Teaching Strategies* (Upper Saddle River, NJ: Prentice Hall, 1991), p. 63.
3. S. J. Rakow, "Assessment: A Driving Force," *Science Scope* 15(6):3 (March 1992).
4. See, for example, E. A. Wynne and H. J. Walberg, "Persisting Groups: An Overlooked Force for Learning," *Phi Delta Kappan* 75(7):527–528, 530 (March 1994).

of the student's knowledge and skills *before* the new instruction; (2) **formative assessment,** the assessment of learning *during* the instruction; and (3) **summative assessment,** the assessment of learning *after* the instruction, ultimately represented by the student's final term, semester, or year's achievement grade.

Grades shown on unit tests, progress reports, deficiency notices, and end-of-term reporting are examples of formative evaluation reports. However, an end-of-chapter test or a unit test is summative when the test represents the absolute end of the student's learning of material for that instructional unit.

ASSESSING STUDENT LEARNING: THREE AVENUES

The three general avenues for assessing a student's achievement in learning are: (1) assess what the student *says*—for example, the quantity and quality of a student's contributions to class discussions; (2) assess what the student *does*—for example, a student's performance (e.g., the amount and quality of a student's participation in the learning activities); and, (3) assess what the student *writes*—for example, as shown by items in the student's portfolio (e.g., homework assignments, checklists, project work, and written tests).

Importance and Weight of Each Avenue

Although your own situation and personal philosophy will dictate the levels of importance and weight you give to each avenue of assessment, you should have a strong rationale if you value and weigh the three avenues for assessment differently than each having equal values.

Assessing What a Student Says and Does

When evaluating what a student says, you should listen to the student's oral reports, questions, responses, and interactions with others and observe the student's attentiveness, involvement in class activities, creativeness, and responses to challenges. Notice that we say you should *listen* and *observe.* While listening to what the student is saying, you should also be observing the student's nonverbal behaviors. For this you can use checklists and rating scales, behavioral-growth record forms, observations with scoring rubrics of the student's performance in learning activities (see sample checklists in Figures 11.3, 11.4 and 11.7 and the sample scoring rubrics in Figures 11.2, 11.8, and 11.9), and periodic conferences with the student.[5] Figure 11.1 illustrates a sample generic form for recording and evaluating teacher observations of a student's verbal and nonverbal behaviors. With modern technology, such as is afforded, for example, by the software program *Learner Profile* and the *Apple Newton,* a teacher can record observations electronically anywhere at any time.[6]

With each technique used, you must proceed from your awareness of anticipated learning outcomes (the instructional objectives), and you must assess a student's progress toward meeting those objectives. That is referred to as **criterion-referenced assessment.**

GUIDELINES FOR ASSESSING WHAT A STUDENT SAYS AND DOES.   Guidelines and steps to follow when assessing a student's verbal and nonverbal behaviors in the classroom are to

- Maintain an anecdotal record book or folder, with a separate section for your records of each student.
- List the desirable behaviors for a specific activity.
- Check the list against the specific instructional objectives.
- Record your observations as quickly as possible following your observation. Audio or video recordings and, of course, computer software programs can help you maintain records and check the accuracy of your memory, but if this is inconvenient, you should spend time during school, immediately after school, or later that evening recording your observations while they are still fresh in your memory.
- Record your professional judgment about the student's progress toward the desired behavior, but think it through before transferring it to a permanent record.
- Write comments that are reminders to yourself, such as "Check validity of observation by further testing," "Discuss observations with student's parent or guardian," "Discuss observations with student," "Discuss observations with school counselor," "Discuss observations with student's mentor" (e.g., an adult representative from the community), and "Discuss observations with other teachers on the teaching team."

Assessing What a Student Writes

When assessing what a student writes, you can use worksheets, written homework and papers, student journal writing, student writing projects, student portfolios, and tests (all discussed later in this chapter). In many schools, portfolios, worksheets, and homework assignments are the tools usually used for the formative evaluation of each student's achievement. Tests, too, should be a part of this evaluation, but tests are also used for summative evaluation at the end of a unit and for diagnostic purposes.

---

5. See also H. Goodrich, "Understanding Rubrics," *Educational Leadership* 54(4):14–17 (December 1996/January 1997).

6. For information, contact Sunburst, 101 Castleton Street, PO Box 100, Pleasantville, NY 10570-0100. Phone (800) 321-7511.

Student _____	Course _____	School _____
Observer _____	Date _____	Period _____
Objective	Desired Behavior	What Student Did, Said, or Wrote

Teacher's (observer's) comments:

Figure 11.1
Sample of a form for evaluating and recording student verbal and nonverbal behaviors.

Your summative evaluation of a student's achievement and any other final judgment made by you about a student can have an impact upon the emotional and intellectual development of that student. Special attention is given to this later in the section Recording Teacher Observations and Judgments.

GUIDELINES FOR ASSESSING STUDENT WRITING. When assessing what a student writes, use the following guidelines.

• Student writing assignments and test items should correlate with and be compatible with specific instructional objectives (i.e., they should be criterion-referenced). Regardless of the avenue chosen, and their relative weights given by you, you must evaluate against the instructional objectives. Any given objective may be checked by using more than one method and by using more than one instrument. Subjectivity, inherent in the assessment process, may be reduced as you check for validity, comparing results of one measuring strategy against those of another.

• Read nearly everything a student writes (except, of course, for personal writing in a student's journal—see subsequent items). If it is important for the student to do the work, then it is equally important that you give your professional attention to the product of the student's efforts. (See also How to Avoid Having So Many Papers to Grade in Chapter 8.)

• Provide written or verbal comments about the student's work, and be positive in those comments. Rather than just writing "good" on a student's paper, briefly state what it was about it that made it good. Rather than simply saying or pointing out that the student didn't do it right, tell or show the student what is acceptable and how to achieve it. For reinforcement, use positive rewards and encouragement as frequently as possible.

• Think before writing a comment on a student's paper, asking yourself how you think the student (or a parent or guardian) will interpret and react to the comment and if that is a correct interpretation of or reaction to your intended meaning.

• Avoid writing evaluative comments or grades in student journals. Student journals are for encouraging students to write, to think about their thinking, and to record their creative thoughts. In journal writing, students should be encouraged to write about their experiences in school and out of school and especially about their experiences related to what is being learned. They should be encouraged to write their feelings about what is being learned and about how they are learning it. Writing in journals gives them practice in expressing themselves in written form and in connecting their learning and should provide nonthreatening freedom to do it. Comments and evaluations from teachers might discourage creative and spontaneous expression.

When responding to a student's journal writing, Gibbs and Earley suggest that the following "don'ts" may be more important than any "dos." *Don't* correct spelling or grammar. *Don't* probe. Resist the temptation to ask for more than the student chooses to share. *Don't* respond with value judgments. Simple empathic statements, such as "I understand your point of view" and "Thanks for sharing your thoughts," can be used to avoid making value judgments. *Don't* require students to share their entries with you or their peers. Pages that students do not want the teacher to read may be folded shut and marked "Personal."[7]

- When reading student journals, talk individually with students to seek clarification about their expressions. Student journals are useful to the teacher (of any subject) in understanding the student's thought processes and writing skills (diagnostic evaluation) and should *not* be graded. For grading purposes, teachers may simply record whether the student is maintaining a journal and, perhaps, a judgment about the quantity of writing in it, but no judgment should be made about the quality.

- When reviewing student portfolios, discuss with students individually the progress in their learning as shown by the materials in their portfolios. As with student journals, the portfolio should *not* be graded or compared in any way with those of other students. Its purpose is for student self-assessment and to show progress in learning. For this to happen, students should keep in their portfolios all or major samples of papers related to the course. (Student journals and portfolios are discussed further later in this chapter.)

Assessment for Affective and Psychomotor Domain Learning

While evaluation of cognitive domain objectives lends itself to traditional written tests of achievement, the evaluation of affective and psychomotor domains requires the use of performance checklists where student behaviors can be observed in action. However, as we said earlier, for cognitive learning as well, educators today are encouraging the use of alternative assessment procedures (i.e., alternatives to traditional paper-and-pencil written testing). After all, as we have said before, in learning that is most important and that has the most meaning to students, the domains are inextricably interconnected. Learning that is meaningful to students is not as easily compartmentalized as the taxonomies of educational objectives would imply. Alternative assessment strategies include the use of group projects, portfolios, skits, papers, oral presentations, and performance tests.

COOPERATIVE GROUP LEARNING AND ASSESSMENT

To reiterate the discussion in Chapter 8, the purpose of a cooperative learning group is for the group to learn, which means that individuals within the group must learn. Group achievement in learning, then, depends on the learning of individuals within the group. Rather than competing for rewards for achievement, members of the group cooperate with each other by helping each other to learn so the group reward will be a good one. Theoretically, when small groups of students of mixed backgrounds, skills, and capabilities work together toward a common goal, they increase their liking of and respect for one another. As a result, there is an increase in each student's self-esteem *and* academic achievement.

When the achievement of a cooperative learning group is recognized, group achievement is rewarded as well as individual achievement. Remembering that the emphasis must be on peer support rather than peer pressure, you must be cautious about ever giving group grades.[8] Some teachers give bonus points to all members of a group to add to their individual scores when everyone in the group has reached preset criteria. When preset standards are established, the standards can be different for individuals within a group, depending on each member's ability and past performance. It is important that each member of a group feel rewarded and successful. Some teachers also give subjective grades to individual students on their role performances within the group (see Figure 11.2). For determination of students' report card grades, individual student achievement is measured later through individual results on tests and other sources of data. The final grade is based on those as well as on the student's performance in the group.

7. L. J. Gibbs and E. J. Earley, *Using Children's Literature to Develop Core Values* (Bloomington, IN: Fastback 362, Phi Delta Kappa Educational Foundation, 1994).

8. See S. Kagan, "Group Grades Miss the Mark," *Educational Leadership* 52(8):68–71 (May 1995); S. Kagan, "Avoiding the Group-Grades Trip," *Learning* 24(4):56–58 (January/February 1996); and D. W. Johnson and R. T. Johnson, "The Role of Cooperative Learning in Assessing and Communicating Student Learning," in Guskey, pp. 25–46.

	9–10	8	7	1–6
Goals	Consistently and actively helps identify group goals; works effectively to meet goals.	Consistently communicates commitment to group goals; carries out assigned roles.	Sporadically communicates commitment to group goals; carries out assigned role.	Rarely, if ever, works toward group goals or may work against them.
Interpersonal Skills	Cooperates with group members by encouraging, compromising, and/or taking a leadership role without dominating; shows sensitivity to feelings and knowledge of others.	Cooperates with group members by encouraging, compromising, and/or taking a leadership role.	Participates with group but has own agenda; may not be willing to compromise or to make significant contributions.	May discourage others, harass group members, or encourage off-task behavior. Makes significant changes to others' work without their knowledge or permission.
Quality Producer	Contributes significant information, ideas, time, and/or talent to produce a quality product.	Contributes information, ideas, time, and/or talent to produce a quality product.	Contributes some ideas, though not significant; may be more supportive than contributive; shows willingness to complete assignment but has no desire to go beyond average expectations.	Does little or no work toward the completion of group product; shows little or no interest in contributing to the task; produces work that fails to meet minimum standards for quality.
Participation	Attends daily; consistently and actively utilizes class time by working on the task.	Attends consistently; sends in work to group if absent; utilizes class time by working on the task.	Attends sporadically; absences or tardies may hinder group involvement; may send in work when absent; utilizes some time; may be off task by talking to others, interrupting other groups, or watching others do the majority of the work.	Frequent absences or tardies hinder group involvement; fails to send in work when absent; wastes class time by talking, doing other work, or avoiding tasks; group has asked that member be reproved by teacher or removed from the group.
Commitment	Consistently contributes time out of class to produce a quality product; attends all group meetings as evidenced by the group meeting log.	Contributes time out of class to produce a quality product; attends a majority of group meetings as evidenced by the group meeting log.	Willing to work toward completion of task during class time; attends some of the group meetings; may arrive late or leave early; may keep inconsistent meeting log.	Rarely, if ever, attends group meetings outside of class or may attend and hinder progress of the group; fails to keep meeting log.

Figure 11.2

Sample scoring rubric for assessing individual student in cooperative-learning project work. (*Source:* Elk Grove School District, Elk Grove, California.)

(Possible score = 50; Scorer marks a relevant square in each of the six categories—the horizontal rows—and student's score for that category is the small-print number within that square.)

STUDENT INVOLVEMENT IN ASSESSMENT

Students' continuous self-assessment should be planned as an important component of the assessment process. If students are to progress in their understanding of their own thinking (**metacognition**) and in their intellectual development, then they must receive instruction and guidance in how to become more responsible for their own learning. During that empowerment process they learn to think better of themselves and of their individual capabilities. To achieve this self-understanding and improved self-esteem requires the experiences afforded by successes, along with guidance in self-understanding and self-assessment.

To meet these goals, teachers provide opportunities for students to think about what they are learning, about how they are learning it, and about how far they have progressed. One procedure is for students to maintain portfolios of their work, using rating scales or checklists periodically to self-assess their progress.

Using Portfolios

Portfolios are used by teachers as a means of instruction and by teachers and students as one means of assessing student learning. Although there is little research evidence to support or to refute the claim, educators believe that the instructional value comes from the process of the student's assembling and maintaining a personal portfolio. During that creative process the student is expected to self-reflect, to think critically about what has and is being learned, and the student is assuming responsibility for his or her own learning.[9]

Student portfolios used by secondary schools fall into three general categories, and the purpose in a given situation may transcend some combination of or all three categories. The categories are the (1) *selected works portfolio,* where students maintain samples of their work as prompted by the teacher; the (2) *longitudinal portfolio,* one that is oriented toward outcome-based goals and that must include samples of student work from the beginning and from the end of the school term to exemplify achievement toward the goals; and the (3) *passport or career portfolio,* one that contains samples of student work that will enable the student to move forward, such as from one school grade level to another or from high school to a career or to postsecondary education.

For example, to demonstrate growth in their reading, writing, and research skills, for an eleventh-grade project in English classes, students at Kent County High School (Worton, MD) produce career portfolios. Each student's portfolio contains an autobiographical narrative or essay; a résumé and cover letter; a character reference letter from a classmate; a career analysis outline; a self-assessment of high school grades and activities; a sample job application; a sample postsecondary school application; a description of a business or company and its employment opportunities; profiles of two colleges or universities; a profile of a community college or technical school; and a career-related annotated bibliography.[10]

Student portfolios should be well organized and contain assignment sheets, class worksheets, the results of homework, project binders, forms for student self-evaluation of and reflection on their work, and other class materials thought important by the students and teacher.[11] As a model of a real-life portfolio, your own career portfolio can be shown to students (see Chapter 12).

Although portfolio assessment as an alternative to traditional methods of evaluating student progress has gained momentum in recent years, setting standards has been very difficult. Research on the use of portfolios for assessment indicates that validity and reliability of teacher evaluation are often quite low. Before using portfolios as an alternative to traditional testing, teachers need to consider and clearly understand the reasons for doing it, carefully decide on portfolio content, establish rubrics or expectation standards, anticipate grading problems, and consider parent and guardian reactions.[12]

While emphasizing the criteria for assessment, rating scales and checklists provide students with means of expressing their feelings and give the teacher still another source of input data for use in assessment. To provide students with reinforcement and guidance to improve their learning and development, teachers can meet with individual students to discuss their self-assessments. Such conferences should provide students with understandable and achievable short-term goals as well as help them develop and maintain an adequate self-esteem.[13]

---

9. J. A. Arter et al., *Portfolios for Assessment and Instruction.* ERIC Digest (Washington, DC: ED388890, ERIC Clearinghouse on Assessment and Evaluation, 1995), p. 1.

10. Southern Regional Education Board, *1995 Outstanding Practices* (Atlanta, GA: Southern Regional Education Board, 1996), pp. 4–5. By permission.

11. Software packages for the development of student electronic portfolios are becoming increasingly available, such as *Classroom Manager* from CTB Macmillan/McGraw-Hill, Monterey, CA; *Electronic Portfolio* from Learning Quest, Corvallis, OR; and *Grady Profile* from Aurbach and Associates, St. Louis, MO.

12. See, for example, S. Willis, "On the Cutting Edge of Assessment," *ASCD Education Update* 38(4):1, 4–7 (June 1996).

13. For a discussion of the biological importance and educational benefits of positive feedback, use of student portfolios, and group learning, see R. Sylwester, "The Neurobiology of Self-Esteem and Aggression," *Educational Leadership* 54(5):75–79 (February 1997).

Oral Report Assessment Checklist

Did the student	Yes	No	Comments
1. Speak so that everyone could hear?	_____	_____	_____
2. Finish sentences?	_____	_____	_____
3. Seem comfortable in front of the group?	_____	_____	_____
4. Give a good introduction?	_____	_____	_____
5. Seem well informed about the topic?	_____	_____	_____
6. Explain ideas clearly?	_____	_____	_____
7. Stay on the topic?	_____	_____	_____
8. Give a good conclusion?	_____	_____	_____
9. Use effective visuals to make the presentation interesting?	_____	_____	_____
10. Give good answers to questions from the audience?	_____	_____	_____

Figure 11.3
Sample checklist: assessing a student's oral report.

Although almost any instrument used for assessing student work can be used for student self-assessment, in some cases it might be better to construct specific instruments with the student's understanding of the instrument in mind. Student self-assessment and self-reflection should be done on a regular and continuing basis so that comparisons can be made periodically by the student. You will need to help students learn how to analyze these comparisons. Comparisons should provide a student with information previously not recognized about her own progress and growth.

Using Checklists

One of the items maintained by students in their portfolios is a series of checklists. Items on the checklist will vary depending on your purpose, subject, and grade level. (See sample forms, Figures 11.3 and 11.4.) Checklist items can be used easily by a student to compare with previous self-assessments. Open-ended questions, such as those found in the checklist in Figure 11.4, allow the student to provide additional information as well as to do some expressive writing. After a student has demonstrated each of the skills satisfactorily, a check is made next to the student's name, either by the teacher alone or in conference with the student.

Guidelines for Using Portfolios for Assessment

Here are general guidelines for using student portfolios in the assessment of learning.

- Contents of the portfolio should reflect course instructional aims and objectives.

- Students should date everything that goes into their portfolios.
- Determine what materials should be kept in the portfolios and announce clearly (post schedule in room) when, how, and by what criteria portfolios will be reviewed by you.
- Give all responsibility for maintenance of the portfolios to the students.
- Portfolios should be kept in the classroom.
- Portfolios should not be graded or compared in any way with those of other students. Their purpose is for student self-assessment and for showing progress in learning. For this to happen, students should keep in their portfolios all papers, or sample major papers, related to the course. For grading, teachers usually simply record whether or not the portfolios were maintained and by checklist whether all materials that are supposed to be in the portfolio are there.

MAINTAINING RECORDS OF STUDENT ACHIEVEMENT

You must maintain well-organized and complete records of student achievement. You may do this in a written record book or on an electronic record book (that is, a computer software program, one commercially developed or one you develop yourself, perhaps by using a computer software program spreadsheet). At the very least, the record book should include attendance records and all records of scores on tests, homework, projects, and other assignments. A high-tech record-keeping and learner profile system is available

Student Self-Assessment Form

Student: _____ Date: _____

Teacher: _____ Number: _____

Draft Title of Paper:_____

Answer the following questions about the draft of your own paper after all group members have shared their papers by reading them aloud to others in the group.

	Yes	No
1. In my introduction, I put forth my thesis.	_____	_____
2. In the beginning I orient the reader by providing relevant background information and sources.	_____	_____
3. I support my interpretive claims by providing (circle those that apply): textual evidence, specific quotations, personal experience, related readings.	_____	_____
4. I explain how my examples support my claim by using words such as *shows, demonstrates, proves,* and *illustrates.*	_____	_____
5. My supporting evidence provides the bulk of my composition.	_____	_____
6. I take a strong, consistent stance and maintain it.	_____	_____
7. I convince my readers that my interpretation is valid.	_____	_____

8. What I like best about my paper is:

9. A part where I need more information is:

10. Other revisions I might make are:

Figure 11.4

Student self-assessment: a sample generic form for an interpretive writing assignment. (*Source:* Adapted from unpublished material by Pam Benedetti, *Using Portfolios to Strengthen Student Assessment in English/Language Arts* (Grades 6–12), Copyright 1991 by Pam Benedetti, p. 29.)

that uses a computer and a bar code scanner to help the teacher plan, customize assessment criteria, observe and collect data anywhere without interrupting the learning process, make reports, and assist in student self-assessment.

Daily interactions and events occur in the classroom that may provide informative data about a student's intellectual, emotional, and physical development. Maintaining a dated record of your observations of these interactions and events can provide important information that might otherwise be forgotten. At the end of a unit and again at the conclusion of a grading term, you will want to review your records. During the course of the school year, your anecdotal records (and those of other members of your teaching team) will provide important information about the intellectual, psychological, and physical development of each student and ideas for attention to be given to individual students.

Recording Teacher Observations and Judgments

You must think carefully about any written comments that you intend to make about a student. Teenagers can be sensitive to what others say about them, and particularly to comments about them made by a teacher.

Additionally, we have seen anecdotal comments in students' permanent records that said more about the teachers who made the comments than about the recipient students. Comments that have been carelessly, hurriedly, and thoughtlessly made can be detrimental to a student's welfare and progress in school. Teacher comments must be professional; that is, they must be diagnostically useful to the continued intellectual and psychological development of the student. This is true for any comment you make or write, whether on a student's paper, on the student's permanent school record, or on a message sent to the student's home.

As an example, consider the following unprofessional comment observed in one student's permanent record. A teacher wrote, "John is lazy." Describing John as lazy could be done by anyone; it is nonproductive and certainly not a professional diagnosis. How many times do you suppose John needs to receive such negative descriptions of his behavior before he begins to believe that he is just that—lazy—and, as a result, acts that way even more often? Written comments like that can also be damaging because they may be read by the teacher who next has John in class and lead that teacher to simply perpetuate the same expectation of John. To say that John is lazy merely describes behavior as judged by the teacher who wrote the comment. More important, and more professional, would be for the teacher to try to analyze *why* John is behaving that way, then to *prescribe* activities that are likely to motivate John to assume more constructive charge of his own learning behavior.

For students' continued intellectual and emotional development, your comments should be useful, productive, analytical, diagnostic, and prescriptive. The professional teacher makes diagnoses and prepares descriptions; a professional teacher does *not* label students as lazy, vulgar, slow, stupid, difficult, or dumb. The professional teacher sees the behavior of a student as being goal-directed. Perhaps "lazy" John found that particular behavioral pattern won him attention. John's goal, then, was attention (don't we all need attention?), and John assumed negative, perhaps even self-destructive, behavioral patterns to reach that goal. The professional task of any teacher is to facilitate the learner's understanding (perception) of a goal and help the student identify acceptable behaviors positively designed to reach that goal.

That which separates the professional teacher from "anyone off the street" is the teacher's ability to go beyond mere description of behavior. Keep that statement in mind always when you write comments that will be read by students, by their parents or guardians, and by other teachers. Now check your understanding of this concept by doing Exercise 11.1.

EXERCISE 11.1

An Evaluation of Written Teacher Comments About Students—A Self-Check Exercise

---

Instructions: The following comments were selected from student records written by teachers about their students. Check *yes* for those you consider to be professionally useful and *no* for those you do not. Then compare your responses against the key that follows. Discuss the results with your classmates and instructor.

Professionally Useful Comments?	*Yes*	*No*
1. Sonja performs her writing assignments much better when done in class than when done as homework.	_____	_____
2. Lucretia was very disruptive in class during our unit on westward expansion.	_____	_____
3. Aram has a lot of difficulty staying in his seat.	_____	_____
4. Arthur seems more responsive during science experiments than during my lectures.	_____	_____
5. Razmik seems to have an excess of nervous energy, and I have a concern about his nutritional health.	_____	_____
6. Su Chin did very well this year in laboratory activities but seems to have reading difficulties.	_____	_____
7. Catalina does not get along well with her peers during group learning activities.	_____	_____
8. Angela seems unable to understand my verbal instructions.	_____	_____
9. I am recommending special remediation for José, perhaps through tutoring.	_____	_____
10. I do not appreciate Dan's use of vulgarity.		

Answer Key

1. This is useful information.
2. Not useful, because there are no helpful specifics. "Disruptive" is merely descriptive, not prescriptive. Also, it could cause Lucretia's future teachers to be biased against her.
3. Could be useful to future teachers.
4. Useful.
5. Useful.
6. Useful, although additional specifics would help more.
7. Useful, although additional specifics would help more.
8. Not very useful; it may tell more about the teacher than it does about Angela.
9. Useful.
10. Not useful.

Note: It can be argued that those identified as "not useful," although not prescriptive, could be signals that the student might benefit from a session with the school counselor.

GRADING AND MARKING STUDENT ACHIEVEMENT

If conditions were ideal (which they are not) and if teachers did their job perfectly well (which many of us do not), then all students would receive top marks (the ultimate in mastery or quality learning) and there would be less of a need here to talk about grading and marking. Mastery learning implies that some end point of learning is attainable, but there probably isn't an end point. In any case, because conditions for teaching are never ideal and we teachers are mere humans, let us continue with this topic of grading that is undoubtedly of special interest to you, to your students, to their parents or guardians, and to school counselors, administrators and school boards, potential employers, providers of scholarships, and college admissions officers.

We frequently use the term *achievement*. What is meant by this term? Achievement means accomplishment, but is it accomplishment of the instructional objectives against preset standards, or is it simply accomplishment? Most teachers probably choose the former, where the teacher subjectively establishes a standard that must be met in order for a student to receive a certain grade for an assignment, project, test, quarter, semester, or course. Achievement, then, is decided by degrees of accomplishment.

Preset standards are usually expressed in percentages (degrees of accomplishment) needed for marks or ABC grades. If no student achieves the standard required for an A grade, for example, then no student receives an A. On the other hand, if all students meet the preset standard for the A grade, then all receive A's. As we said earlier, determining student grades on the basis of preset standards is referred to as criterion-referenced measurement.

Criterion-Referenced versus Norm-Referenced Grading

While criterion-referenced (or competency-based) grading is based on preset standards, norm-referenced grading measures the relative accomplishment of individuals in a small group (e.g., one classroom of chemistry students) or in a larger group (e.g., all students enrolled in the same chemistry course) by comparing and ranking students. It is commonly known as grading on a curve. Because it encourages competition and discourages cooperative learning, for the determination of student grades *norm-referenced grading is not recommended.* Norm-referenced grading is educationally dysfunctional. After all, each student is an individual and should not be converted to a statistic on a frequency-distribution curve. For your personal interest, after several years of teaching, you can produce frequency-distribution studies of grades you have given over a period of time, but *do not* grade students on a curve. Grades for student achievement should be tied to performance levels and determined on the basis of each student's achievement toward preset standards.[14]

In criterion-referenced grading, the aim is to communicate information about an individual student's progress in knowledge and work skills in comparison to that student's previous attainment or in the pursuit of an absolute, such as content mastery. Criterion-referenced grading is featured in continuous-progress curricula, competency-based curricula, and other programs that focus on individualized education.

Criterion-referenced grading is based on the level at which each student meets the specified objectives (standards) for the course or grade level. The objectives must be clearly stated to represent important student learning outcomes. This approach implies that effective teaching and learning result in high grades (A's) or marks for most students. In fact, when a mastery concept is used, the student must accomplish the objectives before being allowed to proceed to the next learning task. The philosophy of teachers who favor criterion-referenced procedures recognizes individual potential. Such teachers accept the challenge of finding teaching strategies to help students progress from where they are to the next designated level. Instead of wondering how Sally compares with Juanita, the comparison is between what Sally could do yesterday and what she can do today and how well these performances compare to the preset standard.

Most school systems use some combination of both norm-referenced and criterion-referenced data usage. Sometimes both kinds of information are useful. For example, a report card for a student in the eighth grade might indicate how that student is meeting certain criteria, such as an A grade for addition of fractions. Another entry might show that this mastery is expected, however, in the sixth grade. Both criterion- and norm-referenced data may be communicated to the parents or guardians and the student. Appropriate procedures should be used: a criterion-referenced approach to show whether or not the student can accomplish the task, and if so, to what degree, and a norm-referenced approach to show how well that student performs compared to the larger group to which the student belongs. The latter is important data for college admissions officers and for committees that appropriate academic scholarships.

---

14. That grading and reporting should always be done in reference to learning criteria, and never on a curve, is well supported by research studies and authorities on the matter. See, for example, from the Suggested Readings at the end of this chapter, pages 18–19 in T. R. Guskey and pages 436–437 in R. J. Stiggins.

Determining Grades

Once entered onto school transcripts, grades have a significant impact on a student's future. When determining achievement grades for student performance, you must make several important and professional decisions. Although in a few schools, and for certain classes or assignments, only marks such as E, S, and I or pass/no pass are used, percentages of accomplishment and letter grades are used for most courses taught in secondary schools.[15]

Although courses taken and grades earned continue to carry a great deal of weight when college admissions officers consider students for admission, SAT scores have become increasingly important in recent years. The increasing importance of SAT scores is the result of a variety of factors, including recent trends in schooling such as (1) the elimination of A–F grading and the traditional grade-point average (GPA); (2) reported grade inflation, whereby in some school districts nearly half the students have A or better averages; (3) the replacement of letter grades with portfolios; (4) the prevalence of home schooling; (5) confusion from weighted grading systems where, for example, a student earning all A grades could have a 4.0 GPA at one school, a 4.5 at another school, and a 5.0 from still another; and (6) the difficulty in trying to compare GPAs of students from one geographical area of the country with students from another who have identical GPAs.

Guidelines for Determining Grades

For determining student grades, consider the guidelines presented in the following paragraphs.

At the start of the school term, explain your marking and grading policies *first to yourself,* then to your students and to their parents or guardians at back-to-school night or in a written explanation that is sent home, or both. Share sample scoring and grading rubrics with students and parents.

When converting your interpretation of a student's accomplishments to a letter grade, be as objective as possible. For the selection of criteria for ABC grades, select a percentage standard, such as 92 percent for an A, 85 percent for a B, 75 percent for a C, and 65 percent for a D. Cutoff percentages used are your decision, although the district, school, program area, or department may have established guidelines that you are expected to follow.

For the determination of students' final grades, we recommend the point system, where things that students write, say, and do are given points (but not for journals or portfolios, except, perhaps, simply for whether the student does one or not); then the possible point total is the factor for grade determination. For example, if 92 percent is the cutoff for an A and 500 points are possible, then any student with 460 points or more (500 × .92) has achieved an A. Likewise, for a test or any other assignment, if the value is 100 points, the cutoff for an A is 92 (100 × .92). With a point system and preset standards, the teacher and students, at any time during the grading period, always know the current points possible and can easily calculate a student's current grade standing. Then, as far as a current grade is concerned, students always know where they stand in the course.

Build your grading policy around degrees of accomplishment rather than failure, and allow students to proceed from one accomplishment to the next. This is *continuous promotion,* not necessarily the promotion of the student from one grade level to the next, but promotion within the classroom. (However, some schools have done away with grade-level designation and, in its place, use the concept of continuous promotion from the time of student entry into the school through the student's graduation or exit from it.)

Remember that *assessment* and *grading* are *not* synonymous terms. As you learned earlier, assessment implies the collection of information from a variety of sources, including measurement techniques and subjective observations. These data, then, become the basis for arriving at a final grade, which in effect is a final value judgment. Grades are one aspect of evaluation and are intended to communicate educational progress to students and to their parents or guardians. For grades to be valid as an indicator of that progress, you *must* use a variety of sources of data for determination of a student's final grade.

Decide beforehand your policy about make-up work. Students will be absent and will miss assignments and tests, so it is best that your policies about late assignments and missed tests be clearly communicated to students and to their parents or guardians. For make-up work, please consider the following.

HOMEWORK ASSIGNMENTS. As discussed in Chapter 8, we recommend that after due dates have been negotiated or set for assignments no credit or reduced credit be given for work that is turned in late. Sometimes, however, a student has legitimate reasons why he could not get an assignment done by the due date, and the teacher must exercise professional judgment in each instance. Although it is important that teachers have rules and procedures—and that they consistently apply

15. For a presentation of other methods being used to report student achievement, see K. Lake and K. Kafka, "Reporting Methods in Grades K–8," and J. Bailey and J. McTighe, "Reporting Achievement at the Secondary Level: What and How," Chapters 9 and 10, respectively, in Guskey.

those—the teacher is a professional who must consider all aspects of a student's situation and, after doing so, show compassion, caring, and understanding of the human situation.

TESTS.   If students are absent when tests are given, you have several options. Some teachers allow students to miss or discount one test per grading period. Another technique is to allow each student to substitute a written homework assignment or project for one missed test. Still another option is to give the absent student the choice of either taking a make-up test or having the next test count as double. When make-up tests are given, they should be taken within a week of the regular test unless there is a compelling reason (e.g., medical or family problem) why this cannot happen.

Sometimes students miss a testing period, not because of absence from school but because of involvement in other school activities. In those instances, the student may be able to arrange to take the test during another of your class periods, or your prep period, on that day or the next. If a student is absent during performance testing, the logistics and possible diminished reliability of having to readminister the test for one student may necessitate giving the student an alternate paper-and-pencil test or some other option.

QUIZZES.   Many teachers give frequent and brief quizzes, as often as every day. As opposed to tests (see next section), quizzes are usually brief (perhaps taking only five minutes of class time) and intended to reinforce the importance of frequent study and review. (However, quizzes should be prepared using the same care and precision described in the sections on testing and preparation of assessment items.) When quizzes are given at frequent intervals, no single quiz should count very much toward the student's final grade; therefore, you will probably want to avoid having to schedule and give make-up quizzes for students who were absent during a quiz period. The following are reasonable options for administering make-up quizzes and are presented here in order of our preference. (1) Give a certain number of quizzes during a grading period, say ten, but allow a student to discount a few quiz scores, say two of the ten, thereby allowing the student to discount a low score or a missed quiz due to absence, or to discount both. (2) Count the next quiz as double for a student who missed one due to absence. About the only problem with this option occurs when a student misses several quizzes. If that happens, then try option three. (3) Count the unit test a certain and relative percentage greater for any student who missed a quiz during that unit. By the way,

we do not advise giving "pop," or unannounced, quizzes; they serve no useful educational purpose.

TESTING FOR ACHIEVEMENT

One source of information used for determining grades is data obtained from testing for student achievement. In this section about testing, we consider first the difference between standardized and nonstandardized tests.

Standardized and Nonstandardized Tests

Standardized tests are those that have been constructed and published by commercial testing bureaus and used by states and districts to determine and compare student achievement, principally in the core subjects of reading, science, social studies, and math. Standardized norm-referenced tests are best for diagnostic purposes and should *not* be used for determining student grades. Space in this book does not allow our consideration of standardized achievement testing. Our focus is on nonstandardized tests that are designed by the classroom teacher for her own unique group of students.

Textbook publishers' tests, test item pools, and standardized tests are available from a variety of sources; however, because schools, teachers, and students are different, most of the time you will be designing (or collaboratively participating in the designing, as is often the case within the departments of large high schools) and preparing tests for your own purposes for your distinct group of students.

Competent planning, preparing, administering, and scoring of tests is an important professional skill. The paragraphs that follow provide guidelines that you will want to refer to while you are student teaching and again, occasionally, during your initial years as an employed teacher.

Purposes for Testing

Tests can be designed for several purposes, and a variety of kinds of tests and alternate test items will keep your testing program interesting, useful, and reliable. As a college student, you are probably most experienced with testing for measuring for achievement, but you will use tests for other reasons as well. Tests are also used to assess and aid in curriculum development; help determine teaching effectiveness; help students develop positive attitudes, appreciations, and values; help students increase their understanding and retention of facts, principles, skills, and concepts; motivate students; provide diagnostic information for planning for individualization of the instruction; provide review and drill to enhance teaching and learning; and serve as informational data for students and parents.

Frequency of Testing

First of all, assessment for student learning should be continual; that is, it should be going on every minute of every class day. For grading or marking purposes, it is difficult to generalize about how often to formally test for student achievement, but we believe that testing should be cumulative and frequent. By cumulative, we mean that the items for each assessment should measure for the student's understanding of previously learned material as well as for the current unit of study. By frequent, we mean as often as once a week. Advantages of cumulative assessment include the review, reinforcement, and articulation of old material with the most recent. The advantages of frequent assessment include a reduction in student anxiety over tests and an increase in the validity of the final summative assessment.

Test Construction

After determining the reasons for which you are designing and administering a test, you need to identify the specific instructional objectives the test is being designed to measure. (As emphasized in Chapter 4, your written instructional objectives are specific so that you can write assessment items to measure against those objectives, and that is criterion-referenced assessment.) So, the *first step* in test construction is identification of the purpose(s) for the test. The *second step* is to identify the objectives to be measured, and the *third step* is to prepare the test items. The best time to prepare draft items is after you have prepared your instructional objectives, while the objectives are fresh in your mind, which means before the lessons are taught. After a lesson is taught, you will then want to rework your first draft of the test items that are related to that lesson to make any modifications necessary as a result of the instruction that occurred.

Administering Tests

For many students, test taking can be a time of high anxiety. Students demonstrate test anxiety in various ways. Just before and during testing some are quiet and thoughtful, while others are noisy and disruptive. To more accurately measure student achievement, you will want to take steps to reduce their anxiety. To control or reduce student anxieties, consider the following discussion as guidelines for administering tests.

Since students respond best to a familiar routine, plan your formative assessment program so that tests are given at regular intervals and administered at the same time and in the same way. In some schools, days of the week are assigned to departments for administering major tests. For example, Tuesdays might be assigned for English and foreign language testing, and Wednesday is the day for mathematics testing.

Avoid tests that are too long and will take too much time. Sometimes beginning teachers have unreasonable expectations of students, even high school students, about their attention spans during testing. Frequent testing with frequent sampling of student knowledge is preferred over infrequent and long tests that attempt to cover everything.

Try to arrange the classroom so that it is well ventilated and a comfortable temperature. When giving paper-and-pencil tests individually, make sure the seats are well spaced. If spacing is a problem, then consider group testing or using alternate forms of the test, where students seated adjacent to one another have different forms of the same test (for example, multiple-choice-answer alternatives are arranged in different order).

Before test time, be certain that you have a sufficient number of copies of the test. Although this may sound trite, we mention it because we have known of too many instances in which the teacher started testing with an insufficient number of test copies. (Sometimes a test is duplicated for the teacher by someone else and a mistake is made in the number run off.)

Before distributing the test, explain to students what they are to do when finished, such as quietly begin a homework or reading assignment, because not all students will finish at the same time. It is unreasonable to expect most students to just sit quietly after finishing a test; they need something to do.

When ready to test, don't drag it out. Distribute tests quickly and efficiently. Once testing has begun, avoid interrupting the students. Items or announcements of important information can be written on the board, or if unrelated to the test, held until all are finished with the test. Stay in the room and visually monitor the students. If the test is not going to take an entire class period (most shouldn't) and it's a major test, then give it at the beginning of the period, if possible, unless you are planning a test review just prior to it. (That seems rather late to conduct a meaningful review, however.) It's improbable that any teacher can effectively teach a lesson with a reasonable degree of student interest in it just prior to or immediately after a major test.

Controlling Cheating

Cheating on tests does occur, but there are steps you can take to discourage it or to reduce the opportunity and pressure that cause students to cheat. Consider the following. Space students or, as mentioned before, use alternate forms of the test. Frequent testing and not allowing a single test to count too much toward a term grade reduce test anxiety and the pressure that can cause cheating and increase student learning by "stimulating greater effort and providing intermittent feedback" to the student.[16] Prepare test questions that are clear, and not ambiguous, thereby reducing student frustration that is caused by a question or instructions that students do not understand. As said before, avoid tests that are too long and that will take too much time. During long tests, some students get discouraged and restless, and that is a time when classroom management problems can occur.

By their sheer nature, performance tests can cause even greater pressure on students and can also provide greater opportunity for cheating. When administering performance tests to an entire class, you should have several monitors, such as members of your teaching team. If that isn't possible, consider testing groups of students, such as cooperative learning groups, rather than individuals. Evaluation of test performance, then, would be based on group rather than individual achievement.

Consider using open-text and open-notebook tests or allowing each student to prepare a page of notes to use during the test. When students can use their books and/or notes, that not only reduces anxiety but helps them with the organization of information and the retention of what has been learned.

The preceding paragraphs provide hints to prevent student cheating. If you suspect cheating *is* occurring, move to and stand in the area of the suspected student. Usually that will stop it. When you suspect cheating *has* occurred, you are faced with a dilemma. Unless your suspicion is backed by solid proof you are advised to forget it, but keep a close watch on the student the next time to prevent cheating. Your job is not to catch students being dishonest but to discourage dishonesty. If you have absolute proof that a student has cheated, then you are obligated to proceed with school and department policy on student cheating, and that may call for a session with the counselor, or the student and the student's parent or guardian, perhaps an automatic F grade on the test, or even a temporary suspension from class.

Allowing Appropriate Time to Take a Test

Again, avoid giving tests that are too long and that will take too much time. Preparing and administering good tests is a skill that you will develop over time. In the meantime, it is best to test frequently and to use tests that sample student achievement rather than try for a comprehensive measure of that achievement.

Some students take more time on the same test than do others. You want to avoid giving too much time, or

Table 11.1 Approximate Time to Allow for Testing as Determined by the Types of Items*

Type of Test Item	Time Needed (in minutes) per Item
Matching	1 per matching item
Multiple-choice	1 per item
Completion	1 per item
Completion drawing	2–3
Arrangement	2–3
Identification	2–3
Short explanation	2–3
Essay and performance	10 or more

* Mainstream students or students with limited proficiency in English may take more time per item.

classroom management problems will result. On the other hand, you don't want to cut short the time needed by students who can do well but need more time to think and to write. As a general guide, use the table of time needed for different types of test items (Table 11.1). This is only a guide for determining the approximate amount of time to allow students to complete a test. For example, for a test made up of ten multiple-choice items, five arrangement items, and two short-explanation items, you would want to plan for about 30 minutes for students to complete the test.

PREPARING ASSESSMENT ITEMS

Preparing and writing good assessment items is yet another professional skill, and to become proficient at it takes study, time, practice, and reflection. Because of the importance of an assessment program, please assume this professional charge seriously and responsibly. Although poorly prepared items take no time at all to construct, they will cause you more trouble than you can ever imagine. As a professional you should take time to study different types of assessment items that can be used and how best to write them, and then practice writing them. As we have emphasized, when preparing assessment items, ensure that they match and sufficiently cover the instructional objectives. In addition, you should prepare each item carefully enough to be reasonably confident that each item will be understood by the student in the manner that you anticipate its being understood. With the diversity of students in today's classroom, especially with respect to their proficiency in oral and written English language and students with special needs, this is an especially important point. Finally, after administering a test you must take time to analyze the results and reflect on the value of each item before ever using that item again.

16. H. J. Walberg, "Productive Teaching and Instruction: Assessing the Knowledge Base," *Phi Delta Kappan* 71(6):472 (February 1990).

Classification of Assessment Items

Assessment items can be classified as verbal (oral or written words), visual (pictures and diagrams), and manipulative or performance (handling of materials and equipment; performing). Written verbal items have traditionally been most frequently used in testing. However, visual items and tests are useful, for example, when working with students who lack fluency with the written word or when testing students who have limited or no proficiency in the English language.

Performance items and tests are useful when measuring for psychomotor skill development. Common examples are performance testing of a student's ability to carry a microscope or hold a jumping rope in place (gross motor skill) or to focus a microscope or to jump rope (fine motor skill). Performance testing also can and should be a part of a wider testing program that includes testing for higher-level thinking skills and knowledge, as when a student or small group of students is given the problem of creating from discarded materials a habitat for an imaginary animal and then display, write about, and orally present their product to the rest of the class.

As noted often throughout this book, educators have rekindled their interest in this last described form of performance testing as a means of assessing learning that is closer to measuring for the real thing—that is, authentic. In a program for teacher preparation, micro peer teaching and the student teaching experience are examples of performance assessment, that is, assessment practices used to assess the teacher candidate's ability to teach (to perform). It seems axiomatic that assessment of student teaching is a more authentic assessment of a candidate's ability to teach than would be a written (paper-and-pencil test) or verbal (oral test) form of assessment.

PERFORMANCE TESTING IS EXPENSIVE AND TIME-INTENSIVE. Performance testing is usually more expensive and time-consuming than is verbal testing, which in turn is more time-demanding and expensive than is written testing. However, a good program of assessment will use alternate forms of assessment and not rely solely on one form (such as written) and one type of written item (such as multiple-choice).

The type of test and items that you use depend upon your purpose and objectives. Carefully consider the alternatives within that framework. To provide validity checks and to account for the individual differences of students, a good assessment program should include items of all three types. That is what writers for professional journals are referring to when they talk about alternative assessment. They are encouraging the use of multiple assessment items, as opposed to the traditional heavy reliance on objective items such as multiple-choice questions.

General Guidelines for Preparing for Assessment

Consider the following six general guidelines when preparing for assessment. (1) Include several kinds of items and assessment instruments (see 12 types that follow). (2) Ensure that content coverage is complete (i.e., that all objectives are being measured). (3) Ensure that each item is reliable—that is, it measures the intended objective. One way to check item reliability is to have more than one item measuring for the same objective. (4) Ensure that each item is clear and unambiguous to all students. (5) Plan each item to be difficult enough for the poorly prepared student but easy enough for the student who is well prepared. (6) Because it is time-consuming to write good assessment items, you are advised to maintain a bank of items, with each item coded according to its matching instructional objective, its domain of learning (cognitive, affective, or psychomotor), perhaps its level within the hierarchy of a particular domain, and whether it requires thinking that is recall, processing, or application. Computer software programs are available for this. Ready-made test item banks are available on computer discs and accompany many programs or textbooks. If you use them, be certain that the items match your course objectives and that they are well written. It doesn't follow that because they were published they are well written. When preparing items for your test bank, use your creative thinking and best writing skills. Prepare items that match your objectives, put them aside, think about them, then work them over again.

Every test that you administer to your students should represent your best professional effort. It should be clean and without spelling and grammar errors. A quickly and poorly prepared test can cause you more grief than you can imagine. One that is obviously hurriedly prepared and wrought with spelling and grammar errors will quickly be frowned upon by discerning parents or guardians. If you are a student teacher, it will certainly bring about an admonishment from your university supervisor and, if the sloppiness continues, your speedy dismissal from the teacher preparation program.

Attaining Content Validity

To ensure that your test measures what is supposed to be measured, you can construct a table of specifications. A two-way grid indicates behavior in one dimension and content in the other (see Figures 11.5 and 11.6). In this grid, behavior relates to the three domains: cognitive, affective, and psychomotor. In Figure 11.5, the cognitive domain is divided, according to Bloom's taxonomy (Chapter 5), into six categories: knowledge or simple recall, comprehension, application, analysis, synthesis (often involving an original product in oral or

CONTENT	BEHAVIORS								TOTAL
SOCIAL STUDIES GRADE 8	**COGNITIVE**						AFFEC-TIVE	PSYCHO-MOTOR	
Ancient Greece	*Knowledge*	*Compre-hension*	*Appli-cation*	*Analysis*	*Synthesis*	*Evaluation*			
I. Vocabulary development		2 (1,2)	1 (2)						3
II. Concepts		2 (3,4)	2 (4)						4
III. Applications	1 (5)	1 (5)	1 (5)	1 (5)	1 (5)	1 (5)			6
IV. Problem solving		1 (6)		1 (6)					2
TOTAL	1	6	4	2	1	1			15

Figure 11.5
Specifications I.

CONTENT	BEHAVIORS							TOTAL
	COGNITIVE			**AFFECTIVE**		**PSYCHOMOTOR**		
	Input	*Processing*	*Application*	*Low*	*High*	*Low*	*High*	
I.								
II.								
III.								
IV.								
TOTAL								

Figure 11.6
Specifications II.

written form), and evaluation. Figure 11.5 does not specify levels within the affective and psychomotor domains.

To use a table of specifications, the teacher examining objectives for the unit decides what emphasis should be given to the behavior and to the content. For instance, if vocabulary development is a concern for this eighth-grade study of ancient Greece, then probably 20 percent of the test on vocabulary would be appropriate, but 50 percent would be unsuitable. This planning enables the teacher to design a test to fit the situation rather than a haphazard test that does not correspond to the objectives in either content or behavior emphasis. Since knowledge questions are easy to write, tests often fail to go beyond that level even though the objectives state that the student will analyze and evaluate. The sample table of specifica-

tions for a social studies unit on ancient Greece indicates a distribution of questions on a test. Since this is to be an objective test and it is so difficult to write objective items to test affective and psychomotor behaviors, this table of specifications calls for no test items in these areas. If these categories are included in the unit objectives, some other assessment devices must be used to test learning in these domains. The teacher could also show the objectives tested, as indicated within parentheses in Figure 11.5. Then, a check later on inclusion of all objectives is easy.

Some teachers prefer an alternative, shown in Figure 11.6. Rather than differentiating among all six of Bloom's cognitive levels, this table separates cognitive objectives into just three levels: those that require simple low-level recall of knowledge, those that require information processing, and those that require application of the new knowledge (refer to Levels of Cognitive Questions and Student Thinking in Chapter 7). In addition, the affective and psychomotor domains each are divided into low- and high-level behaviors. A third alternative, not illustrated here, is a table of specifications that shows all levels of each of the three domains.

TWELVE TYPES OF ASSESSMENT ITEMS: DESCRIPTIONS, EXAMPLES, AND GUIDELINES FOR PREPARATION AND USE

In this section, we present descriptions of, advantages and disadvantages of, and guidelines for preparing and using 12 types of assessment items. When reading about the advantages and disadvantages of each, you will notice that some types are appropriate for use in direct or performance assessment while others are not. Guidelines that follow also include special suggestions for using the item with mainstreamed students.

Arrangement

Description: Terms or real objects (realia) are to be arranged in a specified order.

Example 1: Arrange the following list of events on a time line in order of their occurrence: Maximilian I elected King of Germany; Maximilian I becomes Holy Roman Emperor; Diet of Augsburg establishes Council of Regency, divides Germany into six regions; Charles I of Spain becomes Holy Roman Emperor; Ferdinand I assumes the title of Holy Roman Emperor.

Example 2: The assortment of balls on the table represents the planets in our solar system. (*Note*: The balls are of various sizes, such as marbles, tennis balls, basketballs, and so on, each labeled with a planetary name, with a large sphere in the center labeled the sun.) Arrange the balls in their proper order around the sun.

Advantages: This type of item tests for knowledge of sequence and order and is good for review, for starting discussions, and for performance assessment. Example 2 is also an example of a performance test item.

Disadvantages: Scoring could be difficult, so be cautious and meticulous when using this type for grading purposes.

Guidelines for use: To enhance reliability, you may need to include instructions to students to include the rationale for their arrangement, making it a combined arrangement and short-explanation type of assessment. Allow space for explanations on an answer sheet. Useful for small, heterogeneous group assessment to allow students to share and learn from their thinking and reasoning together.

Completion Drawing

Description: An incomplete drawing is presented and the student is to complete it.

Example 1: Connect the following items with arrow lines to show the stages from introduction of a new bill until it becomes law (items not included here).

Example 2: In the following food web (not shown here), draw arrow lines indicating which organisms are consumers and which are producers.

Advantages: This type requires less time than would a complete drawing that might be required in an essay item. Scoring is relatively easy.

Disadvantages: Care needs to be exercised in the instructions so that students do not misinterpret the expectation.

Guidelines for use: Use occasionally for diversion, but take care in preparing. This type can be instructive when assessing for student thinking, as it can measure conceptual knowledge. Consider making the item a combined completion-drawing, short-explanation type by having students include their rationales for the thinking behind their drawing completion. Be sure to allow space for their explanations. Useful for small, heterogeneous group assessment to allow students to share and learn from their thinking and reasoning together.

Completion Statement

Description: Sometimes called a fill-in item, an incomplete sentence is presented and the student is to complete it by filling in the blank space(s).

Example 1: A group of words that have a special meaning, such as "a skeleton in the closet," is called a(n) _____ .

Example 2: To test their hypotheses, scientists and social scientists conduct _____ .

Advantages: This type is easy to devise, take, and score.

Disadvantages: When using this type, there is a tendency to emphasize rote memory and measure procedural knowledge only. It is difficult to write this type of item to measure for conceptual knowledge and higher levels of cognition. You must be alert for a correct response different from the expected. For example, in Example 2, although the teacher's key has "experiments" as the correct answer, a student might answer the question with "investigations" or "tests" or some other response that is equally valid.

Guidelines for use: Use occasionally for review or for preassessment of student knowledge. Avoid using this type for grading unless you can write quality items that extend student thinking beyond mere recall. In all instances, avoid copying items verbatim from the student book. As with all types, be sure to provide adequate space for students' answers. Try to use only one blank per item. Try also to keep the blanks equal in length. Useful for small, heterogeneous group assessment to allow students to share and learn from their thinking and reasoning together.

Correction

Description: Similar to the completion type, complete sentences or paragraphs are presented, with italicized or underlined words that can be changed to make the sentences correct.

Example 1: The work of the TVA was started by building sand castles. A sand castle is a wall built across a kid to stop its flow. The sand castle holds back the football so the kids do not overflow their backpacks and cause tears.

Example 2: 1, 1, 2, 3, 5, 8, 12, 21, 34, 87, 89

Advantages: Writing this type can be fun for the teacher for the purpose of preassessment of student knowledge or for review. Students may enjoy this type, especially when used only occasionally, for the tension relief afforded by the incorrect absurdities. This type is useful for introducing words with multiple meanings.

Disadvantages: As with the completion type, the correction type tends to measure for low-level recall and rote memory (although this is not necessarily the case in Example 2; if a student is unfamiliar with the Fibonacci number series in mathematics, it would be a relatively high-level question). The underlined incorrect items could be so whimsical that they might cause more classroom disturbance than you want.

Guidelines for use: Use occasionally for diversion and discussion. Try to write items that measure for higher-level cognition. Consider making the test a combined correction, short-explanation type. Be sure to allow space for student explanations.

Essay

Description: A question or problem is presented, and the student is to compose a response in the form of sustained prose, using the student's own words, phrases, and ideas, within the limits of the question or problem.

Example 1: In the story just read, does the author elaborate the setting in great detail or barely sketch it? Explain your response.

Example 2: A healthy green coleus plant sitting in front of you has been planted in fertile soil and sealed in a glass jar. If we place the jar on the windowsill, where it will receive strong sunlight, and the temperature inside the jar is maintained between 60 and 80 degrees Fahrenheit, how long do you predict the plant will live? Justify your prediction.

Advantages: This type measures conceptual knowledge and higher mental processes, such as the ability to synthesize material and to express ideas in clear and precise written language. It is especially useful in integrated thematic teaching. It provides practice in written expression and can be used in performance assessment, as is the case for Example 2.

Disadvantages: Essay items require a good deal of time to read and to score. They tend to provide an unreliable sampling of achievement and are vulnerable to teacher subjectivity and unreliable scoring. Furthermore, they tend to punish the student who writes slowly and laboriously and who has limited proficiency in the written language but who may have achieved as well as a student who writes faster and is more proficient in the language. Essay items tend to favor students who have fluency with words but whose achievement may not necessarily be better. In addition, unless the students have been given instruction in the meaning of key directive verbs and in how to respond to them, the teacher should not assume that all students understand such verbs (such as *explain* in the first example and *justify* in the second).

Guidelines for use

1. When you prepare an essay-only test, many questions, each requiring a relatively short prose response (see the short-explanation type), are preferable to fewer questions requiring long prose responses. Brief answers tend to be more precise, and the use of many items provides a more reliable sampling of student achievement. When preparing short prose response, be sure to avoid using words verbatim from the student textbook.

2. Allow students adequate test time for a full response.

3. Different qualities of achievement are more likely comparable when all students must answer the same questions, as opposed to providing a list of essay items from which students may select those they answer.

4. After preparing essay items, make a tentative scoring key, deciding the main ideas you expect students to identify and how many points will be allotted to each.

5. Students should be informed about the relative test value for each item. Point values, if different for each item, can be listed in the margin of the test next to each item.

6. When reading student essay responses, read all student papers for one item at a time, and while doing that, make notes to yourself; then repeat, and while reading that item again, score each student's paper for that item. Repeat the process for the next item. While scoring essay responses, keep in mind the nature of the objective being measured, which may or may not include the qualities of handwriting, grammar, spelling, punctuation, and neatness.

7. To nullify the "halo effect," some teachers use a number code rather than having students put their

Compare asks for an analysis of similarity and difference, but with a greater emphasis on similarities or likenesses.

Contrast asks more for differences than for similarities.

Criticize asks for the good and bad of an idea or situation.

Define means to express clearly and concisely the meaning of a term, as from a dictionary or in the student's own words.

Diagram means to put quantities or numerical values into the form of a chart, graph, or drawing.

Discuss means to explain or argue, presenting various sides of events, ideas, or situations.

Enumerate means to name or list one after another, which is different from "explain briefly" or "tell in a few words."

Evaluate means to express worth, value, and judgment.

Explain means to describe, with emphasis on cause and effect.

Generalize means to arrive at a valid generalization from provided specific information.

Illustrate means to describe by means of examples, figures, pictures, or diagrams.

Infer means to forecast what is likely to happen as a result of information provided.

Interpret means to describe or explain a given fact, theory, principle, or doctrine within a specific context.

Justify means to show reasons, with an emphasis on correct, positive, and advantageous.

List means just that, to simply name items in a category or to include them in a list, without much description.

Outline means to give a short summary with headings and subheadings.

Prove means to present materials as witnesses, proof, and evidence.

Relate means to tell how specified things are connected or brought into some kind of relationship.

Summarize means to recapitulate the main points without examples or illustrations.

Trace means to follow a history or series of events, step by step, by going backward over the evidence.

Figure 11.7
Meaning of key directive verbs for essay item responses.

names on essay papers. While reading the papers, the teacher is thus unaware of whose paper is being read.

8. While having some understanding of a concept, many students are not yet facile with written expression, so you must remember to be patient, tolerant, positive, and prescriptive. Mark papers with positive and constructive comments, showing students how they could have explained or responded better.

9. Prior to using this type of test item, give instruction and practice to students in responding to key directive verbs that will be used (see Figure 11.7).

Grouping

Description: Several items are presented, and the student is to select and group those that are in some way related.

Example 1: Separate the following words into two groups (words are not included here); those that are homonyms, place in group A, and those that are not homonyms, place in group B.

Example 2: Circle the figure that is least like the others (showing a wrench, screwdriver, saw, and swing).

Advantages: This type of item tests knowledge of grouping and can be used to measure conceptual knowledge, for higher levels of cognition, and to stimulate discussion. As Example 2 shows, it can be similar to a multiple-choice item type.

Disadvantage: Remain alert for the student who has an alternative but valid rationale for her grouping.

Guidelines for use: To allow for an alternative cor-

rect response, consider making the item a combination grouping, short-explanation type, being certain to permit adequate space to encourage student explanations.

Identification

Description: Unknown "specimens" are to be identified by name or some other criterion.

Example 1: Identify each of the plant specimens on the table by its common name.

Example 2: Identify by style each of the three poems shown on the screen.

Advantages: Verbalization (i.e., the use of abstract symbolization) is less significant, as the student is working with real materials; should be measuring for higher-level learning rather than simple recall. The item can also be written to measure for procedural understanding, such as for identification of steps in booting up a computer program. This is another useful type for authentic and performance assessments.

Disadvantages: Because of a special familiarity with the material, some students may have an advantage over others; to be fair, specimens used should be equally familiar or unfamiliar to all students. This type takes more time than many of the other item types, both for the teacher to prepare and for students to do.

Guidelines for use: Whatever specimens are used, they must be familiar to all or to none of the students, and they must be clear, not confusing (e.g., fuzzy photographs or unclear photocopies, dried and incomplete plant specimens, and garbled music recordings can be confusing and frustrating to try to discern). Consider using dyad or team testing rather than individual testing.

Matching

Description: Students are to match related items from a list of numbered items to a list of lettered choices or in some way to connect those items that are the same or related.

Example 1: In the blank space next to each description in Column A (stem column) put the letter of the correct answer from Column B (answer column).

A (stem column)	B (answer column)
_____ 1. Current president of the U.S.	A. George Bush
_____ 2. Most recent past president of the U.S.	B. Bill Clinton
_____ 3. U.S. president during the Persian Gulf War	C. Thomas Jefferson
_____ 4. First president of the U.S.	D. George Washington
	E. etc.

Example 2: Match items in Column A (stem column) to those in Column B (answer column) by drawing lines connecting the matched pairs.

Column A	Column B
ann/enn	conquer
auto	large
min	self
vic/vinc	small
(etc.)	year
	(etc.)

Advantages: Matching items can measure for ability to judge relationships and to differentiate between similar facts, ideas, definitions, and concepts. They are easy to score and can test a broad range of content. They reduce guessing, especially if one group (e.g., answer column) contains more items than the other, are interesting to students, and are adaptable for performance assessment.

Disadvantages: Although the matching item is adaptable for performance assessment, items are not easily adapted to measuring for higher cognition. Because all parts must be homogeneous, it is possible that clues will be given, thus reducing item validity.

Guidelines for use: The number of items in the answer column should exceed the number in the stem column. The number of items to be matched should not exceed 10. Fewer is better. Matching sets should have high homogeneity (i.e., items in both columns or groups should be of the same general category; avoid, for example, mixing dates, events, and names). If

answers can be used more than once, and that is advised to avoid guessing by elimination, the directions should so state. Be prepared for the student who can legitimately defend an "incorrect" response. To eliminate the paper-and-pencil aspect and make the item more direct, use an item such as "of the materials on the table, pair up those that are most alike."

Multiple-Choice

Description: This type is similar to the completion item in that statements are presented, sometimes in incomplete form, but with several options, requiring recognition or even higher cognitive processes rather than mere recall.

Example 1: Of four cylinders with the following dimensions, the one that would cause the highest-pitched sound would be

(a) 4 inches long and 3 inches in diameter
(b) 4 inches long and 1 inch in diameter
(c) 8 inches long and 3 inches in diameter
(d) 8 inches long and 1 inch in diameter

Example 2: Which one of the following is a pair of antonyms?

(a) loud—soft
(b) halt—finish
(c) absolve—vindicate
(d) procure—purchase

Advantages: Items can be answered and scored quickly. A wide range of content and higher levels of cognition can be tested in a relatively short time. This type is excellent for all testing purposes—motivation, review, and assessment of learning.

Disadvantages: Unfortunately, because multiple-choice items are relatively easy to write, there is a tendency to write items measuring only for low levels of cognition. Multiple-choice items are excellent for major testing, but it takes care and time to write quality questions that measure higher levels of thinking and learning.

Guidelines for use

1. If the item is in the form of an incomplete statement, it should be meaningful in itself and imply a direct question rather than merely lead into a collection of unrelated true and false statements.

2. Use a level of language that is easy enough for even the poorest readers and those with limited proficiency in English to understand; avoid unnecessary wordiness.

3. If there is much variation in the length of alternatives, arrange the alternatives in order from shortest to longest (i.e., first alternative is the shortest, last alternative is the longest). For single-word alternatives, consistent use of arrangement of alternatives is recommended, such as by length of answer or alphabetically.

4. Incorrect responses (distractors) should be plausible and related to the same concept as the correct alternative. Although an occasional humorous distractor may help relieve text anxiety, along with absurd distractors they should generally be avoided. They offer no measuring value.

5. It is not necessary to maintain a fixed number of alternatives for every item, but the use of less than three is not recommended. Although it is not always possible to come up with four or five plausible responses, the use of four or five reduces chance responses and guessing, thereby increasing reliability for the item. If you cannot think of enough plausible distractors, include the item on a test the first time as a completion item. As students respond, wrong answers will provide you with a number of plausible distractors that you can use the next time to make the item a multiple-choice item.

6. Responses such as "all of these" or "none of these" should be used only when they will contribute more than another plausible distractor. Care must be taken that such responses answer or complete the item. "All of the above" is a poorer alternative than "none of the above" because items that use it as a correct response need to have four or five correct answers; also, if it is the right answer, knowledge of any two of the distractors will cue it.

7. Arrangement of alternatives should be uniform throughout the test and listed in vertical (column) form rather than in horizontal (paragraph) form.

8. Every item should be grammatically consistent. For example, if the stem is in the form of an incomplete sentence, it should be possible to complete the sentence by attaching any of the alternatives to it.

9. The stem should state a single and specific point.

10. The stem must mean the same thing to every student.

11. The item should be expressed in positive form. A negative form can present a psychological disadvantage to students. Negative items ask what is *not* characteristic of something or what is the *least* useful. Discard the item if you cannot express it in positive terminology.

12. The stem must not include clues that would indicate the correct alternative.

> For example, "A four-sided figure whose opposite sides are parallel is called _____. (a) an octagon, (b) a parallelogram, (c) a trapezoid, (d) a triangle." Use of the word *parallel* clues the answer.

13. There must be only one correct or best response. However, this is easier said than done (refer to guideline 18).

14. Measuring for understanding of definitions is better tested by furnishing the name or word and requiring choice between alternative definitions than by presenting the definition and requiring choice between alternative words.

15. Avoid using alternatives that include absolute terms such as *never* and *always*.

16. Multiple-choice items need not be entirely verbal. Consider the use of realia, charts, diagrams, videos, and other visuals. They will make the test more interesting, especially to students with low verbal abilities or to those who have limited proficiency in English, and consequently, they will make the assessment more direct.

17. Once you have composed a series of multiple-choice items or a test composed completely of this item type, tally the position of answers to be sure they are evenly distributed, to avoid the common psychological habit (when there are four alternatives) of having the correct alternative in the third position. In other words, when alternative choices are A, B, C, and D, or 1, 2, 3, and 4, unless the test designer is aware and avoids it, more correct answers will be in the "C" or "3" position than in any other.

18. Consider providing space between test items for students to include their rationales for their response selections, thus making the test a combination multiple-choice and short-explanation item type. This provides for the measurement of higher levels of cognition and encourages writing. It provides for the student who can rationalize an alternative that you had not considered plausible, especially possible today with the diversity of cultural experiences represented by students. For example, we recall the story of the following math question on a test: If a farmer saw eight crows sitting on a fence and shot three of them, how many would be left? Of course, the "correct" response on the answer key was five. However, one critically thinking student chose none as his response, an answer that was marked wrong by the teacher. However, the student was thinking that those crows that weren't shot would be frightened and would all fly away, thus he selected none as his answer.

19. While scoring, on a blank copy of the test, tally the incorrect responses for each item. Analyze incorrect responses for each item to discover potential errors in your scoring key. If, for example, many students select B for an item for which your key says the correct answer is A, you may have made a mistake on your scoring key or in teaching the lesson.

20. Some mainstreamed students may work better when allowed to circle their selected response rather than writing its letter or number in a blank space.

Performance

Description: Provided with certain conditions or materials, the student solves a problem or accomplishes some other action.

I. Specify the performance objective.

II. Specify the test situation or conditions.

III. Establish the criteria (scoring rubric) for judging the excellence of the process and/or product. Here is a sample rubric for assessing a student's skill in listening.
  A. Strong listener:
     Responds immediately to oral directions
     Focuses on speaker
     Maintains appropriate attention span
     Listens to what others are saying
     Is interactive
  B. Capable listener:
     Follows oral directions
     Usually attentive to speaker and to discussions
     Listens to others without interrupting
  C. Developing listener:
     Has difficulty following directions
     Relies on repetition
     Often inattentive
     Has short attention span
     Often interrupts the speaker

IV. Make a checklist by which to score the performance or product. The checklist is simply a list of the criteria you established in step III. For example, here is a brief checklist for map work:
  Check each item if the map comes up to standard in this particular category.
  _____ 1. Accuracy
  _____ 2. Neatness
  _____ 3. Attention to details

V. Prepare directions in writing, outlining the situation, with instructions the students are to follow.

Figure 11.8
Steps for setting up a performance assessment situation with a sample rubric for listening skill and a sample checklist for map work.

Example 1: Write a retelling of your favorite fable on the computer and create a diorama to go along with it.

Example 2: See Essay Example 2 previously.

Advantages: Performance test item types come closer to direct measurement (authentic assessment) of certain expected outcomes than do most other types. As has been indicated in discussions of the preceding question types, other types of questions can actually be prepared as performance-type items, that is, where the student actually does what he is being tested for.

Disadvantages: This type can be difficult and time-consuming to administer to a group of students. Scoring may tend to be subjective. It could be difficult to give make-up tests to students who were absent.

Guidelines for use: Use your creativity to design and use performance tests, as they tend to measure well the important objectives. To reduce subjectivity in scoring, prepare distinct scoring guidelines (rubrics), as was discussed in scoring essay-type items and as shown in Figures 11.9 and 11.10.[17] To set up a performance assessment situation, see the instructions in Figure 11.8.

Short Explanation

Description: The short-explanation question is like the essay type but requires a shorter answer.

Example 1: Briefly explain in a paragraph how you would end the story.

Example 2: Briefly explain why piano wires vary in length.

Advantages: As with the essay type, student understanding is assessed, but this type takes less time for the teacher to read and to score. By using several questions of this type, a greater amount of content can

---

17. For a presentation on the importance of rubrics, with samples, see M. Schmoker, *Results: The Key to Continuous School Improvement* (Alexandria, VA: Association for Supervision and Curriculum Development, 1996).

Professional Presentation	**14–15** Well organized; smooth transitions between sections; all enthusiastically participate and share responsibility.	**12–13** Well organized with transitions; students confer/present ideas; group shows ability to interact; attentive discussion of research.	**11** Shows basic organization; lacks transitions; some interaction; discussion focuses mostly on research.	**1–10** Unorganized, lacks planning; no transitions; reliance on one spokesperson; little interaction; disinterest; too brief.
Engagement of Audience	**14–15** Successfully and actively engages audience in more than one pertinent activity; maintains interest throughout.	**12–13** Engages audience in at least one related activity; maintains attention through most of presentation.	**11** Attempts to engage audience in at least one activity; no attempt to involve *entire* audience. May not relate in significant way.	**1–10** Fails to involve audience; does not maintain audience's attention; no connection with audience. No relationship between activity and topic.
Use of Literature	**18–20** Strong connection between literature and topic; significant, perceptive explanation of literature; pertinent to topic. At least two pieces used.	**16–17** Clear connection between literature and topic; clear explanation; appropriate to topic. Two pieces used.	**14–15** Weak connection to topic; unclear explanation; one genre; one piece used.	**1–13** No connection to topic; no explanation; inappropriate literature; no literature.
Knowledge of Subject	**18–20** Strong understanding of topic; knowledge factually relevant, accurate, and consistent; solution shows analysis of evidence.	**16–17** Good understanding of topic; uses main points of information researched; builds solution on examination of major evidence.	**14–15** Shows general understanding; focuses on one aspect, discusses at least one other idea; uses research, attempts to add to it; solution refers to evidence.	**1–13** Little understanding or comprehension of topic; uses little basic information researched; forms minimal solution; relies solely on own opinions without support.
Use of Media	**18–20** Effectively combines and integrates three distinct forms with one original piece; enhances understanding; offers insight into topic.	**16–17** Combines two forms with one original piece; relates to topic; connection between media and topic is explained.	**14–15** Includes two or three forms but no original piece; media relates to topic. Explanation may be vague or missing.	**1–13** One form; no original piece; connection between media and topic is unclear.
Speaking Skills	**9–10** Clear enunciation; strong projection; vocal variety; eye contact with entire audience; presentation posture; solid focus with no interruptions.	**8** Good enunciation; adequate projection; partial audience eye contact; appropriate posture.	**7** Inconsistent enunciation; low projection with little vocal variety; inconsistent posture.	**1–6** Difficult to understand; inaudible; monotonous; no eye contact; inappropriate posture; interruptions and distractions.

Figure 11.9
Sample of a scoring rubric for student project presentation. (*Source:* Elk Grove School District, Elk Grove, CA.)
(Possible score = 100. Scorer marks a relevant square in each of the six categories—the horizontal rows—and student's score for that category is the small number within that square.)

	14–15	12–13	11	1–10
Parenthetical References	All documented correctly. Paper's references document a wide variety of sources cited—at least five from bibliography.	Most documented correctly. Few minor errors. At least three sources from bibliography are cited.	Some documented correctly. Some show no documentation at all. May not correlate to the bibliography.	Few to none are documented. Does not correlate to the bibliography. May be totally absent.
	14–15	**12–13**	**11**	**1–10**
Bibliography and Sources	Strong use of library research. Exceeds minimum of five sources. Bibliography is correctly formatted.	Good use of library research. Exceeds minimum of five sources. Bibliography has few or no errors in format.	Some use of library research. Meets minimum of five sources. Bibliography is present but may be problematic.	Fails to meet minimum standards for library research. Bibliography has major flaws or may be missing.
	14–15	**12–13**	**11**	**1–10**
Mechanics/Format	Correct format and pagination. Neat title page, near-perfect spelling, punctuation, and grammar.	Mostly correct format and pagination. Neat. Few errors in title page, spelling, punctuation, and grammar.	Errors in format and pagination. Flawed title page. Distracting errors in spelling, punctuation, and grammar.	Incorrect format. Title page is flawed or missing. Many errors in spelling, punctuation, and grammar. Lack of planning is obvious. Paper is difficult to read.
	9–10	**8**	**7**	**1–6**
Thesis	An original and comprehensive thesis that is clear and well thought out. All sections work to support it.	Comprehensive and well-focused thesis, which is clearly stated. All sections work to support it.	Adequate thesis that is understandable but may be neither clear nor focused. It covers the majority of the issues found in the sections.	Inadequate thesis that is disconnected from the research or may be too broad to support. May be convoluted, confusing, or absent.
	18–20	**16–17**	**14–15**	**1–13**
Completeness/Coherence	Paper reads as a unified whole. There is no repetition of information. All sections are in place, and transitions between them are clearly developed.	Paper reads as a unified whole with no repetition. All sections are in place, but transitions between them are not as smooth.	Paper has required sections. Repetitions may be evident. The paper does not present a unified whole. Transitions are missing or inadequate.	Paper lacks one or more sections and makes no attempt to connect sections as a whole unit. Sections may be grossly repetitive or contradictory.
	23–25	**20–22**	**17–19**	**1–16**
Thinking/Analyzing	Strong understanding of the topic. Knowledge is factually relevant, accurate, and consistent. Solutions show analysis of research discussed in paper.	Good understanding of the topic. Uses main points of information researched. Solutions build on examination of research discussed in paper.	General understanding of topic. Uses research and attempts to add to it; solutions refer to some of the research discussed.	Little understanding of topic. Uses little basic information researched. Minimal examination of the topic. Solutions may be based solely on own opinions, without support.

Figure 11.10

Sample of a scoring rubric for student research paper. (*Source:* Elk Grove School District, Elk Grove, CA.)

(Possible score = 100. Scorer marks a relevant square in each of the six categories—the horizontal rows—and student's score for that category is the small number within that square.)

be covered than with fewer essay questions. This type of question is good practice for students to learn to express themselves succinctly in writing.

Disadvantages: Some students will have difficulty expressing themselves in a limited fashion or in writing. They need practice, coaching, and time.

Guidelines for use: This type is useful for occasional reviews and quizzes and as an alternative to other types of questions. For scoring, establish a scoring rubric and follow the same guidelines as for the essay-type item.

True-False

Description: A statement is presented that students are to judge as being accurate or not.

Example 1: T or F? A suffix is any bound morpheme added to the end of a root word.

Example 2: T or F? Christopher Columbus discovered America in 1492.

Advantages: Many items can be answered in a relatively short time, making broad content coverage possible. Scoring is quick and simple. True-false items are good as discussion starters, for review, and for diagnostic evaluation (preassessment) of what students already know or think they know.

Disadvantages: It is sometimes difficult to write true-false items that are purely true or false or without qualifying them in such a way that clues the answer. In the second sample question, for example, the student may question whether Columbus really did discover America or misunderstand the meaning of "discovering America." Weren't there people already there when he landed? Where, in fact, did he land? What is meant by "America?" Example 2 is poor also because it tests for more than one idea—Columbus, America, and 1492.

Much of the content that most easily lends itself to the true-false type of test item is trivial. Students have a 50 percent chance of guessing the correct answer, thus giving this item type both *poor validity* and *poor reliability*. Scoring and grading give no clue about why the student missed an item. Consequently, the disadvantages of true-false items far outweigh the advantages; *pure true-false items should not be used for arriving at grades*. For grading purposes, you may use modified true-false items (see guideline 11 subsequently), where space is provided between items for students to write in their explanations, thus making the item a combined true-false, short-explanation type.

Guidelines for use:

1. For preparing a false statement, first write the statement as a true statement, then make it false by changing a word or phrase.

2. Try to avoid using negative statements since they tend to confuse students.

3. A true-false statement should include only one idea.

4. Use close to an equal number of true and false items.

5. Try to avoid using specific determiners (e.g., *always, all,* or *none*), because they usually clue that the statement is false. Also avoid words that may clue that the statement is true (e.g., *often, probably,* and *sometimes*).

6. Avoid words that may have different meanings for different students.

7. Avoid using verbatim language from the student textbook.

8. Avoid trick items, such as a slight reversal of numbers in a date.

9. Rather than using symbols for the words *true* and *false* (sometimes teachers use symbols such as + and −), which might be confusing, or having students write the letters *T* and *F* (sometimes a student does not write the letters clearly enough for the teacher to distinguish which it is), have students either write out the words *true* and *false* or, better yet, have students simply circle *T* and *F* in the left margin of each item as indicated by the two previous samples.

10. Proofread your items (or have a friend do it) to be sure that the sentences are well constructed and free of typographical errors.

11. To avoid "wrong" answers, caused by variations in thinking, and to make the item more valid and reliable, students should be encouraged to write in their rationale for selecting true or false, making the item a *modified true-false* item. For example,

When a farmer saw eight crows sitting on the fence surrounding his cornfield, he shot three of them. Five were left on the fence. T or F? ___

Explanation:_____

As stated earlier, for grading purposes, you may use modified true-false items, thus making the item a combined true-false, short-explanation type, and allowing for divergent and critical thinking. Another form of modified true-false item is the "sometimes-always-never" item, where a third alternative, "sometimes," is introduced to reduce the chance for guessing.

Now do Exercise 11.2 to start the development of your skill in writing assessment items.

EXERCISE 11.2
Preparing Assessment Items

Instructions: The purpose of this exercise is to practice your skill in preparing the different types of assessment items discussed previously. For use in your own teaching, select one specific instructional objective and write assessment items for it. When completed, share this exercise with your colleagues for their feedback.

Objective: _____

Grade and subject: _____

1. Arrangement item: _____

   _____

   _____

   _____

2. Completion-drawing item: _____

   _____

   _____

   _____

3. Completion-statement item: _____

   _____

   _____

   _____

4. Correction item: _____

   _____

   _____

   _____

5. Essay item: _____

   _____

   _____

   _____

6. Grouping item: _____

_____

_____

_____

7. Identification item: _____

_____

_____

_____

8. Matching item: _____

_____

_____

_____

_____

9. Multiple-choice item: _____

_____

_____

_____

_____

10. Performance item: _____

_____

_____

_____

_____

11. Short-explanation item: _____

_____

_____

_____

_____

12. *Modified* true-false item: _____

_____

_____

_____

_____

REPORTING STUDENT ACHIEVEMENT

One of your responsibilities as a classroom teacher is to report student progress in achievement to parents or guardians. In some schools student progress and effort as well as achievement are reported. As described in the discussions that follow, reporting is done in at least two, and sometimes more than two, ways.[18] However, for secondary schools, letter grades on report cards are still the most widely used method for reporting student learning.[19]

The Grade Report

Periodically a grade report (report card) is issued. Generally it is done four to six times a year, depending upon the school, its purpose, and its type of scheduling. This grade report represents an achievement grade (formative evaluation). The final one of the semester is also the semester grade, and for courses that are only one semester long it also is the final grade (summative evaluation). In essence, the first and sometimes second reports are progress notices, with the semester grade being the one that is transferred to the student's transcript of records. In some schools reporting is done by computer printouts, often sent by mail directly to the student's home address.

In addition to the student's academic achievement, you must report the student's social behaviors (classroom conduct) while in your classroom. Whichever reporting form is used, you must separate your assessments of a student's social behaviors from the student's academic achievement. Academic achievement (or accomplishment) is represented by a letter and sometimes a number grade (A through E or F; E, S, and U; or 1 to 5, and sometimes with minuses and pluses). Social behavior is reported by a "satisfactory" or an "unsatisfactory," or by more specific items, or is supplemented by teacher-written or computer-generated comments.

In addition to grading and reporting on subject-matter knowledge, some secondary schools are including a broader set of "workplace" or "life" skills that transcend particular subject areas. For example, Academy High School (Fort Myers, FL) uses a "work ethic checklist,"

which is part of the senior portfolio in the school's internship preparation program.[20]

In some instances, there may be a location on the reporting form for the teacher to check whether basic grade-level standards have been met in the core subjects. As an extension to that, some high schools use a two-tiered graduation diploma system, with a basic tier for the student who has reached only minimal standards in the basic core subject areas (usually reading, science, and mathematics) for graduation and a second tier for the student who has reached a standard higher than the minimal.

PARENTAL INVOLVEMENT AND HOME-SCHOOL PARTNERSHIPS

Study after study shows that when parents get involved in their child's school and schoolwork, students learn better and earn better grades, and teachers experience more positive feelings about teaching.[21] As a result of those studies, schools increasingly are searching for new and better ways to involve parents. What follows are suggestions and resources.

Ways to Involve Parents

Although it is not always obligatory, some teachers make a point to contact parents or guardians by telephone or e-mail, especially when a student has shown a sudden turn for either the worse or the better in academic achievement or in classroom behavior. That initiative and contact by the teacher are usually welcomed by parents and can lead to productive conferences with the teacher. A telephone conference can save valuable time for both the teacher and the parent.

Another way of contacting parents is by letter. A letter gives you time to think and to make clear your thoughts and concerns to that parent and to invite the parent to respond at his convenience by letter, by phone, or by arranging to have a conference with you.

In the absence of a computer-link assignment/progress report hot line, most schools have a progress report form that, upon request by a parent, can be sent home with the student. It may be similar to the one from a middle school in Figure 11.11, which shows the student's progress in each of the core subjects. Or perhaps it is like the one from a high school in Figure 11.12, which

18. For a recent research report on various methods used by secondary schools for reporting, see J. Bailey and J. McTighe, "Reporting Achievement at the Secondary Level: What and How," in Guskey, pp. 119–140.

19. See J. W. Valentine, et al., *Leadership in Middle Level Education: Volume 1: A National Survey of Middle Level Leaders and Schools* (Reston, VA: National Association of Secondary School Principals, 1993), p. 61; see also Guskey, p. 121.

20. J. Bailey and J. McTighe, "Reporting Achievement at the Secondary Level: What and How," in Guskey, p. 121.

21. G. Fawcett and T. Rasinski, "Take Parents Where They Are . . . Not Where You Want Them to Be," *Learning* 24(3):43 (October/November 1995).

Weekly Assessment Checklist for _____

	Math	History	Science	Language Arts
Number of tardies				
Number of absences				
Academic grade				
Citizenship grade				

	Usually	Sometimes	Rarely	Never
Homework turned in on time				
Class work satisfactorily completed				
Exhibits acceptable classroom behavior				
Exhibits acceptable use of time in class				
Skill level is adequate to do work				
Participates orally in class discussions				
Participates in classroom learning activities				
Assumes responsibilities for own actions				
Avoids talking excessively or out of turn				
Comes to class prepared with supplies				
Is ready to start working when class begins				
Performs well on quizzes and tests				
Is attentive and focused during class				
Shows good listening skills				
Shows good organizational skills				
Shows up for assigned detentions				
Respects the property of others and of the school				
Respects the rights of others				

Other comments or concerns _____

_____

_____

_____

_____

_____

_____

_____

_____

_____

Figure 11.11
Weekly assessment checklist: middle school sample with teacher input only.

Progress Report: Marina High School

Student: _Anthony von Hauser_   Course: _Algebra 1_   Date: _September 14, 1997_

This progress report form incorporates evaluation by student, teacher, and parent. The form will be completed by the student on Wednesday and by the teacher on Thursday and reviewed by the office and returned to the student on Friday. The student will take the form home for parental review, comments, and signature.

Section I: Self-Assessment: The student is asked to evaluate progress in the course in terms of goals and how closely these goals are being achieved. Do you feel you have made progress since the last progress report?

By taking this algebra class I achieved a greater understanding of it. I feel I have made a lot of progress since I took the class in 8th grade. It is also taught much better, which makes it easier.

Section II: Teacher Assessment: The teacher is asked to assess the student's entry, competency, and achievement to date and make recommendations.

Anthony is doing quite well. He has had to make some adjustments from previous work habits (ie, showing work), but he has made an excellent transition. Anthony has great skills and strong understanding of concepts.

	Present Status: (Rated A–F)		What Is Needed
B+	Class work/ participation	A = Excellent	✔ Emphasis on homework
C+	Homework	B = Above average	____ Improve class participation
A	Portfolio	C = Average	____ More careful preparation for tests
A	Quizzes	D = Below average	
A	Tests	F = Failing	✔ Keep up the good work
A	Overall		____ Contact teacher
			____ Improve portfolio
			____ Other _____
			Office initial ___CM_____

Section III: Parent Evaluation and Comments: Parents are asked to respond and sign this progress report.

I thank you for this timely report. I am delighted that Anthony has started off well and is liking the class. He talks at home a lot about the class and the interesting activities; a tribute to good teaching. I can tell from our conversations at home that he is feeling much better about his math capability. I thank you

Eric von Hauser

Figure 11.12
Progress report: high school subject-specific sample with student and parent input.

requires student self-evaluation, teacher assessment, office signature, and parental response and signature.

You will meet some of the parents or guardians early in the school year during back-to-school night and throughout the year in individual parent conferences. For the beginning teacher, these meetings with parents can be anxious times. But, in fact, it is a time to celebrate your work and to solicit help from parents. The following paragraphs provide guidelines to help you with those experiences.

As you recall from Chapter 1, back-to-school night or meet-the-teacher night is the evening early in the school year when parents and guardians come to the school

and meet their children's teachers. The parents arrive at the student's home base and then proceed through a simulation of their child's school day; as a group, they meet each class and each teacher for a few minutes. Later, in the spring, there is an open house where parents may have more time to talk individually with teachers, although the major purpose of the open house is for the school and teachers to celebrate and display the work and progress of the students for that year. Throughout the school year, there will be opportunities for you and parents to meet and talk about their child.

At back-to-school night, parents are anxious to learn as much as they can about their children's teachers.

You will meet each group of parents for a brief time, perhaps about ten minutes. During that meeting you will provide them with a copy of the course syllabus, make some straightforward remarks about yourself, talk about the course and its requirements, your expectations of the students, and how the parents might help.

Although there will be precious little time for questions from the parents, during your introduction the parents will be delighted to learn that you have your program well planned, are a "task master," appreciate their interest and welcome their participation, and will communicate with them. The parents and guardians will be pleased to know that you are "from the school of the three F's"—that is, you are firm, friendly, and fair.

Specifically, parents will expect to learn about your curriculum goals and objectives, about any long-term projects, about when tests will be given and whether on a regular basis, and about your grading procedures. They will want to know what you expect of them: Will there be homework, and if so, should they help their children with it? How can they contact you? Try to anticipate other questions. Your principal, department chair, or colleagues can be of aid in helping you anticipate and prepare for these questions. Of course, you can never prepare for the question that comes from left field. Just remain calm and avoid being flustered (or at least appear so). Ten minutes will fly by quickly, and parents will be reassured to know you are in control.

As parents who have attended many back-to-school nights at our own children's schools, we continue to be both surprised and dismayed that so few teachers seem well prepared for the few minutes they have with the parents; that considering how often we hear about teachers wanting more involvement of parents, so few seem delighted that parents have indeed come; and that so few teachers take full advantage of this time with parents to truly celebrate their programs. Consequently, we include a model handout (Figure 11.13) that demonstrates the kind of planning a teacher should do for back-to-school night with parents and the sort of information that parents appreciate receiving from their children's teachers.

When meeting parents for conferences, you should be as specific as possible when explaining their child's progress in your class. Again, express your appreciation for their interest. Be helpful to her understanding, and don't saturate the parent with more information than she needs. Resist the tendency to talk too much. Allow time for the parent to ask questions. Keep your answers succinct. Never compare one student with another or with the rest of the class. If the parent asks a question for which you do not have an answer, tell the parent you will try to find an answer and will phone the parent as quickly as you can. And do it. Have the student's portfolio and other work with you during the parent conference so that you can show examples of what is being discussed. Also, have your grade book on hand, or a computer printout of it, but be prepared to protect from the parent the names and records of the other students.

Sometimes it is helpful to have a three-way conference, a conference with the parent, the student, and you, or a conference with the parent, the principal or counselor, and several or all of the student's teachers. If, especially as a beginning teacher, you would like the presence of an administrator at a parent-teacher conference as backup, don't be hesitant to arrange that.

Some educators prefer a student-led conference, arguing that "placing students in charge of the conference makes them individually accountable, encourages them to take pride in their work, and encourages student-parent communication about school performance." But, like most innovations in education, the concept of student-led conferences has its limitations—the most important of which perhaps is the matter of time and scheduling, especially for high school teachers.[22]

Ideas for Teacher-Parent Collaboration

When a parent asks how he may help in the child's learning, the paragraphs that follow offer suggestions for your consideration. Many schools have made special and successful efforts to link home and school. At some schools, through homework hot lines, parents have phone access to their children's assignment specifications and to their progress in their schoolwork, and parents with a personal computer and a modem have access to tutorial services to assist students with assignments.

Helping students become critical thinkers is one of the aims of education and one that parents can help with by reinforcing the strategies being used in the classroom. Ways to do this are to ask "what if" questions and to think aloud as a model for the child's thinking development. Encourage the child's own metacognition by asking questions such as "How did you arrive at that conclusion?" or "How do you feel about your conclusion now?" Ask these questions about the child's everyday social interactions, topics that are important to the child. Ask the child to elaborate on her ideas, accepting the fact that the child may make mistakes but encourage the child to learn from them.

---

22. See D. W. Johnson and R. T. Johnson, "The Role of Cooperative Learning in Assessing and Communicating Student Learning," in Guskey, p. 43; for a discussion of the pros and cons of using the student-led conference and for a conference organizer tool, see J. Bailey and J. McTighe, "Reporting Achievement at the Secondary Level: What and How," in Guskey, pp.137–139. See also L. Countryman and M. Schroeder, "When Students Lead Parent-Teacher Conferences," *Educational Leadership* 53(7):64–68 (April 1996).

Course:	Honors Precalculus (HP)
Instructor:	Mr. Charles Schwing
Text:	Advanced Mathematical Concepts
Description:	This is an accelerated class designed to prepare the student for calculus. As an Honors class (HP), the course requires a higher level of commitment on the part of the student. Grades of *A, B,* or *C* are awarded an extra grade point by St. Francis High School and by the University of California and California State University systems and are given extra weight by many other public and private colleges and universities. A partial listing of topics covered in this class includes analytic geometry, trigonometry, matrices and determinants, probability and statistics, and an introduction to calculus, including the epsilon-delta definition of limit.
Homework:	Homework is assigned daily (with very few exceptions) and should require approximately 30 to 40 minutes to complete. Success in this class is virtually impossible unless assignments are done in a timely and conscientious manner.
Grades:	Points are given for homework, quizzes, and major exams. Grades are computed based on total points, with quizzes and exams comprising 75% of those points. The grading scale is *A* = 88% or above, *B* = 75–87%, *C* = 60–74%, *D* = below 60%. To earn an *F* requires a special "effort" on the part of the student.
Citizenship:	Students begin this class with an *A* in citizenship. Demerits are earned for tardiness and inappropriate behavior. Three demerits result in a one letter drop in citizenship (e.g., from an *A* to a *B*).
Instructor Availability:	I am available for extra help from 7:45 until 8:10 each morning, during blocks C, D, and F, and after school until 4:00. I can be at school before 7:45 or after 4:00 if arranged in advance. It is your child's responsibility to seek me out—I will not chase after a student to come in for help. If extra help is obtained as soon as the need arises, it is usually only a matter of a 10- or 15-minute session. Hours at a time are rarely needed. There is most definitely a positive correlation between the students who come in for help and the grades they receive. If at any time you are concerned about your child's progress, please feel free to call me at school and leave a message. I will get back to you the same day if at all possible.

Figure 11.13
Handout for parents at back-to-school night. (*Source:* Courtesy of Charles Schwing.)

Many resources are available for parents to use at home. The U.S. government, for example, has a variety of free or low-cost booklets available. For information contact the Consumer Information Center, Department BEST, Pueblo, CO 81009 or their Web site, <http://www.pueblo.gsa.gov>.

Other useful resources are N. Berla et. al, *The Middle School Years: A Parents' Handbook* (Columbia, MD: National Committee for Citizens in Education, 1989) and D. Elkind, *Parenting Your Teenager in the '90s* (Rosemont, NJ: Modern Learning Press, 1993). Figure 11.14 lists addresses for additional ideas and resources for home–school partnerships.

Dealing with an Angry Parent or Guardian

If a parent or guardian is angry or hostile toward you and the school, the paragraphs that follow offer guidelines for dealing with that hostility.

Remain calm in your discussion with the parent, allowing the parent to talk out his hostility while you say very little; usually, the less you say, the better off you will be. What you do say must be objective and to the point of the child's work in your classroom. The parent may just need to vent frustrations that might have very little to do with you, the school, or even the child.

- **Alliance for Parental Involvement in Education,** PO Box 59, East Chatham, NY 12060-0059; (518) 392-6900.
- **Center on Families, Communities, Schools & Children's Learning,** 3505 N. Charles St., Baltimore, MD 21218; (410) 516-8800.
- **National Coalition for Parent Involvement in Education,** Box 39, 1201 16th St., NW, Washington, DC 20036.
- **National Community Education Association,** 3929 Old Lee Highway, Suite 91A, Fairfax, VA 22030-2401; (703) 359-8973.
- **National PTA,** 330 North Wabash Ave., Ste. 2100, Chicago, IL 60611-3690; (312)670-6782.
- **Parents for Public Schools,** PO Box 12807, Jackson, MS 39236-2807; (800) 880-1222.

Figure 11.14
Resources for developing home-school partnerships.

Do *not* allow yourself to be intimidated, put on the defensive, or backed into a verbal corner. If the parent tries to do so by attacking you personally, do not press your defense at this point. Perhaps the parent has made a point that you should take time to consider, and now is a good time to arrange for another conference with the parent for about a week later. In a follow-up conference, if the parent agrees, you may want to consider bringing in a mediator, such as another member of your teaching team, an administrator, or a school counselor.

You must *not* talk about other students; keep the conversation focused on the progress of this parent's child. The parent is *not* your rival or should not be. You both share a concern for the academic and emotional well-being of the child. Use your best skills in critical thinking and problem solving, trying to focus the discussion by identifying the problem, defining it, and then arriving at some decision about how mutually to go about solving it. To this end you may need to ask for help from a third party, such as the child's school counselor. If agreed to by the parent, please take that step.

Parents do *not* need to hear about how busy you are, about your personal problems, or about how many other students you are dealing with on a daily basis, unless, of course, a parent asks. Parents expect you to be the capable professional who knows what to do and is doing it.

SUMMARY

Whereas preceding parts of this resource guide addressed the *why, what,* and *how* components of teaching, this chapter has focused your attention on the fourth and final component—*how well.* Assessment is an integral and ongoing factor in the teaching-learning process; consequently, this chapter has emphasized the importance of including the following in your teaching performance:

- Use a variety of instruments to assess the learning of students that focus on their individual development.

- Keep students informed of their progress. Return tests promptly, review answers to all questions, and respond to inquiries about marks given.
- Consider your assessment and grading procedures carefully, plan them, and explain your policies to the students.
- Make sure to explain any ambiguities that result from the terminology used, and base your assessments on the material that has been taught.
- Strive for objective and impartial assessment as you put your assessment plan into operation.
- Try to minimize arguments about grades, cheating, and teacher subjectivity by involving students in the planning, reinforcing individual student development, and providing an accepting, stimulating learning environment.
- Maintain accurate and clear records of assessment results so that you will have an adequate supply of data on which to base your judgmental decisions about achievement.

Because teaching and learning work hand in hand and because they are reciprocal processes in which one depends on and affects the other, the how well component deals with the assessment of both how well the students are learning and how well the teacher is teaching. This chapter has dealt with the first. In the next and final chapter of this resource guide, your attention is directed to techniques designed to help you develop your teaching skills and assess that development, a process that will continue throughout your teaching career.

QUESTIONS FOR CLASS DISCUSSION

1. Other than a paper-and-pencil test, identify three alternative techniques for assessing student learning during or at completion of an instructional unit.
2. Investigate various ways that secondary schools are experimenting today with assessing and reporting student achievement. Share what you find with your class-

mates. Analyze the pros and cons of various systems of assessing and reporting.

3. When using a point system for determining student grades for a class of students, is it educationally defensible to give a student a higher grade than that student's points call for? A lower grade? Give your rationale for your answers.

4. Explain the dangers of using true-false and completion-type items in assessing student learning and using the results for grade determination.

5. Describe any student learning activities or situations that you believe should *not* be graded but should or could be used for assessment of student learning.

6. Some educational analysts suggest that state and national curriculum and performance standards be established for all students to meet—not an easy matter and one that could lead to criticism related to elitism, wrong approach-ism, and possibly disenfranchisement of students. Debate with colleagues your views on the topic of state and national standards after reading one of the following: R. Rothman, *Measuring Up: Standards, Assessment, and School Reform* (San Francisco: Jossey-Bass, 1995); D. Ravitch, *National Standards in American Education: A Citizen's Guide* (New York: The Brookings Institute, 1995). J. Loewen, *Lies My Teacher Told Me: Everything Your American History Textbook Got Wrong* (New York: The New Press, 1995).

7. To what extent do you believe the curriculum and practices of high schools are, or should be, driven or guided by the expectations of institutions of postsecondary education? Discuss your opinion with those of your classmates.

8. Describe any prior concepts you held that changed as a result of your experiences with this chapter. Describe the changes.

9. From your current observations and fieldwork as related to this teacher preparation program, clearly identify one specific example of educational practice that seems contradictory to exemplary practice or theory as presented in this chapter. Present your explanation for the discrepancy.

10. Do you have questions generated by the content of this chapter? If you do, list them along with ways answers might be found.

Suggested Readings

Daniels, H. "The Best Practice Project: Building Parent Partnerships in Chicago." *Educational Leadership* 53(7):38–43 (April 1996).

Davis, S. J. "Teaching Practices That Encourage or Eliminate Student Plagiarism." *Middle School Journal* 25(3):55–58 (January 1994).

Earl, L. M., and LeMahieu, P. G. "Rethinking Assessment and Accountability," in A. Hargreaves (ed.), *Rethinking Educational Change with Heart and Mind*. Alexandria, VA:

ASCD 1997 Yearbook, Association for Supervision and Curriculum Development, 1997, pp. 149–168.

Guskey, T. R., ed. *Communicating Student Learning*. Alexandria, VA: ASCD Yearbook, Association for Supervision and Curriculum Development, 1996.

Hackmann, D. G. "Student-Led Conferences at the Middle Level: Promoting Student Responsibility." *NASSP Bulletin* 80(578): 31–36 (March 1996).

Haladyna, T. M. *Writing Test Items to Evaluate Higher Order Thinking*. Needham Heights, MA: Allyn & Bacon, 1997.

Juarez, T. "Why Any Grades at All, Father?" *Phi Delta Kappan* 77(5):374–377 (January 1996).

Krumboltz, J. D., and Yeh, C. J. "Competitive Grading Sabotages Good Teaching." *Phi Delta Kappan* 78(4):324–326 (December 1996).

Lustig, K. *Portfolio Assessment: A Handbook for Middle Level Teachers*. Columbus, OH: National Middle Schools Association, 1996.

McCarthy, A. R. *Healthy Teens: Success in High School and Beyond*. Birmingham, MI: Bridge Communications, 1996.

McMillan, J. H. *Classroom Assessment: Principles and Practice for Effective Instruction*. Needham Heights, MA: Allyn & Bacon, 1997.

Miller, H. M. "No More One-Legged Chairs: Sharing the Responsibility for Portfolio Assessment with Students, Their Peers, and Their Parents." *Middle School Journal* 28(3):242–244 (January 1997).

National PTA. *National Standards for Parent/Family Involvement Programs*. Chicago: National PTA, 1997.

Overturf, B. J. "Reading Portfolios Reveal New Dimensions of Students." *Middle School Journal* 28(3):45–50 (January 1997).

Popham, W. J. *Classroom Assessment: What Teachers Need to Know*. Needham Heights, MA: Allyn & Bacon, 1995.

Radford, D. L., et al. "Demonstration Assessment: Measuring Conceptual Understanding and Critical Thinking with Rubrics." *Science Teacher* 62(76):52–55 (October 1995).

Schmoker, M. *Results: The Key to Continuous School Improvement*. Alexandria, VA: Association for Supervision and Curriculum Development, 1996.

Shaklee, B. D., Barbour, N. E., Ambrose, R., and Hansford, S. *Designing and Using Portfolios*. Needham Heights, MA: Allyn & Bacon, 1997.

Sills-Briegel, T., Fisk, C., and Dunlop, V. "Graduation by Exhibition." *Educational Leadership* 54(4):66–71 (December 1996/January 1997).

Sobolewski, S. J. "Development of Multiple-Choice Test Items." *Physics Teacher* 34(2):80–82 (February 1996).

Stiggins, R. J. *Student-Centered Classroom Assessment*. 2nd ed. Upper Saddle River, NJ: Prentice Hall, 1997.

Sylwester, R. "The Neurobiology of Self-Esteem and Aggression," *Educational Leadership* 54(5):75–79 (February 1997).

Wiggins, G. "Practicing What We Preach in Designing Authentic Assessments." *Educational Leadership* 54(4):18–25 (December 1996/January 1997).

Chapter

12

Professional Development and Assessment of Teaching Effectiveness

The bad news is that most of us are not born with innate teaching skills; the good news is that *teaching skills can be learned and steadily improved.* Teachers who wish to improve their teaching can do so, and in addition to this resource guide, there are many resources that can help.

This chapter addresses the evaluation and development of your effectiveness as a classroom teacher, a process that continues throughout your professional career. Teaching is such an electrifying profession that it is not easy to remain energetic and to stay abreast of changes and trends that result from research and practice. You will need to make a continuous and determined effort to remain an alert and effective teacher.

Whether you are a beginning or an experienced teacher, one way to collect data and to improve your effectiveness is through periodic assessment of your teaching performance, either by an evaluation of your teaching in the real classroom or, if you are in a program of teacher preparation, by a technique called micro peer teaching. The latter is the focus of the first section of this chapter and is an example of a type of final performance (authentic) assessment for this resource guide.

Specifically, upon completion of this chapter you should be able to

1. Demonstrate growing teacher competencies.
2. Demonstrate your understanding of your responsibilities while in the field components of teacher preparation.
3. Demonstrate your awareness of ways to find a teaching job and to remain an alert and effective classroom teacher throughout your teaching career.

PROFESSIONAL DEVELOPMENT THROUGH MICRO PEER TEACHING

Micro peer teaching (MPT) is a skill-development strategy used for professional development by both preservice (prior to credentialing) and inservice (credentialed and employed) teachers. Micro peer teaching (to which you were introduced in Exercises 7.6, 9.1, and 9.3) is a scaled-down teaching experience involving a

- Limited objective.
- Brief interval for teaching a lesson.
- Lesson taught to a few (eight to ten) peers (as your students).
- Lesson that focuses on the use of one or several instructional strategies.

Micro peer teaching can be a predictor of later teacher effectiveness in a regular classroom. More important, it can provide an opportunity to develop and improve specific teaching behaviors. A videotaped MPT allows you to see yourself in action for self-evaluation and diagnosis. Evaluation of an MPT session is based on

- The quality of the teacher's preparation and lesson implementation.
- The quality of the planned and implemented student involvement.
- Whether the instructional objective(s) was reached.
- The appropriateness of the cognitive level of the lesson.

Whether a preservice or inservice teacher, you are urged to participate in one or more MPT experiences. Exercise 12.1, although formatted differently from previous exercises, should help you better understand the process of micro peer teaching.

EXERCISE 12.1

Pulling It All Together—Micro Peer Teaching IV

Instructions. The purpose of this exercise is to learn how to develop your own MPT experiences. You will prepare and teach a lesson that is prepared as a lesson presentation for your peers, at their level of intellectual maturity and understanding (i.e., as opposed to teaching the lesson to peers pretending that they are public school students).

This experience has two components:

1. Your preparation and implementation of a demonstration lesson.
2. Your completion of an analysis of the summative peer assessment and the self-assessment, with statements of how you would change the lesson and your teaching of it were you to repeat the lesson.

You should prepare and carry out a 15- to 20-minute lesson to a group of peers. The exact time limit for the lesson should be set by your group, based on the size of the group and the amount of time available. When the time limit has been set, complete the time-allowed entry (item 1) of Form A of this exercise. Some of your peers will serve as your students; others will be evaluating your teaching. (The process works best when "students" do not evaluate while being students.) Your teaching should be videotaped for self-evaluation.

For your lesson, identify one concept and develop your lesson to teach toward an understanding of that concept. Within the time allowed, your lesson should include both teacher talk and a hands-on activity for the students. Use Form A for the initial planning of your lesson. Then complete a lesson plan, selecting a lesson plan format as discussed in Chapter 5. Then present the lesson to the "students." The peers who are evaluating your presentation should use Form B of this exercise.

After your presentation, collect your peer evaluations (the Form B copies that you gave to the evaluators). Then review your presentation by viewing the videotape. After viewing the tape, prepare

- A tabulation and statistical analysis of peer evaluations of your lesson.
- A self-evaluation based on your analysis of the peer evaluations, your feelings having taught the lesson, and your thoughts after viewing the videotape.
- A summary analysis that includes your selection and description of your teaching strengths and weaknesses, as indicated by this peer-teaching experience, and how you would improve were you to repeat the lesson.

Tabulation of Peer Evaluations

The procedure for tabulating the completed evaluations received from your peers is as follows:

1. *Use a blank copy of Form B for tabulating.* In the left margin of that copy, place the letters N (number) and σ (total) to prepare for two columns of numbers that will fall below each of those letters. In the far right margin, place the word *Score*.
2. *For each item (a through y) on the peer evaluation form, count the number of evaluators who gave a rating (from 1 to 5) on the item.* Sometimes an evaluator may not rate a particular item, so although ten peers may have been evaluating your micro peer teaching, the number of evaluators giving you a rating on any one particular item could be less than ten. For each item,

the number of evaluators rating that item we call *N*. Place this number in the *N* column at the far left margin on your blank copy of Form B, next to the relevant item.

3. *Using a calculator, obtain the sum of the peer ratings for each item.* For example, for item a, Lesson Preparation, you add the numbers given by each evaluator for that item. If there were ten evaluators who gave you a number rating on that item, then your sum on that item will not be more than 50 (5 × 10). Because individual evaluators will make their *X* marks differently, you sometimes must estimate an individual evaluator's number rating—that is, rather than a clear rating of 3 or 3.5 on an item, you may have to estimate it as being a 3.2 or a 3.9. In the left margin of your blank copy of Form B, in the σ column, place the sum for each item.

4. *Now obtain a score for each item, a through y.* The score for each item is obtained by dividing σ by *N*. Your score for each item will range between 1 and 5. Write this dividend in the column in the right margin under the word *Score* on a line parallel to the relevant item. This is the number you will use in the analysis phase.

Procedure for Analyzing the Tabulations

Having completed the tabulation of the peer evaluations of your teaching, you are ready to proceed with your analysis of those tabulations.

1. To proceed, you need a blank copy of Form C of this exercise, your self-analysis form.
2. On the blank copy of Form C, there are five items: Implementation, Personal, Voice, Materials, and Strategies.
3. In the far left margin of Form C, place the letter σ for the sum. To its right, and parallel with it, place the word *Average*. You now have arranged for two columns of five numbers each—a σ column and an *Average* column.
4. For each of the five items, get the total score for that item, as follows:
   a. *Implementation.* Add all scores (from the right margin of blank Form B) for the four items a, c, x, and y. The total should be 20 or less (4 × 5). Place this total in the left margin under σ (to the left of "1. Implementation").
   b. *Personal.* Add all scores (from the right margin of blank Form B) for the nine items f, g, m, n, o, p, q, s, and t. The total should be 45 or less (9 × 5). Place this total in the left margin under σ (to the left of "2. Personal").
   c. *Voice.* Add all scores (from the right margin of blank Form B) for the three items h, i, and j. The total should be 15 or less (3 × 5). Place this total in the left margin under σ (to the left of "3. Voice").
   d. *Materials.* Add all scores (from the right margin of blank Form B) for item k. The total should be 5 or less (1 × 5). Place this total in the left margin under σ (to the left of "4. Materials").
   e. *Strategies.* Add all "scores" (from the right margin of blank Form B) for the eight items b, d, e, l, r, u, v, and w. The total should be 40 or less (8 × 5). Place this total in the left margin under σ (to the left of "5. Strategies").
5. Now, for each of the five categories, divide the sum by the number of items in the category to get your peer evaluation average score for that category. For item 1 you will divide by 4; for item 2, by 9; for item 3, by 3; for item 4, by 1; and for item 5, by 8. For each category you should then have a final average peer evaluation score of a number between 1 and 5. If correctly done, you now have average scores for each of the five categories: Implementation, Personal, Voice, Materials, and Strategies. With those scores and evaluator's comments you can prepare your final summary analysis.

The following table includes three sample analyses of MPT lessons based *only* on the scores—that is, without reference to comments made by individual evaluators, although peer evaluator's comments are important considerations for actual analyses.

Sample Analyses of MPTs Based Only on Peer Evaluation Scores

| Teacher | Category/Rating | | | | | Possible Strengths and Weaknesses |
	1	2	3	4	5	
A	4.2	2.5	2.8	4.5	4.5	Good lesson, weakened by personal items and voice
B	4.5	4.6	5.0	5.0	5.0	Excellent teaching, perhaps needing a stronger start
C	2.5	3.0	3.5	1.0	1.5	Poor strategy choice, lack of student involvement

For Your Notes

EXERCISE 12.1 FORM A
MPT Preparation

Form A is to be used for initial preparation of your MPT lesson. (For preparation of your lesson, study Form B.) After completing Form A, proceed with the preparation of your MPT lesson using a lesson plan format as discussed in Chapter 5. A copy of the final lesson plan should be presented to the evaluators at the start of your MPT presentation.

1. Time allowed: _____

2. Title or topic of lesson I will teach: _____

3. Concept: _____

4. Specific instructional objectives for the lesson:

   Cognitive: _____

   _____

   Affective: _____

   _____

   Psychomotor: _____

   _____

5. Strategies to be used, including approximate time plan: _____

   Set introduction: _____

   _____

   Transitions: _____

   _____

   Closure: _____

   _____

   Others: _____

   _____

6. Student experiences to be provided (i.e., specify for each—visual, verbal, kinesthetic, and tactile experiences):

   _____

   _____

7. Materials, equipment, and resources needed:

   _____

   _____

For Your Notes

EXERCISE 12.1 FORM B
Peer Evaluation

Evaluators use Form B, making an *X* on the continuum between 5 and 1. Far left (5) is the highest rating; far right (1) is the lowest. Completed forms are collected and given to the teacher upon completion of that teacher's MPT and are reviewed by the teacher prior to reviewing his videotaped lesson.

To evaluators: Comments as well as marks are useful to the teacher.

To teacher: Give one copy of your lesson plan to the evaluators at the start of your MPT. (*Note:* It is best if evaluators can be together at a table at the rear of the room.)

Teacher: _____ Date: _____

Topic: _____

Concept: _____

1. Organization of Lesson	5	4	3	2	1
a. Lesson preparation evident	very		somewhat		no
b. Lesson beginning effective	yes		somewhat		poor
c. Subject-matter knowledge apparent	yes		somewhat		no
d. Strategies selection effective	yes		somewhat		poor
e. Closure effective	yes		somewhat		poor

Comments: _____

_____

_____

_____

_____

_____

_____

_____

_____

2. Lesson Implementation	5	4	3	2	1
f. Eye contact excellent	yes		somewhat		poor
g. Enthusiasm evident	yes		somewhat		no
h. Speech delivery	articulate		minor problems		poor
i. Voice inflection; cueing	effective		minor problems		poor
j. Vocabulary use	well chosen		minor problems		poor

k. Aids, props, and materials	effective	okay	none
l. Use of examples and analogies	effective	need improvement	none
m. Student involvement	effective	okay	none
n. Use of overlapping skills	good	okay	poor
o. Nonverbal communication	effective	a bit confusing	distracting
p. Use of active listening	effective	okay	poor
q. Responses to students	personal and accepting	passive or indifferent	impersonal and antagonistic
r. Use of questions	effective	okay	poor
s. Use of student names	effective	okay	no
t. Use of humor	effective	okay	poor
u. Directions and refocusing	succinct	a bit vague	confusing
v. Teacher mobility	effective	okay	none
w. Use of transitions	smooth	a bit rough	unclear
x. Motivating presentation	very	somewhat	not at all
y. Momentum (pacing) of lesson	smooth and brisk	okay	too slow or too fast

Comments: _____

_____

_____

_____

_____

_____

_____

_____

_____

_____

_____

_____

_____

_____

_____

EXERCISE 12.1 FORM C
Teacher's Summative Peer Evaluation

See instructions within Exercise 12.1 for completing this form.

1. Implementation (items a, c, x, y)   5   4   3   2   1

2. Personal (items f, g, m, n, o, p, q, s, t)   5   4   3   2   1

3. Voice (items h, i, j)   5   4   3   2   1

4. Materials (item k)   5   4   3   2   1

5. Strategies (items b, d, e, l, r, u, v, w)   5   4   3   2   1

Total = _____

Comments: _____

_____

_____

_____

_____

_____

_____

_____

_____

_____

_____

_____

_____

_____

_____

_____

_____

_____

_____

_____

_____

For Your Notes

PROFESSIONAL DEVELOPMENT THROUGH STUDENT TEACHING

You are excited about the prospect of being assigned as a student teacher to your first classroom, but you are also concerned. Questions linger in your mind. Will your host (cooperating) teacher(s) like you? Will you get along? Will the students accept you? Will you be assigned to the school, grade level, and subjects you want? What will the students be like? Will there be many classroom management problems? What about mainstreamed students and students with only limited proficiency in English? Your questions will be unending.

Indeed, you *should* be excited and concerned, for this experience of student teaching is one of the most significant and important facets of your program of teacher preparation. In some programs, this practical field experience is planned as a coexperience with the college or university theory classes. In other programs, student teaching is the culminating experience. Different sequences are represented in different programs. For example, at some colleges, field teaching extends over two or three semesters. In other programs, teacher candidates first take a theory class followed by a full second semester of student teaching. Regardless of when and how your student teaching occurs, the experience is a bright and shining opportunity to hone your teaching skills in a real classroom. During this time, you will be supported by an experienced college or university supervisor and by carefully selected cooperating teachers, who will share their expertise.

Everyone concerned in the teacher preparation program—your cooperating teacher, your university instructors, the school administrators, and your university supervisor—realizes that this is your practicum in learning how to teach. During your student teaching, you will no doubt make errors, and with the understanding and guidance of those supervising your work, you will benefit and learn from those errors. Sometimes your fresh approach to motivation, your creative ideas for learning activities, and your energy and enthusiasm make it possible for the cooperating teacher to learn from you. After all, as we have said many times, teaching and learning are always reciprocal processes. What is most important is that the students who are involved with you in the teaching-learning process will benefit from your role as the teacher candidate in the classroom. The guidelines that follow are offered to help make this practical experience beneficial to everyone involved.

Student Teaching *Is* the Real Thing

Student teaching is the real thing because you have a classroom setting for practicing and honing your teaching skills with active, responsive secondary school stu-dents. On the other hand, student teaching is not real in the sense that it is your cooperating teacher, not you, who has the ultimate responsibility (and the final say) for the classroom.

Getting Ready for Student Teaching

To prepare yourself for student teaching, you should study, plan, practice, and reflect. You should be knowledgeable about your students and their developmental backgrounds. In your theory classes, you learned a great deal about students. Go back and review your class notes and textbooks from those courses, or select some readings suggested in Part I. Perhaps some of the topics will have more meaning for you now.

First Impressions Are Often Lasting Impressions

You have heard that statement before and now you have heard it again! As you get ready for this practical phase of your professional teacher preparation, it is important for you to remember. Remember it as you prepare to meet your school principal and cooperating teacher for the first time; remember it again as you prepare to meet your students for the first time; and remember it again as you prepare for the first observation of your teaching by your university supervisor. You have only one opportunity to make a first impression.

Continuing to Get Ready for Student Teaching

In addition to the preceding, you will need to be knowledgeable about your assigned school and the community that surrounds it. Review the subject areas you will be teaching and the content in those areas. Carefully discuss with your cooperating teacher (or teachers, as you may have more than one) and your university supervisor all of the responsibilities that you will be expected to assume.

As a student teacher you may want to run through each lesson verbally, perhaps in front of a mirror the night before teaching your lesson. Some student teachers read through each lesson, audiorecording the lesson, playing it back, and evaluating whether the directions are clear, the instruction is mind-grabbing (or at least interesting), the sequence is logical, and the lesson closure is concise. Still another student teacher always has a "Plan B" in mind in case "Plan A" turns out to be inappropriate.

Student Teaching from the Cooperating Teacher's Point of View

For your consideration, information about student teaching from the viewpoint of a cooperating teacher is presented here in a question-and-answer format. You may wish to share this section with your cooperating teacher.

What is my role? As the cooperating teacher, your role is to assist when necessary: to provide guidance, to review lesson plans *before* they are taught, to facilitate the learning and skill development of your student teacher, and to help your student teacher become and feel like a member of the school faculty and of the profession.

How can I prepare for the experience? Get to know your student teacher *before* she begins teaching. Develop a collegial rapport with the student teacher.

Who is my student teacher? Your student teacher is a person who is making the transition from another career or from the life of a college student to the profession of teaching. Your student teacher may be your age, older, or younger. In any case, your student teacher may be scared to death, anxious, knowledgeable, and, when it comes to teaching philosophy, somewhere between being a romantic idealist and a pragmatic realist. Do not destroy the idealism—help the student teacher to understand and deal with the realism of everyday teaching.

It is important that you learn about the kinds of teaching experiences that your student teacher has had prior to this assignment so that you and he may build from those experiences. For example, this may be your student teacher's very first teaching experience, or he may have substitute teaching experience, experience teaching in another country, or experience with student teaching in another school prior to this term. Some programs of secondary teacher preparation, for example, require one semester of student teaching in a middle school and another in a high school.

What kind of support, criticism, and supervision should I give? Much of this you will have to decide for yourself. On the other hand, some teacher preparation programs include seminars that train the cooperating teachers in techniques for supervising student teachers. Today, cooperating teachers are often selected because of their effectiveness in teaching and in working with other adults. It is possible that you will be working as a member of a team that includes you, the student teacher, and the university supervisor. Your student teacher may have more than one cooperating teacher, who should then also be included as a member of this professional team. Whatever the situation, your student teacher needs support, helpful suggestions, and productive monitoring. It is unprofessional to place a student teacher into a total "sink-or-swim" situation.

What danger signs should I be alert for? Your student teacher may be quite different from you in both appearance and style of teaching but may be potentially just as effective a teacher. Be slow and cautious in judging your student teacher's effectiveness. Offer suggestions, but do not make demands.

A student teacher who is not preparing well is likely to be heading for trouble. Be certain to ask for and to receive lesson plans *before* they are taught, especially in the beginning and whenever you feel the student teacher is not preparing well.

Another danger signal is when the student teacher seems to show no interest in the school and the students beyond the classroom. The student teacher should be prompt, should be eager to spend extra time with you, should attend faculty meetings, and should be aware of the necessity of performing school clerical tasks. If you feel there is a lurking problem, then let the student teacher or the university supervisor know immediately. Trust your intuition. Poor communication between members of the teaching team is another danger signal.

What else should I know? Your student teacher may be employed elsewhere and have other demands on her time. Become aware of these other demands, but keep the educational welfare of your students paramount in your mind.

See that your student teacher is treated as a member of the faculty, is invited to faculty functions, has a personal mailbox (or is allowed to share yours, with his name on it as well), and understands school policies, procedures, and curriculum documents.

Once your student teacher is well grounded, she should be ready to be gradually alone with the students for increasingly longer periods of time. For a specified time, a student teacher's goal is to work toward a competency level that enables her to begin the class, teach the entire period, and close the class period, while assuming increasing responsibility for everything. This means that you are nearby and on call in case of an emergency but out of sight of the students.

Comments from the University Supervisor

When is the supervisor coming? Is the supervisor going to be here today? Do you see a university or a college supervisor's observation of your student teaching as a pleasant experience or a painful one? Do you realize that classroom observations of your teaching continue during your beginning years of teaching? Being observed and evaluated does not have to be a painful, nerve-racking experience for you. And no, you don't have to become a bundle of raw nerve endings when you realize the supervisor is coming to see you. Whether you are a student teacher being observed by your university supervisor, or a probationary teacher being evaluated by your principal, some professional suggestions may help you turn an evaluating observation into a useful, professionally satisfying experience.

What to Do before an Observation

Successful teachers seem to be able to ameliorate tension and get through an evaluation with skill and tact. Prepare for your evaluative visit by (1) deciding what you do well and plan to demonstrate your best skills; (2) decorating your room and bulletin boards, especially by displaying student work; (3) making sure your work area is orderly (this shows good organization); and (4) selecting an academic aspect of the teaching day that demonstrates some of your best teaching skills. If your university supervisor has previously targeted some of your weak areas, plan to demonstrate growth in those teaching abilities.

What to Do during an Observation

Some supervisors and administrators choose to preannounce their visits. This is certainly true for *clinical supervision* practices. Clinical supervision is based on shared decision making between the supervisor and teacher and is focused on improving, rather than evaluating, teaching behaviors. With the use of clinical supervision, you know when the supervisor or administrator is coming, and you will probably look forward to the visit because of the rapport that has been established between members of your triad (in student teaching situations, your triad is composed of you, your cooperating teacher, and your university or college supervisor).

Features of effective clinical supervision include a preobservation conference, observation of teaching, and a postobservation conference. In the preobservation conference, the student teacher, cooperating teacher, and supervisor meet to discuss goals, objectives, teaching strategies, and the evaluation process. During the observation of teaching, the supervisor collects data on the classroom students' performance of objectives and on the student teacher's performance of the teaching strategies. In the postobservation conference, the student teacher, cooperating teacher, and supervisor discuss the performances. They may compare what happened with what was expected, make inferences about students' achievement of objectives, and discuss relationships between teaching performance and student achievement. The supervisor and cooperating teacher act as educational consultants and may discuss alternative strategies for teaching at this conference or at a later one.

Sometimes your supervisor or administrator may drop in unannounced. When that happens you can take a deep breath, count to ten (quietly), and then proceed with your lesson. You will undoubtedly do just fine if you have been following the guidelines set forth in this book. Additional guidelines for a classroom observation are as follows: allow the observer to sit wherever he wishes; do not interrupt your lesson to introduce the observer, unless the observer requests it, but *do* prepare your students in advance by letting them know who may be visiting and why; do not put the observer on the spot by suddenly involving him in

the lesson, but *do* try to discern in advance the level of participation desired by your observer.

If you have been assigned to a classroom for a student teaching experience, your university supervisor will meet with you and explain some of the tasks you should attend to when the supervisor visits your class. These may vary from the list presented. For instance, some supervisors prefer to walk into a classroom quietly and not interrupt the learning activities. Some prefer not to be introduced to the class or to participate in the activities. Some supervisors are already well known by the students and teaching staff from prior visits to the school. Other supervisors may give you a special form to be completed before they arrive for the visit. This form often resembles a lesson plan format and includes space for your objectives, lesson procedures, motivational strategies, related activities, and method of assessing how well the students learned from the lesson. Remember, keep the line of communication open with your supervisor so that you have a clear understanding of what is expected of you when she visits your classroom to observe your teaching. Without missing a beat in your lesson, you may walk over and quietly hand the observer a copy of the lesson plan and the textbook (or any other materials being used), opened to the appropriate page.

In some teacher preparation programs the student teacher is expected to maintain a *student teaching binder* in the classroom. The binder is kept in a particular location so that the cooperating teacher may refer to it and the college or university supervisor can pick it up upon entering the classroom and refer to it during the observation. Organized in the binder are the current lesson plan, the current unit plan, previous lessons with reflections, tests and their results, assignments, classroom management plan, and a current seating chart with the students' names. The student teaching binder can, in fact, represent the start of your *professional portfolio* (discussed later in this chapter).

Soon after the observational visit, there should be a conference in which observations are discussed in a *nonjudgmental* atmosphere. It might be necessary for you to make sure that a conference is scheduled. The purposes of this postobservation conference are for you and the observer(s) to discuss, rather than to evaluate, your teaching and for you to exit the conference with agreements about areas for improvement and *how* to accomplish those improvements.

What to Do during an Observation Conference

Some supervisors will arrange to have a conference with you to discuss the classroom observation and to begin to resolve any classroom teaching problems. As a teacher or teacher candidate, you should be professional during this conference. For instance, one student teacher asks for additional help by requesting resources. Another takes notes and suggests developing a cooperative plan with the supervisor to improve teaching competencies. Still another discusses visiting other classrooms to observe exemplary teachers.

During other conferences, student teachers may ask for assistance in scheduling additional meetings with the supervisor. At such meetings, the teacher (or teacher candidate) views videos of selected teaching styles or methods, listens to audiotapes, or visits an outside educational consultant or nearby resource center.

Almost all supervisors conclude their conferences by leaving something in writing with the teacher or teacher candidate. This written record usually includes a summary of teaching strengths or weaknesses, with a review of classroom management; the supervisor's recommendations; and, perhaps, steps in an overall plan for the teacher's (or student teacher's) continued professional growth and development.

What to Do after the Supervisor Leaves

In addition to observing the classes of other teachers, attending workshops and conferences, and conferring with college and university authorities, the following are ways to implement your plan for improvement. Be sure you debug your lesson plans by walking through them before implementing them in the classroom. Do what you and your supervisor have agreed on. Document your activities with a record or diary with dated entries. If you maintain a supervisor's binder, this documentation may be kept in the binder along with the supervisor's written comments. If you have a problem with classroom management or organization, review your written classroom management plan and procedures, comparing your plan with the guidelines presented in Chapter 3. Review your plan and procedures with your cooperating teacher, a trusted teaching colleague, or your university supervisor. Obtain help when you need it. Write comments to parents or guardians about students' progress, and leave space for a return message from the adult (see, for example, Figure 11.12 of Chapter 11). Keep positive responses that you receive from these adults, and share them with your supervisor at your next conference.

FINDING A TEACHING POSITION

As your successful student teaching experience draws to a close, you will embark upon finding your first paid teaching job. Your goal of finding that first job should be encouraged by the fact that the projected need for new teachers for the next several years is considerably greater than it is for any other profession.[1] It is predicted that by the year 2007, well more than half of the teachers who were teaching just ten years before, in 1997, will have retired. Guidelines that follow are provided to help you accomplish your goal.

Guidelines for Locating a Permanent Teaching Position

To prepare for finding the position you want, you should focus on (1) letters of recommendation from your cooperating teacher(s), your college or university supervisor, and, in some instances, the school principal; (2) your professional preparation as evidenced by your letters of recommendation and other items in your professional portfolio (discussed next); and (3) your job-interviewing skills.

First, consider the recommendations about your teaching. Most colleges and universities have a career center, usually called a *job* (or *career) placement center*, where there is probably a counselor who can advise you how to open the job placement file that will hold your professional recommendations. This enables prospective personnel directors or district personnel who are expecting to employ new teachers to review your recommendations. Sometimes there are special forms for writing these recommendations. It is your responsibility to request letters of recommendation and, when appropriate, to supply the person writing the recommendation with the blank form and an appropriately addressed stamped envelope. Sometimes the job placement files are confidential, so your recommendations will be mailed directly to the placement office. The confidentiality of recommendations may be optional, and, when possible, you may want to maintain your own copies of letters of recommendation and include them in your portfolio.

Because of the economic depression of the early years of the 1990s, some colleges and universities limited or cut services formerly provided by their job placement centers. If that is the case at your college or university, you may need to maintain and distribute your own file or a professional portfolio.

The letters of recommendation from educators at the school(s) where you did your student teaching should include the following information: the name of the school and district where you did your student teaching; the grade levels and subjects you taught; your proven skills in managing students of diversity in the classroom; your ability to teach the relevant

---

1. See, for example, the Bureau of Labor Statistics projected growth for 15 fields as reported in *Time* magazine, January 20, 1997, pp. 58–59.

subject(s); your skills in assessing student learning and in reflecting on your teaching performance and learning from that reflection; and your skills in communicating and interacting with students and adults.

Second, consider your preparation as a teacher. Teachers, as you have learned, represent a myriad of specialties. Hiring personnel will want to know how you see yourself—for example, as a specialist in middle school core curriculum or as a high school physical education teacher who would also like to coach a sport. You may indicate a special interest or skill, such as competency in teaching English as a foreign language. Or, perhaps, although your teaching field is mathematics, you also are bilingual and have had rich and varied cross-cultural experiences. Have you had a rich and varied background of experience so that you will feel comfortable when you are hired and placed in the one assignment in which you were least interested? The hiring personnel who consider your application will be interested in your sincerity and will want to see that you are academically and socially impressive.

Last, consider your in-person interview with a district official. Sometimes, you will have several interviews or you will be interviewed simultaneously with other candidates. There may be an initial interview with the district's personnel officer, followed by an interview by a department chairperson or a school principal. Sometimes you will be interviewed by a team of teachers from that school with whom you will be working if you are selected for that teaching position. In all interviews, your verbal and nonverbal behaviors will be observed as you respond to various questions, including (1) factual questions about your student teaching, or about particular curriculum programs with which you would be expected to work, and (2) hypothetical questions, such as "What would you do if . . . ?" Often these are questions that relate to your philosophy of education, your reasons for wanting to be a teacher, your approach to handling a particular classroom situation, and perhaps specifically your reasons for wanting to teach at this particular school and in this district. See the interview guidelines that follow later in this section.

The Professional Portfolio (or How to Get Hired by Really Trying)

The concept of maintaining a professional portfolio has even greater significance today, perhaps, than when we first introduced it several years ago in a previous resource guide. For example, a relatively newly recognized benefit of having your personal professional portfolio showing examples of your work is that, when having your students do their own portfolios for use in assessment (as discussed in Chapter 11), you will be able to show them your personal real-life career portfolio. The guidelines set forth here will not ensure that you will be hired for the teaching position that you really want. However, one way to be proactive in your job search is to create a personal professional portfolio to be shared with persons who are considering your application for employment.

The portfolio is organized to provide clear evidence of your skills and to make you desirable to a hiring committee. We emphasize the word *organized* because the portfolio must be more than simply a collection of your accomplishments randomly tossed into a folder. The portfolio must be a deliberate, current, and organized collection of your skills, attributes, experiences, and accomplishments.

Because it would be impractical to send a complete portfolio with every application you submit, it might be advisable to have a minimum portfolio (portfolio B) that could be sent with each application, in addition to a complete portfolio (portfolio A) that you could make available upon request or that you would take with you to an interview. However it is done, the actual contents of the portfolio will vary depending on the specific job being sought; you will continually add to and delete materials from your portfolio. The following are suggested categories and subcategories, listed here in the order that we believe they are best presented in portfolios A and B.[2]

1. Table of contents of portfolio (not too lengthy)—portfolio A only.
2. Your professional résumé—both portfolios.
3. Evidence of your language and communication skills (evidence of your use of English and of other languages, including American Sign)—portfolio A. (Also state this information briefly in your letter of application. See the résumé section that follows.)
   a. Your teaching philosophy (written in your own handwriting so as to show your handwriting). (See Exercise 2.5.)
   b. Other evidence to support this category.
4. Evidence of teaching skills—portfolio A.
   a. For planning skills, include instructional objectives, a syllabus, a unit plan. (See Exercises 4.12, 5.2, and 5.7.)

---

2. See also K. Wolf, "Developing an Effective Teaching Portfolio," and N. P. Lyons, "A Grassroots Experiment in Performance Assessment," both in *Educational Leadership* 53(6):34–37 and 54–67, respectively (March 1996), and Chapter 4, "Creating a Professional Portfolio," in C. Danielson, *Enhancing Professional Practice: A Framework for Teaching* (Alexandria, VA: Association for Supervision and Curriculum Development, 1996). See also Internet site <http://www.teachnet.com/>.

b. For teaching skills, include a sample lesson plan and a video of your actual teaching. (See Exercises 5.6, 5.7, 9.1, 9.3, and 12.1.)

c. For assessment skills, include a sample personal assessment and samples of student assessment. (See Exercises 11.1 and 12.1.)

5. Letters of recommendation and other documentation to support your teaching skills—both portfolios.

6. Other (for example, personal interests related to the position for which you are applying)—portfolio A.

Resources for Locating a Teaching Position

To locate teaching vacancies, you can establish contact with any of the following resources.

ACADEMIC EMPLOYMENT NETWORK. A network employment page can be found on the Internet at <http://www.academploy.com/>. Contact AEN, 2665 Gray Road, Windham, ME 04062. (800) 890-8283. E-mail info@academploy.com.

COLLEGE OR UNIVERSITY PLACEMENT OFFICE. Establishing a career placement file with your local college or university placement service is an excellent way to begin the process of locating teaching vacancies.

LOCAL SCHOOL OR DISTRICT PERSONNEL OFFICE. You can contact school personnel offices to obtain information about teaching vacancies and sometimes about open job interviews.

COUNTY EDUCATIONAL AGENCY. Contact local county offices of education about job openings.

STATE DEPARTMENTS OF EDUCATION. Some state departments of education maintain information about job openings state-wide. See listing in Figure 12.1.

INDEPENDENT SCHOOLS. You can contact non-public-supported schools that interest you, either directly or through educational placement services such as

- IES (Independent Educational Services), 20 Nassau Street, Princeton, NJ 08540 (800) 257-5102.
- European Council of Independent Schools, 21B Lavant Street, Petersfield, Hampshire, GU32 3EL, England.

COMMERCIAL PLACEMENT AGENCIES. Nation-wide job listings and placement services are available from such agencies as

- Carney, Sandoe & Associates, 136 Boylston Street, Boston, MA 02116 (800) 225-7986.
- National Education Service Center, PO Box 1279, Department NS, Riverton, WY 82501-1279 (307) 856-0170.

- National Teachers Clearinghouse—SE, PO Box 267, Boston, MA 02118-0267 (617) 267-3204.

OUT-OF-COUNTRY TEACHING OPPORTUNITIES. Information regarding teaching positions outside the United States can be obtained from

- American Field Services Intercultural Programs, 313 East 43rd Street, New York, NY 10017.
- Department of Defense Dependent Schools, 4040 North Fairfax Drive, Arlington, VA 22203-1634.
- European Council of Independent Schools, 21B Lavant Street, Petersfield, Hampshire, GU32 3EL, England.
- International Schools Service, PO Box 5910, Princeton, NJ 08543.
- Peace Corps, Recruitment Office, 806 Connecticut Avenue, NW, Washington, DC 20526.
- Teachers Overseas Recruitment Centers, National Teacher Placement Bureaus of America, Inc., PO Box 09027, 4190 Pearl Road, Cleveland, OH 44109.
- YMCA of the USA, Attn: Teaching in Japan and Taiwan, 101 North Wacker Drive, Chicago, IL 60606.

PROFESSIONAL EDUCATIONAL JOURNALS AND OTHER PUBLICATIONS. Professional teaching journals (as found in Figure 10.3) often run advertisements of teaching vacancies, as do education newspapers such as *Education Week*. These can be found in your college or university library and on the Internet.

State Sources for Information about Credential Requirements

If you are interested in the credential requirements of other states, check at the appropriate office of your own college or university teacher preparation program to see what information is available about requirements for states of interest to you and whether the credential that you are about to receive has reciprocity with other states. Addresses for information about state credentials can be found in Figure 12.1.

The Professional Résumé

Résumé preparation is the subject of how-to books, computer programs, and commercial services, but a teacher's résumé is specific. Although no one can tell you exactly what résumé will work best for you, a few basic guidelines are especially helpful for the preparation of a teacher's résumé:

- The résumé should be no more than *two* pages in length. If it is any longer, it becomes a life history rather than a professional résumé.
- The presentation should be neat and uncluttered.

Alabama
Teacher Education and Certification
   Section
State Department of Education
349 State Office Building
Montgomery 36130, (205)261-5060

Alaska
Teacher Education and Certification
State Department of Education
Pouch F, Alaska Office Building
Juneau 99811, (907)465-2810

Arizona
Arizona Department of Education
Teacher Certification
1535 West Jefferson
P.O. Box 25609
Phoenix 85007, (602)255-4367

Arkansas
Teacher Certification
Room 106-107-B
Arkansas Department of Education
Little Rock 72201, (501)371-1474

California
Commission on Teacher Credentialing
1020 "O" Street
Sacramento 94244-2700, (916)445-
7254

Colorado
Teacher Certification
State Office Building
201 East Colfax, 5th Floor
Denver, 80203, (303)866-6749

Connecticut
Bureau of School Services
State Department of Education
P.O. Box 2219
Hartford 06145, (203)566-5541

Delaware
Certification and Personnel
Department of Public Instruction
Townsend Building
Dover 19903, (302)736-4688

District of Columbia
Certification and Accreditation
District of Columbia Public Schools,
   Room 1004
415 12th Street, N.W.
Washington, DC 20004, (202)724-4230

Florida
Teacher Certification
Department of Education
Knott Building
Tallahassee 32301, (904)488-2317

Georgia
Certification
Georgia Department of Education
1452 Twin Towers East
Atlanta 30334, (404)656-2406

Hawaii
Office of Personnel Services
State Department of Education
P.O. Box 2360
Honolulu 96804, (808)548-5217

Idaho
Teacher Education and Certification
State Department of Education
Len B. Jordan Office Building
Boise 83720, (208)334-3475

Illinois
Teacher Certification and Place-
   ment
Illinois State Board of Education
100 North First Street
Springfield 62777, (217)782-2805

Indiana
Division of Teacher Certification
   and Placement
State Department of Public Instruc-
   tion
Room 229, State House
Indianapolis 46204, (317)232-6636

Iowa
Teacher Education and Certification
State Department of Public Instruc-
   tion
Grimes State Office Building
Des Moines 50319, (515)281-3245

Kansas
Certification Section
State Department of Education
120 East 10th Street
Topeka 66612, (913)296-2288

Kentucky
Teacher Education and Certification
State Department of Education
18th Floor, Capital Plaza Tower
Frankfort 40601, (502)564-4752

Louisiana
Teacher Certification
State Department of Education
Baton Rouge 70804, (504)342-3490

Maine
Division of Certification
Placement and Teacher Education
State House Station 23
Augusta 04333, (207)289-5944

Maryland
Certification and Accreditation
State Department of Education
200 West Baltimore Street
Baltimore 21201, (301)659-2141

Massachusetts
Bureau of Teacher Preparation, Cer-
   tification and Placement
Quincy Center Plaza
1385 Hancock Street
Quincy 02169, (617)770-7517

Michigan
Teacher Preparation and Certification
   Services
State Department of Education
Ottawa Street Office Building
South Tower, Second Floor
Lansing 48909, (517)373-1924

Minnesota
Personnel Licensing and Placement
State Department of Education
616 Capitol Square Building
550 Cedar Street
St. Paul 55101, (612)296-2046

Mississippi
Teacher Certification
State Department of Education
P.O. Box 771
Jackson 39205, (601)359-3483

Missouri
Teacher Education and Certification
State Department of Education
Jefferson Building, 7th Floor
P.O. Box 480
Jefferson City 65102, (314)751-3486

Montana
Teacher Certification
Office of Public Instruction
Department of Basic Instructional
   Services
1300 Eleventh Avenue
Helena 59620, (406)444-3150

Figure 12.1
Address for requesting information about state credential requirements.

(continued)

Nebraska
Certification and Teacher Education
State Department of Education
301 Centennial Mall South
Box 94987
Lincoln 68509, (402)471-2496

Nevada
Teacher Certification
State Department of Education
400 West King Street
Carson City 89710, (702)885-3116

New Hampshire
Teacher Education and Professional
    Standards
State Department of Education
101 Pleasant Street
Concord 03301-3860, (603)271-2407

New Jersey
Bureau of Teacher Preparation and
    Certification
State Department of Education
225 West State Street, CN 500
Trenton 08625-0503, (609)984-1216

New Mexico
Teacher Education and Certification
State Department of Education
DeVargas and Don Gasper Street
State Capitol Complex, Room 105
Santa Fe 87501-2786, (505)827-6581

New York
Teacher Certification
Cultural Education Center
    Room 5A 11
Madison Avenue
Albany 12230, (518)474-3901

North Carolina
Division of Certification
State Department of Public Instruction
116 West Edenton Street
Raleigh 27603-1712, (919)733-4125

North Dakota
Teacher Certification
State Department of Public Instruction
State Capital, 9th Floor
Bismarck 58505, (701)224-2264

Ohio
Teacher Education and Certification
State Department of Education
Ohio Department Building,
    Room 1012
Columbus 43215, (614)466-3593

Oklahoma
Teacher Education and Certification
State Department of Education
Hodge Education Building
2500 North Lincoln Boulevard
Oklahoma City 73105-4599,
    (405)521-3337

Oregon
Teacher Standards and Practices
    Commission
730 Twelfth Street, S.E.
Salem 97310, (503)378-3586

Pennsylvania
Bureau of Teacher Preparation and
    Certification
Department of Education
333 Market Street, 3rd Floor
Harrisburg 17126-0333,
    (717)787-2967

Rhode Island
Teacher Certification and Place-
    ment
State Department of Education
Roger Williams Building
22 Hayes Street
Providence 02908, (401)277-2675

South Carolina
Teacher Certification
State Department of Education
1015 Rutledge, Room 1004
Columbia 29201, (803)758-8527

South Dakota
Office of Teacher Education and
    Certification
Division of Elementary and Sec-
    ondary Education
Kneip Office Building
700 North Illinois
Pierre 57501, (605)773-3553

Tennessee
Teacher Education and Certification
State Department of Education
125 Cordel Hull Building
Nashville 37219, (615)741-1644

Texas
Teacher Certification
Texas Education Agency
William B. Travis State Office Building
1701 North Congress Avenue
Austin 78701, (512)463-8976

Utah
Teacher Certification
Instruction and Support Section
Utah State Office of Education
250 East 500 South
Salt Lake City 84111, (801)533-5965

Vermont
Certification Division
State Department of Education
Montpelier 05602, (802)828-2445

Virginia
Teacher Education and Certification
State Department of Education
Box 6Q, James Monroe Building
Richmond 23216, (804)225-2907

Washington
Certification and Licensing
Office of the Superintendent of
    Public Instruction
Old Capitol Building
Olympia 98504, (206)753-6773

West Virginia
Office of Educational Personnel
    Development
State Department of Education
Capitol Complex, Room B304,
    Building 6
Charleston 25305, (304)348-2696

Wisconsin
Bureau of Teacher Education and
    Certification
State Department of Public
    Instruction
125 South Webster Street
P.O. Box 7841
Madison, 53707, (608)266-1027

Wyoming
Certification and Licensing
State Department of Education
Hathaway Building
Cheyenne 82002-0050,
    (307)777-6261

Figure 12.1 *(continued)*

- Page size should be the standard 8½ × 11 inches. Oversized and undersized pages can get lost.
- Stationery should be white or off-white.
- Do not give information such as your age, height, weight, marital status, number and names of your children, or a photograph of yourself, because including personal data may make it appear that you are trying to prejudice members of the hiring committee, which is simply unprofessional.
- Sentences should be clear and concise; avoid educational jargon, awkward phrases, abbreviations, and unfamiliar words.
- Organize the information carefully, in this order: your name, address, and telephone number, followed by your education, professional experience, credential status, location of placement file, professional affiliations, and honors.
- When identifying your academic, teaching, and life experiences, do so in reverse chronological order, listing your most recent degree or your current position first. (See sample résumé in Figure 12.2.)
- Take time to develop your résumé, and then keep it current. Do not duplicate hundreds of copies; produce a new copy each time you apply for a job. If you maintain your résumé on a computer disc, then it is easy to make modifications and print a current copy each time one is needed.
- Prepare a cover letter to accompany your résumé that is written specifically for the position for which you are applying. Address the letter personally but formally to the personnel director. Limit the cover letter to one page, and emphasize yourself, your teaching experiences and interests, and reasons that you are best qualified for the position. Show a familiarity with the particular school or district. Again, if you maintain a generic application letter on a computer disc, you can easily modify it to make it specific for each position.
- Have your résumé and cover letter edited by someone familiar with résumé writing and editing, perhaps an English-teaching friend. A poorly written, poorly typed, or poorly copied résumé fraught with spelling and grammar errors will guarantee that you will not be considered for the job.
- Be sure that your application reaches the personnel director by the announced deadline. If for some reason it will be late, then telephone the director, explain the circumstances, and request permission to submit your application late.

The In-Person Interview

If your application and résumé are attractive to the personnel director, you will be notified and a personal or small-group interview scheduled, although in some instances the hiring interview may precede the request

for your personal papers. Whichever the case, during the interview you should be honest, and you should be yourself. Practice an interview, perhaps with the aid of a videocamera. Ask someone to role-play an interview with you and to ask you some tough questions. Plan your interview wardrobe and get it ready the night before. Leave early for your interview so that you arrive in plenty of time. If possible, long before your scheduled interview, locate someone who works in the school district and discuss curriculum, classroom management policies, popular programs, and district demographics with that person. If you anticipate a professionally embarrassing question during the interview, think of diplomatic ways to respond. This means that you should think of ways to turn your weaknesses into strengths. For instance, if your cooperating teacher has mentioned that you need to continue to develop your room environment skills (meaning that you were sloppy), admit that you realize you need to be more conscientious about keeping supplies and materials neat and tidy, but mention your concern about the students and the learning and that you realize you have a tendency to interact with students more than with objects. Assure someone that you will work on this skill, and then do it. The paragraphs that follow offer additional specific guidelines for preparing for and handling the in-person interview.

You will be given a specific time, date, and place for the interview. Regardless of your other activities, accept the time, date, and location suggested, rather than trying to manipulate the interviewer around a schedule more convenient for you.

Before the interview, you will be told whether the interviewer expects a formal teaching demonstration. If so, consider using a videotape of your teaching. Some candidates have used their MPT tapes or tapes made during their student teaching for this purpose.

Dress for success. Regardless of what else you may be doing for a living, take the time necessary to make a professional appearance.

Do not arrive at the interview with small children. If necessary, arrange to have them taken care of by someone. Arrive promptly at the designated location, shake hands firmly with members of the committee, and initiate conversation with a friendly comment, based on your personal knowledge, about the school or district.

Be prepared to answer standard interview questions. Sometimes school districts will send candidates the questions that will be asked during the interview; at other times, these questions are handed to the candidate upon arrival at the interview. The questions that are likely to be asked will cover the following topics:

- *Your experiences with students of the relevant age.* The committee wants to be reasonably certain that you can effectively manage and teach at this level.

JENNIFER DAWSON
510 Newcomb Street, #309, Davis, CA 95616
(916) 552-8996

CREDENTIALS

January 1997	California Preliminary Single Subject Credential in English
	Supplemental authorization in Social Studies
May 1997	CLAD (Culture and Language Academic Development) Certificate
	California State University, Sacramento

EDUCATION

May 1991	Bachelor of Arts Degree in English Literature
	Saint Olaf College, Northfield, Minnesota

TEACHING EXPERIENCE

September 1997 *through* *January 1998* *(Student Teaching III)*	**Douglass Junior High School (Woodland, CA).** *Two 7th-grade 2-hour block interdisciplinary core classes, English and Social Studies.* • Worked with a team to develop interdisciplinary thematic lessons. • Conducted student-led parent conferences. • Employed hands-on learning techniques and simulations.
February 1997 *through* *May 1997* *(Student Teaching II)*	**Davis High School (Davis, CA).** *One period of college preparatory English Literature for juniors.* • Developed book clubs, small-group forums for discussing three novels. • Developed poetry unit in which students published their own poems for class collection.
September 1995 *through* *May 1996* *(Student Teaching I)*	**Los Cerros Middle School.** *One period ESL—13 culturally diverse 7th and 8th graders.* • Bilingual stories and activities; reader's theater presentations.

RELATED EXPERIENCE

Summer of 1997	• Developed and taught a Summer Writing Workshop for small groups of 3rd- through 10th-grade students. Met with students and parents to establish goals.
September 1995–May 1996	• Reader for English department at Valley High School.

OTHER EXPERIENCE

• Volunteer in Juarez, Mexico, through YWAM (Youth with a Mission).
• Coordinator in Glacier National Park for the group, A Christian Ministry, in the National Parks.

Figure 12.2
Sample professional résumé.

You should answer this question by sharing *specific* successes that demonstrate that you are a decisive and competent teacher.

• *Hobbies and travels.* The committee wants to know more about you as a person to ensure that you will be an interesting and energetic teacher to the students, as well as a congenial member of the faculty.

• *Extracurricular interests and experiences.* The committee wants to know about all the ways in which you might be helpful in the school and to know that you will promote the interests and cocurricular activities of students.

• *Classroom management techniques.* You must convince the committee that you can effectively manage a classroom of diverse learners in a manner that will help them to develop their self-esteem.

• *Knowledge of the subject taught at the grade for which you are being considered.* The committee needs to be reasonably certain that you have command of the subject and its place within the developmental stages of students at this level. This is where you should show your knowledge of national standards and of state and local curriculum documents.

- *Knowledge of assessment strategies relevant for use in teaching at this level.*
- *Commitment to teaching at this level.* The committee wants to be assured that you are knowledgeable about and committed to teaching and learning at this level, as opposed to just wanting this job until something better comes along.
- *Your ability to reflect on experience and to grow from that reflection.*
- *Your perceived weaknesses.* If you are asked about your weaknesses, you have an opportunity to show that you can effectively reflect and self-assess, that you can think reflectively and critically, and that you know the value of learning from your own errors and how to do it. Be prepared for this question by identifying a specific error that you have made, perhaps while student teaching, and explain how you turned that error into a profitable learning experience.

Throughout the interview you should maintain eye contact with the interviewer while demonstrating interest, enthusiasm, and self-confidence. When an opportunity arises, ask one or two planned questions that demonstrate your knowledge of and interest in this position and this community and school or district.

When the interview has obviously been brought to a close by the interviewer, that is your signal to leave. Do not hang around; this is a sign of lacking confidence. Follow the interview with a thank you letter addressed to the personnel director or interviewer; even if you do not get the job, you will be better remembered for future reference.

Once you are employed as a teacher, your professional development continues. The sections that follow demonstrate ways in which that can happen.

PROFESSIONAL DEVELOPMENT THROUGH MENTORING

Mentoring, one teacher facilitating the learning of another teacher, can aid in professional development.[3] In what is sometimes called *peer coaching*, a mentor teacher volunteers, is selected by the teacher who wishes to improve, or is selected by a school administrator, formally or informally. The mentor observes and coaches the teacher to help him improve in teaching. Sometimes the teacher simply wants to learn a new skill. In other instances, the teacher being coached remains with the mentor teacher for an entire

school year, developing and improving old and new skills or learning how to teach with a new program. In many districts, new teachers are automatically assigned to mentor teachers for their first year, as a program of *induction.*

During mentoring, the mentor teacher and the teacher being coached meet in a preobservation conference and discuss the skill or skills to be observed. Then the teacher is observed, and a postobservation conference follows, in which the teacher and mentor discuss the observations and plan for the next observation. The cycle continues until the desired skills have been acquired.

Concerned about new-teacher burnout and the accompanying high attrition rate for new teachers (for example, in California, approximately 50 percent of all beginning teachers leave teaching within five years), many states and districts have introduced special induction programs. California sponsors the Beginning Teacher Support and Assessment (BTSA) program. The program has three main components: a mentor teacher who is available to new teachers to offer classroom advice and help; monthly seminars and meetings bringing together new teachers and a master teacher or university professor to discuss problems and solutions and to offer mutual support; and the beginning of explicit standards for beginning teachers in the areas of classroom management, curriculum design, instructional strategies, and assessment. For teachers participating in the BTSA program, the attrition rate has declined.

PROFESSIONAL DEVELOPMENT THROUGH INSERVICE AND GRADUATE STUDY

Inservice workshops and programs are offered for teachers at the school level, by the district, and by other agencies such as a county office of education or a nearby college or university. Inservice workshops and programs are usually designed for specific purposes, such as to train teachers in new teaching skills, to update their knowledge in content, and to introduce them to new teaching materials or programs. For example, Baltimore City Public Schools (MD) provides a systemwide professional development program for middle school teachers of grades 6–8, administrators, and staff at its Lombard Learning Academy Demonstration Center. The Lombard Learning Academy is a school-within-a-school located at Lombard Middle School. Cohorts of five to ten teachers from other schools in the district visit the Academy for five-day periods to observe instruction, practice strategies, and hone their skills in the use of technology.

University graduate study is yet another way of continuing your professional development. Some teachers pursue master's degrees in academic teaching fields,

---

3. See, for example, T. M. Bey, "Mentorships: Transferable Transactions among Teachers," and the several articles about mentoring in *Education and Urban Society* 28(1):11–19 (November 1995), and C. Crowe, "Mentors: Keys to Survival and Growth," *English Journal* 84(4):76–77 (April 1995).

while many others pursue master's degrees in curriculum and methods of instruction or in educational administration or counseling. Some universities offer a Master of Arts in Teaching, a program of courses in specific academic fields that are especially designed for teachers. School districts encourage teachers to pursue graduate work by providing pay raises according to units earned and degrees granted.

PROFESSIONAL DEVELOPMENT THROUGH PARTICIPATION IN PROFESSIONAL ORGANIZATIONS

There are many professional organizations, local, state, and national. Teachers' organizations are usually discipline-specific, such as for reading (International Reading Association), mathematics (National Council of Teachers of Mathematics), social studies (National Council for the Social Studies), or science (National Science Teachers Association). In most states there is a state-wide organization, probably affiliated with a national organization. In addition, there are the National Education Association (NEA), the Association of American Educators (AAE), and the American Federation of Teachers (AFT). In some locales, the NEA and AFT have joined as the collective bargaining organization for teachers.

Local, district, state, and national organizations have meetings that include guest speakers, workshops, and publishers' displays. Professional meetings of teachers are educational, enriching, and fulfilling for those who attend. In addition, many other professional associations, such as those for reading teachers, supply speakers and publish articles in their journals that are often of interest to teachers other than the target audience.

Professional organizations publish newsletters and journals for their members, and these will likely be found in your college or university library. Sample periodicals were listed in Figure 10.3. Additional periodicals of interest to teachers and administrators include *Phi Delta Kappan,* the journal of the Phi Delta Kappa (PDK) professional organization, and *Educational Leadership*, the journal of the Association for Supervision and Curriculum Development (ASCD).

Many professional organizations have special membership prices for teachers who are still college or university students, a courtesy that allows for an inexpensive beginning affiliation with a professional association. For information on special membership prices and association services, write to those of interest to you. Their correct addresses can be found in the most recent journal issues.

PROFESSIONAL DEVELOPMENT THROUGH COMMUNICATIONS WITH OTHER TEACHERS

Visiting teachers at other schools; attending inservice workshops, graduate seminars, and programs; participating in teacher study groups[4] and meetings of professional organizations; and participating in teacher networks[5] and sharing with teachers by means of electronic bulletin boards are all valuable experiences, if for no other reason than talking and sharing with teachers from across the country and around the world. These discussions include a sharing not only of "war stories" but also of ideas and descriptions of new programs, books, materials, and techniques that work. "By sharing stories of the predicaments and dilemmas they face daily, teachers and administrators can help one another to gain insight and perspective, and to grow professionally as a result."[6]

As in other process skills, the teacher practices and models skill in communication, in and out of the classroom. This includes communicating with other teachers to improve one's own repertoire of strategies and knowledge about teaching as well as sharing one's experiences with others. Teaching other teachers about your own special skills and sharing your experiences are important components of the communication and professional development processes.

PROFESSIONAL DEVELOPMENT THROUGH SUMMER AND OFF-TEACHING WORK EXPERIENCE

Whether your school is a year-round school or a traditional one running from late August through the middle of June, in many areas of the country special programs of short-term employment are available to interested teachers. These are available especially, although not exclusively, to teachers of physical education, mathematics, science, and social studies and are offered by public agencies, private industry, foundations, and research institutes. These institutions are interested in disseminating information and providing opportunities for teachers to update their skills and knowledge, with

---

4. See, for example, G. Cramer, B. Hurst, and C. Wilson, *Teacher Study Groups for Professional Development* (Bloomington, IN: Fastback 406, Phi Delta Kappa Educational Foundation, 1996).
5. See, for example, A. Lieberman and M. Grolnick, "Networks, Reform, and the Professional Development of Teachers," in A. Hargreaves (ed.), *Rethinking Educational Change with Heart and Mind* (Alexandria, VA: ASCD 1997 Yearbook, Association for Supervision and Curriculum Development, 1997), pp. 192–215.
6. R. Ackerman, et al., "Case Stories: Telling Tales about School," *Educational Leadership* 53(6):21 (March 1996).

the ultimate hope that the teachers will stimulate in more students a desire to develop their physical fitness, to understand civic responsibilities, and to consider careers in science and technology. Participating industries, foundations, governments, and institutes provide on-the-job training with salaries or stipends to teachers who are selected to participate. During the program of employment and depending on the nature of that work, a variety of people (e.g., scientists, technicians, politicians, businesspersons, social workers, and sometimes university educators) meet with teachers to share experiences and discuss what is being learned and its implications for teaching and curriculum development. For example, in Meridian, Mississippi, supported by local business and industry, teachers from English, social studies, and mathematics are selected and paid a stipend to participate in a Teachers in the Business and Industry World summer internship program.

There are National Science Foundation sponsored summer programs for teachers. The programs are field-centered and content-specific. For example, a program may concentrate on geology, anthropology, mathematics, or reading. At another location, a program may concentrate on teaching, using a specific new or experimental curriculum. These programs, located around the country, may have university affiliation, which means that university credit may be available. Room and board, travel, and a stipend are sometimes granted to participating teachers.

Sources of information about the availability of these programs include professional journals, your local chamber of commerce, and meetings of the local or regional teachers' organization. In areas where there are no organized programs of part-time work experience for teachers, some teachers have had success in initiating their own by establishing contact with management personnel of local businesses or companies.

SUMMARY

Because learning and teaching go hand in hand, and the effectiveness of one affects that of the other, the final two chapters of this resource guide have dealt with both aspects of the *how well* component of teacher preparation—how well the students are learning and how well the teacher is teaching. In addition, you have been presented with guidelines about how to obtain your first teaching job and how to continue your professional development. Although you have not been told everything you will ever need to know about the assessment of teaching and learning, about other aspects of public secondary school teaching, about finding a job, or about continuing your professional development, we hope that we have addressed the essentials. Throughout your

teaching career you will continue improving your knowledge and skills in all aspects of teaching and learning.

We began this resource guide by providing input data about schools and teaching and then proceeded to guide you through additional ways to collect and share data, as well as to process those data into your own plans for teaching. Now you are ready for the highest application of your knowledge and skills—a full-time teaching position, where you are paid for teaching (as opposed to your having to pay to do it).

You have arrived at the end of this text! We thank you for allowing us to be a part of your quest to become a competent teacher. We hope your quest has been and continues to be enjoyable and profitable. Be the very best teacher that you can be. The nation and its youth need you.

—Richard Kellough and Noreen Kellough

QUESTIONS FOR CLASS DISCUSSION

1. Discover what professional teacher organizations are in your geographical area. Share what you find with others in your class. Attend a local, regional, or national meeting of a professional teachers' association, and report to your class what it was like and what you learned. Also share with your class any free or inexpensive teaching materials you obtained.
2. Talk with experienced teachers and find out how they stay current in their teaching fields. Share your findings with others in your class.
3. Describe any prior concepts you held that changed as a result of your experiences with this chapter. Describe the changes.
4. From your current observations and fieldwork related to this teacher preparation program, clearly identify one specific example of educational practice that seems contradictory to exemplary practice or theory presented in this chapter. Present your explanation for the discrepancy.
5. Congratulations! You have reached the end of this resource guide, but there may be questions lingering in your mind. As before, list them and try to find answers.

SUGGESTED READINGS

Cambell, D. M., et al. *How to Develop a Professional Portfolio: A Manual for Teachers*. Needham Heights, MA: Allyn & Bacon, 1997.

Cramer, G., et al. *Teacher Study Groups for Professional Development*. Bloomington, IN: Fastback 406, Phi Delta Kappa Educational Foundation, 1996.

Danielson, C. *Enhancing Professional Practice: A Framework for Teaching*. Alexandria, VA: Association for Supervision and Curriculum Development, 1996.

Fox, D. L. "From English Major to English Teacher: Two Case Studies." *English Journal* 84(2):17–25 (February 1995).

Good, T. L., and Brophy, J. E. *Looking in Classrooms*. New York: Longman, 1997, pp. 443–484.

Huling, L., et al. "Factors in the Selection of Secondary School Teachers." *National Association of Secondary School Principals Bulletin* 80(580):57–64 (May 1996).

Lieberman, A. "Practices That Support Teacher Development." *Phi Delta Kappan* 76(8):591–596 (April 1995).

Sahakian, P., and Stockton, J. "Opening Doors: Teacher-Guided Observations." *Educational Leadership* 53(6):50–53 (March 1996).

Warner, J., et al. *The Unauthorized Teacher's Survival Guide.* Indianapolis, IN: Park Avenue Publications, 1995.

Wolf, K. "Developing an Effective Teacher Portfolio." *Educational Leadership* 53(6):34–37 (March 1996).

Appendix

Sample Unit and Lesson Plans

This appendix displays a variety of sample unit plans and their corresponding representative lesson plans (one for each sample unit), which serve as additional samples and guidelines for your planning. Sample plans (and grade levels) are presented in the following order: art (9–12), biology (9–10), English (11–12), foreign language (9–12), U.S. history (11), mathematics (7 or 8), and music (7–8). For ninth-grade physical science, see Figure 5.7 in Chapter 5.

UNIT AND DAILY PLAN—SAMPLE 1

Art (Grades 9–12)

Title: Art Exploration through Drawing[1]   **Duration:** 4 weeks

Introduction: The study of fine arts affords students opportunity to develop attitudes, acquire knowledge, and improve skills that enhance their ability to express ideas and to develop appreciations of their lives and those of others.

Unit Description: The focus is on the enhancement of skill and knowledge of drawing media, limited to pencil, or other dry media, and pen and ink processes. Through various drawing activities, students explore the media and experiment with ways to develop their own style and expressive technique. Unit assignments provide opportunity for students to explore and share their cultural heritages.

Rationale: At this level in artistic growth, most students regard the ability to draw realistically as the highest level of achievement. Many students pursue art to increase their drawing ability. It is appropriate to spend time assisting students in the mastery of this drawing. Students also develop their skill at talking about and understanding the art of other people. Critical evaluation provides important feedback.

Unit Goals and Objectives

Goals: The teaching goals for this unit are to
  1. Provide opportunities for students to improve their drawing skills.
  2. Present information about drawing media and drawing techniques.
  3. Examine sample drawings by artists from the past and the present and from many cultures.
  4. Encourage students to explore their personal heritage via artists from their culture, their family stories, and their own experiences.
  5. Develop student ability to objectively evaluate personal artwork and the work of others.
  6. Enable students to more clearly understand the creative process and have confidence in their own ability to create.
  7. Provide experiences in cooperative learning.

Objectives: Upon completion of this unit, students will be able to
  1. Use the appropriate vocabulary in describing artworks. (cognitive, knowledge)
  2. Recognize the media used when viewing drawings. (cognitive, knowledge)
  3. Demonstrate an understanding that artists make choices in designing an artwork that ultimately affect the expressive quality of the work. (cognitive, comprehension)
  4. Demonstrate an understanding that artists are influenced by the work of other artists. (cognitive, comprehension)
  5. Use the influences from their own heritage when developing images for drawing assignments. (cognitive, application)
  6. Demonstrate improved mastery of drawing media techniques. (cognitive, application)
  7. Demonstrate skill in determining that aspects of artworks are successful. (cognitive, analysis)
  8. Demonstrate an awareness of the influence of each artist's culture and individual style. (cognitive, analysis)
  9. Make decisions to apply aesthetic, technical, and cultural knowledge to their art projects. (cognitive, synthesis)
 10. Demonstrate objectivity in self-assessment of their own art projects as well as their critiques of the work of others. (cognitive, evaluation)
 11. Demonstrate willingness to cooperatively share and receive ideas about art projects. (affective)
 12. Demonstrate interest in knowing more about a particular heritage. (affective)
 13. Demonstrate appreciation of the complexity of creative processes. (affective)

[1]*Source:* Chris Angi, unpublished material. Reprinted by permission.

14. Demonstrate a valuing of efforts of artists as evidenced by the student's encouraging comments made while critiquing the work of classmates. (affective)
15. Demonstrate improvement in their skill using pencil and pen drawing media. (psychomotor)

Assessment of Student Learning

Preassessment: A preassessment will be used to determine student's view of his or her ability to draw. This includes a simple drawing exercise as well as questions regarding previous drawing experience.

Formative: Performance-based tools will be used as follows:
1. Process portfolio/journal: Students will keep a process portfolio into which will go all finished work as well as preliminary sketches, self-assessment checklists, comments from critiques, and a process journal in which are recorded the details of the process for each assignment. During the third week, student and teacher will together review the portfolio. The culminating activity for this unit (in the fourth and final week) will involve a presentation by the student of selections from his or her portfolio with a discussion on process by both the student and his or her classroom partner.
2. Classroom critiques/peer assessment: During classroom critiques, students will use checklists by which they record their assessment of work by another student. These checklists will be turned in to the teacher and used as feedback when the teacher is working with a student.
3. Collaborative feedback by classroom partner on work in progress.

Summative: Teacher assessment of projects, reports, class participation, and portfolio.

LESSON PLAN: Day 3   **Topic:** Drawing with Pencil

Objective: Upon completion of this lesson the student will be able to demonstrate knowledge by discussing ways that artists use drawing to imagine and communicate ideas.

Materials: Sample drawings to convey concepts prior to developing a product (such as set and fashion designs, storyboard) or illustrating a story (cartoons, book illustrations). White and colored drawing paper (14 × 17); glue sticks; drawing pencils including colors, erasers.

Procedure: *Activity 1 (Introductory Set) (20 minutes):* Teacher shows examples of the ways that artists use drawing in planning designs for creating objects, images, and telling stories. Discuss careers that use these skills.

[Transition] Explain next activity after students glue their 4 × 4 illustration onto paper.

Activity 2 (55 minutes): Attach 4 × 4 drawing (separate drawing given to each student) on 14 × 17 paper. Starting with that drawing, expand into the rest of the paper space with an imaginary transformation—a fantasy work evolving, a remodeling of the space, melting objects, an outdoor environment encroaching on the space. Use pencil (colored pencil use limited to three colors). Have students share their finished drawings.

Activity 3 (15 minutes): Write about the experience in your journal, describing decisions you made, such as why you drew where you did, how you transformed it, changes made while doing it, and so on.

Activity 4 (Closure) (5 minutes): Ask for volunteers to share their journal writing for the preceding activity. Discuss next lesson, which is group critiquing of works.

Homework Reminders: Due _____, your oral and written presentation on an artist or craftsperson. On _____, bring an object of clothing that represents your cultural heritage or personal family history. Reminder for teacher: collect some ethnic articles of clothing. Reminders of portfolio review dates and class presentations/critiques dates.

Teacher Reflections, Evaluation of Lesson, Suggestions for Revision

UNIT AND DAILY PLAN—SAMPLE 2

Biology (Grades 9–10)

Unit Title: Ecology[1]   **Duration:** 3 weeks

Rationale and Description: As emphasized in the *National Science Education Standards* (National Academy Press, 1996), all students in grades 9-12 should develop an understanding of the interdependence of organisms, of the energy flows in ecosystems, and how ecosystems are modified as a result of population growth, technology, and consumption. For many students, high school biology is the only or final opportunity where they can develop the ecological understandings necessary to be informed citizens.

This unit covers basic principles, concepts, and understandings about ecosystems, including the concept of ecosystems, kinds of ecosystems, energy cycles within ecosystems, and ecological ethics. Skills involved in the study of this unit include a number of sciencing skills such as correct use of the microscope, observation and data collecting, summarizing and inferring, and participation in cooperative group activity and learning.

Unit Objectives: Upon completion of this unit the student should be able to
1. Define and identify components of an ecosystem.
2. Give examples of producers, consumers, and decomposers by developing or describing a food chain.
3. Identify trophic levels in an ecosystem.
4. Assess energy consumption up the trophic levels.
5. Distinguish autotroph, heterotroph, herbivore, carnivore, and omnivore and their positions in a food pyramid.
6. Suggest and describe possible impacts of disturbances to ecosystems.
7. Role-play an ecologist by observing and collecting data and examining the interrelationships between biotic and abiotic factors.
8. Describe how materials are recycled in the natural environment.
9. Diagram water, carbon, and nitrogen cycles, tracing the pathways of both between organisms and their environment.
10. Through participation in a jigsaw and writing assignment, develop attitudes regarding ecological ethics.
11. Identify and describe types of ecosystems—freshwater, marine, and major terrestrial biomes.
12. Reconstruct or infer a food chain via an owl pellet lab activity.

Assessments of Student Learning

Formative: quizzes, daily participation, ethics writing assignment, lab practicum, class worksheets, puzzles, and concept maps.

Summative: unit examination and written and oral research project on biomes.

LESSON PLAN: Day 8   **Topic:** Types of Biomes

Objectives: Upon completion of this lesson the students will be able to
1. Restate or paraphrase ideas obtained from dyad reading activity.
2. Identify the three major types of ecosystems.
3. Recall the seven major terrestrial biomes and describe their distinguishing factors.

Materials: Compound microscopes; slides and cover slips; plankton samples

---

[1] *Source:* Raylene L. Ewing, unpublished material. Reprinted by permission.

Procedure: *Activity 1 (Introductory Set) (5 minutes):* Journal write warm-up: "What is a biome?"

Activity 2 (10 minutes): "Say Something" pairs reading (from text section 12.3, pages 257–260): students pair up, one student reads aloud a section, then says something about that section to his/her partner. The other student does the same with the next section and this continues back and forth.

Activity 3 (10 minutes): With input from student dyads, teacher summarizes section 12.3 that the students have just read; students take notes. (summary outline not included here)

Activity 4 (20 minutes): Plankton observation: Each student is to prepare a slide of plankton and view under the compound microscope at all powers of magnification; worksheet (not included here) to be completed and turned in at end of period.

Activity 5 (Closure) (5 minutes): Review major points on impact of climatic changes (e.g., temperature and rain) on ecosystems.

Homework Reminders: Remind students of biome project time line and due date for written report and oral presentation. Rough draft due anytime this week for nongraded assessment.

Teacher Reflections, Evaluation of Lesson, Suggestions for Revision

UNIT AND DAILY PLAN—SAMPLE 3

English (Grades 11–12)

Unit Title: Stylistics and Grammar[1]   **Duration:** 12 days

Introduction: This unit is designed to couch several principles of grammar in a meaningful context through the examination and imitation of various authors' writing styles. Specifically, students will (1) learn about standard English usage and commonly used literary devices, (2) apply standard English usage and literary devices in their imitative writings of M. Angelou, E. Hemingway, and U. K. Le Guin, and (3) develop reading, writing, thinking, and studying skills.

Rationale and Unit Goals: This unit is part of a language arts–based writing curriculum about understanding and applying proper standard English usage (grammar, punctuation, and literary devices) in writing. Through multicultural readings, the students develop comprehension of how English grammar affects various authors' styles of writing. As students learn about grammar and style by imitating various styles, they experiment with new writing voices, thereby developing a personal style and voice to be used and recognizably changed throughout the student's writing career in modern and meaningful situations.

Unit Description: At the beginning of the unit, a classroom bulletin board displays the three authors studied in this unit: M. Angelou, E. Hemingway, and U. K. Le Guin. The board is divided into three sections with each author's photo, list of works, and main points of style shown. As students imitate these authors, several of their works will be placed on the board as examples. At the end of the unit, students may opt to have any of their original works placed in the class's literary publication.

Unit Objectives: Upon completion of this unit students will be able to (1) describe and appraise three authors' styles and (2) create a lengthy piece of writing employing proper grammar and voicing elements of style.

Unit Assessments of Student Learning: Unit assessment of student learning is based on each student's unit portfolio, worth 100 points (1/8 of the semester grade), that includes the following items:
- Imitation of M. Angelou (5 points for turned in on time; 15 points for quality)
- Imitation of E. Hemingway (5 points for turned in on time; 15 points for quality)
- Imitation of U. K. Le Guin (5 points for turned in on time; 15 points for quality)
- Student creating writing in own style or imitating favorite author (10 points for rough draft; 20 points for final product)
- One-page explanation of own style (5 points for quality)
- Class participation (5 points)

Summative: Journal and vocabulary are assessed in separate domain from portfolio.

LESSON PLAN: Day 1   **Topic:** What Is Style?

Objective: Upon completion of this lesson the student will be able to define style and analyze Maya Angelou's *I Know Why The Caged Bird Sings* for grammar and style.

Materials: TV/video cart; Maya Angelou video and photo.

Procedure: *Activity 1 (Introductory Set) (10 minutes):* Journal write warm-up: "What is style? How would you describe your own personal style? Of clothing, personality, and writing?"

   Activity 2 (10 minutes): From discussion of journal write topic (student sharing of their ideas in dyads, then to large group), lead students to definition of style in writing as including the following elements: grammar, punctuation, dialect, sentence structure, voice, word choice, and tone.

[1] *Source:* Linda Spharler, unpublished material. Reprinted by permission.

Activity 3 (15 minutes): Introduce Maya Angelou—her life—show photo, followed by video presentation of her writings.

Activity 4 (15 minutes): Brainstorm elements of Angelou's style: use of descriptive words, many colorful adjectives, adverbs, verbs, dialect, autobiography, complex sentence structure.

How does this style lend to the feeling of the story? (*I Know Why the Caged Bird Sings* already read by the students.)

Activity 5 (Closure) (5 minutes): Give assignment and syllabus of unit, expectations re portfolios.

Homework Reminders:

1. Write a one-page scene imitating Maya Angelou's writing style. Underline all adjectives once and adverbs twice.
2. Vocab presenters for tomorrow.
3. Group/peer reviews due in two days.

Teacher Reflections, Evaluation of Lesson, Suggestions for Revision

UNIT AND DAILY PLAN—SAMPLE 4

Foreign Language—Spanish (Grades 9–12)

Unit Title: The Uses of *Ser* and *Estar*[1]   **Duration:** 10 days

Rationale: *Ser* and *estar* are verbs that both mean "to be." However, these two verbs are widely different in their concepts, and they can never be interchanged without a basic change of meaning. Because of the frequency of their use, it is important that students understand when to use each verb. This unit is a focus on the uses of the two verbs.

Goal: The goal of this unit is for each student to be able to correctly use the verbs *ser* and *estar*.

Objectives: Upon completion of this unit the student will be able to (1) correctly translate English sentences containing forms of "to be" into their Spanish equivalents, and (2) compose oral presentations correctly using the correct forms of *ser* and *estar*.

Content Outline:
1. Read and discuss the *Enfoque* at the beginning of the chapter (3 days).
2. *Estructura* (5 days)
   a. General view of *ser* and *estar*.
   b. *Ser* and *estar* with adjectives.
   c. Other uses of *ser* and *estar*.
3. Read and give oral presentations on *Creación* to reinforce vocabulary words and grammatical concepts (2 days).

Assessment of Student Learning: Students' answers to oral and written homework drills; content of oral presentations; vocab quiz and unit test.

Materials: Handouts on vocab words for *ser* and *estar* drills; scoring rubric for student oral presentation; vocab quiz; unit test.

LESSON PLAN: Days 3–4   ***Topic:*** Conjugation of the Irregular Verb *Ser* in the Present

Goal: To help students develop skills and confidence necessary to carry on a simple conversation in Spanish using the correct conjugations of the verb *ser*.

Objectives: Upon completion of this lesson the student should be able to
1. Recognize the correct conjugations of the verb *ser* in the present tense. Students will orally conjugate *ser* in the present tense. Students will write sentences using the correct conjugations for the verb in the present tense. Students will apply the correct forms of the verb in dialogues. (cognitive)
2. Create and perform skits using the present tense of the verb *ser*. (psychomotor)
3. Cooperate in group learning. (affective)

Materials: Overhead projector; textbooks; set of Spanish/English dictionaries

Procedure: *Activity 1 (Introductory Set) (5 minutes):* Tell students that although they have not officially learned the conjugations for the irregular verb *ser*, they have been using the verb correctly in expressions that they already learned. Give some examples, and ask volunteers for additional examples. (record on board)
   Activity 2 (3 minutes): Students brainstorm in think-write pairs to come up with all the correct conjugations for *ser* in the present tense.
   Activity 3 (3 minutes): Dyads share their conjugations and peer-correct.

[1] *Source:* Adapted with permission from original unpublished material by Reva Larson.

Activity 4 (5 minutes): Teacher lists all six verb forms for *ser* in the present tense (on overhead). Models orally a sentence using one of the verb forms and then calls on students to use the verb forms in sentences (orally).

Activity 5 (8 minutes): In their cooperative learning groups (CLGs) students role-play that they are friends greeting each other at a party. They may do this standing in different places in the room. Must speak in Spanish and must apply the verb *ser* to their conversations. Teacher roams, monitors, and helps groups.

Activity 6 (until end of period): In CLGs, students plan and create 15-minute skits that will be presented to the entire class starting tomorrow. Students may use their textbooks and Spanish/English dictionaries to create dialogues in whatever situation they choose for their skit, such as friends meeting at a restaurant, at a party, at a job interview or work situation, in a family meeting, and so on. The skit must consist of at least 10 lines per person and must employ the verb *ser* at least 10 times overall. Their dialogues may be either read or memorized, their choice.

Assessment: Individual students will be assessed (using a teacher-prepared checklist) on participation in all aspects of this lesson.

Teacher Reflections, Evaluation of Lesson, Suggestions for Revision

UNIT AND DAILY PLAN—SAMPLE 5

U.S. History (Grade 11)

Unit Title: Forming a New Nation, 1763–1800[1]   **Duration:** 18 days

Rationale and Unit Goals: As emphasized in the History–Social Science Framework for the State of California, students should draw their earlier studies of the Enlightenment and the rise of democratic ideas as the context in which this nation was founded. From their study of this unit, students will develop their

1. Comprehension of the events leading up to the American Revolution.
2. Understanding of the principles stated in the Declaration of Independence.
3. Understanding of the transformation of the U.S. from a confederation to a nation.
4. Understanding of the Preamble to the Constitution and the Bill of Rights.
5. Understanding of the Federalist Era in American history, 1789–1800.
6. Skills in reading, writing, studying, and thinking.
7. Interpersonal skills through group work.
8. Positive attitudes about America's past.
9. Understanding of the importance of the time period studied in this unit and how it relates to their lives today.

Unit Objectives: Specifically, upon completion of this unit of study, students will be able to

1. Identify several important individuals and terms associated with the road to and victory of the Revolutionary War, the transformation of the U.S. confederation to a nation, and the beginning of the United States.
2. Locate on a map the location of several significant sites, events, and battles of the Revolutionary War, the Western land claims ceded to Congress between 1784 and 1802, and Indian land cessions and other treaties between 1784 and 1810.
3. Explain the causes of the Revolutionary War.
4. Work cooperatively with their classmates.
5. Use their historical imaginations to write a paper about how life would be different today had the British won the Revolutionary War.
6. Explain why some people supported the new Constitution and others opposed it.
7. Explain George Washington's role in helping the U.S. get off to a good start.

Unit Content Outline

I. Forming a new nation, 1763–1800
   A. The road to revolution and victory
      1. The British take a collision course
      2. Declaring independence
      3. How British power was overthrown
   B. From confederation to nation
      1. New state governments
      2. The Continental Congress
      3. A weak confederation
      4. Writing a nation's constitution
      5. The states ratify
   C. The United States begins
      1. The nation in the 1790s
      2. George Washington sets a course
      3. Foreign affairs and the new nation
      4. John Adams and the rise of parties

Student Projects

1. (Initiatory) Students collaborate on a bulletin board with the theme of "Early America, 1763–1800."

[1]*Source:* Dan Androlowicz, unpublished material. Reprinted by permission.

2. (Developmental) Each student writes a paper explaining how the U.S. might be different today had the British won the Revolutionary War.
3. (Culminating) College Bowl–type tournament between heterogeneous teams of six members, each followed by a unit test for all students except the winners of the tournament.

Unit Assessments of Student Learning: *Preassessment* by informal observation of students and their individual contributions to the bulletin board project. *Formative assessment* by informally assessing students during class discussions, daily homework, and chapter tests. *Summative unit assessment* by unit test.

Materials: Textbook and Teacher's Edition, *A History of the United States* (Ginn); student handouts, class sets for handouts 14, 16–22, and 25 from teacher's edition of text; overhead transparencies of handouts 14 and 16 and of map (p. 69); handouts and overhead transparencies of Eastern U.S. map; copies of tests for Chapters 4, 5, and the unit test.

Films: The House of Representatives: Voice of the People (Prentice Hall Media) and *George Washington: Man and Myth* (National Educational Television Film Service).

Copies of directions for essay.

Materials for bulletin board: construction paper, scissors, rulers, crayons and markers, glue, stapler and staples, and precut letters and numbers for "Early America, 1763–1800." Copies of "Documents of Freedom" for each student.

LESSON PLAN: Day 1   **Topic:** Designing a Bulletin Board

Teacher Goals:
1. To help students improve their interpersonal skills through group work collaboration on a theme bulletin board.
2. To find out what students already know or think they know about the period in U.S. history, 1763–1800.

Objectives:
1. Students will cooperate on the development of their bulletin board.
2. Students will share what they already know about this period of U.S. history.

Materials Needed: Construction paper, scissors, rulers, crayons and markers, staplers and staples

Procedure: *Anticipatory Set (approximately 10 minutes):* Start class by asking students to share what or who they think of when they think about the last half of the eighteenth century in early American history. (Use think-write-pair-share.)

Have each pair share with the whole class while teacher records on writing board. [Transition 1: Have someone record on paper or overhead transparency all student contributions from the writing board, to be kept for comparisons later; explain to students that we will return to these.]

Instruction (10–15 minutes): Explain directions and organize students for the bulletin board project. Today is bulletin board project planning; tomorrow they will put it together. Establish teams but let students decide what teams, their team's name, and individual roles of team members. Teacher records these decisions.

Guided Practice (25 minutes): Teams begin work on the project; teacher monitors group progress and serves as a resource.

Closure (5 minutes): Stop and review progress on project; identify problem areas and possible resolutions. Clean up; place teams' project materials in designated classroom location.

Homework Reminders: Study Chapter 4 of text.

Teacher Reflections, Evaluation of Lesson, Suggestions for Revision

UNIT AND DAILY PLAN—SAMPLE 6

Mathematics (Grade 7 or 8)

Unit Title: Percents, Ratios, and Proportions[1]

Duration: 3 weeks

Instructional Goals: Upon the completion of this unit, seventh-grade prealgebra students will be able to
1. Interrelate mathematical topics, specifically percents:fractions, ratio:proportions, decimals:percents.
2. Develop problem-solving skills further.
3. Appreciate the connection between mathematics and the world around us.

Rationale: This unit will develop skills and concepts necessary for students to function in the real world. In addition, the information provides a stronger base of algebraic knowledge vital in the continuation of higher-level mathematics. Percents and ratios are constantly used in many areas, such as media (newspaper, magazine, TV), merchandise ads, credit card accounts, bank accounts, etc. Without proper knowledge of these mathematical figures, statistical information in the media appears as riddles embedded in a story. Students will work both individually and cooperatively to translate percents, ratios, and proportions into more understandable terms. They will also review the use of decimals, fraction reduction, and conversions between forms. In a society with unstable budgets, variable interest rates, and multiple tax brackets, it is essential that our future consumers are provided with the proper computation and problem-solving skills to make smart economical decisions. Although many seventh graders are not yet required to make such decisions, they need to become aware of the connections between the real world and the skills taught in mathematics.

Method of Evaluation: The class level of understanding will be frequently assessed using a collaboration of the following methods:
1. Cumulative tests will be given two to three times during the trimester. These tests will consist of short-answer and calculation problems taught in the previous units. These tests will be approximately 100 points. If a student does not pass or desires a higher grade, he or she may come in for lunch or before school tutoring until he or she is prepared to retake the test.
2. A team contest will be given at the beginning of at least two to three class periods during each week. The team contest will consist of problems reviewing recently taught skills. Each individual in the team must participate and write up the questions and solutions. The first team to present a completed and correct version of all of the problems will receive a choice of three bonus points or three pieces of candy or any combination of the two. The remaining teams must continue to complete the solutions. After about ten minutes, I will do the problems on the overhead. Each team with a correct packet will receive bear stamps toward future bonus points.
3. During the week, students will also be assigned homework exercises. At the beginning of each class period, students will be responsible for correcting their own homework using the solutions placed on the overhead. Three students have been chosen to check for the completion of homework daily. To receive three points, students are only required to finish the assigned work with the proper heading.
4. Individual projects will be assigned each unit. These projects give the student the opportunity to apply skills taught and to investigate mathematics in the real world. The weight of these projects will be equivalent to one test (100 points).
5. Each students is assigned a problem of the week (referred to as POW). These problems are written up by the department chair and issued in every class on Mondays. The problems are challenging word problems demanding a variety of skills and problem-solving methods. Students are encouraged to get assistance from parents, older siblings, or other teachers. They are not only asked to give the answer but a complete write-up of how they went about solving it. The problems are collected on Friday. They are worth a total of 10 points with partial credit given for effort.

---

[1]*Source:* Kim Rabang, unpublished material. Reprinted by permission.

If at any time in the trimester, the majority of the class ($\geq$ 10 students) does not understand the skill or the students' team contest reflects a lack of understanding, I will review the skill before moving on to the next lesson.

A student may also come in for lunchtime tutoring for extra help.

Students may also work within their teams to discuss problems.

Grades will be calculated according to a traditional percentage scale:

$$100\text{–}90\% \ = \ A$$
$$89\text{–}80\% \ = \ B$$
$$79\text{–}70\% \ = \ C$$
$$69\text{–}60\% \ = \ D$$
$$59\text{–}0\% \ \ = \ F$$

Instructional Objectives: At the end of this unit, students will be able to

Cognitive objectives:
1. Define ratios, percents, and proportions.
2. Review fractions and reducing fractions.
3. Convert a fraction to a decimal.
4. Compute sales tax and compounded interest.
5. Define exponents.
6. Convert exponential notation to factor notation and standard notation.
7. Find a percent of a number and the number when a percent is known.
8. Solve proportions including rate problems.
9. Use formulas to solve problems.
10. Translate word problems into mathematical terms.

Affective objectives:
1. Evaluate answer to be of a reasonable value.
2. Work cooperatively to achieve given tasks.
3. Translate newspaper and magazine ads to understandable terms.

Psychomotor objectives involving the use of manipulatives:
1. Use pie charts and 100-square grids to find the percent of an object.
2. Use ruler and map to calculate mileage from one place to another.
3. Use calculator to assist in problem solving.

Approximate Duration of Unit: Three weeks
1. This unit includes approximately 12 lessons, 2 lab days, 1 to 2 game days.
2. Shortened days and advisory days have also been taken into account.

Approximate Day Schedule

Monday	Tuesday	Wednesday	Thursday	Friday

		Day 1
		Team Contest
		Exponents
		pg. 121/2–36 even
			Day 2
			Review Exponents
			Ratios
			Pg. 251/26–30 all
			Pg. 251/36–64
			even
				Day 3
				GAME DAY
				POW 8 due
				Answer homework
				questions
				play quizzer
				reviewing skills:
				  exponents
				  combine like
				  terms
				  ratios
				  fraction reductions

Day 4 Team Contest Review ratios Introduce proportions Pg. 253/6–34 even ditto 1 & 2	**Day 5** Team Contest problem solving with proportions Map activity ditto 3 & 4	**Day 6** review for test pretest	**Day 7** TEST DAY	**Day 8** LAB DAY Marcy Cook Algebra Tiles POW 9 due
Day 9 Team Contest review POW 7 Introduce percents find number of a % find % of a number pg. 263/8–34 even pg. 265/6–20 even Find newspaper ad with %	**Day 10** Team Contest percent estimations review percents percent ditto 1, 2, & 3	**Day 11** Team Contest Lane Co. estimations problem solving pg. 266/2–44 even	**Day 12** problem solving with ratios, proportions, & percents percent of increase & decrease pg. 269/4–32 even	**Day 13** LAB DAY design a room Lane County problem solving POW 10 due
Day 14 Team Contest REVIEW				

Lesson Plan: Day 1   *Topic:* Exponents

Definition: An *exponent* is a number used to tell us how many times a factor is multiplied by itself. An exponent is written as a superscript next to the base; i.e., X^3 where 3 is the exponent and X is the base.

Objectives: At the end of this lesson, students will be able to
1. Define exponents.
2. Convert numbers in exponential form to standard and factor form.
3. Use calculators to compute numbers in exponential form.

Model Used: Direct Instructional

Set Induction: Introduce lesson by writing out 3^{10} in factor form. Respond to students' reactions. "Today, we are going to study a very important part of algebra. Exponents are special abbreviations we use in mathematics. Without them, we would have much more writing to do."

Materials Needed: None

Student Activities

Student Activities	Time Line	Teacher Strategies
1. Team contest.	10 min.	1. Review 2-step algebra with like terms.
2. Introduce exponents.	5 min.	2. Give $+/-$ examples, ask students to define exponents.
3. Talk about application.	5 min.	3.
4. Use calculators to compute exponents.	10 min.	4. Guided practice.
5. Practice.	10 min.	5. Work cooperatively.
6. Go over POW.	10 min.	6. Q & A.
7. Homework: take from page 121 in book.		

Positive/Negative Examples
    $+$: X^5, 5^3, 20^{10}, 2^3, 3^4, 32^0,
    $-$: $X \cdot X$, $3(2)$, $3(3)(3)(3)(3)(3)$
A base with its exponent is pronounced as X to the 5th power.
There are certain exponents with special names. The superscript "2" is equivalent to "squared," and the superscript "3" is equivalent to "cubed."

Closure
Ask students why we use exponents in mathematics.
Ask students if $5(5)(5)=5^3$.

Evaluation: During the class practice time, I will be walking around to make sure problems are completed properly. Students should be able to answer the closure question properly if they have comprehended the lesson. There will also be a team contest the following day to test for comprehension of the skill.

Teacher Reflections, Evaluation of Lesson, Suggestions for Revision

UNIT AND DAILY PLAN—SAMPLE 7

Music (Grades 7–8)

Unit Title: Jazz[1]

Duration: 1 week

Goals: Students will learn the nature of jazz music, including its history, instrumentation, and famous jazz musicians.

Objectives: Upon completion of this unit students will be able to
1. Identify instruments typically used in playing jazz. (cognitive)
2. Identify at least four famous jazz musicians. (cognitive)
3. Identify music as jazz. (cognitive)
4. Trace the history of jazz. (cognitive)
5. Demonstrate an interest in jazz music. (affective)
6. Tap out jazz rhythms. (psychomotor)

Rationale: Jazz music has had a prominent place in American history. Learning that music has several different styles gives a broader understanding and appreciation of music. Learning about jazz and its rhythmic style helps build a foundation for music appreciation and participation.

Content: Presentation of the history of jazz music and its relation to music history as well as to American history in general; listening to several examples of jazz music and its different styles as well as instrumentation; tapping out jazz-style rhythms; names and pictures of famous jazz musicians.

LESSON PLAN: Day 1   **Topic:** Introduction to Jazz Music

Introductory set: Before students enter the classroom, have pictures of jazz musicians with their instruments posted around the room. Have upbeat jazz music playing as students enter.
  Activity 1 (10 minutes): As students enter the room, they are to move directly to their seats and, using think-write-pair-share, answer these questions: What instruments do you hear being played? What do you hear that is distinctive about this music? About the rhythm, for example, how are drums and bass being used?
  Activity 2 (10 minutes): Pairs share their conclusions with the whole class. Teacher records contributions on overhead transparency.
  Transition Activity 3 (5 minutes): Teacher demonstration of swing rhythm. Clap or tap examples. Play an example where swing is obvious; have students clap or tap along.
  Activity 4 (10 minutes): Teacher talk about how and when jazz began; about American South in early 20th century, New Orleans and its many cultures; about instruments commonly used in jazz bands, pointing to the pictures of famous musicians and their instruments.
  Transition Activity 5 (1 minute): Play a saxophone solo for students.
  Activity 6 and Closure (until period ends): Teacher talk about concept of solo playing and improvisation by playing portions of recorded solos of C. Parker, L. Armstrong, D. Ellington, etc. As class end approaches (and if space permits), allow students to get up and dance to the music or, if they choose, to tap and clap.

Materials: Pictures; musical selections and tape player; my saxophone.

Assignments and Reminders: Our next lesson is about different jazz styles. Your assignment for this week is to be attentive to jazz that you might hear on the radio or elsewhere and written notes about what you are hearing to share with us in class.

---

[1]*Source:* Adapted with permission from original unpublished material by Staci L. Webb.

Assessment of Student Learning: Teacher observations of student participation in tapping (clapping), dyad and brainstorming responses.

Teacher Reflections, Evaluation of Lesson, Suggestions for Revision

Glossary

ability grouping The assignment of students to separate classrooms or to separate activities within a classroom according to their perceived academic abilities. *Homogeneous grouping* is the grouping of students of similar abilities, whereas *heterogeneous grouping* is the grouping of students of mixed abilities.

accommodation The cognitive process of modifying a schema or creating new schemata.

accountability Reference to the concept that an individual is responsible for his behaviors and should be able to demonstrate publicly the worth of the activities carried out.

advance organizer Preinstructional cues that encourage a mind-set, used to enhance retention of materials to be studied.

advisor–advisee A homeroom program that provides each student the opportunity to interact with peers about school and personal concerns and to develop a meaningful relationship with at least one member of the school staff.

affective domain The area of learning related to interests, attitudes, feelings, values, and personal adjustment.

alternative assessment Assessment of learning that is different from traditional paper-and-pencil objective testing. See *authentic assessment.*

American Federation of Teachers (AFT) A national professional organization of teachers founded in 1916 and currently affiliated with the American Federation of Labor and Congress of Industrial Organizations (AFL-CIO).

anticipatory set See *advance organizer.*

assessment The relatively neutral process of finding out what students are learning or have learned as a result of instruction.

assignment A statement telling the student what she is to accomplish.

assimilation The cognitive process by which a learner integrates new information into an existing schema.

at risk General term applied to students who show a high potential for not completing school.

authentic assessment Assessment that is highly compatible with the instructional objectives. Also referred to as *accurate, active, aligned, alternative, direct,* and *performance* assessment.

behavioral objective A statement of expectation describing what the learner should be able to do upon completion of the instruction, with four components: the audience (learner), the overt behavior, the conditions, and the level or degree of performance. Also referred to as *performance* and *terminal* objective.

behaviorism A theory that equates learning with changes in observable behavior.

block scheduling The school programming procedure that provides large blocks of time (e.g., two hours) in which individual teachers or teacher teams can arrange groupings of students for varied periods of time, thereby more effectively individualizing the instruction for students with various needs and abilities.

brainstorming An instructional strategy used to create a flow of new ideas, during which the judgments of the ideas of others are forbidden.

CD-ROM (compact disc, read-only memory) Digitally encoded information permanently recorded on a compact disc (CD).

classroom control The process of influencing student behavior in the classroom.

classroom management The teacher's system of establishing a climate for learning, including techniques for preventing and handling student misbehavior.

closure In a lesson, the means by which a teacher brings the lesson to an end.

coaching See *mentoring.*

cognitive disequilibrium The mental state of not yet having made sense out of a perplexing (discrepant) situation.

cognitive domain The area of learning related to intellectual skills, such as retention and assimilation of knowledge.

cognitive psychology A branch of psychology devoted to the study of how individuals acquire, process, and use information.

cognitivism A theory that holds that learning entails the construction or reshaping of mental schemata and that mental processes mediate learning. Also known as *constructivism.*

common planning time A regularly scheduled time during the school day when teachers who teach the same students meet for joint planning, parent conferences, materials preparation, and student evaluation.

competency-based instruction See *performance-based instruction.*

comprehension A level of cognition that refers to the skill of understanding.

computer-assisted instruction (CAI) Instruction received by a student when interacting with lessons programmed into a computer system.

computer literate The ability at some level to understand and use computers.

computer-managed instruction (CMI) The use of a computer system to manage information about learner performance and learning-resources options in order to prescribe and control individual lessons.

concept map A visual or graphic representation of concepts and their relationships; words related to a key word are written in categories around the key word, and the categories are labeled.

constructivism See *cognitivism.*

continuous progress An instructional procedure that allows students to progress at their own pace through a sequenced curriculum.

convergent thinking Thinking that is directed to a preset conclusion.

cooperative learning A genre of instructional strategies that use small groups of students working together and helping one another on learning tasks, with an emphasis on support among group members rather than on competition.

core curriculum Subject or discipline components of the curriculum considered as being absolutely necessary, including English/language arts, mathematics, science, and history/social studies.

covert behavior A learner behavior that is not outwardly observable.

criterion A standard by which behavioral performance is judged.

criterion-referenced assessment Assessments measured against preset standards rather than nationally-normed standards.

criterion-referenced measurement The measurement of behaviors against preset standards rather than against the behaviors of others.

critical thinking The ability to recognize and identify problems and discrepancies, to propose and test solutions, and to arrive at tentative conclusions based on the data collected.

curriculum What is planned and encouraged for teaching and learning, including both school and nonschool environments, overt (formal) and hidden (informal) curriculums, and broad as well as narrow notions of content (its development, acquisition, and consequences).

curriculum compacting The procedure of allowing a student who already knows the material about to be studied to pursue enriched or accelerated study.

curriculum tracking The practice of students' voluntary or involuntary placement in different programs or courses according to their ability and prior academic performance.

deductive learning Learning that proceeds from the general to the specific. See *expository learning.*

detracking An effort to minimize or eliminate separate classes or programs for students according to their differing abilities.

developmental characteristics A set of common intellectual, psychological, physical, social, and moral and ethical characteristics that, when considered as a whole, indicates an individual's development relative to others during a particular age span.

developmental needs A set of needs unique and appropriate to the developmental characteristics of a particular age span.

diagnostic assessment See *preassessment.*

didactic teaching See *direct teaching.*

direct experience Learning by doing (applying) that which is being learned.

direct intervention Teacher use of verbal reminders or verbal commands to redirect student behavior, as opposed to the use of nonverbal gestures or cues.

direct teaching Teacher-centered expository instruction.

discipline The process of controlling student behavior in the classroom. The term has been largely supplanted by the terms *classroom control* and *classroom management.* The term is also used in reference to the subject taught (e.g., the disciplines of language arts, science, mathematics).

discovery learning Learning that proceeds from identification of a problem, through the development and testing of the hypotheses, to the arrival at a conclusion. See *critical thinking.*

divergent thinking Thinking that expands beyond original thought.

early adolescence The developmental stage young people go through as they approach and begin to experience puberty, usually occurring between ages 10 and 14.

eclectic Utilizing the best from a variety of sources.

effective school A school where students master basic skills, seek academic excellence in all subjects, demonstrate achievement, and display good behavior and attendance.

elective High-interest or special-needs courses that are based on student selection from various options.

empathy The ability to understand the feelings of another person.

equality Considered to be same in status or competency level.

equilibration The mental process of moving from disequilibrium to equilibrium.

equilibrium The balance between assimilation and accommodation.

equity Fairness and justice, with impartiality.

evaluation See *assessment.*

exceptional child See *special-needs student.*

exploratory course A course designed to help students explore curriculum experiences based on their felt needs, interests, and abilities.

expository learning The traditional classroom instructional approach that proceeds as follows: presentation of information to the learners, reference to particular examples, and application of the information to the learner's experiences.

extrinsic motivators Rewards from outside of the learner, such as parent and teacher expectations, as well as gifts, certificates, and grades.

facilitating behavior Teacher behaviors that make student learning possible.

facilitative teaching See *indirect teaching.*

family See *school within a school.*

feedback Information sent from the receiver to the originator that provides disclosure about the reception of the intended message.

flexible scheduling Organization of classes and activities in a way that allows for variation from day to day, as opposed to the traditional fixed schedule that does not vary from day to day.

formative assessment Evaluation of learning in progress.

full inclusion The commitment to education of each special-needs learner, to the maximum extent appropriate, in the school and classroom that he would otherwise attend.

goal, course A broad generalized statement telling about the expected outcomes of the course.

goal, educational A desired instructional outcome that is broad in scope.

goal, teacher A statement telling what the teacher hopes to accomplish.

hands-on learning Learning by doing, or active learning.

heterogeneous grouping A grouping pattern that does not separate students into groups based on their intelligence, learning achievement, or physical characteristics.

hidden curriculum The accepted or implied values and attitudes and the unwritten rules of behavior students must earn to participate and to be successful in school.

high school A school that houses students in any combination of grades 9 to 12.

holistic learning Learning that incorporates emotions with thinking.

homogeneous grouping A grouping pattern that usually separates students into groups based on their intelligence and past school achievement, or physical characteristics.

house See *school within a school.*

inclusion The commitment to educate each special needs child in the school and, when appropriate, in the class that child would have attended had the child not had a disability. Inclusion is used in place of the earlier term *mainstreaming.*

independent study An instructional strategy that allows a student to select a topic, set the goals, and work alone to attain them.

indirect teaching Student-centered teaching using discovery and inquiry instructional strategies.

individualized instruction See *individualized learning.*

individualized learning The self-paced process whereby individual students assume responsibility for learning through study, practice, feedback, and reinforcement, with appropriately designed instructional packages or modules.

inductive learning Learning that proceeds from specifics to the general. See *discovery learning.*

inquiry learning Like *discovery learning,* except the learner designs the processes to be used in resolving the problem, thereby requiring higher levels of cognition.

instruction Planned arrangement of experiences to help a learner develop understanding and to achieve a desirable change in behavior.

instructional module Any free-standing instructional unit that includes these components: rationale, objectives, pretest, learning activities, comprehension checks with instructive feedback, posttest.

instructional scaffolding See *concept map.*

integrated (interdisciplinary) curriculum Curriculum organization that combines subject matter traditionally taught separately.

interdisciplinary team   An organizational pattern of two or more teachers representing different subject areas; the team shares the same students, schedule, areas of the school, and the opportunity for teaching more than one subject.

interdisciplinary thematic unit (ITU)   A thematic unit that crosses boundaries of two or more disciplines.

internalization   The extent to which an attitude or value becomes a part of the learner; that is, without having to think about it, the learner's behavior reflects the attitude or value.

interscholastic sports   Athletic competition between teams from two or more schools.

intervention   The teacher interrupts to redirect a student's behavior, either by direct intervention (e.g., a verbal command) or by indirect intervention (e.g., eye contact or physical proximity).

intramural program   Organized activity program that features events between individuals or teams from within the school.

intrinsic motivation   Rewards from within a person, such as a student's internal sense of accomplishment.

intuition   Knowing without conscious reasoning.

junior high school   A school that houses grades 7 to 9 or 7 to 8 and that has a schedule and curriculum resembling those of the (senior) high school (grades 9 to 12 or 10 to 12) more than it does those of the elementary school.

lead teacher   The teacher in a teaching team who is designated to facilitate the work and planning of that team.

learning   The development of understandings and the change in behavior resulting from experiences; see *behaviorism* and *constructivism* for different interpretations of learning.

learning activity center (LAC)   An instructional strategy that utilizes activities and materials located at a special place in the classroom and that is designed to allow a student to work independently and at her own pace to learn one area of content.

learning modality   The way a person receives information; four modalities are recognized: visual, auditory, tactile (touch), and kinesthetic (movement).

learning resource center   The central location in the school where instructional materials and media are stored, organized, and accessed by students and staff.

learning style   The way a person learns best in a given situation.

looping   Sometimes called banding or multiyear teaching, looping is when a teacher remains with the same cluster of students for two or more years.

magnet school   A school that specializes in a particular academic area, such as science, mathematics and technology, or the arts; also referred to as a *theme school*.

mainstreaming   Placing a special-needs student in regular education classrooms for all (full inclusion) or part (partial inclusion) of the school day.

mastery learning   The concept that a student should master the content of one lesson before moving on to the content of the next.

measurement   The process of collecting and interpreting data.

mentoring   One-on-one coaching, tutoring, or guidance to facilitate learning.

metacognition   The ability to plan, monitor, and evaluate one's own thinking.

micro peer teaching (MPT)   Teaching a limited objective for a brief period of time to a small group of peers, for the purpose of evaluation and improvement of particular teaching skills.

middle grades   Grades 5 to 8.

middle-level education   Any school unit between elementary and high school.

middle school   Schools that have been planned and organized especially for students of ages 10 through 14 and that generally have grades 5 to 8, with grades 6 to 8 being the most popular grade-span organization. There are many variations, though; for example, a school might include only grades 7 and 8 and still be called a middle school.

minds-on learning   Learning in which the learner is intellectually active, thinking about what is being learned.

misconception   Faulty understanding of a major idea or concept; also known as *naïve theory* and *conceptual misunderstanding*.

modeling   The teacher's direct and indirect demonstration, by actions and by words, of the behaviors expected of students.

multicultural education   A deliberate attempt to help students understand facts, generalizations, attitudes, and behaviors derived from their own ethnic roots as well as others. In this process, students unlearn racism and ethnic prejudices and recognize the interdependent fabric of society, giving due acknowledgment for contributions made by its members.

multilevel instruction   See *multitasking*.

multimedia   The combined use of sound, video, and graphics for instruction.

multiple intelligences   A theory of several different intelligences, as opposed to just one general intelligence; other intelligences that have been described are linguistic, musical, logical-mathematical, spatial, kinesthetic, interpersonal, and intrapersonal.

multipurpose board   A writing board with a smooth plastic surface used with special marking pens rather than chalk; sometimes called *visual aid panels.* A multipurpose board may have a steel backing, which allows it to be used as a magnetic board as well as a screen for projecting visuals.

multitasking   When several levels of teaching and learning are going on simultaneously in the same classroom, when students are working on different objectives, or when different students are doing various tasks leading to the same objective; also called *multilevel instruction.*

naïve theory   See *misconception.*

National Education Association (NEA)   The nation's oldest professional organization of teachers, founded in 1857 as the National Teachers Association and changed in 1879 to its present name.

norm-referenced   Individual performance is judged relative to overall performance of the group, as opposed to criterion-referenced (e.g., grading on a curve).

orientation set   See *advance organizer.*

overlapping   A teacher behavior where the teacher is able to attend to more than one matter at once.

overt behavior   A learner behavior that is outwardly observable.

paraprofessional   An adult who is not a credentialed teacher but who works with children in the classroom with and under the supervision of a credentialed person.

partial inclusion   Placing a special needs student in a regular education classroom part of the day.

peer tutoring   An instructional strategy that places students in a tutorial role, where one student helps another learn.

performance assessment   See *authentic assessment.*

performance-based instruction   Instruction designed around assessment of student achievement against specified and predetermined objectives.

performance objective   See *behavioral objective.*

portfolio assessment   An alternative approach to assessment that assembles representative samples of a student's work over time as a basis for assessment.

positive reinforcer   Encouraging desired student behavior by rewarding those behaviors when they occur.

PQRST   A study strategy where students review the reading to identify the main parts, create questions, read to the material, state the main theme or idea, and test themselves by answering the questions they posed earlier.

preassessment   Diagnostic assessment, or assessment of what students know or think they know prior to the instruction.

probationary teacher   An untenured teacher. After a designated number of years in the same district (usually three), the probationary teacher receives a tenure contract upon rehire.

procedure   A statement telling the student how to accomplish a task.

psychomotor domain   The domain of learning that involves locomotor behaviors.

realia   Real objects used as visual props during instruction, such as political campaign buttons, plants, memorabilia, artwork, balls, and so forth.

reciprocal teaching   A form of collaborative teaching, where the teacher and the students share the teaching responsibility and all are involved in asking questions, clarifying, predicting, and summarizing.

reflective abstraction   See *metacognition.*

reliability   In measurement, the accuracy with which a technique measures that which it does measure.

schema   A mental construct by which the learner organizes his perceptions of situations and knowledge (plural: schemata).

school-within-a-school   Where one team of teachers is assigned to work with the same group of about 125 students for a common block of time, for the entire school day, or, in some instances, for all the years those students are at that school; sometimes referred to as a *house, cluster, village, pod,* or *family.*

secondary school   Traditionally, any school housing students for any combination of grades 7 to 12.

self-contained classroom   A grouping pattern in which one teacher teaches all or almost all subjects to one group of children; commonly used in the primary grades.

self-paced learning   See *individualized learning.*

senior high school   See *high school.*

sequencing   Arranging ideas in logical order.

simulation   An abstraction or simplification of a real-life situation.

special needs student   A student who deviates from the average in any of the following ways: mental characteristics, sensory ability, neuromotor or physical characteristics, social behavior, communication ability, or multiple handicaps. Also known as *exceptional child* and *special education student.*

SQ3R   A study strategy in which students survey the reading, create questions, read to answer the questions, recite the answers, and review the original material.

SQ4R   Similar to SQ3R, but with the addition of recording. The students survey the reading, ask questions about what was read, read to answer the questions, recite the answers, record important items into their notebooks, then review it all.

student teaching   The field-experience component of teacher preparation, often the culminating experience, in which the teacher candidate practices teaching children while under the supervision of a credentialed teacher and a university supervisor.

summative assessment   Evaluation of learning after instruction is completed.

teacher leader   See *lead teacher.*

teaching   See *instruction.*

teaching style   The way a teacher teaches, including any distinctive mannerisms and personal choices of teaching behaviors and strategies.

teaching team   A team of two or more teachers who work together to provide instruction to the same group of students, either alternating the instruction or teaching simultaneously in team teaching.

team teaching   Two or more teachers working together to provide instruction to a group of students.

tenured teacher   A teacher with a tenure contract, which means that the teacher is automatically rehired each year thereafter unless the contract is revoked by either the district or the teacher and for specific and legal reasons; see *probationary teacher.*

terminal behavior   What has been learned as a direct result of instruction.

thematic unit   A unit of instruction built on a central theme or concept.

theme school   See *magnet school.*

think time   See *wait-time.*

transescence   The stage of human development, usually thought of as ages 10 through 14, which begins before the onset of puberty and extends through the early stages of adolescence. Students in this stage of development are referred to variously as the *transescent, preadolescent, preteen, in-betweenager,* and *tweenager.*

transition   In a lesson, the planned procedures that move student thinking from one idea to the next or that move their actions from one activity to the next.

transitional activities   An activity for students who have finished a learning activity to do while watching for others to finish, and intended to keep all students academically occupied, thereby allowing no time in which some students have nothing to do but to wait while others catch up.

untracking   See *detracking.*

validity   In measurement, the degree to which an item or instrument measures that which is intended to measure.

village   See *school-within-a-school.*

wait-time   In the use of questioning, the period of silence between the time a question is asked and the questioner (teacher) does something, such as repeating the question, rephrasing the question, calling on a particular student, answering the question herself, or asking another question.

whole language learning   A point of view with a focus on seeking or creating meaning that encourages language production, taking risks, independence in producing language, and using a wide variety of print materials in authentic reading and writing situations.

withitness   The teacher's ability to intervene in a timely manner and redirect a student's inappropriate behavior.

young adolescent   The 10 to 14-year-old who is experiencing the developmental stage of early adolescence.

Name Index

Subject Index